TO THE POINT

Class Formation, 1869. Cadets formed ranks by section; and, after reporting attendance to the guard, the section marcher moved his section to the classroom in the Academic Building to the right of the photograph.

TO THE POINT

The United States Military Academy, 1802–1902

GEORGE S. PAPPAS

Foreword by General Edward C. Meyer

PRAEGER

Westport, Connecticut
London

Library of Congress Cataloging-in-Publication Data

Pappas, George S.
  To the Point : the United States Military Academy, 1802–1902 /
  by George S. Pappas : foreword by Edward C. Meyer.
      p.   cm.
  Includes bibliographical references and index.
  ISBN 0–275–94329–1 (alk. paper)
  1. United States Military Academy—History.   I. Title.
U410 L1P37   1993
355′.0071′173—dc20   92–36632

British Library Cataloguing in Publication Data is available.

Library of Congress Catalog Card Number: 92–36632
ISBN: 0–275–94329–1

First published in 1993

Praeger Publishers, 88 Post Road West, Westport, CT 06881
An imprint of Greenwood Publishing Group, Inc.

Printed in the United States of America

The paper used in this book complies with the
Permanent Paper Standard issued by the National
Information Standards Organization (Z39.48–1984)

10 9 8 7 6 5 4 3 2 1

55.00

This work is for

Thomas K. McManus
Class of 1927
United States Military Academy

Few graduates have loved
their Alma Mater more

Few have better shown
true dedication to
Duty, *Honor*, Country

Contents

Illustrations   xi

Foreword by General Edward C. Meyer   xiii

Preface   xvii

Acknowledgments   xix

1775–1802

1. The Foundation Is Laid   3

1802–1817

2. Struggle for Survival   25

3. Existence in Name Only   45

4. Right Man at the Right Time?   61

5. Deliver Your Sword to the Bearer   75

1817–1828

6.   The Rebuilding Begins   99

7.   Governed by the Rules and Articles of War   119

8.   Still in a State of Progressive Development   129

9.   Members of One Brotherhood   149

10. Living Armory of the Nation   167

1829–1833

11. I Have the Honor to Tender My Resignation   185

12. I Believe It the Best School in the World   205

1833–1852

13. A Firm Hand Is Needed   221

14. Preparing for the Ultimate Test   239

15. We Follow, Close Order, Behind You   261

1852–1865

16. The Ante-Bellum Army   281

17. When Shall We Meet Again?   287

18. Adhere to Your Purpose   323

1865–1902

19. All Institutions Are Imperfect and Subject to the Law of Change   353

20. Guard Well Your Heritage   387

1902

21. The Corps and the Corps and the Corps   419

APPENDICES

A.   Superintendents, U.S. Military Academy   423

B.   Commandants of Cadets   427

C.   Deans of the Academic Board   431

D.   The 1780 Map of West Point: An Unintentional Historical Hoax   433

E.   Comments on Sources   437

    Bibliography   447

    Index   467

Photo essay follows page 181.

Illustrations

PHOTOGRAPHS

(All illustrations are from the West Point Library Special Collections Division unless otherwise noted. Except for the frontispiece, all photographs follow page 181.)

Class Formation, 1869 (*frontispiece*)

The Revolutionary War Blockhouse below Kinsley Hill
    (West Point Museum)

Cadet Uniform in 1802 (The Company of Military Historians)

Cadet Uniform circa 1816 (The Company of Military Historians)

West Point in 1826

West Point in 1826 (West Point Museum)

South Barracks, 1830s

Central Area of Barracks in 1854

Cadet George Derby in Furlough Uniform, 1844

Cadet Lieutenant, circa 1845

Sheet Music of the 1850s

Lieutenant George Crook, Cadet Philip Sheridan, and Lieutenant John Nugen

The West Point Hotel and Road from the Landing, 1855

A Cadet Drawing of a Room in the 1860s

Central Barracks, 1860

Cadet Hop in the 1860s

A Cadet Fire Team Mans the Pump Engine, 1863

The Hudson River Looking North from Trophy Point, 1864
    (West Point Museum)

The Cadet Chapel and the Library, 1867

Cadets on a Wagon in Front of the Mess Hall, 1867

Kosciuszko Monument in 1868

The Riding Hall, 1868

The Snow Plow, 1872 (West Point Museum)

Cadet Guard in the Summer of 1873

Looking West from the Old Cadet Chapel in 1875

A Cadet Room, 1st Division, Central Barracks, 1880

The Normal Cadet Room in Central Barracks, 1880

Academic Section Formation, 1880

The Ill-Fated Custer Monument, 1880

The Back of the Library from the East Porch of the Administration Building,
     1882

Cadet Hop Cards, 1852 to 1880

Cadet Hop in the Mess Hall, 1883

A Room in the Cadet Hospital, circa 1885

Parade at Summer Camp, 1886

Artillery Drill in the Late 1880s

Thayer Monument in Front of the Gymnasium, 1887

Cadet Class in 1890

Class in Practical Military Engineering, circa 1890

Two Yearlings Accost a Plebe Sentinel, Summer Camp, 1891

A Cadet Takes the Five-Foot Hurdle Bareback, 1895

Walking the Area, 1894

Christmas Hop, 1898

Observance of the Centennial of the Military Academy,
     June 11, 1902

MAPS

(All maps are from the West Point Library Special Collections Division.)

West Point in 1830   184

The Academy in 1844   220

West Point in 1863   280

The Military Academy in 1891   352

Foreword

The point of most books written about the United States Military Academy has been the quality of its product. Bradley, Patton, Eisenhower, MacArthur, Abrams, Pershing, Grant, Lee, Schwarzkopf, and hundreds of other heroes of past wars in which Americans have fought have been the centerpiece of books on leadership in peace and war. Their formative years at West Point are always heralded as a key contributor to their success.

To the Point is not about its graduates but about the institution, the United States Military Academy, which will celebrate its two-hundredth birthday on March 16, 2002. It is an institution that had a marked influence on the development of a nation, the birth of an army, and the birth of a professional officer corps.

George Pappas tells us about the central role that Jonathan Williams and Sylvanus Thayer played in ensuring that West Point would become not only a military academy, but also a quality engineering school to provide for the growing needs of our nascent nation.

His vignettes of the interrelationship of the Superintendent of the Academy, the Secretary of War, and the President remind us of how small our nation was in the early 1800s. He also reminds us of the continuing confrontation between the Congress and the President, even in such a seemingly inconsequential issue as discipline at West Point.

His word pictures of the physical growth of West Point are a microcosm of the growth of cities throughout our nation. The first chapel, cadet barracks, the first hotel, the outdoor plumbing all reveal the struggle to grow in periods of little funding from Washington and form a picture of the challenges our forefathers faced throughout the nation.

But the heart of this book is the Military Academy itself. The development of instructors; the development of the curriculum; the development of the cadet; the importance of "honour"; the creation of a library; the role of discipline, including good and bad examples; the daily exams; the weekly academic reports; life in the barracks; Benny Haven's Tavern—these and many other vignettes of West Point are brought to life throughout Pappas's skillful use of unparalleled research.

Historical figures flit through the pages as asides, not as centerpieces—Sylvanus Thayer's evaluation of Jefferson Davis as "a recreant and unnatural son" when he was found off limits and drinking at Benny Haven's Tavern; Edgar Allan Poe's being dismissed from the Academy for "gross neglect and disobedience of orders"; attacks on the need for the Academy by Congressman Davy Crockett.

Little-known historical incidents titillate: the agreement in 1825 between the Secretary of War and the Secretary of the Navy that the source of second lieutenants for the Marine Corps would be graduates of West Point, or the letter from James Monroe to Sylvanus Thayer requesting advice on how to improve the University of Virginia. The visits of distinguished foreign and American visitors, such as the Marquis de Lafayette or General Winfield Scott, provide insights into the mores of the era.

One might wonder how to judge whether the institution that had such a difficult beginning was ever able to succeed. Pappas does a superb job of answering that question by identifying the graduates who performed outstandingly in the War with Mexico, the Civil War, the War with Spain, as elected officials, as founders of colleges, as builders of railroads, canals, bridges, and roads across our nation—all of this and more during West Point's first hundred years.

General Winfield Scott, not a Military Academy graduate, said, "I give it as my fixed opinion that but for our graduated cadets, the war between the United States and Mexico might, and probably would have lasted some four or five years, with, in its first half, more defeats than victories falling to our share."

That quotation, which is a part of every living graduate's consciousness, is probably a good way to end this foreword on a high point. However, the foreword to a book about West Point should not end without a little barracks humor. George Pappas explains the origin of today's cadet slang, terms such as "found," "boodle fight," "turnback," and even "plebe." He makes many references to the cadet uniform—a very visible emblem, even today, of West Point. He tells us that in 1853 Academy authorities adopted fly-front trousers despite the objections of many West Point ladies. One of the little-known facts he includes is that the gray uniforms were adopted after the War of 1812, not to commemorate Winfield Scott's victory at the battle of Chippewa, but because they were significantly cheaper than blue uniforms. Thus, if it had not been for the penury of the early founders, the Long Gray Line would today be the Long Blue Line.

An extraordinary series of events in the early years of our republic led to the need for a military academy. Extraordinary men developed the institution that has provided leadership for our nation for nearly two centuries. Thank God for that institution, and thank George Pappas for providing us with his extraordinary history in *To the Point*.

Edward C. Meyer
General, U.S. Army, Ret.

Preface

Many friends have asked me why I decided to prepare a new history of the Military Academy when so many have already been published by both graduates and historians. There were two reasons for my decision. First, while working on my book about the Cadet Chapel, I noted that a recent history written by an eminent historian included many errors of fact and perpetuated unfounded myths about West Point. To satisfy my own curiosity, I began looking at older histories to determine where some of these legends had originated. I was amazed and appalled to find that some resulted from authors' deliberately withholding information or changing facts to attain a predetermined objective. Countless cadets and graduates perpetuated unfounded myths and even rumors, passing such stories on from generation to generation. Both the inaccurate accounts of early authors and institutional legends often have been accepted by later historians and writers who failed to ascertain the veracity of these statements. Many of these inaccuracies are pointed out in this work. This led to my determination to research every available source to produce a history of the Academy based upon facts and actual occurrences, not on legend, cadet "sinkoids," or hearsay.

My second reason was the early discovery of new materials not previously available to or not used by other historians. Perhaps the best example of such materials are the Henry Burbeck papers, given to the USMA Library in 1987. These papers provided the first definitive information about the pre-1802 West Point academy of the Corps of Artillerists and Engineers. Regimental, battalion, and artillery company muster rolls provided additional information. The data from these sources was supplemented by material found in Quartermaster waste books, Court Martial records, pay vouchers, medical returns, and other similar obscure sources. The hundreds of cadet and graduate letters, diaries, photo albums, and scrapbooks in the USMA Library Special Collections are another example of materials seldom used by other writers. Cadet letters are the primary source for descriptions of the fires that destroyed the old Long Barracks in 1827 and the Academic Building in 1838 and other events in the early years of the Military Academy. Cadet and graduate letters also provide a wealth of information to supplement the cold and uninteresting official records. Descriptions of the post and narratives of events from these sources provide an excellent description of West Point's colorful past. Cadet scrapbooks have been a gold mine of information, for they contain photographs, programs of special events, copies of orders, periodical articles, newspaper clippings, delinquency reports, punishment awards, rolls for class formations, and guard reports—materials often not included in the USMA archives. I have been asked often how I would define my work, how it differs from other histories of the Military Academy. I believe it can be best described as a history of the Academy as seen through the eyes of the cadets and graduates who made that history.

Acknowledgments

Few writers have had as much help as I have been given during the last four years. Every individual on the following list has contributed to my efforts. Some have assisted my research; some have provided material support by long and objective oral interviews; others gave advice and moral support. Several have read my manuscript and given me astute and positive comments. Others gave me materials from their personal files. To each and every individual I give my heartfelt thanks and appreciation.

My work has been made incalculably easier by the help of many individuals. Thomas K. McManus has given me complete support and advice and has served more or less as my father confessor; without his help and encouragement this work probably would not have been started, let alone completed. Lieutenant General Dave R. Palmer while Superintendent assisted in every possible way, including submitting to an extensive series of oral interviews. His successor, Lieutenant General Howard Graves, has continued Dave's support.

Brigadier General Paul Berrigan; Lieutenant General Garrison H. Davidson, former Superintendent, USMA; Thomas K. McManus, and Colonel Arthur Roth, all Class of 1927, were my advisors, "murder board," readers, and energetic supporters. General Berrigan and Mr. McManus made it possible for each member of the West Point Class of 1992 to recieve a copy of my history from the Class of 1927 in observance of the sixty-fifth anniversary of its graduation.

Colonel John K. Robertson has been a blessing. He has been one of my readers, provided computer support and advice, shared his own research in early West Point history and his in-process catalog of officers stationed at the Academy, *Who Was Who, 1802–1990*. During his own research in the National Archives,

Robie obtained for me many documents verifying information in the Henry Burbeck papers.

The entire staff of the USMA Library Special Collections Division has provided exemplary support. Mrs. Marie T. Capps, before retiring as Manuscript and Map Librarian, guided me to many relatively obscure references and made many useful suggestions. Alan Aimone has shared his own research and, between my many trips to West Point, set aside new materials he knew would be of interest to me and has been one of my readers. Mrs. Judith Sibley, another reader, has provided exemplary assistance in tracking down answers to my many questions. Mrs. Dawn Crumpler and Mrs. Gladys Calvetti have also assisted me in retrieving information from myriad sources in Special Collections.

I have been blessed by help from my many readers. Dr. Robert Ferrell, former Visiting Professor of the USMA Department of History and Professor Emeritus of the University of Indiana, gave me many suggestions and provided very sound advice. Brigadier General Roy Flint, former Dean of the USMA Faculty; Lieutenant Colonels James Johnson and James Rainey, USMA Department of History; Brigadier General Jack L. Capps, former Professor of English, USMA; Lieutenant General Marshall S. Carter; Colonel Paul Child, former Editor, *Assembly*; Colonel Larry Donithorn, Superintendent's Staff; Major and Mrs. Mark Snell, Department of History, USMA; and Colonel William L. Wilson, Superintendent's Staff have provided advice and comments after reading my manuscript. Their help has prevented me from making mistakes that would have been hard to explain and assisted me in clarifying many statements I have made.

The entire staff of the U.S. Army Military History Institute, Carlisle Barracks, Pennsylvania, has provided uncommon assistance. Dr. Richard Sommers, David Keogh, and Pamela Cheney of the Manuscript Division assembled material prior to my arrival, enabling me to begin work immediately upon entering the Institute. John Slonaker and Linda Brenneman provided additional assistance.

Susan Christoff and Mrs. Dorothy Rapp, USMA Archives, have given me special help in using the many official records in the Archives, often spending much time in digging out answers to my many questions.

Major General David Bramlett, former Commandant of Cadets, compared today's Corps with the Corps in previous years, as well as participating in oral history interviews. General Bramlett's astute comparison of changes in the Corps and in Academy procedures was of much help.

Mrs. Leah Schwarz was a reader and copy editor. She also assisted in reproducing the many copies of my manuscript required for other readers.

Special thanks is due to Colonel Julian M. Olejniczak, Editor of *Assembly*. Jay has given me sound advice. Most important, he has enabled me to publish many articles based upon my research. The comments and information provided by many *Assembly* readers have given me information that would not otherwise have been available.

In addition, the following individuals have all provided help and advice beyond any normal requirement: The Reverend Richard Camp, Cadet Chaplain;

Cadet Sean Cleveland; Brigadier General Elliott Cutler, former Professor of Electricity; Colonel Robert Doughty, Professor of History, USMA; Dr. Sidney Forman, former USMA Librarian; Brigadier General Gerald E. Galloway, Jr., Dean of the USMA Faculty; Mrs. Carolyne Gaspard, Cadet Hostess; The Reverend Robert Geehan, Assistant Cadet Chaplain; Cadet Robert Goldsmith; Lieutenant General Howard Graves, Superintendent, USMA; Stephen Grove, USMA Historian; Kenneth Hedman, USMA Librarian; Master Sergeant Warren Howe, USMA Band; Colonel Seth Hudgins, Executive Vice President, Association of Graduates; Colonel Robert Lamb, former Executive Vice President, Association of Graduates; Michael Moss, Director, USMA Museum; Andrew Mowbray, Mowbray Publishing Company, Providence, Rhode Island; Colonel Roger Nye, former Professor, Department of History, USMA, and Chairman, Friends of the West Point Library; Mrs. Dave R. Palmer; Dr. Carole Petillo, Professor of History, Boston College; Colonel Alfred Rushton, Jr., Director of Admissions, USMA; Colonel John Shelter; Colonel Rolland Sullivan, Association of Graduates; Egan Weiss, former USMA Librarian; Brigadier General Sumner Willard, former Professor of Foreign Languages, USMA; Mrs. Charity Willard, former Secretary, Friends of the West Point Library; and a countless number of graduates and friends of the Military Academy who commented on my many articles in *Assembly*, which were based on this work, and who provided me with much information not found in the official records, letters, or diaries.

My thanks and appreciation go to Ron Chambers and Alicia Merritt of Praeger Publishers. Ron's enthusiasm and Alicia's selfless help have been outstanding.

I have a special reason for thanking Michael Koskie, an unusual reason. Michael came up with the titles for this first volume of Military Academy history, *To the Point*, and for the forthcoming second volume, *More to the Point*, which will describe the events from 1902 to date.

And last—but far from least—I must thank my wife, Pat, for her understanding over the past four years. I know that I have spent time researching and writing that should have been devoted to her and household projects. Her uncomplaining support has truly made my work—and life—much more enjoyable.

To each and every individual I can only express my heartfelt thanks. Without their help—especially for the advice given over a four-year period—I doubt that this work would be the comprehensive, factual, and firsthand history it is. Thank you, each of you, for all of your help.

1775–1802

. . . a Military school for instructing the art of Gunnery, Fortification, Pyrotechny & every thing relative to the art of War.

HENRY BURBECK

1

The Foundation Is Laid

Although West Point today is known to almost every American, such has not always been true. Nearly two hundred years ago, a group of farsighted men struggled to establish a military academy. Opposing them were individuals who believed that state militias could handle any military emergency; after all, state forces had defeated the well-trained British regulars. Other opponents felt that such an institution would develop a military elite that could some day take over the government. Only after two disastrous defeats by the Indians, an internal insurrection, and a threat of war with France was there support for establishing an academy to prepare young Americans as professional military leaders.

The idea of a military academy can be traced almost to the very beginning of the Revolutionary War. The occupation of Boston by British army units in July 1774 resulted in the convening of the first Continental Congress in Philadelphia in September. In April 1775, colonists fired on British forces at Lexington and Concord. Massachusetts, realizing that it alone could not cope with the British forces, asked other colonies for help. In May, Ethan Allen captured the British fortress at Ticonderoga; in June, colonial forces severely mauled the British at Bunker Hill. When militia from several colonies gathered in Boston, Congress faced the serious problem of selecting a qualified officer to command these forces. After much discussion, George Washington was chosen.

Upon assuming command of the Continental Army in June 1775, Washington encountered the same problems he would face throughout the conflict with Great Britain: insufficient troops, inadequate military supplies, a shortage of funds, and a lack of trained, professional soldiers, especially officers. Despite congressional pressure, Washington could not take the offensive. He was forced to reorganize—actually, to organize—his forces.

Washington was especially handicapped by a lack of experienced, trained officers. Although a few officers had served in the British army, Charles Lee and Richard Montgomery for example, and many others had fought in the French and Indian wars, the majority were militiamen elected by the members of their units. Senior officers were appointed by state officials, often for political expediency. Washington's efforts to reorganize the colonial forces at Boston were complicated by the loyalty of troops to their home states. This, for example, prevented him from transferring officers from a Massachusetts regiment to a Connecticut unit despite the resolution of Congress taking all troops into service of, as Congress put it, the "United Colonies."

Another factor influencing Washington's organizational efforts was the short term of enlistments of state units, one year or less. Many soldiers, officers, and even complete units would depart when their period of service had been completed, regardless of the military situation. Although the British did not attack at Boston, other commanders were less fortunate than Washington; the disintegration of the American Army in Canada resulted in the failure to take Quebec.

Although there was abundant food to supply the troops around Boston, other supplies were lacking. Powder and lead were in extremely short supply. Powder was strictly rationed, so much so that for a time sentinels on a thirteen-mile ring within gunshot of British troops had no powder at all. Artillery of all types was needed. Clothing varied. Some regiments were in uniform; some wore buckskin tunics; but many officers and men had only their civilian clothing. Individual weapons differed from unit to unit and even from man to man. Better equipped units were armed with the same weapons. In others, men carried personal firearms and edged weapons. Although many men and officers were able to cast bullets for their weapons, others did not have the necessary bullet molds. The variety of weapons increased the difficulty of supplying the troops and often prevented any direct attack on the British. What was needed were trained officers who knew how to equip and feed an army.

Adding to Washington's problem was the variation of administrative practices in state units. Although most had adopted British regulations, there was little uniformity in administration. Some state contingents were well trained and disciplined; others were the exact opposite. Sanitation varied greatly, and medical care was almost nonexistent. What Congress considered to be an army was described by Washington in a February 1776 letter to Joseph Reed as "men without arms, without ammunition, without anything fit for accommodation of a soldier."

During his first months, Washington begged for men, arms, and powder while attempting to train and discipline those troops who remained long enough to learn at least the fundamentals. Frustrated, Washington wrote to Reed, "Could I have foreseen what I have, and am likely to experience, no consideration upon earth should have induced me to accept this command."

There was another reason for trained officers: the length of the war, which proved to be eight long years after Bunker Hill. Only disciplined officers who felt that they were members of a profession could take the humdrum, the obnoxious, the long periods of inactivity followed by sudden emergencies that often befell an army in a long war.

Although the colonists hoped that the British government would ease its policy toward the colonies, the opposite occurred. The British decided to increase the effort to reduce the rebellion by sending more troops and supplies. In addition to coping with organizational problems, Washington had to raise a force to compete with the increasing number of British regulars. Washington's plan called for incorporating state units in a "Congressional" or "Continental" army under direct jurisdiction of the Continental government instead of being under state control. The size of this army, 20,000 men and officers, would not be large enough to oppose the British forces; but Washington planned to ask the states to provide militia units.

Washington's reports to Congress in late 1775 and early 1776 stressed this need to train both officers and men. Although these American soldiers were not all that was desired, the deficiencies of officers were even greater. A few exceptional leaders at company and regimental levels provided a steadying influence, but leadership at all levels was generally indifferent. It was evident that developing good officers would be more difficult than providing well-trained soldiers.

In September 1776, Congress sent a committee to "inquire into the state of the army and the best means of supplying its wants." The committee report of October 3, 1776, in addition to agreeing to Washington's proposal, stated that "some of the troops in the Camp were badly officered, and not subject to the command which good troops ought ever to be. The Articles of War and General Orders were frequently transgressed, and the Commander-in-Chief had the mortification to see, that some of his officers, instead of suppressing disorderly behavior, encouraged soldiers by their examples to plunder and commit other offenses, or endeavored to screen them from just punishment by partial trials."

Among the many resolutions adopted by the committee was the first official recommendation concerning a military academy: "Resolved, That the Board of War be directed to prepare a Continental Laboratory, and a Military Academy, and provide the same with proper officers." This was a novel concept, one whose time had come, yet one that would have to wait passage for another quarter century, long after the end of the American Revolution.

During its visit to the Army headquarters at Newburgh, the committee had talked with Washington and many officers. Colonel Henry Knox, the Chief of Artillery, gave his recommendations for improving artillery, including his concern for officer education: "And as officers can never act with confidence until they are masters of their profession, an Academy established on a liberal plan would be of the utmost service to the Continent, where the whole theory and practice of fortification and gunnery should be taught; to be nearly on the same plan as that at Woolwich [the British artillery school], making allowance for the difference of circumstances; a place to which our enemies are indebted for the superiority of their artillery to all who have opposed them." Almost at the same time in Philadelphia, John Adams, never a soldier and always distrustful of the military, declared that a military academy was essential if "the United States is ever going to have a fighting force to be confided in."

Like other contemplative bodies, Congress responded by appointing another committee, albeit this time "to prepare and bring in a plan of a Military Academy at the Army." There is no indication that such a plan was ever submitted. Many early War Department records were burned in a November 1800 fire; early records at West Point were also destroyed by a fire that burned the Academic Building, which included the adjutant's office, in February 1838. Congressional records include no further mention of a military academy after appointment of the planning committee in 1776.

A Corps of Invalids, established in 1777 to care for and, if possible, to employ disabled veterans, had the additional task of functioning as "a school for propagating military knowledge and discipline." The Corps of Invalids guarded supplies in Philadelphia and Boston until ordered to West Point in 1781 to assist artillery units garrisoning the fortifications. There is no indication that it ever met its schooling requirement.

General Washington continued to be plagued by shortages of supplies and ammunition. The short enlistments of state units constantly affected the size and efficiency of his army, but there was a gradual lessening of the need for officers, especially those schooled to meet the technical requirements of artillery and engineers. The arrival of experienced volunteers from Europe provided the cadre required to train their American counterparts. Von Steuben, Kosciuszko, Pulaski, De Kalb, Du Portail, and others filled this requirement of Washington's army. Unfortunately, many other eager European volunteers had little qualification other than a noble title. Congress nevertheless was generous in giving them commissions, passing over qualified American officers. Among them was Benedict Arnold, an outstanding combat leader whose discontent led to treason.

Assisted by the volunteers and trained in the school of combat, the American Army matured and improved. The arrival of French troops in 1779 and continued errors of the British brought an end to the struggle after eight long years of conflict.

In April 1783, Washington asked his officers at Newburgh and New Windsor to submit recommendations for a peacetime military establishment. Many of the voluminous reports included comments on the need for a military academy. With the coming of peace, the emerging history of West Point took a turn from being a dire need to a period of analysis and thoughtful reexamination. Without the pressures of the Revolution, it was possible to consider the need for a professional corps of officers. Gradually, this concept was expanded to include the establishment of an academy to train these officers.

The eventual founding of an academy owed much to the recommendations submitted to Washington. Brigadier General Ebenezer Huntington, who had served as an infantry officer since 1775 and who would continue in service until his retirement in 1800, urged that the fortifications at West Point be continued in a state of readiness and that the installation be used as a depot for arms and munitions, and "with a small additional expense, an academy might be here instituted for instruction in all branches of the military art." Although some officers advocated the establishment of academies at various arsenals throughout the United States, the Quartermaster General, Colonel Thomas Pickering, disagreed vehemently, stating that "it might be expedient to establish a military school or academy at West Point. . . . Those students should be instructed in what is usually called military discipline, tactics, and the theory and practice of fortification and gunnery. The Commandant and one or two other officers of the standing regiment and the Engineers, making West Point their general residence, would be masters of the Academy; and the Inspector General superintend the whole."

Steuben offered a far more comprehensive proposal based upon three academies: one at West Point, and two in other parts of the country. Each would provide instruction in natural and experimental philosophy (physics and mechanics), eloquence and "belle lettres," civil law, the law of nations, history and geography, mathematics, civil architecture, drawing, French, horsemanship, fencing, dancing, and music. Students were to be prepared for infantry, cavalry, artillery, or engineer service. Strangely, Steuben's proposal did not make it mandatory for any graduate to enter the Army.

Washington's report included his own recommendations, summarized as "Sentiments on a Peace Establishment." He listed four specifics:

> First: A regular and standing force . . . as . . . necessary to awe the Indians, protect our Trade, prevent encroachments . . . guard us . . . from surprises. . . .
> Secondly: A well-organized Militia; upon a Plan that will pervade all the States, and introduce similarity in their Establishment, Manoeuvres, Exercises, and Arms.
> Thirdly: Establishing Arsenals of all kinds for Military Stores.
> Fourthly: Academies, one or more for the Instruction of the Art Military.

Congress was struggling with far more serious and timely problems involving the discharge of the Continental Army and ignored Washington's recommendations. Attempting to provide an interim solution, it proposed that troops be furloughed with a promise of financial settlement. A settlement was important to both men and officers. Many had not been paid in months, some not for years. Washington's recommendation concerning retired pay was disregarded because any military payment was complicated by the necessity of lessening the debt incurred during the conflict and the need to establish some way to raise money without depending on state assistance.

This congressional inaction caused dissension in the Army. An address prepared by officers at Newburgh carried a threat that the Army might not disband if its demands were not met by Congress, a threat made ominous by the statement, "If peaceful requests should fail, the Army could march west and defy Congress to destroy it." Washington stopped this effort by a personal appeal; officers voted to let him handle the problem. When his report about this episode arrived, Congress acted immediately by giving officers full pay for five years and enlisted men full pay for four months.

Even this action failed to completely satisfy the troops. Congress hesitated to furlough the troops before peace terms had been signed; this caused more problems. Groups of enlisted men demanded some payment before leaving for home penniless, as Washington stated, as "a sett of beggars." Officers asked for some financial payment. Congress finally approved furloughs for most officers and enlisted men. The desire to go home prevailed over demands for immediate payment, and the Continental Army dispersed, leaving only 700 men available for garrison duty. These events added to the existing antagonism toward and fear of a regular army.

Facing Congress was the question of determining what permanent military establishment was necessary. A committee chaired by Alexander Hamilton reviewed the problem, relying primarily on the advice and recommendations of Washington and Steuben, although their belief in a strong permanent force was known. There was little doubt that Congress would not agree to the establishment of a large regular military force. Memories of British regulars before and during the Revolution were still too fresh to be forgotten. Problems encountered in disbanding the Continental Army had increased fear and distrust of a standing army. The new nation faced a severe financial crisis. There was opposition from those who maintained that British regulars had been defeated by state forces placed under federal control and that these state forces could be used again.

Washington, Steuben, and Hamilton's committee were extremely conservative in recommending the size of a regular army. Washington recommended a force of about 2,600 men to defend against Indians on the frontier and a navy to guard the coast. This force would be backed by a militia consisting of men between the ages of eighteen and fifty. Steuben's recommendations were similar. The report submitted by the Hamilton committee incorporated the Washington and Steuben proposals. Even this skeleton organization was rejected. Instead, Congress decided that the states would provide whatever forces were required.

On June 1, 1784, Congress, ever antagonistic toward establishing any military force, directed the senior officer remaining on duty, Henry Knox, to discharge all men and officers other than 55 at West Point and 25 at Fort Pitt, despite the fact that the total strength of the Army was less than 700 men and officers. Fortunately, common sense prevailed, and the next day a resolution was passed calling on four states—Connecticut, New Jersey, New York, and Pennsylvania—to provide state troops to protect the northwest frontier. Only Pennsylvania met its quota.

Not until almost a year later did it become apparent that state units enlisted

for only twelve months could not protect the frontier. Despite still strong antagonism toward a regular army, Congress in April 1785 authorized a "body of
troops consisting of 700 noncommissioned officers and privates to be raised for
a term of three years, unless sooner discharged, for the protection of the Northwest frontiers, to defend the settlers on land belonging to the United States from
the depredations of the Indians and to prevent unwarrantable intrusion thereon,
and for guarding the public stores." In October 1786, it authorized an additional
1,340 troops. Once again, the source was the states, and again the result was
failure. Only two companies of artillery were formed. The entire army of less
than 1,000 men was scattered in small forts on the frontier and in a few eastern
arsenals and fortifications.

One of the eastern posts was West Point, a major depot for weapons, ammunition, and other supplies. Another was a new arsenal at Springfield, Massachusetts, a pet project of Henry Knox, then Secretary of War. Remembering
the problems that he had faced in obtaining cannon and ammunition as Washington's Chief of Artillery, he had advocated the development of a foundry,
magazine, and storage depot at Springfield. The Arsenal became the focal point
of danger in December 1786 when malcontents forced the Massachusetts Supreme Court to adjourn to prevent the collection of debts and to resist taxation
under state laws. Led by Daniel Shays, 2,000 rebellious resisters moved against
the Arsenal, hoping to obtain arms. No federal troops were available. Militia
units commanded by General William Shepherd, using artillery from the Arsenal
without federal approval, put down the rebellion.

Shays' Rebellion was a shock to Congress and the entire nation. It was apparent to Knox and other supporters of a strong regular army that the United
States was not only too weak to oppose any enemy, it was not even strong
enough to prevent internal disorder. This episode strengthened efforts to replace
the Articles of Confederation with a stronger government.

The discussions leading to the new Constitution in 1787 were perhaps vehement when involving military matters. Delegates favoring a strong central
government supported the need for a regular army, while those favoring state
control opposed such a force. Opponents again played on fear of a standing
army and emphasized that militia had defeated British regulars. A proposal to
include in the Constitution a provision limiting the regular army to no more
than 2,000 men was unsuccessful. Washington, in an aside, suggested an amendment that would make it unconstitutional for an enemy to attack with any larger
force. The military provisions of the Constitution were a compromise that divided control of the military between Congress and the President. One of the
most important changes designated the President as Commander in Chief; the
Secretary of War was responsible to the President, not to Congress. Federal
advocates were satisfied, but state forces capable of being used during an emergency were also authorized. The Army was to be backed in a traditional manner
by the citizen soldier, the "Minute Man."

After ratification of the Constitution by the states, there was no immediate change in the existing military structure. Knox continued as Secretary of War; the Army was maintained at slightly more than 700 men, with the capability of calling for state troops. In April 1790, the Army was increased to 1,216 men. This force soon proved insufficient to counter Indian problems on the northwestern frontiers, and 1,500 state militia were called into service. In a major engagement in Ohio, the combined force was badly mauled. Regular units proved to be reliable; militia troops did not. As a result, a second infantry regiment was authorized; and, in late 1791, a second campaign was undertaken against the Indians, again with militia added to the regular force. The result was disastrous. The militia fled; regular troops, standing fast, were decimated. The Indians inflicted over 50 percent casualties.

Two successive disasters led to a more realistic army strength of 5,000 men and officers organized as a "Legion" under the command of Anthony Wayne. Instead of the traditional separate infantry, artillery, and cavalry, the Legion's four sublegions each included infantry, dragoon, rifle, and artillery units. Each was a combined arms team capable of operating separately. After a period of intensive training in tactics and field fortification, Wayne led his troops and 1,600 Kentucky militia against the Indians, defeating them in August 1794 at the battle of Fallen Timbers near present-day Toledo, Ohio.

During this entire period, there was little effort to establish a military academy despite the need for professional training of engineers and artillerymen. Instead, foreign officers with the required expertise received commissions. Fortifications on the East Coast were improved, and new forts were built under the guidance of foreign engineers. By this time, Forts Putnam and Clinton and other Revolutionary War fortifications at West Point were in poor shape. Only work on Fort Putnam was authorized. New and higher walls were constructed, and nine bombproof arches were erected over the barracks and magazine. Stone replaced the wood and earthen walls of the Revolutionary War. Restoration was never completed; Congress did not provide the required funds.

Although the need for training American officers was recognized, fear of a military elite nullified efforts to establish military schools. President Washington, intending to include a recommendation for a national military academy in his December 1793 message to Congress, encountered Jefferson's argument that such an institution would be unconstitutional. Washington nevertheless included such a suggestion, remarking that "a material feature in the improvement of the system of military defence ought to afford an opportunity for the study of those branches of the [military] art which can scarcely ever be obtained by practice alone." To provide troops to garrison the new and improved installations, a Corps of Artillerists and Engineers was authorized in 1794 with four battalions, each with eight cadets in addition to officers and enlisted men. The intent was to bring young men into service as cadets, train them, and then commission them as lieutenants. The Secretary of War was directed to procure books, instruments, and apparatus for the unit. Although there was no mention that a military academy was to be established, it would appear that such was the intent. At least one company and often as many as four (one battalion) were stationed at West Point. The scant records available do indicate that there was instruction at West Point in the Revolutionary War "Old Provost" building near Execution Hollow.

Without any documentary evidence, one can only guess what the curriculum was. Consulting artillery manuals of the period, there is reason to believe that cadets—and young officers as well—were not only taught how to fire cannon but also how to make powder, forge metal parts of artillery carriages, make wooden carriages, and train matrosses and artificers. Engineering instruction was probably limited to the construction of simple fortifications capable of being built on the western frontier.

Once again, there was reliance upon foreign expertise and French artillerymen or engineers were commissioned as the senior officers of the new unit. Stephen Rochefontaine became lieutenant colonel; Lewis de Tousard, John Rivardi, Constant Freeman, and Henry Burbeck, majors. Only Freeman and Burbeck were Americans. Junior officers, cadets, and enlisted men were primarily American.

The weakness of having French senior officers became apparent when relations with France deteriorated as French efforts to enlist American support against England intensified. France disrupted American shipping and imprisoned ship crews. American efforts to negotiate a treaty with France, similar to the Jay Treaty with Britain, failed. War with France was not only possible but appeared imminent. In April 1798, at President John Adams' request, Congress provided funds for expanding coastal fortifications, building a navy, and organizing a second regiment of Artillerists and Engineers. It empowered the President to appoint no more than four teachers of the arts and sciences to instruct cadets of the two regiments of Artillerists and Engineers, fifty-six cadets in all. Burbeck replaced Rochefontaine as commander of the 1st Regiment of Artillerists and Engineers. Tousard was retained, although most of the other French officers were discharged. Many of the artillery companies were stationed on the frontier. Burbeck was with two companies at Fort Mackinac when promoted to command his regiment.

The new second regiment increased requirements for training newly commissioned officers and cadets. Some training was undoubtedly on-the-job learning by experience; but the number of students at the small school at West Point increased. For a time, the entire second regiment was stationed there while men were uniformed and trained in the basic school of the soldier. They were taught infantry movements as well as artillery drill, for artillery companies on the frontier fought as infantry more often than as artillerymen.

The physical appearance of the post had changed little since the Revolutionary War. The small hamlet of Buttermilk Falls was a mile south of the post, but no roads connected West Point with towns to the north or south. Contact with the outside world was by water. Boats docked at the small point below and east of the present site of Eisenhower Hall. Near the landing were warehouses and storage buildings that stored the chain that had stretched across the Hudson narrows to Constitution Island during the war and many captured British weapons, including cannon taken at Saratoga. Magazines at Fort Clinton and, later, at Constitution Island held a vast quantity of powder. Although perishable supplies were moved to the upper level of today's Plain, other materials were kept in a quartermaster building near the dock and issued as required.

This was not an efficient arrangement; it was dictated by the capacity of the steep and narrow path to the upper area and by the lack of draft animals. Anything that had to be taken to the upper area was moved by manpower—including a few cannon. The path reached the upper level where the Commandant's residence now stands. A small knoll was to the right of the path, and to the northwest were a storage building and sheds. Closer to the head of the path were other structures, including a guardhouse and a makeshift hospital. A short distance from the path lay the ruins of a Revolutionary War barracks.

The level ground of the present Plain was covered with low, yellow-pine trees, none higher than twelve feet. Areas had been cleared near buildings, and there were small drill fields near the barracks. The ground was pockmarked by small knolls and hollows. The largest, both in area and depth, was southwest of the present location of Battle Monument. Still known as "Execution Hollow," it had been used for executions during the Revolutionary War. The wartime prison, known as the "Old Provost," on the western edge was used for classes until it was destroyed by fire in 1796, possibly by discontented student officers.

A few buildings from the Revolutionary War period extended along the foot of the bluff on the western edge of the level area, not in a regimented row but sprinkled randomly in a north-south direction. The largest, the "Academy," built after the Old Provost was destroyed, was on the site of the present Superintendent's Quarters. A pond, fed by a stream that trickled down the hill below Fort Putnam, was south of the Academy. A small headquarters building was on the eastern side of the pond. The last and largest set of officer's quarters in this haphazard row, used by the senior officer of the garrison, was on the site of the present Cadet Store. Small buildings, including a laboratory, extended from this house to a "model yard" near the present Bartlett Hall. Wooden models, made by Rochefontaine and Rivardi, were used to demonstrate different types of fortifications and artillery siege techniques.

Behind these structures, a tumbledown wall extended from the storage buildings near the river, behind the ruined barracks and the row of officers' quarters, to the senior officer's house. From here, the wall extended east to the edge of the bluff, falling down to the river. Immediately south of the wall stood North's tavern and a store. The area enclosed by the wall marked the limits of the Revolutionary War post, although Fort Putnam and several redoubts were well outside the wall. The land within the wall did not become government property until 1790 when the Moore lands, granted by patent in 1746, and the Congreve lands, granted in 1733, were purchased at a total cost of $11,000. The purchase was approved by Congress, not with the intent that a military academy should be located at West Point but to provide an arsenal and storage depot for weapons and ammunition.

During the years from 1796 to 1800, funds were provided for renovation or replacement of the Revolutionary War buildings. A new academic building was erected to replace the structure that burned in 1796. A new barracks was erected near Execution Hollow. Warehouses and other buildings were built to house supplies and arms. Magazines were incorporated in the Fort Clinton casemates, and more than 1,000 barrels of powder were moved into these magazines from Constitution Island. Forts and redoubts were strengthened and repaired. Cannon were emplaced at Forts Putnam and Clinton and on Constitution Island. The garrison at West Point varied from one company to a full regiment. From time to time, units from other posts replaced some of the troops at West Point to provide better training for all components of the two regiments of Artillerists and Engineers. Part of the training for officers included academic instruction in both artillery and infantry tactics, using the Steuben manual for infantry maneuvers.

Duty at West Point, except for academic instruction, was similar to duty at any other post of that time. Most of the day was devoted to training. There were formal parades and ceremonies. Guard mount was held daily in front of the flag pole at Fort Clinton. The pole was erected in 1795 when the Secretary of War for the first time authorized a flag to be flown at West Point. The flag was received with ceremony and flown from sunrise to sunset. Morning and evening guns were fired as the flag was raised or lowered.

The band, which varied in size and in its instruments depending upon the number of units in the garrison, played at parades and ceremonies. The band of the 1st Regiment of Artillerists and Engineers, supported by monetary subscription by the officers, had twenty members dressed in scarlet jackets with dark blue facings and yellow epaulets, black gaiters, and helmets with scarlet plumes. Band uniforms followed the British custom of reversing the color of the coats worn by troops. In artillery units, the jackets of both men and officers were dark blue with scarlet facings. Each artillery company had its assigned "field music," fifes and drums. In January 1799, the field music of four companies of the 1st Regiment of Artillerists and Engineers, then the West Point garrison, were ordered to "beat the assembly" on the south side of the barracks. The "Hell Cats" reveille apparently outdates the actual establishment of the U.S. Military Academy by several years!

The hair of men and officers was powdered. A May 1796 requisition asked for flour to be used as hair powder by the men; one can imagine the result on a very hot day or if it rained during a formation! The Fourth of July and Washington's Birthday were observed with artillery salutes and music, and an extra gill of liquor was issued to each man. Military justice was prompt—and severe. A regimental court martial sentenced one soldier to be punished with the "water cure." An officer who killed another officer in a duel was merely cashiered.

Little recreation was available for the soldiers. Fishing, hunting, and hiking filled many leisure hours. A "bathing place" was established near the warehouses. Although the nearest community was Buttermilk Falls a mile south of the post, there was at least one tavern immediately beyond the southern wall of the military reservation. Soldiers lived in the old Revolutionary War barracks or in the new barracks completed in 1796. There was a small hospital, a contractor's store, and a building for bachelor officers. The daily ration allowance was 15.5 cents per man per day.

Experiments were conducted in the Revolutionary War laboratory building. Supply records for the laboratory indicate that experiments related primarily to testing powder and shot. The quality of instruction for cadets and officers depended on the abilities and experience of officers of the garrison for the four teachers approved in 1794 had not been appointed. From time to time, officers with special qualifications were ordered to West Point as instructors. For example, Colonel Henry Burbeck ordered Lieutenant Steven Worrell of the 2nd Regiment of Artillerists and Engineers to West Point as an instructor. Drawing, fortification engineering, ordnance techniques, and some French were included, even at this early date. The ability to at least read French was essential, for most of the artillery and engineering texts available were written by French officers.

While this infant military school was developing, the Army was experiencing constant increases and decreases in its size and number of units. In 1792, the Army was reorganized as a legion with four sublegions totaling 4,800 men and officers. The legion was abolished in 1796 and replaced by four regiments of Infantry, two companies of Light Dragoons, and the two regiments of Artillerists and Engineers of four battalions of four companies each. The reorganization decreased Army strength by nearly 2,000 officers and men. War Department orders separating officers specified that they be "deranged"! A later order directed that officers be separated, not deranged. Officers separated received six months' pay and allowances.

The threat of war with France in April 1798 brought an increase of three additional regiments of Artillerists and Engineers. Twelve regiments of Infantry and six companies of Light Dragoons were added in July. The eight companies of Light Dragoons were consolidated into a regiment, the first mounted regiment of the new Army. This force was increased again in 1799 by twenty-four regiments of infantry, another regiment of Artillerists and Engineers, and three mounted regiments. This, however, was only a paper force that was never mustered because the threatened war never materialized.

In the midst of strained relations with France, a group of irate taxpayers in eastern Pennsylvania rebelled against the war tax. With only a force of 500 regulars available, President John Adams called on the Pennsylvania militia to help quell the insurrection. The rebellion emphasized the need for an adequate regular force capable of meeting internal unrest as well as countering any foreign threat.

By early 1800, diplomatic negotiations ended the trouble with France. All of the temporary forces were discharged; nearly 3,400 men and officers were dismissed and the Army reduced to four Infantry regiments, two regiments of Artillerists and Engineers, and two troops of Light Dragoons. After four years of frenzied increases, the Army was at the exact authorized strength with which it had started. This reorganization resulted in the recall of Colonel Burbeck, Commander of the 1st Regiment of Artillerists and Engineers, from Fort Mackinac, Michigan, to become Chief of Artillery in command of both regiments of Artillerists and Engineers. Burbeck had served with Revolutionary War artillery and was a major when the war ended. He realized early the necessity of educating Army officers. In a letter written to Henry Knox on April 17, 1782, Burbeck discussed the need for discipline and proficiency of officers and stressed the importance of formal training. He had entered the new Army as a captain in 1786, was promoted to major, and became commander of his regiment in 1798 when Rochefontaine was discharged. In December 1800, Burbeck assumed command of all troops on the eastern seaboard, reporting directly to the Secretary of War. This channel was to prove an advantage to Burbeck, for the new Secretary of War, Henry Dearborn, was an old friend. Dearborn and Burbeck had served together during the Revolution and maintained contact afterward.

One of the first tasks faced by Burbeck was building his two regiments to full strength. Realizing that many of the Infantry and Dragoon officers "deranged" during the mass discharges in 1800 represented a pool of trained talent, Burbeck commissioned many of them as lieutenants in his regiments. Nearly half of the artillery lieutenants commissioned from 1799 to 1802 had served with other branches during the French crisis. All required retraining to serve as artillerymen. Burbeck's solution was to send them to West Point for schooling. He had been stationed there several times and had observed the attempts to educate young officers and cadets. The school needed strengthening; Burbeck provided that by assigning qualified officers from his two regiments as instructors. His first selection was Captain William Amherst Barron, a graduate of Harvard and classmate of John Quincy Adams. Barron, however, was in charge of engineer construction at Portsmouth, New Hampshire, and the transfer would have delayed completion of the harbor project. Burbeck therefore assigned Lieutenants Stephen Worrell and Peter Dransey as assistant instructors to George Baron, the acting Professor of Mathematics. President Adams had appointed Baron teacher of the arts and sciences for the regiments of Artillerists and Engineers, filling one of the four instructor positions authorized in the Act of 1798.

The position of superintendent was offered to Benjamin Thompson, Count Rumford of Bavaria, a Massachusetts Tory who had served in the British army. Known for his experiments with artillery, heat, and chemistry, Thompson had established a military school in Bavaria. He did not accept the offer. To supervise school activities and specifically to develop a course of instruction, Burbeck then ordered Lieutenant Colonel Lewis Tousard to West Point from the laboratory at Frankford Arsenal in Philadelphia.

Burbeck's close relationship with Secretary Dearborn enabled him to resubmit recommendations he had made to the previous secretary concerning the organization of the two regiments of Artillerists and Engineers. Included was a strong statement concerning the establishment of a military academy "for instructing the arts of gunnery, fortification, pyrotechny, and everything relative to the art of war; and that there be taken from the line of artillerists and engineers one field officer and four captains well versed in science, especially in mathematics and natural philosophy, to be employed in superintending the laboratory and instructing the officers of the line and the cadets, whom the commanding officer of each separate district shall send, in rotation, for the purpose of being instructed; and that the whole superintendency and instruction be afforded by these officers. That the said field officer be, ex officio, Inspector of Artillery & Fortifications, & have, as his assistants, the said Captains."

Burbeck included recommendations for establishing an ordnance laboratory and a small corps of engineers "continually to be increased in number as the exigencies of the Country shall require & be separate from the artillerists."

Secretary of War Dearborn fully supported Burbeck's efforts. Tousard's assignment was one result. As Inspector of Artillery, he was directed to "give all the assistance in your power in the instruction of such officers and cadets as may be at West Point for the purpose of learning their duty. Such ordnance materials and apparatus, as may be necessary for experiments in Gunnery, may at all times be used under your direction, or by such other person as may be appointed as a Teacher to the Officers and Cadets at that Post."

During the early months of 1801, Burbeck's correspondence with subordinate commanders included comments about the school and its proposed students. A letter to Major Constant Freeman, who commanded a battalion at Charleston, stated, "As to Cadets, I am not in favor of appointing any to companies. I think they ought to be appointed by the Secy of War & put to school to learn every Branch of their duty." Burbeck's idea was not adopted until 1812; cadets continued to be assigned to companies. Muster rolls showed cadets "on command at West Point," the equivalent of a temporary duty assignment in today's army.

An April 1801 letter to the commanding officer at West Point, informing him of Tousard's appointment with station at West Point, stated, "It is contemplated to establish a Military School at West Point." It soon became apparent that Tousard's duties would involve frequent travel. Major Jonathan Williams, assigned to the 2nd Regiment of Artillerists and Engineers, was ordered to report to the school. The order indicated that President Thomas Jefferson had been consulted, for it stated: "The President having decided in favor of the immediate establishment of a Military School at West Point, and also on the appointment of Major Jonathan Williams as Inspector of Fortifications, it becomes necessary for the major to be at West Point as soon as possible for the purpose of directing the necessary arrangements at that place for the commencement of the school." This order provides the first indication that Jefferson had dropped his opposition to a military academy. Another letter to Major Freeman instructed him to provide his cadets with a newly designed uniform and pay them because "The Secretary is making arrangements to establish a Military School at West Point where all cadets will be ordered for instruction."

Improvements were ordered to prepare buildings at West Point for the expected influx of officer and cadet students and the faculty. Quarters for staff and faculty and a barracks for cadets were to be renovated, but "No expense must be incurred that shall not be actually necessary to render the . . . buildings comfortable; outside painting should be attended to on the score of economy." It is apparent that War Department funds had not included any appropriation for the institution of a military school. Troops, including the band of the 2nd Regiment, were ordered to West Point to support the new school activities.

One order established a military chain of command that was to be a problem for many years. The senior officer of troops present was to command both the troops and the post; the superintendent of the school was not to have any jurisdiction over the garrison.

A War Department order of July 24, 1801, directed *all* cadets and selected junior officers of the 2nd Regiment of Artillerists and Engineers to "repair to West Point by the first of September next." Cadets and officers of the 1st Regiment had already been given similar orders; many had already reported for duty. Burbeck explained these orders to Major Freeman: "It is the determination of the Secretary of War that Cadets shall receive some instruction relative to their duty before they receive an appointment, and for that reason, he has ordered them to West Point to attend a military school, which he is about establishing."

The twelve companies of 1st Regiment already at West Point had a total authorized strength of eighteen officers and twenty-four cadets. Orderly books indicate that most officers were present, but that fewer than half of the cadets authorized were assigned. Students performed other duties in addition to attending class. Even cadets were required to serve as junior officers. An orderly book of one company indicates that Cadet Joseph Cross was detailed as Judge Advocate for a court martial. Cadets drew supplies for their companies from the post quartermaster and served as officers of the guard.

As each company in the two regiments was authorized two cadets, there would have been a total of fifty-six cadets if all spaces had been filled. The destruction of both early War Department and West Point records makes it difficult to determine what officers and cadets actually reported for instruction. Letters, memoirs, and some unit returns do provide some names.

Burbeck's papers, acquired by the West Point Library in 1987, provide much information about students of the 1799–1802 period. Lieutenants Alexander Macomb, Lewis Howard, Robert Osborn, Robert Parkinson, James Rand, George Ross, Thomas Van Dyke, and James Wilson are known to have reported as students in 1800–1801. Cadets ordered to "repair" to West Point included Walker K. Armistead, Silas Clark, Joseph Cross, Samuel Gates, William Gates, Henry B. Jackson, Louis Landais, Simon M. Levy, John Lillie, William Murray, Ambrose Porter, Joseph Proveaux, Joseph G. Swift, and Josiah Taylor. One other cadet was appointed in March 1801 but not ordered to West Point: Joseph B. Wilkinson, a sophomore at Princeton. Other cadets may have been ordered to report. Several company muster reports in the Burbeck papers indicate cadets "on command at West Point" without providing names. Eight student officers and fourteen cadets can definitely be identified by name.

Apparently, more than the fourteen cadets reported. From 1795 to 1797, at least three battalions of the Corps of Artillerists and Engineers were stationed at West Point; each battalion consisted of four companies; each company was authorized two cadets. Twenty- four cadets would have been present if all spaces were filled. The number of companies at West Point diminished in 1798 and 1799, with only three or four assigned. In 1800, Burbeck apparently had the entire second regiment moved to West Point, four battalions each with four companies. If all cadets had been appointed, thirty-two cadets might have been enrolled. In addition, most of the junior officers were required to attend classes.

One of the difficulties of determining the actual number of cadets at West Point in the early years is that no consolidated register of students was maintained. Cadets and student officers were carried only on rolls of companies. Very few musters or orderly books survived the West Point and War Department fires. There is an indication that many commanders retained reports from subordinate units, probably consolidating these reports before forwarding them to the War Department. The Burbeck papers contain many company musters that were submitted to Burbeck as regimental commander.

Another indication that more than fourteen cadets were expected is found in the renovations directed in May 1801 by Secretary Dearborn who ordered barracks to be prepared for twenty-five cadets. A letter from Tousard to Colonel Burbeck in September asked for additional troop support since "a Military School would in my opinion require a more respectable company." Tousard emphasized, "A great number of cadets are here and more are expected." One reason for the additional troops was Tousard's belief that additional men were required to serve as waiters for cadets and staff officers. Not to be ignored are the cadets authorized for Infantry regiments and troops of Dragoons, a total of forty for the Infantry and four for the Dragoons. There is, however, no definite indication that infantry or dragoon cadets were ordered to West Point at this time.

Regiments of the different branches were authorized a different number of cadets. Infantry regiments had ten cadets. There was no dragoon regiment; only two troops existed, each with two cadets. Because of their technical duties, each Artillerist and Engineer regiment was authorized thirty-two cadets.

The fourteen cadets known to have reported were an interesting group, a cross-section of the officer corps. Several were sons of officers: Samuel and William Gates, Henry Jackson, and John Lillie. Some had been appointed from enlisted ranks: Simon Levy had been a sergeant and Josiah Taylor sergeant major in the 1st Infantry Regiment; Silas Clark a sergeant and Ambrose Porter sergeant major in the 2nd Regiment of Artillerists and Engineers. Swift had been appointed directly from civil life. Lillie's father, Major John Lillie, had commanded the West Point garrison until his death in September 1801, shortly before his son's appointment. Lillie was the youngest of the group, ten years and seven months old at the time of his appointment.

Lewis Landais had been born in France; his brother, Philip, had also been a cadet until commissioned in 1796. No information has been found concerning their education or reason for coming to the United States. Their father may have been an engineer during the Revolutionary War, but this cannot be verified. Their appointments as cadets and commissioning as lieutenants is another indication of the reliance upon foreign-born officers in technical assignments.

Colonel Tousard had developed a proposed curriculum, and classes officially began on September 1, 1801. The school must have provided instruction in subjects not directly related to the artillery or even to engineering. An orderly book of an artillery and engineer company at West Point gave the password for August 5, 1796, as "electricity"; for October 17, the password was "astronomy"; for July 20, 1797, "philosophy." Might not one consider this a forerunner of modern West Point "plebe knowledge"?

A requisition of June 14, 1796, signed by Tousard as commander of the garrison, asked for one ream of extra folio paper, two dozen pieces of red tape (Army administration required documents to be bound and sealed with red tape; hence the term "bound up in red tape"), four pewter ink stands, six boxes of wafers (probably red wax wafers used to seal tape about a document), and twelve papers of thinning sand. A receipt also signed by Tousard acknowledged the delivery of 1,796 round shot for 32-pound cannon.

A February 1796 memorandum required officers and cadets to "attend in the Study Room" from 11:00 A.M. to noon and from 4:00 to 5:00 P.M. "to receive the first lecture on Theorical [theoretical] part of Fortification." The memorandum indicates the instruction given and the methods used:

> The morning meeting will be spent in explaining the different principles of Fortification and copying the author (Mr. Muller) [The text referred to is John Muller's *A Treatise Containing the Elementary Part of Fortifications* . . . , London: 1793]. In the afternoon officers will draw the plans relative to the explanation given in the morning. The officers will be furnished in the Room with pen, ink and paper in the morning and the books from which the study is originated. In the afternoon they will be provided with paper, pencil, ruler and mathematical instruments for drawing. Mr. Warren, Tem'y. Engineer, will attend the evening sitting and will explain the principles of Drawing. The officers may meet an hour sooner if they please for their own information. The rule to be observed in the Room for the preservation of good order will be that the senior officer present will be the Moderator and will preserve over the other officers that superiority, which military subordination has established among military men.

Another memorandum dated June 26, 1797, required lieutenants to attend instruction at the model yard daily. Captains were directed to "take turns to

Instruct the Gentlemen in the exercise of the field pieces, Howitzers, Mortars, Seacoast pieces, etc."

Some officer students resented being required to study and refused to attend class; Professor Baron reported them to the Secretary of War. Dearborn then informed Colonel Burbeck that "some subalterns, who were ordered to that post for the purpose refuse to attend and receive the instructions offered them by the wisdom of the government. Its importance and usefull [sic] designs must not be permitted to be frustrated in this manner. The instruction offered in the Academy is necessary for an officer, and those who will continue to refuse it must be considered unfit for the service. You will please to take order accordingly."

Burbeck sent a copy of the letter to Tousard with instructions to see that discipline was firmly established. He added his own comments, "I am exceedingly surprised that any officer should refuse attending any institution that would give him insight in his profession. I should rather suppose that they would attend with alacrity and be happy in an opportunity to improve themselves in their duty as artillery officers. It is the determination of the Secretary of War that the officers shall be detailed from the two Regiments of Artillery in rotation for the purpose of Instruction and should any officer refuse to attend so useful [an] establishment, you will report him to me."

Another incident was more serious. Cadet Swift, welcomed by Lieutenants William Wilson and Lewis Howard when he reported for duty in October 1801, was asked to join the Artillery mess. Apparently this was not acceptable to Professor Baron, who sent a servant to direct Swift to mess with other cadets. Swift refused to follow instructions given by a servant. Baron went to the Artillery mess and asked Swift if he had refused to obey orders. Swift replied, "No, sir, but I refuse to receive a verbal order by any servant." Baron called Swift a mutinous young rascal. Swift sprang at Baron, intending to strike him; and Baron ran to his quarters and locked the door. Charges were preferred that could have resulted in Swift's dismissal.

In the interim, Baron was charged with conduct unbecoming an officer, tried by court martial, and discharged. Swift was also tried, found guilty of using disrespectful words to his superior officer and admonished but returned to duty. Had this decision not been reached, Swift would not have been the first graduate of the U.S. Military Academy after its establishment in 1802.

Jonathan Williams, in charge of the school from May 1801 until the Military Academy was established in 1802, described it in an 1808 report to Congress: "The institution was established at West Point in the year 1801, under the direction of a private citizen, and was nothing more than a mathematical school for the few cadets that were then in service. It was soon found that the government of young military men was incompatible with the ordinary system of schools, and, consequently, this institution ran into disorder, and the teacher into contempt." Williams undoubtedly referred to the earlier refusal of some officers to attend class and to Baron's dismissal.

Williams was unduly harsh in his assessment that the institution was only a mathematical school. Fortification and drawing were also taught. Tousard, when at West Point between visits to other artillery installations, instructed cadets and student officers in French. There was training in artillery and infantry tactics and techniques. The student body was small, but no smaller than that of the new academy in 1802.

Four of the known fourteen cadets from the Burbeck school—Cross, Landais, Murray, and Taylor—were commissioned in 1801, all in the regiments of Artillerists and Engineers. One, Silas Clark, was discharged. The remaining nine continued their studies after 1802. Seven of them graduated from the U.S. Military Academy: Swift and Levy, the first two graduates in the Class of 1802; Armistead and Jackson in 1803; Samuel Gates in 1804; and William Gates and Proveaux in 1806. Lillie and Porter were discharged in 1805. Landais in a letter to Colonel Burbeck thanked him for his commission as lieutenant in the 1st Regiment of Artillerists and Engineers, stating, "I have already served almost three years as a cadet."

Henry Burbeck has received no recognition for his role in establishing the military school at West Point. As a young captain in 1782, he had urged Henry Knox to consider establishing a school to professionally educate officers. As the senior artilleryman, he realized the need for trained artillerymen and engineers in his two regiments and started the school using only his regimental resources. His close friendship with Secretary of War Dearborn enabled him to persuade the Secretary to order cadets to West Point in 1801. His efforts convinced President Jefferson that a military academy should be established. His recommendation that engineers be made a separate branch was incorporated in the Act of 1802. Burbeck's conviction that all cadets should attend the academy before being commissioned did not become law until 1812. His belief that Artillery and Engineer officers required scientific and technical training not available in colleges of that period was the basis for establishing the small academy for cadets of the two regiments of Artillerists and Engineers. The existence of this academy, small as it was, made it easier to convince the President that a national military academy was a vital necessity for a professional army. Sylvanus Thayer is honored as the "Father of the Military Academy." Perhaps Henry Burbeck deserves to be called its godfather.

March 16, 1802, has been accepted as the date of the founding of the U.S. Military Academy. In one respect, this must be accepted as true. The institution established and developed from 1796 through 1801 was never entitled to be called the U.S. Military Academy; it was never authorized by Congress. It was a school organized for the sole purpose of preparing cadets for service as officers of the regiments of Artillerists and Engineers.

Swift, in his memoirs, and Burbeck's biographer, Asa Bird Gardner, both indicate that the Military Academy founded in 1802 was a continuation of the school existing at the time. Cullum in the first volume of his *Register of the Officers and Graduates of the United States Military Academy* lists each of the six graduates who attended the earlier school as appointed "Cadet U.S. Military Academy, 1801" although the Academy had not been formally established by Congress at the time the cadet warrants were issued. An 1817 report submitted to the Acting Secretary of War by Brigadier General Joseph Swift, Chief of Engineers and USMA Superintendent, states: "I have the honour to submit the following statements in relation to the United States Military Academy . . . 1st. Of the number of cadets appointed and admitted for education at the military academy, West Point, from October 1801, the period when the institution was opened." The report shows eight cadets appointed in 1801. Swift, officially recognized as the first USMA graduate in the Class of 1802, states in his memoirs that there were three earlier graduates. In all probability, he was referring to cadets of the earlier academy commissioned in 1801.

Why has there been almost no recognition of the pre-1802 academy? Early West Point historians, particularly Edward C. Boynton and George Cullum, were handicapped in their research because early Academy records had largely been destroyed in the 1838 fire. Most of their research was done at West Point. Cullum did have access to War Department files but again was handicapped because many early Army records had also been destroyed by fire. Cullum relied greatly on answers to a questionnaire he sent to all graduates. The Swift and Burbeck papers were not available. Orderly books, ordnance and quartermaster records, and other similar documents at Schuylkill Arsenal in Philadelphia were not transferred to the West Point Library until many years after the Boynton and Cullum histories appeared. What was written was based upon available material. Unfortunately, many historians and writers have accepted the Boynton and Cullum accounts without question.

Although there is every justification to assert that a military academy did exist before 1802, there is no reason to dispute the observance of March 16, 1802, as the date on which the United States Military Academy was founded, for it was then that Congress for the first time authorized the establishment of *the* United States Military Academy. It was the result of efforts of many men, extending over a quarter century: Washington, Hamilton, Knox, Steuben, Dearborn, Burbeck, and many others. Their vision and perseverance prepared the foundation upon which Congress could specify "That the said corps when so organized, shall be stationed at West Point, in the State of New York, and shall constitute a military academy."

1802–1817

I totally despair of any alteration in the system that will raise the Academy to that state which the honour of the nation and the advantage of the Army indispensably require.

JONATHAN WILLIAMS

2

Struggle for Survival

Little immediate change occurred when the Act of Congress created the Corps of Engineers, which was to "constitute a Military Academy." No sign was erected at the gate; there was no gate. The nine cadets and several young officers in Burbeck's school for Artillerists and Engineers continued their studies. The same instructors taught the same subjects. Jonathan Williams, who was transferred to the new Corps of Engineers as its senior officer, continued as Superintendent of the new Academy.

Contact with the outside world was still primarily by water. Near the dock was a new stone building used to store supplies until they could be moved up the hill and also to provide shelter for passengers in inclement weather. The path to the plateau above was still narrow and unimproved. Erosion caused by severe winters was corrected by using nearby rocks and dirt. At the top of the path was a set of officers' quarters occupied by the Artillery commander, Lieutenant Robert Weir Osborn. It was also used for the Artillery officers' mess. The class building, the "Academy," was on the western edge of the plain near the site of the present Superintendent's home. South of the Academy near a pond was a small building once used for offices but now quarters of the military storekeeper, Major Fleming. Other houses lay in a rough line to the south. The last was Major Williams' quarters.

To the east were a model yard, more quarters, and a building used as a laboratory. In the In the spring of 1802, Cadets Swift and Armistead planted twelve elm trees around the model yard. The trees were still standing during the Sesquicentennial Observance in 1952 but were removed during the 1970s because of Dutch elm disease and new construction.

A hard-surface walk, possibly of brick, extended diagonally from the garden gate of Major Williams' quarters northeast across the Plain to the cadet barracks near Execution Hollow. On the west side were the ruins of the Old Provost, burned in 1796.

Many early commentaries indicate that these barracks were the "Long Barracks" of the Revolutionary War period. This claim must be questioned. Contemporary documents and maps indicate that barracks were built in many places: inside the parapets at Forts Putnam and Clinton and near the present professors' quarters on Washington Road. Maps by Kosciuszko, Villefranche, Le Bourg, and Greenleaf show these barracks. The 1805 map prepared by Lieutenant Alexander Macomb for use in rebuilding the wall around the military post includes "ruins of old barracks" on the approximate site shown in the Villefranche and Kosciuszko maps. Possible additional verification for this site appeared in the 1920s. As a boy, Lieutenant General Marshall S. Carter, whose father was Professor of Natural and Experimental Philosophy, found uniform buttons and other relics near this location.

Kosciuszko and Villefranche show another large barracks west of Fort Clinton. Greenleaf has no barracks in this area but places another at about the site of the present Bartlett Hall. Le Bourg shows several small buildings west of Fort Clinton, which are identified as "casernes pr 1000 hommes." None of these maps show or identify a prison building on the west edge of Execution Hollow later known as the Old Provost. The 1780 Barbe-Marbois map published in 1815 showing the prison caserne but no barracks has been accepted as an authentic Revolutionary period map. Merle Sheffield convincingly asserts that it was based upon the Zoeller 1808 map and that its authenticity must be questioned. (See Appendix D.)

Although the belief that the Revolutionary War Long Barracks were near the Execution Hollow site is suspect, the Burbeck papers and other documentation indicate that barracks were erected on this site for cadets and enlisted men. If Revolutionary barracks were on this site, they were either completely renovated or razed and a new barracks built on the same site by Major Rivardi in 1795 or 1796. Swift estimated that these barracks were approximately 240 feet long. The wooden, three-story building was U-shaped with porches running between the two end wings and facing south. Cadets were quartered here until new barracks were built in 1815 and 1817.

It is not difficult to deduce how the legend of the Revolutionary War Long Barracks may have originated. The Rivardi building, much longer than either the 1815 or 1817 structures, would have been called the Long Barracks to differentiate it from the newer buildings. Rivardi's barracks burned in December 1827. By the time Park's history was published in 1840, the ruins of the Rivardi building were assumed to have been the Revolutionary Long Barracks. Boynton and Cullum accepted that assumption; their accounts were considered factual.

Much of the Plain was still covered by scrub pine trees. The only cleared areas were the drill field near the barracks, another field near Fort Clinton, garden plots adjacent to quarters, and an area in front of the row of buildings along the western edge of the Plain. Swift described Fort Clinton on the east side of the plateau as "a dilapidated work of Generals Dreportail [Du Portail] and Kosciuszko, engineers in the Revolutionary War. This work was garnished with four twenty-four pounder cannon on sea coast carriages. The fort also enclosed a long stone magazine filled with powder many years of age." Over 1,000 barrels of powder were stored in the magazine, much of it moved from Constitution Island in 1795–1796.

Below the eastern rim of the plateau was a sheltered glade where Kosciuszko had planted a garden. Swift and Lieutenant Macomb repaired the garden during the summer of 1802. The small fountain at the base of the rock was cleared, and water again trickled down into the basin. Swift and Macomb planted flowers and vines and built several seats, making it possible to use the garden as "a pleasant resort for a reading party."

At the western edge of the post near the river stood two long yellow buildings housing captured Revolutionary War stores. The chain that had stretched across to Constitution Island during the war lay near the buildings. East of the storehouses were the armory and the home of the armorer, Zebulon Kingsley. Nearby was the hospital. About one-half mile to the west was the "Red House," home of John Moore. Because George Washington often stayed here during visits to West Point, the glen in which the house was located was called Washington's Valley. The area between the Moore house and the post was known as German Flats because American troops of German descent had camped here during the Revolutionary War. In 1817, a cemetery was laid out in this area, and remains of Revolutionary War dead, which had been interred in several locations on the Plain, were moved here.

Towering above the Academy on a rocky crag, Fort Putnam had been renovated and improved in 1796–1800. Extensive work had been required. The dirt and wood revetments had deteriorated from neglect and exposure to the elements. The renovation, which was not completed, replaced these revetments with strong stone walls and casemates. Strangely, the land on which the fort was located did not become government property until 1824, when the Gridley tract was purchased for $10,000. In 1802, however, the fort was in good condition, although only two twenty-four pounder cannon were in place.

The view from Fort Putnam was beautiful. On a clear day, one could see Newburgh to the north. Below were the military buildings and quarters all painted with the standard yellow issue paint. Splashes of bright colors from flowers in gardens interrupted the verdant greens of foliage and grass. Gray rocks and many rocks dotting the Plain peeped through the scrub pines.

From Fort Putnam, the entire bend of the river was visible, dominated by the silent guns. Seeing ships slowly make the difficult double turn made obvious the reason for the West Point and Constitution Island fortifications. Fully manned and armed and with the chain stretched across the river, the forts would make it almost impossible for ships to pass.

To the east, near the site of the present Administration Building, was North's tavern, a problem both before and after the Academy was established. After an altercation with North in 1794, Captain Stelle, according to Swift, "levelled a field piece at North's house and suffered a severe penalty therefor [*sic*] in a law suit." Soldiers and cadets sought "rest and relaxation" here, often with disastrous results. Cadet regulations that prohibited imbibing alcoholic beverages or that restricted cadets from leaving the military post did little to lessen the attraction of the tavern.

A dispute arose concerning the possible location of the tavern on government property. Congress in 1811 directed a commission to determine exactly where the southern boundary of the military post ended and North's land began. The report did fix the boundary but did not eliminate the tavern. In 1819, North sold the tavern and adjoining land, including the site of Fort Putnam, to Oliver Gridley. Cadets and soldiers continued to frequent the tavern surreptitiously until the government purchased Gridley property in 1824.

A rough road extended south from the post past North's tavern along the bluff past the home of J. D. Kinsley about a half mile from the post. The road narrowed as it continued on to the hamlet of Buttermilk Falls. A small mill dominated the small community. Inhabitants included Revolutionary War veterans and farmers. Several veterans had been members of the Corps of Invalids that had been moved to West Point in 1781. Their remaining in the area after leaving military service was the start of what has since become almost a tradition. Many officers and enlisted personnel remain in the West Point vicinity after retirement. Civilian employees of the post often do the same. For example, many Italian stone masons who were employed at West Point during the great expansion from 1903 to 1910 stayed in the area. Tailors and shoemakers, brought to the post from New York City, also became local inhabitants.

One of the Revolutionary War veterans living in Buttermilk Falls was Molly Corbin. Wounded in battle and cited for extreme bravery, Molly was sent to the Corps of Invalids at West Point where she received half of male pay. When she was denied the ordinary daily ration of rum, she caused so much trouble that her ration was reinstated.

The Act of 1802 creating the Corps of Engineers stated "That the said corps when so organized shall be stationed at West Point, in the State of New York, and shall constitute a military academy." It also specified that "the principal engineer, and in his absence, the next in rank, shall have the superintendence of the said military academy." The senior engineer was to be a major, and with authorization for promotion to lieutenant colonel and for increasing the number of officers in the Corps of Engineers from seven to ten at a later date.

The separation of the Corps of Artillerists and Engineers into two distinct branches must have caused confusion. Officers for the new Corps of Engineers were selected with care. Colonel Henry Burbeck, as Chief of Artillery, was involved because Engineer officers would come from his regiments of Artillerists and Engineers. It can be assumed that Jonathan Williams participated in the selection as senior Engineer officer.

The new Corps of Engineers had only seven officers and two cadets. Major Williams was the senior officer; Major Decius Wadsworth, second in command. Captains William Amherst Barron and Jared Mansfield and Lieutenants Peter Dransey, Alexander Macomb, and James Wilson were other officers transferred to the Corps of Engineers; Barron and Mansfield, in April 1802; Wadsworth, in July; and Macomb in November.

With this small group, Williams not only had to place the Military Academy in operation but continue supervising the construction or renovation of fortifications already underway in major harbors. Since no enlisted men had been authorized for the Engineers, the Artillerist unit continued to serve the Academy needs. In July, Cadets Joseph Swift and Simon Levy, who had been carried on Artillerist company rolls, were transferred to the Corps of Engineers. The remaining seven cadets at West Point were assigned to companies of the Regiment of Artillerists.

Jonathan Williams, whom Burbeck had recommended to President Jefferson to be Superintendent of the small Artillerists and Engineers academy, was a grandnephew of Benjamin Franklin. A Harvard graduate, he had served in France as a representative of the American government during the Revolution. Because of an early interest in science and in military art, Williams collaborated with Franklin in several experiments. In 1799, he published a well-received treatise on thermometrical navigation based on some of these experiments. He contributed to the *Transactions* of the American Philosophical Society, of which he was an officer. In 1800, he translated de Scheel's *A Treatise of Artillery* from the French for the War Department. Williams was interested in the practical applications of experiment and theory. His knowledge of fortification construction probably surpassed that of any other American.

These many qualifications enabled Burbeck to easily convince Jefferson in 1801 that Williams should be appointed Superintendent of the Artillerist and Engineer academy and Inspector of Fortifications with the rank of major in the Regiment of Artillerists and Engineers. His direct commission as one of thirteen field grade officers in the small Army with no military background whatsoever was to prove a handicap. Despite this disadvantage, his scientific and technical qualifications and his short experience as Superintendent of the Artillerist and Engineer academy resulted in Williams being appointed the senior officer in the new Corps of Engineers. Undoubtedly, the requirement that the senior Engineer officer would also serve as the Superintendent of the new Academy was a factor in his selection.

Temporarily, Lieutenants Dransey, Macomb, and Wilson became officer students, joining the nine cadets from the Burbeck academy. Dransey and Wilson had been instructors at that institution, but Williams decided to assign Barron and Mansfield to academic duties at West Point. A classmate of John Quincy Adams and a former mathematics tutor at Harvard, Barron had been Burbeck's first choice for a professorship in the Artillerists and Engineers academy but could not be spared from his work at Portsmouth, New Hampshire. Williams then assigned him as Professor of Mathematics. Mansfield, a friend of President Jefferson and a former instructor at Yale, became Acting Professor of Natural and Experimental Philosophy.

It has often been maintained that the Academy was established to educate only Corps of Engineer cadets. Denton states, "the military academy was not considered to be a nursery for all officers, it was not designed to train a nucleus which could be expanded into a larger army, it was not to be a school of application and training through which all officers, of all branches, whether regular or militia were to be rotated; it was rather a part of a small, technical service, limited by law to twenty members." Such was not true, for the Academy from its beginning included cadets from other branches.

It is possible that the interpretation of the wording of the 1802 Act was a misinterpretation of the word "constitute." Denton and others have used "compose"; this would indicate that the Corps of Engineers would compose, or be, a military academy. An alternate meaning is given in the *American Heritage Dictionary* and other lexicons: "to establish formally; found (an institution, for example)" invalidates the contention that the Academy was intended to educate only engineers. Much of the insistence that the Academy was intended to be a school for engineers can be attributed to Boynton and Cullum, who ignored the fact that cadets from other branches attended the Academy from its beginning.

Nothing in the Act of March 16, 1802, indicated that cadets of branches other than the Corps of Engineers were to attend the Academy, but the Act did not prohibit attendance. The War Department accepted the latter interpretation and required cadets from Corps of Artillerist companies to attend the Academy. Cadets were carried on the rolls of their parent units and returned to them after completing the course of instruction. There can be little doubt that Henry Burbeck was the proponent of this arrangement. His interest in educating cadets and young officers in the regiments of Artillerist continued unabated.

For many years, it was maintained that only Engineer officers required technical proficiency. As late as 1814, the Secretary of War insisted, "The rule of Commissioning Infantry or Artillery appointments is liable to much qualification. Science being the basis of engineering, an extended preliminary knowledge of mathematics, etc., is of course a prerequisite. A less degree of this knowledge is necessary to Artillery and Infantry officers." As a result, although two cadets in the class of 1803 were commissioned in the Regiment of Artillerists, the first Infantry cadet was not commissioned until 1806; the first Dragoon, in 1809. During its first ten years, the Academy graduated seventy-one cadets. Thirty-eight were commissioned in the Artillery; fourteen in the Infantry; fifteen as Engineers; and one as a Dragoon. Two refused commissions after completing the course of instruction. This does not support the contention that the Academy was a school only for Engineer cadets.

Burbeck had long urged that all cadets, regardless of branch, be educated at the Academy. In an 1801 letter to Major Constant Freeman he stated, "As to cadets, I am not in favor of appointing any to companies. I think they ought to be appointed by the Secy of War & put to school to learn every Branch of their duty, the practical part with theory, and when vacancies happen in the Regiment, the one best qualified ought to fill it." Not until April 1812, at the urging of the War Department, did Congress direct that "cadets heretofore appointed in the service of the United States, whether of artillery, cavalry, riflemen, or infantry, or that may in the future be appointed . . . be attached at the discretion of the President of the United States, as students to the military academy." The Act stipulated that "when any cadet shall receive a regular degree from the academical staff, after going through all the classes, he shall be considered as among the candidates for a commission in any corps, according to the duties he may be judged competent to perform." The 1812 Act formally charged the Corps of Engineers, still considered to constitute a military academy, with the task of educating and training cadets for all branches.

One reason there were so few Engineer graduates was that only two cadets were authorized for the Corps of Engineers. The Regiment of Artillerists in 1802 was authorized forty. Each of the two Infantry regiments had ten cadets. Officer allocations also differed. Total Engineer officer strength, initially seven, was restricted to ten; the Regiment of Artillerists was authorized sixty-seven and each infantry regiment forty-four. No cadet could be commissioned in a branch unless a vacancy existed. Vacancies occurred only when officers were promoted, resigned, transferred, or died. Because of the small number of cadet spaces and the few officer vacancies occurring, fewer cadets were commissioned in the Corps of Engineers than in other branches.

Williams' first major problem developed because the Act of 1802 did not assign any enlisted men to the Corps of Engineers. Consequently, the War Department in its infinite wisdom directed that a detachment of the Regiment of Artillerists be stationed at West Point to support the Academy. Assuming that as senior officer he commanded all military personnel at West Point, Williams found that Artillerist officers refused to obey his orders because he was an Engineer officer and could not command line troops. Williams appealed to the War Department, which solved the problem by transferring Artillerist officers elsewhere, leaving the enlisted detachment under Williams' control. The War Department regulation prohibiting Engineer officers from command was a hangover from the Revolution, when most engineers were foreigners considered to be untrustworthy. President Jefferson upheld the War Department ruling on the basis that Engineers should not command troops of other branches because their technical and scientific duties did not leave time for them to cope with routine Army matters.

Captain Barron arrived in April and became Acting Professor of Mathematics. Captain Mansfield reported in May to become Acting Professor of Natural and Experimental Philosophy. Williams and his small faculty began the first of many changes in the curriculum necessary to establish an engineering school. Mathematics was to be the keystone of Academy instruction; this emphasis continued for over 150 years. Few schools taught more than the most fundamental mathematics. Cadets proved woefully weak in this basic subject. For many years, cadets were taught elementary math to develop a foundation for advanced study. Their text was C. H. Hutton's *Mathematics*.

The only scientific text used was W. Enfield's *Natural Philosophy*, a very basic study of physics and mechanics. Little laboratory equipment was available. Cadets recited or discussed lessons with the instructors. "Hands on" training was used in engineering instruction. Cadets surveyed the West Point terrain with transits and stadia rods. Using the basic triangulation method, they found that Fort Putnam was 400 feet above the Plain, which was determined to be 190 feet above the Hudson River. Surveying classes have continued, and cadets have measured the Fort Putnam elevation countless times. Many, however, often found the Plain to be below the level of the river!

There were classes in fortifications and artillery tactics and techniques, based on Vauban's *Traité de Fortifications* in its original French. Cadets assigned to the Burbeck academy had received some French instruction from Tousard, but newly appointed cadets had little if any knowledge of French. This shortcoming and the fact that most fortification, engineering, and military texts were in French emphasized the need for instruction in that language. There was a laboratory of sorts, the test facility used by the Burbeck academy. The old model yard from the Burbeck academy containing models of fortifications constructed by Roche-fontaine and Tousard was used to demonstrate fortification principles.

Instruction in artillery techniques was not handicapped by a language difference. The text was de Scheel's *Treatise of Artillery*, which Williams had translated for the War Department. Artillery howitzers and mortars were available. Infantry instruction was based on Steuben's *Regulations for the Order and Discipline of Troops*.

There were basic differences between the infant academy and colleges of the time. There was no instruction in Latin or Greek, and no knowledge of either language was required for appointment. There was no religious study, although services were conducted by visiting clergymen or an officer of the Post. Other colleges followed the English example. Harvard was patterned after Emanuel College at Cambridge; William and Mary after Queens College at Oxford. The Academy followed the French example of Ecole Militaire and Ecole Polytechnique, which Williams had visited often before and during the Revolution. Colleges emphasized arts and letters with little or no mathematics or science. The Academy followed an opposite pattern, with emphasis on mathematics and physical sciences and almost no study of the humanities.

Academy classes were small, and every student officer or cadet was expected to be prepared to recite every day. Classes in the colleges were also small. With small student bodies, there was no need to lecture to large groups. At West Point, use of the blackboard, initiated in the Burbeck academy, continued, especially in mathematics and natural philosophy. The normal class procedure had one student reciting to the instructor while a second worked at a blackboard. There were few lectures—a decided contrast with other colleges.

The greatest difference between West Point and other colleges was the availability of a library. The small library of the Burbeck academy had been provided with books, instruments, and apparatus by the 1794 Congressional Act. Books were primarily texts by the "most approved Authors on Tactics and the Petite Guerre." Other books were obtained by assessing officers one day's pay each month. This library, the first federal library, was the ancestor of the USMA Library. Unfortunately, the 1796 fire that destroyed the Old Provost burned most of the books in the library housed in the building. Few replacements had been added by 1802.

Williams' first request for permission to purchase books and apparatus was approved by Secretary of War Dearborn in a July 1802 letter: "You will observe the notes made by the President on the margin of your list. You will please to inform yourself what part of the Books and Instruments can be procured at New York or Philadelphia and their cost, in addition to those you propose to spare from your own Library, which you will please make a Bill of, and when you shall have obtained the necessary information respecting what may be procured as above, you will be pleased to make a list of such as it will be necessary to send to Europe for." The notes made by Jefferson on a list of books, truly an unimportant document, are perhaps the most significant indication of his great interest in the Academy.

To supplement the small library, Williams permitted cadets to use his manuscripts concerning his studies and experiments with Franklin, books bequeathed to him by Franklin, and books and manuscripts he had obtained during his long stay in France and England before and during the Revolutionary War. Several of Williams' books remain in the West Point Library. At least one, the first of three volumes of the 1750 edition of M. Belidor's *Architecture Hydraulique*, bears Franklin's signature, undoubtedly one of the books left to Williams by his great-uncle. Other officers made personal books available. Swift remembered that Captain George Izard of the Artillerist detachment permitted him to use his collection of charts and books. Izard had been educated at the French Military School in Metz, and his library included works on French military concepts and techniques.

Williams' interest in the library continued throughout his superintendency. On many trips to visit fortification projects, he purchased books for the library as well as for his personal collection. Visits to Boston, New York, Philadelphia, and Charleston enabled him to visit many bookshops. In his memoirs, Swift recalled a trip to Albany in October 1802. Before returning to West Point, he and Williams went to the Leavenworth and Whiting bookstore, where Williams purchased Neetat's *General History* and works of Hogarth for the library. Captain Barron purchased books from Swift's private collection for the library in 1803.

Williams emphasized the importance of a personal library to the cadets and officers. The importance of a personal professional library continued as an unpublicized part of West Point training. During the Civil War, many graduates carried small libraries on campaigns. Western posts during the Indian Wars had few books available other than those in libraries of officers. In several of his works, Charles King mentions the books of officers and their importance to other officers, families, and enlisted men. As late as 1944, graduating cadets were provided with wooden book boxes in which they could pack books obtained as cadets. The boxes were made in such a way that they could be stacked and used as bookcases. Current military moving regulations exempt books and professional books from the weight allowances. In later years, many graduates and their families donated collections to the West Point Library, the U.S. Army Military History Institute at Carlisle Barracks, and college and university libraries.

Regulations are a necessity for every military installation. The Burbeck academy undoubtedly had rules governing its activities, but no consolidated list of such regulations has been found. The first rules for the newly activated U.S. Military Academy were issued by the Secretary of War, not the Superintendent. Entitled "Regulations for West Point," Dearborn's list was more a directive to Colonel Williams. He directed that housing be provided Williams, other officers of the Academy staff, officers of the garrison, cadets, and the military storekeeper. A building was designated as an academic facility and another building as a store to be operated by a contractor. No public building would be used by a sutler.

Far more important were Dearborn's orders concerning the relationship between the Superintendent and the troops of the garrison. The long-standing antipathy toward Engineer officers to commanding troops prevailed. The principal officer of the Corps of Engineers—the Superintendent—was to direct "the general superintendence of the police, exclusive of the civil jurisdiction," but he was not "ever to have any direction or command of the Troops of the Garrison except in cases of emergency when no commissioned Officer of the Troops shall be at the Post." The troop commander would have no role in matters relating solely to the Academy.

This division of command was complicated by the requirement for the troop commander to provide "a reasonable number of men . . . for aiding in making such practical experiments as may be made from time to time, and for such other reasonable aid as shall be required by the said superintendent." This support was tempered by the statement that "at no time shall it be considered reasonable for the superintendent to require more men than can be spared from the common and usual duties of the Garrison." Troop support would be provided, but Dearborn gave the troop commander an excuse to refuse any support requested.

Dearborn's directive stated that "commissioned Officers of the Corps of Engineers will sit on Courts Martial, when the circumstances of the Garrison render it necessary." Again, this provision emphasized the lower status of Engineer officers, for they could be members of a Court Martial only if the number of officers of other branches available was not sufficient to constitute a court. This provision did have one benefit: cadets were no longer eligible to sit on a Court Martial as in the Burbeck academy.

This War Department directive, undoubtedly issued with President Jefferson's approval, continued the policy established during the Revolutionary War when almost all professional engineers in Washington's army were foreigners. National pride could not condone American soldiers under the command of foreigners, especially technicians who theoretically had no command experience. The policy continued after the signing of the Constitution because most of the engineers in the two regiments of Artillerists and Engineers were foreigners. When French officers were discharged during the difficulty with France in the 1790s, the policy was continued on the basis that engineers could not take time from their professional duties for administrative or command responsibilities.

Problems caused by this decision were not restricted to West Point; the same confusion occurred at other posts. Although the headquarters of the Corps of Engineers was at West Point, its officers were sent elsewhere to supervise harbor fortification construction work. Artillery troops manned these fortifications and often assisted in construction. Even the senior officer of the Army, Major General James Wilkinson, disagreed with this policy. He had placed Major Decius Wadsworth, second senior officer in the Corps of Engineers, in command of Fort Adams, Massachusetts, when Artillery Major Daniel Jackson resigned. Secretary Dearborn countermanded the order, informing Wilkinson that "it is the wish of the Executive that the gentlemen who have received appointments in the Corps of Engineers should devote their time and attention exclusively to the theory and practice of their professional pursuits uncomplicated with military command." Friction between branches caused by this policy, acerbated by the professional ego of Engineer officers, would not be eliminated until long after the War of 1812.

A part of this restriction still exists. Academy professors have command only of their own departments. They cannot command the Academy or the post in the absence of the Superintendent. The Commandant of Cadets or the senior line officer at West Point takes command when the Superintendent is absent. The same restriction applies when a professor is on sabbatical duty at another installation.

Despite all of these problems—developing a curriculum; obtaining adequate instructors, books, and laboratory equipment; improving housing for officers, men, and cadets; and at the same time supervising the construction of fortifications along the coast—Williams determined to conduct the first examination of cadets deemed qualified for commissions. Not until after 1812 were cadets considered graduates of the Military Academy. Prior to the Act of April 29, 1812, cadets who completed the course were considered promoted rather than graduated. After public examinations conducted by Williams, Mansfield, and Barron, two cadets, Joseph Swift and Simon Levy, were commissioned second lieutenants in the Corps of Engineers.

None of the officer faculty looked forward to spending the winter on West Point's windblown rocky promontory. Poorly heated frame buildings provided slight shelter from the cold and wind. The experience of the Burbeck academy indicated drifting snow would seal off most of the buildings, often for days. No horses or oxen were available to remove snow. Cadets and enlisted men would have trouble getting to their messes, and officers and cadets would find it difficult to reach the academic building.

Williams therefore asked Dearborn to approve a vacation period from December to mid-March. Dearborn agreed with the stipulation that cadets could be required to return to West Point at any time during this period. This decision established the pattern followed until 1817. By December, only the Artillerist detachment remained.

Before disbanding for the winter, Williams assembled all Corps of Engineer officers and cadets on November 12. Present were Major Wadsworth; Captains Barron and Mansfield; Lieutenants Wilson, Macomb, Swift, and Levy; and Cadets Walker K. Armistead and Joseph G. Totten. Armistead had transferred from the Burbeck academy; Totten had been appointed a cadet only eight days earlier. None of the Artillery student officers or cadets was present. The fact that Williams included Armistead and Totten was an indication that he planned to have the two cadets commissioned as Engineer officers after their Academy schooling.

The group discussed Williams' proposal to establish a scholarly association, The United States Military Philosophical Society. The proposal was adopted unanimously. There was little chance of dissension; such seldom occurs when a commander presents a plan. Williams' prestige undoubtedly was a factor in the decision.

All officers and cadets of the Corps of Engineers were to be members "of right." Any officer of the military services and any civilian could apply for membership. Society officers were to be officers or cadets of the Corps of Engineers. The purpose of the Society was to promote military science. Meetings were to be held twice monthly, normally in the academic building.

A second meeting on November 29 elected officers. Williams was chosen president, and five other officers were selected for other positions. Members agreed that Williams should ask President Jefferson for his approval and patronage because that would give the Society semi-official status. Williams wrote Jefferson on December 12 asking for his support and providing a description of the Society's purpose "to select and preserve as far as possible the Military Science, which must still exist among the veterans of our revolutionary contest, and those of our fellow citizens who have gathered scientific fruits in the course of their travels." Activities of the Society were not to concern the organization or internal functions of the Army; they were restricted to the arts and sciences. Williams' careful delineation was important, for it prevented the Society from becoming involved in any internal military controversy or external politics.

Jefferson approved the project, stating, "A friend to Science in all its useful

Branches, and believing that of the Engineer of great utility, I sincerely approve of the Institution of a Society for its improvement. . . . Altho' it is not probable that I may be able to render it any service, yet, I accept thankfully the Patronage you are pleased to propose, and the more justifiably as the perfect coincidence of its objects with the legal duties of the Members, will render the respects shown to the Society always consistent with the duties which I owe to their military Institution.''

This letter reflects Jefferson's support of the new Military Academy, a great change from his earlier attitude toward such an institution. In 1793, Jefferson as Secretary of State had argued that Washington's proposal to establish an academy was unconstitutional. Less than ten years later, he supported the legislation that established the U.S. Military Academy. One can only guess what caused this change of attitude. He undoubtedly remembered well his discussions with President John Adams concerning the need for a professional army during the crisis with France. He had observed Adams' problems in obtaining congressional approval for increasing the strength of the Army and Navy and for appropriations for fortifications. He had seen the difficulty of finding qualified officers who were United States citizens.

There also can be little doubt that Dearborn contributed to Jefferson's transformation. Dearborn, in turn, was greatly influenced by Burbeck. Most of Burbeck's recommendations concerning an academy were incorporated in the 1802 Act. Did Dearborn discuss this proposal with Jefferson? Undoubtedly. Did Burbeck participate in such discussions? Possibly. His close friendship with Dearborn and the adoption of many of his proposals support this supposition. Unfortunately, extant records of the War Department and personal papers of this period provide no documentary evidence.

Another factor that may have contributed to Jefferson's change of position may have been his desire to establish a national university that would differ from contemporary colleges by eliminating the study of classics and adding scientific research to the curriculum. He encountered opposition because many Congressmen sincerely believed that colleges could provide education for any profession. Idealist, philosopher, and innovator that he was, Jefferson was also a realist. He sensed that there would be much less opposition to a military academy, an institution that would incorporate his views. Whatever the cause, Jefferson's support resulted in the establishment of the Military Academy at West Point, and his patronage of the United States Military Philosophical Society assured the Society of acceptance by the academic community.

By the end of the first week of December 1802, all cadets and most of the officers had left West Point. Only the Artillerist detachment remained. Williams spent most of the winter months working with Barron and Mansfield to develop a curriculum. He and his two faculty members were not satisfied with the results of the first year. They were aware of the deficiencies: the need for a curriculum that would provide a professional education, the inadequate library, too few qualified instructors, and primitive laboratory facilities. They agreed that the location of the Academy at West Point was a disadvantage because of its isolation from other places of learning.

Williams presented their recommendations to Dearborn in early January 1803. In answer to his urgent request to move the Academy and headquarters of the Corps of Engineers to Washington, the Secretary replied that, although President Jefferson agreed that this was desirable, it was doubtful that the move could be made unless Congress would amend the 1802 Act. The amendment was not forthcoming, and both the Corps of Engineers and the Academy remained at West Point.

Expansion of the curriculum was approved. Williams urged that a teacher of French be authorized, pointing out that engineering texts and many military treatises were in that language. He asked for the appointment of a teacher of drawing, explaining the importance of accurate drawings in planning fortifications and military structures. Dearborn was able to obtain congressional approval in February 1803.

Once again Williams raised the question of command for Engineer officers, stressing the difficulty of obtaining enlisted support for cadet activities. He reminded Dearborn of his September 1802 report concerning waiters for officers and cadets and the reluctance of the Artillery commander to provide men for this duty.

"On the subject of waiters," Dearborn replied, "it was my instruction that the officers of the Corps of Engineers should be furnished with waiters from the Military in such manner as would be most convenient not as a matter of courtesy, but as a common right, and the cadets should undoubtedly be furnished with a reasonable number." But Williams' request that senior Engineer officers should be authorized to command troops of other branches was not approved. To provide support for the Academy, Congress authorized the Corps of Engineers to recruit a force of one artificer and eighteen men who would receive "the same pay, rations and clothing as are allowed privates in the Army of the United States." These men were to assist in experiments and maintain the instruments used. The wording of the Act emphasized that the detachment was part of the Corps of Engineers and not an Army unit. This was the only force an Engineer officer could command.

Officers and cadets returned to West Point in late March 1803, and instruction began on April 1. Before a week had passed, the War Department transferred many officers elsewhere to supervise the repair and renovation of harbor fortifications. Williams was sent to Wilmington, North Carolina, and Charleston, South Carolina; Major Wadsworth, to Fort Adams on the lower Mississippi. Lieutenant Wilson took charge of work at Fort Mifflin near Philadelphia and fortifications at Norfolk. Lieutenant Macomb was responsible for renovations in New York harbor and at Portsmouth, New Hampshire. By law, Captain Barron, the senior Engineer officer at West Point, became Acting Superintendent during Williams' absence. To assist him, he had only Captain Mansfield. Lieutenants

Levy and Swift remained at West Point as students, joining several Artillery officers sent there by Burbeck.

Before departing, Williams interviewed applicants for positions of teachers of drawing and French. Dearborn cautioned him to avoid selecting "intemperate men, foreigners, and men far advanced in years." Because he was unable to find a qualified instructor in drawing, Williams selected Francis D. Masson to fill both positions. Although Masson was a Frenchman, Williams was able to convince Dearborn that he was fully qualified. Masson was attached to the Corps of Engineers with the "pay and emoluments of a Captain." He filled the dual position until Christian E. Zoeller was appointed teacher of drawing in 1808 and continued as teacher of French until 1812.

En route to Wilmington, Williams stopped in Washington to review his selection of Masson with Dearborn. He again raised the question of command for Corps of Engineer officers, stressing that all the Engineer officers, except Levy and Swift, had been officers in one of the regiments of Artillerists and Engineers and were accustomed to command procedures, that in his opinion reluctance to authorize command for Engineer officers was the result of experience during the Revolutionary War when most professional engineers were foreigners, and that American engineers were now educated at the Academy. Dearborn would make no comment in support of Williams or against him.

Returning from Wilmington in June, Williams again called on Dearborn to find that the Secretary, with the President's approval, would not change the official position that an Engineer officer could not command troops of other branches. Since it was clearly apparent that there would be no change, Williams resigned on June 20, stating that the prohibition destroyed all credibility of Engineer officers in the eyes of the remainder of the Army. Dearborn asked Williams to reconsider, but he refused.

The positions of both Dearborn and Williams were understandable. Other than Mansfield, all Engineer officers had been transferred from the Corps of Artillerists and Engineers, retaining their original dates of appointment and the seniority this implied. Engineer officers were eligible to sit on a court martial that might pass judgment on an enlisted man or officer of other branches. The troops at West Point were needed to assist in maintaining the post and training cadets; yet the senior Engineer officer was required to formally ask for enlisted support, even though the Artillery commander was junior in rank. At harbor installations, building or renovating fortifications was the responsibility of an Engineer officer; some work was done by troops over whom the Engineer had no control. Williams' argument was based on the simple fact that if the Corps of Engineers was a part of the·Army, its officers should have the same rights as officers of other branches.

Major Decius Wadsworth, now the senior Engineer officer, became the Superintendent, but he was still at Fort Adams. Captain Barron as ranking Engineer at West Point was the Acting Superintendent. Barron had no objection to the

War Department command policy. His commission was based primarily on his mathematical competence, and he anticipated no situation involving troop command. Captain Mansfield and Masson were his faculty.

Barron's lack of experience, guidance, and organizational ability was apparent. He had little knowledge of administration or discipline, although his academic ability was unquestioned. The curriculum was not improved from that of the previous year, yet Masson did provide the first instruction in drawing and French. Three cadets were commissioned in March and April 1803, all before Williams' departure. Walker K. Armistead became the third graduate commissioned in the Corps of Engineers. Henry Burbeck Jackson and John Livingston were assigned to the Corps of Artillerists. Armistead and Jackson had been cadets in the Burbeck academy; Livingston entered the Academy in June 1802. Armistead remained at West Point. Jackson and Livingston were assigned to Corps of Artillery posts.

Barron's problems in disciplining both student officers and cadets were eased by support from Dearborn, who gave him authority to discharge cadets who did not conduct themselves in a "decent, sober, and correct manner." This early reference to sobriety was necessary because of the proximity of North's tavern outside the south wall. Barron convinced the War Department that cadets should not be younger than fourteen or fifteen years of age when appointed. The fourteen-year age limit remained the minimum for many years.

Barron was less successful in adding books to the small library. Although able to purchase some books from Lieutenant Swift's private collection and fourteen copies of Adams' *Geometrical and Geographical Essays* to supplement the Hutton basic mathematical text, he had no funds for any significant purchases. No meetings of Williams' Military Philosophical Society were held. Primarily Barron devoted most of his efforts to administration and teaching.

The year 1803 was significant for another reason: the first cadet resignation was submitted and approved. Ambrose Porter, one of the cadets transferred from the Burbeck academy, resigned on February 22. His departure and the commissioning of Armistead, Jackson, and Livingston in March and April left thirteen cadets at West Point.

Four cadets were appointed by July and four more before classes were dismissed for the winter. This haphazard appointment method added to the problems faced by Barron, Mansfield, and Masson. It was almost impossible to organize a curriculum when cadets with varying educational backgrounds arrived throughout the year. This continued until 1816 when Joseph Swift, then Superintendent, persuaded the Secretary of War that all newly appointed cadets should report to West Point in September.

Captain Mansfield was ordered to Detroit in May 1803 to become the Surveyor-General of the Northwest Territory, where he remained until October 1812. This left only Barron and Masson officially assigned as instructors. After the winter recess, Lieutenants Swift and Levy left to supervise harbor fortification construction, and Barron no longer had them to assist in teaching cadets. This was the situation awaiting Major Wadsworth when he returned in May 1804.

Wadsworth found change at West Point. Cadets were billeted in the Long Barracks built by Rivardi in 1796. The thirteen cadets and the few student officers occupied only part of the barracks areas. The remainder was occupied by enlisted men of the Artillery detachment and the eighteen sappers of the Corps of Engineers. Rooms had almost no furniture. Cadets, officers, and enlisted men slept on pallets on the floor. Each room had a fireplace. The possibility of fire was a constant concern, and buckets of water were permanent fixtures in each room. Chairs, tables, or other furniture were not provided. Furniture or boxes used as chairs or tables were obtained by the occupants.

Cadets had no common uniform. Those assigned to the Artillery wore the same uniform as an Artillery officer. Engineer cadets wore the uniform of an officer of the Corps of Engineers. Artillery cadets wore a high-collar, dark blue coat with red facings and gold buttons; Engineer cadets, a similar coat with Engineer facings. In winter, blue pantaloons and vests were worn; summer pantaloons and vests were made of white linen. Black cocked hats were worn throughout the year. Either the half-boot of an officer or the black gaiters of enlisted men were to be found, depending on the desire or financial assets of the individual cadet.

The pay of Engineer cadets was sixteen dollars a month and two rations each day. Artillery cadets received only ten dollars and the double ration. From this small salary, each cadet had to purchase his uniforms and pay for his meals. There was no common mess. A fortunate few cadets boarded with Mrs. Thompson, widow of a Revolutionary officer, or with married officers. Most cadets took their rations in cash, twenty-seven cents a day, and bought provisions from local tradesmen. Some cooked their meals; others hired soldiers to do the cooking. Because the pay did not always arrive on time, cadets were often in debt to merchants and spent more for food than the total of their pay and ration allowances. The condition of their uniforms and personal possessions reflected their penury.

Classes were held in the Academic Building, a small frame structure on the western edge of the Plain with two rooms on the ground floor. With so few cadets, only one room was used for instruction. Three rooms on the upper floor were officers' quarters. Cadets sat on low benches facing the blackboard, which was used extensively by the instructor. This method, not common at other colleges, had been developed by Professor George Baron in the Burbeck academy period and was retained by Williams. Cadets used the single blackboard for recitations. A War Department order in June 1803 directed the military storekeeper to "furnish the room occupied as a school room with a suitable number of Chairs for the officers, with hand irons, shovel & tongs, and such other articles as may be necessary."

French, mathematics, and natural philosophy classes were taught here, although philosophy experiments were conducted in the old laboratory building on the south edge of the Plain. There were no surveying classes during 1803 and 1804. Apparently Williams' resignation had removed the only qualified surveying instructor. There was some instruction in fortifications, either in the classroom or at the model yard. The models, which had been constructed by Rivardi and Rochefontaine in the 1790s, were still an important educational medium.

Some tactical instruction was provided. Infantry drill still used the Steuben manual. Artillery training was based upon current army tactics, although no American manual had been published. Officers from the Artillery detachment conducted most tactical training with assistance from student officers.

Recreational facilities were almost nonexistent. The bathing area near the north dock was available. Hiking, fishing, and hunting were permitted. Fish and game provided a welcome addition to meals. The small library had few books other than works related to the curriculum. Occasional newspapers from New York City or from a cadet's home town were eagerly read by many cadets and officers. A few cadets visited the warehouse housing the Revolutionary War arms captured from the British. This was not a museum; it was, at best, an arsenal. Studying captured artillery and infantry weapons, however, did give cadets and officers the opportunity to compare foreign arms with those made in the United States. Of course, North's tavern continued to be an attraction.

From across the Hudson, Fort Putnam dominated the vista. Smaller redoubts broke the expanse of trees and brush. Fort Clinton loomed over the edge of the embankment dropping to the river. Most of the Plain was still covered by scrub pine trees through which one could glimpse the Academy buildings and quarters, which were yellow, apparently the only paint available from military supplies.

That Barron had been unable to handle disciplinary problems was evident in regulations Wadsworth published on July 20, 1804, requiring "punctual attendance at the Academy" by both officers and cadets. Absences were to be reported to the Superintendent. A parade and roll call was scheduled daily at nine in the morning in front of the Academic Building. All "the gentlemen attached to the Military Academy as well as all the officers, cadets, and privates of the Corps of Engrs. (except the French instructor and the waiters) be pleased to attend."

Regulations required officers, cadets, and enlisted men to wear the uniforms of their corps, "but as some of the gentlemen may not have provided themselves dress, the order will not until a reasonable time shall have elapsed, be strongly enforced." Formation for parade and drill was prescribed and musicians ordered "to give some taps on the drum ten minutes before the nine o'clock which will be the signal for officers to attend." Wadsworth required that "subaltern officers . . . will render themselves responsible for the decent appearance of the men and their regular behavior within and out of quarters and will therefore visit the Barracks as often as may be necessary to inspect their conduct and mode of living."

Wadsworth included the first published schedule of classes in these regulations. Captain Barron taught mathematics and the theory of fortifications each morning, except Saturday and Sunday. In the afternoons Masson alternated classes in drawing and French. Saturdays were devoted to tactical instruction. Although not specified by the regulations, Wadsworth undoubtedly continued the Sunday religious service. Occasionally a visiting clergyman conducted the service; at other times, the senior officer substituted. Weather permitting, Catholic cadets and officers crossed the river to attend Mass in Cold Spring.

All cadets attended the same classes and received the same instruction regardless of their previous education or time they had at the Academy. No attempt was made to establish a prescribed curriculum for a definite period. No plan was derived to establish a course length beyond one year. Cadets were to be commissioned when the instructors considered them qualified. Swift and Levy had been commissioned in 1802 after only seven months instruction. In March 1803, Armistead was commissioned after ten months at the Burbeck school and one year at the Academy; Jackson, in April after one year's study at the Burbeck institution and eleven months at the Academy; and Livingston after only ten months at the Academy. In the Class of 1804, Samuel Gates had one year at the Burbeck school and two at the Academy, while his classmate, Hannibal Allen, had only thirteen months at the Academy. All were considered to be qualified when tested by the faculty.

It was evident to the entire Corps of Engineers and to other officers as well that both the Academy and the fortification construction needed the firm guidance of Jonathan Williams. General Wilkinson, the senior officer in the Army, urged Dearborn to place the Corps of Engineers on an equal status with other branches of the Army but with little success. Many Engineer officers wrote Williams, begging him to return to service. One letter described the condition of the Military Academy: "Never was West Point so much in want of you as at this moment. Morals and knowledge thrive little, and courts martial and flogging prevail. The Military Academy, instead of being the seat of knowledge and the place of application, is fast turning into that of ignorance and idleness."

Even Wadsworth was convinced that only Williams could improve the situation, although the restoration of Williams to command would definitely eliminate Wadsworth's chance for promotion to lieutenant colonel. In November 1804, Wadsworth proposed to officers at West Point that they appeal to President Jefferson to reinstate Williams. Little attention was given to sending correspondence "through channels." Direct contact with the Secretary of War and the President was commonplace.

Although Dearborn officially would not change his position, he placed Lieutenant Swift in command of both the post and the Artillery garrison at Fort Johnston, North Carolina. This delegated command to a very junior officer while still denying that authority to the Chief of Engineers. Pride perhaps kept Dearborn from making this concession. Williams was equally adamant and refused all offers to recall him to duty.

There were many indications that a compromise might be possible. Wilkinson continued to discuss the problem with Dearborn and Jefferson. There were frequent letters between Wilkinson and Williams discussing both sides of the controversy. It is significant that Major Wadsworth was not promoted; this retained the lieutenant colonel space for Williams should he agree to return. When ordered to New Orleans in February, Wadsworth resigned. Captain Barron was now the senior officer of the Corps of Engineers and Academy Superintendent.

Finally, on March 29, 1805, Wilkinson made a proposal to Williams that was acceptable. "I am authorized by the Secretary of War," wrote Wilkinson, "to inform you that, if agreeable to you, the President will re-appoint you to the command of the Corps of Engineers on the express condition that you are not to interfere with the discipline, police, or command of the troops of the line but by his orders, to which alone you are to be subject, and that in all other respects you are to enjoy the honors of your rank." Williams agreed to return.

Wilkinson issued an order on April 17, 1805, which explained the status of officers of the Corps of Engineers. They were not to have command of line troops unless by special order of the President. Most important was the statement that "this suspension of official command, though deemed essential to the interests of a particular corps, does not subvert any inherent principle, or fundamental right, because the superior officers of Engineers are held liable to be called into general command whenever the public service may require, and the will of the President may direct." This was a compromise, one in which the capable hand of Jefferson can be detected. Dearborn's stand was supported; Williams' argument was accepted in principle if not in fact.

Five days later, Williams accepted reappointment as Chief Engineer. Writing to Dearborn he stated, "I beg leave to assure you that this honorable mark of favor has made a deep impression on me, and it is with heartfelt gratitude that I again offer to devote my life to the service of my country." As assurance to the Secretary of War, Williams added, "The explanation which has taken place has put the subject on a correct footing, which will not in future admit of mistake, and it is my wish so to come into service again that the whole might be buried in oblivion."

3

Existence in Name Only

When he arrived at West Point, Williams found Captain Barron, Masson, two other officers, and twenty-four cadets. Lieutenant Alexander Macomb served as adjutant and instructor of tactics. Additional cadets were appointed in May and December. One, Alden Partridge, was to have great impact upon the Military Academy.

The first task facing Williams was to establish a more suitable curriculum. He assigned Barron to teach mathematics and Masson to teach French and drawing. With Mansfield gone and no other qualified instructor available, natural and experimental philosophy was dropped. Macomb would conduct infantry drill and artillery instruction, assisted by Artillery officers of the garrison. The schedule called for infantry drill from 5:00 to 6:00 A.M.; mathematics from 8:00 A.M. to 11:00 A.M.; French and drawing on alternate days from 11:00 A.M. to 1:00 P.M.; study from 2:00 P.M. to 4:00 P.M.; and artillery drill, practical gunnery, surveying, or the study of fortifications after 4:00 P.M. This was essentially the schedule instituted by Major Wadsworth the year before.

There were other problems. Williams wanted to increase the holdings of the library but found little money available. Congress in 1803 had provided $2,000 for "purchasing maps, plans, books and instruments for the department of war and the military academy." This amount was halved in 1804 and reduced to $500 for 1805.

Williams was appalled at the appearance of the cadets. Their uniforms were a mixture resembling those seen at a costume ball. In 1802, cadets had worn the uniform of the Regiment of Artillerists and Engineers; in 1803, the uniform of the Corps of Engineers or the Corps of Artillerists. He now found that some cadets wore uniforms they had purchased before reporting. There were militia uniforms, and one cadet wore the coat of a general officer. Many uniforms were threadbare because cadets were spending most of their salaries for food or mess charges. Williams asked the Secretary of War to prescribe a standard uniform regardless of the branch to which cadets were assigned. He also requested permission to establish a "commons," a mess for all cadets, which would be operated under his supervision. He asked for a band, "even a drum and fife." Artillery units had assigned musicians; the Corps of Engineers had none. He explained his budget problems and asked for help.

Secretary Dearborn agreed with most of Williams' recommendations. He directed that cadets wear the uniform of their branch. This was desirable because many cadets served with units before reporting to West Point and had uniforms. This at least placed cadets in a common uniform differing only by the color of the coat facings. To ease the budget problem, he ordered the purchase of ten sets of imported instruments and a gross of lead pencils, using War Department funds. Field musicians were approved.

Significantly, Dearborn agreed with Williams' recommendation to establish a common mess. In July the first "mess house" opened on a trial basis. Captain Barron presided at every meal. The fare was plain but wholesome, a decided improvement over what cadets had obtained on their own. The trial period disclosed that the daily cost for each cadet was thirty cents, three cents more than the ration allowance. When this was reported to the War Department, the overage was considered too great, and Williams was ordered to discontinue the mess. He protested strongly, forwarding to the Secretary a report by Major Barron (he had been promoted to major in June to fill the vacancy created by Wadsworth's resignation), who indicated that, from his viewpoint as a professor, cadets should not have to devote time to the purchase and preparation of food. He described the financial problems encountered by cadets who spent far more than their daily ration to obtain meals that were unappetizing and unhealthy. The cost left them with little money for uniforms or other necessities. Finally, he wrote, the cadet "finds that his time has been broken, and his progress in science impeded." These arguments were unsuccessful, and the mess was closed.

Williams sent a strong request to Dearborn, asking for "an allowance of clothing to cadets as non-commissioned officers." This too was refused because the cost was considered to be excessive. Williams asked Colonel Burbeck for help, and Burbeck did provide some enlisted Artillery uniforms. This eliminated some of the tattered clothing, but it added another uniform variation.

Despite these administrative problems, Williams and his faculty continued to teach cadets the basic subjects considered so necessary. Three cadets—George Bomford, William McRee, and Joseph Totten—were commissioned in the Corps of Engineers in July. Another first took place when Cadets John Lillie and Ambrose Porter were discharged; both had transferred from the Burbeck academy.

Williams revived the American Military Philosophical Society. By law, only a few subjects could be taught at the Academy. Williams considered the Philosophical Society a means of supplementing the curriculum, a way to expose cadets to academic matters beyond the narrow scope of the Academy curriculum. He considered the activities of the Society to be a part of cadet education and wrote President Jefferson to ask if War Department funds could support the Society. Jefferson refused the request but offered suggestions for increasing membership. Jefferson's hope that Society activities would be successful encouraged Williams.

In November an election of officers retained Williams as president. Most important was the election of members; sixty-seven prominent military and political personages were selected, including James Madison, Commodore Edward Preble, Captain Stephen Decatur, William C. C. Claiborne, Henry Knox, George Clinton, and C. C. Pinckney. The Society eventually included many other distinguished men: John Quincy Adams, James Monroe, John Marshall, DeWitt Clinton, Thomas Cushing, Benjamin Latrobe, Robert Fulton, Eli Whitney, Joel Barlow, and Bushrod Washington. Academicians from other institutions asked to join. These included Professor John Williams of Harvard, historian John Ramsey of South Carolina, and Samuel L. Mitchell, professor of natural history at Columbia. The Army, Navy, Marine Corps, and militia were all well represented. Navy officers who asked to join included William Bainbridge, Charles Stewart, Isaac Hull, and John Rogers.

To support Society activities, Williams donated several shares of Eagle Fire Insurance Company stock. Members contributed funds, enabling Williams to undertake many projects. One of the more important was the establishment of a Society library at West Point to supplement the Academy library. The Society library grew, largely through gifts of its members and friends. General John Armstrong, Minister to France, sent a copy of Jomini's *Traité de Grand Critique*. Other gifts included works of Francis Bacon, Newton, Saxe, Vignola, Villeneuve, and the ten-volume treatise by Montalembert. In addition to books and pamphlets on mathematics, fortifications, architecture, and natural science, the Society library included an extensive collection of manuscripts. One of the most significant was the gift of Captain Richard Whiley: eight volumes containing all the orders issued by General Anthony Wayne during his Indian campaigns.

As a result of Williams' efforts, the Corps of Engineers and the Military Academy cadets had access to the finest collection of technical books in the United States. In addition to the libraries of the Academy and the Military Philosophical Society, they could use private libraries of faculty members or Engineer officers. Williams, Swift, Barron, Mansfield, Masson, and Hassler, who arrived in 1807, all had excellent personal libraries. Despite the lack of academic excellence, the Academy achieved a reputation within the academic community because of the quality of the combined Academy and Society libraries.

Under Williams, the Society published pamphlets on military topics. Included were Major Alexander Macomb's treatise on military law, the first full-length study published in the United States. So important was this book considered that the War Department purchased copies for all garrisons and units. "A Short Essay on The Military Constitution of Nations," originally published in the

National Intelligencer, was republished in pamphlet form. Other publications included Williams' translation of Kosciuszko's *Manoeuvres of Horse Artillery*, Robert Fulton's *Torpedo War and Submarine Explosions*, and Zebulon Pike's *An Account of Expeditions to the Source of the Mississippi*.

Scholarly papers were presented at meetings at West Point, New York City, and Washington. Subjects were not restricted to military matters but encompassed scientific research, exploration, history, and civil engineering. Hassler reviewed Gallatin's "Report on Canals." Lieutenant Joseph Totten discussed maps that he had had prepared in the Indiana Territory and a "plan of the ancient works at Marietta." Alden Partridge's paper on barometric measurement of the Hudson River highlands was discussed. Williams made many presentations, including a proposal for a floating battery to defend the New York harbor and his paper on the barometrical measurement of the Blue Ridge and Allegheny mountains. Major Barron discussed the breach-loading fusil developed by Montalembert. Members recommended the adoption of the fusil by the War Department because of its superiority over the muzzle-loading musket.

Many papers concerned official work by Corps of Engineer officers. Williams promised that "the Corps of Engineers, who have been dispersed over the union, will present to this Society descriptive accounts of all the works they have erected, attended with such observations as their own experience may have suggested." One such by Williams during the construction of fortifications in New York Harbor compared the martello tower with the traditional star-shaped fort. Williams advocated the martello circular conformation and used it in Castle Williams on Governors Island.

By 1807, the Society had achieved national importance, with growing membership and prestige. That year two officers were elected who were not members of the Corps of Engineers. Charles C. Pinckney of South Carolina was elected vice president and William Popham, former aide to General Von Steuben, treasurer. Much of the Society's success was the result of Williams' enthusiasm. His departure from military service in 1812 and the war with Great Britain brought a decline in activities of the Society, and it ceased to exist in 1813.

A similar fate befell the Military Service Institution of the United States a century later. Founded by Major General Winfield Scott Hancock in 1878, the Institution was a flourishing activity that sponsored many fine publications, including a bimonthly journal. Its prestige within military circles, the academic community, and other professions paralleled the reputation of Williams' Military Philosophical Society. Unfortunately, its activities were stopped during World War I, and it ceased to exist shortly thereafter.

For nearly ten years, the Military Philosophical Society was one of the leading scientific institutions in the United States. Its contribution to scientific learning was considerable. Williams considered it to be a semi-official part of the Military Academy. Cadets were exposed to discussions involving the work of scientists, explorers, academicians, artists, and military men of the United States and Europe. The Society library provided materials that the Academy library could not obtain because of budget limitations. More important was the prestige the Society gained for the Military Academy, a reputation for scientific study that far exceeded the scope of its limited curriculum. At the end of its tenth year, the Academy had graduated only seventy-one cadets. Although they made considerable contributions to the Army, their work was not widely known. Thanks to the Military Philosophical Society, the Academy became known in many parts of the country, and sons of many prominent men applied for cadet appointments.

In many ways, 1805 and 1806 were the most critical years of Williams' superintendency. Support from the Secretary of War fluctuated from positive to negative. In October 1805, Dearborn required cadets to purchase their uniforms, stating that he "had not been able to find any authority for continuing to provide clothing for cadets." To standardize cadet pay, he directed that all cadets be appointed to the Regiment of Artillerists regardless of their possible assignment after graduation. The logic directing this order concerned cadet pay. Engineer cadets received $16 a month; Artillery cadets, $10. Assigning all cadets to the Regiment of Artillerists would save the government $6 per cadet.

This decision, coupled with the War Department refusal to support a common mess, was a hardship to cadets. Dearborn justified these economies by saying, "I conceive their pay and emoluments are in full proportion to the officers generally. Among other considerations, it should be recollected that these young gentlemen are receiving their education at the expense of the United States." This decision established a policy continued to the present: each cadet pays for his uniforms.

Williams asked that Mansfield be returned from his surveying tasks in the Northwest Territory. Although Mansfield retained his rank as an officer of the Corps of Engineers, he was paid from other funds. His absence meant one less Engineer officer to assist in accomplishing the many tasks assigned to the branch. Retention of his Engineer commission made that space unavailable to another officer or graduating cadet. The request was refused.

In 1806, the largest graduating class was examined and commissioned. Five cadets were assigned to the Corps of Engineers and ten to the Corps of Artillerists. One of the Engineer cadets, Alden Partridge, was commissioned first lieutenant, one of the few times a graduating cadet was given a rank higher than second lieutenant. Partridge was retained at West Point as assistant teacher of mathematics.

Son of a Revolutionary War veteran, Partridge attended Dartmouth College for two years before being appointed a cadet in December 1805. He remained at West Point for his entire military career. Partridge was a welcome addition to the small staff. As teacher of mathematics, he enabled Barron to devote his efforts to more advanced mathematics and natural philosophy. His presence also made it easier for Williams to divide his time between duties at West Point and work on the fortifications of New York harbor.

In response to a request from Colonel Williams, Secretary Dearborn provided four artillery field guns and two mortars. Lieutenant George Bomford, an 1804 graduate, and Partridge taught cadets artillery procedures using de Sheel's tactics as a text. Bomford also gave lessons in pyrotechny and the preparation of fixed ammunition for artillery pieces. Infantry drill was still based on the Steuben manual.

Williams continued to urge moving the Academy either to Washington or the New York City area. In a letter to Secretary Dearborn in May 1806, Williams indicated that he considered West Point to be only a temporary station for headquarters of the Corps of Engineers and the Military Academy and that he would not request improvements that would be necessary if West Point were to be a permanent headquarters.

He listed improvements needed to make the barracks more habitable, repairs that would provide thirty-two rooms. The Academic Building required extensive work because the ground floor area was in such poor condition that it could not be used. The second-floor fireplace needed repair. Officers' quarters all needed extensive renovation. Williams listed several buildings that were not salvageable and recommended that they be demolished. A smithy and carpenter shop were needed. He proposed that the water supply flow through hollow logs and that a stone wall should be erected around the post to replace the rotting wooden fence. The wharf required repair. All in all, the buildings at West Point were in extremely poor condition. Although it is possible that Williams may have overstated the needed repairs as a means of securing approval for moving the Academy, his statements were verified in letters and memoirs of many cadets.

Williams used the same letter to the Secretary of War to review personnel requirements. Major Mansfield's return having already been refused, he asked for a replacement and repeated his request for a chaplain. He indicated that more privates were needed for general work and duty as waiters. A larger band was a necessity or at least two drums and several fifes to provide music for dress parades. A clock was needed in the cadet area to assure that cadets arrived at formations on time. He asked for a bell sufficiently large to be heard throughout the post as a way to sound an alarm. Apparatus and supplies were needed for philosophical and pyrotechnic experiments.

The move of the Military Academy almost became fact. New York State offered land on Staten Island at no cost to the government. One argument in favor of this location was the possibility of adding naval instruction to provide trained cadets who could become naval officers. This was in agreement with Jefferson's concept of a truly national military academy as a substitute for a national university. A bill presented in Congress was dropped when several Congressmen argued that West Point was the site of the Military Academy by law and that the law should not be changed.

Williams spent much of his time supervising fortification construction in New York harbor. He traveled back and forth in the cutter, *Engineer*, spending as much time as required to supervise activities at either West Point or New York.

During his absence, the Academy was under the supervision of Major Barron, senior officer present and second ranking officer of the Corps of Engineers. Barron had shown his ineptitude for supervision or command during the period after Williams' resignation. He was inclined to neglect supervisory duties, although he was an excellent instructor. As a result, discipline deteriorated. Secretary Dearborn recognized Barron's shortcomings as Acting Superintendent and informed Williams, "Although I have a high opinion of Major Barron as a gentleman of science and integrity, I would prefer your judgment in all cases relating to necessary expenses, the particular qualification of respective students, and in short on every subject which requires the exercise of correct judgment and sound common sense."

At end of 1806, Lieutenant Charles Gratiot preferred charges against Barron for "Neglect of the Military Academy during the absence of Lieut.-Colonel Williams, thereby not advancing the interest and wishes of the public, and destroying the reputation of the institution." Barron was given the choice of resigning or standing trial for "conduct unworthy the Gentleman and Soldier." Investigation of Gratiot's charges had given Williams proof that Barron was "suffering prostitutes to be the companion of his quarters and table, thereby setting an example injurious to the morals of youth and disgraceful to the institution." Barron resigned and left West Point in June 1807. Williams ordered Captain Joseph Swift, the first Academy graduate, to West Point as Acting Superintendent.

Major Barron's resignation did not have any effect on the operation of the Academy, but it did cause dismay in the small group of officers in the Corps of Engineers. The reasons for his departure added more emphasis to the need for high moral character of officers, one of the points Williams stressed throughout his superintendency. In correspondence with the Secretary of War and Colonel Burbeck concerning the commissioning of cadets, he often indicated that a cadet "is free from the slightest imputation against temperance." In another letter to Burbeck in May 1808, Williams told Burbeck that "I keep nothing secret from you" after informing Burbeck that a cadet had "provoked a challenge & then not only refused but complained to the Comdg Officer & had the officer who challenged reported to him and arrested."

Williams stressed the importance of "honour" from the beginning of his superintendency. He sincerely believed an officer's word must be accepted without question and often discussed this with cadets and officers of the Corps of Engineers. There were many reasons for Williams' emphasis on honesty. Every officer, regardless of his branch, was required to sign reports with the statement "I certify on honour that the above is a faithful statement." This statement was required on strength muster rolls, supply inventories, pay records, payment forms, and other reports. Accurate accounting was even more important to Engineer officers because they were accountable for large funds dispersed to civilian contractors who built fortifications and other structures. Absolute honesty was essential in maintaining financial records because Engineer officers received a small percentage of the total project expenditure for performing this additional duty.

The high moral standards and character important to Williams were the bases for many of the regulations he established. He was against intemperance; many cadets were punished for overindulgence. North's tavern was a problem; North refused to stop selling liquor to cadets or soldiers. Dueling challenges were common throughout the Army and the civilian community. Williams did much to stop this practice at West Point and in the Corps of Engineers.

Williams considered religion to be an important part of cadet education. Although his efforts to have a chaplain were unsuccessful, he tried to instill appreciation for religion by requiring services each Sunday with an officer reading the service if no minister was available. He also made it possible for Catholic cadets to attend services in nearby Catholic parishes.

Much of the instruction concerning character and morals was given by example rather than classroom sessions. Williams and his officers displayed a devotion to duty that superseded personal comfort or gain. The action taken concerning Major Barron's dereliction undoubtedly made a profound impression upon both cadets and other officers. The foundations Williams established were continued by his successors.

Barron's departure had little impact on instruction. In February 1807, President Jefferson had appointed Ferdinand R. Hassler as Acting Professor of Mathematics, and he took over much of Barron's instruction. Hassler was a Swiss educated at the University of Gottingen and in Paris. As Attorney General of the Canton of Berne, he had made statistical surveys and supervised public works. Perhaps his most important accomplishment before coming to the United States was a geodetic survey of Switzerland. Hassler brought with him an excellent personal library of scientific and professional works, as well as copies of many of his own studies.

Jefferson had selected Hassler at the recommendation of his fellow countryman Secretary of the Treasury Albert Gallatin. With a well-deserved reputation as a mathematician, philosopher, and astronomer, Hassler seemed to be an excellent choice, but he was not a good instructor. He had never been a teacher and had little concept of teaching methods. He had no understanding of discipline, something cadets soon realized. They took advantage of Hassler's absorption in his teaching and often dropped into class one by one, recited what they had studied the night before, and left whenever they chose.

Hassler remained at West Point until the end of the academic term in 1809. In 1810, he became Professor of Mathematics and Natural Philosophy at Union College at Schenectady. He left this position in 1811 to direct the United States Coast Survey, a task that occupied him until his death in 1843.

Swift described Hassler in his memoirs as an excellent instructor, a view not held by many others. Swift said that "Mr. Hassler's mind was of a desultory cast, in fact it seemed to be crowded with ideas. At the blackboard he would occasionally branch off into notions of extending the use of the lecture . . . to surveys of the mountains of the country, and . . . would point out the geographical form that nature had made of the mountains and valleys and watercourses in a sort of opposition to the artificial boundaries of the states."

One individual who benefitted from Hassler's instruction was Alden Partridge, who was an assistant instructor of mathematics. When he entered the Academy, Partridge had a better mathematics background than most cadets because of his Dartmouth education. Williams and Barron had shown him the engineering applications of mathematics. Hassler, expert in astronomy and geodetic surveys, developed Partridge's ability. His study with Hassler enabled Partridge to undertake his own research, measuring the heights of Catskill mountains by barometrical observation and conducting experiments at West Point concerning artillery and infantry ammunition.

Ordered to return to West Point from Fort Johnston where he had been in charge of fortifying Charleston harbor, Swift arrived before the start of the academic year and moved his family into quarters. Having Swift at West Point enabled Williams to spend more time supervising fortifications in New York harbor and inspecting work at other ports. Swift improved discipline. This was one of the reasons Williams had ordered him to West Point. His instructions to Swift included, "You will please to consider it a leading principle to supporting your command to pay a marked attention to the professors, and to require not only a strict observance of their instruction, but a gentlemanlike deportment towards them from all the officers and cadets."

Seventeen cadets were appointed during 1807, bringing the total on the rolls to forty-one. One of the new cadets was a Dartmouth graduate who had known Alden Partridge. Sylvanus Thayer was appointed a cadet in March 1807 and reported to West Point before the start of the academic term. The number present actually varied, for the War Department often ordered cadets to duty elsewhere. Williams also sent cadets to installations for practical work under the Engineer officer supervising construction.

There was little change in the schedule. Mathematics, now taught by Hassler and Partridge, filled the morning hours. Masson taught drawing and French on alternate afternoons with military subjects every afternoon between the end of Masson's class and supper.

In June the British ship *Leopard* fired on the American frigate *Chesapeake* off Norfolk Roads. In addition to the furor in Congress and outrage throughout the nation, the action led to an intensive effort to improve instruction at the Academy. Worsening relations with Britain and France and their refusal to permit neutral trade with their respective opponents made it apparent that the American military and naval forces were completely inadequate. Rather than attempt to build a much stronger Navy, Jefferson decided to invoke the Embargo Act. Coast defenses were strengthened, and a fleet of small gunboats suitable for use in coastal waters was built. Williams ordered all of the Engineer officers at West Point except Partridge to important harbor sites. Williams, still occupied with the New York forts, tried to supervise Academy activities by frequent visits.

In March 1808, Williams submitted a report to Jefferson recommending many improvements. Jefferson asked Congress to consider adopting Williams' proposal, stating that "the scale on which the Military Academy at West Point was originally established is become too limited to furnish the number of well instructed subjects, in the different branches of artillery and engineering, which the public service calls for." Emphasis on both artillery and engineering requirements was further indication that the Academy was not established solely as a school for engineers.

Congress adopted none of Williams' recommendations. The size of the Corps of Engineers remained unchanged; no additional civilian instructors were authorized; and the proposed move of the Academy to Washington was disregarded. Congress did pass the Act of April 12, 1808, increasing the number of Artillery, Infantry, and Cavalry regiments. Included was an increase in the number of cadets; the 156 new spaces brought the total to 200.

By the end of 1808, forty-one new cadets had been appointed. Williams and Partridge solved housing and feeding more than twice the number of cadets present the previous year by moving enlisted troops out of cadet barracks and by boarding cadets with families on post. Williams appointed Christian Zoeller teacher of drawing. This enabled Williams to have Masson teach engineering in addition to French. There was no provision for a third civilian instructor, but Williams convinced Dearborn that the Academy would benefit from this action. Dearborn provided funds to pay Zoeller until such time as Congress approved the third civilian position. By the end of the term, fifteen cadets had been examined and commissioned. One was Sylvanus Thayer.

March 1809 brought cadets and officers back from the winter recess. Jefferson left office; with him went Secretary of War Dearborn. Dearborn had supported most Academy activities. Appreciation of Jefferson's support of the Military Academy was shown when the officers of the Corps of Engineers commissioned Thomas Sully to do a full-length, life-size portrait of Jefferson. The portrait today hangs in the Library.

The new President, James Madison, appointed Dr. William Eustis, a Revolutionary War surgeon, to replace Dearborn. Eustis and Madison brought with them the old distrust of a regular military force. Eustis maintained direct control over almost every military activity and made parsimonious allocations of funds. He directed that the one horse-drawn artillery unit sell its horses because mounts were too expensive. He refused to authorize the purchase of fresh fruit for hospitalized soldiers in Louisiana. He refused permission for regiments to recruit men needed to bring units to authorized strength. At a time when relations with Britain were deteriorating, the Army had fewer than 7,000 of its authorized 10,000 men.

Williams' relationship with Eustis was anything but cordial. Shortly after Eustis was appointed, Williams urged him to adopt the martello tower as the standard harbor fort instead of the classic star-shaped fortification. Eustis refused to listen. In May 1809, Williams submitted a plan for reorganization of the Army based primarily on the need for command by Engineer officers. He proposed that the Corps of Engineers be combined with the Corps of Artillerist units manning harbor fortifications and that the remaining Artillerist companies be incorporated into the Light Artillery, then a separate branch. Williams' proposal was ignored. In 1813, Williams described Eustis in a letter to Swift, "in a word it seems to have been incompatible with his ideas of self-dignity to receive advice."

Eustis's tenure almost doomed the Military Academy. In 1809, he approved the appointment of only four cadets, this during his first month in office. The following year, he made only two appointments, and none in 1811. He ordered many cadets to duty elsewhere and curtailed Academy funds. In November, he informed Williams that the three civilian instructors would have to exist on salaries authorized for two; War Department contingency funds would no longer be used for Zoeller's salary. This problem eased when Hassler resigned to become a professor at Union College. Zoeller also resigned in 1810, leaving only Masson and Partridge as instructors.

Even day-to-day living was affected. In May 1809, Eustis ordered troops to West Point, theoretically to survey the condition of several thousand muskets stored there for many years. Williams was directed to house the troops in barracks. To do this, he moved cadets into officers' quarters, the library, and the Academic Building. The move was supposed to be temporary, but the units remained at West Point until 1812.

After directing Williams to order all possible Engineer officers to harbor installations, Eustis wrote to Lieutenant Colonel Mansfield in January 1810, ordering him to return to West Point because "the want of a sufficient number of able instructors at the Military Academy & the importance of the institution to the public interest require the services of all the Officers of the Corps of Engineers." Mansfield was given the alternative of resigning his commission; this he did.

At first glance, Eustis's letter would appear to be an attempt to support the Academy as an academic institution. In view of other orders, which destroyed Williams' capability for efficient operation and supervision of the Academy, this interpretation of the letter to Mansfield may be incorrect. It is possible that Eustis's only intent was to return Mansfield to duty with the Corps of Engineers and then to order him to one of the harbor projects.

Eustis did provide some support by issuing regulations for the operation of the Academy based on recommendations Williams had made to Secretary Dearborn and then to Eustis. These regulations required cadets to be between fifteen and twenty years of age. Each cadet appointed was required to serve a minimum of four years unless sooner discharged. Qualification standards were established: each cadet was to be "well versed in the English language, in Writing & Arithmetic ... of good moral character and of sound Constitution." Cadets would receive a certificate after being examined for a commission, the first directive that a diploma be given at graduation. A common uniform was to be required regardless of a cadet's branch. Furloughs were not authorized except for "Sickness, Domestic casualties, or at the special request of Parents or Guardians." Pay and allowances would cease during furloughs. The academic recess from December to March was continued. Most important, the Superintendent was authorized to issue internal regulations "provided that no existing Regulation be altered or counteracted without special order of the Commandant of the Corps of Engineers."

Two weeks after issuing these regulations, Eustis sent Williams an order that destroyed all of Williams' efforts to bring prestige to the Academy. He directed that "after the cadets shall have completed their Academical Education, it is intended that they shall be attached to Companies and perform Duty as Soldiers in the Lines, in order to their becoming Candidates for promotion to Commissions." Ironically, cadets were to be quartered and rationed with officers of companies to which they had been assigned even though they were relegated to the status of enlisted men. This directive was based on the fact that cadets remained assigned to their companies while studying at the Academy.

Any interpretation that this letter only intended to make certain that cadets were familiar with enlisted duties before being commissioned was nullified by Eustis's next letter. He made his intention clear in his June 4 order that cadets "shall wear precisely the same uniform (the cloth may be of superior quality) with the Company to which they are attached, the same arms, and perform the duties of Privates with such exceptions and exemptions as the Commanding Officer may permit; that they may also perform the duties of Corporals and Sergeants if found qualified, and that when they shall be nominated for commissions, their appointment may be considered and styled promotions." There was no doubt that Eustis intended to have cadets serve as enlisted men before being commissioned.

Unable to convince the Secretary that this order should be rescinded, Williams resorted to a direct appeal to President Madison. In addition to asking Madison to revoke the order, he informed the President that he was convinced that "under its present want of necessary buildings, requisite professors, and almost everything that should constitute a seminary of Military Science" the Military Academy could not meet the requirements of the Army.

Williams faced another problem involving Lieutenant Partridge, who had been stationed at West Point since his graduation in 1806. Why he had not been sent periodically to supervise fortifications or other construction, as were other Engineer officers, is not known. He had studied mathematics at Dartmouth; this had created a favorable impression on Williams and other faculty members. He had been commissioned a first lieutenant at graduation, one of the few in the entire history of the Academy to start at that rank. During Williams' frequent absences, he was the Acting Superintendent, as the only Engineer officer at West Point, although his primary duty was teaching mathematics.

Williams apparently was satisfied with Partridge's performance of his administrative and tutorial duties. Nevertheless, for some unknown reason, Williams ordered Captain Charles Gratiot to West Point in June 1810. This automatically made Gratiot, senior to Partridge, the Acting Superintendent.

Williams fully realized that Partridge would object to losing command status. To eliminate this potential problem, he very carefully issued orders defining the duties of both Gratiot and Partridge. Gratiot was to command the post and all activities except those of academic nature. Gratiot was informed that "all the rules established for the particular administration of academical superintendence necessarily fall under the professors' charge, and, of course, Lieutenant Partridge, the chief professor, must be supported, and in no instance interrupted, in enforcing the execution of them, or in giving theoretical or practical instruction to cadets." Realizing that there would be overlap between these command functions and academic supervision, Williams stated that in such cases "the Colonel Commandant relies upon the judgment of the commanding officer, which, joined to the disposition of the professors generally, will, it is presumed, insure a complete cooperation. It must be understood, however, that while officers of the corps are engaged as professors, they must be considered . . . not liable to any military order which might interrupt or impede their academical duties; but this is not to exempt them from obeying all orders which the police and good government of the post, and gradations of military rank, may render necessary."

This regulation gave Partridge control of all academic activities and assured him that Gratiot would not interfere. As Williams had anticipated, Partridge objected to this arrangement and asked that his previous command status be restored. His letter reveals much about his character and egotism. He cited "conditions upon which I am willing to continue my duties in the Academy." He asked that "all Academy regulations, and also the cadets, be exclusively and in every respect under my direction." If Williams did not agree, Partridge asked for leave. All of this would appear to be a rehearsal for what would occur in 1817.

Williams refused Partridge's request with a stern rebuke and denied his request for leave. Partridge then obtained a doctor's certificate, stating that he was "very much affected with a febrile disease, and rendered thereby unfit for duty." Williams regretfully approved the leave.

To assist Gratiot, Williams ordered Lieutenant Sylvanus Thayer to West Point. Admirably qualified for academic duty, Thayer had attended Dartmouth in the class behind Partridge. Although Partridge had left Dartmouth after two years, Thayer had remained to graduate. To assist Thayer, Williams detailed four cadets to act as assistant instructors, a practice that would continue for over 125 years.

Working with Gratiot and Thayer, Williams prepared internal regulations to govern the operation of the Academy in accordance with authority given by Secretary Eustis in April. To be eligible for a commission, a cadet was required to complete studies including arithmetic, logarithms, algebra, geometry, trigonometry, mensuration of heights and distances, planometry, stereometry, surveying, artificer's work, conic sections, and French. Military training included the manual of arms, management of artillery field pieces, and the "various evolutions of infantry and artillery perfectly."

A certificate was to be given each cadet meeting these requirements. Regulations stated that "whenever a cadet shall have completed the above course of studies, he shall be entitled to a certificate . . . after which, if he wishes, he shall be excused from attending the Academy, but may pursue such studies as he choses at his quarters." This rule indicated that no prescribed time would be required for graduation and confirmed the practice of graduating a cadet as soon as he mastered the curriculum. Although not stated, it was understood that cadets would be commissioned as branch vacancies became available.

Other rules prescribed hours for study and drill and disciplinary requirements. The commanding officer was authorized to appoint a cadet as Adjutant, and all cadets were subject to duty as an Officer of the Day. Violation of the regulations was reason for punishment. Disobedience would result in dismissal, although a cadet so charged could request a court of inquiry. A recommendation for dismissal was to be referred to the Secretary of War "that he may assign such duties as he may think proper to the dismissed cadet at any other post or place."

Giving qualified endorsement to Secretary Eustis's directive that cadets would serve as soldiers, the regulations stated: "Cadets are required by law to perform any duty that a soldier may be commanded to perform, and, that there may be no misapprehension of this obligation, it is here declared that they are liable to be ordered on all kinds of military duty . . . as well as upon any other duty that may tend to increase their military knowledge."

Eustis continued to chip away at the Academy. He ordered almost all cadets to other posts where they either assisted fortification construction or were tutored by Engineer officers. Williams objected, pointing out to the Secretary that he found no law authorizing cadets to be tutored by individual officers. His objection failed to convince Eustis. No class graduated in 1810—one result of Eustis's actions.

Another action by Eustis undercut the Superintendent's disciplinary authority. In July 1810, Cadets Burchstead and White resorted to blows, and the Officer of the Day was called to stop the fight. Burchstead was ordered to his quarters. Burchstead refused and, drawing his sword, threatened the officer. A Court of Inquiry found Burchstead guilty of mutiny, an offense subject to court martial. Burchstead was dismissed and sent under arrest to Fort Columbus on Governors Island, where Colonel Burbeck was to try him, since Burchstead was an Artillery cadet. Eustis set aside Burchstead's dismissal, permitted him to continue his studies, and commissioned him an Infantry ensign in March 1811.

Eustis then ordered Gratiot and Thayer to report for duty at harbor installations. Thayer, fortunately, was assigned to New York to assist Williams, where he remained for nearly two years. This association enabled Thayer to absorb many of Williams' concepts about education, military science, and organization of the Military Academy, for Thayer later adopted many of Williams' ideas when he became Superintendent.

Nineteen cadets were graduated in 1811; none were at West Point when commissioned. Eustis, however, appointed no new cadets. Although there were thirty-two cadets in service, only six were at West Point. The only instructor was Partridge, now a captain. Masson was on leave. The curriculum essentially was the same as in 1802. The buildings and quarters were badly in need of repair. After ten years, the Academy seemed doomed. Eustis appeared to be doing everything possible to hasten its closing without officially ending its existence. This he could not do without congressional approval.

In its first ten years, eighty-nine cadets had been appointed. Seventy-one had completed the course and been commissioned. Fifteen had been assigned to the Corps of Engineers; thirty-eight, to the regiments of Artillery; one, to the Dragoon regiment; and fourteen to Infantry units. Two were not commissioned although they did complete the course. The energy, enthusiasm, and drive of Jonathan Williams had developed a reputation for the Academy as an institution of scientific learning. Its library was recognized as the finest technical library in the United States, due to efforts of the Military Philosophical Society as much as to books purchased with appropriated funds. The actions of the Secretary of War, however, nullified everything that Williams had accomplished. At the end of its first ten years, the United States Military Academy virtually existed in name only and appeared to be destined for oblivion.

4

Right Man at the Right Time?

As the new year of 1812 started, it became shockingly apparent to Congress that, with war with Britain clearly approaching, the armed forces of the United States were unprepared for any conflict. The small Navy, only 16 ships, was vastly inferior to the 400 ship British Navy, already tested against the French. U.S. seamen were well trained. The Army, by contrast, was far from combat ready. Its 7,000 men and officers were scattered in small installations from Fort Mackinac to Florida; from New Orleans to New England. Thanks to Secretary Eustis, arms and equipment were obsolete and in poor condition. Almost every unit was understrength. Regiments were commanded by Revolutionary War veterans over sixty years of age. Senior officers had little training for commanding large forces; no force of any size had been assembled since Anthony Wayne's Legion fought Indians in Ohio. With most installations manned by company-size garrisons, there had been little opportunity or reason to schedule battalion or regimental training. Both staff control and logistic supply were inadequate. Training was lax and varied from unit to unit.

On January 11, a worried Congress increased the size of the Army by ten regiments of infantry, two of artillery, and one of light dragoons. In addition to prescribed officers and men, each artillery regiment included forty cadets; each infantry regiment, ten; and the single dragoon regiment, twenty-four. Had this law been implemented by Eustis appointing young men to fill the cadet spaces, facilities at West Point would have not been unable to house, feed, or educate the additional cadets.

The law was little more than a paper exercise. Recruits would not volunteer for the five-year term, and few regiments were activated. Eustis did appoint a few cadets who were assigned directly to units, not to the Military Academy.

Captain Partridge and Professor Florimond Masson, brother of Francis Masson who had resigned in 1808, taught a handful of cadets.

Exactly how many cadets were present cannot be determined, another informational gap caused by the destruction of West Point and Army records. Forty years later, Thayer wrote Cullum that only four cadets remained on the rolls by April 1812 and that "there could have been no cadets at West Point at term time except De Russy." Eighteen cadets were commissioned from January to June; all except De Russy were in the field with artillery or infantry companies. Rene De Russy, the only cadet at West Point, was commissioned in June, the last graduate of 1812. Partridge was on leave; there were no cadets; the Military Academy had ceased to exist in all but name.

On April 29, 1812, Congress passed a bill that placed the Academy on a foundation that assured its continued development. An academic framework was provided, with professors of Natural and Experimental Philosophy, Mathematics, and the Art of Engineering added to teachers of Drawing and French already authorized. The Academy remained under the Chief of Engineers, but all of the academic positions could be filled either by Engineer officers or by civilians who would receive the "pay and emoluments" of officers. A ninety-four man company of bombardiers, sappers, and miners was to be commanded by Engineer officers. Twenty-five thousand dollars was provided to erect or renovate buildings and for obtaining apparatus, books, and "all necessary implements."

Most important were the stipulations concerning cadets. All cadets "heretofore appointed in the service of the United States, whether of artillery, cavalry, or infantry, or that may in future be appointed as herein after provided, shall at no time exceed two hundred and fifty; that they may be attached at the discretion of the President of the United States as students to the military academy." Cadets were to be organized into companies. Four musicians were allocated to each company. Cadets would be "trained and taught all the duties of a private, non-commissioned officer, and officer." Three months of each year were to be devoted to a summer camp where cadets would learn duties "incident to a regular camp." Appointment age was between fourteen and twenty-one, and each applicant "shall be well versed in reading, writing, and arithmetic." Each cadet would serve five years unless sooner discharged. All cadets would receive the pay of Engineer cadets.

After completing the course, a cadet was to be considered "as among the candidates for a commission in any corps, according to the duties he may be judged competent to perform." If no vacancies existed in a corps, the graduated cadet could be attached to that corps with brevet rank "of the lowest grade as a supernumerary officer until a vacancy shall happen."

This Act was as important as the 1802 Act establishing the Military Academy. What Burbeck had recommended nearly twenty years earlier and Williams had requested was now law: cadets would no longer be assigned to units; they were appointed to the Military Academy; cadet spaces were deleted from regimental manpower authorizations. Equally important, a cadet would be commissioned only in a branch for which he was qualified; the determination of a cadet's qualifications would be made by the Superintendent and faculty.

An applicant had to meet standards for reading, writing, and arithmetic established by the faculty. For many years, applicants were examined at West Point before becoming cadets. Age limits were prescribed; the Secretary of War could no longer change these requirements without congressional approval.

Three months were to be devoted to summer camp, a pattern that is still followed. In 1812, the requirement may have been a disadvantage. If the winter vacation were to be continued, less than six months could be devoted to academic instruction. The camp requirement nevertheless provided military training uninterrupted by academics or weather. Conversely, concentrating military instruction in the summer months lessened the need for military training during the academic term.

Organizing cadets into companies made it possible to teach cadets the duties of privates and noncommissioned officers. Company officers initially were to be Engineer officers, the first assignment of tactical officers, "Tacs," to cadet companies. The organization specified would systematize a cadet's existence if nothing else, providing some idea of the military system he would encounter after graduation.

Nothing in the Act specified the academic departments to be established; this was left to the Superintendent. The mere fact that professorships were authorized provided the basis for an expanded curriculum, the curriculum Williams had advocated. Professors were to have the equivalent rank of lieutenant colonel. An assistant professor with the rank of captain was authorized for each department, "which assistant professor shall be taken from the most prominent characters of the officers or cadets." The specification that cadets could be assigned as assistant professors enabled the Superintendent to use cadets if qualified officers were not available. Cadets served as instructors periodically until 1942.

Williams offered Jared Mansfield the professorship of Natural and Experimental Philosophy. Mansfield accepted and indicated that he would return to West Point from his survey position in the Northwest Territory in time for the academic term. Williams had written to Mansfield in March 1809 that he wanted Mansfield "here to take the direction of the Academy." He informed Mansfield, "If I had not been well assisted by Lieut. A. Partridge I should not have been able to have got through in the Government of the young men, of whom we have 40 at a time at West Point, but by prompt and decisive measures with mild & gentle treatment to all the deserving, we have gone on far better than I could have expected." Williams indicated his future plans by informing Mansfield, "I want you to superintend the whole, & devote yourself to researches & demonstrations in what is strictly understood as Physics with an apparatus inferior to none in Europe." Eustis dashed Williams' hopes by refusing to recall Mansfield and then by his ultimatum that led to Mansfield's resignation. Williams perhaps sensed the difficult years ahead as he ended his 1809 letter: "This is what I want, but my zeal is almost burnt out, & without the fuel of public patronage it will certainly be extinguished."

Mansfield accepted Williams' new offer but, as a civilian, could not be placed in charge of the Academy. By law, only the senior Engineer officer present could exercise overall supervision. Captain Partridge continued as principal Assistant Professor of Mathematics. Florimond Masson returned as teacher of French, and Christian Zoeller as teacher of Drawing. With an increased number of cadets, funds for buildings and equipment, and approval for selecting instructors for each of the academic departments, it appeared that Williams could develop the institution he had envisioned for ten years.

Williams had resigned in 1803 because Engineer officers were denied command of troops of other branches. He had been reappointed in 1805 with the assurance that he would be responsible only to the Secretary of War and the President and that the President could authorize him to command troops of other branches. In May 1812, Eustis placed Williams under the command of Brigadier General Joseph Bloomberg whose district included West Point and the harbor defenses of New York. Two weeks later, war was declared with Britain. On the same day, Williams complained to President Madison that he now had fourteen superior officers compared to the three over him in the peace establishment. He asked the President to authorize him to command the New York harbor defenses. Madison not only complied, he directed Bloomfield that "whenever exigencies of the service may require the talents and knowledge of the officers of the Corps of Engineers beyond the line of their immediate profession, you may assign to those under your command such duties in the line of the Army as may comport with their rank." Bloomfield informed Williams of these instructions.

Williams immediately placed Major Armistead in charge of the Corps of Engineers and prepared to move to Governors Island to assume command of the New York defenses. Before he could do this, eighteen junior officers of the Regiment of Artillerists signed a memorial objecting to Williams being placed in command of artillery troops. Addressed to Colonel Burbeck, the Chief of Artillery, the memorial was left on a table in General Bloomfield's quarters. Bloomfield, in a quandary, placed the matter in Eustis's hands. While waiting for a decision, Bloomfield informed Eustis, "I have deemed it correct to exercise the discretion with which the pleasure of the President has honoured me, to suspend calling Colonel Williams or any of the Corps of Engineers to exercise the duties in the line of the Army contemplated in your communication of the 23d of June last, until I shall be favoured with the further orders of the President in this unpleasant business."

Williams considered this a breach of faith and submitted his resignation to both Secretary Eustis and President Madison. Six weeks passed without word from Washington. Then, on August 29, Williams was informed that his resignation was accepted, effective July 31.

Swift in later years accused Burbeck of supporting if not instigating the Governors Island memorial. To the contrary, the Burbeck papers include no documents to support Swift's allegation. Burbeck's correspondence with Williams shows a cordial relationship between the two men during Williams' entire period of service. It would appear that Williams' old opponent, Eustis, saw the controversy as a means of ridding himself of Williams. One can guess that President Madison at first refused to accept Williams' resignation and, with problems of the newly declared war facing him, finally agreed to Eustis's demands.

Williams retired to his home in Philadelphia but was called from retirement almost immediately to become executive member of the Committee of Defense of the Delaware River and Bay, responsible for the security of Philadelphia. The Governor of New York commissioned him a brigadier general of militia. He was frequently consulted regarding the harbor defenses of New York City and Military Academy affairs. As a token of respect and affection for their departed commander, officers of the Corps of Engineers commissioned Thomas Sully to do the full length portrait of Williams that today hangs in the USMA Library. In 1814, Williams was elected to Congress, where he served until his death on May 16, 1815.

The first graduate of the Military Academy, Joseph G. Swift was now the senior officer of the Corps of Engineers. The Senate confirmed him as Chief of Engineers with the rank of colonel in December 1812. Ten years after completing his cadet studies, Swift as senior Engineer officer was also the Academy Superintendent. Other officers of the Corps were Walker K. Armistead, George Bomford, Rene De Russy, Charles Gratiot, Alexander Macomb, William McRee, Alden Partridge, Sylvanus Thayer, and Joseph G. Totten. All except Macomb were Academy graduates; as a young lieutenant, Macomb had studied at both the Burbeck school and the Military Academy. All were between twenty-three and thirty years of age. All would participate in the development of the Academy during the next half century. Four would serve as Chief of Engineers and three as Superintendent.

Ironically, after Williams' resignation, several Engineer officers commanded troops of other branches. Both McRee and Macomb commanded artillery units. McRee was chief of artillery of General Wade Hampton's Northern Army; and Macomb, commander of the 3rd Regiment of Artillery. All nine Engineer officers served at one time or other as chief engineer of one of the northern armies in combat. All were promoted in either brevet or permanent rank. Swift and Macomb became brevet brigadier generals; McRee and Gratiot, brevet colonels; Armistead, a permanent lieutenant colonel; Bomford and Totten, brevet lieutenant colonels; Thayer, a brevet major; and De Russy, who was commissioned in June 1812, a permanent captain. Meanwhile, Alden Partridge, who had been promoted to captain in 1810, remained at West Point and received little recognition and no promotion during the war.

Swift, as Chief Engineer of General Wilkinson's Army on the Canadian border, could not be released from his duties; Partridge remained in charge of the

Academy. He was also Professor of Mathematics. Mansfield was Professor of Natural and Experimental Philosophy; Masson, teacher of French; and Zoeller, teacher of Drawing. Thirty-two cadets remained on the rolls after the Class of 1811 was graduated, although many may have been elsewhere. Nine cadets were appointed during 1812; eighteen were graduated, including some cadets not attending the Academy; and eleven were dismissed.

In many ways, the Military Academy was dormant during 1812; instruction differed little from the Williams period. Much of Partridge's time was devoted to supervising the repair of buildings in preparation for the arrival of a greater number of cadets in the coming year. The barracks built in 1795 required much work, but they remained cold, drafty, and extremely uncomfortable when renovation was completed. To provide room for cadets, enlisted men moved into an old warehouse converted into barracks. Quarters of officers and enlisted men needed repair. One officer's wife complained that her home was in such poor condition that cows could thrust their heads through cracks in the walls. The academic building needed a new chimney and interior work. A few small buildings were erected, and a new pier replaced the dilapidated moorings at the north end of the post. Little improvement was made to Fort Putnam, but the magazine in Fort Clinton was repaired to better store powder. Little effort was made to upgrade the armament of either fort. Significantly, the fortifications at West Point were no longer considered important because Williams' New York harbor defenses appeared to be capable of preventing the British fleet from entering the Hudson River.

The company of bombardiers, sappers, and miners was used for all post details. Although its authorized strength was ninety-four men, it usually was understrength because recruiters had to compete with competition from line and militia units. In 1814, it was sent to the Northern Army commanded by Major General Jacob Brown.

The last members of the Class of 1812 were commissioned in June. Fewer than twenty cadets remained for summer training and the start of the fall academic term. In December, most of the cadets left West Point for home or other more pleasant winter surroundings. Partridge left for his annual trip to Vermont.

Returning in early April, he found cadets already reporting for duty. By mid-April, eighty-six new cadets had joined the twelve from the previous year to make the Corps of Cadets larger than at any previous time. The increase in appointments was the result of the Act of April 1812 and the appointment of John Armstrong as Secretary of War in January 1813. Armstrong was sincerely interested in the Academy and gave every indication that he would support it fully.

Armstrong realized that Swift could not properly perform his duties as Chief of Engineers or supervise the Military Academy while on duty with combat units in northern New York and in Canada. In November 1813, after the battle of Chrystler's Field, he ordered Swift to New York to assume command of New York harbor defenses, including artillery troops manning the fortifications. During his stay in the north, Swift had met an energetic young artilleryman, Winfield Scott. A close friendship developed, a friendship that grew with the years and brought Scott into contact with the Military Academy.

Swift apparently realized that he did not have the experience and knowledge to head an educational institution. Despite duty with combat units in the 1812–1813 attacks against Canada, he took time to seek advice and information from sources outside the Army. John T. Kirkland, president of Harvard, provided copies of college regulations, a list of books in the Harvard library, and a review of teaching methods used. Thayer provided information concerning Dartmouth. Although Swift may have discussed teaching methods with Partridge and Mansfield, there is no evidence that such occurred. Swift returned to New York in November 1813 to command forces defending the city and harbor. This enabled him to supervise Academy activities and to make frequent trips to West Point.

Partridge remained in charge of the Academy. Swift had little choice other than to leave Partridge at West Point. No other Engineer officer was available; all were serving with combat units or supervising construction. There was no reason to question Partridge's capability. He had been at the Academy since his graduation in 1806, and Williams had often praised his work. Swift had known Partridge during his tour at West Point in 1807.

Mansfield, who had been ill, reported to West Point in August. Swift offered the professorship of Engineering to Major Pierre L'Enfant, planner of the District of Columbia, but L'Enfant declined. Partridge, who had been Acting Professor of Mathematics, became Professor of Engineering and was replaced by Andrew Ellicott, the astronomer of the United States. Swift now had the framework to develop the curriculum envisioned by Jonathan Williams.

Not content with this concept, Swift took steps to add other subjects. Writing to Partridge from Sacketts Harbor in October prior to his move to New York, Swift directed that "the handwriting and spelling of the Cadets must be attended to. You will therefore cause each of their exercises as you may deem essential, to be written in blank books in a fair hand, keeping the books clean to be examined every Saturday morning." In 1814, a teacher of writing, Benjamin O. Tyler, came from Washington periodically to give penmanship lessons to the cadets.

Swift wanted cadets to learn more about their country and other nations. In early 1813, he requested Secretary Armstrong to appoint a chaplain who would also "lecture in Geography, History and Ethics." Nothing came from this request. In June 1813, he asked for a "Chaplain, Surgeon, and Professor of History, Geography and Ethics." Armstrong agreed and appointed the Reverend Adam Empie as Cadet Chaplain and Acting Professor of Geography, History, and Ethics and Dr. Samuel Walsh as Surgeon.

Many writers have considered Swift a figurehead Superintendent who delegated his duties to Partridge. His actions from the time he was promoted to Williams' position do not support this theory. In 1812 and 1813, while serving as Chief Engineer of Major General James Wilkinson's army during the invasion of Canada, Swift found time to take an active and energetic role in Academy affairs. He was instrumental in revising the curriculum and selecting faculty members. Realizing the desirability of reviewing instructional methods of other institutions, he asked for advice from their presidents and faculty. His knowledge of the poor condition of Academy buildings and profound interest in the welfare of both the cadets and the staff enabled him to obtain support from the Secretary of War.

Much of the criticism of Swift has centered on the fact that he chose to stay in New York from 1813 until ordered to West Point in 1816. He had reasons for staying. The United States was at war; the British fleet had penetrated Chesapeake Bay to capture Washington and attack Baltimore. The war along the Canadian frontier was bringing more disaster upon American forces. It was not impossible that the British might attack New York; and, as its harbor commander, Swift had to devote most of his efforts to improving the defenses and training his troops. Nevertheless, he made weekly or biweekly trips to West Point, taking a supervisory role in Academy affairs.

Although the Act of April 1812 had prescribed age and scholarship requirements for appointment, these were often ignored. George D. Ramsay, Class of 1820, was appointed a cadet in 1814 at the age of twelve. Many years later in response to Cullum's request, he indicated that his early education "consisted of some little knowledge of the Latin and Greek. I had read Caesar's commentaries, Sallust, and had made some little progress in Greek grammar. Of Mathematics I knew nothing." Physical requirements were almost nonexistent. Ramsay recalled Cadet Daniel Mulhallon who had only one arm; Mulhallon resigned in 1818. Benjamin Tyler, the writing instructor who visited West Point often during 1814, wrote Partridge in 1817: "I had a long talk yesterday with Poulk the one eyed Cadet [Cadet Edward Polk, separated in 1816 and believed to have deserted]." According to Ramsay, Cadet J. J. Shuler brought his wife with him when he reported. He surreptitiously found lodgings for her with Mrs. Kinsley south of the Post, and sneaked off nights to see her until he graduated in 1822. Another married a Kinsley daughter while a cadet but later resigned.

When Professor Mansfield and his family arrived in August 1813, they found the Academy much as it had been when Mansfield left for Ohio in 1803, although there were some changes. They landed at the new stone dock at the north end of the Post and climbed the same winding, narrow path to the Plain. Mansfield's daughter recalled wild roses and sweet briar lining the path. Near the top of the hill, but below the Plain, were two small cottages, Chaplain Empie's quarters and the home of Mrs. Thompson, who still maintained a mess for a few cadets. Near these was a frame building housing commissary supplies, Major Burton's "store."

A hillock marked the end of the path; east of the hillock was a small building occupied by a soldier named Blane. Before a regular tailor shop was established,

Blane repaired cadet clothing. Northwest of the hillock was the warehouse converted into troop barracks.

The row of buildings along the western edge of the Plain was little changed. The Mansfields were assigned the first house, a duplex, the same quarters they had occupied in 1802–1803. Dr. Samuel Walsh, the surgeon, and his family occupied the northern half. Next to it was the renovated Academic Building. A small house, occupied by Captain Partridge, stood on the edge of a deep hollow with a small mound in its center, the present site of the Superintendent's garden. Behind it was a large pond fed by water trickling down the hill from Fort Putnam. The pond provided the ice supply for a long time; ice cut here was stored in the ice house in Execution Hollow. It is possible that ice was also taken from the lower part of Execution Hollow where water would accumulate when winter snow melted. Another small hollow in front of the Academic Building was filled with wild rose bushes. In the 1860s, the two hollows and the pond were filled.

The next house, possibly the oldest at West Point, was a mess hall operated by Captain Partridge's uncle, Isaac Partridge, after a common mess was approved by the Secretary of War. Professor Ellicott lived in the next house to the south. In the rear of the Ellicott house was a small building used by the barber. It later became a school for post children. The last house on the row, built before the Revolution and occupied by Jonathan Williams, was occupied by the French teacher, Florimond Masson, and his large family. The house was razed in 1839.

The stone boundary wall surveyed by Macomb ran along the back of this row of buildings and then turned east until it reached the river near the site of the present library. The old laboratory building and other small structures present in 1802 were gone, as was the model yard. Immediately south of the wall was North's tavern, still an attraction for cadets and enlisted personnel.

Fort Clinton stood above the Hudson with only a few cannon in place. It was used as a powder magazine. It included the "Black Hole," a prison for enlisted offenders. Cadet barracks were not too far distant, northwest on the edge of Execution Hollow. There was one change from Mansfield's memories of his previous tour; barracks were now occupied only by cadets. In 1803, cadets had lived on the second floor and enlisted artillerymen on the first. The only hard surface roadway on the Post was a brick walk stretching from the barracks to the old Williams house.

Most frame buildings were painted yellow. Many years later, Mansfield's daughter commented that "they seemed to have known no color but yellow in those days." Things have not changed much: today, the tendency to paint all government buildings a certain color causes comments about "Quartermaster buff" or "GI white." The buildings were neat and in far better condition than when Mansfield had last seen them in 1803.

Many areas of the Plain were still covered with scrub pine. Clear spaces had been made near Fort Clinton, the cadet barracks, and in front of the Academic Building. Parades, drills, and summer camp were held near the academic area.

The flag pole was moved from Fort Clinton to the hillock at the head of the path from the dock in 1813 and remained there until 1820.

Mansfield brought with him a white horse and a chaise, the only horse at West Point in many years. When he learned that there was no stable, he had it taken across the river to Garrison. During summer vacation, he and his family would ride the carriage through Danbury to his old home in New Haven.

Despite the eighty-six cadets appointed in 1813, only one cadet was graduated. George Trescot, who had entered the Academy in March, was commissioned in October after his seven months' instruction in mathematics, French, and drawing. Mansfield, for self-determined health reasons, taught no philosophy classes that year nor in 1814. Partridge conducted infantry and artillery training during the summer. Academic instruction at the Academy was no better than it had been in 1803.

Knowing that more cadets would be appointed in 1814, Swift submitted a series of requests. Secretary Armstrong approved some of the more important projects. He agreed with Swift that the buildings at West Point were inadequate and approved the plan for new barracks, an academic building, and a mess hall. Probably assisted by Partridge and possibly by both Mansfield and Ellicott, Swift carefully studied the entire area before selecting a location for the buildings. His decision would affect physical development of the Academy to the present day.

The existing facilities were completely inadequate. The Long Barracks, built in 1796, had been intended to house possibly as many as 100 cadets. After the company of bombardiers, sappers, and miners moved to the converted warehouse barracks, cadets occupied both floors, sleeping on narrow pallets. By 1814, the barracks could not accommodate the 200 cadets. In warm weather, they could use the stoops, but such was impractical on cold nights. Some cadets lived with officers and families, a necessary imposition.

Because the Academic Building was used as a library and a headquarters as well as a classroom, professors and instructors also taught classes in their homes. Messing facilities were crowded. The mess hall, a converted house, was far too small to feed cadets at a single sitting. Additional rough tables and benches filled the rooms used for the cadet mess. Mrs. Thompson continued to board a few cadets, but even her help did little to improve the situation.

Almost every building failed to meet the added requirements. Officer and enlisted quarters, laboratory space, a carpenter shop, a new store building, gun sheds, and even storage structures were badly needed. Fortunately, Secretary Armstrong agreed with General Swift, and funds were provided for a major construction program, starting with new barracks, a mess hall, and an academic building.

Instead of locating the buildings near the old Long Barracks or near the Academic Building on the west edge of the Plain, Swift decided to have the buildings erected in an east-west line along the south edge of the Plain approximately on the site of the present-day Eisenhower Barracks. Old buildings along this line, some built during the Revolution and others during the Burbeck period, would be razed. The mess hall would be the western building with the academic building between it and the barracks. One disadvantage was the proximity of North's tavern, less than a hundred yards south of the barracks. Work began in late spring; walls were in place by winter.

In March 1814, Swift asked that Pierre Thomas be appointed swordmaster. His request was approved in April, and Thomas became the first Master of the Sword. His duty was instructing cadets in the use of either the mounted saber or the dismounted sword. Fencing, for such was his teaching, was the first required athletic instruction at the Academy.

Swift's request for history and geography books and apparatus for natural philosophy brought criticism from Secretary Armstrong. "Until your Philosophy Professor is well enough or willing to do his duty, I see no reason for buying an apparatus for his use." Mansfield had been at West Point for nearly a year and not taught a single class. Armstrong indicated that he intended to recommend that Mansfield be dismissed, but this did not occur. "Morse's American History, Plutarch's Lives, and Morse's Geography will be enough under the head of History and Geography," Armstrong wrote. He refused Swift's request for Gibbon's works, calling these "luxuries of leisure, the mushrooms and truffles of literary sensualists." Armstrong also opposed providing books and paper to cadets because cadets would take better care of books if they were their own property.

As Swift had anticipated, a large number of cadets were appointed during 1814: 149. With cadets already present, the Corps now totalled 243, only seven less than its authorized strength. Many, however, were not at West Point. The War Department ordered several to Washington for duty as clerks. Swift assigned several to assist Engineer officers at harbor defense projects. Nevertheless, the old Long Barracks were filled and the small academic building jammed with students.

In August 1814, General Swift approved Captain Partridge's suggestion that the cadets travel to Governors Island. The trip was made in a sloop, which docked at the island. Cadets lived in tents but messed on board their transport. During their stay, the cadets observed the execution of a deserter, forming part of a hollow square with troops of the garrison. Next morning, they embarked and returned to West Point.

The prescribed uniform for cadets was a dark blue coat with gray trousers in summer and dark blue in winter. Wartime restrictions made it difficult to obtain good, blue-wool cloth. Many units, including Winfield Scott's brigade, were issued gray uniforms. For the same reason, cadets were given gray uniforms in late summer 1814. In September 1816, Swift recommended that the gray uniform be retained as the permanent uniform, indicating that "the price of the uniform $18 to $20 better suits the finance of the Cadets than one of Blue would." He added, "the Uniform and Undress for Cadets . . . has been Grey for the last fifteen months." Many years later, Scott claimed in his memoirs that the gray uniform was adopted to commemorate his victory over the British at the Battle of Chippewa. Such was not the reason for the permanent change from blue to gray; the main factor was cost. Cadets were not the only gray-clad figures at West Point. Captain Partridge wore a gray coatee with three rows of buttons despite the regulation for Engineer officers to wear blue. The 1816 cadet uniform coat may have been patterned after Partridge's coatee. Partridge's nickname, "Old Pewter," may have come from his gray uniform.

Thirty cadets graduated between March and July. No attempt was made to require these graduates to complete a course of study as required by the Act of April 1812; no examinations were held to determine their qualifications. Cadets were commissioned to meet the requirements of the War Department. Three had been at West Point less than a year; one for only four months. None of the remaining twenty-seven had more than a year's study. Perhaps the best interpretation of such haphazard graduation is that this was an example of early graduation to meet wartime requirements. Accelerated programs shortening the course were instituted during every conflict from 1861 through 1946; but, as Denton states, "never quite so drastically, nor with such blatant disregard for established principles."

Although the graduating cadets were not examined, a comprehensive examination was given to all others prior to the start of the vacation period in December. Mansfield wrote Swift to praise Partridge and Ellicott, telling Swift that their capabilities were "not exceeded by any Professors in United States." In his year-end report to Secretary of War James Monroe, who had replaced Armstrong in September, Swift indicated that the examinations demonstrated progress made by the cadets in studies and military exercises. The Academy appeared to have recovered from its neglect under Eustis.

Cadet life was far from easy. There was no water in barracks, and younger cadets were required to carry water from a nearby stream. There were no furnaces or stoves; open fireplaces provided heat. Again, younger cadets carried wood to their rooms where it was sawed or split into usable lengths.

Although vacation started in December, many cadets chose to remain at West Point. The winter of 1814–1815 was bitterly cold, and cadets suffered in the drafty barracks. There were no cots. Cadet Simon Willard recalled that cadets were "obliged to wrap themselves in blankets & lie on the floor with their feet to the fire to keep from freezing." Apparently no plan had been made to care for cadets during this vacation period. Willard stated, "No provision having been made by the Government to provide fires or food, they were obliged to cut their own fuel in the neighboring forest & drag it home on sleds or pack it in on their backs." Cadets bought their food and cooked it in fireplaces. Willard commented that "as neither had the faintest idea of culinary art either theoretical or practical, the results of their various combinations would have ruined the digestive apparatus of an Ostrich."

Formations continued and some classes were taught during this period, although discipline was relaxed. Winter formations were not military. No overcoat was prescribed, and cadets stood in ranks wearing civilian coats or wrapped in blankets. They were not alone; Captain Partridge was never known to wear an overcoat.

Partridge used the winter months for extensive artillery training. Disregarding deep snow, he had cadets drag a field piece to the edge of the river and fire toward Newburgh. Cadet George Ramsay recalled him as "an accomplished tactician of his day, and rendered the battalion drills interesting and instructive by forming diminutive armies and fighting over renowned battles and always accompanied by an intelligible and interesting lecture." He was so fond of military instruction that he often drilled a single squad. Much interested in military history, Partridge wrote to Williams in July 1810 requesting history books for the library, "Being fully sensible of the advantage of a knowledge of History to a Military Man . . . I take the liberty, Sir, of enclosing a list of Books." Williams agreed, and obtained a few histories.

Ramsay described Partridge as a "commander, professor capable of teaching all branches, and when need be Chaplain." He was not only the senior officer present but the senior instructor by tenure. Partridge had been instructor, assistant professor, and Professor of Mathematics from his graduation in November 1806 until he became Professor of Engineering in September 1813. Often he was Acting Superintendent during Williams' or Swift's absences. Williams had confidence in Partridge's ability. Swift appeared to have the same trust and openly expressed the opinion that Partridge was "the right man at the right time."

5

Deliver Your Sword to
the Bearer

Shortly after Christmas 1814, Partridge went to Washington, theoretically to discuss new regulations for the Academy with Secretary of War Monroe. The regulations he presented did not concern internal operations of the Academy but instead incorporated changes in its basic organization, administration, and relationship of the Superintendent with the Chief of Engineers, the Secretary of War, and the President.

Both Williams and Swift had complained of the requirement for the Superintendent to be many places at one time: West Point as Superintendent, supervising engineering construction throughout the United States, and Washington to advise the Secretary of War. They had often discussed this problem informally with Partridge, a normal procedure involving the Superintendent and the senior Engineer officer at West Point. Partridge, believing he had the answer to this dilemma, persuaded Monroe to accept his solution. Regulations approved by Monroe on January 3, 1815, provided for a *permanent* Superintendent responsible to the Secretary of War. The Chief of Engineers was to be Inspector of the Academy and responsible for examining the operation and management of the institution and reporting his findings to the Secretary of War. No officer other than the Superintendent would exercise command at West Point unless so ordered by the Secretary of War. Qualified cadets were to be commissioned in "such Corps as the Superintendent may think him best qualified for." The same day, Monroe sent Partridge a letter informing him that he was "hereby appointed Superintendent of the Military Academy at West Point, agreeable to the provisions of the regulations for that institution, which I have this day approved and transmit to you."

There were only two things wrong with these regulations. First, the Acts of

1802 and 1812 made the Chief of Engineers responsible for the operation and management of the Academy. The new regulations placed the Superintendent directly under the Secretary of War and removed the Chief of Engineers from any command with or direct connection with the Academy. Second, the Act of 1812 provided for commissioning cadets only with the approval of the academic staff. The provisions to the contrary in the Partridge-sponsored regulations were clearly illegal.

Partridge had made one other extremely serious error. He had discussed the proposed regulations with Secretary Monroe without Swift's knowledge or approval. Swift's reaction was predictable. He immediately went to Washington and pointed out the errors to Monroe. On January 22, Monroe informed Partridge that the new regulations were suspended.

Partridge waited two weeks before trying to explain his actions to Swift. He indicated that his proposed regulations had been based on previous discussions with Swift and his belief that Swift had agreed to them informally. He denied that he was trying to cause problems, insisting that his experience as an instructor and his service as Acting Superintendent for more than five years qualified him to determine what was best for the institution. Partridge gave every indication that he felt he alone knew what should be done to assure the successful operation of the Military Academy.

Swift was too intelligent not to see the advantage of having a permanent superintendent. In discussions with Monroe, he agreed that such was desirable. However, he insisted that the Chief of Engineers must retain control of the Academy and that the academic staff should determine cadets qualified for graduation and branch assignment.

On February 28, Secretary Monroe issued regulations replacing those advocated by Partridge. The Chief of Engineers was designated Inspector of the Military Academy "responsible to the Secretary of War for the successful progress of the institution." He was to forward all reports to and receive orders from the Secretary concerning the Academy. "From the Inspector only the Superintendent of the Academy will receive orders and to him only will the Superintendent make all reports and communications pertaining to the Academy." No officer of any rank could command at West Point unless subordinate to the Chief of Engineers.

The regulations specified that a permanent Superintendent would be appointed to "direct the studies, field exercises, and other academic duties." Professors, academic officers, and cadets were under his command. When cadets had been examined and considered qualified, they would receive diplomas signed by the professors and the Superintendent. Each diploma would specify the branch of the Army in which the cadet was being commissioned.

It seemed that Partridge had been successful in all of his efforts. Such was not to be. He no longer had Swift's confidence. In a letter to Professor Ellicott, Swift stated, "I now care not for his [Partridge's] opinion or convenience." Swift asked several senior Engineer officers to accept appointment as Superintendent.

All refused. Most were involved in harbor defense construction or were with units on the Canadian border. Swift had little option other than to appoint Partridge Superintendent under the provisions of the February regulations. Those regulations were specific concerning any direct communication between the Superintendent and the Secretary of War. Swift undoubtedly felt that Partridge could not act on his own and could be fully supervised by frequent trips to West Point.

To further implement the regulations, Swift and Monroe in early 1815 decided that the United States could learn much from European engineers and their experiences during the Napoleonic wars. They selected Colonel William McRee and Captain Sylvanus Thayer to visit schools in Europe and, while there, to purchase books for the Military Academy and War Department libraries. Before departing in May, they were interviewed by Monroe.

Initially, Partridge resumed his duties with no signs of displeasure and with no change to his normal routine. He continued his artillery instruction. An unfortunate accident occurred when a 12-pounder gun served by cadets exploded. Cadet John Payne was severely injured and eventually lost an arm. Ramsay indicated that a premature explosion caused the gun to burst. If so, the cadet crew had not properly sponged the tube, possibly because of cold freezing the sponge, a reflection on Partridge's qualifications as an artillery instructor.

Sunday religious services had been held regularly from the beginning of the Academy. Until the Reverend Adam Empie was appointed Chaplain in 1813, the senior officer present conducted services or a visiting clergyman presided. After Empie's arrival, Sunday services were supplemented by daily prayers at morning roll call and evening parades regardless of the weather. After roll call or at the end of parade, the cadets formed a hollow square. Ramsay described the Reverend Empie, "the Parson moving to the centre, reverently kneeling down, sometimes in the snow." At times, Empie would oversleep and arrive at the barracks too late to offer morning prayer. "This," said Ramsay, "was always considered a triumph and sometimes unmistakably manifested."

At Swift's insistence, a more comprehensive course of study was started in 1815. In a May letter, Swift informed the Secretary of War that "the plan of education can be more easily increased in the current year than at any future period." The Secretary later directed that English grammar be added because "it is deemed indispensable to give them [cadets] a correct and intimate knowledge of the structure of their own language." He added, "Altho a critical knowledge of the Latin & Greek languages is not considered essentially necessary, yet when the cadets have studied those languages before their appointments, it is believed that the review of those languages during the last year of study will add to the reputation of the institution and cannot fail to be useful to the cadets." The chaplain was to assume "the duties required by these additions."

Mansfield instructed older and more advanced cadets in natural and experimental philosophy. Ellicott taught mathematics and astronomy. Mathematics was expanded to include spherical trigonometry and conic sections. Partridge supervised engineering studies. Claudius Berard, who replaced Florimond Masson in January 1815, taught French; and Christian Zoeller, drawing and surveying. Ramsay remembered that younger cadets were taught separately in only French and arithmetic.

The teaching work load was eased with the assignment of officers as assistant professors. Lieutenants John Wright and Stephen Long joined the Mathematics Department, and Lieutenant David B. Douglass was assigned to the Natural and Experimental Philosophy Department. Partridge was assisted by Brevet 2nd Lieutenant William Eveleth.

By midsummer 1815, the new buildings had been completed and were occupied by cadets. All three buildings were built of stone and stuccoed. The barracks, later designated as "South Barracks," was a two-story, U-shaped building. The two wings contained twelve rooms used as offices and officers' quarters. The fifty rooms of the center section were assigned to cadets, three cadets to a room. The old Long Barracks were also used by cadets until "North Barracks" was completed in early 1817. Erected at a right angle north of South Barracks, the building, also of stuccoed stone, contained forty rooms in its four stories. Four cadets were assigned to each room. The total capacity of the two barracks was at least 310, greater than the authorized number of cadets. Each room had a fireplace, indispensable as the only means of heating the building. Although no furniture was provided, cadets apparently were permitted to obtain cots and tables at their own cost. Cadet Abraham Wendell retained a list of equipment that he intended to purchase at the suggestion of Captain Partridge. Included were a cot and mattress, sheets, pillow, three blankets, a table and two chairs, a pitcher, water bucket, wash basin, two tumblers, a mirror, and a candle stick and snuffer. Many cadets continued to sleep on the floor until 1838 when cots were provided.

Immediately to the west was the Academy, a two-story, T-shaped stone building. The east wing on the ground floor was used by Partridge's Engineering Department; the west wing was a laboratory. The center room, used as a Chapel on Sundays, was used for mathematics instruction on weekdays. The library was located in the center room of the second floor. The Philosophical Department occupied the space above the laboratory; and the adjutant's office, the room above the Engineering Department.

The new mess, which Swift called the Refectory and Partridge the Commons, was west of the Academy. Cadets were fed in large rooms on the first and second floors. The kitchen was a one-story building in the rear. The mess steward, Partridge's uncle Isaac Partridge, lived in the west end of the building. Rooms in his quarters were the only accommodations available for visitors to West Point. A room at the opposite end of the building was used as a reading room or as a courtroom when required. Newspapers from eastern cities were available here.

Cadets were messed for $10 a month. The surroundings were austere. Ramsay recalled that the mess had "no table cloths, no glass tumblers, tin cups instead, no chairs, and the tables and benches were painted in red ochre which made its impress on the sleeves of our gray uniform coats and on the unmentionable seats of honor of our trousers." Cadet Horace Webster remembered, "Mr. Partridge, a most excellent man, kept the Hall for a year or two from the time I joined [October 1814], to the satisfaction of the reasonable persons concerned."

Mrs. Thompson continued to board a few cadets in her home below the level of the Plain. Cadets fortunate enough to mess here undoubtedly enjoyed their meals more than those at Isaac Partridge's Commons. Mrs. Thompson's waitress, Souverine, was a native of Santo Domingo. She, her husband, "Black George," and their family were the only blacks at West Point. Cadets familiarly called Souverine "Shove-her-in." Then as now, cadets surreptitiously carried food from the mess, a practice called "hooking." Ramsay stated that "each participant was expected to carry from the mess table the sinews of war. To one, bread and butter would be assigned, to another sugar, and to others a limited supply of knives, forks, and plates." Occasionally, a chicken or turkey would be purchased or otherwise obtained and roasted by suspending the carcass from a string before the fireplace.

Bachelor officers and professors were required to eat with the cadets. When some objected to this requirement, Secretary of War William Crawford, who replaced Monroe in August 1815, indicated that "the regulation requiring the unmarried professors, teachers & assistants to eat with the cadets is believed to be conformable to the general usage of colleges and ought not to be considered onerous." Partridge also was expected to attend.

Partridge issued special regulations for the Commons. Breakfast was "to beat of 7 O'Clock. Dinner at 1 O'Clock, and supper a little after sundown." Cadets were to be marched to and from meals and "the utmost order and silence must be observed both in going and returning." This requirement contrasted with the way cadets assembled for parade. They did not form in front of barracks but, instead, ambled across the Plain to the parade area in front of the Superintendent's quarters, where they were organized by cadet officers. Partridge's mess regulations continued, "There must be perfect order at table; no talking except what is absolutely necessary in asking for things." Each table had an assigned cadet "to carve the victuals and help others to such as they may wish." When the meal was over, "All must rise from table by word of Command, the carvers first, and return by files in the most perfect order."

As the academic term of 1815 neared an end, a definite change in Partridge's attitude gradually surfaced. He became very dictatorial and even autocratic in his supervision of the Academy. Convinced that the February 28 regulations gave him full charge of all activities, Partridge often entered a classroom and took over instruction regardless of what subject was being taught. He continued to conduct all military exercises. Cadet quarters were inspected several times daily. Even bachelor officers were closely supervised. In March, Captain Douglass, second in seniority to Partridge, was admonished for being absent from his quarters on several evenings; Partridge considered visiting Professor Ellicott no justifiable excuse.

Unrest that had previously not been apparent surfaced. Cadets submitted a series of petitions to Partridge asking for privileges or complaining about Partridge's actions. In April 1815, seventeen young officers who had graduated in March petitioned Partridge, "Sir as we shall probably be soon ordered hence, we beg leave to suggest to you that it would be useless for us to commence the study of Mathematicks, and if it would be no infringement of the regulations, & is agreeable to you, we would prefer studying history and other useful books at our quarters, to attending the Academy." Apparently Partridge had decided that the young officers should continue their studies while waiting for assignment orders. Whether he agreed to their request is not known.

Another of this group, Lieutenant Henry Smith, objected to Partridge ordering him to parade as a sergeant. Smith felt that he should have the duties of an officer at a parade. Other new graduates complained about Partridge ordering them to perform various duties. Their objections were based upon the fact that Partridge, as an Engineer, theoretically could not give them orders because they had been commissioned in the Artillery. Partridge could not bring himself to treat the young officers other than as cadets; this they resented. Word of the controversy undoubtedly reached Washington because one of the young graduates was James Monroe, nephew of the Secretary of State.

In June, 132 cadets signed a petition to Partridge concerning the attitude and actions of the enlisted detachment. "We are fully sensible," said the petition, "that a private soldier has his rights as well as those of a higher grade, and that it is the duty of the officer commanding them strictly to guard against any infringement of those rights. But in doing this, we are also of opinion that he ought to be particularly cautious that he should give too much of liberty to them and thereby destroy that subordination which is the life of an Army." In the opinion of the cadets, a cadet should rank a private and should expect respect from enlisted men. Complaints of insolence had been made, but the charges were usually resolved in favor of the enlisted men. "Encouraged by this leniency," continued the petition, "they have become insolent, and we must abide with it. But Sir the spirit of a Cadet cannot brook such degradation, and until we are stripped of our warrants we shall consider ourselves entitled to a suitable respect."

There were many reasons for this situation. Partridge used enlisted men as guards in the cadet barracks, and cadets had to report to the sentry whenever leaving or entering the building. Cadets in confinement for a misdemeanor were supervised by enlisted guards. There was no officer commanding the enlisted detachment; Partridge himself assumed these duties. What action Partridge took concerning this petition was not recorded.

A series of regulations issued by Partridge led to other petitions from cadets. One order prohibited cadets from accepting invitations to visit homes or attend parties in Newburgh. The same order specified that "the practice also of assembling together on the Point for the purpose of having Petty Balls [*sic*] or Dances must cease. These are injurious to the Institution, without any advantage from them. Every cadet will find as much as he can possibly attend to if he does his duty correctly and makes the necessary progress in his Studies."

Another cadet requested permission to bathe each morning, "believing that it would be beneficial to our health and knowing that it would add to our pleasure." Cadets asked, "Sunday is the only day in which we are not engaged in our Academic Studies, if you should think proper to allow that day for walking or other recreation with the limits of the Point, we flatter ourselves that we should give you no cause to regret your decision." This petition again asked that enlisted men stop insulting cadets.

Several cadets complained about preferential treatment given other cadets in appointing cadet officers. Many cadets cited their own seniority as reason for questioning Partridge's appointments. Several petitions signed by more than twenty cadets requested that the cadet selected by Partridge be replaced because he "is the person who of all others is most disappreciable to us. If you will please appoint from the squad any other that you may think proper you will greatly oblige Your humble & Obdt Servants."

Cadets bitterly resented favoritism in selecting individuals to be graduated and commissioned. Ramsay commented about this in his letter to General Cullum many years later, "I remember that several cadets were allowed to accomplish the course prescribed for two years in one, thus anticipating by one year their time of graduating. Whether they were strictly confined to the programme of studies I can't say; but it is hardly to be presumed that unless qualified by previous study, they could have fully and satisfactorily mastered in one year course prescribed for two." It is possible that Partridge may have acted in response to orders from the Secretary of War to provide graduates by a specific date, but this does not justify the favoritism shown. Cadet John Webber was so upset at seeing cadets commissioned who were junior to him in length of service and possibly less qualified academically that he submitted his resignation to the Secretary of War. His request was refused, and he graduated with the Class of 1815.

One unusual complaint was made to Partridge. Addressed to "Honbl Sir," it was submitted by an enlisted man. "After what has happened, it cannot be supposed I am willing any longer to continue as a soldier in the service of the U.S. Altho the best youth of my life as yet has been spent in her service. I well know Sir, the duty of a private soldier. I know the duty of an officer. And yet altho the situation which has caused my requesting my resignation is of such a Nature that no Gentleman would put up with, Yet you think to the contrary. I therefore request you would accept this my resignation," said the author, whose signature cannot be deciphered. What caused the complaint is unknown.

The requirement that all communications for the Secretary of War had to be sent through the Chief of Engineers applied only to the Superintendent, not to other officers, professors, or cadets. Eventually, a series of complaints concerning Partridge was sent to Swift or directly to the Secretary. At first, the complaints were ignored, but the flood of accusations continued. Professors and instructors accused Partridge of interfering with their academic duties, being arbitrary and dictatorial in his supervision of all Academy activities, and failing to follow congressional laws, regulations, and directives of the Secretary of War. The military storekeeper, Captain Samuel Perkins, submitted the most serious charges, including depositions from cadets alleging cruel punishment by Partridge and allegations of the irregular leasing of government land and the sale of timber on government property.

Other aspects of Partridge's activities disturbed Swift. Despite instructions to Partridge to prevent cadets from going into debt, many owed large sums to the storekeeper or civilian merchants. Swift instructed Partridge to devise a four-year course of instruction several times; he had not complied. Partridge's involvement with the mess and leasing public lands had been ordered stopped. Isaac Partridge was removed from his steward's position in March but remained in the area. The combination of these shortcomings and the flood of complaints finally brought action from Swift and the Secretary of War.

In November, Partridge went to Washington. No record was made of the reason for the trip nor has any report been found that there were discussions with the Secretary of War and Swift. Such conversations must have taken place because Partridge on his return sent a message to the cadets, "As the time has now arrived when I must part with you all for a season, perhaps some of you forever, I should do injustice to my feelings were I to be entirely silent on so interesting an occasion." He praised cadets for progress in their studies, correct deportment, and the good order and harmony that existed. "You have come," Partridge said, "from almost every part of the United States and (with few exceptions) entire strangers to each other. You have lived together like members of the same family, like a band of brothers." He expressed the hope that all would "persevere in a line of Conduct so honorable to yourselves and show to the world that the members of the United States Military Academy are not more distinguished for Scientific acquirements than for correct deportment and the cultivation of filial and social affection of virtue and the discarding of every vice."

During Partridge's absence, Captain Douglass assembled the academic staff to devise the four-year curriculum desired by Swift and to develop a code of conduct for the staff. Giving priority to these tasks, the group prepared a course of instruction that provided for first year instruction in French, drawing, and mathematics covering algebra, geometry, and plane trigonometry. The second year would include more French, geometrical and topographical drawing, and mathematics instruction in navigation, spherics, infinite series, and conic sections. Because they considered cadets not ready to study more than the two year course, the staff listed "the study of Natural and Experimental Philosophy, Engineering, Geography, Belles-Lettres, History and Ethics" as subjects for the third and fourth years, the exact year to be determined at a later date. The group classified all cadets based on standings in each subject and the progress each cadet had made since his appointment. The purpose of this classification was to provide a means of assigning cadets to first or second year courses. Draft regulations for the conduct of the academic staff were prepared.

On his return, Partridge ignored most of the staff recommendations. Only the cadet classification was retained. No effort was made to implement the modest four-year course nor was the proposed curriculum forwarded to Swift. The proposed staff regulations were ignored because they would lessen Partridge's control of academics and the deportment of instructors.

From December 4 through 8, the Board of Visitors began the examination and inspection of the Academy. Their oral reports to Swift were highly complimentary of cadets and their military and academic accomplishments. Only one Board member, DeWitt Clinton, sent a written report to the Secretary of War. Clinton was very critical of the administration of the Academy. He criticized the lack of any examination for appointment, pointing out that cadets were not divided into classes, that there was no prescribed course of studies and no final examination. Clinton recommended regulations be issued defining the relationship between the Superintendent and the academic staff. The lack of proper administrative supervision was evident even to an outside observer such as Clinton.

Partridge left for Vermont after the Board of Visitors had departed. During the remainder of the winter, complaints continued to reach General Swift and the Secretary of War. When President Madison learned about the situation, he suggested that Swift replace Partridge with another officer. Swift stated that no other qualified officer was willing to accept the appointment. Swift was subsequently accused of retaining Partridge because he was convinced that Partridge was "the right man in the right place." He was also criticized as being unfit or unqualified to be Superintendent. Swift's actions from the time he became Chief of Engineers in 1813 do not justify this criticism. Every action he took concerning the Academy, with the exception of retaining Partridge, led to improvement.

For over a year, Swift had tried to obtain approval to expand the Academy. He recommended expanding the curriculum and proposed establishing two additional academies, one in Washington and the other in Pittsburgh. At each, 150 cadets would be educated at public expense and required to enter military service. An additional 250 cadets would pay for their education but would not be expected to enter government service. Swift's concept was supported by Mansfield and Ellicott. The proposal bore a remarkable resemblance to Steuben's 1783 concept, although neither Swift nor the two professors appear to have been aware of Steuben's plan. The proposal was not favorably considered by Congress. Charges of sectionalism, fear of too strong a military clique, and the old distrust of a professional officer corps prevented approval.

The stream of complaints and allegations reached the point where they could no longer be ignored. In February 1816, Crawford ordered a Court of Inquiry to investigate Partridge's conduct. Members of the Court were Colonel Henry

Atkinson and Lieutenant Colonels James House and Joseph Totten. Captain John O'Connor, who was translating a French treatise on fortifications for the War Department, was appointed recorder. The composition of the Court is interesting; only Totten was an Engineer. Atkinson was an Infantry officer; House an Artilleryman. Perhaps no other Engineer officers senior to Partridge were available; perhaps the Secretary wanted other branches represented.

The charges investigated were many and varied. O'Connor informed Partridge that Professor Ellicott had alleged that Partridge had violated the law by curtailing the required three-month summer camp and that many cadets charged Partridge with "maltreatment (alleged) of the young gentlemen of the Academy." Partridge was also charged with permitting uniforms to be sold to cadets at much higher prices than they would cost in New York City. Captain Perkins, the Assistant Deputy Quartermaster at West Point, had charged Partridge with misappropriation of public lands, fuel, and buildings; granting a monopoly to Isaac Partridge and Oliver Burton; failing to properly safeguard military stores and property; failing to hold required examinations; permitting soldiers to be employed by Isaac Partridge; illegally leasing land to Benjamin and David Havens; using enlisted personnel for his own benefit; failure to maintain proper discipline among enlisted soldiers; and fraudulent accounting for wood purchased for use by cadets and officers. Nearly fifty witnesses were listed by O'Connor, including forty cadets. Partridge was provided with copies of all documents relating to the charges.

The Court met at West Point from March 15 through April 12. Every witness was questioned in detail by both Partridge, who was his own defense counsel, and the Court. Surprisingly, Partridge was an astute spokesman and consistently proved witness testimonies to be incorrect. This was especially true of cadet statements that he had inflicted cruel treatment as punishment for misdemeanors. He forced cadets to retract charges that he had punished them by forcing them to ride a cannon, by long confinement in "the dark hole," a cell in Fort Clinton, or by requiring cadets to wear a derogatory placard while being marched before ranks of other cadets. These allegations have been accepted by many writers despite the fact that neither Ramsay nor Webber recorded such penalties in their memoirs. It is interesting that the cadet depositions submitted by Captain Perkins contained many common verbatim statements and that all began with a phrase indicating that the deposition was submitted in response to a request from Perkins.

Most of Perkins' allegations were disproved. Partridge had leased public land but with prior approval of the Secretary of War. All charges of fraud were refuted, and most of the other allegations were countered by evidence presented by Partridge.

The Court announced unanimous findings on its final day. Partridge was exonerated of misusing money received from individuals cutting wood on post, but the Court questioned whether Partridge had any authority to permit wood to be cut for other than military use. No authorization was found permitting enlisted soldiers to cut wood on public lands or paying them for this work. The charge of not properly guarding public land was nullified because of the small number of soldiers available for guard duty, but Partridge was censured for not properly guarding stores when "a single sentinel might have been kept over the public property." He was also censured for permitting soldiers to be employed by Isaac Partridge and receiving compensation "to his own benefit or that of Mr. Partridge." The charge of illegally leasing public land was dropped when it was shown that authority had come from the Secretary of War and General Swift. Partridge was exonerated of the charge that he had personally benefitted from the receipts of Isaac Partridge, the store operated by Mr. Burton, or the tailor shop.

Partridge was unable to counter allegations concerning his supervision and administration of the Military Academy. The findings of the Court emphasized Partridge's arbitrary and autocratic methods. Regarding charges of favoritism in commissioning cadets, the Court found that "The Law & Regulations require an examination by the Superintendent & Professors, and a certificate of qualifications. They have never been complied with by Capt. Partridge but in *one* instance." The Court censured Partridge for shortening the summer camp period, pointing out that "the only power that should venture to set aside the Law is that next below the power that made it,—The President."

With regard to the charge of failing to maintain discipline in the enlisted detachment, the Court was even more definite in its criticism of Partridge's supervision, maintaining that "if the multifarious duties of the Superintendent have prevented personal Inspection and command, he was bound to assign them to a Subordinate, but he could not divest himself of the Responsibility as Commanding Officer." Partridge was also criticized for failing to keep proper orderly books and other records.

All of the Court's findings were not derogatory. Their final statement indicated that "Capt. Partridge has been extremely attentive to & solicitous about the Health, Morals, and Improvement of the Youths under his charge; and that in the correction of faults & offenses he has been uniform, punctilious, Dispassionate & Forbearing." The Court added that "the Reports & Complaints of Intentional Ill-treatment & unjust Punishment of the Cadets by Capt. Partridge, are not sustained by a Shadow of evidence, and it appears Discontents have been Encouraged, and even Opposition to Legal Authority invited, to gratify personal animosities!"

Ignoring the admonitions and censure of the Court, Partridge felt its findings were a complete vindication of all of his activities. The transfer and later resignation of Captain Perkins further convinced Partridge that the War Department supported him fully. He failed to consider the possibility that Perkins had been relieved because his charges against Partridge were for the most part unsubstantiated. Thus convinced, Partridge returned to his normal method of supervising all Academy activities, feeling that his position as permanent Superintendent was quite safe.

His opinion was wrong. In February 1816, even before the Court of Inquiry met, President Madison asked Swift to assign Partridge to some duty away from West Point. Swift indicated that it would be difficult to move Partridge at such short notice and without any specific reason. Madison agreed. Secretary Crawford at the same time urged Swift to replace Partridge with another Engineer officer, and Swift made his usual reply that no other officer was willing to be assigned as Superintendent.

In March, Crawford rescinded the 1815 regulations that authorized appointment of a permanent Superintendent. New regulations prescribed that the Superintendent would be an "officer of the Corps of Engineers who shall have charge of the military exercises." This gave Swift an opportunity to assign an officer senior to Partridge as Superintendent while retaining him as Professor of Engineering. Although the intent was to bar any professor from military command at West Point, the new regulations failed to directly state this prohibition, and Partridge continued to hold the two positions. The regulations required semi-annual examinations in July and December, with a Board of Visitors to participate in the July examinations and report their findings directly to the Secretary of War.

In May, Swift finally sent the Secretary a four-year course of studies, which essentially was the same as the draft prepared by the faculty the previous November. It did have additional details for the third and fourth years. At Crawford's insistence, grammar was added to the first year studies and a review of Latin and Greek and additional grammar in the fourth year. Crawford approved the proposal in July with instructions regarding administration and military studies.

Realizing that the course submitted was very general, Crawford directed the Superintendent and faculty to determine how each year's course was to be conducted. Changes to the course were permitted, and subjects could be transferred from one year to another "as necessary to produce quality." The academic staff was to have no control over military exercises; these were to be directed by the Superintendent "and shall be attended to at such times as will interfere the least with their [cadets'] academic duties."

Crawford specified that a cadet who was examined and found qualified in the course of studies for that year would be advanced to the next year's subjects. If a cadet proved unqualified, he would be put back into the next lower class to repeat those studies in which he was not proficient. This system is still in effect today. The term for requiring a cadet to repeat a year was "turn back." Cadets soon adopted "turnback" as a title for the cadet involved, a term still used.

Since the founding of the Academy in 1802, the faculty had to accept young men who had been appointed cadets without the desired educational qualifications. Crawford was determined to change this situation in some way, realizing that it was politically motivated. The ideal solution would have been to modify and intensify the requirements, but this Crawford could not do unless Congress changed the law. As an immediate step, he directed that a list of names of those who were not qualified be prepared, standards set by law be rigidly enforced, and cadet warrants not be issued until after entrance examinations at West Point had been concluded. Previously, warrants had been sent to newly appointed cadets before the examinations. This often caused problems with parents of cadets who were found unqualified to attend the Academy and with Congressmen to whom these parents complained. Crawford hoped to ease the situation by not appointing cadets until they passed the entrance examinations.

Swift asked Crawford to appoint the five-member Board of Visitors for the July examinations, but Crawford for some reason failed to do so. Swift went ahead with the scheduled testing, but found no cadet qualified for a diploma.

In September, a General Order directed that the official uniform of the Corps of Cadets would be gray. Although the cadets had worn gray for nearly fifteen months, this had been a temporary expedient required because blue cloth was not available. Cost was the primary reason for retaining the gray uniform. Although Swift had urged that gray be retained, he was displeased with the design selected, which apparently had been submitted by Partridge. "I do not like the uniform," Swift informed Partridge in mid-September, "& am not pleased of the manner in which it has been established." At Swift's request, the design was changed, and the gray uniform became a symbol of the Military Academy.

Partridge began a new tactic by complaining to the Secretary of War about the decline of discipline at the Academy. Why did he make these complaints? Perhaps it was an attempt to obtain greater control over Academy personnel, the academic staff as well as cadets and enlisted soldiers. Partridge undoubtedly was aware that instructors and cadets were complaining directly to the Secretary and Swift. This he probably considered a breach of discipline. If his complaints were intended to obtain official support, Partridge failed badly. His letters irritated Secretary Crawford, who maintained that "his letters to this department, complaining of the relaxation of discipline in the Academy, reflect no honor upon his judgement, his energy or his zeal." Crawford believed that a "complaint of the relaxation of discipline, by an officer whose duty compels him to enforce it, is considered not only ridiculous, but disgraceful."

Crawford decided the time had come to remove Partridge. In early September, he directed Swift either to go to West Point as Superintendent or to appoint the next senior officer of the Corps of Engineers to that position. Emphasizing that the Acts of 1802 and 1812 supported his instructions, Crawford agreed that during war the "principal officers of that Corps could be more usefully employed than in superintending the military academy. But the departure from the requirements of the law should cease with the emergency which produced it." If Swift did not want to be Superintendent, he was to order Colonel McRee to assume that duty. Since McRee was in Europe with Major Thayer, Swift was to proceed to West Point and assume the duties of Superintendent until McRee returned.

Swift, serving on a Court Martial in Maryland, was unable to comply immediately with Crawford's order. In October, Crawford reminded him that he should go to West Point as soon as possible. Later that month, the Secretary informed Swift that President Madison had directed that "the Professors of the Academy be confined exclusively to their duties as professors, and restrained from interfering in any manner with the military exercises of the Academy." His obvious intent was to prohibit Partridge, as Professor of Engineering, from serving as Superintendent.

Swift still delayed. When Partridge received a copy of the order, he promptly resigned his professorship to retain control as Superintendent. Swift must have agreed with this move, for he approved the resignation and delayed assigning another officer as Superintendent. The resignation was accepted by Acting Secretary of War George Graham who had replaced Crawford.

James Monroe was elected President in November 1816. One of his first acts was to direct the Adjutant General to inform Major Thayer in France that he would become Superintendent when he returned. Thayer was to report for duty by the start of the new term in April or in early May. Strangely, Swift was not informed of Monroe's action.

In December, Swift finally reported to West Point to assume the duties of Superintendent. Partridge should have been assigned duty elsewhere, but Swift did not transfer him. After his arrival, Swift supervised the second examination, although the War Department again had failed to invite a Board of Visitors. He was pleased with the results despite the fact that no cadet was considered qualified for a diploma. Partridge had urged Swift to commission cadets whom Partridge felt deserved a diploma, a return to the favoritism previously used by Partridge. That Swift refused is an indication of his intention to set the Academy on a proper course. He informed Secretary Graham of the examination results and indicated that, after members of the First Class (seniors) had received more instruction in descriptive geometry, at least twenty cadets should be ready to graduate, probably by June.

For the second time in its short history, the Academy had graduated no class. Responsibility for the 1810 hiatus can be attributed to Secretary Eustis and his failure to appoint cadets or otherwise support the Academy. The reasons for the failure to graduate a class in 1816 are more complex. This was the year the new four-year course of instruction was initiated. It is possible that cadets were unable to progress sufficiently with the expanded curriculum to qualify for a diploma. Another reason was the time taken by the Court of Inquiry, almost half of the spring term. Partridge, then Professor of Mathematics, taught no classes while the Court was in session. Other professors, instructors, and many cadets were involved as witnesses. Another factor was Partridge's constant interference with teaching by other professors and instructors and his refusal to follow any system or course of instruction advocated by the academic staff. Partridge's actions may have been the primary reason for the failure to graduate a class in 1816, but Swift must also be held at least partially responsible because he had not removed Partridge.

Before making his report of the examination results, Swift requested approval of a trip to Washington. Although he was told to come in February or March, he went to the Capital in January. During his stay, he talked to President Madison and obtained approval to leave West Point. Secretary Graham's effort to get Partridge away from the Academy failed, for Swift ordered Partridge to resume his functions as Superintendent.

An unfortunate accident marked the start of 1817. On New Years Day, Partridge asked Swift for permission to fire an artillery salute at noon. Swift consented, and Partridge ordered the 1st Company of cadets to assemble as the firing detail. After checking the four guns, he ordered two to be recleaned since they did not meet his requirements. At noon, he began the salute. Two 12-pounders and an 18-pounder each fired one round. Hearing some talking among the gun crews, Partridge, who was at the right of a 24-pounder, repeated his "order for each one to pay particular attention to his own duty." As he turned back toward the fourth gun, the 18-pounder fired prematurely killing Cadet Vincent Lowe. The accident, similar to that which had injured Cadet Payne two years earlier, was caused by improperly sponging the tube after firing the previous round.

Contrary to some accounts, Lowe was not killed by concussion. Partridge reported to Swift that Lowe's left arm was "very much shattered—his face burnt, and his Breast and right arm injured" and that his clothes were burning. Sending for the surgeon, Partridge put out the fire. Lowe was taken to the hospital but was dead on arrival. In 1818, the Corps erected a monument to Lowe's memory. Each cadet contributed fifteen dollars, a large sum at that time. Names of other cadets who died at West Point were added to the monument over the years.

Dissension and complaints continued when Swift was away from the Academy. Partridge, aware of the situation, became convinced that Captain Douglass was urging other faculty members to take a stand against him. He informed Douglass that if he disobeyed any of his orders, he would be placed under arrest. The faculty claimed certain rights and privileges; Partridge insisted that he had absolute authority over officers, cadets, and enlisted men. He wrote Swift that "all the noise and pretensions about the rights of the Academic Staff are a complete farce. They have their rights, but those rights do not free them from military discipline nor from the obedience to military orders."

Partridge displayed even more his belief that he and he alone was able to operate the Military Academy. He reverted to his practice of attending classes and, whenever the mood struck him, taking over instruction. It may be true that he was qualified to teach mathematics and engineering, but his capability in other subjects was questionable. Nevertheless, Partridge insisted on teaching Mansfield's classes in Natural and Experimental Philosophy. This was a tactical error. Mansfield had supported Partridge from the time he reported for duty in 1813 and had taken no sides in the dissension leading to the 1816 Court of Inquiry. Partridge had now antagonized his only major faculty supporter.

Another step taken by Partridge further irritated Mansfield. Partridge insisted that advanced cadets should be permitted to study the required subjects at their own rate instead of being held to the level of the average cadet. Despite objections from the professors that this would make a shambles of the four-year course, Partridge put his concept into effect in March 1817. He informed several cadets in classes of higher mathematics that they could also study Natural and Experimental Philosophy. The cadets applied to Mansfield for the necessary instruction. Mansfield refused because he felt he could not carry the additional workload. Partridge went ahead; he held evening classes for the selected cadets. All of the faculty objected on the basis that Partridge as Acting Superintendent no longer had any academic status.

Mansfield was outraged. His letters to Swift and Graham complained bitterly about Partridge's actions. After informing the Secretary of Partridge's invasion of academic activities, he made other allegations, including tyrannical treatment of cadets and officers, misuse of government property, and selling wood from government land for personal gain. Many of his charges had been investigated by the 1816 Court of Inquiry.

Another ally joined Mansfield and other faculty members. Captain John O'Connor, the recorder for the Court Inquiry, came to West Point in December 1816 to complete his translation of Guy de Vernon's *Treatise*. O'Connor had developed a strong dislike of Partridge during the Court hearings; this dislike increased to hatred. A close friend of William Crawford, who had left the War Department to become Secretary of the Treasury, O'Connor gave him detailed reports about the Academy and Partridge's activities. Without doubt, Crawford passed this information to the Secretary of War and probably to President-Elect Monroe.

Swift, in Washington for the inauguration, learned that Monroe planned to inspect coastal defenses in northeastern states and the Academy. As Chief of Engineers, he was to join the party. Swift and Graham made plans for rebuilding Washington public buildings burned during the war and discussed conditions at the Academy.

In May, O'Connor returned to Washington and reported to Graham for reassignment. He submitted a report to Graham concerning "the state of the cadets and the Military Academy and the actions and conduct of Capt. Partridge." The report, requested by Graham, was addressed to the President.

About this time, McRee and Thayer returned from Europe and reported to Swift in New York City. When Graham learned of their arrival, he directed Swift to order Thayer to West Point as Superintendent at the request of the President. Swift discussed the directive with Thayer, emphasizing his confidence in Partridge and his feeling that Partridge was the only Engineer officer qualified to be Superintendent. Thayer, because he personally did not want to head the Academy, recommended that Swift wait until the President's visit to West Point in hopes that Monroe would revoke the order. In the meantime, Thayer would remain in New York.

Monroe, escorted by Swift, arrived at West Point for the first official visit of a President to the Academy. During his stay, the five professors submitted a report discussing the organization of the Academy and the problems caused by Partridge's interpretation of the regulations. In a discussion with the President, with Swift present at the President's request, Mansfield presented his many complaints about Partridge. He later provided a twelve-page report to support his oral comments.

Swift attempted to counter the many allegations made by Mansfield and the other professors without success. Monroe was determined that Partridge be removed and tried by court martial. Swift informed Partridge of the President's directive and offered him the option of being transferred or going on leave until a court could be convened. Swift, however, did not issue orders placing Partridge on leave and appointing Thayer as Superintendent until mid-July.

After Swift and Monroe departed, Partridge accosted Mansfield concerning the report given to the President; Swift had given him a copy. Mansfield stated that he had proof to support every allegation. Partridge promptly informed Mansfield that if the professors did not obey his instructions, he would place them under arrest. Within a month, Mansfield and Ellicott were under arrest for disobeying orders and restricted to the Post. In late July, Partridge arrested the military storekeeper, Mr. Snowden, and indicated that he shortly would arrest Claudius Berard, teacher of French.

Partridge threatened to prefer charges against O'Connor for conspiring against him by spreading "false and malicious statements." Mansfield, learning of Partridge's intention, informed O'Connor, who promptly sent the information to his friend, Secretary of the Treasury Crawford. Crawford told O'Connor that there was no need to worry.

Swift finally ordered Thayer to West Point in late July. At the same time, he informed Partridge that the President would not alter his determination to have him court martialed and assumed that Partridge would take leave when Thayer arrived. Preparing to leave for Vermont, Partridge terminated the cadet summer camp and informed Swift of his action. The letter to Swift indicated that Partridge did not accept the fact that he was no longer Superintendent, for he assumed that Thayer would be his assistant and Acting Superintendent only during his absence.

Thayer arrived at West Point and assumed command on July 27, 1817, and gave Partridge a copy of his orders. A day or so later, Partridge left West Point on leave, theoretically to prepare for his court martial. Neither Thayer nor Swift was aware that he intended to return in the fall.

Thayer immediately began to make changes to make operation of the Academy more efficient. He requested that additional officers be assigned for military instruction and administration of the Corps of Cadets. This was an indication that he, as Superintendent, would not be directly involved in the instruction or supervision of cadets. He released Mansfield, Ellicott, and Snowden from arrest.

He made plans with the Academic Board for the classification of cadets, including those newly appointed. Swift forwarded the request to Graham, who readily concurred.

If Partridge had followed Swift's advice and accepted a transfer elsewhere, there is every possibility that there would have been no Court Martial. Almost every allegation made by Mansfield, O'Connor, and other members of the Academic Board was merely a reiteration of the charges investigated by the 1816 Court of Inquiry. Swift on August 6, as part of his letter forwarding Thayer's request for additional officers, recommended to Graham that another Court of Inquiry investigate the charges made against Partridge. Such a Court could only censure but not convict.

Swift informed Partridge of this possibility in early August when Partridge requested permission to return to West Point. Swift refused and told Partridge that his return would be against the orders of the President and could only hurt his case. Swift had misjudged Partridge's reaction to this news. Instead of retiring to Vermont or taking another assignment, Partridge did the exact opposite—he returned to West Point. Perhaps more than any other of his actions, this showed his conviction that he could not be removed and was indispensable. If Swift had any concept of reinstating Partridge later—and there is no evidence to substantiate this belief—informing Partridge that he had requested an inquiry instead of a trial was the worst possible action he could have taken.

Partridge landed at the north dock on August 28 to be met by Lieutenant Charles Davies, Assistant Professor of Mathematics, and several cadets. He received an enthusiastic welcome from other cadets as the word of his return spread. Reporting to Thayer, Partridge asked to have his quarters made available. Thayer replied that this was impossible because he had assigned them to Captain Douglass, although Douglass had not yet moved. Partridge informed Thayer that he was senior to Douglass and that, in compliance with War Department policy, he was entitled to those quarters. Thayer still refused. Ignoring Thayer's brevet rank, Partridge told Thayer that, as senior Engineer officer at West Point, he could assume command if he chose. Thayer refused to assign the quarters to Partridge, who then left Thayer's office.

The next morning, Partridge again asked Thayer to assign him his old quarters, and Thayer again refused. Partridge informed Thayer that he was assuming command. He wrote an assumption order, which was read to the cadets. Thayer quietly left, returning to New York to inform Swift of Partridge's action and to send a written report to the Secretary of War.

Partridge took command with an iron fist. He placed Captain Douglass under arrest and preferred charges against Thayer for violation of War Department orders by not assigning quarters in the approved manner, for unjust and arbitrary conduct, and for conduct unbecoming an officer and gentleman. He forwarded the charges to Swift with a letter explaining what had taken place from his viewpoint. He urged Swift to come to West Point immediately to take command and, in a postscript, urged him to "not fail to order a general and full investigation into my conduct as well as the conduct of all those against whom I have preferred charges."

If Swift was surprised when Thayer reported, he was astounded when Thayer reported what had occurred. He immediately issued an order to place Partridge under arrest and for Thayer to resume command. The order was taken to West Point on September 1 by Swift's aide, Lieutenant George Blaney. The directive to Partridge was succinct and clear: "On receipt of this you will deliver your sword to the bearer, Lieut. Blaney, my Aide de Camp, and consider yourself in arrest. The charges against you will be furnished in due season." He instructed Blaney to remain at West Point until Swift arrived.

The next day, Swift accompanied Thayer to the Academy, ostensibly to provide any support Thayer might require and to personally make certain that Partridge had complied with his order. Meanwhile, Thayer's report to the Secretary of War reached Graham, who ordered Swift to arrest Partridge and Lieutenant Davies and send them to Governors Island to await further orders.

Swift and Thayer discussed whether cadets who had enthusiastically welcomed Partridge should be punished. On September 7, Swift informed Graham that he and Thayer agreed that no punishment was warranted but that cadets should be informed that "implicit obedience was their only course." He directed Thayer to dismiss any offender immediately. Swift recommended with Thayer's concurrence that no charges be preferred against Davies because his action was due to youthful ignorance and impetuosity.

Partridge asked Swift for permission to remain at West Point for a few days to remove his books and furniture, claiming that he had been ill for several days. Swift refused, ordering Partridge to go to New York immediately. Swift would no longer support Partridge in any way. Swift's actions surprised Partridge, and he still refused to accept the facts. Believing that he was irreplaceable and convinced that he was the victim of a conspiracy, he decided to carry his fight to the public. A letter to the editor of the New York *Columbian* published on September 12 denied all allegations made against him and bitterly attacked the individual responsible. No name was given; he might have referred to Swift, Thayer, Mansfield, Douglass, Ellicott, or O'Connor.

On September 5, Partridge handed Swift a note preferring charges against Captain Douglass, adding additional charges against Mansfield and Ellicott, and requesting that Berard be placed in arrest. Swift ignored the charges. Thayer released the faculty members and officers under arrest as soon as Partridge left for New York. His final departure was made in style. Without permission, cadets and the band escorted Partridge to the dock, where he embarked with the full honors due an officer of high rank. Thayer very wisely took no action against those involved.

The War Department moved rapidly, issuing orders for Partridge's trial on September 25. Officers appointed to the Court were an indication of the seriousness and importance placed on the trial by the War Department. Major General Winfield Scott, one of the most senior officers in the Army, was to be

President of the Court. Colonel J. R. Fenwick of the Light Artillery; Colonel J. S. Jessup, 3rd Infantry; and Colonel H. Leavenworth, 2nd Infantry, were assigned as members. Significantly, there was no Engineer member.

The General Court Martial met at West Point from October 23 through November 11. Four charges had been preferred against Partridge. After hearing witnesses and receiving documentary evidence, the Court found Partridge not guilty of the ten specifications of the first charge, neglect of duty and unofficerlike conduct. There were four specifications of the second charge, unofficerlike conduct to the prejudice of good order and military discipline, based on Partridge's teaching classes in Natural and Experimental Philosophy and writing the editor of the New York *Columbian*. The Court found him not guilty of all specifications of this charge. On the third charge, two specifications of disobedience of orders, he was judged guilty. He was found guilty of two of four specifications of the fourth charge, mutiny, by his actions from August 29 through September 2.

Based upon its findings, the Court sentenced Partridge to be cashiered but recommended to the President that he remit the punishment "in consideration of the zeal and perseverance which the prisoner seems to have displayed in the discharge of his professional duties up to the period of August last." The Court stated that it "cannot conclude this trial without pronouncing its opinion that the first two charges and most of the specifications under those charges appear to the court but frivolous and vexatious." President Monroe approved the findings and sentence of the Court on November 27 and directed Partridge to report to the Chief of Engineers for assignment.

At his request, Swift placed Partridge on extended leave. Partridge never returned to duty, resigning his commission on April 15, 1818. Partridge began a lifelong campaign to vilify all who were involved in his trial and, later, almost anything or anyone connected with the Academy. He started in March 1818 before his resignation by preferring thirteen charges against General Swift. The charges ranged from misuse of government funds to "repeatedly violating his word and promises." The charges were ignored by the Secretary of War.

What caused the change in Partridge from an officer held in high esteem by both Williams and Swift, an officer who had almost alone held the Military Academy together during its most trying years? Perhaps it was the blow to Partridge's ego when he saw his former cadets and officers junior to him receive promotions and recognitions during the war while he, restricted to his duties at West Point, was not promoted and received little public recognition. Perhaps there was no change; perhaps Williams and Swift never knew the real Partridge. Williams spent very little time at West Point after Partridge was assigned to the faculty, and when he was at the Academy, Partridge might have acted very differently than when Williams was elsewhere. It is difficult to accept any contention that Partridge could have changed from a competent and esteemed officer and academician to the dictatorial autocrat he is alleged to have been during Swift's assignment as Chief of Engineers.

There is another factor that must be considered in any attempt to analyze

Partridge as a man or condemn him for his actions. Cullum in the third volume of his *Biographical Register* laid the foundation for considering Partridge a bad commander and a poor Superintendent. Cullum included Ramsay's memoirs as a part of his discussion of Partridge, but he omitted or changed any positive references to Partridge or any indication that he had benefitted cadets and the Military Academy. Thayer praised Cullum in a March 1863 letter for his efforts to contact graduates to obtain an accurate account of the Academy during its early years. But Thayer cautioned Cullum about preconceived opinions, "It is only after every ascertainable & pertinent fact shall have been established by a general concurrence of those who are competent to testify that I would be willing to express *decided & definitive* opinions in the premises. Until *then* I intend to keep my mind open to conviction. May I not take the liberty to recommend a similar reserve on your part?" Cullum disregarded Thayer's advice in the *Register* and other writings. To him, nothing Partridge did was good; everything was bad.

Partridge did make positive contributions to the Academy. Had he not been at West Point during Eustis's tenure as Secretary of War, the Academy might not have survived. He must be considered an outstanding "caretaker" Superintendent. When the Corps of Cadets was increased to 250, Partridge insisted that small classes be retained even though this meant an increased workload for the small faculty. Thayer retained this concept. His interest in drill excellence established a trend that continued. The reputation of discipline early graduates took with them to the Army was directly attributable to Partridge, for he and he alone supervised all military activities. His disciplinary methods, for the most part, were welcomed by the cadets, and he was truly popular with them. Thayer has often been given credit for organizing the Corps of Cadets into two companies. Partridge did this before 1815. After the new barracks were ready for occupancy in the fall of 1815, one company was quartered there, the other in the old barracks near Execution Hollow.

Findings of both the 1816 Court of Inquiry and his final Court Martial indicate that Partridge was the victim of prejudice. Both courts commented on unfounded, frivolous, and vexatious charges; both acquitted him of most allegations. Perhaps the findings of the Court of Inquiry, which Partridge was convinced had vindicated him completely, were the cause of his dictatorial actions during his final year at West Point. Only a truly great man, an outstanding and understanding individual, would not have his ego increased by such decisions or continue unchanged. Partridge was not that man. Perhaps he was too human to do other than he did.

There was no excuse whatsoever for his actions in late August 1817; he disobeyed the orders of Swift, the Secretary of War, and the President. Partridge clearly believed that he and he alone was capable of operating the Military Academy and that he knew better than anyone else what course the Academy should follow. He assumed that he had Swift's backing and could not believe or even begin to believe that he was actually being replaced.

But he was replaced by decision of the President, the Secretary of War, and—at long last—by General Swift. His departure left a void and the Academy in confusion. This Thayer faced in September 1817 with confidence and with the intention of developing the Military Academy into the institution visualized by Jefferson when he approved the Act of March 16, 1802. The old era was ended; the new was about to begin.

1817–1828

My mission was to create, to construct, to build up from the foundation under difficulties coming more from within than from without; and then to preserve and defend what had been accomplished . . .

SYLVANUS THAYER

6

The Rebuilding Begins

"My mission," Sylvanus Thayer wrote General George Cullum in March 1865, "was to create, to construct, to build up from the foundation under difficulties coming more from within than without." Thayer actually had the task of re-establishing the Military Academy for it had never fully recovered from the hiatus caused equally by Secretary of War Eustis's neglect and Partridge's supervision. Attempting to categorize the problems facing Thayer from the viewpoint of sequential importance is almost impossible because of the interrelationships of these requirements.

A sound and comprehensive curriculum had to be established, but such a curriculum would require a competent faculty in sufficient numbers to instruct the 250 cadets. Faculty morale was low after contending with the dictatorial actions of Alden Partridge. Cadet discipline needed refining to eliminate the weaknesses developed by Partridge's favoritism. Administrative procedures were almost non-existent, and relationships between the enlisted detachment and the faculty and cadets had to be improved. Cadet and post regulations needed revision. The library was inadequate. Apparatus and models were in short supply. Cadet financial procedures had to be developed. The physical condition of the post was not adequate to support all the activities despite the new barracks, mess building, and academy.

After his return from Europe in May 1817, Thayer reported to Swift in New York where he remained while Swift escorted Monroe on his inspection tour of the East Coast. In all probability, Monroe met Thayer during his visit to New York, although no documentary evidence verifies such a meeting. It is logical to assume that such a meeting would have taken place in view of Monroe's announced intent to replace Partridge with Thayer and that Swift and Thayer received instructions from Monroe regarding Thayer's assignment.

Swift delayed ordering Thayer to West Point until the end of July. Thayer spent nearly ten weeks in New York before assuming the superintendency. He probably used this time to familiarize himself with the exact situation of the Academy. Swift's letter books, which included copies of all correspondence with the War Department and Partridge, were available. The Chief of Engineers office records included copies of the 1816 Court of Inquiry report, Academy budget requirements, lists of cadets appointed, and plans for the new buildings. That Thayer had reviewed all available records is evidenced by the prompt action he took after assuming the superintendency on July 28.

Thayer's first official act was to release Ellicott, Mansfield, and Douglass from arrest; this did much to lessen the problem of faculty morale. He wisely consulted senior faculty members as he began his first changes and asked them to prepare plans for their courses, showing details for each year of a four-year curriculum. Thayer's request pleased Mansfield, Ellicott, and Douglass, who had tried unsuccessfully to persuade Partridge that this was necessary. This action also pleased Secretary of War Graham, who had asked for such a plan months earlier.

Despite the confusion and delay caused by Partridge's return, cadet classification continued almost on schedule. The extensive testing found forty-three cadets, about one-fifth of the total number enrolled, to be deficient. Thayer reported to Graham that "twenty-two of these gentlemen have been here more than three years and some of them longer without having advanced beyond the first year's course. The remaining twenty-one have been here more than two years, and some three and four years, without having made any progress whatever in the course of studies."

Recommendations made to Graham illustrated one of Thayer's outstanding characteristics: fairness. He and the academic staff carefully reviewed each cadet's record before sending Graham a list of twenty-one cadets considered to be incapable of meeting course requirements. "Most of them are deficient in natural abilities," Thayer informed the Secretary, "and all are destitute of those qualities which would encourage a belief that they could ever advance through the four year course of studies. The public money would be wasted, therefore, by retaining them here any longer." Thayer recommended that these cadets be discharged for academic deficiencies.

Cadets who survived the classification examination were placed in classes based upon their academic ability rather than their tenure as cadets. Twenty-two who had failed the examination were considered to have some improvement capability. These Thayer recommended should be permitted to join the new appointees. After admission of the new cadets, the Corps of Cadets was divided into four classes; each class could be projected to graduate four years later.

Thayer's intention to discharge cadets who did not meet the academic standards of the classification examination was approved by Graham and President Monroe. Graham proposed to Thayer that they be permitted to resign if they had caused no disciplinary problems. Obviously, this procedure would nullify some of the political pressure that might result if cadets were summarily discharged.

Graham indicated that cadet resignations would be accepted immediately. Some cadets resigned voluntarily; others delayed. Rawlins Lowndes, Class of 1820, many years later wrote General Cullum that "among the orders was, every now and then, a batch of resignations accepted, very much to the dismay and astonishment of those whose names were mentioned." When these cadets objected, Thayer gave them the option of facing a court martial, an option that all refused.

Thayer also recommended to Graham that two cadets from Chile be discharged. Luis and Mateo Blanco had been brought to the United States by Commodore Horace Porter to enter the Academy in May 1816. How this was accomplished is unknown, for Congress had not approved an official program for accepting foreign cadets. The two brothers, Thayer wrote Graham, "are extremely deficient in the first rudiments of education, reading, writing, and orthography." Their lack of interest, inability to learn, and refusal to conform to disciplinary standards were cited as further reasons for their separation. Graham agreed, and the first two foreign cadets were discharged.

Several cadets on leave failed to report back to the Academy for the classification examinations. All were informed upon their return that their resignations would be accepted. At least one resignation caused problems. General Charles Pinckney of South Carolina, whose son was on leave at the time of the examinations, wrote to Swift, asking that his son be reinstated since his return had been delayed by "the unhealthy season & dangerous travelling in that climate." Swift asked Thayer to permit young Pinckney to rejoin his class.

This episode brought out another of Thayer's characteristics: he would not yield to pressure and would show no favoritism. He wrote General Pinckney that the faculty reported that his son had made little progress in his studies. The general refused to accept this explanation, and the son was permitted to return at the direction of President Monroe. He remained only a few months, resigning in March 1818.

The classification tests and the recommendations made to the War Department had complete faculty participation and approval. Thayer's comments to Graham included a letter of support from the academic staff. In less than two months, Thayer had brought faculty morale from the despair and resentment of the Partridge regime to enthusiasm and full support of his actions.

Thayer shrewdly intended to delegate responsibility for academic matters to the professors. Although he chaired meetings of the Academic Board and participated fully in discussions, he expected each professor or senior teacher to have full and uninterrupted control of all matters relating to his department. Thayer had no intention of teaching, another decided contrast with Partridge; he took no direct part in any instruction, academic or military.

Thayer considered the Academy an institution established to educate potential officers for all branches of the Army. Writing Swift from France in May 1816, he stated that the objective of such an institution was to give "suitable instruction to those who are designed for the Engineers & Artillery." This differed from Williams' concept that the Academy was primarily an engineering school. Thayer was impressed by Napoleon's use of artillery and realized the value of the support that artillery could give other troops. Thayer was a realist and knew that some cadets would never develop the technical and scientific skills required of engineers and artillerymen. These cadets would become infantry or cavalry officers.

Each class was divided into small sections of ten to fifteen cadets. Classification results were used in assigning cadets to sections. Sections were numbered, and cadets with the best test results were placed in the first section; those with the lowest in the last section. New cadets were assigned alphabetically and later reassigned based on merit. Thayer also numbered the classes. The Plebe Class, freshmen, was designated as the Fourth Class; the seniors, the First Class. Class and section designations are still used.

Partridge had insisted that cadets be divided into small sections, but Thayer's method differed from Partridge's haphazard section assignment. Thayer's system enabled the more competent cadets in a first section to progress more rapidly than cadets in the last section. Higher sections studied each subject in greater detail than the last section, which covered only minimum requirements. This was accomplished by using different texts, higher sections using a more comprehensive work. Most texts were in French or, later, English translations of French works.

Sections were rearranged periodically, and cadets were reassigned every two or three months, based on recitation and test grades. Changes later were made monthly. Fourth Classmen were divided alphabetically, except for French sections, which were based on knowledge of French, Latin, and English grammar. Fourth Class sections remained unchanged until January examinations provided a means for reassignment by academic standing. For many years, new cadets were on probation and received cadet warrants only after passing the examinations.

Every instructor reported the progress of cadets in his section to Thayer each Sunday. These written reports included a summary of the cadet's progress during the week and a description of his strong points or weaknesses. This enabled Thayer to review the progress of each cadet on a weekly basis.

Initial cadet reaction to the new section arrangement is unknown. One may guess, however, that it initially was anything but enthusiastic. By June this attitude changed to acceptance and even interest. The first change in attitude came when the standings of the first three men in each subject were posted on a bulletin board outside the south entrance to North Barracks. Cadets soon learned that they could determine their own standings by reporting to the Superintendent.

What Thayer accomplished by this simple system of section assignment based upon merit had impact upon a cadet's entire military career. His branch was based on his class standing. Even more important, relative seniority was based on class rank. In the days when promotions were slow and made only when vacancies existed because of transfers, promotions, resignations, or deaths, seniority at graduation often determined a man's seniority at a later date. Rank standing became apparent when General John J. Pershing's officer serial number system was adopted after World War I. Comparative class standing could be determined by comparing a graduate's serial number with those of his classmates.

There is no record of why Thayer devised the merit system to assign cadets to sections. It is possible that he based his concept on similar methods at Ecole Polytechnique, the French Military Academy, because sections based on student merit were not uncommon in Europe. Thayer's best friend and Dartmouth classmate, Harvard Professor George Ticknor, visited German colleges at the same time Thayer was in France. On his return, Ticknor divided language classes into sections to permit better students to progress more rapidly. He forced modern languages into the Harvard curriculum, a decided contrast to Princeton and Yale, which taught only Latin and Greek. Harvard in the early 1800s was considered to be an extremely liberal institution. One wonders if traditional Princeton and Yale also considered West Point to be liberal.

Whatever the source of Thayer's concept, it proved to be extremely successful. Letters of cadets during the nineteenth century often expressed concern about standings and the importance of high academic ranking. Cadet Isaac Stevens described the cadet attitude in a letter to his sisters: "We go to the section room with long and solemn faces. I assure you we know that by study and severe application alone we can keep our places. I admire the spirit which pervades the whole class. The common remark is, 'I intend to bone it with all my might.' *To bone it* means *to study hard*. Everyone seems determined to rise, or keep his present standing at any rate." Stevens' use of "bone" is an early example of cadet slang; cadets still use "bone" to indicate hard study.

Posting grades weekly continued for many years. Initially, only grades of the top three men in each section were posted at the entrance to North Barracks. Later, lists included all cadets in each section. After Central Barracks was built in 1851, grades were posted in the sallyport facing the Plain. Cadet interest was evident by the large number of cadets in the sallyport each Saturday after grades were posted. Posting grades was discontinued in the 1970s.

Thayer's faculty consisted of seven men: Claude Crozet, Professor of Engineering; Jared Mansfield, Professor of Natural and Experimental Philosophy; Andrew Ellicott, Professor of Mathematics; Lieutenant David Douglass, Assistant Professor in Mansfield's department; Lieutenant Charles Davies, Assistant Professor of Mathematics; Christian Zoeller, Teacher of Drawing; and Claudius Berard, Teacher of French. All had been inherited from the Partridge regime; all had encountered Partridge's wrath.

Mansfield was the senior faculty member. He had been Professor of Mathe-

matics for eighteen months in 1802 and 1803, and had been appointed Professor of Natural and Experimental Philosophy in 1812. George Ramsay, Class of 1820, in his memoirs described Mansfield as extremely nearsighted and "of such delicate structure as to convey the idea of decrepitude." This sight problem proved to be an advantage to the cadets. Mansf
::%s:SATURNo use the same letters shown in a textbook on their blackboard recitation figures. Cadets refreshed their memories by glancing at the book on which Mansfield focused his attention. Albert Church, Class of 1828, described Mansfield as "very old, yet quite enthusiastic in his branch of study, generally a mere listener to demonstrations, complimentary to a good one, but coldly silent to a bad one." Both Ramsay and Church recalled Mansfield as much respected and beloved by the cadets. The first section of the Class of 1828, the last that Mansfield taught, had his portrait painted by Sully; it now hangs in the Library.

Andrew Ellicott, Professor of Mathematics, Ramsay described as "the exact opposite in figure to his philosophical compeer [Mansfield], and would well have personified Falstaff in person." Ramsay remembered Ellicott as very jolly with a good sense of humor. Acknowledged as a leading astronomer, Ellicott, like Mansfield, had supervised boundary surveys. As an instructor, he confined himself to mathematics through spherical trigonometry. He insisted that cadets construct figures on the blackboard with precision, using a cord and straight edge. To make notes, Ellicott used a small slate, sponge, and chalk attached to his buttonhole. When a post office was authorized in 1815, he became the first postmaster. Ellicott headed the Department of Mathematics until his death in 1820; he was succeeded by Captain David B. Douglass.

A Yale graduate, Douglass had a long and varied career as a Military Academy instructor. From January 1815 to August 1820, he was Assistant Professor of Natural and Experimental Philosophy; from 1820 until 1823, Professor of Mathematics. In April 1823, he became Professor of Civil and Military Engineering after Crozet resigned, a position he held until he left the service in 1831. Despite his reputation as an engineer and scholar, Douglass was not an outstanding instructor. Church recalled that "his style was somewhat diffuse, and there was a great want of logical sequence in his language."

Despite his inability to communicate orally, Douglass was an excellent planner, writer, and leader among the faculty. This was shown by his actions during Partridge's trip to Washington in October 1815. As senior Engineer officer at West Point and Acting Superintendent, Douglass guided faculty members in developing a four-year curriculum and classifying cadets. Although Partridge nullified this effort on his return, Douglass had shown ability as a planner and the capability of working with other faculty members, including those senior to him.

An important action taken by Swift in 1815 was obtaining the appointment of Claude Crozet as Assistant Professor of Engineering. In 1817, during the final period of the Partridge regime, Crozet replaced Partridge as Professor of Engineering. A graduate of the French Ecole Polytechnique, Crozet had served in Napoleon's army and was captured during the disastrous retreat from Moscow. After his release, he joined Napoleon on his return from Elba and fought at Waterloo. He fled to America after Napoleon's defeat, bringing with him letters from Lafayette, which enabled him to apply for a position at the Military Academy.

When Crozet arrived at West Point prepared to teach engineering, he was amazed to find not one cadet capable of studying that subject. Edward Mansfield, Class of 1819 and son of Professor Mansfield, in 1863 recalled that "the surprise of the French engineer instructed in the Polytechnique may well be imagined when he commenced giving his classes certain problems and instructions, which not one of them could comprehend or perform." Crozet taught his classes mathematics and drawing to provide the foundation for more advanced studies later.

Among the preliminary studies was Descriptive Geometry, a subject not taught elsewhere in the United States and only in a few schools in Europe. So new was this subject that no textbooks were available, not in French let alone English. Fortunately, Crozet had a complete set of the drawings used at the Ecole Polytechnique. To complicate his problems, Crozet had begun to learn English only six months before his arrival at West Point. Richard Delafield, Class of 1818, remembered "instruction had to be conveyed through the medium of Cadets who understood something of French." Crozet soon learned to use the blackboard, a common teaching aid at the Military Academy. "The first problems," recalled Edward Mansfield, were "drawn and demonstrated on the blackboard, by the Professor; then drawn and demonstrated by the pupils, and then accurately copied into permanent drawings."

As Crozet's English and cadets' mathematical background improved, he began to teach engineering, assisted by Cadet Constantine Eakin, Class of 1817, who remained as an assistant professor for three years after his graduation. Three other cadets, Richard Delafield, Ethan Allen Hitchcock, and Andrew Talcott, were appointed Acting Assistant Professors of Engineering. Delafield copied a series of ninety-two drawings to be used in classes studying Descriptive Geometry, Architecture, Shading and Perspective, and fortifications; the drawings were obtained by the Academy Library in 1989. Delafield and Hitchcock, as Third Classmen in 1815, had been appointed Acting Assistant Professors of Drawing, among the first cadets to serve as instructors.

Christian Zoeller, Swiss Teacher of Drawing (heads of the Drawing and French departments were not designated professors until 1846), had served at West Point from 1808 to 1810, resigned, then returned in 1812. He taught surveying, terrain sketching, and some technical drawing. A capable surveyor, Zoeller had assisted in the survey of the Alps in the Cantons of Bern, Lausanne, and Leman prior to coming to the United States. Cullum considered him to be a poor instructor who lowered himself to the level of his students by constantly joking with them.

Claudius Berard, Teacher of French, received an excellent classical education before emigrating to the United States in 1807. In 1812, he had been appointed

Professor of Greek and Latin at Dickinson College. Three years later, he accepted the position at the Military Academy, where he remained until his death in 1848. Church remembered Berard as an excellent instructor of his own section but "never comprehending the importance of a merit roll." As a result, many of the better French students were left in lower sections. In 1826, Berard prepared his own grammar for cadet use, *A Grammar of the French Language*. For reading exercise, he used the first volume of *Histoire de Gil Blas*. Among civilian colleges, only Harvard and a few others taught French. At West Point, French was considered essential because the only available mathematical and scientific texts were in that language.

Like Lieutenant Douglass, Charles Davies had a long and varied career as a West Point instructor. An 1815 graduate, he was appointed Assistant Professor of Mathematics in 1816. In 1821, he became Assistant Professor of Natural and Experimental Philosophy. From 1823 until his resignation in 1837, he was Professor of Mathematics. Returning to West Point in 1841 as Paymaster and Treasurer, he resigned again in 1845 to become Professor of Mathematics and Philosophy at the University of New York. He later became Professor of Higher Mathematics at Columbia College. Davies was a prolific writer and authored many mathematical and scientific texts which were used in public schools and colleges throughout the United States.

Church called Davies "enthusiastic, energetic, a clear and logical demonstrator, and an admirable teacher"; Latrobe agreed with this analysis. Cadets nicknamed him "Tush" because of his protruding front teeth. Latrobe described Davies' energetic action in putting out a fire in South Barracks in 1819, action that added "Rush" to his nickname, which became "Rush-Tush." Using the blackboard extensively, Davies was able to pass his own knowledge of mathematics to cadets easily and thoroughly. Almost without exception, he was fondly remembered by his former cadets many years later.

With only a seven-man faculty, Thayer realized that he needed additional instructors if small sections were to be maintained. He decided to use cadets as acting assistant professors when officers were not assigned. Authorized to appoint cadet instructors by the Act of April 1812, Partridge used cadets in 1815. Throughout his superintendency, Thayer appointed cadets as instructors, five or six each year. Although assigned primarily to teach mathematics and French to the Fourth Class, cadet instructors also taught Drawing, Natural and Experimental Philosophy, Engineering, and Chemistry. Only once was a cadet appointed Acting Assistant Instructor of Tactics: George Webb during the temporary absence of Lieutenant George Gardiner in 1817–1818.

Appointment as an instructor was to be "considered an honorable distinction"—Academy regulations so specified! Cadet instructors received ten dollars a month for this service. There were other advantages: instructors did not have to march to class and were excused from some duties. Toward the end of Thayer's superintendency, cadet instructors were designated by three rows of fourteen buttons on their dress coats, a contrast to the eight buttons in each row for other cadets.

Many cadets distinguished in later years were assistant instructors during the Thayer period. Richard Delafield, later Superintendent, was Acting Assistant Professor of Drawing in 1815, Engineering in 1817, and Natural and Experimental Philosophy in 1818. George Whistler, John H. Latrobe, Dennis Mahan, Alfred Mordecai, Robert Parrott, William H. C. Bartlett, Robert E. Lee, Pierre G. T. Beauregard, and Henry Hallack all were appointed instructors during their cadet years. Cadets from southern states were usually appointed to teach French; cadets from northern states taught mathematics or scientific subjects.

The use of cadets as instructors was discontinued toward the end of the nineteenth century, but reinstituted in 1941 and 1942 when the great increase in Army strength as World War II approached caused a shortage of instructors at the Military Academy. Twenty cadets taught French, English, Drawing, or Mathematics in 1940–1941. In the 1942 school year, thirty-two cadets were appointed instructors.

Additions to the faculty did not come immediately. His September request for officers brought no help but did enable Thayer to retain Lieutenant Constantine Eakin, who had graduated in July 1817, as an Assistant Professor of Natural and Experimental Philosophy and Lieutenant George Gardiner, Class of 1814, as Commandant of Cadets. Gardiner was also instructor of artillery and infantry tactics. Thayer's reorganization began with eight academic instructors assisted by four cadets. Classes were underway using a very rough-structured four-year curriculum.

Although he did not teach any classes, Thayer kept fully informed of cadet progress. Weekly reports submitted by each instructor gave daily cadet grades, a total for the week, and comments concerning student strengths and weaknesses. The grading system instituted was based on a 3.0 maximum grade and 0.0 for complete failure. A 2.0 grade was considered satisfactory; anything less was unsatisfactory. Cadets receiving unsatisfactory marks were "deficient" or "D." This system was used until the late 1970s when it was changed to the 4.0 system more common to other colleges and universities. Test and semi-annual examination grades added to weekly totals provided a final term standing.

The faculty agreed to hold the first comprehensive examination at the end of the first term, despite restructuring difficulties. Thayer had two reasons for insisting that this be done: he anticipated that some cadets would fail the examination, and the examination would in itself be a crucial test of the Thayer system. Working seven hours a day from December 17, 1817, through January 3, 1818, Thayer and his faculty examined each cadet in each subject. Thayer was pleased with the results.

Fewer than twenty cadets were found deficient; these Thayer recommended for discharge. The cadets were given the option of resigning. Forwarding the results to Secretary Calhoun, Thayer indicated that he believed the progress made was due to the high "degree of attention to study which is believed to be unexcelled at this institution." One reason for this increased study, he believed, was cadet interest in weekly grade reports and section assignment based on merit. Thayer asked Calhoun to give appropriate recognition to cadets after the annual June examination.

Pleased and impressed with Thayer's report, Calhoun agreed to publish the names of the first five cadets on the merit roll of each class annually in the Army Register, believing that this would "encourage scientific attainments and promote emulous exertions among cadets." Calhoun's innovation would be continued for many years. As Thayer anticipated, Calhoun's decision created great excitement in the Corps of Cadets and led to increased study.

The importance of the merit system initiated by Thayer became apparent after the June examinations. Twenty-three cadets were commissioned based on their final class standings. The first two men were assigned to the Corps of Engineers. Those next in rank went to the Artillery. The bottom of the class were commissioned in the Infantry. Realizing the importance of final class standing, cadets applied themselves more diligently to their studies.

Throughout the fall and winter, Thayer and his faculty developed a series of proposals for improving Academy operations. Despite the normal teaching load and the added task of conducting examinations, the plan was completed in late January 1818 and forwarded to Calhoun. Twenty-three propositions discussed personnel, salaries, faculty organization, organization and supervision of the Corps of Cadets, commissioning of graduates and former cadets, duties of a Board of Visitors, and the relationship of the Superintendent with the Chief of Engineers. Calhoun submitted the proposals to the Board of Engineers, General Simon Bernard, a French officer hired in 1816, and Colonel William McRee, Thayer's companion on his European trip.

Several of the propositions placed Thayer at odds with the Chief of Engineers. Thayer recommended that the Superintendent be an officer of any branch of the Army, not necessarily an Engineer. The faculty would be selected from officers of the Army "or elsewhere." Tactical officers would be a part of the academic staff. The Superintendent would be responsible to the President through the Secretary of War, not through the Chief of Engineers, who would be designated Inspector of the Academy. To justify these proposals, Thayer emphasized the necessity of separating the Academy from the Corps of Engineers. Unspoken was Thayer's intention to have the Academy provide officers for all branches of the Army, an intent expressed to Swift many months earlier. Bernard and McRee agreed with the proposed separation, but Calhoun did not concur. Calhoun did agree to appoint faculty and tactical officers from all branches of the Army.

Faculty organization and numbers were an important proposal. Natural and Experimental Philosophy, Engineering, and Drawing would each have one assistant professor; Mathematics, three. The Chaplain would continue as Professor of Geography, History, and Elements of Civil Law. Two teachers of Drawing were recommended; one to teach elementary drawing and the second, military drawing. A riding and sword master would be added, the first indication that horsemanship was considered important to the cadet's education. A new department was to be headed by a Professor of Languages, Oratory, and Belles Lettres. Thayer maintained that the new department would improve knowledge of English and oratory, enable cadets who had studied Latin and Greek to continue that study, and give cadets the opportunity to study literature. This suggestion was similar to that made by Secretary of War Crawford in 1816.

McRee and Bernard disagreed. In their opinion, the Academy curriculum should be restricted to subjects absolutely necessary, that only mathematics, sciences, and French were considered essential for cadet education as officers. They considered history, geography, civil law, classical languages, and "Belle Lettres" merely an addition or accessory to a military education.

Other propositions concerned the pay of the faculty and tactical officers. The salary of the Professor of Natural and Experimental Philosophy was equivalent to the pay of an Engineer lieutenant colonel, while that of the Professors of Mathematics and Engineering was equal to that of a major. Similar disparities existed between the salaries of assistant professors. Thayer recommended a uniform schedule with equal pay for equal rank. Although Bernard and McRee agreed with the proposal, nothing was done; faculty salaries were not standardized until 1850.

Thayer requested the assignment of officers as surgeon, paymaster and treasurer, quartermaster, and adjutant with appropriate clerical assistants. A surgeon was already assigned, but the treasurer's tasks were an additional duty for a faculty member. Paymaster functions were provided by the Corps of Engineers. An adjutant was attached provisionally. The quartermaster officer would assume the responsibilities of the military storekeeper—care of military materials and the old Revolutionary War relics still at West Point—and the added duty of maintaining buildings and other government property. Bernard and McRee concurred with this recommendation.

Another proposition recommended forming an Academic Board consisting of the Professors, the principal French instructor, and the artillery instructor. Strangely, the principal drawing teacher was not included. The Superintendent would preside over the Academic Board, whose "duty it should be to fix and improve the System of Studies and Instruction, to conduct and decide upon all examinations, and to specify in detail the duties of the several instructors." Thayer based this proposal on a similar council at Ecole Polytechnique. Bernard and McRee disagreed because they believed the Academic Board should only propose changes in the operation of the Academy that would be submitted to the Secretary of War for approval.

Several of the propositions concerned cadet organization already in effect. Thayer made six proposals concerning the commissioning of cadets. Not more than two cadets "distinguished in a remarkable degree for their scientific attainments" would be recommended for commissions in the Corps of Engineers; no other cadets would be considered for an Engineer commission. To make it possible for cadets in each graduating class to become an Engineer, the number of Engineer officers would be increased.

The Academic Board would recommend assignment to specific branches, indicating all branches for which a cadet was considered qualified. The War Department would make assignments based upon vacancies existing in each branch. When there were no vacancies, graduates would be assigned "by Brevet in the lowest commissioned grade as a supernumerary officer." A cadet had no branch choice except in exceptional cases when he had a valid reason to be assigned to another branch. Bernard and McRee disagreed and recommended that assignment be based upon the academic standing at graduation. Despite this disagreement, the Academic Board retained its control of branch recommendations until after the Civil War.

Several proposals concerned the commissioning of cadets who did not graduate. Recognizing that some cadets who did not meet academic requirements "have nevertheless exhibited a prospect of their being useful and active officers with proper cultivation in the field," Thayer recommended that they be attached to various branches when they left the Academy, but they would not be commissioned until the class to which they belonged had graduated.

Cadets who resigned would not be eligible for commissions until after their class had been "promoted." Thayer used the term "promoted" to indicate graduation from the Academy. Cadets who were dismissed would not be eligible for a commission until five years after their class graduated. A cadet dismissed "for an act in itself dishonorable" should not be eligible for a commission at any time. Thayer explained the reason for these propositions briefly and emphatically; "The object of this and the following propositions . . . is to guard carefully the point of rank in favor of those who persevere in their studies."

Two other propositions were included that seem at variance with the general tone of the other recommendations. Thayer asked that waiters be employed, one for every twenty cadets. He recommended that musicians be enlisted, as directed by the President. No explanation was given for these two requests, but there was ample justification for their being included. The mess steward, who operated the cadet mess by contract, received $10 a month for each cadet. He was unable to provide the necessary waiters without reducing the quality and/ or quantity of food. There was no authorization for the band and field music. In earlier years, a band was furnished by an artillery regiment. Because these bands were not maintained by official funds, officers undoubtedly objected to contributing monthly to support a band not with the unit. Thayer's recommendation obtained a band, the first authorized and supported by the government.

Many of the propositions were eventually approved; many were not. Thayer enforced some immediately with tacit approval of Secretary Calhoun. Thayer, as Superintendent, had been appointed by and was responsible to the President, not to the Chief of Engineers. The Academic Board was formally organized in March 1818. A Board of Visitors was again authorized. Bernard and McRee did not agree with appointing the Chief of Engineers as Inspector of the Academy, recommending instead the periodic appointment of an individual or commission to conduct an inspection. Calhoun agreed with Thayer and appointed the Chief of Engineers Inspector of the Military Academy in April 1818.

Other propositions could not be adopted without congressional action. Some became effective at later dates; others were never approved. Despite the small number of propositions immediately adopted, this document was important because it defined Thayer's philosophy concerning the operation and mission of the Military Academy. He stated clearly that the institution had the mission of educating officers for the entire Army, not for the Corps of Engineers alone. Thayer's belief in the merit system was emphasized; cadets would be commissioned based upon their academic standing. The Academy would be the primary source of officers for the entire Army; if no vacancies existed in the officer corps, graduating cadets would be commissioned with brevet rank. Former cadets could not be commissioned until after their class had graduated. The importance of honor and character was emphasized by prohibiting any cadet dismissed for a dishonorable act from ever being commissioned. The propositions were a blueprint of the course Thayer would follow throughout his superintendency, a course supported by the faculty and Secretaries of War.

The Academic Board met formally for the first time on March 30, 1818. After several sessions, it recommended changing the reporting date of newly appointed cadets from September to June, extending the annual summer camp period, and limiting summer vacations. Having new cadets report in June made it possible to teach them military drill before the start of academics. Summer camp would extend from the June examinations until September. Limiting summer vacations made certain cadets would receive important summer military training, lessening the need for military training during the academic year.

Thayer submitted these recommendations to Swift who, as Inspector of the Military Academy, approved the decisions of the Academic Board. He postponed implementation for one year because appointment of the new Fourth Class had already been announced and orders issued to report in September.

As the academic year neared an end, Thayer faced a different problem. As part of economy measures, Congress directed the Army to stop giving the Superintendent brevet-rank salary and double rations. This meant that Thayer, a brevet major, would receive only captain's pay. He asked Swift for help, stating "while receiving brevet pay and double rations, I have found my expenditures, although regulated by the most rigid economy of which I was capable, to exceed my means of payment." Much of this problem was caused by the number of important visitors Thayer was required to entertain. Swift did not answer Thayer's letter.

About the same time, Thayer was informed that Congress would not act on the recommendations made for improvement of the Academy, no Quartermaster would be authorized, and no funds provided for maintaining the buildings and grounds. Thayer was not receiving the support and assistance he needed to continue his development of the institution.

On May 12, 1818, Thayer submitted his resignation to Swift, stating "I shall not have it in my power hereafter to be useful in any considerable degree to the military academy." The resignation was to be effective at the conclusion of the June semi-annual examinations. Swift did not answer the letter, and there is no indication that he forwarded it to the Secretary of War.

Thayer's resignation, although ignored, must have had some effect. In late May, Calhoun approved most of the changes in regulations recommended by Thayer, abolished summer vacations, and concurred that summer camp would extend from mid-June to September. Additional support came from both Swift and Calhoun.

June examinations were conducted over a three-week period. Each cadet was tested individually by oral presentations or blackboard recitations. Examination grades were combined with weekly marks received, and each class was ranked based upon a cadet's total grade. For example, the Second or Junior Class had thirty-eight members. In Natural and Experimental Philosophy, twenty were recommended for promotion to the next class; nine were advanced but required to study philosophy texts; six would be advanced if they passed another philosophy examination in January; and three were turned back to repeat the entire year with the next class.

Similar procedures were followed in each course and for each class. The number of cadets turned back or dismissed was greater in the Third and Fourth Classes. However, four plebes did so well in the examinations in French and mathematics that they were advanced directly into the Second Class; one was Andrew Donelson, nephew of Andrew Jackson.

For the first time, the Academic Board provided the Secretary of War with a list of graduates ranked in order of merit for the entire four-year course. To provide a basis for this ranking, the Academic Board weighted the subjects, taking "into consideration the relative value and importance of the several studies." Mathematics and scientific subjects were given a weight of two; drills and military conduct, one and a half; French and drawing, one; and descriptive geometry one-half. The actual grades received for each subject were multiplied by the weight number and a total computed. This method gave greater importance to scientific and military subjects than to the preparatory subjects studied during the first two years. Although the weights assigned varied from time to time, this method was followed until 1961 when the system of using semester hours common in other colleges and universities was adopted.

Thayer participated fully in the examinations. As Superintendent and chairman of the Academic Board, he sat in the center of the table facing cadets being tested. Many cadet letters and memoirs described his calm and dignified manner in questioning cadets and commented on his seemingly unending knowledge of the subjects being reviewed. A similar procedure was followed throughout his superintendency. His thorough and knowledgeable participation would indicate that he must have studied the courses tested because he had little background in these studies, either as a cadet or at Dartmouth. Descriptive Geometry, for example, was taught at West Point by Crozet for the first time in the United States. The mere fact that Thayer prepared himself for the June 1818 examination by self-study is in itself amazing. That he continued to do so as the subjects taught cadets increased in scope and technical content is an indication of his perseverance and mental capacity. It is even more astounding considering the many tasks facing him from the very outset of his superintendency.

In his first year, he had been involved in academic matters even though he taught no classes. Cadets had been tested and classified based upon their academic abilities. A four-year course had been instituted. Two semi-annual examinations had been conducted. Working with the faculty, Thayer prepared lists of books to be ordered from Europe to supplement those he had purchased during his two-year stay in France and England. With his encouragement and assistance, lists of apparatus for the Philosophy and Engineering courses were prepared.

His work was not restricted to academic affairs. By December 1817, he had prepared a budget request for the Secretary of the Army, asking for funds to build quarters for officers and instructors. He recommended building a hospital, gun shed, laboratory, and observatory and adding an addition to the mess building. The total amount requested was $32,500. By contrast, he asked for nearly $19,000 for books, instruments, and apparatus. Supplies and housekeeping repairs totaled over $12,000 with $7,500 for firewood. Nearly three years would pass before the funds needed for construction were provided. Most of the other funds were provided by Secretary Calhoun.

Of great importance to Thayer was discipline in the Corps of Cadets. Realizing that a sudden change in regulations would be impractical, he moved slowly by changing or adding a few rules at a time. One of his first steps was to reorganize the two cadet companies, appointing cadet officers and noncommissioned officers from the First and Second Classes. Each company had a captain, three lieutenants, a first sergeant, four sergeants, and four corporals. A colonel, an adjutant, and a sergeant major were also appointed. Chevrons indicated rank. Officer chevrons were made of gold lace, and noncommissioned officers wore yellow "ribband." The cadet colonel wore three chevrons on each arm; captains, two on each arm; the adjutant, one on each arm; and lieutenants, one on the left arm. The sergeant major wore two chevrons on each arm; sergeants, one on each arm; and corporals, one on the left arm.

Cadet officers were responsible for the conduct of cadets in their companies and for the police of barracks. Violations of regulations were reported to the Commandant of Cadets in writing and published at evening parade. A cadet reported for a violation could offer a written excuse. If the excuse was accepted, the report was removed. If the excuse was inadequate or if no excuse was submitted, the report stood as published. Punishments were based on the seriousness of the reported violation. For minor infractions, punishment was extra drill or guard duty. The next level of misconduct was punished by restriction to quarters or confinement in the light or dark prison in North Barracks. Serious misdemeanors could result in court martial and dismissal. The demerit system was not used at this time.

Requiring written excuses had another unstated purpose: it was a medium for developing honor and integrity. The excuse submitted by a cadet was judged based upon its validity; there was no check of its veracity. Honor had been stressed at West Point even in the Partridge era, an emphasis deemed necessary because of the large funds controlled by engineers and artillerymen working on fortifications. Thayer went one step further by emphasizing that a cadet's statement would be accepted as truth, that a man's word was his bond.

Thayer stressed devotion to duty as a necessary attribute of an officer. Cadet officers had specific duties, which they were expected to perform at all times. Supervision of barracks and maintaining good order were the responsibility of cadet officers, particularly in the first months of Thayer's superintendency when he had so few officers available to supervise cadets. In October 1817, Cadet Adjutant Ragland published an order indicating that "the officer commanding the Corps of Cadets regrets the necessity of an order on the neglect of duty." Barracks superintendents were not maintaining order. Disorderly conduct was contrary to existing regulations. Ragland's order stated that cadet "officers who are accountable for its suppression seem to have forgotten or are extremely neglible in the discharge of their duty." The order directed that "they must show hereafter more evidently than they have done their capacity to command or they will be reduced to the Ranks."

Barracks were assigned by company, 1st Company to North Barracks and 2nd Company to South Barracks. Cadets selected their roommates; there was no requirement that roommates had to be classmates. Newly appointed cadets often were welcomed by cadets from their home state and invited to room with upperclassmen.

Cadet rooms were Spartan in appearance and comfort. There was no running water and no central heating. Water was carried in buckets from the well near South Barracks, usually by plebes. Cadets devised a yoke enabling a cadet to carry two pails without spilling water on the floors. One of the yokes hung in the office of the head barracks policeman in the 1940s, a cause of wonder to twentieth-century cadets. Fireplaces in each room provided the only heat in the barracks. Cadets carried wood to their rooms from a woodyard near the barracks. In winter, it was mandatory that at least one bucket of water be kept beside each fireplace. Fires were not uncommon, and the cadets were organized into fire companies to put out all-too-frequent blazes.

There was little furniture in the rooms. Cadets had to buy all furnishings; nothing was provided by the government. Prohibited from receiving money from home, few had the means to obtain furniture. Fortunate cadets had a table and chairs; the less fortunate used boxes, barrels, or trunks. Beds were permitted but not required, and most cadets slept on the floor. Each cadet was authorized one basin and one candlestick. A tinder box and a water bucket were the only other common items. Muskets were placed in a corner; books were kept in or on boxes.

Furniture variation and rooms of different sizes and shapes made any standard arrangement impossible. A regulation that bedding be folded during the day and placed in a bedding sack was the only uniform requirement. Fireplaces were important to cadets because they provided heat and, more important, better light than candles.

Cadet finances were a major concern to Thayer. He was determined that cadets would not go into debt but would save enough of their meager salaries to buy officer uniforms at graduation. During the Partridge period, cadets had received their monthly salaries from the paymaster. Many went into debt by obligating funds before receiving their pay. This Thayer promptly stopped. In October 1817, he instituted a "checkbook" system. A cadet checkbook was not a checkbook in the current sense of the word but a voucher book showing receipts and expenditures. This basic system, with many changes, was used until the 1970s. To purchase any item from the storekeeper, permission had to be obtained from the Superintendent personally. If a cadet had insufficient funds or if his credit line was below a desired level, Thayer refused the request. This stringent supervision was unpopular with many cadets because it prevented selling pay vouchers at a large discount to obtain ready cash. Popularity was not one of Thayer's objectives. He stressed integrity in every phase of cadet life regardless of cadet opinion of his actions.

A cadet's day was full. Reveille sounded at dawn summer and winter. Twenty minutes after reveille, cadets were drilled by squad until breakfast at 7:00 A.M. The twenty minutes between reveille and drill were used to prepare rooms for inspection. There was no drill between November 1 and March 1. Classes were held from 8:00 A.M. to 1:00 P.M. Lunch was at that time. At 2:00 P.M., classes resumed. Except for the November to March hiatus, company or battalion drills took place from 4:30 to parade time. Supper was immediately after parade. Evenings were spent studying until 9:00 P.M. when it was required that "candles be extinguished."

Cadets had little recreation. Cadet August Canfield wrote his brother that "the only time we have for recreation is about 1/2 hour at noon and Saturday afternoons. At these times even we cannot go off the Point without getting permission." Walking, hiking, and fishing continued to be the most popular activities. In winter, cadets skated on the Plain, on a large pond near the present Superintendent's garden, or on the river when the ice was thick. In summer, cadets swam in a cove near Gees Point.

This cove was also used for bathing since there were no tubs or showers in the barracks. Bathing periods were scheduled, and cadets marched to the cove.

Enterprising cadets devised a primitive shower near the present entrance to the cemetery. A rough trough drew water from a spring trickling down the rocky hill to a shower at the end of the trough. After Thayer saw the contraption in use, he officially authorized its use. Cadet Harvey Brown recalled that he had "taken this bath on a morning when icicles were hanging from the trough." No record has been found indicating that officers also used the shower.

Thayer encountered the same problem in developing discipline within the Corps he had faced in devising the academic program: shortage of officer instructors. He was fully aware of this problem when he assumed the superintendency. One of his first actions was to request instructors in infantry and artillery tactics. Only one was provided; Lieutenant George Gardiner, an artilleryman, reported for duty in early September 1817 to become the first Commandant of Cadets. Thayer might have detailed academic officers to assist Gardiner, but he insisted that instructors should devote all their time to academic matters. There was one other officer who might have aided Gardiner, Lieutenant John Wright, who commanded the detachment of sappers and bombardiers, but Wright was fully occupied with post caretaker requirements.

Thayer's disciplinary measures were not popular. Strict regulation of every hour of every day applied equally to all cadets was a contrast to the easy, uneven discipline of the Partridge era. All cadets except the new Fourth Class had served under Partridge, some for more than five years. They resented the changes, open resentment of which Thayer was fully aware.

To further complicate matters, Partridge continued to cause problems. He was kept informed of activities at West Point by several cadets; his nephew, Lieutenant Wright; and the military storekeeper, John Burton, son-in-law of Partridge's uncle, Isaac Partridge. Partridge used their information for a series of newspaper articles, accusing Thayer and Swift of mismanagement of the Academy and mistreatment of cadets. In December 1817, Partridge preferred charges against Thayer for malfeasance in office, submitting the charges to Swift, who forwarded them to Secretary Calhoun. No action was taken. Partridge continued to criticize the Academy and Thayer vehemently until his death in 1854. His letters to cadets during the early years of Thayer's superintendency fostered their resentment of the new regime.

The cadet adjutant, Thomas Ragland, also served as post adjutant until the arrival of Lieutenant James Graham in October 1817. Ragland, who had been one of Partridge's favorites, issued orders, kept records, and supervised the one clerk in the Academy headquarters. He also commanded the band and field music. During Lieutenant Gardiner's absence in October, Cadet Colonel George Webb, another Partridge favorite, was appointed Acting Instructor of Tactics, the only instance in Academy history that a cadet held this position. Ragland and William Fairfax, also high in Partridge's favor, were appointed Acting Assistant Professors in Mathematics.

It is possible that Partridge recognized the abilities and talents of Ragland, Webb, and Fairfax and that this recognition led to their being called his favorites.

Nevertheless, Thayer's appointment of these cadets is perhaps the best example of his impartiality. Despite their standings with Partridge, Thayer recognized and rewarded their abilities.

The arrival of Captain George Bliss, 6th Infantry, in April 1818 relieved Thayer of any need to directly or indirectly supervise cadet activities. Thayer had specifically requested assignment of Bliss, whom he had met during the war. Thayer had been impressed with his disciplinary control of troops. As senior line officer, Bliss also was appointed Commandant of Cadets. He arrived in time to make preparations for the summer encampment. Working with Gardiner, now the Instructor of Artillery Tactics, he planned training for the entire summer.

Thayer's first year as Superintendent had brought many changes to the Academy. Cadets had been tested and classified based upon their academic capabilities. Organization and discipline were improved. Two semi-annual examinations had been conducted, and the results received favorable comment from the Secretary of War and the President. Additional officers had been assigned. Thayer had the confidence and cooperation of his academic and tactical staffs. His impersonal and equitable supervision of Academy affairs appeared to be successful despite some cadet resentment. Rebuilding had begun; Thayer could now proceed with his plans.

7

Governed by the Rules and
Articles of War

Tents were pitched in the level space in front of the old Academy building in the summer of 1818, near the present location of the Superintendent's quarters. For the camp period, organization of the Corps of Cadets was expanded to four companies. There were two purposes for this change: four-company organization gave more cadets a chance to serve as officers, sergeants, and corporals, and the larger number of companies made it much easier for Bliss and Gardiner to conduct battalion maneuvers.

Cadets formed in front of barracks under full pack and marched to the camp site with the band leading the way. After removing their packs, cadets returned to their rooms to move bedding and other possessions. Each wall tent had a wooden floor, the only provision for comfort. There were no cots; cadets slept on the floor. There were no lockers or trunks; possessions were kept in large bags. As in barracks, bedding was folded after reveille and placed in a bag. Gray winter trousers were left in barracks; white linen trousers were worn during the summer with the heavy, wool coatees.

Each company was assigned a line of tents. At one side of the camp were tents for the Commandant and other officers. At the opposite side, latrines were dug. Sentinels patrolled all four sides of the camp twenty-four hours a day. Guard was alternated daily, and the new and old guard were changed at formal guard mount. Cadets rotated as Officer of the Day. Major Thayer went through the entire roster of upperclassmen because this gave him the opportunity of getting to know cadets more intimately. Cadet George Ramsay recalled the cadet on duty "was invited to dine with him [Thayer], a thing before unheard of. It was our first introduction to a dinner party and a pretty severe ordeal as we had not had at the Point any instruction in the polite accomplishment of dining out."

Cadets were inspected in ranks under arms each morning and afternoon. Tents were inspected several times a day. Parades were held late each afternoon. After officers marched front and center, the cadet adjutant published orders of the day. Then the Corps passed in review and marched back to camp. After removing belts, cartridge boxes, and swords and sashes, cadets marched to supper.

Hours between meals were fully occupied. Infantry drill was emphasized, and Captain Bliss developed cadets into a well-drilled unit. Training emphasized the school of the individual soldier and movements of squads, platoons, companies, and a battalion at parades and ceremonies. Cadets learned to fire their muskets and soon were able to load their weapons quickly. Lieutenant Gardiner supervised artillery drill. There still were no horses, and cadets manhandled artillery pieces from place to place. Many cadets in letters or in memoirs mentioned the strenuous task of moving cannon to the edge of the bluff, loading it there, and firing up river. Gardiner was unable to teach artillery tactics; there were no books available for such instruction. Another year would pass before cadets learned movements used in the field.

There were occasional important visitors. General Winfield Scott was a frequent visitor. A formal review was always held to honor the visitor. In addition to the review, cadets fired an artillery salute.

Life in camp was far from comfortable. In the hot, humid climate of West Point in summer, woolen coats and bedding soon became musty. When rain continued for more than one or two hours, clothing was damp and uncomfortable. Camp was intended to duplicate to the greatest degree possible the actual conditions of a troop encampment. This it did, with the exception of the wooden tent floors. Caring for muskets and swords occupied any cadet free time. Muskets of the period were not blued, and cadets worked hard and long to keep the barrels shiny and free from rust. Bayonets and brass insignia required much work. More than one cadet was reported for improperly shining his equipment. Strangely, shoes were polished by bootblacks. Cadets had to carry water from the well near South Barracks to camp; the yokes were fully used for this purpose.

One of the few breaks in the strenuous summer routine was the Fourth of July observance. Companies formed in front of camp and marched to the parade ground near the barracks, where they were formed in a hollow square to listen to appropriate speeches. After a national salute fired by a cadet artillery crew, companies returned to camp and then marched to supper. This was a special and relatively sumptuous meal, served under trees near the mess, weather permitting. Wine was served at this festive occasion, and a few cadets usually had too much to drink. Although drinking was not permitted normally, the regulations were relaxed on this date and at Christmas dinner during the early years of Thayer's superintendency.

Regulations were never eased for cadets who headed for Gridley's tavern after dark (North, owner during the Partridge era, sold the tavern to Gridley about 1816). It was easy to slip through the wooden wall near the barracks to hasten to the tavern near the site of the present Administration Building. Many cadets went there only to have a special meal, but others went for ale or rum. Punishment was quick and severe for any cadet caught out of camp and off the limits of the Post.

Benny Havens in 1818 occupied a small building on Gees Point, where he had built a dock, the only place that barges going up river could tie up to wait for good winds to navigate the double bend of the Hudson River. How Havens obtained permission for this operation is not known, but it can be assumed that it was part of the lease he obtained during the Partridge period. Very few cadets frequented his tavern despite its location. It was too difficult to clamber down the bluff in the dark, and Gridley's was far more accessible.

The new Fourth Class reported at the end of August to be examined by the Academic Board. Those who passed were assigned to cadet companies. The reason for Thayer's desire to change the reporting date to June became apparent. With no military training, plebes required intensive instruction before being able to properly march with their companies. Reporting only days before summer training ended, new cadets received little instruction before the return to barracks. Tactical officers and upperclassmen worked with them during every possible minute, from the start of academics until normal drills and parades stopped in November. Throughout the winter, they continued to practice rudimentary drill in halls, on stoops of barracks, or outdoors when weather permitted. Despite this effort, there was still a visible difference between plebes and upperclassmen when parades were resumed in the spring. Had the new class reported in June, the plebes would have undergone intensive training during the remaining camp period that would have eliminated the need for continued drill after the start of academics—drill that took the time of both plebes and their upperclass instructors.

Twenty-three cadets had graduated in the Class of 1818 and were commissioned in branches recommended by the Academic Board and the Superintendent. Secretary Calhoun had waited for recommendations from the Board before making other appointments. Calhoun filled some other vacancies with three former cadets who had been dismissed. Two, who had been underclassmen when dismissed, were commissioned at least a year before their former classmates graduated.

Appeals to Calhoun were unsuccessful. Thayer then sent a strong protest directly to President Monroe asking that the three non-graduate commissions be revoked. Monroe refused to act on the request because it had not been forwarded through the Secretary of War. When the protest was resubmitted through proper channels, the President denied the request because it would be unfair to the three individuals concerned, undoubtedly making this decision with Calhoun's advice.

Monroe's action conflicted with his February 1818 approval of Thayer's recommendation that a former cadet "shall on any account receive an appointment in the Army of the United States until after the promotion of the class to which he belonged." Why Calhoun ignored the 1818 regulations is not known. Monroe agreed to consider recommendations of the Academic Board in the future, a solution with loopholes because the President could appoint officers as he chose at any time he desired. Monroe's agreement set a precedent rarely ignored. The problem ended in August 1861 when Congress passed a law incorporating the restrictions on commissioning former cadets cited in the 1818 regulations.

There were changes in the academic staff during the summer. The Reverend Thomas Picton was appointed Cadet Chaplain in August with additional duty as Professor of Geography, History, and Ethics. One or two officers were added to the faculty, but additional instructors were still needed. Five cadets were selected; three for math, one each for drawing and French.

In August, Christian Zoeller informed Thayer that he intended to resign as Professor of Drawing. At Thayer's suggestion, Secretary Calhoun withheld approval until a replacement could be obtained. In January 1819, Zoeller was replaced by Thomas Gimbrede, who held the position until his death in 1832. Church described Gimbrede as an excellent artist but not a good instructor. Gimbrede designed and in 1824 corrected the first diploma used at the Academy. The design is still used, changed only by replacement of the eagle at the top of Gimbrede's design with the Academy coat of arms in 1899. The original diplomas were lithographed using the stone prepared by Gimbrede, a professional lithographer. Under his supervision, the first Academy print shop was established, and many texts by Academy instructors and translations of French works were published for cadet use.

Thayer and the Academic Board carefully reviewed the records of thirty-two cadets who failed the June examinations and were turned back one or more classes. At the end of August, fifteen were informed that they would be permitted to resign or would be discharged if they did not. Most of the fifteen had been at West Point at least three years and, like those cadets who had resigned the previous January, were believed incapable of completing the course. This opinion was substantiated by their poor academic progress during the period between the January and July examinations.

The action of the Board indicated that January examination results would be used as a warning to cadets with academic problems as well as providing a report of each cadet's progress. June examination results would determine the final standings of cadets in each subject, recommendations for promotion to lieutenant and assignment to a particular branch, and cadets who should be turned back or discharged for deficiency in their studies. The framework and methodology established would remain almost unchanged for many years.

One change was made after the return to barracks; cadets were reassigned to companies based on height. Taller cadets were placed in the 1st Company, shorter cadets in the 2nd. This established the long tradition of "flankers" and "runts." Sizing was followed after the expansion of the Corps of Cadets into a battalion of four companies in 1824 and continued into the 1970s despite interim increases in the size of the Corps from a battalion to a regiment and then to a brigade.

Bliss, Gardiner, and Thayer evaluated summer training. Bliss indicated some shortcomings, such as the need of more drill for plebes and the poor condition of artillery pieces. One comment by Bliss caused Thayer to ask the Secretary of War for shorter muskets because the younger cadets had difficulty using the long 1816 regulation musket. The request was approved, but the replacements, which had been shortened by cutting the barrels, were unsatisfactory. In 1830, the Springfield Arsenal developed a special cadet musket that was a finely made, scaled-down version of the regulation firearm. This was the first of several special cadet muskets.

In October, ceremonies dedicated a monument to Lieutenant Colonel Eleazer D. Wood, Class of 1806. Wood had been killed leading an assault on British siege works at Fort Erie in September 1814. The monument was the gift of his commander, Major General Jacob Brown, who was present for the ceremony. Originally placed in front of South Barracks overlooking the parade ground, the monument was moved to the hillock on the northwest corner of the Plain. Many early drawings show the monument in this location, including the two engravings made by George Catlin in 1826. Richard Delafield was refused permission to move the monument to the cemetery during his first superintendency, but it was moved there at the turn of the century.

The hard summer camp was a contrast to the easy, holiday atmosphere of camp during the Partridge era. Cancellation of the long vacation was not popular among cadets. The stern discipline and rigid regulations imposed by Captain Bliss led to resentment of all of his actions. The daily routine was no easier after the return to barracks. Drill continued before and after classes, four hours daily. This schedule was far more rigorous than Thayer had planned in his initial proposals for the cadet course. He was pleased with the progress Bliss had made with the Corps and therefore agreed with Bliss's daily drill schedule.

Cadets grew more restless. Discussions in barracks compared cadet life under Thayer with the relaxed discipline under Partridge. This comparison would be a problem to Thayer until the last cadet from the Partridge period was graduated or discharged. In late October, Bliss recommended to Thayer that daily drill continue after November 1, although drill had ceased at the end of October in previous years. There were reasons for this recommendation. The weather was unusually mild for that time of year, and drills and parades could be continued until it snowed. The primary reason was the need for additional drill for plebes. After six weeks, they had progressed to the stage where training could be expanded to company drill, training that required all cadets in ranks. The resentment of older cadets became apparent by their attitude and the way that they reacted to commands.

On November 22, trouble erupted as tempers flared at parade. The result was an explosion that would bring congressional action that would settle definitely and permanently the status of the Corps of Cadets as a part of the Army. Cadet Edward L. Nicholson, a Third Classman who had entered the Academy in 1814, misbehaved in ranks. When Captain Bliss corrected him, Nicholson reacted slowly and insolently. Outraged, Bliss grabbed Nicholson by his cross belts, pulled him out of ranks, cursed him in the language of a drill sergeant, and ordered him to barracks.

Two days later, five cadets reported to Thayer and announced that they represented the Corps of Cadets in condemning Bliss for a long list of alleged outrages, including his unwarranted attack on Nicholson. To support their stand, they handed Thayer a petition signed by 179 cadets. Thayer calmly refused to accept the petition. He informed them that any cadet who had a grievance was welcome to discuss the problem with the Superintendent, but he emphasized that he would not tolerate any unmilitary action such as a petition. The committee was dismissed with a warning only.

It would have been easy for Thayer to chastise the committee on the spot. He did not for many reasons. The "round robin" had been used many times during the Partridge era, and most of the cadets involved had signed earlier petitions. Thayer was well aware of the great differences between the discipline instituted by Bliss and the lax supervision of Partridge. He realized that cadets were young men with little knowledge of proper military procedure. Looking at the five cadets, he must have been inwardly disturbed. Two, Thomas Ragland and Wilson M. C. Fairfax, had been cadet instructors and Ragland, as cadet adjutant, had also been post adjutant until an officer replaced him. Another of the five, Nathaniel W. Loring, was cadet captain of the 2nd company. Four were First Classmen; Charles R. Holmes had been a cadet only since September.

Thayer knew that the four First Classmen had stood high in Partridge's favor and that Ragland was one of the leaders who organized the uproarious greeting and farewell given Partridge when he took command from Thayer in 1817. He had ignored this and instead recognized Ragland's abilities from the outset of his superintendency. Thayer's fairness was never more apparent than in his dignified, calm, objective, and proper treatment of the cadet committee.

The next morning, the five cadets again reported to Thayer. Ragland, acting as spokesman, handed Thayer another petition with the threat that unless Thayer received their grievances, the entire Corps was ready to mutiny. He also wanted to prefer charges against Captain Bliss for four instances of "unofficerlike conduct" in physically and verbally abusing cadets. Thayer listened and then icily ordered the five cadets to leave the post within six hours for the "places of their respective guardians where they will remain until further notice." He then directed an order be read to the Corps of Cadets stating that round robin petitions were "not only in a military but in a civil point of view, a crime of the first order."

The five cadets left the post but went to Gridley's tavern outside the south gate. When Thayer learned this, he ordered them to leave the area immediately.

Protesting that they were only waiting for the evening boat to New York, they were rowed to Peekskill. In the interim, Thayer wrote to Lieutenant Colonel Walker K. Armistead, who had become Chief of Engineers when Swift resigned ten days before, informing him of the action he had taken and asking for a Court of Inquiry to be convened as soon as possible.

Thayer's account is revealing. He placed the blame entirely on "certain Cadets who were old offenders having been the instigators of the disturbances which took place last year," obviously referring to the four First Classmen. The committee, Thayer informed Armistead, "waited on me to demand the arrest of that officer & even dare to threaten me with rebellion in case of a non-compliance with their wishes." Thayer made it clear that "the pretty general dislike of the young gentlemen to Capt. Bliss arises in part from his strict discipline forming as it does a complete contrast to that of former times." Although Thayer made no effort whatsoever to place the blame on anyone other than the five cadets, he made it clear to Armistead that the "radical cause of the disturbance to which the Mil. Acady. is liable is the erroneous & unmilitary impressions of the Cadets imbibed at an inauspicious period of the institution when they were allowed to act as tho' they had rights to defend as a corps of the Army & to intrude their view and opinions with respect to the conduct of the Acady." Thayer assured Armistead that "there has been no positive act of mutiny or disorder."

Armistead immediately reported the incident to Secretary of War Calhoun. The five cadets, who had gone to New York City instead of their homes, also sent a long letter to Calhoun. They then went to Washington and submitted an even longer and more vindictive document to the Secretary. Calhoun and President Monroe supported Thayer fully. The Court of Inquiry convened by Armistead submitted a report completely in agreement with Thayer's actions. After reviewing the findings of the Court of Inquiry, Calhoun wrote to Thayer in early January 1819: "I have the pleasure to state that your conduct as Superintendent of the Military Academy in the unpleasant occurrences which induced that investigation have been satisfactory and approved."

Captain Bliss was not so fortunate. Calhoun stated that "as Captain Bliss does not appear to possess sufficient control of his temper" he would return to his regiment. Captain John R. Bell of the Light Artillery replaced Bliss. Calhoun and President Monroe deplored the action of the cadets who had signed the petition and the attitude of the five committee members. "The redress of Military grievances must never be exhorted or obtained by combinations which are alike mutinous," Calhoun informed Thayer. Acting on Thayer's comments concerning the reasons for the episode, Monroe directed that the five cadets be reinstated because their "youth and inexperience were probably the cause of their irregular conduct."

The decision should have ended the matter, but the five cadets were not content merely to be reinstated. They sent their complaints to Congress. The House of Representatives asked Calhoun to submit a copy of Academy regulations and a report of legislative action required to improve the "organization and government of said academy; the better to secure a strict obedience to all proper orders and a suitable respect for the rights of those whose duty it may be to yield obedience."

Ragland refused to accept Monroe's generous reinstatement, and his four companions agreed to demand a General Court Martial. The court convened at West Point at the end of May for a brief session before it adjourned because its members decided that Army regulations did not indicate that cadets were subject to trial by court martial. Thayer referred the decision to the Secretary of War, who in turn asked Attorney General William Wirt for a legal opinion. After long and careful study of Army regulations and other statutes, Wirt informed Calhoun that "the corps at West Point form a part of the land forces of the United States and have been constitutionally subjected by Congress to the rules and articles of war and to trial by courts-martial."

The court reconvened at the end of September. Ragland presented a long and detailed defense. The court again declared itself unable to try cadets despite the ruling of the Attorney General. President Monroe ordered the court to be dissolved, although he fully supported the ruling by the Attorney General. "The President," Adjutant General David Parker informed Thayer in November, "is of the opinion that the Professors, teachers, and Cadets are governed by the rules and Articles of War although the institution is intended for instruction and is preparatory for Military promotion, it is nevertheless evidently governed by Martial law."

Monroe took unusual action, ordering Thayer to read Calhoun's letter of January 15, 1819, to the Corps of Cadets, the staff, and the faculty. He also decided that the five cadets had been punished sufficiently by their long suspension and again ordered them to be reinstated. The class to which Ragland, Fairfax, Loring, and Vining belonged had graduated in July 1819; Holmes' classmates were now Third Classmen. The five decided to refuse reinstatement, resigned, and again took their case to Congress. After lengthy hearings, a congressional committee in April 1820 stated that Thayer, Armistead, Calhoun, and Monroe had reacted properly.

The episode, though ended officially, was not completely over. Partridge used it as the basis for another series of allegations. One publication attributed to him, "Exposé of Facts Concerning Recent Transactions Relating to the Corps of Cadets of the United States Military Academy at West Point," was published at Newburgh, New York, in late 1819. Ragland and his committee members submitted this as evidence to both the General Court Martial and the congressional committee. Partridge made certain that the pamphlet was widely distributed. It resulted in many newspaper accounts.

During the eighteen months that the affair continued, activities at the Academy continued in a normal manner. Captain Bell replaced Bliss in January 1819. Additional officers reported for duty and were assigned to academic departments or to the Commandant's staff. Three semi-annual examinations were conducted.

The cadets who had been placed on probation because of low grades in Natural and Experimental Philosophy were found to be proficient at the January 1819 examinations. Several cadets in the Second Class requested permission "to attend the recitations of the First Class with a view to offer themselves for examination with that class in June." The request was denied.

Thayer and the Academic Board constantly reviewed the curriculum, making changes in the content of various courses and moving some subjects from one year to another in the four-year course. Descriptive Geometry was moved from the First Class year to the Third to ally it with other mathematical subjects rather than with engineering. The time in the First Class course vacated by the move was filled by a new course in Geography, History, and Ethics taught by Chaplain Picton. The method of teaching this course differed from the methodology used in all other departments. The entire class as a group attended each lecture because Chaplain Picton had no assistant instructors and because he had ecclesiastical duties. Because these changes were made in March, it was decided that the Second Class would study geometry to prepare for the revised First Class course starting that fall. Other modifications provided greater flexibility in teaching cadets to enable more capable cadets to study subjects in greater detail.

The Board of Visitors participated in the July 1819 examinations. Twenty-nine cadets were found qualified to graduate. Four of the Second Class cadets who had requested permission to attend First Class instruction were examined as part of the First Class and found qualified. Two of the four had already been advanced from Fourth Class to Second Class studies the previous year and thus graduated from the Academy in two years. During the Thayer era, only five other cadets graduated ahead of the class with which they entered the Academy. The rearrangement of the curriculum made it impossible for a cadet to "skip" a class.

In its report to the Secretary of War, the Board of Visitors praised the overall operation of the Academy, discipline and appearance of cadets, and academic progress shown in the examinations. Several recommendations were made to the Secretary. The Board noted "the inability of the Corps of Engineers to act as a constituent part of the Academy as contemplated by Law" and criticized the Corps of Engineers as being too small "to furnish the number of officers required for the Instruction of the Cadets in Military exercises." The need for additional officer instructors was emphasized, although the Board complimented cadet instructors for their excellent work.

The Board urged that an astronomical observatory be provided and astronomy, chemistry, and mineralogy be added to the curriculum with two qualified professors provided for these courses. The Board noted that "the want of practical knowledge is severely felt" and recommended that a cadet be taught "the practical as well as the scientific part of his profession." Realizing that it would be impractical and impossible because of lack of time to incorporate the military instruction of a "School of Application" into the West Point curriculum, the

Board recommended that "one especially devoted to that purpose be established elsewhere." This recommendation was accepted in 1824 when the Artillery School of Instruction was established at Fortress Monroe, Virginia.

By the end of his second year as Superintendent, Thayer had a curriculum and methods of instruction keyed to cadet abilities. Section assignments based on merit enabled instructors to vary the prescribed curriculum to provide a challenge to cadets. Rather than offer a standard group of courses supplemented by electives, Thayer chose to prescribe a finely tailored course that appeared to be rigid in concept but was actually flexible in operation. With one exception, the addition of the Chemistry and Mineralogy course in 1822, the curriculum instituted by Thayer during his first two years remained essentially unchanged until his departure in 1833.

Thayer's close association with the members of the Academic Board was disturbed by Professor Mansfield, who began a new series of complaints prior to the July 1819 examination. Mansfield felt that the Academic Board should have more control over Academy operations, much the same attitude he had taken during the Partridge period. Apparently he still resented the fact that he was only a professor even though Jonathan Williams had once asked him to head the institution. He now complained to Secretary Calhoun that the Academy needs "less military and more civilian influence." He also felt that there was too much influence by the French schools and compared West Point with "Academies of despotic countries." His complaints were ignored.

Sylvanus Thayer had met every severe threat to his superintendency with flying colors. The Ragland episode resulted in the ruling that the Corps of Cadets was part of the Army. The Board of Visitors praised the revised curriculum. Mansfield's complaint had failed. Thayer had the support of the Secretary of War and the President. In two short years, Thayer had established the foundation on which the Military Academy would develop basically unchanged for over 150 years.

8

Still in a State of Progressive Development

The June 1820 examinations showed the results of Thayer's efforts to transform the curriculum into an orderly, comprehensive course of study designed to develop officers with a technical background. Thirty First Classmen were qualified for graduation. Eleven had entered the Academy in 1814, eight in 1815, and nine in 1816. Their departure left only three cadets who had served under Partridge.

The Board of Visitors, which included retired General Joseph Swift, the first Academy graduate, did not restrict its report to comments on the examinations. The Board inspected all phases of Academy operations. After the tempestuous Ragland affair, it is not surprising that its primary interest was discipline and the method used to instill and continue that discipline. The Board recommended that the Superintendent be relieved of "the tedious duty of adjudging crimes and awarding punishment" and that instead "a court of council be authorized to assemble for the trial of all such delinquents whose cases might involve their dismissal or permanent disgrace." Many years later a similar concept was adopted. Boards of tactical officers were established to investigate serious violations of regulations and award punishments, subject to approval of the Commandant and the Superintendent. The Battalion "Batt Board" of pre–World War II cadets and the Regimental Board of the 1950s were tribunals of this type.

The Board of Visitors pointed out that there were differences between the regulations published by the War Department and those actually used at the Academy. "It is evident," the Board reported, "upon an inspection of the former that many of them must have of necessity become inapplicable from the changes that the institution has undergone." It recommended that the regulations be clarified and each cadet given a copy.

Thayer was praised for the disciplinary "improvement that has taken place and is still going on under the direction of the present Superintendent." Particularly noteworthy was "the manner and decorum of Cadets at meals; and their deportment to each other has been altered since the adoption of regular reports." The Board commented on the undesirable proximity of Gridley's tavern and recommended the purchase of the Gridley tract. "So long as this small property remains in private hands," the Board reported," it will continue to be, as it has long been, a location for shops and taverns, and continue to injure morally and physically the youth attached to the Military Academy."

Although Thayer had attempted no major building program, realizing that better relations with Congress were necessary to have such a program approved, he did have many projects under study. The Board commented about several of these projects as well as indicating a need for many buildings. These projects included the installation of a pipe system to bring water from a large pond in the hills to the Plain and the construction of a road north to link the Academy with other communities.

The Board recommended approval of a hospital, library, chapel, hotel, gun shed, arsenal or artillery laboratory, and observatory. Many of these buildings had been requested by Swift during his superintendency, but Thayer had submitted no request, although their need was apparent. Knowing the difficulty of getting funds, Thayer in 1819 had asked only for additional quarters. The Board urged that the request be approved. These recommendations indicated that Thayer realized the benefits that could be obtained from the reports of Boards of Visitors. His discussion of his own projects with Board members brought the strong recommendations in their report.

The most effusive praise concerned the curriculum. "The introduction of the analytical method into the course of Natural and Experimental Philosophy and into the preparatory course of Mathematics in consequence will probably form an era in the public education of the United States," stated the report. The Board commented favorably on the teaching of French and the benefits gained by adding descriptive geometry. The merit system and the improvement in knowledge and teaching methods of young instructors received favorable comment. The Board suggested that courses in astronomy and in chemistry and mineralogy be added.

The Board recommended that the course in Geography, History, Ethics, and Natural Law taught by the Chaplain be divided into two courses. The Chaplain would continue as Professor of Ethics, Belle Lettres, and Oratory. History, Geography, and Natural Law would become a separate department. Although no criticism was directed at the Chaplain in his role as Professor, it was evident that the Board believed that a qualified instructor was required to teach geography, history, and law. "It is vital to its interest that this Department be headed by a man of strong and comprehensive powers," said the report. "The studies of History, Government, and Man," continued the Board, "are mingled in the constitution of the field over which he presides . . . and they should be lectured upon and discussed with an ability commensurate with their importance."

The stress given these subjects reflected the interest and expertise of two of its members, Samuel L. Mitchell and James Renwick. Renwick was Professor of Natural Philosophy at Columbia College, a position Mitchell had filled before he was elected to the Senate. Their knowledge was reflected in emphasizing the importance of these subjects, although the Board report did approve stressing mathematics and science. "The course of Moral Philosophy . . . " said the Board report, "constitutes a primary branch of the system. The others relate more particularly to the details of the profession of arms—this, to its high and momentous operations." In the opinion of the Board, Moral Philosophy was "the course which is to communicate the finish to education, the tone to character, and to give a determining cast to the habits of thought. Its importance is forcibly obvious, and with its importance, the necessity of establishing over it a man of refined and polished manner with the highest order of intellect and the most profound erudition."

Comments about the Drawing course were not favorable. "There appears to be a deficiency of instruction in those kinds which are applicable to Military purpose," said the Board. More instruction in topographical and geometric drawing was considered necessary. The Board recognized the artistic capabilities of Professor Gimbrede and was pleased with "the talents shown by many of his class in the Crayon Drawings to which their attention has been devoted."

Another area of concern to the Board was what is today called "morale and welfare." These comments probably represent the interest of Swift and Brigadier General James Jessup, the Quartermaster General of the Army. Recommendations suggested ways to improve the uniform, cadet amusement, and teaching the cadet the "courtesies of society."

Comments concerning the cadet uniform reflected Jessup's special interest. The gray kerseymere (wool) vest was not regularly worn because regulations permitted wearing of a white vest instead. The Board recommended that only the white vest be authorized. Unfavorable comment concerned the length of the trousers legs for both the winter gray and the summer white trousers, which were so short "as to leave an unsightly gap between it and the regulation shoe." The use of a fatigue uniform during camp received favorable mention because it would save the cadets' dress uniforms and cost less to launder. The cadet headgear was criticized because the dress hat was "heavy, and affords no shelter either from the sun or rain." The Board noted that "there is no half dress cap, and the Cadets in consequence wear, except when on duty, common hats." The Corps must have had a ragamuffin appearance in winter for no uniform overcoats or hats were worn. Shoes were considered to be of good quality but the cost of $3.00 or $4.00 a pair was considered too expensive.

Interest in morale was evidenced by comments concerning recreation. This interest was to some degree the result of the Ragland controversy, for the report stated, "a good discipline may be much promoted by providing amusement calculated to break into the tedium of study and duties." The Board suggested music as an appropriate recreational activity, pointing out that the Academy had an excellent band, an instructor in music, and a cadet organization for musical improvement. Greater use of the library was encouraged. "The Cadets might, however, be directed to other innocent objects of amusement much to their benefit and comfort, and to the advantage of the institution," commented the Board. Dancing was cited as one example and the need for an instructor was noted. This recommendation represented another difference from the official attitude during the Partridge period when cadets were forbidden to attend or hold any dance.

The Board recommended that some means be devised for cadets to "acquire that species of experience which would enable them upon leaving the Academy to associate easily with a new community." More attention, in the opinion of the Board, should be given to social and moral intercourse "by which the Cadets may enjoy the courtesies of society . . . the usefulness of men in society depends much upon easy and good manners."

The Board carefully studied the food "furnished to Cadets at the mess-house." A menu posted in the mess hall for each meal enabled cadets to determine if the meal served agreed with the menu. The Board indicated that food was abundant and wholesome. It noted that the kitchen "possesses no apparatus for roasting, although roast meat is a part of the regulation diet." The steward substituted baked meat, which the Board considered less wholesome and less palatable. The Board recommended that Academy officials review the mess operation to make certain that the steward did not use substitutes or change the menu, "the choice of which he is governed entirely by means of his own advantage." Board interest in the mess operation was probably generated by General Jessup.

The Board had one unusual comment concerning the qualifications of graduates for duty in non-military fields. "It should be universally known through the Nation," the Board stated, "that the object of the instruction which is given at the Military School at West Point, is, not only to prepare young men to fill the vacancies which occur in the Corps of Engineers, Artillery, and Infantry of the Army, but also to prepare them to occupy other useful stations in the service of the General Government." This concept was very different from the original mission of the Academy, even when preparing young men to serve as officers was not restricted to officers for the Corps of Engineers. In many ways, this comment by the Board reflects what may have been Thomas Jefferson's prime motive in supporting the establishment of the Military Academy: it would replace the National Academy of Science he so greatly desired. Board comments indicated a growing belief that the graduates of the Academy should serve the federal government in positions for which they were qualified that would most benefit the nation.

The report of the 1820 Board of Visitors is important and of special interest for several reasons. The Academy had been under Thayer's supervision for almost three years, and almost every facet of its operation reflected Thayer's touch. The diverse backgrounds of the Board members provided probably the most widespread professional interest of any other Board of the nineteenth century. That comments and strong recommendations in the report show the sincere interest of every member of the Board is best evidenced by one phrase in the report, "The Board of Visitors would not fulfil their duty, did they not bear testimony to the improvement which has taken place and is still going on under the direction of the present Superintendent." The report can be considered another blueprint of Thayer's plans for future development.

No Board of Visitors or other external commission can make a detailed inspection of a facility without being briefed by institution officials and receiving informal comments at social functions. The 1820 Board was no exception; its report incorporated Thayer's concepts and intents for the future development of the Academy and the Corps of Cadets.

The favorable analysis of the 1820 Board did much to counter adverse comments in newspapers generated by the Ragland controversy. The report also contributed to the defeat of a congressional resolution to abolish the Academy. Increases in the number of newly appointed cadets failing entrance examinations and cadets dismissed academically or for bad conduct brought attacks on West Point in newspapers and state legislatures. The Board report showed the Academy in a positive way, improved its reputation throughout the country, and countered many unfavorable articles.

Within a year, Thayer had initiated some projects commented on by the Board. A small lake, the present Delafield Pond, was converted into a reservoir. Water was piped from the lake down the steep hillside to the area of the Plain and then to quarters, the mess building, and an outlet near cadet barracks. Water was not piped into buildings until about 1826, according to Professor Church in his memoirs. Indoor bathrooms were not installed until 1863 or 1864. Outlets near quarters and other buildings provided water carried to its destination in buckets. Reservoir water was an improvement because it lessened the need for water from wells or streams trickling onto the Plain.

The proximity of Gridley's tavern and hotel continued to cause problems. Church summarized the magnitude of the problem insofar as cadets were concerned. "It was but a step through the wood yard to the hotel entrance." The high wood fence was no obstacle to a cadet who wanted to add variety to his mess-hall fare or who desired liquid refreshment. "Scarcely a night passed," said Church," in which one or more parties did not enjoy the excellent suppers set forth by this enterprising host." All efforts to dissuade Gridley from serving cadets were unsuccessful. Thayer finally found one way to obtain at least limited cooperation. The only docks in the area were on the post. Gridley had permission to use the docks to receive supplies delivered by water. By closing the post, Thayer stopped the supply route; and since there were no suitable roads leading to the Academy or Buttermilk Falls, Gridley had to agree not to serve cadets.

This would continue for a brief period, and then the entire procedure would be repeated.

Thayer's complaints to the War Department and the comments of every Board of Visitors brought approval in 1824 to buy the Gridley tract, which included all the land from the Hudson River to Fort Putnam. The possibility of a hotel being built on Academy grounds was being discussed at that time, and some preliminary work was done on the site. Because a great part of tavern receipts came from Academy visitors lodging there, Gridley realized his days were numbered and agreed to sell his land and its buildings for $10,000.

About this time, Benny Havens' lease was canceled, and he moved his barge-supply activities to Buttermilk Falls, where he built a dock and tavern. Havens apparently had no intention of attracting business from cadets or other post personnel, but cadets soon found their way there, although not in the numbers that had headed for the Gridley tavern.

As soon as the tavern-hotel was taken over, Thayer converted it into a badly needed hospital, which was used until a new hospital was built in 1830 on the present site of Lee Barracks. Part of the original tavern was moved to the back of the new hospital and used as officer's quarters until it was razed in the late 1880s.

Shortly before the June examinations, Thayer received informal word from a friend in the War Department that General Andrew Jackson had asked Secretary Calhoun "to have his nephew Donelson promoted into the Engineer Corps, and his other nephew Butler in the Artillery." There is no indication that Calhoun formally forwarded this request. Andrew Donelson, second in his class, was one of the cadets advanced from the Fourth Class to the Second Class in 1818. After the examinations, he was recommended for one of the two Engineer vacancies. Butler ranked high enough academically to be assigned to the Artillery. No favoritism was shown in recommending these assignments.

For some reason, assignments for the Class of 1820 irritated Professor Mansfield, and he began another string of letters criticizing the Academy. He complained to friends in Washington that there were too many French instructors and that Thayer was arbitrary in his decisions. He argued that Academy personnel, including cadets, should not be subject to military law. Mansfield went so far as to recommend drastic changes in Academy operation: military law and "despotic command" should be abolished; the Academy should be controlled by a joint board consisting of the Superintendent and the department heads; the academic staff should be abolished because "more than two thirds are Foreigners"; the number of cadets "supported by the nation" should be reduced to 100 or 150 and any over that number should pay for their education and not be required to go into public service; and "fixed and determinate laws" should prescribe the exact duties of the professors and the commander. Mansfield's tirade irritated General Alexander Macomb, now Chief of Engineers, but no steps were taken to stop Mansfield from complaining.

Mansfield's wife considered his complaining an ingrained habit. "It would be happy for me and for him," she said, "if with his complaints he had lost the habit of complaining, but I fear it is an infirmity which time cannot remove." He apparently complained about everything: weather, food, family, friends, and even animals.

Mansfield continued his tirades until he resigned in 1828. It would appear that his primary problem was the twofold resentment of military discipline when it applied to himself and his egotistical conviction that his abilities qualified him to be the governing influence in any institution with which he was associated. He complained while working on the Northwest Territory surveys. He complained about the "despotic" actions of Alden Partridge. Although he had initially supported Thayer enthusiastically, he now complained about Thayer and used wording almost identical to that of his complaints about Partridge. That his letters had little impact did not lessen the irritating effect on Thayer.

There was another side to Mansfield. He was an affectionate family man despite his constant complaining. He was generous with his time and assisted cadets with their studies. He often invited cadets to his home, knowing that they would appreciate a good home-cooked meal.

Mansfield supported efforts to improve landscaping around the Plain by planting trees. Church told the story that Mansfield, hearing someone chopping down one of the trees Swift had planted as a cadet, rushed out of his quarters to stop the man. He was told that the Superintendent, Captain Partridge, had ordered all of the trees to be felled for firewood. Mansfield sent the man away, went to Partridge to ask that these trees be spared, and "by offering to advance money from his own pocket . . . succeeded in saving them." Mansfield was instrumental in building an art collection for the Academy. In January 1821, he wrote to Jefferson, asking him to pose for a portrait by Sully, the artist who had painted the portrait of Jonathan Williams. This is the Jefferson portrait hanging in the Library today.

Thayer implemented another of the 1820 Board of Visitors' recommendations by adding Chemistry to the curriculum in October with Military Surgeon James Cutbush teaching the course to both the Second and First classes. Mineralogy was included in 1821. In 1823, the course was presented only to the First Class and some geology was added. By 1827, it was evident that the surgeon was not qualified to head the Department of Chemistry and Mineralogy, and Lieutenant William F. Hopkins, appointed Assistant Professor after he graduated in 1825, became the Acting Professor.

During the summer of 1820, Thayer was notified that funds would be provided to build officers' quarters. Thayer had work started on a house for the Superintendent and others for faculty and staff officers on the west side of the Plain, away from the cadet area. Construction continued for over five years, resulting in a row of stone houses facing the river, today's Professors Row, and the Superintendent's quarters. Thayer, who had lived in the old academy since 1817, moved temporarily into visitor rooms in the mess building. The duplex houses for professors were built with stone excavated on the site or obtained by removing some of the many large boulders scattered on the Plain. Using the boulders achieved the dual purpose of providing building material and, at the same time, clearing some of the obstructions from the level area.

The new Superintendent's quarters, a two-story, simple, rectangular structure, was completed in 1821. Many changes and additions have been made over the years, and the present building has little resemblance to the 1820 original structure. Thayer had two offices in the basement. One, a very simply furnished small room, was the office he used when he met with cadets. The other, a study as well as an office, was his work area.

Many cadet letters and memoirs described Thayer's office and, at the same time, revealed one method he used to keep informed of the status of each cadet. Cadets could call upon or be ordered to report to the Superintendent between seven and eight o'clock in the morning, the time between breakfast and class. Thayer's desk had a large number of pigeonholes facing Thayer, compartments not visible to the cadets. Thayer's clerk, Timothy O'Maher, monthly or more often when Thayer directed, prepared summary memoranda about each cadet, showing the status of his cadet financial account, the number of delinquencies for which he had been reported, his academic marks, and anything and everything else of interest. Thayer had only to glance at the proper pigeonhole to know immediately current information about a cadet.

Cadets credited Thayer with an incredible memory. The secret of his ability to counter any cadet request with detailed information was not revealed until 1879 when Church included a description of Thayer's desk in his memoirs. At the suggestion and through the efforts of Major General and Mrs. Frederick A. Irving—General Irving was Superintendent from 1951 to 1955—the Thayer office has been restored to approximately its original state.

Thayer's information concerning cadets went far beyond the brief memoranda pasted in his desk. Every Saturday afternoon, each instructor reported to Thayer with a written report showing the progress of each cadet in his sections. Instructors reported in the study, not the office used by cadets. Thomas Cram, Class of 1826 and an assistant professor from 1829 to 1836, recalled that Thayer always asked many questions about the proficiency of cadets and their behavior in class. "In this way," said Cram, "the superintendent obtained a pretty accurate insight into the moral deportment and mental acquirement of every cadet." Frequent reports from the Commandant and tactical officers added more details to Thayer's knowledge of cadet activities.

Many legends have developed concerning the Superintendent's quarters and its adjacent garden. The house is rumored to have, not one, but several ghosts. In the late 1960s, Sam Koster, son of the Superintendent, maintained that he was awakened one night by "a lady in a long white dress." When the boy asked what she was doing in his room, the apparition walked through the closed door and disappeared. Molly, Thayer's housekeeper, is believed to be another of the spirits still in the quarters. Molly is described as "an old, milky iridescent maid, a tall, dark woman" who periodically delights in rumpling the coverlet in one of the bedrooms. A third reported spirit is a male servant, a black man, who wanders in the upstairs halls.

Another legend or myth is the belief that the beautiful copper beech tree formerly in the garden was planted by Jonathan Williams in 1802. No evidence has been found to support this contention although no exact information has been located for the exact time the tree was planted. There is much negative evidence against the 1802 planting. Jonathan Williams did not live in the present building nor in any house on or near that site. When he was at West Point, which was relatively infrequently, he occupied quarters near the present site of Washington Hall. For many years, a large pond, fed by springs, was on the site of the garden. Church said that "another skating pond was in what is now the garden of the Superintendent, holding water nearly all year." The pond was not filled in until the 1860s, primarily because so much of the rich mud on the bottom of the pond had been removed to use in gardens that the water became stagnant.

Planting trees was a memorable and noteworthy event in the early days of the Academy. Swift in his memoirs describes trees that he and Armistead planted near the present site of Washington Hall. These trees are also mentioned by Church, Latrobe, and Ramsay in their memoirs. Mrs. Davies described trees planted in front of the quarters on the western edge of the Plain. Other letters and memoirs tell of cherry trees planted in the yards of officers' quarters and the problem of keeping cadets from picking their fruit. Not one of the many collections of letters and memoirs in the West Point Library mentions the copper beech being planted in the garden. Had the tree been planted by Williams or another early superintendent, this event would have been noted by cadets or officers in their letters or later recollections. Mrs. Davies did mention Thayer planting a horse chestnut on a mound in the middle of a hollow across the road from his quarters, but this was not the copper beech.

Maps from 1805 to 1863 show the pond on the site of the present garden. Maps prepared in 1874, 1883, and 1891 show no pond; it had been filled by that time. An 1891 map, with great detail, locates many trees along officers' row, the barracks, and elsewhere on the Plain. Included is a tree beside the quarters, possibly the copper beech. Art works and the earliest photographs show no copper beech before the Civil War.

When was the copper beech planted? One may hazard a guess. In the period after the Civil War, a wave of Anglophilia swept many parts of the United States, particularly the East Coast; and things English became a fashion and even a fixation. The copper beech is not native to North America; it is English by origin. Several of the large estates on the east bank of the Hudson River have copper beech trees planted at this time; some can be seen from the Galilee Porch of the Cadet Chapel. The close relationships with many inhabitants on the eastern shore started by Thayer continued through the years. It is possible that one of the individuals who planted a copper beech on his estate brought one to a Superintendent as a gift. A copper beech planted at the entrance to the Highland

Falls cemetery about 1875 is not as large as the tree in the Superintendent's garden, but this may be due to different soil and watering conditions.

Conjectures are only theories at best. It has not been possible to determine the exact date the copper beech was planted. Evidence does verify that it could not have been planted by Williams or in all probability at any time before the Civil War. The story that Williams was responsible did not surface until the early 1980s; there is no indication of why or by whom the legend was started. Webster defines a legend as "any story coming down from the past, esp. one popularly taken as historical though not verifiable." The allegation that Williams planted the copper beech in 1802 is an example of a legend not based upon fact. The beautiful old tree fell in a small wind storm in July 1989. Counting its rings indicated an age of about 118 years, showing that it must have been planted about 1871. Regardless of the controversy about its origin, the beautiful copper beech will be missed by the many graduates who stood beneath its lofty branches.

Venerable Professor Andrew Ellicott died in August 1820. After his burial in the West Point cemetery, Thayer and the Academic Board discussed possible successors. Noted oceanographer and navigator Nathaniel Bowditch declined appointment despite his long friendship with Thayer. Few if any other civilian educators were considered; very few Americans had the necessary scientific background needed, and the search concerned Academy graduates primarily. Two members of the faculty were qualified: Captain David Douglass, Assistant Professor of Natural and Experimental Philosophy, and Lieutenant Charles Davies, Assistant Professor of Mathematics. Douglass was selected because he had taught at the Academy for a longer period, and Davies was moved into Douglass's old position. Two years later, Douglass became Professor of Engineering when Claude Crozet resigned, and Davies was appointed Professor of Mathematics.

There were other personnel changes. Brevet Major William Worth reported as the new Instructor in Infantry Tactics in March 1820 and was also designated Commandant of Cadets, positions he would hold for over eight years. Worth later was venerated almost as much as Thayer for his contributions to the development of the Corps of Cadets. It was his recommendation to Thayer that resulted in establishing the demerit system about 1825. Also at Worth's recommendation, Thayer ordered two tactical officers, Lieutenants Zebina J. D. Kinsley and Henry W. Griswold, to live in North and South Barracks.

This decision was made after a fire in December 1821. When the alarm was sounded, cadets left their beds to man the primitive pump, set up a bucket brigade, and brought the blaze in the mess building under control. The fire, apparently incendiary in nature, had demolished most of the roof. Not until after the fire had been extinguished did the cadets and officers discover that a cannon had been dragged to the front of the Superintendent's quarters during the confusion, loaded, and apparently fired. The fuse, however, had gone out. It was never learned who had moved the cannon.

There were other reported incidents, some true and some not. *The New England Galaxy* printed a letter from a cadet, previously published in the *New York Evening Post*, alleging that cadets had "assailed the guard-house" in an effort to free a cadet who had been dismissed only to find there was no cadet there. This episode supposedly concerned three cadets who had been tried by Court Martial for gambling and sentenced to be discharged. The cadets, sent to a hotel on the east shore of the river to await review of the sentence by the President, had returned without approval and were placed in the guardhouse. The article, signed by "A Scholar of West-Point," cannot be verified. Possibly it is another of Partridge's diatribes.

There were other indications that cadets resented the discipline under which they lived. A battalion order published in late December 1820 stated, "It is with the bitterest regret and mortification that the Comdg. Offr. states, that the Corps of Cadets exhibits at the present moment, a scene of riot and insubordination bordering on mutiny." The events of the previous month, the order continued, were "replete with every offence, characterizing a total disregard of every military principle, of any military virtue, and he sincerely regrets, devoid in some instances of every principle of the gentleman and man of honor."

Apparently the incident involved resentment toward cadet officers who had reported other cadets for violating regulations. "An officer on duty knows no one," stated the order, "to be partial is to dishonor both himself and the object of his ill-advised favours." The order was an appeal to the sense of duty and honor on the part of cadet officers and sentinels and emphasized that partiality or favoritism would not be condoned.

Reasons for the cadet attitude are unknown. Letters to families and friends showed little resentment. The only criticisms expressed concerned the lack of time for recreation. Thayer was strict, but he also was fair and even partial to those cadets who regretted violating regulations. Cadet Samuel Southerland in December 1820 "having refused obedience to the order of yesterday" was dismissed. Another order, written within hours of the dismissal, showed Thayer's lenient attitude: "Cadet Southerland being sensible of his error in refusing to recite to Cadet Washington [a cadet instructor], and having promised future obedience, the order directing his dismission is hereby countermanded." Other similar orders ended or reduced punishments.

Thayer's method of handling discipline was firm and fair. He used infractions as a means of stressing duty. Cadet explanations of reported delinquencies were accepted without question, an unspoken emphasis on honor. A cadet pledge of future obedience to orders, as in the Southerland case, was a means of developing a sense of honor in the cadets. This unspoken and unwritten policy may have been the origin of the cadet honor system.

Punishments for most infractions were not strict. A cadet might be confined for short periods in the "light" or "dark" prisons. These were not actually jails or guardhouses but rooms in North Barracks. The light prison had windows; the dark did not. Confinement, directed only for more serious offenses, was not continuous; the cadet being punished was required to attend classes and other formations. Cadets might be restricted to their rooms, which meant that they could not leave their rooms during "release from quarters," a relatively short time each day.

There were other punishments for minor infractions. Extra tours of guard duty were a common award. Normally, underclassmen had guard duty every fourth or fifth day and were posted at the entrances to barracks and in other parts of the cadet area from after parade until taps. They were not excused from classes or drill the next day. Extra tours on guard were somewhat of a hardship because they necessitated unauthorized study by candlelight after taps had sounded. Extra guard duty during the summer was a hardship, a twenty-four hour tour involving walking a specified post for several four-hour periods.

Extra drill was another punishment for minor infractions, a punishment that became more frequent as years passed. This involved being drilled in the area of barracks by a cadet Officer of the Guard. Extra drill soon devolved into requiring the punished cadet to walk back and forth in the area under the supervision of an Officer of the Guard, the origin of "walking the area."

For a brief period, Thayer assigned cleaning the Plain as punishment; "policing the area" was the official term. In their memoirs both Church and Latrobe mention such punishment as removing small rocks from the Plain. A cadet rumor or "sinkoid" maintains that similar punishment was meted cadets in the post–World War II period when cadets were ordered to pick up rocks on the new golf course for minor infractions.

There were some unusual punishments. One cadet was punished by not being permitted to take part in parades; one wonders if he considered this a punishment! On rare occasions, cadets were ordered confined in the post guardhouse in old Fort Clinton. Cadets Granville Cooper and George Tallmadge were confined in the dark prison after using "profane oaths & in such a manner as to be heard by persons passing the Barracks." While confined, they were disorderly "by breaking and otherwise injuring the wall, door, & Mantlepiece of said room." The cadet Officer of the Day was ordered to move them to the Fort Clinton prison. They were charged with "unsoldierlike and disorderly conduct, and conduct tending to mutiny," and the cost of repairing the room was deducted from their pay. Neither Cooper nor Tallmadge graduated.

Cadet rank was important to the young men, but cadet officers and noncommissioned officers often were punished for breaking rules, usually reduction to the grade of private. There were exceptions to "breaking" a culprit. Cadet Lieutenant John Pratt was punished for being "absent from his quarters at prohibited hours . . . and outside the limits of the Post without leave." Apparently he either did not head for the tavern or was apprehended on the way for his only punishment was that "his Rank in the Battalion is in consequence suspended for two weeks" and restriction "to his Room for one week at all hours in which he may not be called from it by Academic or Field Duties." Pratt was fortunate; being caught at Gridley's meant almost automatic dismissal. So many cadets were caught "running" to the tavern that Thayer had a cadet sentinel posted at the gate. This slowed but did not stop the almost nightly forays.

Cadet regulations were made more explicit and more restrictive. In addition to rules concerning the care of weapons and equipment, there were many "Thou Shalt Not" regulations governing all aspects of cadet life. Musical instruments were not to be played between 8:00 A.M. and 3:00 P.M. Cadets could not visit other rooms "during the hours of Study & recitation." They could not enter another cadet's room without knocking and receiving permission to enter. After taps at ten o'clock, "any Cadet who shall keep on view a light . . . without permission shall be reported by the Officer of the Day."

There were many restrictions concerning deportment. Cadets were not to throw "shot or stones on the Plain or at either of the Barracks or Buildings." Another order prohibited "playing at ball in or about the Barracks or other Public Buildings and all other amusements by which the buildings are liable to injury." Athletic games were permissible away from the cadet area. Many writings mention "football" as a favorite athletic pastime; this was probably a form of soccer.

Thayer and his staff were concerned about the moral welfare of cadets, and many of the restrictive regulations were intended to develop a high sense of morality. "Games of Chance are strictly forbidden," stated one order. Strangely, chess was included in this restriction for several years. Card playing was considered to be "most immoral in its tendency." The prescribed punishment was dismissal for "any Cadet who shall be convicted of Card Playing either at his Quarters or elsewhere, or of having Cards in his possession, of procuring them or causing them to be procured." To make certain that cadets were not tempted to play cards when visiting officers' quarters or attending a party, the Superintendent informed the staff and faculty that he expected them to "accordingly exclude card playing from their social parties."

Physical welfare was the basis for other restrictions. "The practice of chewing, snuffing, & smoking tobacco," stated a December 1823 order, "being deemed pernicious to the health of the students of the Military Academy, and as being altogether unnecessary & inconsistent with a due respect to economy is hereby forbidden and prohibited." In addition to prohibiting cadets from imbibing at Gridley's tavern, regulations specified that "any Cadet who shall be convicted of having in his possession Spirituous Liquors, or of bringing them or causing them to be brought into the Barracks without the written permission of the Superintendent will be dismissed."

One regulation applied to a typical habit of that time: "The practice among the Cadets of spitting on the floors of the section rooms and Academies must immediately cease. The rooms have all been furnished with spit boxes, and the instructors will be vigilant that this order is duly observed." Similar boxes were placed in barracks.

Orders were issued concerning cadet appearance. Twice a month, cadets were required to have their hair cut "in such a manner as not to project beyond the upper edge of the coat collar." The first restriction on beards and mustaches prescribed that "the beards will not be suffered at any time to appear upon the face and necks below the lines drawn direct from the lower extremity of the ear to the corner of the mouth nor upon any part of the upper lip." This restriction became a routine part of many 100th Night Shows that lampooned "No horse, no wife, no mustache."

The tactical staff tried to make this rigid life more comfortable for cadets. Boot blacks shined cadet shoes; an 1825 order prohibited them from entering cadet rooms for any reason. "Cadets will place their shoes in the hall by the side of the door," stated this order, "from whence they will be taken by the blacks and returned arranged in the same order as they were found." Wash women cleaned cadet clothing, which could be taken to them by a cadet or picked up once every two weeks by a detail.

It was no longer necessary for cadets to request permission to bathe. They could use the primitive shower during their free time or swim in the cove near Gees Point. During summer months, cadets were marched to the cove or to the "shower-bath" after supper, supervised by cadet officers. Because of concern that accidents might occur, cadet supervisors were directed, "While bathing they will hold themselves in readiness & such others as they may select to meet any accident which may occur."

The two cadet companies were expanded to four during the summer camp period. In 1824, at Major Worth's recommendation, the battalion organization of four companies was adopted for the entire year. This gave more cadets an opportunity to serve as cadet officers and noncommissioned officers. The rank of cadet colonel had been dropped after two or three years. Cadet captains were now ranked in order of seniority. For a time, officer appointments were rotated periodically to give every First Class cadet a chance to serve as an officer. With the expansion to four companies, there was no longer any need to rotate cadet officers.

At the same time, companies were given letter designations from A through D, conforming to the Army change made in 1816. The four-company organization also brought a reassignment of cadets based on height. Tall men were placed in the flank companies, A and D, and short men in B and C.

Worth and Thayer decided that cadets should room only with their classmates. This policy was adopted because arrangement of studies by year and scheduling of classes made it inconvenient for cadets with different schedules to room together. This change developed a feeling of belonging to a class for the first time. Class spirit increased and many undergraduate class activities took place. Beginning in 1853, graduated classes began to return to the Academy, a tradition still maintained.

The 1820 Board of Visitors' report had commented on the cadet mess and its quality. To make certain that the mess steward provided good meals and followed the posted menu, Thayer made the Commandant responsible for supervising the mess. He also directed Major Worth to periodically review cadet financial records. The intent of assigning the Commandant these and other extra duties was to make him responsible for all aspects of cadet life other than academics.

This division of responsibility divorced the academic staff from any responsibility for cadet activities other than studies. The only exception was requiring instructors to report cadets for delinquent conduct in class. The division has caused friction between the Department of Tactics and the Academic Board over the years. The Commandant often feels that his activities are of paramount importance. Needless to say, the professors feel the same. Often, a superintendent has had to intervene and make decisions that caused dissatisfaction on one side or other.

Worth and Thayer realized that more area was required to properly train cadets in infantry and artillery tactics and techniques. The only suitable area was the Plain, and only parts of it could be used because of hollows, boulders, and stones. Most of the scrub pine had already been removed. To provide a better site for summer camp, the Fort Clinton area was cleared and small hollows filled. Summer camp had been located near the Superintendent's quarters through 1820. After clearing away many of the rocks and boulders in the area in 1821 or 1822, the camp site was moved to the west side of Fort Clinton on the northeastern corner of the Plain. Here it remained until 1942, when the new training facilities at Popolopen Lake became available. Hedges were planted around the camp site to close off the area from public view and interference. Moving the site away from the vicinity of officers' quarters eliminated the bustle and noise of cadet activities. The old location became the parade ground. Guard mount and drill continued to be held near barracks.

Many of the boulders were too large to be moved. Most of these were demolished by hand, but some were shattered with gunpowder. One large boulder near the site of the present library was spared at the request of cadets and graduates. Church recalled in his memoirs that it became traditional for the graduating class the night before leaving the Academy "to form in procession with their drawing-boards, tables, &c., on their shoulders, and march to this rock upon which these articles, then their private property, were piled and set on fire, and around the brilliant flames, with hands joined and tuneful voices, the class would dance and sing until every article was consumed."

Enlisted men from the bombardier detachment did most of the work when other duties permitted. At one period, the inability of the detachment to provide a rock-picking detail required a daily detail of twenty cadets to be used. This procedure stopped after the new camp site had been cleared. Thayer was not pleased with the record of the detachment. Too many men were tried for various offenses, particularly drunkenness. In 1821, he asked for the temporary assignment of an Artillery company. In 1823, he disbanded the bombardier detachment, and Secretary Calhoun ordered Company A, 2nd Artillery to be stationed at West Point. An artillery company continued to be the Academy support unit until long after the Civil War.

Comments of a Board of Visitors were not needed to give Thayer concern about the cadet mess. He was aware of its deficiencies and took steps to improve its operation. After directing Major Worth and his tactical officers to supervise the mess, Thayer decided to replace the mess steward. In June 1820, he found an excellent and experienced individual to run the mess. William B. Cozzens signed a contract agreeing to "supply the Cadets commons at the Military Academy, West Point, with provisions for two years" and to pay $5,000 for this concession. The money from this contract was placed in a special Post fund to be used for improvements at the Academy. These were the funds used to build the hotel on the northern edge of the Plain in 1829.

A supplementary agreement attached to the formal contract described the meals that Cozzens would serve: "Breakfast. Good Coffee with milk and sugar, fresh bread and butter, smoked beef or ham and radishes in season for them. Supper. Young Hyson tea of a good quality, with milk and sugar and fresh bread and butter. Dinner for Sunday, Tuesday and Thursday, fresh meat either Beef, Veal, or Mutton well roasted, with good bread and potatoes and two of the following vegetables properly boiled, Viz., Beets, Onions, Cabbage, Turnips, or Carrots; but as a substitute for one of them, (except potatoes which shall always be given) green Peas or Beans shall be furnished in season for them. For Monday and Saturday, corned beef and pork, well boiled, good bread with the same vegetables as for Sunday, also a pudding with sauce. For Wednesday, good meat soup, boiled meat and rice, with bread and vegetables as on Sunday, also a pudding with sauce. For Friday, fresh fish when it can be procured, with bread, vegetables Etc. or a dinner as specified for Sunday when fish cannot be procured."

The supplement included other stipulations. Cozzens would provide provisions "of a good quality" and bread made of "Superfine flour." At least seven waiters would be hired to "attend at table on the cadets while eating." He would provide and furnish three large rooms "with two beds in each for the accommodations of Strangers." A parlor was required "furnished as a sitting room for Strangers who are to be accommodated on the same terms as at respectable houses in the vicinity of the Post." Cozzens agreed to sell bread to the families living in quarters "at New York prices." Officers assigned to the Academy or garrison could board with Cozzens. This specification was joyfully welcomed by the bachelor officers living in cadet barracks.

What Cozzens had agreed to maintain was actually a triple establishment. He would operate the cadet mess, maintain a separate officers' mess, and operate a small hotel, a facility immediately used by official visitors and by the "strangers" cited in the contract. Generals Winfield Scott and Jacob Brown were frequent guests. Many members of various Boards of Visitors stayed here during annual examinations. When the new hotel was built in 1829, Cozzens became its host. He and his sons, Theodore and Sylvanus, managed the hotel until 1879.

Mrs. Thompson continued to board twelve cadets, including the cadet instructors. Being assigned to her table was considered a great privilege. Latrobe, one of the twelve boarders, stated, "Here we enjoyed the comforts and observances of a private family, at a table at which Mrs. Thompson or one or more of her daughters were always present." Mrs. Thompson moved to a house on officers' row vacated when the storekeeper's establishment moved to a building near the mess hall. After Mrs. Thompson's death, her daughters continued to board cadets until the last died, about 1875.

Thayer was also concerned about proper amusements for cadets. The suggestion that a dancing instructor be obtained included in the 1820 report of the Board of Visitors probably resulted from a comment made by Thayer to one of the Board members. Within a year, dancing classes were scheduled. Latrobe said that "the superintendent allowed our fencing master [Pierre Thomas] to give dancing lessons, and on the days or evenings to which we were allowed to go we had a jolly time. The ladies were few, but there were enough to make up a dance, and make it pleasant for us." Thayer's interest in dancing and its importance in the overall development of the cadet is shown by his obtaining a noted dancing master from Boston in 1823. Papanti traveled to West Point each summer and spent several weeks instructing cadets. Through 1944, dancing was taught to the new Plebe Class during summer camp. Plebes were formed in company groups and marched to class carrying their "hop" shoes. In most classes, few if any young ladies were present; many cadets learned to dance with roommates as partners.

Other recreational activities were encouraged. Although playing ball games near the barracks was prohibited, cadets could play "at football" near Fort Clinton or north of the large boulder near the site of the present Library. Latrobe makes curious mention of a game called "baseball" played in this area. Unfortunately, he did not describe the game. Could it be that cadets in the 1818–1822 period played the game that Abner Doubleday may have modified later to become the present sport?

Hiking, swimming, and fishing were common during the summer months. Many cadet memoirs describe climbing Crow's Nest and the view from that peak. Swimming was restricted to the cove near Gee's Point. Edward Mansfield indicated that he often swam from the cove to Constitution Island and back. A few boats were available for fishing; they were also used by enterprising cadets heading for Benny Havens' tavern or to cross the Hudson to Garrison or Cold Spring.

Skating was a popular sport during the cold winter months. A shallow hollow near South Barracks that froze easily and regularly was the principal skating area. Cadets who were invited by officers or their families also skated on the pond beside the Superintendent's quarters.

Thayer encouraged cadets to use the Library, but it had few books other than those supporting the curriculum. To provide others, Thayer approved the establishment of the Amosophic Society, a literary and debating association whose members included cadets of every class. Latrobe said, "How the society got its name I never found out, but suppose that the founders, knowing like Shakespeare, 'little Latin and less Greek,' but believing there might be something good in both, divided the name between the two languages by taking a part from each." Books were purchased using funds from monthly dues. Latrobe cites Gibbon's *Decline and Fall of the Roman Empire* and Humes's *Essays* as two of the books purchased. Presenting original compositions, excerpts from poetical works, and debates were routine society activities. The Amosophic Society was absorbed by the Philomatheu Society in 1823. Another rival group, the Ciceronian Society, was formed that year. They combined to form the Dialectic Society in 1824, an organization that still exists although not as a literary and debating society.

The relatively remote location of the Military Academy gave it a rather mystical charisma as far as most Americans were concerned. Newspapers were available only in the largest cities, and their coverage of Military Academy activities was, for the most part, reports of rumors and hearsay. There were many accounts of debates in Congress and state legislatures concerning possible abolition of the Academy. The number of newly appointed cadets who did not pass the lenient entrance examination and cadets dismissed for academic deficiencies or misconduct and continued allegations by Partridge made many newspaper accounts uncomplimentary.

Thayer searched for some method to present true facts about the Academy to the public. Thayer considered the Military Academy to belong to the American people; and, realizing the need to make them more knowledgeable about their Military Academy, he scheduled a series of "marches" to various parts of the East Coast. He planned to have cadets visit large cities, knowing that the resulting publicity would be positive.

A short march was made in 1819. The Corps crossed the river to Cold Spring and marched in easy stages to Poughkeepsie and Hudson, returning to West Point by boat. In 1820, the Corps moved by boat to Staten Island, where it camped for five days before marching to Philadelphia. Notifying the Chief of Engineers of the trip, Thayer indicated that the time required would be about two weeks and that "the expenses of the march to the Public are not to exceed Four hundred & fifty dollars, which will be paid from the appropriation for the Academy, should that appropriation admit of it, otherwise from the Academy Fund."

The following year, a longer and more extensive march was scheduled. Led by Major Worth—Thayer did not make any of the marches—the Corps traveled by steamboat to Albany. The cadets marched 170 miles to Boston through Lenox, Springfield, Leicester, Worcester, Framingham, and Roxbury. Some marches were made at night because of extremely hot weather. The Corps was welcomed wildly by Bostonians and invited to camp on Boston Common. Bostonians presented a stand of colors to the Corps, the first time it had its own flag. The cadet battalion visited Harvard College; another trip took the Corps to Bunker Hill, where they camped for a night. Perhaps the most memorable part of the Boston stay was a march to Quincy to pay a formal call on former President John Adams.

Major Worth had written Adams to request that the cadets "might be allowed to pay him their respects," and Adams had replied that the visit would give him great satisfaction. Adams spoke briefly to the Corps. "It was interesting," reported Worth to Thayer, "to see one of the conscript fathers of the land—the wisdom of a century, addressing itself in the affecting language of patriotism, with a tremulous tongue and a palsied hand, to the youth of another generation, exhorting them to love of Country." One phrase of Adams' short talk was almost a duplication of Thayer's own philosophy. "I congratulate you," said Adams, "on the great advantages you possess for attaining eminence in letters and science as well as arms. These advantages are a precious deposit, which you ought to consider as a sacred trust, for which you are responsible to your Country."

After three weeks of public dinners, parties, and dances, the Corps began its return. The cadets marched to Providence and then to New London, where they embarked for the short sail to New Haven. After one day there, they sailed on to New York for two days of festivities. On September 16, almost two months after their departure, the Corps returned to West Point to begin the fall academic term.

The cadets were tired after their long trip, tired by the long marches and the constant round of social activities. Although pleased with the outcome of the expedition, Thayer decided that no further trips should be scheduled. The entire Corps had spent most of the summer without normal summer training. He also felt that the numerous social activities had an improper impact upon the cadets, including some activities he considered immoral.

The objectives of the two trips, however, were outstandingly successful. Cadets made a favorable impression wherever they stopped. American citizens from Albany to Boston to New York, in large cities and small hamlets, and on farms along the route of march had seen the Corps at its best. Drills, parades, and ceremonies had placed the cadets before the eyes of a large section of the American public. The precise, well-disciplined drill of the Corps was compared with that of militia units and came out well ahead. Newspaper coverage, not only in the area, but throughout the United States was extensive and highly complimentary. Exactly how successful the marches were became evident the following year when an unequalled number of young men applied for cadet appointments.

Thayer had now been Superintendent for five years. He had restructured the curriculum into a four-year scientific course. Cadets had been sectioned based upon merit. Military training had been improved, and the Corps was recognized as a highly disciplined unit. Initially faced by near-mutinous cadet resentment, Thayer had changed this attitude by his fair treatment of every cadet. Attacks against the Academy by Partridge, Congress, and state legislatures had seemingly been nullified. More Americans knew about West Point; the Corps had achieved an excellent reputation as a result of the two long marches. Boards of

Visitors were extremely complimentary after their inspections. Thayer had accomplished much during his first five years, but more remained to be done. As the 1822 Board of Visitors stated, the Academy was "still in a state of progressive improvement, and steadily advancing toward that point of perfection, which every friend of his Country must wish to see it reach."

9

Members of One Brotherhood

Newly appointed cadets now reported to West Point by the end of June instead of in September. After examination by the Academic Board and Thayer, those who passed the tests were accepted. Despite the very lenient examinations—essentially only an assurance that the young men were able to read, write, and do basic arithmetic problems—the number of candidates who failed was shocking. Few appointees from small communities or farms had any formal schooling. Sons of prominent men and young men from large cities had attended school as an accepted routine. Consequently, the Corps had far more cadets from "good families" than from poorer homes or rural districts.

To Thayer this was wrong. He sincerely believed that the Academy should reflect a cross-section of the American public. He realized that an entrance examination was necessary, and he believed that the examinations being given were not adequate because many cadets who passed were not able to absorb Academy instruction. He knew this could be corrected only by teaching fundamentals to a potential cadet.

Beginning in 1822, new cadets were required to report by the second week in June. For two weeks, they were taught subjects covered in the July examination. Most of the instruction was given by cadets or young officers, new graduates awaiting assignment orders. Church remembered that instruction consisted of four hours of arithmetic daily, two hours of basic drill, and one hour of reading and writing.

Examinations, recalled Church, were simple. Appointees were asked only two or three mathematics questions. "We were required to read and write in the presence of the Academic Board," said Church, "with more time given to reading than to writing." The results achieved Thayer's objective. As Church reported,

"Very few comparatively were rejected. Over one hundred of my class were admitted." Thayer's innovation continued for many years until the educational level of appointees eliminated the need for pre-examination instruction. Cadets called appointees "things" until they passed the tests and became plebes.

Young men who passed the entrance tests did not become full-fledged cadets immediately but remained on probation until January. Five months of instruction and the semi-annual examinations indicated whether each individual could absorb the lessons ahead. This first winnowing often included a large percentage of a class, but the remainder were considered to have the ability and attributes necessary to master the remainder of the course.

After the entrance examinations, the new cadets were drilled, drilled some more, and then drilled again. It was expected that each new plebe would be able to join in company and battalion drills by midsummer. Under the watchful eyes of Major Worth and his tactical officers, upperclassmen taught the new cadets the basic school of the soldier, squad drill, and platoon movements.

Some unusual methods were used to instruct the new cadets. Latrobe in his reminiscences stated, "How well do I remember the parallel lines of shallow trenches, twenty-eight inches apart, on the east side of North Barracks, over which the squads were marched back and forth, again and again, until they were supposed to be able to step that distance uniformly in the daily drill." Cadets were also taught by a system called "lock step." A cadet would lift one foot at the count of "one," standing on the other foot until the instructor said "two." The cadet then put the other foot down one pace to the front and waited for the next command. Latrobe indicated, "It took a good deal, no doubt, to bring me up to the cadet pattern, and the work was done by those who, having gone through the mill themselves, seemed to take a malicious pleasure in grinding me between the same stones."

Cadets learned many fine techniques that added to the precision of their movements. Major Worth taught cadets doing the manual of arms of the period to press the butt of the musket against the left hip. "It was 'good form,' " said Latrobe, "in coming from 'support' or 'present' to strike the butt audibly with a rapid flourish of the left hand." Cadets cut away bits of wood from under the first and second bands, the metal loops holding two pieces of the stock together. This caused a sharp, clearly audible crack when the barrel rattled against the wooden stock during execution of the manual of arms. This practice was continued by cadets as long as musket or rifle stocks were made of wood. In the early 1900s, stocks of Springfield 1903 rifles were altered to produce the sound; the same was done with the World War II Garand M1 rifle. Graduates taught this procedure to crack drill units wherever they served, and the crack of a rifle or musket during the manual of arms became a mark of excellence throughout the Army.

Maliciousness or hazing was not the reason for this intense drilling. Perfection was the objective. Church recalled that "at this time there was nothing in the Corps of Cadets approaching what is now [1879] called 'hazing.' Every one admitted to the corps was regarded as a member of one brotherhood." Church cited some practical jokes played on new plebes as a routine during summer camp, but these stopped after the move back to barracks.

This feeling of brotherhood reflected the pride and esprit of the Corps. The trips to Philadelphia and Boston were partially responsible for the development of this spirit. Thayer, Worth, and the academic staff were equally responsible. The merit system and the administration of fair and equal justice to all gave each cadet a sense of accomplishment as he passed each of the semi-annual examinations. Letters to families and friends often expressed pride in passing tests, high class standing, and few delinquency reports. Many admitted that discipline was hard, hard but fair. Cadet life may have been Spartan, but it created a common bond among cadets and graduates.

Thayer attempted to improve living conditions in barracks. Cots were authorized although not required. He might have made their use mandatory, but he knew many cadets did not have sufficient funds in their accounts to buy a cot. After passing the entrance examinations, cadets were required to deposit with the Academy Treasurer all money in their possession. Cadets from wealthy families usually had a large balance in their accounts because of the initial deposit, and they were able to purchase cots with Thayer's approval. When they left the Academy, these cadets either sold or gave their cots to underclassmen. Eventually, cots were provided from military stores, but cadets continued to buy mattresses and bedding until World War II.

Both Latrobe and Church provided descriptions of South Barracks. The three-story barracks had rooms placed back to back and opening on outdoor galleries or stoops extending along the length of the building. The east and west rooms on all floors were used for official purposes. On the ground floor, the east room was used as an office for the Commandant. The west room was the Academy Quartermaster's office. The end rooms on the second and third floors were assigned to bachelor officers, two to each room.

Outdoor stairways led from the ground to each floor, one stairway at each end of the building. A large wood box at each end of the gallery provided wood for nearby rooms. Cadet rooms were small, "not one-third as large as those now in the new barracks [Central Barracks built in 1851]," said Church. Latrobe estimated the rooms to be about eleven feet square. Three cadets were assigned to each room. Latrobe and his roommates had a room that, according to Latrobe, "Speaking only of mine, was furnished with three cots, that were nothing more than camp stools widened and lengthened to accommodate a person six feet tall." One cot was on either side of the fireplace, the third near the window at right angles to the other cots. Church and his roommates were not as fortunate and slept on mattresses placed in the same relative location as the cots. Bedding was folded and placed in bags during the day.

The door from the gallery and one window were opposite the fireplace. Between the door and window was a rack for three muskets and accoutrements. A shelf over the fireplace was used for books, tinderbox, candlesticks, and personal items. Clothing was kept in trunks. Most rooms had some type of table and three chairs or low stools, andirons, and a fireplace fender. In such a room, said Latrobe, "three tall men were 'cabinned, cribbed, confined.' "

Both Church and Latrobe commented on the cold temperatures during the winter. "Many a winter's night," said Church, "we were obliged to sit at our tables with blankets at our backs, scorching on one side and freezing on the other." Candles, one for each cadet, and the fireplace provided the only light for studying. The door to each room had a window in its upper section; the window had to be raised before the door could be used. Church recalled, "Many a bumped head and harsh word resulted from failing in the hurry of exit to raise the upper part sufficiently."

There was always danger of fire. The large sheet-iron fender was intended to lessen this possibility. It was the responsibility of the room orderly—each cadet served as room orderly for a week, and his name was posted on the mantel— to place the fender against the fireplace opening whenever the room was vacant. Many room orderlies were reported for "fender not up."

To combat the frequent fires resulting from neglect, cadets were organized into fire companies. Church indicated that fires were "speedily extinguished by prompt passage of buckets filled with water along an instantaneously formed line to the pumps." One pump was in front of the south entrance to South Barracks, the other near a cistern in front of North Barracks. A small, hand-pumped engine was available but seldom used.

Fireplaces were important for another reason. Almost nightly, cadets would toast bread smuggled from the mess hall. They often cooked a full meal. Church remembered that "we made jolly fires in winter, and before which many a turkey was roasted for late suppers." Cadets were often reported for foraging a chicken for this purpose, a delinquency that brought stiff punishment.

Cadets considered North Barracks preferable to South. Latrobe was fortunate enough to be reassigned after his plebe year "to my great delight." A four-story building, North Barracks had no exterior galleries or stoops. A long hall ran down the center of each floor with rooms opening off either side of the hall. Interior stairways led from floor to floor. A guardroom was in the first room near the south entrance. This was the only entrance; the north door was permanently closed. A room near this entrance was used as a post office. All other rooms on the first floor were used for class instruction, except one assigned to the Dialectic Society for its meetings and library.

The upper three floors were used by 1st Company cadets and then by cadets in A and B Companies after the Corps was reorganized as a battalion. Rooms were larger, about eighteen feet square with four or five cadets in each room. A thin wall divided the room into a sleeping area and a study space. Chairs and a table filled most of the study area and a large woodbox stood in a recess near the fireplace. The gun and accoutrements rack was beside the door.

Neither Church nor Latrobe located the "light" or "dark" prisons in the barracks, although frequent mention is made in letters that these two cells were in one of the barracks. It is possible that they may have been first floor rooms near the guard room in North Barracks. There is no record of a basement in either barracks, the logical place for the two prisons.

Differences in the two buildings are interesting because they were built at approximately the same time, South Barracks in 1815 and North Barracks in early 1817. Each represented a completely different barracks concept. What caused the different arrangements is unknown. Apparently the South Barracks design was considered to be more desirable because a similar design was used when old Central Barracks was built. Rooms were arranged in four-story "divisions," each division opening onto stoops at ground level.

There were few comforts to ease the life of a cadet. Most rooms had a small mirror, kept on the shelf over the fireplace. Each cadet had a wash basin and a glass. Water was kept in pails; at least one was required to be full in case of fire. Cards, of course, were prohibited. Thayer did remove the restriction on chess playing during free hours. It is quite possible that the original restriction came from the Commandant, for Thayer himself was an excellent chess player. Cadets in North Barracks had a slight advantage over those in South Barracks; they could slip out of their rooms to the Dialectic Society room on the first floor to get a book without running into the cadet guard posted outside barracks doors.

Cadet Thomas Cram indicated that a room orderly was responsible for complying with all regulations. This included cleanliness of the room, correct arrangement of furniture, arms, and accoutrements, banking the fire at night with ashes, placing the fender in front of the fireplace, and extinguishing candles at Taps. Cadets cleaned the area around each barracks, carried water from the well or pump, and emptied "slop water" from their rooms into large tubs in the halls of North Barracks or on the stoops of South Barracks.

"The only menial services allowed to be performed for the cadets by other than themselves," recalled Cram, "were the washing of clothes, bringing up wood [from piles outside each barracks to the wood stacked on the stoops or in hallways], trimming the hall lamps, making the morning fire, removing the ashes also the slops from the tubs, and blacking shoes." All other work was done by cadets. Only men tending the fires—"barracks policemen," a term still used—were permitted to enter cadet rooms. Washerwomen and bootblacks could not enter a room at any time.

It is remarkable that few of the cadet letters of the period or memoirs written in later years complained about the puritanical existence. They described their life as hard, but this was done with an unwritten sense of great pride. Cadet esprit was astounding considering their way of life and their overly full daily schedule.

A cadet's time was fully occupied on weekdays. Drill before breakfast, more drill and parades before supper, and compulsory study time filled all but one hour of time not devoted to academics. Classes extended from 8:00 A.M. to noon and from 1:00 P.M. to drill at 4:00 P.M. every day except Sunday. An inspection in ranks and quarters on Sunday morning was followed by chapel services in the Academic Building. Two hours of leisure after dinner were followed by a dress parade. Study was required every evening except Sunday from dinner to Tattoo at 9:00 P.M. Understandably many cadet letters apologized for a lack of time to write home.

Thayer's curriculum was settling into a pattern that provided maximum flexibility to permit cadets in higher sections to study in more depth than those in the lower groups. In 1822 and 1823, the First Class had only two sections, each with approximately twenty cadets. Each section studied the same assignments in all subjects except Engineering where the 1st Section covered more material on fortifications and stone cutting than did the 2nd Section.

The subjects studied by the Second Class showed greater differences between sections. In Natural and Experimental Philosophy, the 1st Section studied mechanics, astronomy, and physics. The 2nd and 3rd Sections were taught only mechanics and physics, and these in less depth than the 1st Section. Different texts were used by each section. All sections covered the same material in drawing classes. The Third and Fourth Classes had four sections; each received different instruction in mathematics and French, the only two subjects taught to these classes.

This was the curriculum pattern followed throughout Thayer's superintendency. Material taught by various departments differed from year to year. Occasionally, a subject taught in one class would be moved to another class the following year, a change requiring at least two years to complete to assure that every class covered the entire prescribed curriculum during its four years at the Academy. Astronomy, surveying, and mapping were given more emphasis toward the end of the 1820s, and drawing began to include more engineering applications. Church in 1879, after more than thirty years as Professor of Mathematics, stated that "the course of studies, at this time, was theoretically the same as now. Thayer, after the labor of years, had succeeded in organizing a course which he deemed best fitted for an American military education—a course calculated to cultivate the powers of thought rather than store the memory."

The method of instruction used at the Academy differed from that of other colleges. The blackboard presentations and daily recitations were unique. Church indicated that the instructors at the time he was a cadet had to learn the true use of the blackboard and "the strict and detailed manner of instruction."

Text books were a serious problem. The best texts that could be found for algebra and trigonometry were poor translations of Lacroix's French works. Most texts in English were of poor quality, even those translated from French or German. The Library had an increasing number of foreign writings, obtained from contacts Thayer had made during his stay in France. Paris bookseller A. J. Kilian periodically shipped books to the Academy. From time to time, he provided foreign journals, surveying instruments, apparatus of various types, and other materials required for West Point instruction. Although most of the books ordered were French, Thayer obtained materials in English and German.

It is interesting to note that these shipments included copies for the Secretary of War's library in Washington. That library later provided the nucleus of the Army War College Library whose older books, including many ordered by Thayer, today are in the U.S. Army Military History Institute at Carlisle Barracks.

Although most foreign works provided the latest and best information on a subject, it was a disadvantage to require cadets to study texts in another language; and more and more books written by faculty members were used. Davies, Crozet, and Berard translated French texts into English. Davies was the most prolific author of the three and published a series of mathematical and scientific books that were used throughout the United States. In time, most of the texts used in scientific and technical studies were written or translated by members of the Academy faculty. These books were also used by other institutions offering scientific courses.

To print official papers and texts for cadets, a small lithographic printing plant was established. Some extremely fine works were published with illustrations by Gimbrede or cadets. Gimbrede's design for the Academy diploma was placed on a lithograph stone, and the printing plant printed diplomas for over 150 years. Hop cards and other materials were also prepared. The printing plant continued to print books for cadet use for over 100 years.

In descriptive geometry, a small text prepared by Professor Crozet with few illustrations was used. Shading, shadows, perspective, stone cutting, and construction were taught by lecture. Notes were taken by cadets who then made drawings during the evening study period. The next morning, the cadet drawings were checked by the instructor, and the cadets recited using the drawings to explain their recitation.

Church indicated that "the real teachers, in these subjects, were those cadets who made careful notes, finished their drawings early in the day, made the demonstrations to their classmates, and lent their drawings for copying." A primitive light table was used. A large, clear pane of glass was placed on top of the wash stand in a cadet room, and a lighted candle was held under the glass. Copying was acceptable to instructors. Several years later, however, each cadet was required to do his own work.

Thayer considered French to be only a means of providing cadets with the ability to use the French scientific works. No effort was made to teach conversational French. Church indicated that a good knowledge of grammar, a thorough knowledge of the verbs, and a "full translation from French into English were all that was required." Several Boards of Visitors commented on this fallacy and urged that cadets be taught to speak as well as translate the language. Despite Thayer's intent, cadets did learn to speak French "tolerably well." During each recitation period, several cadets were given problems involving grammar to be answered on the blackboard. While these cadets were doing their blackboard work, others would read aloud from the text and then translate what they had read. Their pronunciation was corrected by the instructor.

The course in Natural and Experimental Philosophy included mechanics, physics, electricity, optics, and astronomy. Material taught by this department probably changed more often and more drastically than in other academic departments because of rapid and radical discoveries in these subjects during the early nineteenth century. Church stated that there were few apparatus available during Thayer's time, and what equipment the Academy had often did not function properly. Church believed that Thayer's cadets had to study harder to learn the Philosophy material than cadets of 1879 did to learn the "more extended course of today."

Thayer was intensely interested in the academic program. He visited different sections to listen to cadet recitations. This increased his knowledge of each cadet's ability and provided an indication of the knowledge and capability of each instructor. There is little question that Thayer himself studied every subject to prepare for examining cadets at the semi-annual examinations.

Because the Academic Building so carefully designed by Swift and Partridge was now totally inadequate, eight first-floor rooms in North Barracks were also used for classes. Some classes, drawing for example, were taught in the mess building. The Academy had only three large rooms on the ground floor and four on the second. A large room in the center of the first floor was used as a chapel on Sundays and for lectures to an entire class on weekdays. The chemistry laboratory was on the west end of the first floor; the engineering workroom on the east. On the upper floor, the library was in a room above the chapel. The Natural and Experimental Philosophy Department occupied the west end of this floor; the Adjutant's office, the eastern section. Some small offices were also located on the second floor.

In February 1823, Thayer was promoted to Brevet Lieutenant Colonel at the recommendation of Winfield Scott, who informed Secretary Calhoun that in his opinion "if any officer, since the peace, has earned a brevet, Major Thayer is certainly that individual. The Academy has been placed in a state of the most perfect organization & efficiency under his administration, & has, in the last five years, given to the Army a majority of the good officers in it." Calhoun and Monroe concurred and Thayer was promoted in recognition of "Distinguished and Meritorious Service as Superintendent."

Thayer was authorized to draw a triple ration allowance, which enabled him to entertain the increasing number of official and casual visitors coming to West Point with minimum personal expense. Thayer greeted all official visitors and casual tourists alike. Often he took visitors on a tour, including an impromptu inspection of barracks. Cram in his memoirs remembered Thayer "exchanging a pleasant word with the occupants, always introducing us by name to the stranger."

Cram remembered many of the "gentlemen of distinction" who came from every part of the country to visit West Point. All were greeted by Thayer "in a manner that evinced his hospitable propensities as well as the urbane side of his character." Thayer was equally at ease with statesmen, lawyers, physicians, clergymen, historians, poets, scientists, and merchants. "In almost every branch," said Cram, "he seemed to possess and to be ready to exhibit when called upon, an unlimited knowledge of the particulars as well as a general intimacy with the principles of the subject under discussion. Cadets and officers alike were proud of Thayer as a host.

General Winfield Scott was a frequent visitor. He had first visited West Point as President of the Court Martial trying Captain Partridge. During that relatively short stay, he developed an affection for the Military Academy that increased with time. During Thayer's superintendency, Scott would often stop at West Point en route to or on the way back from an official trip to other Army installations. At times, the Corps was turned out for a formal review; at other times his visits were informal. Scott normally stayed with Thayer instead of boarding with Cozzens. In 1874, Professor Charles Davies said of Scott's visits, "Here he loved to come for rest and recreation. He regarded the members of the Academic Board as the honored professors of a national school, and the Cadets, as the younger branch of his military family."

In August 1825, the Marquis de Lafayette came to the United States as guest of the nation. Landing in New York, he was persuaded by Thayer and General Swift to visit West Point en route to his first official stop in Albany. Lafayette accepted the invitation. His expected morning arrival on September 15 was delayed several hours by fog that caused his steamer to run aground south of Bear Mountain. Thayer and the official party waiting at the dock were relieved when the boat finally docked shortly after noon. Lafayette was welcomed by Thayer, Generals Scott and Brown, who had come from Washington to greet Lafayette, and the officers and staff of the Academy.

After being introduced briefly to the group, Lafayette, accompanied by Thayer, rode up the hill in an open carriage. A cadet battery of two guns fired a twenty-one gun salute as the carriage reached the level of the Plain. The Corps was formed for parade, facing the Superintendent's quarters with the Band, on the right, in its new white uniforms, trimmed with red epaulets, facings, braid, and buttons. The Corps was in full dress uniform, buttons and brass even more highly polished than usual. After the party dismounted and moved to the reviewing site, the Corps passed in review.

Refreshments were served in the quarters of Scott and Brown in the mess building before the party walked to the library in the Academic Building. Here the entire Corps and all of the officers stationed at West Point were introduced individually to Lafayette, who shook hands with each man. Thayer then hosted an excellent dinner prepared by Cozzens' staff. Wine was served with the meal, and there were many toasts by the more than 400 diners. One wonders if cadets were served wine, possibly to join in the toasts. Lafayette presented the Academy with a fine clock, which is in the Superintendent's quarters, still keeping accurate time. Some reports indicate that Lafayette also gave Thayer about 100 books. Official records of the Library have no record of such an acquisition but, if the books were received, some may still be on Library shelves. Shortly after six o'clock, Lafayette and his party reboarded the steamer and departed for Albany.

There were other foreign visitors. The Duke of Saxe-Weimar spent three days at West Point in 1825, visiting classes, inspecting barracks, reviewing the curriculum with various professors, and even attending chapel. Noting that Thayer was modeling the Academy after the French Ecole Polytechnique, the Duke indicated that he felt Thayer could never rival the French institution because Thayer could not find in the United States "such excellent professors as were assembled in that institution." Cadets were not impressed by the German visitors. Samuel Heintzelman noted in his diary that a "whole passel of German officers" were on post. The Duke impressed Heintzelman as a "sorry looking chap."

Thayer must have been pleased that the Academy had gained stature, not only in the United States, but abroad as well. It appeared that the Academy was functioning well and smoothly. Cadet discipline was excellent, although cadets continued to slip off post to Gridley's tavern. The purchase of Gridley's land late in 1824 appeared to end that temptation, for Havens had not opened his tavern in Buttermilk Falls. There were few academic problems, although Mansfield continued to complain. Relations with the Secretary of War and the President were excellent. Calhoun and Monroe continued to support Thayer in every way. There were only two major problems facing Thayer: continued attacks on the Academy in the press and Congress, and the reinstatement of cadets by either Calhoun or Monroe.

Although unfavorable newspaper reports were far less numerous than before the Philadelphia and Boston trips, many still reflected adversely on Thayer and the institution. Each time a Board of Visitors' report was published, an anti-Academy comment could be expected, usually instigated by Partridge. Thayer expressed his concern often to General Macomb, Chief of Engineers, who advised Thayer not to worry about these reports. Some Congressmen, however, absorbed what was published and periodically sponsored a bill to abolish the Academy. One such Congressman was William Eustis, the same man who as Secretary of War brought the Academy to the brink of extinction. His activities as a Congressman give credence to opinions that his actions had been a deliberate effort to abolish the Academy with or without congressional or presidential approval.

Information about attacks on the Academy came to Thayer from many sources. Andrew Donelson, nephew of Andrew Jackson and an 1820 West Point graduate, writing Thayer in 1823 to introduce a new cadet reporting for the entrance examinations, cited his "pleasure that your exertions have extended the course and given more perfect organization to the school. It is more popular in this section of the country [Tennessee] than it has ever been before." Donelson was pleased to report that one of the Academy's most severe critics, Newton Cannon, had not been re-elected to Congress. Other information came from other graduates and Thayer's civilian friends.

Boards of Visitors partially nullified continued attacks in Congress. Confident that a visit to the Academy by the opposition would eliminate misconceptions and counter Partridge's allegations, Thayer recommended to Macomb that at least one opponent "be invited to be a member of each Board of Visitors." Adoption of the suggestion did not eliminate opposition to the Academy, but it did lessen the attacks.

Thayer's second problem, reinstatement of cadets who had been discharged for academic or serious delinquencies, was more serious than the efforts to abolish the Academy, although the attacks were irritating. Thayer had faced this reinstatement problem since the beginning of his superintendency. Heavy political pressure on Calhoun, Monroe, Madison, and John Quincy Adams often resulted in the reinstatement of a discharged cadet. The return of that individual created disciplinary problems in the Corps of Cadets, especially when the cadet had been discharged—with the approval of the Secretary of War and the President—for a serious violation of Academy regulations.

Perhaps the most critical reinstatement was Monroe's decision to return the five cadets involved in the Ragland affair, who were reinstated despite Thayer's vehement opposition. Periodically, Thayer was notified that a cadet was reinstated because of his youth or because his previous conduct had shown no "vicious traits." This problem was not solved in Thayer's time.

Perhaps Thayer did not object to one reinstatement. In February 1824, several cadets apprehended at Gridley's tavern were tried by Court Martial for intoxication and sentenced to be discharged. While the sentence was forwarded to the President for approval, a group of cadets signed a voluntary temperance pledge. Their spokesman asked Thayer to request the President to reinstate the cadets involved. Thayer was impressed, as were Calhoun and Monroe, and the dismissed cadets returned to the Academy. The wording of the pledge is interesting: "We do set our countenances against it and do pledge on our word and honor that we will not in any time use these spiritous liquors so long as we remain members of the Institution except when sanctioned by the Superintendent."

The exception "when sanctioned by the Superintendent" referred to the special meals on the Fourth of July and Christmas when liquor was served in the cadet mess. This leniency often caused problems because a few cadets invariably overindulged. Seldom were these cadets punished; their classmates kept them under control or officers closed their eyes to cadet antics on those days.

In early 1825, Thayer decided to institute another disciplinary procedure, which he hoped would bring fewer delinquencies by cadets and lessen the number of reinstatements. Working with the Commandant, Thayer devised the demerit system—the basis of the system used today. A specific number of demerits would be given a cadet for a particular deficiency. Only the most serious infractions would result in a Court Martial. The number of demerits received in a year would be weighted, used in determining the cadet's class standing, and included in the Register of Cadets published annually. The new system gave Thayer a means of countering complaints of supposed injustice received from cadet families and provided the Secretary of War with the comparative standing of a cadet recommended for discharge for improper conduct. Eventually, Thayer established 200 demerits as the maximum number a cadet could receive annually without being dismissed.

Cadets, as might be expected, resented the new system, which they felt infringed on their rights. Thayer was convinced to the contrary, and the system remained in force. Cadet resentment boiled over during the Fourth of July outdoor banquet at which champagne was served. The celebration became riotous as more than the usual small number of cadets drank too much liquor. A snake dance was organized. Major Worth was hoisted on cadet shoulders and carried to the barracks. Thayer was outraged. After talking to Worth, Thayer issued orders that no liquor of any type would be served to cadets on post at any time, including the Fourth of July and Christmas.

Cadets objected to this restriction even more than they disliked the demerit system and countered by increasing their surreptitious forays to Benny Havens' new tavern at Buttermilk Falls despite its distance from the Academy, more than a mile. Realizing that they might be required to identify other cadets if they were caught at the tavern, they developed the habit of drinking with faces turned away from each other. If they were caught by tactical officers, they could say that they had not "seen" Cadet Blank drinking without violating their honor.

Benny and his father had operated a tavern for river boatmen at Gees Point on the northeastern edge of the post on land leased from Captain Partridge. In 1824, when their lease was canceled and the Gridley tavern and land were purchased by the government, they moved to Buttermilk Falls and built a new tavern near the foot of Buttermilk Creek. Benny still worked for the post sutler, John DeWitt, whose store was near the present site of the central sallyport of Eisenhower Barracks. In 1825, Benny's employment ended suddenly when DeWitt discharged him after he was caught selling rum to a cadet. DeWitt may not have been involved, but he did not escape Thayer's wrath. The sutler store was closed, and a new store was placed under and operated by Academy personnel.

Many cadets "ran" to Benny's, not for liquor, but for food. Initially, Benny sold cadets only cakes, candy, buckwheat flapjacks, and cider in summer or cider flip in winter. A few cadets demanded something stronger, and Benny changed his cider flip to an ale flip for their benefit. As time passed, Benny Havens became a tradition as more and more cadets made the long walk to his tavern. Many memoirs praised Benny for his treatment of cadets. If tactical officers approached, he warned his cadet customers and pointed another way out of the tavern. Because most cadets had little money, he was willing to serve them on credit. He was also willing to barter his wares, and many cadets made a moonlight requisition for blankets to trade for food or drink. Havens would not accept uniforms or shoes, knowing cadets could only purchase these with money from their accounts. Blankets were acceptable because they could be sent from home.

Benny's recipe for flip was recorded. It was a mixture of ale or cider and well-beaten eggs, sweetened and spiced. A hot poker gave the mixture "a delicious caramel-like flavor, but if left in too long, a burnt tasted was the result." One of the pitchers used, a brown earthenware jug, with decorations on the sides and a dog sniffing over the rim as a handle, was given to the Officers Mess many years later by a Highland Falls resident.

In 1838, Army doctor Lucius O'Brien visited his friend, Cadet Ripley A. Arnold. Arnold led the doctor to Benny's several times during his stay; cadets had little difficulty leaving the post at night. O'Brien was so taken with Benny's establishment that he wrote several verses for a song to the tune of "Wearin' of the Green," selecting a good Irish tune as any true Irishman would do. O'Brien's song was adopted by the Corps and became one of its traditional airs. Many verses were added over the years saluting the ladies, historical events, and the Academy. The song has been included in many Dialectic Society Hundredth Night Shows and in old summer camp Color Line skits. Verses were still being added in 1944 when the cadet yearbook added three new verses saluting World War II forces.

One of the first cadets apprehended at Benny's tavern was Jefferson Davis. During the summer of 1825, Davis and five others were caught drinking porter and hard cider. As an alibi, they told tactical officer Captain Ethan A. Hitchcock that they had wandered to Benny's seeking shelter after a rainstorm collapsed and soaked their tent. Despite such a noteworthy excuse, the culprits were tried by Court Martial and sentenced to be dismissed. Major Worth and Captain Hitchcock asked Thayer to remit the punishment of Davis and Samuel Hayes because of their soldierly talents. Thayer reluctantly agreed; the two were reinstated, but their three companions were dismissed.

Thayer had an extremely low opinion of Davis as a cadet, officer, and Secretary of War. In 1855, he wrote George Cullum, "Neither he nor my opinion of him has changed since I knew him as a cadet. If I am not deceived, he intends to leave his mark in the Army & also at West Point & a *black* mark it will be I fear. He is a recreant & unnatural son, would have pleasure in giving his Alma Mater a kick & would disown her, if he could." As a cadet, Davis distinguished himself only by making frequent trips to Benny's. Only ten in his Class graduated below him; he lacked only eleven demerits to be dismissed for misconduct.

There were no other taverns readily accessible on the west side of the Hudson. Occasionally, cadets would row across the river to taverns in Cold Spring or walk across the ice in winter. One cadet was marooned when the ice broke up before he could return. Cadets also crossed the river to dine with friends. One cadet asked Thayer for permission to accept an invitation to a dinner. For several good reasons, Thayer denied the request, but the cadet decided to go without permission, eluded the sentries around summer camp, and rowed across the river. To his consternation, he found the Superintendent sitting across from him at dinner. Thayer had no harsh words for the young man and spent the evening in small talk with the stunned cadet. After dinner, the cadet excused himself, rowed back to West Point, again eluded the sentries, and returned to his tent.

He expected to hear his name in orders the next day, but he was not reported then or later for breaking limits. Years later, he learned that Thayer had severely reprimanded the Commandant and the tactical officer on duty for permitting cadets to leave the limits of the post so easily.

With Calhoun's approval, Thayer obtained several benefits for cadets during this period. Four months leave for the graduating class was approved in 1824. The policy of giving an extended leave to graduates in peace time continued for over 100 years. Both Calhoun and Thayer appreciated the additional load placed upon cadets selected to be assistant professors. At Thayer's request, each cadet instructor was given twenty dollars a month for his work, double the previous amount; and they were authorized to keep a waiter, an unusual benefit. Some cadets brought servants with them during Jonathan Williams' superintendency, but this was stopped during the Partridge era.

At Worth's suggestion, Thayer approved the appointment of a tactical officer as Officer in Charge for specified periods. This was a roster detail, rotated weekly at first and eventually changed daily. The Officer in Charge, the "OC" in cadet terminology, was the Commandant's representative for the period designated. Use of this term eliminated the ambiguous situation of a tactical officer and a cadet both being called the Officer of the Day, the practice before the new term was adopted.

In 1825, the Secretaries of War and the Navy agreed that the source of Marine Corps second lieutenants would be graduates of the Military Academy. Two members of the Class of 1826 were assigned to the Marine Corps. They were not the first graduates to become Marines; one 1814 graduate and two in 1817 were already serving in the Corps. The agreement lasted only a short time.

The 1826 Board of Visitors was memorable for Thayer. Sam Houston was president of the Board, and Thayer's old friend and Dartmouth classmate George Ticknor was a member and stayed with Thayer during the examinations. He wrote to his wife in detail daily, providing an excellent description of the Academy, its activities, and Thayer. Thayer had gone to the dock to meet Ticknor, but Ticknor had already walked up the hill to Cozzens' by another route. Thayer arrived a short time later and took Ticknor to his quarters.

"It is better that you did not come with me," wrote Ticknor. "There is no house but that of our old friend, Cozzens, where ten rooms are, indeed, reserved for the Board of Visitors, and they are made as comfortable as they can be in such a place." Cozzens' rooms were filled when more visitors arrived. All rooms had been assigned to Board members, and the new arrivals had to sleep on the floors of the parlors. Among the late arrivals were five ladies who were upset when they learned that they would have to sleep on the floor of a back parlor instead of being assigned a room with their husbands. Thayer housed the Brazilian minister, General Revello, General Macomb, and Ticknor. At one point, Ticknor noted, "forty or fifty persons slept at Cozzens' last night." He compared his quiet, comfortable quarters in the Superintendent's home as "a most luxurious contrast to what is going on at Cozzens'; where, in fact, I think affairs would hardly go on at all if Cozzens were not one of the best tempered and most obliging creatures in the world." Ticknor's description emphasized the need for a hotel in the immediate area.

Ticknor gave his wife an excellent description of the examination. The Board met briefly the first day to elect Sam Houston as its president and then moved to the examination room in the Academic Building. "Thirteen men were under the screw for four hours, on a single branch," wrote Ticknor, "and never less than four on the floor, either drawing on the blackboard or answering questions every moment." Each cadet was tested for about one hour. "The young men," said Ticknor, "are addressed as Mr. So-and-so." Thayer adjourned the tests for dinner, and the examinations were then resumed until seven o'clock, a total of about nine hours of questions and answers.

When not being questioned, cadets sat on benches facing two long tables. At one table were the members of the Board of Visitors with Sam Houston in the center; at the other table, the Academic Board sat with Thayer in the center. The full Academic Board participated in every examination, joined by instructors of a subject when cadets were tested in that subject. Thayer participated fully in every test. Two large blackboards faced the tables, and two cadets stood at each blackboard. One cadet would recite on the problem he had solved on the board, while the other three prepared problems given them. In this way, three cadets were always working while the fourth was questioned. One officer sat between the two tables to ask questions. Usually this was an instructor, but occasionally a professor would take the chair.

Ticknor estimated that each cadet was examined a minimum of one hour in each subject. After five days, he wrote his wife that "the fact is that each of the forty cadets in the upper class will tonight have had about five hours' personal examination." He was much impressed by the thoroughness of preparation by each cadet and the way the cadets "unite, to a remarkable degree, ease with respectful manners toward their teachers." No one left the room during the examination without Thayer's permission or without bowing to the Superintendent, "the cadets and Staff to obtain permission and the members of the Board from respect. All goes on as if by instinct or clockwork."

Ticknor was impressed by one cadet tested in military engineering, a subject Ticknor found "less interesting than usual." He described the cadet as having uncommon character and qualifications. The cadet, William Bartlett, had stood first in his class at every examination; and, as Ticknor learned from Thayer, he had the record of "never in any one instance, even where discipline is so excessively severe, or rather exact,—never having once been reported for any irregularity or neglect." In simple words, Bartlett had received no demerits during his four years as a cadet. "It is a pleasure to look upon him, and listen to the beauty and completeness of all his examinations. Thayer says he has heard him at common recitations above a hundred times, and never knew him to miss a single question." Bartlett would soon begin an academic career that would cover a period of over forty-five years.

One day after dinner, the Board was taken to the Library to view drawings made by cadets of the Third and Fourth Classes. "There were perhaps four hundred on the greatest variety of subjects, heads, figures, landscapes, topographical drawings," wrote Ticknor, "and though each cadet was obliged to produce his specimens and have them hung with his name on them, there was hardly an ordinary piece among them, and not a single bad one." Ticknor indicated that he was very surprised by the quality of the drawings because "the amount of instruction and practice allowed them is not great—about two hours a day for not exceeding sixteen months."

Ticknor described the daily afternoon parades. On Sunday, the Chief of Engineers, General Macomb, ordered a review at nine o'clock. The Corps, commanded by Major Worth, was drawn up in front of Thayer's quarters. When the reviewing party came forward, its members were honored by an artillery salute. The Corps, wrote Ticknor, "went through a considerable number of very graceful and picturesque evolutions with wonderful exactness." Ticknor indicated that he did not agree with Macomb's order but "made no opposition." After the review, the Board attended chapel services, where the chaplain "by way of edifying General Macomb, read him the commandments—thinking, no doubt, that the General had forgotten the one about the Sabbath day."

More guests arrived that afternoon to swell the total number housed by Cozzens. They included Governor Holmes of North Carolina, Governor Pickens of Alabama, and several members of their suites. Ticknor reported that more guests were expected the next day, including several ladies. "How they will get along," he wrote to his wife, "I do not well see."

Thayer and Ticknor spent what little free time they had talking. In addition to remembering mutual acquaintances, the two old friends discussed many aspects of Academy affairs. Thayer withheld nothing. He was very frank in his analyses of Academy matters. In talking about his staff or members of the Washington government, he restricted his comments to their actions and said nothing against any individual personally. One discussion impressed Ticknor, who told his wife, "It was very interesting, and satisfied me more and more of the value and efficiency of his system. One proof of it which I have just learned is very striking. Before Thayer came here it was not generally easy to find young men enough to take cadet's warrants to keep the Academy full. But for the last two or three years there have been, annually, more than a thousand applications for warrants, and there is at this moment not a small number of sons of both the richest and the most considerable men of our country at the Academy." Ticknor believed this "gratifies Thayer very much, and consoles him for the considerable privations and the great and increasing labor he is obliged to undergo."

After two weeks of examinations, the Board prepared its report for the War Department with Ticknor serving as secretary. Several Board comments were noteworthy. Members considered the six-months probationary period for a new class advantageous and noted that an average of one-fourth of a class failed the examinations at the end of their probation. The Board estimated that about one half of a class failed to graduate. One of every seven cadets entering the Academy spent five years completing the course, some for academic reasons, some for sickness.

Considering the six-months' probation requirement to be "the most important single provision among the rules of the Institution," the Board urged the War Department to accept recommendations of the Academic Board to dismiss cadets who failed the examination because "to set aside the decisions of the Academic Board except in very extraordinary circumstances would have no other effect than to expend the public means on those who cannot be educated by them; to lower the Standard of Merit; to bring decisions of the Academic Board into disrespect with the Cadets and the public; and gradually reduce the whole tone of the Institution."

The report included favorable comments about discipline. It noted the thorough supervision of cadet activities, with special comment on the effectiveness "during the hours of study when each room is visited at least four times every day to ascertain the good order of its furniture and the presence and diligence of its occupants." After discussing the demerit system and punishments, the Board stated that "the decisions of the Superintendent should be fully sustained by the Government at Washington, and the Sentences of Court Martial, on Cadets, when approved by the President, be remitted by Pardon only on the most urgent reasons." This comment, although not worded as such, referred to the common practice of reinstating dismissed cadets by the Secretary of War or the President.

Analyzing the curriculum, the Board stated that "Mathematics, Natural Philosophy, Engineering, and Military Tactics, occupying above three quarters of each day, as they occur during four years given to study here, constitute the *main course* on whose success this Institution is always to depend." To support this main course, the Board considered French, Drawing, Chemistry and Mineralogy, and a miscellany of several subjects to be a "*subsidiary course* whose purpose it is to furnish the needful means for full success in the principal one."

Miscellaneous subjects considered part of the subsidiary course were English Grammar, Geography, History, Rhetoric, National Law, Constitutional Law, and Political Economy. The Board noted that some of these subjects were taught every year, but that "in no one year have all of them been taught because it was impossible to find place for them all." It recommended that these subjects be dropped from the curriculum "because they should be acquired either before the Cadets come to this Academy or after they leave it and because the superficial knowledge of them that can be here acquired is a contradiction to the exact thoroughness that prevails in every other department."

The Board reported "a suitable Chapel with fireproof rooms for the Library and the different collections of Instruments used here is greatly needed," a recommendation made by previous Boards. The Board recommended the construction of buildings for a riding school and gymnastics, a gun shed, and a new hospital, stressing deficiencies of the building then used, the old Gridley tavern. Other recommendations concerned replacing cadet instructors with graduates; allocating more funds for books, instruments, and apparatus; establishing the admission age between fifteen and eighteen years; making entrance academic requirements more difficult; and assigning additional instructors.

Several comments and recommendations concerned Thayer. The Board urged that he be provided with a clerk "to be employed in the office of the Adjutant and Superintendent, because in the office of the Adjutant an oppressive amount of writing is already done, and because the Superintendent for want of a clerk has never been able to preserve copies of his official communications to the Government." Another recommendation urged that "the rank and pay of the present Superintendent be increased, not on account of the claims of this distinguished officer . . . because it is well known he rather declines than solicit such a recommendation." The Board said it made the recommendation "on account of the public service, which they are persuaded cannot be suitably sustained by his present income." Another comment concerned the return of Academy supervision to the Chief of Engineers as Inspector instead of being directly under the Secretary of War. The Board strongly recommended that the Superintendent of this Academy be made responsible to the Secretary of War with no intermediate responsibility to the Chief of Engineers. The 1825 Board of Visitors had made a similar recommendation, but added "the Superintendent if necessary should be made a part of the general Staff of the Army," reflecting Thayer's opinion that officers assigned to the Academy should be selected based upon ability rather than branch of the service.

The report of the 1826 Board should be considered an account of the exact status of the Academy and its actual needs. Ticknor, because of his long and close friendship with Thayer, must have received many frank comments concerning problems he faced and the needs of the Academy. As secretary of the Board, Ticknor would have discussed these with his fellow members. The unique analysis of the West Point curriculum may have been Thayer's own estimate of the value of the course of instruction, but it may have been Ticknor's personal analysis as a Harvard professor.

Thayer must have been pleased with the report, for Ticknor had included many of his plans. More important, it also presented a summary of his philosophy concerning the operation of the Academy and cadet discipline. The three-week examination period had been busy, but Thayer found time for many long discussions with Ticknor concerning Academy operations, politics, world events, the arts, science, and personal matters. Ticknor's visit was of great benefit to Thayer. He had found command a lonely duty, isolating the commander from his compatriots. Ticknor gave Thayer an opportunity to relax and confide in an old friend. After his departure, Thayer resumed his routine supervision of Academy activities.

10

Living Armory of the Nation

Although no changes resulted immediately after the report of the 1826 Board of Visitors reached the Secretary of War, benefits came from elsewhere. Members of the Board spread word of the Academy's method of instruction, excellent discipline, and scientific curriculum. Thayer's reputation in academic circles, already nationwide, was enhanced even more. Harvard had conferred an honorary Master of Arts degree on Thayer in 1825; an honorary doctorate would come from St. John's College in 1830 and from Harvard in 1857. Others followed after his departure from West Point.

Efforts were made to have Thayer promoted. In March 1826, Winfield Scott recommended to the President that he promote Thayer to brevet colonel and Major Worth to brevet lieutenant colonel. Scott stated that "it is believed that he has, at length, given to the school, an excellence equal to the most celebrated in the world. All the young officers of the Army (now more than one hundred and fifty) who have graduated in his time; all the persons who have been appointed to assist in the annual examinations; and besides hundreds of the most distinguished persons, natives and foreigners, who have at different times visited West Point, bear testimony to the pre-eminent merits and services of Lieutenant Colonel Thayer." Despite Scott's eloquent recommendation and that of the 1826 Board of Visitors, a promotion was not forthcoming.

July 4, 1826, passed without any visible evidence of cadet resentment when no "spiritous liquors" were served at the special outdoor dinner. There was resentment, however, and it was evidenced by the increasing number of cadets patronizing Benny's tavern and found smuggling liquor into camp and barracks. Thayer became so concerned that he made a special trip to Washington, hoping to discuss this problem with President John Quincy Adams. Unfortunately, the

President was away, and Thayer had to be satisfied with reviewing the problem with Secretary of War James Barbour, who had replaced Calhoun in March.

Thayer discussed another problem with Barbour. General Macomb, Chief of Engineers and the Inspector of the Academy, had gradually involved himself in more and more Academy activities. Macomb was not a graduate, although he had been stationed at West Point at the Burbeck academy in 1801 and served under Jonathan Williams for a short period after 1802. In Thayer's opinion, Macomb was abusing his authority by becoming involved in everyday activities at West Point. Thayer asked Barbour to eliminate the connection between Macomb and the Academy, but Barbour refused, stating that this would require both Presidential and Congressional approval. He did, however, agree not to be overly persuaded by Macomb and promised to support Thayer in his management of the Academy.

Shortly after his return to West Point, Thayer received a request from James Monroe for advice concerning the University of Virginia; Monroe had been recently appointed a regent. His answer to Monroe provides a summary of Thayer's educational concepts. He recommended that a university president should not be a professor, be given extensive power to supervise all phases of university operations, and receive the advice of the professors "but not be shackled by them or controlled by their votes." This was the philosophy Thayer followed as Academy Superintendent.

Concerning the duties of professors, Thayer stated that they should be primarily concerned only with academics. An individual not directly involved in teaching should be in charge of administration. Realizing that funding might not be available for administrative personnel, Thayer suggested using young graduates who might also serve as junior instructors.

Thayer advocated the use of small sections instead of large group lectures. In his opinion, a one-hour lecture should be followed by three or four hours of section work, preferably at the blackboard. "You know," he wrote, "that this is the system of instruction which has been practiced at West Point for the last ten years with what success I leave it for others to say." To support such a system in a civilian institution would require additional instructors, and Thayer recommended young graduates who would not receive a large salary but could be induced to accept such positions as an "opportunity of prosecuting their studies under able professors." What Thayer advocated is essentially the system used in so many universities today where graduate students teach undergraduates.

Thayer urged Monroe to insist that the supervision of students be paternal in nature. Severe punishment, in Thayer's opinion, reflected adversely on the institution. He recommended a system of prevention that would include keeping the student fully occupied to the best of his individual ability; using time not required for recitations, study, meals, and sleep for athletics and other supervised amusements; removing all pecuniary matters from student hands, with supervision of their finances under a treasurer or bursar; and persuading the state legislature to ban taverns from the immediate area. This is another view of Thayer's concept for relations between the Academy staff and cadets.

An unsigned letter of this period is interesting. A New York City society, the "Grecian Ladies" expressed to Thayer "their heartfelt gratitude for your kindness in allowing them to transplant, from Brooklyn to New York, the Cross erected to the cause of unhappy Greece." Apparently the Cross was to be erected where it was clearly visible from the river because the ladies indicated that they would provide "a beautiful lamp & oil to feed it for the top of the Cross, for a point of light to the numerous vessels which navigate the H. River." The letter indicated that the Cross would be shipped in a few days, and "Yes sir, posterity shall know that in the darkest hour of her struggle Colonel Thayer gave protection to this frail emblem of Religion & Liberty." There is no indication in Academy records that the Cross was ever erected, nor is there any mention of this incident in either the Academy archives or the Thayer papers.

Throughout the fall, problems connected with the ban on liquor increased. As Christmas neared, Thayer and Worth became more and more apprehensive. In some manner, they learned that Jeff Davis and other Southern cadets had passed word throughout the Corps that they would explain "the mysteries of eggnog" on Christmas Eve. Davis and two other cadets would obtain ingredients from Benny Havens. In an effort to stop the proposed revel, Thayer and Worth ordered all tactical officers on duty Christmas Eve, not only on duty but awake and patrolling the cadet area. Cadet division supervisors were directed to remain awake until released by the tactical officers. Cadets on duty as Officer of the Day and Officers of the Guard were instructed to be especially vigilant and to prevent other cadets from leaving barracks. This information was announced to the cadets but did nothing to stop them.

Davis and his cohorts headed for Benny's for the ingredients and smuggled them into North Barracks where Davis lived. Two rooms were to be used for the festivities, one on the second floor and another on the fourth. Most of the cadets in North Barracks, regardless of class, were invited to participate and most did. Some, including Joseph Johnston and Robert E. Lee, refused the invitation. Cadets living in South Barracks were also invited, but most did not feel it worth the risk of slipping past the guard.

The party started after midnight when the hosts assumed that the officers and cadet guards had decided that nothing was going to happen. At first, things were quiet, but rum added to the eggnog in increasing amounts soon dissolved all inhibitions. The increasing noise attracted Captain Ethan Allen Hitchcock, who had been patrolling the lower floors.

Hastening to the center of activity, Hitchcock found a room filled with cadets, all with mugs in hand. As he began to order various cadets by name to return to their respective rooms under arrest, Davis came into the room to warn the cadets that Hitchcock was on the prowl. Hitchcock immediately ordered Davis to his room under arrest; Davis complied without a word. This was probably the most positive action Davis took during his entire cadet career because it took him away from the event soon to take place.

Several cadets who had too much to drink used highly abusive language, addressed to Hitchcock but also describing Thayer, Worth, and other officers. Hitchcock ordered these cadets to their rooms under arrest, but they refused to obey with more vindictive words. Threats were made to Hitchcock. Realizing that the situation was getting out of hand, he left and went to his own room to decide what to do.

In the meantime, Lieutenant William A. Thornton, who lived on the fourth floor and was responsible for patrolling the third and fourth levels, was also in trouble. Periodically, he had walked the halls. Each time he left his room, a cadet sentinel outside the party room alerted the boisterous group who would lower their voices and extinguish the candles lighting the room. As the party went on, the noise increased, and the sentinel's alarm went unheeded. As Thornton approached, two cadets reeled out of the room toward him. Thornton, raising his lantern, recognized the cadets and ordered one to his room under arrest. He was obeyed instantly and quietly. The second cadet, twirling a saber, told Thornton to get out of his way. Thornton replied by demanding that the cadet give him the saber and go to his room under arrest. Instead, the cadet hammered the floor with the saber and cursed Thornton. Finally, the cadet went into the nearest room.

Thornton started down the stairs, intending to find Hitchcock. He was startled by the sound of a drum outside the barracks beating the reveille call accompanied by the shrill notes of a fife playing an unrecognizable air. Cadets from the second floor had gone to the guard room and taken the fife and drum despite the objections of the cadet on duty there. The raucous and discordant sounds brought cheers from participants, who opened windows or smashed panes to watch the performance in the assembly area. Many cadets not involved in the affair dressed and started to form as if it was an actual reveille formation.

Resuming his descent, Thornton encountered a cadet whom Hitchcock had ordered to his room. Instead, the cadet had had more to drink and gone into the hall to get wood for the fireplace. Seeing Thornton, he threw a small log at him. Thornton, hit, dropped his lantern and fell to the steps. His assailant staggered back to the party to report his successful attack, which he said had prevented Thornton from entering the room.

Halls on all floors were now in pandemonium. Drunken cadets reeled from room to room, shouting and banging on doors. Many carried swords and some had muskets and bayonets. Hitchcock, on the second floor, was also hit by a small log. He continued his efforts to bring order without success. As he approached one room, the door was slammed in his face. He knocked, following the regulation that no one entered a cadet room without knocking. The three cadets in the room, all viciously drunk, refused to admit him. He continued to knock. Finally, one cadet picked up his musket, which was loaded, and fired, intending the round to go through the thin door. Instead, his unsteady hand and blurred aim sent the bullet into the wall beside the door.

Hitchcock did the sensible thing; he immediately went downstairs to the guard room. Plebe guard James G. Overton came to attention. Thornton sent him to South Barracks to get Cadet Lieutenant Nathaniel Eaton, Officer of the Day. Eaton was not in the south guardroom, and Overton returned to report to Hitchcock. Hitchcock asked if Overton knew where Major Worth lived and sent him running to the Commandant's quarters to report what had happened and ask for help.

Several of the revelers heard Hitchcock's orders. Apparently he gave his instructions in such a way that the eavesdroppers thought he had sent Overton to get the bombardiers, mistaking Hitchcock's "Fetch the 'Com' here" for "Fetch the bombardiers." It is odd that cadets still referred to the enlisted detachment as "bombardiers," for it was now a company of the 2nd Artillery stationed at West Point after Thayer disbanded the detachment of bombardiers, sappers, and miners. The rumor spread rapidly, and more and more cadets poured into the halls, determined to stop any efforts of the enlisted detachment to prevent further disorder.

Meanwhile, Lieutenant Thornton, who had only been bruised by the wood thrown at him, managed to return to his room on the fourth floor. He went to a rack, pulled his sword from its scabbard, and determined to go back into the hall armed for his own protection. As he started toward the door, Hitchcock entered. He questioned Thornton and told him what had happened on the lower floors and his effort to get the word to the Commandant. As they talked, the drum and fife began to sound Reveille outside the barracks. This time it was the enlisted musicians beating the call at the normal hour.

Cadets began to stream out of South Barracks and, to a much lesser degree, from North Barracks. Major Worth had not appeared, but Hitchcock, Thornton, and the two tactical officers from South Barracks watched the cadets form in ranks. Most of those from North Barracks were in various states of undress and unshaven, with many clearly suffering from overindulgence. Cadet officers stood waiting for the sergeants to call the roll as more cadets from North Barracks straggled into ranks. By the time the formation was over, few cadets were absent.

Worth, after being awakened and given the news, had dressed and gone next door to the Superintendent's quarters. He found Thayer in uniform waiting for him. Together, they looked across the Plain and watched the reveille formation. Before Worth left, Thayer decided to conduct an investigation and to conduct the examinations as scheduled.

After roll call, cadet companies were dismissed. Cadets in North Barracks began to clean the halls and rooms, seemingly determined to restore neatness once again. Breakfast call sounded, and the two companies marched to the mess hall. Two cadets who had been among the instigators of the eggnog party, still feeling the effects of rum, started an argument that developed into a brawl. Walter Guion, a hot-blooded Mississippian, threw a fork at Daniel Whitehurst, a South Carolinian. Whitehurst grabbed a sharp table knife and swung at Guion. Guion grabbed another knife and thrust back across the table. Two cadet officers, at considerable risk, disarmed the cadets. Cadet Captain James Bradford called the Corps to attention and dismissed the cadets from the mess hall. The riot was over.

Twenty-two cadets were in their rooms under arrest. At least seventy more were known to be implicated, based on the identifications made by Hitchcock, Thornton, and cadet officers, approximately one-third of the Corps. Thayer and Worth must have been shaken and shocked when this information was reported. Most of the culprits were from North Barracks, only a few from South. Thayer notified General Macomb, who immediately directed a full Court of Inquiry to be convened. Thayer ordered Major Worth to serve as senior member with assistance from two other officers. The investigation was conducted simultaneously with the January examinations.

Two weeks later, results of the examination and findings of the Court were handed to Thayer. Cadets who had participated in the riot were identified by name. By coincidence, a number of this group were recommended for dismissal by the Academic Board for academic deficiency, misconduct during the previous six months, or both. They were to be dismissed in the normal manner. That decreased the list submitted by the Court to seventy cadets. Thayer had to determine the action to be taken.

Thayer and Worth, reviewing the list of cadets and the violations determined by the Court of Inquiry, divided the names into several categories based on the seriousness of offenses committed. Names of seven cadets who had physically assaulted an officer or cadet officer acting in the line of duty were placed on a list to be tried by Court Martial. A second group included four or five cadets who had introduced liquor into barracks. Cadets who had incited others to riot were in a third group. In the last category were cadets known to have damaged government property. While this discussion was taking place, one of the cadets deeply involved, William Burnley, broke arrest and headed for Havens' tavern. This was noted beside his name.

The outcome of this lengthy analysis was a list of nineteen cadets who would be charged and tried by Court Martial. Thayer realized that charging ninety cadets, or even seventy, would endanger the Academy. Too many were sons of influential citizens, who could bring congressional pressure on the Army. He knew there was still a feeling in Congress that the Academy should be abolished, and preferring charges against one-third of the Corps would give these opponents the fuel they needed. Knowing the exact status of every cadet, Thayer was aware that many of the offenders might not pass the examinations; his estimate proved correct. However, charging seventy cadets was still undesirable. That was one reason for the lengthy and careful deliberation that reduced the number of cadets to be charged to nineteen.

Thayer considered what would happen if no charges were preferred or if he punished cadets with demerits and extra duties. He realized that this would make it almost impossible to administer discipline to the Corps; it would be a return to the riotous attitude of the Partridge era. He therefore decided to prefer charges against the nineteen cadets most deeply involved. The remaining fifty-three would be punished in other ways. Strangely, Jefferson Davis was not one of the nineteen. His prompt obedience to Captain Hitchcock's order saved him from serious charges.

The nineteen cadets were tried and sentenced to be dismissed. The Court recommended that a number of cadets be pardoned by the President. John Quincy Adams reviewed the records and approved the immediate dismissal or resignation of twelve of the cadets. Seven sentences were revoked, based upon the clemency recommendations of the Court. Adams sent his approval to Thayer in May 1827 with an explanation of his decisions.

Thayer had been right in believing that the dismissal of a large number of cadets, even though the charges were serious, would cause problems. Adams was shocked to find that nineteen cadets had been tried and sentenced to be dismissed. Had seventy cadets been tried, he would have "blown his top," to use modern vernacular. The President indicated that he had "an obligation of duty to read and deliberately to consider the record of proceedings of the Court on every trial." He said that the events involved—drinking, breaking limits, visiting other rooms without permission, rioting, assaulting officers, and destroying government property—raised the question of "whether the system of discipline established at that Academy, and which has hitherto been one of its highest recommendations, shall be maintained."

Fortunately, Adams concluded that discipline should be continued. He indicated that each offense in itself might be comparatively minor but that "no one can doubt the wisdom and parental tenderness of the regulations by which they [the acts with which the nineteen cadets were charged] are constituted offences, or the necessity when after they have been so constituted, and are set at defiance of visiting the violation of inflexible punishment. It is not the character of the act itself, it is the spirit in which it is perpetuated, the pernicious tendency, the contuminous temper, the reckless rushing into vicious indulgence, which call for unyielding animadversion."

The President addressed the entire Corps of Cadets, saying, "The confirmation of so many sentences of dismission from the Academy, of Young Men from whom their Country had a right to expect better things, is an act of imperious though painful duty." His last sentence was an admonition to every cadet; "Convinced, that these considerations must yield to the necessity of a rigorous example, he [the President] hopes it will not be lost upon the Youth remaining at the Academy; that they will be admonished to the observance of all their duties by the reflection that when violated by them, while the offence is imputable only to themselves, the punishment of necessity is shared with them by the dearest of their friends."

Little is known about measures to restore discipline taken from Christmas 1826 to July 1827. Whatever steps were taken, cadet reaction was not enthusiastic.

Cadets continued to frequent Benny Havens' establishment, but fewer in numbers and less frequently. The Fourth of July came and went with no outward demonstration of cadet resentment and without wine at dinner. Apparently the prompt and strict measures taken by Thayer and Worth had impressed the cadets. President Adams' words contributed to the changed attitude of the Corps.

Cadet reaction to the charges must have pleased both Thayer and Worth. During the trial, not one cadet charged denied his participation. True, several made impassioned statements attempting to justify their actions, but none refused to answer questions of the Court. Cadets called as witnesses also answered questions without hesitation. Cadets punished by Thayer did not complain, possibly because they realized that they were fortunate in receiving relatively minor punishment. The reaction of the Corps indicated that cadets had felt a sense of duty to answer questions of the Court. Whenever a cadet made a statement, either as a defendant or as a witness, his statement was accepted by the Court as the truth without any hesitation whatsoever, an indication of respect for the honor of the individual concerned.

By the end of the summer, there was little indication that the riots had taken place. Academics began in September with new faces among the faculty. William H. C. Bartlett was appointed Assistant Professor of Engineering. Thomas W. Twiss joined the Department of Natural and Experimental Philosophy, and Thomas J. Cram, the Department of Mathematics. There were two new instructors in Drawing and one in French. Two new tactical officers were assigned. Cadets Charles Mason and Robert E. Lee were among the six cadets appointed Acting Assistant Professors.

There was continued improvement in instruction, not drastic changes but slight adjustments within the courses taught by a department. New texts were adopted; some came from Europe, but most were the work of Academy professors. The number of books in the library had grown to nearly 3,000 volumes. The small library of the Dialectic Society, housed in a first-floor room in North Barracks, was also growing but at a slow rate since the dues of its cadet members and some donations by officers were its primary source of revenue. The Academy Library continued to order books for the War Department Library. In December 1828, twenty-six books from European and American publishers were shipped to Washington with a note that twelve other volumes requested were out of print. The Library also sent books to the Artillery School of Practice at Fortress Monroe. Established in 1824, the School needed books badly, and Thayer was glad to help.

Thayer learned that Lieutenant Dennis Hart Mahan, Assistant Professor of Civil and Military Engineering, wanted permission for a furlough in Europe. Mahan had graduated at the head of the Class of 1824 and, at Thayer's request, had agreed to remain as an instructor. Not a strong individual, Mahan suffered from the frigid winters and cold springs at West Point. He thought his health would improve if he could spend at least a year abroad.

Thayer recommended approval and the Secretary of War concurred. Mahan requested that he be appointed a courier to carry dispatches to "our Ministers at the Courts of Europe." The reply was a request for Mahan to come to Washington after the completion of the June examinations. There Mahan was given a letter ordering him to Europe to procure "in the course of your travels, information that may be highly important and valuable to this country." Mahan was instructed to "study roads, canals, bridges, the improvement of rivers and harbors, construction, labor-saving machinery, etc. which would be new to this country and of sufficient importance to render its acquisition desirable." The order emphasized that Mahan was already familiar with subjects in which the Army was interested.

Mahan would remain in Europe for nearly four years. Periodic reports were made directly to Secretary of War Barbour. In addition to providing the information required by his orders, Mahan requested and received permission to attend the French Artillery and Engineering School at Metz. As a student officer, he was able to obtain lithographed text books and drawings used at the school, publications not available through booksellers. During his stay in France, he visited the Paris dealer Kilian, who continued to send books to the West Point Library. Although his physical condition improved only slightly, Mahan returned to West Point in June 1830, refreshed and eager to resume his teaching.

A curious aftermath of the December 1826 disturbances was a resurgence of religion at the Academy. Chapel attendance had been compulsory since the founding of the Academy in 1802, but cadets attended chapel without any religious fervor. To the contrary, during the tenure of Chaplain Thomas Picton from 1818 to 1825, cadets ignored his long and tedious sermons. Sitting on backless benches in the room used as a chapel, cadets gazed into space, nodded, slept, and even read books. Cadet Augustus Canfield wrote to his family that "there is not one here who professes Christianity. The two who did have left."

A new chaplain was assigned in early 1825, Dr. Charles P. McIlvaine. A fine speaker, McIlvaine vigorously tried to change the cadet attitude toward religion, but he soon found that he had an indifferent parish at best, a hostile audience at worst. Almost a year passed before any cadet came to him for help. A young cadet, disconsolate at the death of his father, asked the Chaplain for solace. McIlvaine talked with him, carefully and sympathetically, and gave him a religious tract to read. In some way, the tract reached Cadet Leonidas Polk, one of the leaders of the Class of 1827. He became interested, obtained more religious literature, and then discussed religion with Chaplain McIlvaine.

It has been said that McIlvaine converted Polk; perhaps it should be said that he revived in Polk religious feelings that had become dormant. Polk's change became evident one Sunday when, after preaching for about an hour, McIlvaine turned from the altar to find Polk kneeling in prayer. Polk wrote his brother, "This first step was my most trying one, to bring myself to renounce all of my former habits and associations, to step forth singly from the whole corps acknowledging my convictions of truth."

Discussions in barracks now often concerned religion. Other cadets joined Polk for visits to the Chaplain's quarters. When McIlvaine started a series of prayer meetings in his home, attendance grew so rapidly that the sessions were moved to the chapel room in the Academic Building. Polk assisted this religious revival by holding prayer sessions in the "light prison" in North Barracks, the only room available. Thayer, remaining as neutral as possible, gave approval. Polk asked for permission to hold nightly meetings of worship, and Thayer approved the request. Polk would resign after graduation, enter the Episcopal ministry, and be elected bishop.

Although Thayer realized that the new religious attitude of many cadets was a beneficial influence, he relied on discipline to develop a sense of responsibility, duty, and honor in the Corps. He believed that good discipline, as he had written to Monroe, was paternal in nature. He never expressed his definition of discipline, either as Superintendent or in later years, but it is evident that he believed that there was no such thing as bad discipline. His definition involved just and equal treatment, and fairness in dealing with subordinates, officers and cadets alike.

His paternal supervision of all phases of cadet activities brought improvements. Winters at West Point were a hardship on all who lived there, in barracks or in quarters. Cadets in ranks were always cold because there was no uniform overcoat. Winter formations barely resembled a military activity. Cadets wrapped themselves in blankets or wore civilian overcoats. Thayer tried for several years to have a uniform overcoat prescribed, but the Quartermaster General insisted on testing different designs and materials; this took time. Finally, in time for the winter of 1828–1829, authorization was given to a cadet overcoat made of gray wool with flat brass buttons stamped with the word "cadet." A short cape dropped from the collar to the waist. The design was intentional because it enabled the wearer to toss the cape over his head in extremely bad weather.

There were other uniform changes. The only cadet hat authorized was the full dress shako, a leather helmet weighing more than five pounds. Because the hat was extremely uncomfortable, many cadets wore a civilian "round hat" off duty. Thayer secured approval of a cloth forage cap for wear when not in full dress uniform. To improve the appearance of a cadet in full dress uniform, Thayer had a strap added to the trousers. The strap, fastened under the shoe, kept trousers at the proper distance above the shoes. He was concerned about the rapid wearout time for most uniform items. The only coat or jacket authorized was the high-collar, brass-button, full dress coat. Cadets were required to wear a coat at all drills and fatigue duties. Consequently, both coat and braided trousers had to be replaced three or four times a year, an unnecessary expense in Thayer's opinion. He obtained approval for a fatigue jacket and undress gray trousers without braid. Cadets appreciated the changes and additions to the uniform. Many wrote home telling of the pleasure of wearing a light cap instead of the heavy shako. Others expressed delight that the overcoat had the short cape.

Thayer was flexible and did not hesitate to make a change if change would bring improvement. In only one thing was he completely inflexible: the ban on liquor. Thayer was not a teetotaler. Quite the contrary, he was an oenophile who truly enjoyed good wine. Many guests who dined at his West Point quarters commented on the excellent selection of wines served. Many years later, one of Thayer's cadets called on him at Braintree, Massachusetts, and was asked to stay for dinner. Thayer poured wine, telling him that this was "some that I laid down at West Point in 1825."

There was one reason for Thayer's insistence that cadets not imbibe. The Army of that period still issued a liquor ration to enlisted men. There were many instances when drunkenness made men and officers completely unreliable. Senior officers tried in vain to prevent overindulgence with varying degrees of success. Winfield Scott, in 1829 during the Blackhawk campaign, ordered that anyone found drunk would be required to dig a grave "at a suitable burying place, large enough for his own reception, as such graves cannot fail to be wanted for the drunken man himself or some drunken companion." Thayer may have seen examples of individuals unable to do their required duties during his service on the Niagara frontier during the War of 1812. This may have been the reason for his restriction on cadet drinking. The War Department stopped the issue of "spiritous liquors" in 1832.

Worth and Thayer watched Christmas 1827 approach with trepidation. Would the anniversary of the 1826 melee bring a repeat performance? Their concern was not evident to the cadets; normal activities continued. Christmas Eve arrived and passed with no outbreak of any kind, nor was their any expressed resentment by cadets when Christmas dinner was served without wine or any other liquor.

On the day after Christmas, pandemonium of a different nature broke out. The enlisted barracks, the old "Long Barracks" near Execution Hollow, caught fire and burned to the ground. Apparently an enlisted man or a soldier's wife—some families were quartered in the barracks—either failed to bank the fire in a fireplace or had not placed a fender in front of the fire. Sparks ignited furniture in the room, and the fire spread rapidly throughout the wooden building. Cadet Samuel Heintzelman blamed the fire on a sleepy sentinel. The entire Corps of Cadets rushed to assist in evacuating women and children. Cadet fire companies assisted the soldiers attempting to put out the blaze but without success. Fire fighting efforts were handicapped by a lack of sufficient water. Barrels of water on the lower stoops were frozen; those in the halls could not be reached because of the fire. In a very short time, the barracks had burned to a heap of smoldering ashes. One of the last reminders of the Burbeck academy was gone.

Officers and married enlisted men opened their quarters to the families who had lived in the barracks. Other buildings were converted into quarters until a new barracks and houses were built below the brow of the hill above the dock. This started the trend of separating enlisted quarters from those occupied by officers, as well as moving the center of enlisted activities away from the cadet area.

The destruction of the barracks solved one of Thayer's problems. He had urged that a hotel be erected for several years. Where to locate the building was a problem. It should not be near the cadet area but within easy walking distance regardless of weather conditions. The hotel should be near the path leading up from the dock since most visitors to West Point came by boat. Destruction of the barracks made its site available.

Thayer made one more effort to obtain appropriated funds to build the hotel but without success. He then asked the Secretary of War for permission to use his Post Fund, and Secretary Barbour approved the request. The Fund had grown over the years. Rental from Benny Havens and others using government land had been deposited in the Fund. Other sources were revenue from the sale of wood cut on the military reservation and the concession payment from the mess steward. Work was started during the summer of 1828 and completed in time for the hotel to accommodate the 1829 Board of Visitors. The initial cost was approximately $18,000.

Rather than operate the hotel as a government activity, Thayer recommended that it be leased to a qualified individual, and Secretary Barbour agreed. This relieved Thayer and his successors of any direct operation of the hotel. The lease money was returned to the Post Fund, initially $2,000 a year. The hotel in 1829 was a building fifty by sixty feet with thirty-seven rooms with thick, stone outer walls to keep the interior cool in summer and to prevent the loss of heat in winter. Floors were made of wide, oak boards fastened with hand-forged nails from the West Point Foundry at Cold Spring. Heat was provided by fireplaces or woodburning stoves. A kitchen range was imported from France, but many meals were still cooked over an open fire in the kitchen fireplace. Three wings were added later, one in 1850 and two in the 1870s.

Considered one of the finest establishments in the East, the hotel was open to friends and families of cadets and to the general public. It became fashionable for New Yorkers to spend a weekend at the hotel, sitting on the veranda to watch cadet parades. The hotel register is a veritable autograph album of famous Americans and foreign visitors. It includes the faded signatures of cabinet members, foreign dignitaries, artists, writers, and many new cadets arriving to become members of the Corps from 1829 to the end of the 1920s. Winfield Scott lived in the hotel after his retirement until his death in 1866. Mrs. Ulysses Grant came to the hotel after her husband died. Mrs. Arthur MacArthur stayed there to be near her son Douglas while her husband was in the Philippines. While the hotel was being built, Thayer interviewed applicants for its lease. He finally selected William Cozzens, the mess steward. Cozzens operated the hotel until he was replaced by Stephen Roe. Cozzens built his own hotel in Highland Falls on what is now the West Point South Post. The comfort of the West Point Hotel accommodations, excellence of its meals, gaiety of its social functions, and colorful cadet parades kept the hotel full.

Problems were anticipated, but Thayer wisely solved most before they occurred. Cadets were not to enter or dine at the hotel unless they were guests of residents and had the permission of the Superintendent. Under no circumstances would the management serve liquor to cadets. Cadets could use only the "public areas" of the hotel; rooms were off limits. Full-dress uniform was to be worn at all times when at the hotel. Visiting hours were specified. There were a few violations of these regulations; most were for being at the hotel at unauthorized times.

Another significant event took place in 1828. The Corps had asked Thayer in 1827 for permission to erect a monument to Thaddeus Kosciuszko, the Polish officer who had supervised building the West Point fortifications during the Revolutionary War. Thayer approved the request. A cadet committee wrote to General Swift, asking for his advice and assistance. Members of the committee included Charles Mason and Robert E. Lee; Mason graduated first in the Class of 1829 and Lee, second. Cadet contributions and donations from officers and friends of the Academy provided the $5,000 needed. John Latrobe, former cadet of the Class of 1822, designed the simple monument, a plain Doric column. A bronze statue of Kosciuszko was added in 1913 by the Polish clergy and laity of the United States.

In November 1828, Andrew Jackson was elected President. It was evident to Thayer and the entire nation that changes could be expected. What Jackson's policy would be concerning the Military Academy was unknown. His two nephews were graduates, Andrew J. Donelson in the Class of 1820 and Daniel Donelson in 1825. Both ranked high in their classes; Andrew was second and Daniel, fourth. Both resigned from the Army shortly after being commissioned. Andrew wrote Thayer from time to time to keep him informed about the anti-Academy attitude in Tennessee. He also expressed his appreciation for improvements that Thayer had made during his years as a cadet and after his graduation.

What Jackson's personal opinion of the Academy and Thayer would be was the unknown factor. Thayer had no direct contact with Jackson. His only knowledge of the man were reports of his service in the War of 1812 and the Seminole Wars. There had been the indirect indication that Jackson wanted Thayer to make certain that his nephew Andrew Donelson was commissioned in the Corps of Engineers, but Thayer did not have to react because Donelson ranked high enough in his Class to be recommended for the appointment without any special consideration. Thayer's main concern was not so much what Jackson would do as President but rather who would become Secretary of War.

Thayer had been fortunate, for he had served under John Calhoun and James Barbour, Secretaries of War who supported him in almost every way. Presidents Thomas Jefferson, James Madison, James Monroe, and John Quincy Adams had agreed with his efforts and backed him in problem matters, such as the Ragland affair and the eggnog Eve riot aftermath. Thayer could look back on more than ten years when he faced only two problems insofar as the War Department and the Presidents were concerned. One was the reluctance to provide funds needed for improvements; the second, continual reinstatement of cadets dismissed for academic deficiencies or misconduct. Thayer had been disappointed when Adams ignored his recommendation to institute a system for punishing cadets for serious offenses without trying them by Court Martial. Thayer had discussed the proposal with Adams in August 1828, possibly the last meeting he had with Adams as President. Taking the entire ten years as a whole, Thayer could not complain about support from Washington.

Thayer had no reluctance to administer justice by Court Martial for serious offenses. Most offenses involved drinking or breach of arrest. One exception occurred in December 1828 when Cadet Jeremiah Dargan was tried for mutiny, charged with assaulting his Tactical Officer, Lieutenant W. A. Thornton, on the stairway in North Barracks and again in Thornton's room. He was found guilty of both specifications and the charge of mutiny and sentenced to be shot. Because of Dargan's "youth and inexperience," the Court recommended that the sentence be commuted to "dismissal from the service of the United States, with disgrace." In approving the sentence and recommendation of the Court, the President stated, "The purpose of punishment is example. From the Cadets of the United States Military Academy, the favored children of their country, she will expect that in their bosoms, of the two punishments presented, one by the judgement of the Court and the other their recommendation of the Prisoner to mercy, the last is the most severe. It is approved. Let it be carried into effect."

One other 1828 event undoubtedly eased Thayer's worries. General Macomb, Chief of Engineers, was appointed General in Chief of the Army. Strangely, although he would be the senior officer and in effect command the Army, promotion removed him from direct contact with the Academy. Charles Gratiot, Class of 1806, became Chief of Engineers. Gratiot had little liking or respect for his classmate, Alden Partridge. Thayer knew Gratiot well and admired Gratiot's reputation as an excellent military, civil, and scientific engineer.

In December 1828, President Adams sent his last annual message to Congress, a summary of his administration. His comments about the Academy represented an appreciation of the purpose of the Academy and the accomplishments of its graduates. "Of these great national undertakings," said Adams, "the Academy at West Point is among the most important in itself and the most comprehensive in its consequences. In that institution a part of the revenue of the nation is applied to defray the expense of educating a competent portion of her youth, chiefly to the knowledge and the duties of military life. It is the living armory of the nation." Adams, after defining improvements made by other agencies of the government, stated that "the instruction acquired at West Point enlarges the dominion and expands the capacities of the mind. Its beneficial results are already experienced in the composition of the Army, and their influence is felt in the intellectual progress of society." He concluded with the comment, "The institution is susceptible still of great improvement from benefactions proposed by several successive Boards of Visitors, to whose earnest and repeated recommendations I cheerfully add my own."

The Revolutionary War Blockhouse below Kinsley Hill. The blockhouse was part of the West Point fortifications designed to repel any land attack from the south. Illustration by Archibald Robertson.

Surtout Summer Dress Winter Dress

Cadet uniform in 1802. The blue coatee with red facings and blue shoulder straps edged in gold was similar to the uniform worn by junior officers of the Regiment of Artillerists. The cockade on the hat was black; the plume was red. Cadet officers in the center and right of the illustration wore a white leather sword belt and had one gold-lace epaulet on the left shoulder. Brass buttons were emblazoned with the eagle and cannon of the Regiment of Artillerists. The cadet on the left wears a dark blue surtout, or overcoat, with a red collar and edging. Illustration by H. Charles McBarron.

Cadet Uniform circa 1816. The gray uniform was adopted in 1814 because of wartime shortages of blue, wool cloth. Made of gray sattinett cloth, the uniform included brass bullet buttons and Austrian loops on the pantaloons. The round hat bore a black leather cockade with a brass eagle. Cross belts were white leather. Black leather stocks were worn inside the collar. Vests were gray in winter and white in summer. During the summer months they were made of white Russia sheeting or white jean. The coatee resembled the full dress coat of today, the only major change being the collar. Illustration by H. Charles McBarron.

Winter Parade Summer Dress Winter Undress

West Point in 1826. The Long Barracks are shown on the right. Engraving by Jaques G. Milbert.

West Point in 1826. The row of houses on the left includes the quarters of the Superintendent and the Commandant. The Thompson house is hidden by the trees at bottom left. Cadets have formed for parade facing the quarters. An engraving from George Catlin's oil painting.

South Barracks, 1830s. This building was built in 1815 and demolished in 1849 as the new barracks designed by Delafield were nearing completion.

Central Area of Barracks in 1854. This is one of a series of photographs taken by noted photographer Victor Prevost during a spring 1854 visit to West Point. During this visit, Prevost photographed the May solar eclipse, using telescopes in the Library observatory.

Cadet George Derby in Furlough Uniform, 1844. This is one of the earliest photographs of a cadet. Derby wears the furlough uniform: a blue frock coat, white trousers, white shirt, and black cravat. He carries a cane. The cap worn was either the officer's undress kepi or a straw hat resembling the more modern boater.

Cadet Lieutenant, circa 1845. This drawing by Cadet George Derby shows a cadet ready for parade. He wears the shako adopted in 1839. The plume of black cock feathers became regulation in 1842.

Sheet Music of the 1850s. Words for *The Cadets Graduating Song* of 1848 were written by Mrs. Winfield Scott.

Lieutenant George Crook, Cadet Philip Sheridan, and Lieutenant John Nugen. The photograph was taken either before or immediately after graduation in 1852 because both Crook and Nugen, who graduated that year, wear lieutenants' uniforms while Sheridan, an 1853 graduate, is in cadet uniform. This is one of the earliest photographs of a cadet in full dress uniform.

WEST POINT HOTEL, AND ROAD FROM THE LANDING.

The West Point Hotel and Road from the Landing, 1866. The hotel, built during Thayer's superintendency, was replaced by the Hotel Thayer at the south end of the post in the late 1920s. In the illustration, officers watch a cadet ride as it moves from the north dock up the hill to the Plain. A woodcut from *Gleason's Pictorial Drawing Room Companion*.

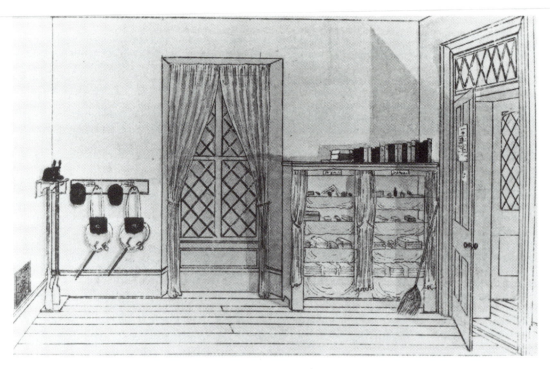

A Cadet Drawing of a Room in the 1850s. One view shows the sleeping alcove where clothing was hung on hooks hidden by the curtains. The second shows racks for full dress shakos, muskets, cartridge boxes, and bayonets on the left and the notorious "clothes press" detested by cadets. It was used for small articles of clothing; books were shelved on the top shelf.

Central Barracks, 1860. Children of the West Point garrison were taught drawing by Professor Robert Weir. This sketch was drawn by William Bailey, son of Professor of Chemistry, Mineralogy, and Geology Jacob Bailey.

A CADET HOP AT WEST POINT.

Cadet Hop in the 1860s. Woodcut from *Harper's Weekly*. This is probably a summer hop since cadets wear white trousers.

A Cadet Fire Team Mans the Pump Engine, 1863. Several engines were housed in various parts of the Post. This engine had a shed in back of the hospital, the building in the background.

The Hudson River Looking North from Trophy Point, 1864. Oil by Professor Robert Weir. The siege guns used in cadet training are in the right foreground.

The Cadet Chapel and the Library, 1867. The Chapel was moved to the cemetery in 1911 after the new Chapel was completed. The move was made possible by the spontaneous and unsolicited contributions of graduates who did not want to see their Chapel razed. The new Library is on the site of the domed building in the photograph; Bartlett Hall occupies the Chapel site.

Cadets on a Wagon in Front of the Mess Hall, 1867. Cadets messed in the portion of the building to the right of the tower behind the wagon. The tower rooms and the larger rooms to the left were used by members of the West Point Army Mess. In 1887, the building was named Grant Hall in honor of Ulysses S. Grant.

Kosciuszko Monument in 1868. This was a favorite gathering spot for cadets, who often came here in early evening before call to quarters to relax or enjoy a song fest.

The Riding Hall, 1868. In the background are the Chapel and the domed Library. At this time, the Riding Hall was considered to be the largest indoor riding area in the United States. It stood on the site of the present Thayer Hall.

The Snow Plow, 1872. An oil by Professor of Drawing Robert Weir. Miss Augusta Berard in her re-membrances wrote, ''Among the most vivid recollections of my childhood is the picturesque appearance of a weather-beaten soldier, one of the old Bombardiers, equipped in a long, loose blue overcoat . . . breaking with a team of oxen attached to a clumsy sledge or drag, the almost impass-able drifts after a winter snow storm.''

Cadet Guard in the Summer of 1873. Several sentry boxes were sited around the camp to provide shelter for guards during rains. These boxes were still used when old summer camp ended for the last time in 1943. In the background is the remainder of the Fort Clinton parapet.

Looking West from the Old Cadet Chapel in 1875. The building with the clock tower is the Academic Building, erected in 1838. Next to it is Central Barracks. The white houses at the end of the road were officers' quarters.

A Cadet Room, 1st Division, Central Barracks, 1880. Cadet battalion staff officers were assigned quarters consisting of two rooms. The curtains on the windows and clothes press are "turkey red" material. Although cadet officers had some leeway in study room arrangement, they did comply with regulations by folding their bedding on their cots, as seen through the doorway to the right.

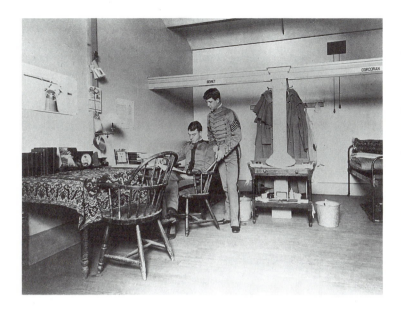

The Normal Cadet Room in Central Barracks, 1880. Each cadet had his clothing and bed in one side of the alcove. Uniforms were hung on the dividing partition. This photograph was taken from in front of the window facing the area; the door to the hall was to the left of the table and a fireplace across the room on the right. Plebes carried water from the water taps in the area and poured it into the pails by the washstand.

Academic Section Formation, 1880. This scene would have been the same for any period between 1867 and 1900. The Section Marcher stands in front of his section. After reporting any absentees to the cadet guard, he would march the section to its classroom. After class, the section re-formed in the Academic Building hallway to be marched back to barracks.

The Ill-Fated Custer Monument, 1880. Erected in 1879 with funds provided by friends and admirers of George Custer. Mrs. Custer objected to the portrayal of Custer, insisting that the features were those of an old man. After long and bitter correspondence with the Superintendent, the General Commanding the Army, and the Secretary of War, Libby Custer succeeded in having the statue removed in 1885. The pedestal was placed on Custer's grave in the cemetery.

The Back of the Library from the East Porch of the Administration Building, 1882. The latter building, erected in 1870, was a gray stone building with black wrought-iron adornments.

Cadet Hop Cards, 1852 to 1880. Hop cards or dance programs were used at cadet hops from the 1850s to the late 1950s. The upper left card used in 1852 is a hand-written list of dances with the names of cadets the young lady would dance with during the evening. The second card was used in 1863. The other cards are from the 1870s and 1880s.

Cadet Hop in the Mess Hall, 1883. The officer at left center is possibly General William T. Sherman; the bearded officer conversing with him may be the Superintendent, General John M. Schofield. Drawing by Harry Ogden.

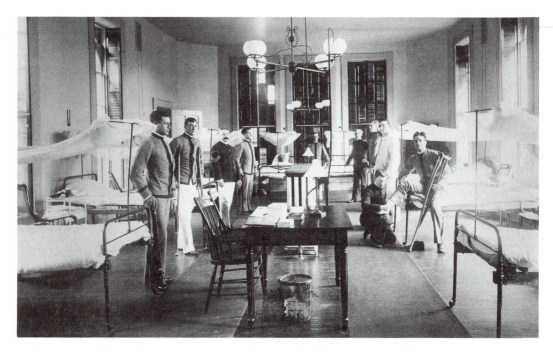

A Room in the Cadet Hospital, circa 1885. The "old" Hospital stood on the site of the present Lee Barracks. The knoll on which it was located was leveled when the new barracks were built. Enlisted men had their own hospital near their barracks and quarters.

Parade at Summer Camp, 1886. The cadet officers have moved "front and center" and have doffed their full dress hats to the Officer-in-Charge, who has removed his own full dress, plumed helmet in return.

WEST POINT—IN BATTERY—LIGHT ARTILLERY DRILL.—DRAWN BY R. F. ZOGBAUM.—[SEE ARTICLE ON DOUBLE PAGE.]

Artillery Drill in the Late 1880s. The horses are guided into place by enlisted men mounted on the off-side horses. Cadet gunners in gray jackets and white trousers run to unhitch the piece and swing it into firing position. Drawing by Rufus Zogbaum, noted military historian and artist.

Thayer Monument in Front of the Gymnasium, 1887. The Gymnasium, on the site of today's Washington Hall (the Cadet Mess Hall) was built in 1885. The statue of Sylvanus Thayer was dedicated by Academy graduates in November 1877, the same day that Thayer's remains were interred in the West Point cemetery.

Cadet Class in 1890. The center cadet standing near the blackboard is reciting his solution to a problem in descriptive geometry. He holds a pointer in his right hand, which he will use to show points in his solution.

Class in Practical Military Engineering, circa 1890. The class, wearing white fatigues, has raised the cannon tube using an A-frame and block and tackle. The officer at the left is the instructor. The photograph was taken near summer camp; the building whose roof can be seen in the right background is the West Point Hotel on Trophy Point.

Two Yearlings Accost a Plebe Sentinel, Summer Camp, 1891. The plebe stands at the *plebe* position of attention—left arm along the side of the body, palm of the hand facing outward, with the little finger touching the seam of the trousers. Testing this position shows one that it automatically pushes the shoulders back. The plebe wears the single shoulder belt of the period instead of the crossed belts worn today. The position of the two yearlings is typical: coats unbuttoned, caps anything but straight, arms akimbo.

FIVE-FOOT HURDLE BAREBACK.

A Cadet Takes the Five-Foot Hurdle Bareback, 1895. Cadets were taught to ride bareback as well as with the military saddle. This included jumping, as shown in this illustration by Frederick Remington, charging with the saber, firing a revolver, and attacking dummy figures on the ground. Staying on the horse while bareback was difficult even at the trot and a challenge at a faster pace or while jumping.

Walking the Area, 1894. Punishment tours for disciplinary infractions were instituted by Sylvanus Thayer. Initially, such punishments were extra tours of guard duty; later the penalty was changed to walking back and forth across the area because guard was an official roster duty that should not be considered punishment. Nothing would stop the area bird from making his rounds. Drawing by Rufus Zogbaum.

Christmas Hop, 1898. This scene shows the outer lobby on the second floor of Cullum Hall. The Ballroom is shown in the background. Drawing by Howard Chandler Christy.

Observance of the Centennial of the Military Academy, June 11, 1902. President Theodore Roosevelt, escorted by Superintendent Albert L. Mills, passes between an honor guard of the entire Corps of Cadets to enter Cullum Memorial Hall.

1829–1833

I am now continuing my course of reformation, have dismissed some cadets, suspended others, and shall persevere until I produce that state of discipline which is as indispensable in an institution of this nature as in a regular army. This course may in the end occasion my removal, but in the mean time I shall have done some good and performed my duty.

SYLVANUS THAYER

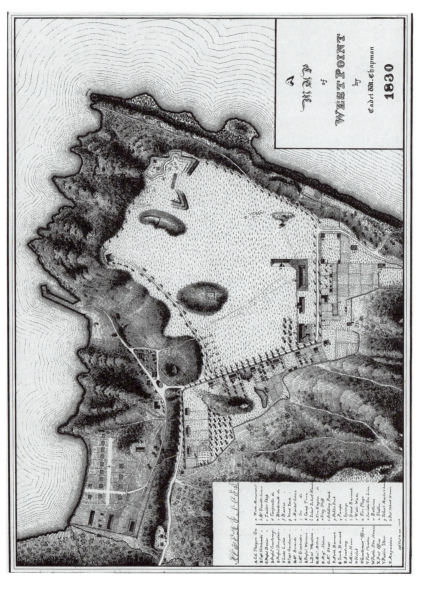

West Point in 1830. This map drawn by Cadet William Chapman, Class of 1830, as part of his drawing and surveying studies, shows the improvements made by Joseph G. Swift, Alden Partridge, and Sylvanus Thayer during their superintendencies. In the lower center of the map are (P) North Barracks, (Q) South Barracks, (R) the Academy (or Academic Building), and (S) the Mess Hall constructed by Partridge and Swift between 1815 and 1817. Quarters along the west edge of the Plain and facing north toward the Hudson River were built by Partridge and Thayer. The new West Point Hotel (T), erected in 1829, is shown on the northernmost bluff of the Plain.

11

I Have the Honor to Tender My Resignation

When Andrew Jackson was inaugurated on March 4, 1829, Democrats throughout the country rejoiced that a man of the people was now President. Jackson's actions fostered this belief, for he rewarded his supporters with appointments to government positions. This was not unusual. Patronage for political purposes was common in most states. Jefferson had been the first President to use the system but with restraint. Senator William Marcy of New York applied the term "spoils system" to Jackson's activities by stating in a congressional debate that "they see nothing wrong in the rule that to the victor belong the spoils of the enemy."

Opponents of a strong national military force and supporters of the militia concept assumed that they could count on the backing of the new President. It is true that Jackson had hoped to rely on the militia for defense of the nation. That hope, however, was based upon the belief that the militia would be composed of well-trained units. The Battle of New Orleans taught Jackson that poorly trained units could be effective only in a prepared position; such units could not be relied upon in a mobile situation. That lesson was emphasized during Jackson's battles with the Florida Seminole Indians in 1818. His Regular Army units were the primary means of defeating superior Indian forces; his militia were for the most part unreliable.

Never adequately trained, the militia degenerated into organized and disorganized units during the Jackson presidency. The unorganized militia in theory included every man of military age but in actuality was non-existent. The organized militia consisted of active companies with only a part of their theoretical strength. Volunteer membership all too often was sought because of social desirability rather than military patriotism. As Russell Weigley indicated in *Towards an American Army*, "With no militia save a few more or less fancily uniformed drill companies, there was no alternative to reliance on the regular army."

As the militia became increasing ineffective and militarily amateurish, the Regular Army became more and more professional. The results of the Thayer rebuilding of the Military Academy brought to the officer corps the status of a profession rather than a trade. With that status came a sense of responsibility, a sense originating from Thayer's emphasis on duty. Thayer's professionals possessed intellectual skill, skill developed by intense study as cadets. By the time Jackson became President, West Point graduates had begun to develop the Army into a highly trained, corporate body ready to respond to national requirements. A few militia units— very few—reached a state of reasonable training because many Academy graduates who had left the Army volunteered to serve with the militia.

As Jackson began his first term, Thayer was more concerned with improving the Military Academy faculty than worrying about relationships with the new President. Jared Mansfield, Professor of Natural and Experimental Philosophy and irritant to every superintendent, had resigned in August 1828 because of poor health and age. David Douglass, Professor of Military and Civil Engineering, was becoming more and more dissatisfied with the low pay of the West Point faculty. During the summers from 1826 to 1828, he was employed as a consulting engineer for the State of Pennsylvania. His request to the Chief of Engineers for permission to work with the Morris Canal Company of New Jersey was not approved. Douglass was upset; the $4,000 salary for two months' work was important to him. It was apparent to Thayer that Douglass would probably leave in the near future.

To replace Mansfield, Thayer selected Lieutenant Edward H. Courtenay, Class of 1821, who had already served four years on the faculty. He knew that Courtenay would be supported by William H. C. Bartlett, who was serving with the Corps of Engineers. Thayer planned to have him reassigned to the Academy when he had completed his work at Fortress Monroe, Virginia, and Fort Adams at Newport, Rhode Island. Courtenay would resign in 1834 to be succeeded by Bartlett, who would remain as head of the Natural and Experimental Philosophy Department until 1871.

Although Douglass did not resign until 1831, Thayer had already picked his successor, Dennis Hart Mahan. Mahan, on an extended stay in Europe, would become Acting Professor on his return in 1830 and succeed Douglass eight months later, remaining until his death in 1871.

Thayer saw little reason to select new men to head the Drawing and French Departments. He was pleased with Drawing Teacher Thomas Gimbrede and French Teacher Claudius Berard (heads of these two departments were not granted professorial rank until 1846). There was little reason to select a new Professor of Mathematics. Charles Davies, who became Professor in 1823, was an able instructor. His assistants included Albert E. Church, Class of 1828. Church remained on the faculty as Assistant Professor from 1828 to 1831 and from 1833 to 1837. At that time, Davies resigned, and Church became Professor, a position he held until his death in 1878.

The Commandant of Cadets, William J. Worth, had been reassigned in 1828 and replaced by Captain Ethan Allen Hitchcock. Hitchcock had been at West Point from 1824 to 1827 as a tactical officer and an artillery instructor. In early 1827, Hitchcock disagreed with Thayer's action in obtaining the Secretary of War's approval for appointing "Academic" Boards of Inquiry with authority to dismiss cadets. When first appointed Superintendent, Thayer had been authorized to dismiss cadets for misconduct without a Court Martial. This authorization was later withdrawn, and cadets could be dismissed for misconduct only by being tried by Court Martial. Using a Court of Inquiry instead of submitting a cadet to trial would, in Thayer's opinion, be more efficient. He had prepared the necessary document and obtained the approval of the Secretary of War. Hitchcock maintained that this was contrary to the Articles of War and that a Court of Inquiry could only be requested by an accused person or directed by the President.

The disagreement was not resolved, and Hitchcock refused to serve on such a court. When Thayer insisted, Hitchcock requested that he be reassigned to his regiment, the 1st Infantry at Fort Snelling, Minnesota. While waiting for orders, he went to Washington to discuss the matter with the Secretary of War but with no success. Convinced that Secretary Barbour was unfamiliar with the Article of War involved, Hitchcock then went to President John Quincy Adams and explained the legal points involved. Adams assured him that, if the authorization was illegal, he would revoke the order. The fact that a young captain was able to discuss a disagreement with his commanding officer with both the Secretary of War and the President is an indication of the informality and simplicity with which the government operated at that time, a great difference from procedures of today.

Hitchcock was given temporary duty as a recruiter in New York City. While there, he talked with Major Worth several times. Colonel Thayer called on him twice to try to persuade Hitchcock that his opinion was in error; neither man would admit that the other was right. Finally, in the fall of 1828, Hitchcock was ordered to take a group of recruits to Fort Snelling. By the end of November, he had reached Fort Crawford at Prairie du Chien, Wisconsin, where he remained several weeks waiting for the Mississippi River to freeze because traveling on the ice was the only practical way of going north during the winter months.

Hitchcock was surprised one day when the commanding officer, Major Stephen W. Kearney, handed him a newspaper with an article stating that Worth had been reassigned to his regiment, the 1st Artillery, and that Hitchcock had been designated to replace him. The next mail, several days later, brought orders from the War Department and a warm note from Thayer asking him to report as soon as possible. Hitchcock left in January and, after a two-month journey by horseback, stagecoach, and wagon, reached West Point in early March. Hitchcock wrote in his memoirs, "I was received by Major Thayer with the greatest possible kindness, and without any allusion whatever to the cause of my having been sent away from the Academy." He later learned that the Secretary of War, instead of nullifying the authorization for Thayer to convene Courts of Inquiry, had directed that no additional courts would be formed under that order.

The disagreement between Thayer and Hitchcock and Hitchcock's assignment as Commandant of Cadets to replace Worth provide insight into Thayer's character. His discussions with Hitchcock and his refusal to admit that he was wrong indicate stubbornness, tenacity, and a certain degree of egoism. That he did not mention the matter to Hitchcock after Hitchcock reported for duty is an indication that he wanted to avoid admitting that he had been wrong. His cordial welcome to Hitchcock and the close relationship that existed during Hitchcock's tour as Commandant are further proof of Thayer's fairness in all of his dealings with subordinates, officers and cadets alike. Worth had recommended Hitchcock as his replacement; that Thayer was willing to accept Hitchcock shows that Thayer placed the welfare of the Academy above any personal feelings. This willingness also graphically displays Thayer's characteristic of not wanting sycophants on the staff and faculty. He listened to arguments against his opinion; but, once he had reached a decision, he expected that decision to be followed.

There were indications that Thayer could count on support from the Jackson administration. Cadet Isaac Rowland was dismissed after the June 1829 examinations for academic deficiency. His father complained to Secretary of War John Eaton, charging favoritism and expressing a feeling of disgrace and dishonor. Eaton expressed his belief in the fairness of the Military Academy administration and defended the use of the merit system, stating that "I will only remind you that the merit roll is not the work of one person, but the result of the deliberations of the whole Academic Board, gentlemen of character, who having no dependence on the students and no interest of their own to consult except what is a correct charge of their public duties are entitled to the confidence of the War Department." Eaton's refusal to reinstate the cadet seemed to indicate that there would be little change from the overall policy of previous administrations.

Increased interest in the Military Academy brought requests for information regarding appointment as a cadet. To reduce the work required in answering each request individually, Thayer recommended to the War Department that a printed form be prepared to answer these requests. The form described the procedure for obtaining an appointment (all appointments were then made by the Secretary of War), the entrance requirements, and clothing a newly appointed cadet should bring with him. This procedure was continued; and, as time passed, the information provided increased to several pages, then to a booklet, and finally to the present admissions kit prepared by the Academy Director of Admissions.

Thayer initiated periodic reports, informing parents of their son's progress and his academic status. Grades were not sent to parents; the report showed a cadet's class standing in each subject, the number of cadets in the class, and the number of demerits received. At first, these reports were first sent to parents after the examinations in January and June. Thayer increased the frequency to quarterly and, in the early 1830s, to monthly reports. This practice has been continued to the present day with many changes in material included in the reports.

Internal administration was formalized. By 1831, instructors were required to submit a weekly printed report when they met with Colonel Thayer on Saturday. The report form was simple. Each cadet's daily grades were entered and totaled, and remarks concerning a cadet could be added by the instructor. A separate report was prepared for each section. There was a definite advantage in having reports submitted by section instead of having individual cadet grades provided. Thayer could immediately determine the relative rank of a cadet within his particular section. Weekly reports were supplemented by periodic reports from a department head, giving the relative rank of every cadet in a particular subject.

Many of the officers on the staff and faculty were not married. Church in his memoirs indicated that "among the assistants, at this time [1828] and for three years after, there was not a married officer. Bachelors messed in the cadet Commons at a cost of about fifteen dollars a month, one-fourth of their salaries. In late 1829, Cozzens informed his officer boarders that he could no longer continue the mess at that price. Many of the young officers objected, and the mess was disbanded. A few continued with Cozzens at greater cost. Many cooked their own meals in a makeshift kitchen in South Barracks. Others messed with Mrs. Kinsley in her home south of the Post. Church described their trek, "Three times a day in all kinds of weather, for over a year, we trudged through the woods to our meals at her house." Efforts to obtain commutation for rations and quarters with the eloquent plea that they had decided to make an "account of the many inconveniences to which we have been subjected which we believe to be unequalled at any other military post in the United States" was unsuccessful. Although the Secretary of War approved the request for commutations, the Quartermaster General refused to make the payments because he considered the Military Academy not to be a regular military post.

The problem eased somewhat when the new hospital was built in 1830. A stone building on the present site of Lee Barracks, it replaced the inadequate facilities of the old Gridley tavern. The north end of the building was set aside as bachelor officer quarters. The officers messed in the old tavern building. After it was moved and turned into quarters for the fencing master, bachelor officers either cooked their own meals in their quarters, ate at the new hotel, or boarded with Mrs. Kinsley. A regular officers mess was not established until 1841.

Social life at West Point had improved. Church recalled that the many private parties before the hotel was built were "plain and inexpensive." Most social entertainment was hosted in officers' homes, but an occasional dance took place in either the cadet mess or the chapel room in the Academic Building. Music by band musicians included quadrilles, Spanish dances, and an occasional waltz. Dancing always ended with a Virginia reel; and "by half-past ten or eleven all were again home, and most in bed, as honest people should be."

Church and many other young officers enjoyed these parties. A few did not. Hitchcock disliked the formal dinners and evening parties, where "the chief object seemed to be to bring out a dozen different bottles of wine, bottle by bottle, of each of which there must be a long account given, setting forth its history, the date of vintage, date of importation, date of bottling, &c., &c." Apparently Thayer was not the only oenophile at West Point.

Cadet Charles Mason, classmate of Robert E. Lee, described a November 1829 party to his sister. "Know," wrote Mason, "that a Lady Professor [sic] gave a ball last night to the ladies and officers of the post—but more particularly for the benefit of her nieces, the Misses Totten." The ball was held in the cadet mess, where two large rooms had been thrown open to provide space for the festivities. The hostess decorated the room with paintings and portraits, one of which Mason said, "informed us how our hostess looked twenty years since." Plants were placed in window wells and at both ends of the rooms. At one end was a large sideboard "loaded with that part of the entertainment that required mastication or solution."

The far end of the room was closed off by a curtain. When the curtain was drawn, "our 'corps de ballet' . . . seemed to be dancing a dead march to a low-mournful-wailing air . . . two or three German plants were evidently in tears at the affecting spectacle; they had heard that funeral strain years before on the banks of the Rhine." Despite this comment, Mason called the music "divine." He was more concerned with refreshments than with the entertainment. In addition to oysters, chicken salad, and several kinds of sandwiches, there was "an abundance of confectioneries for those who still preserve their childish fondness for sweets—kisses with sentimental verses for love sick youths."

Mason described the drinks in detail; "There was lemonaid for the ladies and the teetotalers, champaign for the dull who would feign to be witty, sherry &c. for those who were just forgetting their first flame, and champaign with brandy for those who had no love whatsoever." Mason did not tell his sister which beverage he drank. In all probability he openly limited himself to the "lemonaid," while surreptitiously downing some of the "champaign." There was dancing after the performance. Mason danced a waltz and then left for his bed in North Barracks.

The opening of the hotel in 1829 was celebrated with a ball to which "young ladies from Newburgh, Poughkeepsie, &c." were invited. Church and others described some of the many parties at the hotel. Balls were sponsored by a group of "managers," officers and cadets who made the necessary arrangements and presented the guests to the Superintendent and Commandant. There were no separate cadet balls during Thayer's superintendency. Later, recalled Church, at the end of each month "the cadets began to have their 28th balls, they were not called hops at first."

There were other amusements. Band concerts during the summer were held between the hotel and camp; in winter, in the chapel room. Hitchcock described one concert, saying that he "was so much affected by the music at a concert in the evening that I was obliged to leave the hall. Music has often overcome me." There were other musicals. Often officers' wives or daughters sang or provided piano music. Bandmaster Willis taught music to families and a few cadets. One, John H. Hewitt, who failed to graduate with the Class of 1822, became a noted composer of popular songs and oratorios. His "All Quiet Along the Potomac Tonight" was a popular song during the Civil War.

Groups often met for "readings," reviews of books, poetry, or essays. Claudius Berard taught French to officers and their ladies, and some of their evening classes discussed French literature. Although Thomas Gimbrede taught drawing to some families, there is no indication that the art classes had any social meetings. Many artists came to West Point to sketch the beautiful scenery and cadet activities. One of the first was George Catlin, who made several paintings of the Academy in 1826. He and others who visited in later years received a warm welcome from officers and their families.

The Dialectic Society met once or twice a month for debates and discussions. A new organization, The Associate Society of West Point, was established in August 1830 "for the promotion of Science, Literature, and the Arts." Although the founders hoped to expand the Society to other places throughout the country, there is no indication that they were successful. After a few meetings at West Point, the Society quietly dropped from the scene.

Cadets were included in many officer social activities, and they in turn invited officers and their families to cadet activities. There was little differentiation between members of various cadet classes. Plebes—members of the Fourth Class were given this name about 1824—and upperclassmen were all welcome at social activities. Church, Cullum, and others mentioned this in letters and memoirs. The strict discipline, difficult academics, and Spartan life developed a bond as strong as brotherhood, a bond that led graduates and historians to label the cadets of this period as the "band of brothers."

Church explained this relationship in a February 13, 1879, letter to General Cullum; "I think a higher standard of honor and a better 'esprit de corps' prevailed at this time than I have known since. The name of cadet, whether belonging to the last admitted plebe or to the graduating first class man, was honored by all and indignity offered to the former would have been resented as even, by the Corps as one offered to the latter." The fact that most classes during Thayer's superintendency graduated only about half of those who entered as plebes—in some classes only one third completed the course—drew the survivors together in an inseparable bond that often lasted a lifetime.

Appointments were still made by the Secretary of War, who undoubtedly acted upon the recommendations of Congressmen and Senators. Although there was no firm requirement for appointing cadets from each state or congressional district, it became an unwritten rule to select new cadets from as many states and districts as possible, undoubtedly for political reasons. A brief comparison of the appointments made from 1818 through 1820 with those made from 1828 through 1830 shows this trend. The twenty-three graduates in the Class of 1818 represented eleven states; thirteen from seven states in the north, eight from three southern states, one from the west, and one from the District of Columbia. In 1819, the twenty-nine graduates came from thirteen states; eighteen from six in the north, seven from four southern states, three from two in the west, and one from the District of Columbia. There were thirty graduates in 1820 from eleven states. Thirteen came from five northern states; sixteen from five southern states; and one from the west.

Ten years later, more states were represented in the classes graduated from 1828 to 1830. Thirty-three in the Class of 1829 were appointed from sixteen states and the District of Columbia; twenty from eight northern states, eight from six southern states, four from two in the west, and one from the District of Columbia. The Class of 1829 came from fifteen states. Thirty had been appointed from nine northern states; thirteen from five in the south; one from each of two western states; and one from the District of Columbia. The forty-two men in the Class of 1830 represented eighteen states. Twenty-one were from nine northern states; fifteen from six in the south; three from three western states; and three from the District of Columbia.

During this period, there was no increase in the number of cadets authorized, the 250 stipulated by the Act of April 1812. Northern states consistently produced more graduates than the southern states; the west had the fewest. In the earlier period, New York had the most graduates, twenty-three. Massachusetts was represented by nineteen, and Virginia by seventeen. In the 1828–1830 classes, New York again had the largest representation, eighteen graduates. Twelve came from Pennsylvania; eight from Maryland and Connecticut; and seven from Virginia and Kentucky.

It is not surprising that more graduates came from these states than others with smaller representations because they had better educational facilities, both secondary schools and colleges. Consequently cadets from these states had little trouble passing the simple entrance examinations and surviving the rigid first year curriculum. Cadets from some southern states and most western states often did not qualify. Many who passed the entrance examinations later failed academically. Had the efforts of Thayer and the Academic Board to stiffen the entrance requirements been successful, there would have been even fewer cadets from many of the western and southern states.

It might be expected that the Jackson spoils system would change the source of cadet appointments with more appointments going to western states and other Jacksonian areas. Except for an increase in the number of cadets from Tennessee, there is no indication of any great change. Jackson's two nephews had already graduated. Nine cadets from Tennessee graduated between 1820 and 1827. Between 1828 and 1836, fourteen graduates had been appointed from Tennessee. One, George L. Welcker of the Class of 1836, was the first western cadet to graduate at the head of his class. From 1818 to 1836, fourteen class leaders came from northern states; three from the south; and only Welcker from the west. Strangely, none came from Virginia despite the large number of graduates from that state. Robert E. Lee, second in the Class of 1829, was the closest to that distinction.

The 1828 election brought a host of Jackson Democrats to Congress. One, David Crockett from Tennessee, was an outspoken antagonist of the Military Academy and the Regular Army. Tennessee politicians had consistently tried to abolish the Academy. The State legislature had passed acts demanding that Congress eliminate this aristocratic institution. Jackson's nephew, Andrew Jackson Donelson, had informed Thayer in 1823 that Tennessee's most vehement advocate of abolishment, Newton Cannon, had not been elected. Crockett now resumed Cannon's attacks.

At the same time, similar antagonism developed toward all colleges, institutions that were considered to be exclusive and catering to the rich and privileged. Kentucky in 1825 started a wave of hostility followed by many other states when it reduced state support of colleges. Private colleges could exist without state or federal assistance, but the Military Academy could not. It depended on the largess of Congress and the support of the Secretary of War and the President for its very existence. Secretary Eustis had almost eradicated the Academy in 1810; it had been saved by a war and congressional support. The Academy now faced a battle with Congress but this time with the support of Secretary of War Eaton.

Perennial gadfly Alden Partridge joined the attacks on the Academy. He had never lessened his personal campaign, and he took Jackson's election and the anti-military sentiments of the Democrats as an indication that he could attain his objectives. He had always condemned Thayer's Academy as a school for aristocrats and its graduates as an elite who prevented good men from being commissioned. In March 1830, Partridge opened fire with a pamphlet he called "The Military Academy at West Point Unmasked or Corruption and Military Despotism Exposed." Although the pamphlet was authored by "Americanus," there was no question that Partridge was its author.

The pamphlet had three sections; one addressed to the Congress, the second to the President, and the third to the American people. There was little new information in the first two sections; they merely repeated what Partridge and others had said many times. Partridge maintained that the Academy was unconstitutional because worthy enlisted men and civilians could not be commissioned since only Academy graduates could become officers. He charged that Academy regulations were against the law and that more officers were on the faculty than authorized. One reason for this, wrote Partridge, was the fact that the Superintendent taught no classes, took no part in drill, and actually did nothing of value. He criticized cadet punishments and recommended that the Academy be abolished, officers be appointed from the states in proportion to its number of congressional representatives or from qualified enlisted men, and all newly appointed officers be sent to a training school at West Point for six months only.

The second section leveled charges at Thayer, Berard, and Douglass, the only officers remaining at West Point who had participated in his ouster. Thayer's administration was compared with Partridge's service with emphasis on Partridge's ability to teach mathematics or engineering and conduct artillery and infantry instruction. The third section was a scathing denunciation of the Congressional Committee studying the Military Academy and its operation. Partridge again criticized almost every facet of Academy activities and asserted that the Academy fostered a military aristocracy. What benefit might have been obtained by placing the pamphlet in the hands of Congressmen was nullified to a large extent by his remarks about the Committee.

Ironically, the Committee investigation had been the result of Partridge's discussion with James Blair, a member of the House Committee on Military Affairs. He had persuaded Blair to introduce a resolution calling for an investigation of the Academy. Blair was supported by Crockett, who was against any government institution, military or civilian. His convictions differed from those of another Tennessee politician, Sam Houston, who had been President of the Academy Board of Visitors.

The only result of this turmoil was a Committee request that the War Department provide information concerning cadet appointments, financial status of the Academy, sons of prominent political figures who had been appointed, and the number of foreign citizens appointed.

While the War Department and Thayer were gathering the information requested, Crockett introduced a series of resolutions to abolish the Academy. Most of his charges were based on the Partridge pamphlet, but the diatribes in the pamphlet brought the exact opposite reaction Partridge had assumed would ensue. Most Congressmen, even those who had first supported the earlier Blair-Crockett efforts, were not interested in supporting Crockett.

Thayer was concerned and asked Secretary of War Eaton and General Gratiot, the Chief of Engineers, for advice. He also wrote to Joseph Vance, a senior member of the House Committee on Military Affairs who had a cadet son. Vance recommended that Thayer do nothing because he felt that things would improve. "Blair," wrote Vance, "who is a highly honorable man has become completely disgusted with Partridge and expresses his opinion openly that he believes he is a vindictive and disappointed man."

Gratiot gave Thayer similar advice: "Since the appearance of Partridge's pamphlet, I do not perceive that his object has had the least success." Gratiot assured Thayer that friends supported him and that the pamphlet was unworthy of Thayer's notice. Gratiot proposed that Thayer assemble information concerning Partridge's service at West Point; he would add this material to other records in his files to use "on any future occasion if required." Gratiot also asked Swift for copies of letters he had received from Partridge "in which is expressed a final determination to prosecute as long as his revengeful feelings are not truly glutted." Gratiot intended to fight smoke with fire if Partridge continued his attacks on the Academy. A West Point classmate of Partridge, Gratiot had not let this association blind him to the true basis of Partridge's vengeful actions. He was determined that neither the Academy nor Thayer should be harmed by these unwarranted attacks.

The War Department report to the Committee answered all questions raised. A complete list of cadets appointed, graduated, and dismissed was provided. Expenditures were summarized to show that annual costs per cadet were less than the cost of educating an English cadet at Sandhurst. The only request for which no information was available was for a list of cadets whose families were too indigent to educate their sons in any other way. The reason given was that there was no regulation requiring newly appointed cadets to provide information concerning family "pecuniary circumstances." Four foreign-born cadets had attended the Academy. John Wyndham, a former British Army officer, had graduated in 1806. Luis and Mateo Blanco, Chilian cadets who had been accepted on the recommendation of Captain David Porter, were dismissed in early 1818. Juan Perez, from the Republic of Colombia, entered in 1823 and left with the Class of 1826 after completing the full course of studies. His expenses were paid by the Colombian government.

The report created little interest in Congress or elsewhere. Crockett persuaded Congress to print 6,000 copies for nationwide distribution. Academy supporters opposed this expenditure until Representative J. W. Taylor of New York insisted that it be published to counter accusations in the Partridge pamphlet. "Much has been said here and elsewhere," argued Taylor, "of the enormous abuses which had been practiced at the academy, and as to its being an institution for the sons of the rich, especially of members of Congress." He pointed out that only thirteen sons of Congressmen had been or were cadets, five sons of Senators, four sons of governors, and seventeen sons of "a person holding office in the District of Columbia." The report was published; interest declined even more; and another vehement effort to abolish the Academy had failed.

Cadets were aware of the controversy. George Cullum wrote his friend Alfred Huidekoper that "a little stir has been made here lately by the appearance of a pamphlet under the title of 'Military Academy Unmasked or Corruption and Military Despotism Exposed.' These are pretty hard names to begin with, but still not quite so hard as some contained within it." Cullum attributed the pamphlet to Partridge and stated, "He represents the Academy as a nursery of a Military Aristocracy and likely to prove very fatal to the liberties of the United States. I would advise the poor fellow, whoever he is, not to be so frightened before he is hurt." Cullum placed the blame on "Southerners who are now trying to break up the Academy and by this means gain their support to some of his Schools which he has established in South Carolina."

Cullum's letter revealed two trends developing within the Corps of Cadets. Interest in political matters was increasing, and there were signs of sectionalism. Cadets had always had newspapers available, either those from large eastern cities or those sent from home by parents or friends. The reading room in the mess building made newspapers available. There was only one restriction: cadets had to obtain Thayer's permission to subscribe to a paper. This was not an attempt to censor or control reading material; Thayer felt the restriction necessary to his efforts to guide cadets to fiscal solvency. Despite exposure to political discussions in newspapers, cadets had shown little tendency to debate political problems. Perhaps the controversy caused by the Partridge pamphlet and Crockett's antagonism toward the Academy were a catalyst, for cadets became more and more interested in national and state politics.

There was at the same time a growing feeling of sectionalism. A certain amount of sectional bias had always existed, but this had been shown only by comparing class standings of northern and southern cadets. The western bloc added a third side, leading to cadets discussing issues affecting three separate sections of the country. This growing sectionalism had little impact on the brotherly feeling among the cadets. If anything, it strengthened the bond of fellowship.

Cullum wrote his friend Huidekoper at least once a month as a cadet and for many years after he graduated. He wrote his family often, but the letters to his close friend provided a different insight into cadet life. Cullum missed feminine companionship and often asked Huidekoper about young ladies at home. He described cadet dances and other social activities with emphasis on the ladies present. He mentioned home events that he missed at West Point. In February 1830, Cullum wrote nostalgically that he missed sleigh rides at home in Pennsylvania. "It is almost too provoking," he said, "to hear sleigh bells jingling about the Barracks without the hope of participating in the enjoyment of a fine sleigh ride." He asked Huidekoper to "take a few turns around Patterson for me."

Social activities described by Cullum included teas in officers' homes. He was a frequent visitor at Professor Douglass's quarters and was quite upset when he learned Douglass would be leaving the Academy. Lieutenant and Mrs. Bradford Alden often asked Cullum to their home. He mentioned in one letter a discussion with Mrs. Alden concerning the possibility of his boarding with them: "Mrs. Alden would like that I should come to board with them at the same price that I get boarding at the Mess House which is $10 a month." This was an unusual comment because nothing in regulations indicated that cadets could board at any place other than the Thompson house and the cadet mess. Cullum's letters gave no further information concerning Mrs. Alden's suggestion.

Cullum did not hesitate to complain to Huidekoper about inconveniences and requirements he did not appreciate. He expressed a dislike of chapel services. "I am obliged to sit for two long hours on a bench without a back," he wrote in 1829, "squeesed up among a parcel of Cadets, and squeesed up still more with my belts, as we have all to wear our side arms to church." Another time, he wrote, "I have just returned from church after hearing rather a dry sermon." Many times, he compared chapel services with those at home, and the West Point services were a poor second.

From his letters, details of academic procedure appear, details which were lost when the 1838 fire destroyed so many records. In the summer of 1832, Cullum reported, "We are now instructing the plebes in firing cannon which affords us no small quantity of amusement. Not being accustomed to hearing so many pieces discharged at once so near them to make as much fuss as though they had an arm or two shot off. Some get so frightened that it is almost impossible to get them again to do their duty before two minutes." After artillery drill, upperclassmen reported to the laboratory for instruction "in making all sorts of things for doing mischief such as cartridges, fire balls, Congreve rockets &c., &c." Cullum described making signal rockets, "which are very pretty to see when set off but I can assure you are not so pleasant to make."

After dinner at noon, dancing classes took two hours. Cullum said they were not much fun without ladies, but "we cannot complain for want of them in the evening" at cotillions at the hotel. After dancing class, cadets formed for drill and then for evening parade. Summer was as busy as winter, the only difference being less studying at night. "Nothing is here taken for granted"; Cullum ended one letter, "we must give a reason for everything. This is not a very easy task, but it is much the best way of learning as it impresses it more deeply on the mind, and gets a person in the way of thinking and reasoning a great deal."

A sad event was described by Cullum in another letter, the funeral of Bandmaster Willis, "the great performer on the bugle," who was buried with full honors. There was a military escort of twenty cadets, who "marched in front with reversed arms." The band, playing "some of the most solemn airs I ever heard," was followed by officers, cadets, and civilian friends. After the burial service, "three volleys of musquetry were fired over and in the grave." The services were very impressive to young Cullum, who ended his description with "but the affect was destroyed by returning with the musick of 'Hasten to the Wedding' and some other such tunes. This is a military practice but I think it a very wrong one."

Cadet letters displayed wide knowledge of Academy matters. Little mention was made of reinstatement or reappointment of cadets dismissed for academic deficiency or misconduct, possibly because this had become a continuing pattern as a means of repaying political obligations. Monroe, Madison, John Quincy Adams, and many Secretaries of War had used this means of patronage.

Secretaries Calhoun and Barbour made reinstatement an almost routine matter. Thayer objected vociferously but with little success. Denton estimates that Calhoun and Barbour reappointed thirty-one dismissed cadets, approximately ten percent of the total number of appointments made from 1822 through 1828. The vast majority of reappointments were cadets who had failed academically. During Jackson's first administration, approximately twenty-one cadets were reappointed.

Jackson not only reappointed cadets who had been dismissed for academic deficiency, he also remitted sentences of cadets dismissed by Court Martial for misconduct. There had been a few remissions during the previous administrations, but Jackson and Secretary of War Eaton set aside nearly half of the dismissals by Courts Martial. Initially, Eaton approved Court Martial judgments, but by early 1831 he began to set aside some sentences of dismissal while approving others.

In February, he approved the dismissal of Cadet Edgar Allan Poe, who had been tried for gross neglect of duty and disobedience of orders. According to cadet legend, orders for parade stated that cadets would form "with cross belts under arms." Poe was alleged to have reported wearing only cross belts and carrying his musket. There is no truth to this legend. Poe had failed to report for various formations thirteen times between January 7 and 27 and refused to attend chapel or class when specifically ordered to do so.

In early April, Eaton reviewed several cadet cases tried earlier that month. One involved Cadet George W. Featherstonhaugh, who had been tried for ninety-five violations of regulations involving arson, absence from formations, refusal to obey orders, and unsoldierly conduct. Four other cadets had been tried for playing cards. Eaton studied the records carefully before stating that "the Secretary of War deeply deplores the necessity of being obliged frequently to examine Records of Courts Martial instituted for the trial of young gentlemen of the Military Academy." In his opinion, there could be no apology for the trouble caused because the rules and regulations of the Academy were "few, simple and easy to be understood. To disregard them is wholly inexcusable." Eaton scathingly warned that cadets who disregarded the rules and regulations consistently should "voluntary leave a service for which they manifest no taste, and give place to others, who will obey the Rules of the School and the admonitions which are set before them."

Eaton commented on the conduct of H. Ariel Norris, who had persuaded the other three cadets to play cards. Because Norris was older and theoretically more mature, Eaton blamed him for misleading younger cadets. He agreed that the Court had taken the proper steps in recommending dismissal of all four cadets "lest their misconduct might have the injurious tendency to lead others into similar practices and error." Despite his deprecatory comments, Eaton set aside the findings of the Court in the hope that "the present example may prove a warning for the future." The four cadets were returned to duty.

Featherstonhaugh did not fare as well. Noting that he "stood charged, not with the violation of one Regulation, the commission of a single fault, but with an habitual disregard of those Rules by which he has pledged himself to be governed," Eaton did not remit his sentence because "others in the future will have an equal claim upon the Department for forgiveness the consequence of which would be a destruction of everything like wholesome order." Featherstonhaugh was dismissed, but Eaton's words of admonition would soon be ignored.

Norris and another cadet, Thomas W. Gibson, were real problems. Gibson, appointed from Indiana, had been Poe's roommate. During his eighteen months as a cadet, he was tried for major violations four times, sentenced to be dismissed five times, and reinstated four times. His fifth sentence of dismissal was approved by Secretary of War Lewis Cass, who replaced Eaton in August 1831. Gibson's first trial was for breaking cadet limits; Eaton reinstated him. He was then tried twice for drinking and twice more reinstated.

Gibson was a troublemaker and arsonist. In October 1831, he and Cadet Robert Allen set fire to a small building near the barracks. Once the fire was underway, Gibson disabled all the pumps near the building, and it burned to the ground. When Thayer attempted to gather evidence and testimony that would warrant a trial, he was shocked to find that cadets refused to testify against either Allen or Gibson. Thayer had no recourse but to ask the Secretary of War to convene a Court of Inquiry. Gibson, Allen, and eight others known to have been witnesses refused to testify before the Court. Secretary Cass ordered them tried by Court Martial on charges of contempt of authority and refusing to obey the orders of the Court of Inquiry. All were found guilty and sentenced to be dismissed.

President Jackson reviewed the case and set aside the sentences of the Court Martial. He stated that "believing themselves, though erroneously, bound in honor not to disclose the facts made known to them, what under other circumstances would constitute an unjustifiable contempt of court authority, becomes in this case a misapprehension of duty." Jackson's reasoning might have applied to Gibson and Allen. Had they obeyed the ruling of the Court of Inquiry, they would have incriminated themselves. The other eight cadets, however, had not participated; their testimony would have been directed toward Gibson and Allen, not themselves.

During the investigation and the subsequent Court Martial, Gibson and Allen were under arrest and restricted to their rooms. Gibson broke arrest and persuaded another cadet, Alexander Wolcott, to set fire to the ice house in Execution Hollow. The two were apprehended and tried by Court Martial, Wolcott for setting the building on fire and Gibson for aiding and abetting him. Both were sentenced to be dismissed. While waiting for review by the Secretary of War and the President, Gibson persuaded Wolcott to desert; both were arrested at the steamboat landing. Their desertion attempt had backfired. The sentences had been removed. They faced another Court Martial.

Wolcott was tried for desertion and sentenced to be dismissed and to serve one month in solitary confinement at Fort Columbus, Newport, Rhode Island. Gibson was tried for the second case of arson and for assisting Wolcott to desert. He was sentenced to be dismissed. Thayer, the faculty, and many cadets were shocked when the Secretary of War set aside Wolcott's sentence of confinement, although he let the dismissal stand. Gibson's sentence was again nullified, and he was reinstated.

During this turmoil, Hitchcock and Thayer gathered evidence concerning the first arson. A new Court Martial was convened to try Gibson for setting the fire and disabling the pumps. The Court found him guilty and sentenced him to dismissal. This time the sentence was approved; apparently three sentences of dismissal in an eight month period were too much for Cass and Jackson.

In July 1831, Thayer received approval from the Chief of Engineers for a refinement of the demerit system. Possible deficiencies were divided into seven categories with from one to ten demerits to be awarded depending upon the seriousness of the violation. After the first year, the value of each demerit was increased by one-sixth in the second year, one-third in the third year, and one-half in the fourth year. The logic for the change was the belief that a plebe was not as informed about the disciplinary system as upperclassmen. First Classmen were expected to set the example for other cadets and were therefore subject to more demerits for deficiencies. Any cadet receiving more than 200 demerits in any one year would be considered deficient in conduct and recommended for discharge.

Cadet Norris, who had been reinstated by President Jackson, had 222 demerits for the year ending in June 1831. It appeared that he had benefitted somewhat from Jackson's leniency, for he had only 181 demerits the following year. This was an election year, and Jacksonians throughout the country were planting hickory trees on village commons to show their support of the President. One night, Norris left his tent in summer camp, carefully crossed camp limits, and planted a hickory tree in the middle of the Plain. Thayer and Hitchcock were outraged. Norris was tried by Court Martial for being absent from his tent at tattoo and at reveille the next morning but not for planting the tree on the parade ground. His sentence of dismissal was removed by Jackson after personal appeal by Norris and political supporters in New York City. There is little doubt that an outsider informed Jackson about Norris's planting the hickory tree during his absence from camp because this was not mentioned in the Court Martial record.

Secretary Eaton's words in approving the Featherstonhaugh sentence in April 1831 proved a prediction of what was taking place: "Others in future will have an equal claim on the Department for forgiveness the consequences of which would be a destruction of everything like wholesome order." Cadets dismissed for misconduct knew that if they appealed to the President or had relatives or friends ask for clemency, they would probably be reinstated regardless of the offense committed. Many old grads jokingly say that "the Corps Has [Gone to Hell]!" That certainly applied to the situation in 1832. Discipline had deteriorated to the point where cadets neglected their studies, according to Hitchcock, to determine "means by which they might escape the penalties of idleness and neglect of duty." The attitude of many cadets had changed and "instead of looking upon the professors and officers as their friends working for their advancement in life, they regarded them rather as enemies seeking on occasion to punish them."

Hitchcock and Thayer discussed the situation, and Thayer asked General Gratiot for advice. The situation was critical; something had to be done. Thayer had to find a way to convince Jackson that he should stop reinstating recalcitrant cadets. Hitchcock finally suggested a possible solution. He asked Thayer for permission to go to Washington "to see the President personally and convince him, if I could, of the importance of having the regulations of the Academy duly observed." Thayer agreed and directed Hitchcock to tell Jackson that if the Academy regulations did not meet with his approval, he should have them revised. Hitchcock was to tell the President that "it was absolutely necessary that the rules should be enforced, for the value, if not the existence, of the institution" depended on their being enforced.

In late November, Hitchcock discussed the situation with the President. After he finished his explanation, Jackson began a tirade concerning Thayer and his tyranny. Apparently, some cadets who had asked the President for clemency accused Thayer of being dictatorial. Hitchcock tried to tell Jackson that he had been misinformed. Jackson then stated that Cadet Norris had only done what people everywhere were doing. Hitchcock replied that "it was incongruous for boys in a public school to employ themselves in making political demonstrations." The discussion ended with Jackson asking Hitchcock to tell General Gratiot to see him at once. Gratiot later told Hitchcock that Jackson had directed General Jessup, the Quartermaster General, and General Jones, the Adjutant General, to review Academy regulations and recommend changes that should be made.

While Hitchcock was in Washington, Secretary Cass appointed a Court Martial to meet at West Point to try any cases presented to it. The appointment of a Court by the War Department was in itself unusual because previous Courts at West Point had been appointed by the Chief of Engineers. Even more unusual was its composition: three general officers, three colonels, one lieutenant colonel, three majors, and four captains. The Court tried several cases and then adjourned. It was rumored among the faculty and cadets that the Court had come to investigate Thayer's conduct of Academy affairs. Such appeared not to be true.

Hereafter, Courts Martial were ordered by the War Department and included only officers not assigned to the Academy. This was considered a sign of distrust by the War Department and the President. However, there is a more logical explanation. Several cadets appealing to Jackson for clemency accused Thayer and the faculty of favoritism, maintaining that a Court consisting of staff and faculty officers would be biased in its findings. This new procedure eliminated that argument and may have caused the reduction in the number of reinstatements.

Another change required a Court to investigate and report all facts involved in a case even when the accused pleaded guilty. This would provide the Secretary with sworn statements if a cadet appealed the findings instead of being presented only with cadet opinion in the request for clemency. This change also contributed to the reduced number of sentences set aside.

After Hitchcock returned to West Point and reported to Thayer, Gratiot wrote that Jessup and Jones had recommended to the President that no changes be made in Academy regulations. For a brief period, there were no reinstatements. Thayer was unwilling to adopt a wait-and-see attitude. Instead, he wrote a long personal letter to Secretary Cass, stating that "I am led to believe that there is something at this institution which does not altogether meet with the President's approbation, but I am at a loss to conjecture whether the dissatisfaction, if such really exists, relates to persons or things." He cited reports of fourteen successive Boards of Visitors and frequent inspections, all favorable to the Academy and its officers. Thayer, indicating that some individuals might consider Academy regulations too strict, said, "I flatter myself that opinion is confined principally to those who have not witnessed their operation and the spirit and manner in which they are administered." He ended his letter by saying, "You know better than I can tell you that any regulations however perfect in themselves and however well administered by the authorities here are incapable of producing the desired result so long as the impression continues (and I assure you that the impression is deep and general) that they do not meet with the full approbation of the Executive, or while it is believed that a dismissed cadet can get reinstated whether by the influence of powerful friends or by direct and personal application to the President."

Secretary Cass replied with a soothing letter. He said that Jackson did not have "the slightest shade of unkindly feeling toward you. He has the greatest respect for you and he has expressed it to me many times." Only five weeks before, the President had told Hitchcock that Thayer was a tyrant with more power than "the autocrat of the Russias!" Cass's final words were intended to assure Thayer that his concerns were unfounded. "The state of affairs at the academy is good. Temporary difficulties have disappeared and I imagine when they existed they were greatly overrated. Dismiss the whole subject from your mind."

The next day, before his letter reached Thayer, Cass acted on a complaint made by Cadet Frederick A. Smith, who had been reported for giving an unauthorized serenade to a young lady on the Post. This was a relatively minor offense, and he was punished only by being given demerits. Smith complained that he was punished based on suspicion only. Smith's action was odd because all he had to do to have the report removed was to deny the accusation. Instead he asked the Secretary to cancel the report because it was unjust to be accused without evidence.

Without asking for a report, Cass wrote Thayer that the proceedings involving Smith had been wrong and ordered the demerits removed. What Cass did, intentionally or not, was indicate that a cadet could expect to have punishments removed by not answering reports directly. This destroyed Thayer's efforts to instill in cadets a realization that their word was accepted without question in rebutting delinquency reports or making any official statement. All Smith had to do was to deny that he had been involved or admit that the report was correct.

Cass's action undermined the sense of honor Thayer had so carefully developed in the Corps of Cadets.

Almost at the same time, Secretary Cass informed Thayer that the President agreed that the minimum age requirement for an appointment should be sixteen years. Thayer had recommended this age limit to Madison and John Quincy Adams because he felt more mature young men were needed instead of boys. The age limits of from sixteen to twenty-one would remain in effect for many years.

Thayer encountered another problem the day after Christmas. At the request of Cass and Jackson, General Gratiot sent Thayer a copy of the *Charleston Mercury*, describing a meeting of the Young Men's States Rights and Free Trade Association. The group adopted a resolution supporting the Ordinance of Nullification passed by the South Carolina legislature, an act declaring the protective tariff law unconstitutional. The Association also passed a resolution supporting the alleged resolution of Academy southern cadets "who have expressed their determination to adhere to South Carolina." The resolution stated that southern cadets had aroused the wrath of the administration and were "likely to be expelled from their present situation." Gratiot directed Thayer to determine the facts as soon as possible.

Five days later, Thayer reported to Gratiot that there was no justification for the Charleston allegation, there had been no meetings of southern cadets, and there was no indication of any such sentiments in the Corps of Cadets. On January 2, Thayer sent Gratiot a copy of a letter from a Charleston cadet to the editor of the *Charleston Mercury*, denying that any southern cadets supported the South Carolina cause, stating that the cadets, regardless of personal feelings in the matter, "feel bound, on account of their peculiar situation, by every principle of honor and of duty, to withhold those sentiments and to remain neutral." All southern cadets had read and approved the rebuttal. Thayer informed Gratiot that the cadet had written the letter on his own volition, without any interference or suggestion from Thayer.

Thayer must have been pleased by this expression of a high sense of duty and honor, an indication that his efforts to develop this feeling in the Corps had been successful. Although the knowledge that sectionalism existed among the cadets was disturbing, the unanimous support of the cadet writer by southern cadets lessened his concern that sectional feelings might divide the Corps into segmented groups. Such did not happen at this time and did not occur even in the last months before the start of the Civil War.

Word of the Charleston article spread throughout the Corps. Cullum answered his friend, Alfred Huidekoper, who asked if cadets involved would be tried, "You wish to know something about the affair of the South Carolina cadets and the Court Martial. I can tell you it is all a humbug; no meeting has been held by them, neither have any of them been Court Martialed." Cullum indicated that the rumor might have originated when the Secretary of War appointed the

Court in early December to try other cadets for various offenses. He told his friend there had been many complaints "to Gen. Jackson about the injustice of the sentences of Courts composed of West Point officers." Cullum explained that the War Department–appointed Court would set a precedent to govern future cases. Evidently, little took place at West Point that was not known by the Corps.

Cullum told Huidekoper that he might see the letter written by the Charleston cadet in newspapers, asserting "we have no Nullifiers here." Cullum added his opinion of the attitude at West Point: "I am proud to say that 49/50ths would unsheath the sword in defense of the United States against nullification, Indians, or anything else." He added praise for Jackson's message to the Senate about the South Carolina situation and ended his letter by saying, "The Crisis is near at hand. God grant that we may yet escape the horrors of a civil war."

The events of the last six months of 1832 exhausted Thayer. His unsuccessful battle to sustain dismissals of cadets was frustrating. This more than anything else caused him to write his personal letter to Secretary Cass. Cass's comment that the President had nothing personal against Thayer was nullified by Hitchcock's report that Jackson had called Thayer a tyrant. After receiving the Secretary's letter and listening to Hitchcock's report, Thayer discussed resigning with his old friend General Gratiot and gave him a letter of resignation to hold until he could prepare a cover letter addressed to Gratiot.

After the January examinations had been completed, Thayer decided that a cover letter was unnecessary because of the "very friendly and satisfying communication from the Secretary of War in consequence of which I request you to present my resignation without further delay." Thayer sent Gratiot a short letter stating, "I have the honor to tender my resignation as superintendent of the military academy and to request that I may be relieved with as little delay as practicable."

12

I Believe It the Best School in
the World

Thayer's resignation was handed to the Secretary of War at an inopportune time. Cass and his small staff were struggling to handle the dangerous problem of troop assignments in the South during the South Carolina crisis, a step required by the President's public statement that he would use force if necessary to stop the nullification attempt. There were also other problems, including the settlement of pension claims and preparing to submit Indian treaties to Congress. He took no immediate action on Thayer's resignation, merely telling General Gratiot to tell Thayer that it would be acted on at the proper time. That he was surprised and, to a certain degree, shocked is evident, for he also told Gratiot that he could not understand the resignation, which assumed that "an officer possesses the right to decline a service which constitutes an integral part of his legitimate duties." This statement is puzzling because Cass routinely processed requests for reassignment by other officers. Nearly two months passed before Cass informed Gratiot that Thayer's resignation would become effective after the June examinations.

Ten days before he was notified that his resignation was accepted, Thayer was promoted to brevet colonel. The War Department issued other orders affecting the Academy. General Order 48 reduced graduation leave from four to three months, a specification that remained in effect during peacetime for many years. The same order required an officer to serve at least three years with his regiment before being assigned to special duty. This had a direct impact on the Academy because it was customary to assign distinguished graduates as instructors immediately after graduation. This same restriction applied to the War Department staff and other staffs as well, but the West Point faculty interpreted this to be another Jackson attack on the Academy.

Of much more concern to the Academic Board was the statement that an officer could not be requested by name for any staff assignment, including duty at West Point. Assignment requests would indicate only the number of officers required. If this directive was enforced, a request might result in a completely unqualified officer being assigned.

A third restriction limited tours of staff duty to two years. This decreased faculty by at least one year and, in most cases, two or three years. Rapid turnover of instructors would curtail the development of academic teaching ability in these men and lessen the capability of the Academic Board to select instructors for long or repetitive assignments.

A fourth restriction prohibited officers from visiting Washington unless en route to or from their assigned posts. This also applied to cadets. Apparently Cass and Jackson had tired of receiving calls and complaints from officers and cadets; but, again, the unofficial attitude at West Point assumed that the restriction was intended to prevent official visits such as Hitchcock's trip the previous November. This assumption was in error because the order authorized trips "necessary for the public service or for any just right of the individual concerned."

The majority of Academy officers and many cadets considered that everything was directed against West Point instead of understanding that these measures applied army-wide and would be beneficial in the long run if enforced. The impact on the Academy would be severe. There is no indication that the special duty restrictions were ever rigidly enforced. Academy requirements continued to be filled selectively. It can only be assumed that General Gratiot convinced Secretary of War Cass and the President that these restrictions would damage the capabilities of the Academy faculty.

Cadets were greatly upset by the order. George Cullum, now a First Classman, wrote his sister that "an order was published signed by that greatest of all jacknapes, our worthy Commander in Chief General Macomb, depriving all officers who have not done three years of duty with their regiments, of the privilege of being put on extra duty." Cullum protested that the restriction on visiting Washington "beats West Point tyranny; a man not allowed to visit the seat of his government!" Understandably, he complained about the decrease in graduation leave. Cullum, with his ear to the sentiments of faculty friends, provided an accurate picture of the prevailing attitude at the Academy.

There have been many conjectures about the reasons for Thayer's resignation. Many early writers asserted that Jackson disliked the Military Academy and the Regular Army and believed the militia to be the best means of defending the United States. Others stated that Jackson's attitude against Thayer and the Academy was influenced by his nephew and personal secretary, Andrew Jackson Donelson. These theories appear not to be fully supported by facts.

Donelson was an 1820 graduate of West Point, second man in his class and a cadet officer. He entered the Academy in July 1817, serving under Partridge for only a short time. After graduation, he was Jackson's aide-de-camp in Florida for two years. After resigning his commission, Donelson wrote Thayer frequently, often to report on the status of anti-Academy sentiment in Tennessee. Nothing in this correspondence indicates any antagonism toward Thayer. To the contrary, Donelson praised Thayer for the changes made in Academy operations and the resulting improvements.

Jackson was not antagonistic toward either the Army or the Academy. He had learned early that relatively untrained militia could be relied upon in battle only if entrenched in a strong, stationary position as he had insisted at the Battle of New Orleans. He believed in a small but highly trained regular establishment, depending on militia only to support this force. His attitude toward the Academy is best illustrated by a letter he wrote to Andrew Donelson when his younger brother considered asking for a cadet appointment but was not certain this was the course to take. His advice to Andrew was not to persuade his younger brother to accept an appointment unless he truly wanted to become a cadet and follow a military career. If he did not have this intent, it was better to leave the space to some other young man who had the desire. This advice could well be given today to any young man considering applying for appointment. If Daniel Donelson wanted to attend a college, Jackson offered to help with expenses. He ended his letter with "I believe it the best school in the world."

Daniel Donelson entered the Academy and graduated as the fifth man in the Class of 1825. Further evidence of a favorable family attitude toward the Academy came when Andrew Donelson's son entered the Academy to graduate as the second man in the Class of 1848, his father's standing twenty-eight years earlier. He served on the Academy faculty twice for a total of eight years.

There is no question that Jackson reinstated many cadets as a means of repaying political obligations. There are indications that he considered many reasons for dismissal to be trivial offenses; it must be agreed that many of the violations were relatively minor, leaving cadet quarters in barracks or camp, for example. Jackson did approve the dismissal of cadets for many major infractions. Even Cadet Norris, despite Jackson's early leniency and Norris's political connections, was dismissed when he failed to meet what Jackson considered fair regulations.

There are other indications that Jackson and his Secretary of War tried to support Thayer to some degree. The requirement that Courts Martial would be appointed by the War Department and consist of officers not on duty at West Point may have been intended to stop charges of bias by a Court consisting only of officers on duty at the Academy. Jackson and the Secretary had received enough charges of this nature from dismissed cadets to justify the steps taken to end that allegation.

The basic problem was the inability of the Superintendent to award severe punishment for more flagrant violations of regulations without having a cadet tried by Court Martial. The development of the new demerit system with a limit of 200 demerits annually eliminated part of the problem because cadets could be and were awarded demerits for many offenses previously tried by Court

Martial. This policy was instituted only after it had been approved by the Secretary of War, probably with the full knowledge and concurrence of Jackson.

Much emphasis has been placed on the Norris hickory tree episode. Norris was tried for being absent from his tent and leaving camp limits; no mention of the tree planting was included in the court record. Jackson called Thayer a tyrant for punishing Norris for planting the tree; this information must have come from Norris personally. Hitchcock in his diary indicated that Jackson stopped his tirade when Hitchcock gave him the true story. It is possible that this was the first time Jackson had been given Thayer's side of the episode. Jackson had a volatile temper, as shown by his outburst against Thayer; he then showed his fairness. After hearing Hitchcock's explanation, he must have realized that he may have been wrong in accusing Thayer of tyranny, for he ordered a study made of Academy regulations to determine if changes to the existing rules were needed. Had Jackson intended to make major changes in Academy operations, this would have been the time to do so; but no changes were made.

Thayer's promotion would indicate that there was little personal animosity on the part of either Jackson or Cass. It has been stated that Thayer submitted his resignation because he disliked the President, that he resented Jackson's actions, and that he believed it to be better for the Academy. Thayer never criticized Jackson, not during his superintendency or in his voluminous correspondence after he left the Academy. He did not hesitate to criticize Jefferson Davis as a cadet, officer, and Secretary of War. He described Partridge in extremely vindictive terms. But not once did he offer any adverse criticism of Andrew Jackson nor did he make negative comments about any of the Secretaries of War or Presidents under whom he had served. About as close as he came to criticism was the statement, "Politics is a poor business as a profession."

There were many indications of support by the Jackson administration. During Jackson's first four years in office, approval and funds were provided for a new hospital and other buildings. In 1832, Thayer was authorized to erect a building "for military and other exercises" and the funds to begin construction of a chapel. More than $15,000 was provided to repair existing buildings and quarters, almost as much as the amount provided for the exercise building. Funds were increased annually to purchase books, instruments, models, and other items needed for instruction. This support not only equaled that provided by previous administrations, it was far greater.

Thayer was given the opportunity of selecting his next station from the best assignments available to an Engineer officer, including the harbor defenses of New York or Boston. Thayer chose Boston to be near his family home in Braintree. Had any animosity existed in Washington, Thayer would have been given no option; he would have been assigned to Engineer works in Florida or Mississippi or along the Mississippi River. Nothing that occurred during Thayer's last few months at West Point indicates any vindictiveness on the part of Andrew

Jackson. To the contrary, Thayer was treated courteously and many of his requests were approved by the Secretary of War.

The news that Thayer had resigned was a shock to Academy officers, cadets, and graduates. Each member of the First Class called on Thayer individually to express his regrets. Many underclassmen did the same. There were no demonstrations by cadets either to protest Thayer's departure or to rejoice that he was leaving. Cullum indicated to his friend Huidekoper that most of the cadets were truly grieved.

Shortly after Thayer announced his departure to the staff and faculty, all of the officers met to discuss the news and what should be done. There was concern that many instructors and tactical officers might be reassigned because of the restriction imposed by General Order 48, but this did not happen. Other than Hitchcock, only three officers were reassigned, one from each of the three academic departments; and those three were completing a normal tour of duty. This countered a cadet rumor that Jackson intended to remove all officers who had served under Thayer.

The group discussed possible reasons for Thayer's resignation. Cram in a letter to Cullum many years later listed the suppositions discussed. The possibility that Donelson had influenced Jackson was one rumor. The weakness of the rumor is shown by the statement that Donelson as a cadet had taken sides with the "turbulent Partridge cadets"; he had not. Cram admitted in his letter that he did not know if this was true. Another fallacy in the faculty opinion was the concept that Generals Jones and Jessup had come to investigate Thayer's use of the Post Fund to build the hotel. This was untrue, for they had been sent to West Point by Jackson to discuss Cadet Regulations to determine if any changes were needed. Other suppositions were equally unfounded. Cullum blamed Jackson for Thayer's departure, using Cram's letter and other similar statements as the basis for his conclusions.

At the meeting, the officers unanimously agreed to request Thayer to sit for a portrait by Sully, and a subscription list was started. Cram in his letter to Cullum indicated that within a few hours every officer on the Post "had agreed to bear his proportion of the cost of the painting." Professor Davies, the senior member of the Academic Board, and Lieutenants Cram and Tillinghast were selected to call on the Superintendent to obtain his approval. Thayer received the committee in his basement study. When Davies told him the purpose of their visit, Cram said Thayer "was deeply moved by this evidence of esteem, and for some seconds—with eyes full of tears—could not reply." Thayer expressed his thanks and asked that one of the committee return that evening to receive a formal reply.

Tillinghast was selected and returned only to learn that Thayer would not approve the proposal. He said that "any expression of approbation or disapprobation from officers in respect to a commanding officer about being relieved is unmilitary and contrary to the spirit of military discipline." Thayer believed that any approval would reflect adversely on his friends and himself. He asked the committee to destroy the resolution and the subscription list immediately. Cram called Thayer's decision "the degree of his sense of military propriety in respect to resolutions of military gentlemen."

Professor Robert W. Weir later painted two portraits of Thayer. Many years later, Dr. Edward S. Holden, the USMA Librarian, discovered that Sully had painted a portrait of Thayer in 1831 and that the portrait was at Dartmouth College. Thayer must have sat for Sully, but there are no records of where or exactly when this was done. Holden indicated that "through the kindness of the President of Dartmouth, the USMA has been permitted to make a copy in oil of the original." This was completed in time for the Centennial Observance of the founding of the Academy in 1902.

In the ensuing weeks, cadets often mentioned in letters that Thayer walked carefully around the Post. An early riser who often passed cadet barracks before reveille, Thayer extended his walks in different directions each day. He seemed to be making a mental comparison of the Academy with what it had been when he arrived sixteen years earlier. There was a new dock and stone house for the sentry and visitors who landed in inclement weather. The path to the level of the Plain had been widened and graded. To the west, on the shore level, were the new enlisted barracks and quarters for married soldiers in the area once known as Camp Town. The old, dilapidated hospital building had been renovated and was now used as quarters. In the distance were the two warehouses in which Revolutionary War relics were stored. On the bluff above was the cemetery with the white Cadet Monument shining in the sun.

To the left of the path on the level of the Plain was a knoll on which stood the Wood Monument. It had been moved there from its original location in front of South Barracks. The flag pole was near the monument. Between the knoll and the path was a small, irregular plot of earth. When word spread that Thayer was leaving, an old man named Cronk, who had a farm above Buttermilk Falls, brought an elm sapling to Thayer and asked permission to plant the tree. Thayer offered to provide an enlisted detail to help, but Cronk declined, saying that he wanted to plant the tree himself "as a tribute of friendship to a great and true man." The tree was planted in this irregular plot, the triangular spot between today's Howard and Ruger Roads.

To the left on the level ground on the site of the old Ordnance Compound were two small buildings occupied by a shoemaker, a tailor, and the post office. The cottage formerly occupied by Mrs. Thompson became quarters after she moved to a house near the cadet mess. A carpenter shop was in a building nearby.

From Wood Monument, Thayer could see the row of new duplex quarters, Professors' Row, and a small set of quarters near the west gate. The sluice used for cadet bathing was not visible; it was beyond a bend near the gate. Water had been piped to the quarters and barracks from a reservoir dammed at the present Delafield Pond under the direction of Lieutenant Church shortly after his graduation in 1828. There were no indoor bathrooms with running water. Water was carried from taps near the quarters or barracks. There were outhouses behind each set of quarters and larger "sinks" near the barracks and summer camp area.

Walking from Wood Monument toward his home, Thayer passed the Commandant's quarters north of his own residence. A wide dirt road extended south from these houses. Across the pond next to his quarters were two sets of brick quarters occupied by professors. Next to these was the old wooden house occupied by Mrs. Thompson and her daughters. Before Mrs. Thompson moved into these quarters, one wing was moved to the northwest near the rocky slope. It was used as the post school; the schoolmaster lived on the upper floor. A white picket fence ran along the road in front of the row of quarters. Between the fence and the road were a wide gravel walk and a row of elm trees. A row of what Church called "ugly Lombardy poplars," elms, and maples bordered the western edge of the road. The grove of twelve elms planted by Swift and Macomb in 1802 stood across the road from Mrs. Thompson's home in front of the cadet mess. This was the site of Fourth of July dinners.

The road made a sharp left turn just beyond the mess and extended to the edge of the bluff of the river. The mess building had been renovated and improved during Thayer's superintendency. Across the road were several sets of small quarters for faculty members and a small cadet garden whose vegetables supplemented the produce of a larger garden near the cemetery. A small bakery near the garden provided bread and pastries for the mess and for sale to families. Immediately east was the Academic Building and next to it, South Barracks. There were a few small quarters across the road and a building used as a "market house" for farmers bringing produce to sell to post personnel. North Barracks was perpendicular to South Barracks, extending north into the Plain. There were still springs near each barracks as well as pumps for the water piped from the reservoir.

To the south was the old Gridley tavern, now used as quarters. The wood yard, the means of so many cadets escaping to Gridley's tavern, was still north of that building. Thayer had erected buildings at the intersection of the road in front of the barracks with the road leading south to Buttermilk Falls. One was the gun shed, a structure consisting of twenty doors facing north to permit easy entrance for guns. This was the first time cannon could be sheltered during bad weather. Across from the gun shed was a new laboratory with thick brick walls. The small rooms used by cadets making pyrotechnics had thick walls as a safety precaution. A small stable and a blacksmith shop were located in the southern corners of the woodyard. The few horses kept here were carriage horses. It would be some time before horses would be available for artillery and cavalry training.

The new stone hospital and several other buildings were located across the road to the southwest. About a thousand yards south was the south gate to the Post. The road continued on through the Kinsley property to Buttermilk Falls.

A small path near the gate curved up the hill toward the ruins of Forts Webb and Wyllys, Revolutionary War redoubts.

A road extended along the bluff, through Fort Clinton, to the hotel. Another path near the north turn of the road led to Kosciuszko's Garden, a favorite retreat for cadets. About fifty yards north, approximately on the site of the present West Point Army Mess, was a small house that had been the quarters of Bandmaster Willis until his death. Across the road on the edge of a small depression was a brick building used as the office of the Post Quartermaster.

Fort Clinton had deteriorated greatly in the forty years since it was restored during the French crisis. It was no longer used, and its magazines were barred; powder once stored here had been moved to a new magazine beyond the warehouses in the Camp Town area. Kosciuszko's Monument stood on the northeast parapet of Fort Clinton.

The road from Fort Clinton continued to the hotel and then curved to join the road leading to the dock. The hotel stood on a promontory overlooking the Hudson River. A narrow winding path, called "Chain Path" because it led to the spot where the Revolutionary chain had been moored, wound slowly down the bluff to the river and along the bank to Gees Point. This today is "Flirtation Walk."

Ruins of the Long Barracks and the old Provost near Execution Hollow had been removed. A stone ice house was nestled in the hollow, low enough to keep it away from most sunlight. The summer camp site extended along the west edge of Fort Clinton toward the hollow. A path, from the road north of the hollow to the cadet barracks area, had been developed to provide ready access to the barracks area by buglers and other enlisted men living in the Long Barracks. Cadets used it as the best way to get to the hotel.

The parade ground occupied the area from the path to the road in front of Thayer's quarters. Cadets formed for parade in front of the barracks, followed the band north along the edge of the path, and wheeled to form a line facing Professor Row. Thayer could watch the parades from his veranda or walk across the road to take a review. Normally, the Commandant of Cadets was the reviewing officer.

Other than quarters, enlisted barracks, work buildings, and other similar structures, there had been no major construction during Thayer's tenure. Plans were underway to build a chapel and a building for indoor military drills and other exercise. The chapel would be located on the site of the woodyard. The exercise building was being designed, but its exact location had not been determined.

Most of the Plain had been leveled and small hollows filled. Hollows near camp and the barracks were gradually being filled. Debris from the ruins of the Long Barracks and the old Provost had been dumped in the camp hollow. Most large boulders had been removed. Some were used in building projects, others pulverized to use on roads or as land fill. Only one large boulder remained near the proposed site of the chapel.

Many trees had been planted around the Plain, near the quarters, and around the hotel. Almost every set of quarters had at least one cherry tree, which was a constant temptation to cadets. There was grass in the parade area, but the remainder of the Plain was rough ground, suitable for artillery drill but little else. Lawns in and around the quarters were also sown, and many of the quarters had gardens. As he made his daily rounds, Thayer must have been pleased with the appearance of the Post; it had a pleasant and warm appearance despite its military function.

Preparing for the June examinations, his last official duty as Superintendent, Thayer must have reflected on the changes made in the curriculum during his tenure. He had taken command of an Academy without any firm curricular plan and developed that institution into the leading engineering and scientific school in the United States. Its graduates had already had a profound and positive impact on the Army. Their contributions were not restricted to military activities. Many graduates had put their uniforms aside to contribute to the engineering development of the nation and to aid in establishing other scientific schools. Thayer must have felt that he had achieved the goals he had been given: "to create, to construct, to build up from the foundation under difficulties coming more from within than from without; and then to preserve and defend what had been accomplished against the assiduous attacks of its enemies." This he had done; he was now ready to turn the Academy over to his successor, Major Rene E. DeRussy.

Few officers have assumed command under the disadvantages DeRussy would face. His predecessor had achieved national recognition for his development of the Military Academy into one of the finest academic institutions in the United States. His friends included Winfield Scott, Gouverneur Kemble, John Calhoun, James Monroe, George Ticknor, and Hamilton Fish. Among the Academy graduates were sons of Monroe, Henry Clay, and the Vice President, Martin Van Buren. He had survived constant criticism by the press and Congress. Colleges had honored him with honorary degrees, and he had been recognized militarily by two promotions. Was Thayer a superman or only a man?

It is difficult to analyze Sylvanus Thayer as an individual. So much has been written about him that the countless pages used tend to shroud the man in an aura of near-saintliness. He has been called a genius, an outstanding academician, a father figure beloved by his officers and cadets. Much of this hero worship must be attributed to George Cullum, who first called him the "Father of the Military Academy." Cullum went to extremes to preserve the Thayer legend. He withheld material giving credit to Partridge when he published his history of the Academy in the third volume of his *Register*. There are indications that Cullum also preserved the unproven story that Thayer resigned because of his dispute with Jackson. Loss of many early records led many earlier historians to accept Cullum's statements. In recent years, newly discovered personal papers have provided a different view of much of the Thayer legend. Unfortunately, his niece destroyed many of his personal papers after his death, letters to his family and other material that might have provided better insight into the inner man.

Sylvanus Thayer was a quiet man with great natural dignity. That he had natural scholastic ability is quite evident. He was the valedictorian of his Dartmouth Class. Although he was the third man in the Academy Class of 1808, this is not an indication of his academic rank because there was no list of merit during the Partridge period. His scholarship is better indicated by his accomplishments as Superintendent. He participated fully in all Academic Board discussions and gave keen professional advice to his professors. Ticknor and others recorded his scholastic supervision of annual examinations. His knowledge of every subject in which cadets were tested showed comprehensive knowledge of all levels of each course. Thayer spent two years at West Point from 1810 to 1811, teaching some classes during this period. Despite his knowledge and teaching ability, Thayer taught no classes as Superintendent, a contrast to Partridge, who tried to teach any class at any time. He was a member of the American Academy of Arts and Sciences, the American Philosophical Society, the Military Philosophical Society, and many other scholarly groups. His talents were recognized militarily by chairmanship of the Board of Engineers for Coastal Defenses and membership on many Engineer, Artillery, and Ordnance special panels analyzing new methods and techniques. There are many other examples of his professional, scientific, and scholastic abilities too numerous to mention.

Thayer was a quiet man who had the respect of every member of his staff and most of his cadets. Like the captain of a naval ship of war, Thayer was a loner who had no close friends among his officers. He never married. One story maintains that the young lady of his affections married another man after Thayer entered the Academy, but the story cannot be verified. He enjoyed female company, and many writings describe the warm attitude he displayed toward all ladies regardless of their age. Despite his efforts to stop cadet intemperance, Thayer was not a teetotaler. More than most men of that period, he enjoyed fine wine, perhaps a taste he had developed during his two-year sojourn in France. The dinners and other entertainments he hosted at West Point were commented upon enthusiastically by individuals he had invited to attend. It is curious, however, that none of the descriptions of Thayer indicate that he was popular or well liked.

It is quite possible and very probable that Thayer deliberately made little effort to be popular. Knowing that favoritism and partiality had caused many of Partridge's problems, Thayer insisted on fairness and impartiality in all associations between officers and cadets. He himself set the example by treating every officer, cadet, enlisted man, and family member equally, fairly, and even coldly. Every officer, enlisted man, and most cadets respected him. Local residents, wealthy landowners and small farmers alike, admired him greatly. He was admired and respected, but there is no indication that he was well liked.

Cadets at that time, as now, coined nicknames for officers and enlisted men they particularly liked. Worth was "Haughty Bill." Drawing Teacher Gimbrede was called "Jim Brede" because many cadets pronounced his name in this way. Most of the officers of Thayer's time had cadet nicknames. Even Partridge, who was popular with at least the cadets whom he favored, had the nickname "Old Pewter," possibly because of his non-regulation gray uniform. Thayer, however, was always referred to as "the Colonel," or "the Superintendent," or "Colonel Thayer." No record has been found of any cadet or officer calling him anything else.

Most existing cadet letters memoirs speak of Thayer with respect; none show either like or dislike. This is odd because these same cadets did not hesitate to indicate officers who were popular or that some, such as Lieutenant Kinsley, were not. A few descriptions of Thayer indicate that he was not well liked by the cadets. It is best to ignore H. Ariel Norris and other cadets who were dismissed during Thayer's superintendency. As might be expected, they had little good to say about Thayer; but these dissatisfied cadets expressed no dislike of him as an individual. Perhaps the most accurate and completely acceptable statement was made by Cadet Robert E. Lee in a letter to his family. Lee said that cadets disliked Thayer and accused him of espionage because he always seemed to know everything that took place within the Corps and because he had complete information about every cadet at his fingertips. He maintained that Thayer would listen to any accusation against a cadet regardless of the source. Lee also called Thayer an austere man who refused to accept sentiment or emotion in others.

Without doubt, Thayer knew more about each cadet than the cadet may have known about himself. He also was aware of much that went on in the Corps, as evidenced by his advance knowledge of Jefferson Davis's eggnog party. He was equally informed about activities of each of his officers. Not well known were his many gestures of kindness and help to cadets and officers. He often counseled cadets with academic problems or consoled them when a family member died. Despite restricting furloughs, Thayer often gave a cadet leave to go home when problems there justified this unusual action. He often wrote unsolicited letters of recommendation for his cadets many years after they graduated. His voluminous correspondence with Cullum, written over a period of twenty years, shows that Thayer watched the careers of all of his cadets, including those who resigned their commissions. When a member of the Class of 1820 wrote Thayer in 1853 asking about one of his classmates, Thayer sent him a summary of what each classmate had done since graduation. Thayer may have been austere, dignified, and even aloof; but he was also a very compassionate, understanding, and warm individual.

Thayer was often accused of being an extremely hard disciplinarian. Those accusations must be accepted as being true. He was hard: hard on the cadets, hard on the officers, but equally hard on himself. He was a firm believer in discipline—not good discipline—just discipline. It is quite evident that Thayer maintained there was no such thing as bad discipline; if discipline was considered bad, it could not be called discipline. Perhaps General John M. Schofield's definition of discipline, ''That discipline which makes the soldier of a free country reliable in battles is not to be gained by harsh and tyrannical treatment,'' best defines the discipline in which Thayer believed.

Coupled to this belief in discipline was Thayer's insistence on high standards of honor and duty. A cadet's word was always accepted as truth, and no effort was ever made to show that a cadet had lied when he made an official statement. Duty was considered even more important. Thayer expected cadet officers to report delinquencies of other cadets as a routine duty. He expected a cadet sentinel to prevent other cadets from crossing his posts without permission; this was the sentinel's duty. He expected cadet subdivision inspectors to maintain order in their assigned section of barracks; this was their duty. He expected each cadet room orderly to keep his room neat and to prevent disturbances in the room, even by his roommates. This was his duty.

Much has been written about Thayer's reasons for insisting on high standards of duty and honor but always from the standpoint of their impact upon the Corps of Cadets. After the War of 1812, most Americans disliked and distrusted the Army, feelings inherited from their fathers, who considered a regular military force nothing more than continuation of the British imposition on colonists. Thayer knew that when he accepted the Academy superintendency his normal career no longer existed. He and his contemporaries often discussed the need for professionalism in the Army, a professionalism that would bring greater acceptance by Americans. In Thayer's opinion, one indication of true military professionalism was a high standard of both duty and honor. By instilling this sense in young cadets, Thayer hoped that as graduates they would disseminate their own sense of duty and honor throughout the Army. He believed that this, coupled with the education and professional training gained as cadets, would gradually change military service from a trade to a profession. When Thayer resigned in 1833, much of what he had hoped was already taking place. By the end of the Mexican War, his graduated cadets had accomplished this unspoken mission. Professional officers and even graduates who had resigned from the Army had the respect of the average American and even more from colleges, scientists, and engineers throughout the country.

Another accusation aimed at Thayer by Partridge and others accused him of being unable to control cadets as evidenced by the eggnog riot, arson, assault of officers, and other types of cadet demonstrations. That these events occurred is true. What was ignored by the accusers and many writers since was the fact that cadets represent their contemporaries elsewhere in the country. At the time Thayer faced these problems, other colleges encountered the same unrest. Young Americans, particularly Jacksonians, rebelled against anything institutional. Harvard had an insurrection more disastrous than the West Point eggnog riot. Students dropped cannon balls from upper story windows and sprayed professors with ink and water. In another Harvard demonstration, bonfires were fed with wooden bombs that exploded and injured instructors. A series of rebellions at the University of Virginia continued until an instructor was murdered. Cadet dislike of chapel services was also mirrored elsewhere. At Princeton, a student riot caused by religious dislike resulted in broken glass, fires in buildings, and student unrest. Princeton had at least six violent demonstrations between 1800 and 1830. Thayer was not alone in facing evidence of student dissatisfaction.

Thayer believed, as he wrote to James Monroe, that the head of an educational institution should administer his duties in a fatherly manner. This was perhaps the reason that Thayer wanted to know everything possible about each cadet and about the Corps as an entity. His concern for cadet welfare was shown in many ways. His early discussions with Gouverneur Kemble concerning the possible use of gas to heat and light barracks was based on his realization that the fireplaces and candles were not adequate for warmth or study. Knowing that cadets suffered from cold winters without any prescribed overcoat, he finally obtained approval and design of a cadet overcoat despite the bureaucratic tendency to make no change. He also obtained approval for a better and more comfortable shoe. Perhaps his greatest uniform improvement was the fatigue uniform and soft cap instituted to save cadet funds. The gradual increase in availability of cots was another Thayer contribution. Sleeping on a pallet on the floor was hardly conducive to the rest needed by cadets. A more balanced diet came when Thayer brought Cozzens to West Point as mess steward. His many actions to improve cadet life show the humane side of his very complex character.

Thayer was a perfectionist and, to some degree, an egoist as well. He believed, as one cadet wrote home, that there was a reason for everything; and, since there was a reason, everything should be done well. Proper recognition and reward were given to those who excelled. This was the purpose of the academic merit list and publication of names of the first five men in each class in the *Army Register*. He gave recognition to cadet instructors by special privileges not available to other cadets. The demerit system was another innovation based upon Thayer's sense of perfection. Cadets of the First Class were expected to receive fewer demerits in their senior year than plebes. His egoism is shown to some degree by the quiet way that he accepted compliments for his accomplishments, a manner that indicated that one could expect nothing other than near perfection.

Although Thayer may have thought that he had ended his military career by accepting the superintendency, his advice was often asked by other officers. Several times, new tactics manuals were reviewed at West Point and tested using the Corps of Cadets as a maneuver group. Thayer was always asked to participate and his comments often brought changes in the original proposals. After his resignation, he was consulted about military affairs and individuals. His astute analysis of human character is shown in many of his letters to Cullum. In a letter to Cullum immediately before the first Battle of Bull Run, Thayer predicted that the force making the first attack would lose the battle because relatively untrained troops, the militia, would break and run when fired upon. His prediction proved true; Union forces attacked, were repulsed by the Confederates, and fled in panic.

The system Thayer instituted would endure for many years. His curriculum continued without major changes for over a hundred years. His disciplinary methods were retained even longer. The academic merit list, the demerit system, and much of the Academy terminology are still used today, modified but still basically the same. Thayer may not have been the founder of the Military Academy, but he certainly deserved Cullum's appellation of being its father. He found a disorganized institution filled with undisciplined cadets who were taught only a smattering of academic and military subjects by discontented instructors. As he prepared to leave West Point, he could look on a well-drilled, well-trained, highly educated Corps of Cadets taught by a qualified faculty. He had accomplished his mission.

Major DeRussy came to West Point for the June examinations. He sat beside Thayer but took no direct part in testing the cadets. One evening, Thayer hosted the Board of Visitors at a dinner in the hotel. Joel R. Poinsett, a friend of Thayer and President of the Board, remarked that the examinations were the best he had ever witnessed. Unfortunately, he made what he intended to be a compliment, saying that he did not understand how the cadets could be so well prepared without previous knowledge of the test material. This was reported to Thayer by a member of the faculty after dinner.

Thayer ordered the class involved to be assembled the next morning to be retested. He carefully explained the reason to the cadets; he felt this necessary to remove any possible stigma caused by Poinsett's unfortunate remark. Cadet attitude was described by Cadet Francis H. Smith: "The examination was resumed and continued with the deepest interest, each member of the class feeling that an appeal was made to his honor as well as his pride." The re-examination over, Poinsett praised the cadets highly and expressed his chagrin at the misinterpretation of what he had intended to be a compliment.

Before leaving the Academy, each member of the graduating class went to Thayer to make a personal farewell. Thayer made it known throughout the Corps that he wanted no demonstrations when he departed—no band, no honors, no review by the cadets. He remembered all too well the riotous departure given Partridge and the equally flamboyant welcome when he returned. Thayer was so determined to leave quietly that he did not announce when he would depart.

Always an avid walker, he began to walk to the north dock each evening at the time the down-river steamer passed the Academy. Many officers and cadets often walked to the dock to welcome guests or watch the steamer pass. One evening, Lieutenant Cram and several others were at the dock when Thayer walked up. The steamboat pulled in and moored to discharge passengers and cargo. This done, the captain signaled a final warning in preparation for leaving. Cram wrote that Thayer suddenly turned, said only two words, "Goodbye, gentlemen," and stepped on board after quietly shaking hands with each officer and cadet. The steamboat pulled away as the watchers stood in astonished silence. Thayer was gone; he would not return.

1833–1852

I give it as my fixed opinion that but for our graduated cadets, the war with the United States and Mexico might, and probably would have lasted some four or five years, with, in its first half, more defeats than victories, falling to our share.

WINFIELD SCOTT

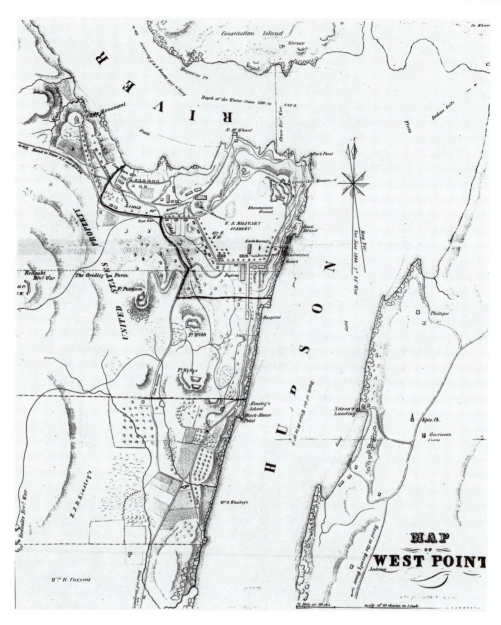

The Academy in 1844. This map from Colton's 1844 *A Guide to West Point and Vicinity* shows the Exercise House built in 1836–1838 and converted into the Academic Building after the 1815 building burned in 1838. Clearly shown are the Cadet Monument in the Cemetery and enlisted quarters in Camptown. The 1836 Chapel and the 1841 Library are east of the Academic Building; to the south is the Cadet Hospital. South of the Post are the Kinsley School, conducted by Zebina J. D. Kinsley, Class of 1819, for older officers' children and to prepare candidates for the Academy entrance examinations. Blockhouse Point was the site of a Revolutionary War blockhouse.

13

A Firm Hand Is Needed

Selection of Major Rene DeRussy to succeed Thayer was a surprise. He was the last man to graduate in the Class of 1812, not because he had the lowest grades but because class rank during the Partridge period was based only upon the date of commissioning. He had served with distinction in the War of 1812 and was promoted to brevet captain. After the war, he continued the building of fortifications in New York Harbor, first as Assistant Engineer and then as Supervising Engineer from 1818 to 1821. After working on fortifications on the Gulf of Mexico, he returned to New York for a second tour from 1825 to 1833.

It has been alleged that he was appointed by President Jackson because he graduated before Thayer became superintendent and had no direct contact with Thayer or the Academy. This contention ignores several facts. Both Thayer and DeRussy were appointed cadets on March 20, 1807, and were together until Thayer graduated in February 1808. Thayer returned as an instructor during DeRussy's last year as a cadet. DeRussy and Thayer probably met often during DeRussy's service in New York because contact between the Academy faculty and Engineer officers supervising New York fortifications was routine.

There are other reasons for questioning the allegation. It was mandatory that the superintendent be a senior Engineer officer. There were only four Engineer officers senior to DeRussy. Joseph Totten, an 1805 Academy graduate, senior to DeRussy, had won two brevet promotions during the War of 1812, had supervised the construction of many fortifications, had been a member of several Boards of Visitors, and had far more administrative experience than DeRussy. Many thought that he would be selected, but his seniority as brevet colonel and the importance of his duties in Boston may have eliminated him from consideration. Charles Gratiot, a brigadier general and Chief of Engineers, obviously could not be considered. Another possibility was John Abert, Class of 1811 and a brevet lieutenant colonel, but he could not be appointed because he held a commission in the Topographical Engineer Corps; the superintendent by law had to be an Engineer officer. The fourth senior officer was Thayer.

It was common during this period for an officer to decline an assignment, and there was precedent for refusing appointment as superintendent. McRee had done so in 1817 prior to the selection of Thayer. Totten may have declined the superintendency. Whatever the reason for not appointing Totten, only DeRussy was available if seniority was a primary factor in selecting Thayer's replacement.

There were only eighteen Engineer officers junior to DeRussy although fifty-two graduates had been commissioned in the Corps of Engineers from 1812 to 1832. Thirty-four had transferred to other branches of the Army, resigned, or died on active duty. Of the eighteen remaining, five were captains and thirteen, lieutenants. All eighteen may have been considered too junior to be appointed. Three later became superintendents: Henry Brewerton, Richard Delafield, and Robert E. Lee; and three were appointed professors: William Bartlett, Edward Courtenay, and Dennis Mahan. Their junior rank at the time probably eliminated them from consideration regardless of their qualifications.

The prohibition against appointing officers of other arms was part of the 1802 Act establishing the Military Academy. Thayer and others had asked that the restriction be removed, but Congress had not accepted the recommendations. There were many regular officers, especially those in Artillery regiments, who were admirably qualified for the position. Qualified or not, they could not be considered.

There were few immediate changes after Thayer's departure. DeRussy had arrived at West Point before the annual examinations. He sat quietly beside Thayer as members of the faculty and the Board of Visitors tested each cadet. Thayer participated fully in his usual manner, displaying his comprehensive knowledge of each subject. DeRussy listened quietly as the Board of Visitors questioned Thayer about every aspect of Academy operations. He watched cadets display their ability to perform infantry and artillery movements for the visitors. More than ten days of observation gave him an excellent overview of Thayer's Academy.

Thayer continued to brief DeRussy during two weeks before his unannounced departure. DeRussy was with Thayer when cadets came to his office. He joined Thayer in reviewing results of the examination as each professor discussed the grades given various cadets. Hitchcock escorted DeRussy through the barracks and the Cadet Mess. He joined tactical officers in their inspection of tents in summer camp, watched formal guard mounts, drills, and parades. Professors discussed their courses with him. By the time Thayer departed, DeRussy had been given nearly a month of orientations and discussions, a comprehensive review of all aspects of Academy operations, as well as an understanding of some of the problems he would face and the improvements he should consider.

Hitchcock left a few days after Thayer. Major John Fowle, the new Commandant of Cadets, arrived on July 10. His appointment was more astounding than DeRussy's selection as superintendent. Fowle was not an Academy graduate. He had been commissioned a second lieutenant in the 9th Infantry Regiment in April 1812. Wounded during the War of 1812, he was transferred to the Paymaster Corps. His post-war service was on the frontier or on recruiting service. From 1824 to 1827, he was on an extended leave. In March 1833 he was promoted to major and transferred to the 3rd Infantry, less than three months before he became Commandant. Fowle's service in Minnesota and Michigan and on recruiting duty showed little if any special qualification for his assignment to West Point.

Contrary to some expectations among the faculty and the Corps of Cadets, there were no drastic changes in the faculty or the tactical staff. One tactical officer and three assistant professors were reassigned during 1833. They were not replaced immediately, and DeRussy was confronted with the same problem encountered constantly by Thayer: a shortage of qualified tactical officers and instructors. Forced to continue using cadets as acting assistant professors, DeRussy complained strongly to Secretary of War Cass. His protests were ignored in the same way that many of Thayer's complaints had been treated.

Rumors continued to spread through the Corps of Cadets. The selection of Major Fowle to be Commandant led to the assumption that other changes would be made. Cadet William Frazer, Class of 1836, wrote to his brother that "Jackson was going to clear every officer off of the Point, professors and all, but Major DeRussy told him that he would try them another year and find out those that were fit to stay." He then added a vindictive note, saying that "Jackson is not agoing to have the cadets treated like a parcel of dogs by those lazy drunken officers, which has been the case too long." This comment was one result of Jackson's leniency in reinstating cadets dismissed for misconduct.

The rumors caused widespread discontent among the cadets. Many letters to parents and friends complained of prejudice on the part of professors and instructors or mistreatment by tactical officers. Much of this discontent can be attributed to slackened discipline. Although Thayer's 1829 regulations were still unchanged—War Department approval was required for any revision and DeRussy had not initiated any changes—the regulations were not strictly enforced. One significant example was DeRussy's approval for wine and champagne to be served at the Fourth of July dinner. Several cadets wrote to parents about rampant overindulgence by many of their friends. Despite the regulation that cadets were not to have any money, many wrote home asking for funds. One or two even indicated that they needed cash to obtain "flapjacks at Havens'." In all probability, the flapjacks were accompanied by Benny's cider flip.

A strong superintendent could have coped with an inept commandant who had no prior contact with the Academy or its cadets. Such an individual might have been guided by example and instruction. Unfortunately, DeRussy was not a strong leader, and he failed to give Fowle the direction so badly needed. He also failed to set an example for either Fowle or the cadets, joining in cadet activities, including the Fourth of July celebration. One cadet commented on his dancing at cadet balls; another compared him with Thayer in an unfavorable manner.

Young tactical officers gradually tightened discipline. Cadets who had expected minor punishment for major misdemeanors found themselves facing trial by Court Martial. The courts recommended dismissal in many cases, but cadets continued to make personal appeals to Jackson and Cass; they were often reinstated.

One dismissal was referred to Attorney General Benjamin F. Butler in late 1833. After reviewing the case, Butler ruled that the court had been instructed to impose the maximum sentence possible and ignored the evidence presented by the Trial Judge Advocate in its findings. This, stated Butler, was "an error that involves a serious violation of principle." The cadet involved was reinstated.

The ruling of the Attorney General had far greater ramifications. Members of a court were appointed by the War Department and instructed in their duties by the Judge Advocate General. Apparently instructions given after Butler's ruling directed courts to impose punishments other than the maximum when evidence so indicated. Several trials of cadets who had gone beyond cadet limits after taps brought far more lenient punishment than the automatic dismissal of the Thayer period. Cadet Lucien D. Cabanne was sentenced to ten days in the light prison, attending all of his normal duties during this period, and required to perform fifteen extra tours of guard duty for leaving his post while on guard duty. William D. Grandin was sentenced to dismissal for being absent from the post for two days, but the court recommended that this sentence be commuted to thirty days in the light prison and twenty extra tours of guard duty. Other sentences of dismissal carried a recommendation that the sentence be remitted because of the youth and inexperience of the cadets involved or because a tactical officer testified in favor of the cadet.

Despite this more liberal attitude, many cadets sentenced to be dismissed appealed directly to the Secretary of War or the President. In many instances they were reinstated. By 1835, Jackson had tired of receiving complaints and pleas for reinstatement from cadets, their fathers, or influential politicians. After receiving an appeal from Cadet Marcus M. Hammond, who had been dismissed for organizing a combination against authority, the President ordered him reinstated but directed DeRussy to read a strong warning to the Corps. Hammond, he indicated, had been guilty of a serious military offence. "I had hoped that a lenient system of administration would be found sufficient for the Military Academy—But I have been disappointed; and it is now time to be more rigorous in enforcing its discipline." Jackson emphasized that in the future the sentence of a court, when legal and proper, would be confirmed. Punishments would be remitted only when recommended by a court or when circumstances "appear so very favorable as to justify such a measure." Jackson meant what he said and did not again interfere with Academy discipline.

DeRussy was fortunate in one respect; the faculty he inherited continued to supervise academic matters in the Thayer tradition. Mahan, Bartlett, Berard, and Davies formed a cadre that molded new professors, young officer instructors, and cadet assistants into a viable and competent faculty. Thayer's curriculum remained unchanged.

Some cadets criticized the emphasis on mathematics and science. Isaac Stevens, who would graduate first in the Class of 1839, wrote to a friend that the curriculum "is not calculated generally to strengthen and improve the mind as much as a four years' course of study should." Although he recognized that some individual capabilities were highly developed, he considered others to be neglected. "Its effect," he said "is to cast the mind in a strong mould without embellishing or polishing it." To Stevens, the curriculum neglected general information essential to a man of liberal education. In his opinion, there would be an advantage in studying political economics and elementary principles of composition, history, and literature.

Stevens made up for this deficiency by reading and participating in Dialectic Society activities. He found many history books in the Academy library. The Dialectic Society library provided volumes on other subjects. His family sent him novels and other works. He wrote to his sister that he had read all of Sir Walter Scott's novels and the writings of Franklin, Plutarch, Addison, Rollins, Sparks, and Burke. Among discussion topics of the Dialectic Society were "In jury trials, ought the twelve jurors be required to be unanimous?," "The importance of a good style of writing to an officer of the Army," and "The proper study of mankind is man."

There were academic problems caused by cadet complaints. In 1834, Cadet John Sanders sent a petition to Secretary Cass in the name of several members of the First Class, complaining about Professor Mahan and the course in Military and Civil Engineering. The cadets complained about the course content, especially the time devoted to civil engineering compared to the time allocated to military engineering. They took exception to the changes in class standing resulting from the January examinations in Mahan's course. They accused Mahan of misconduct in the classroom and "an unnecessary exhibition of temper."

Mahan was never popular with cadets during his long tenure as a professor. As is often true of brilliant individuals, he was intolerant of those who were unable to keep pace with his rapid thinking. To cadets he appeared to be cold and extremely sarcastic. He demanded perfection; few of his students could meet that demand. Cadets respected Mahan the scholar and detested Mahan the man.

Sanders' letter caused Cass to appoint a Court of Inquiry to investigate the charges against Mahan. After meeting with cadets and Mahan, the Court mildly censured both sides. Mahan, it stated, was "irritable, sarcastic, & uncourteous in his official intercourse with the First Class of the Corps of Cadets." The Court ruled that although Mahan had told his students that he "was willing to give them personal satisfaction for any differences they might have with him of a private nature," his statement was not made with any intention of accepting a challenge to a duel.

The Court did not find that Mahan's conduct was caused by any intention to deliberately "offend, insult, or wound" the feelings of cadets under his supervision. It attributed his words and actions to his irritable disposition but placed equal blame on the frequent improper conduct of the cadets. The findings of the Court were a Solomon-like solution: "There was no deliberate intention by either party in the controversy to do wrong, yet it is manifest that the conduct of both had been improper & perhaps deserving of reprehension."

DeRussy's poor administrative ability soon became apparent to Academy officers and to the War Department as well. Required monthly reports to the Chief of Engineers and Secretary of War were often late. Part of the responsibility belonged to the professors, who were consistently late in submitting their weekly and monthly reports to DeRussy.

Adjutant, Captain Charles F. Smith, who had served Thayer as an instructor in Infantry tactics and adjutant for more than four years, was unable to fully accomplish his work because of these problems. Major Fowle's inexperience brought similar delays involving the supervision of cadet tactical instruction and discipline. Smith was able to get better cooperation from young tactical officers and instructors, but he could not persuade the professors to meet their deadlines. This required strong direction by DeRussy, direction that he apparently could not or was reluctant to give.

DeRussy's indecisiveness was frustrating to both his subordinates and higher headquarters. This inability to make a decision finally caused a real problem. As was normal in any hospital of that period, visiting hours were restricted. Chaplain Thomas Warner ignored the regulations, and Chief Medical Officer William V. Wheaton reported this to DeRussy, who decided to prefer charges against Warner. Before a Court Martial could be appointed, DeRussy decided to withdraw the charges. Because Court Martial members were appointed by the War Department, the matter was known to the Secretary of War, but no official action was taken.

Chaplain Warner resented the steps taken by Wheaton and DeRussy. In his opinion, Wheaton's rules should not apply to a cleric giving solace to members of his congregation. A few months later, Warner visited Winfield Scott's family at the hotel and told Mrs. Scott that a cadet had died because of negligence by the hospital staff. Mrs. Scott passed the information to her husband. A Court of Inquiry was appointed. Its findings cleared the surgeon and DeRussy, as his commanding officer. The findings also stated that Warner had been wrong in giving the Scotts a rumor when he had no direct knowledge of what had actually transpired. The Court indicated that Warner had acted without malice. This incident further damaged DeRussy's status with both the Chief of Engineers and the Secretary of War.

Another indication of DeRussy's inability to make a decision involved the construction of a chapel and exercise hall. Funds for both had been appropriated and initial planning was underway before Thayer's departure. Because of DeRussy's reluctance to approve the plans, work on the chapel did not start until 1834. Plans for the exercise hall were changed to provide a new Academic Building with exercise rooms on the ground floor. Construction finally started in late 1836.

Cadet letters and later memoirs do not indicate that the Corps was aware of any of these problems. DeRussy was well liked by cadets, who found him amiable and very cordial, a contrast to Thayer's reserved manner. The strict academic schedule was continued, and cadets had no more free time than during the Thayer period. They still complained about the food in the Mess Hall, and many made after-hours forays to Benny Havens.

One step DeRussy took in hopes of lessening visits to the Havens tavern was the establishment of a "soda shop." A plebe in the Class of 1836 reported in an article for *The Military and Naval Magazine* that he had treated other cadets at the soda shop, "a place of luxury I had no idea existed in this barren spot." However, the new establishment did not stop unauthorized visits to Havens for flapjacks and cider flips.

The Cadet Mess was still under Cozzen's management despite his operation of the hotel. His dual responsibilities enabled him to obtain food for both places at advantageous prices. This may have improved food in the Cadet Mess. Cadets were still assigned to specific tables and marched to and from meals. The first captain gave the order to take seats after the cadets entered to stand behind their places. When the time allocated for the meal had passed, he ordered the Corps to rise, and cadets left the mess hall to march back to barracks or camp.

Visitors provided a change to the routine. Chief Black Hawk was brought to West Point en route to Washington at President Jackson's order. Cadet Walter Sherwood wrote that Black Hawk and his associates had spent several days at West Point. Winfield Scott and his family were frequent visitors, often unofficially. Mrs. Scott spent most of each summer in the hotel to escape the hot, humid Washington weather. The Academy had become a popular tourist attraction; hundreds of visitors took passenger steamers from New York to spend a day at West Point. Cadet Bushrod Johnson wrote that the Academy was considered to be the second best resort in the eastern United States.

The 1830 Polish insurrection roused much interest in the Corps of Cadets. William Frazer told his brother of the 1833 Fourth of July dinner where cadets and guests, including Winfield Scott, drank "many elegant toasts," one to "Poland the Land where Justice sleeps and Liberty lies bleeding." The following November, Frazer wrote to his brother, describing a visiting Polish officer who was ill and without funds and anxious to get to South Carolina, where he expected to find employment. The First Captain appealed to the Corps to contribute "12 1/2 cents apiece and the officers would make up the rest. There was not a dissenting voice."

The Class of 1835 established a tradition that still exists when it decided to have class rings made. These first rings had no common design, the only similarity being the motto, "Danger brings forth friendship," carved on the stone. The Class of 1836, as far as is known, had no ring. The custom was revived by the Class of 1837 and has been followed since. Tiffany, the New York jewelry firm, has stated that the Academy was the first college to adopt the custom. The practice did not become common in other institutions until about 1900.

Academy rings have varied over the years. Prior to 1897, the ring had no standard design, although it included an engraved seal or signet of the class motto. In 1897, it was decided that a plain stone would be used and that classes could vary the design of embossed insignia in the metal portion of the ring. After 1898, only the Academy motto, "Duty, Honor, Country," would be used. In 1917, possibly because of wartime restrictions, a standard design was used for all rings with the Academy crest on one side and the class crest on the other; choice of stone was optional. It became traditional for a cadet to wear his ring with his class crest facing him until graduation; after graduation, he wears the Academy crest facing him. This symbolism indicates that his class is foremost to the cadet; the Academy is more important to the graduate.

After World War I, a second tradition developed. Many cadets gave their fiancées a miniature of their class ring as an engagement ring. The miniature, about half the size of the cadet ring, often is given to a cadet's mother. Interesting variations have been made from time to time. Several fathers and sons who are graduates have given the wife and mother a miniature with two class crests; some brothers have done the same. The class ring and its miniature have become one of the most cherished West Point traditions.

Cadet pranks continued unabated. In January 1836, six cadets moved the "old waker," the reveille gun, from the flag pole at the northwest corner of the Plain to a spot between North and South Barracks after a rousing in-barracks party. Cadet John Bratt reported that, after loading the gun, they "gave a salute of one gun." Only four windows on the west side of the barracks remained unbroken. They then dismantled the piece and reassembled it on the fourth floor of barracks, pointing out a hall window toward South Barracks. A few cadets, who wanted to fire another salute, loaded the powder into the tube. Fortunately, John Sedgwick inserted a handkerchief before the cartridge, and the gun could not be fired. The next morning after order had been restored, a detail of nearly twenty soldiers finally moved the gun back to its original position.

In December 1835, a small Army force was massacred by Seminole Indians as the unit marched peacefully between two posts. The affair, known as Dade's Massacre, aroused the entire country. News of the debacle reached West Point in January 1836 with electrifying results. Five of the officers killed were graduates. Captain George W. Gardiner, Class of 1814, had been the first Commandant of Cadets from 1817 to 1818. Lieutenants William E. Basinger, 1830; Robert B. Mudge, 1833; and Richard Henderson and John L. Keais, 1835, were known to the faculty and most cadets.

For the first time, cries of "Early Graduation!" were heard at West Point. The entire First Class volunteered for immediate assignment to Florida. Secretary of

War Cass reluctantly replied that "the application of the First Class to be ordered to Florida is honorable but is denied."

Cadet James Mason wrote to his sister expressing the feelings of his classmates, "their glorious death excited our sympathies as well as our admiration." He added that it was difficult to realize that all the expectations and hopes of the young officers' parents should be ended in this way as they "had just completed their education, had just entered upon their profession at a time when life was most agreeable." The impact on the Corps increased when word was received of the deaths of Lieutenant James F. Izard, Class of 1828, and Lieutenant Colonel Alexander R. Thompson, Class of 1812 and son of Mrs. Thompson, who still boarded cadets.

The Seminole War dragged on for over seven years. Twenty officers were killed in action; thirteen were graduates. Dade and his command were not forgotten. In 1845, a monument financed by contributions from cadets and graduates was erected in their memory near the present site of Cullum Hall. When Cullum Hall was built in 1896, the monument was moved across the road from the Library. After World War II, Dade Monument was moved to the cemetery to be replaced by the statue of General George Patton.

Although interest in the Florida campaigns did not diminish, cadets and faculty officers discussed the Texas insurrection and possible success of the fight with Mexico. United States intervention was a topic of debate. Southern cadets were in favor of extending immediate help to the Texans; northern cadets were reluctant to become involved. Western cadets were divided. Many from states along the Mississippi agreed with the southern sentiments but for different reasons. They could see a commercial advantage in helping Texas, while the southern cadets believed it to be a means of supporting slavery. More than anything else, the Texas fight for freedom strengthened sectionalism in the Corps of Cadets.

Cadet Isaac Stevens wrote to his uncle that southern cadets "have a great contempt for our Yankee Farmers and even pretend to compare them with their slaves." A Massachusetts man, Stevens said that if any man compared him with slaves, he would consider it an insult and act accordingly. Cadet debates included topics of interest to cadets from northern and southern states. Stevens told his father of one Dialectic Society discussion on the justice of lynch laws. "We got very warm, indeed," he wrote, "the debate came very near merging into the discussion of abolition. This, you are aware, is a very tender subject, and, for our society, a very improper one."

The attitude of southern cadets must have been known throughout the Corps. George Thomas used almost the same words as Stevens, indicating that cadets from the south had contempt for those who worked for a living. The southern attitude was honed by knowledge that many northern cadets had better educational backgrounds. Virginian Richard Ewell expressed a jealous feeling when he wrote that many "Yankees here know the whole mathematical course. A person who comes here without a knowledge of mathematics has to contend against those who have been preparing themselves for years under the best teachers and who have used the same class books." Ewell stated that the Yankees took the lead in every class. Although the feeling of sectionalism increased, it had little effect on the feeling of comradeship between cadets. Friendship was more important than political issues.

The period from 1830 to 1840 brought further development of cadet slang. Some of the terms initiated remained in use for over a hundred years. One of the earliest terms was "found," meaning a cadet had been found deficient. Another was the appellation "turn back," a reference to a cadet who had been turned back to join a lower class because he had been found deficient in one or more subjects. "Board fight" described the normal classroom routine of going to a blackboard to demonstrate a problem. The word "bone" indicated hard study or special effort to reach a goal. An outgrowth of this word was "fileboner," an individual trying to advance in academic standing. From the Thayer period, "plebe" was the accepted designation for a Fourth Classman.

A rather unusual term was "sub-diver." This developed from the division arrangement in South Barracks. Each of the two tactical officers quartered in the barracks was assigned supervision of two or more divisions and was known as a division inspector. Cadet officers were assigned as sub-division inspectors, a position shortened to "sub-diver." The title continued until old Central Barracks was razed. A few acronyms began to be used even though that word was nonexistent at the time. "OC" referred to the Officer in Charge, a tactical officer assigned general supervisory duties for one day or a short period of time. The cadet Officer of the Day was the "OD"; and the Officer of the Guard, the "OG." Cadet slang and acronyms increased until nearly a hundred terms were used after World War II.

The Cadet Chapel was completed and consecrated in 1836, the first building at West Point with a specific architectural style, the classic design popular in the United States during the 1830s. Although the simple Doric columns supporting the gabled roof of the porch are Greek in origin, the circular ceiling of the interior and the arched windows are Roman. Above the altar is the mural, "Peace and War," by Robert W. Weir, Professor of Drawing from 1833 to 1876.

In 1899, the Daughters of the Revolution presented the black marble tablets on the walls bearing the names of Revolutionary War generals in incised gold letters. Included are Washington, Gates, Greene, Kosciuszko, Lafayette, Lincoln, Marion, Putnam, Stark, St. Claire, and Wayne. In an inconspicuous place on the rear wall is a plaque bearing only "Born 1740" and the rank, "Major General." This plaque recognizes Benedict Arnold's outstanding services in the invasion of Canada and at the Battle of Saratoga. The omission of his name and date of death is a silent reminder of his treasonous effort to turn the West Point fortifications over to the British. Other plaques were installed at a later date in memory of officers killed in the War of 1812, the Florida Indian Wars, the Mexican War, and the War with Spain. The last tablet added in 1955 honors the first two Academy graduates, Joseph Swift and Solomon Levy.

Later, cannon captured during the Revolutionary War were imbedded in the east wall; guns taken in the Mexican War, in the west wall. Flag cases on the side walls at one time held flags captured during the Revolutionary and Mexican Wars. The Mexican standards were returned to Mexico in 1946; the Revolutionary flags, removed for restoration and preservation, are in the West Point Museum.

The Chapel stood on the present site of Bartlett Hall until increases in the size of the Corps of Cadets made it inadequate. As a part of the massive building program from 1904 to 1911, a new chapel on the hill above the cadet complex was consecrated in 1910. The original plans for the building program included destruction of the old Chapel. When graduates learned that their chapel would be razed, a spontaneous effort was made to prevent its destruction. As a result, the "old" Chapel was moved stone by stone to the cemetery in 1911. The ease with which the necessary funds were contributed at a time when an officer's pay was quite meager was an indication of the unspoken importance of religion to cadets and graduates.

Another problem remaining from the Thayer era was Partridge's attempts to have the Military Academy abolished. He persuaded several state legislatures to pass resolutions calling for the Academy to be dissolved. Periodic resolutions presented in Congress failed to pass. DeRussy contributed little to their defeat. That these efforts were unsuccessful was due to the efforts of General Gratiot, Chief of Engineers, and President Jackson. Although many Jacksonians considered the Academy to be undemocratic and an institution for the rich, Jackson did not share their sentiments. His refusal to support his party's efforts to pass legislation abolishing the Academy was a major reason that such efforts were unsuccessful.

By the end of the summer of 1836, construction of the new Academic Building was underway. The plan finally adopted include a large hall on the ground floor for military exercises and cadet physical training, sixteen recitation rooms, a large drawing academy, and quarters for all of the assistant professors. Sufficient classrooms would eliminate any need to use rooms in North Barracks and the Cadet Mess for classes. The new building was across the road from the Chapel and parallel to South Barracks, on the present site of Pershing Barracks. Centering all cadet activities along the southern edge of the Plain established a pattern that has been followed to the present day.

Resignation of many graduates after one year of service provided the anti-Academy group with a strong argument for abolishing the institution. There was some justification for this position. Each cadet agreed to serve five years when he accepted his appointment. Four years of this period of compulsory servitude were spent as a cadet. Consequently, many graduates resigned their commissions after a single year of active duty. Railroads, canal firms, engineering concerns, other colleges, and state governments actively sought graduates because their engineering training surpassed that offered by any other institution of the time. The salaries offered far surpassed the pay of a junior Army officer. Recognizing the seriousness of this problem, the Secretary of War recommended in December 1836 that Congress extend the term of service of a cadet. Eighteen months later, the term was increased to eight years, four as a cadet and four as an officer.

The extended service requirement had little impact on the number of young men seeking cadet appointments. The reputation of the Academy as an engineering school and the attractions of military life brought an increasing number of applications. The law had another impact, however, because it related to officer promotions.

The small Army provided only a fixed number of officer spaces. When a cadet graduated, he was assigned to the Corps of Engineers, the Ordnance Corps, or to a regiment of Artillery, Infantry, or Dragoons. Promotions were made within the regiment or corps to which he was assigned, not by branch. Vacancies occurred only after another officer was promoted, resigned, transferred to another unit, or died. In many instances, graduated cadets, assigned to units with no vacancies for second lieutenants, were commissioned only as brevet lieutenants. By law, each company of Artillery, Infantry, or Dragoons could have only one supernumerary or brevet lieutenant.

Before the increase in mandatory service to eight years, resignations of graduates after only one year of commissioned service gave some assurance that graduates would receive a regular commission instead of only brevet rank. After the new law was enacted, the number of regular commissions available dropped. Over forty percent of the graduates in 1840 were given brevet commissions. This was not an immediate problem to the men concerned because they received the same pay and allowances as a regular officer. The greatest disadvantage was date of rank. A brevet second lieutenant might not be given a regular commission for months or even for more than a year, placing him behind his classmates who held regular commissions. With promotions based only on seniority, a year's difference in date of rank as a regular second lieutenant often resulted in several years passing before being promoted again.

Cadets were concerned about the possibility of receiving only a brevet commission. Knowing that class standing would be the determining factor, competition for grades became as keen as it had been during the Thayer era. More and more time was devoted to studies, so much so that the Board of Visitors expressed concern that cadets did not have enough free time for exercise.

There were actually two reasons for the increased effort. One was the hope that a high enough class standing would be earned to receive a regular commission because brevets usually went to the lowest men in a class. The second reason was the Academic Board recommendation of the branch or branches for which it considered each cadet to be qualified. Recommendations to the Corps of Engineers and the Artillery normally went to the men standing highest academically, although the Engineers often received brevet commissions because that branch was so small. The greatest number of men in each class normally were assigned to the Artillery, which consistently had more regular vacancies.

Cadet letters during this period often mentioned the reasons for increased study and the hope for high enough ranking to be commissioned in the Artillery.

Martin Van Buren was sworn in as President in March 1837, bringing the Jacksonian era to an end. Van Buren's selection for Secretary of War was Joel Poinsett, the member of the Board of Visitors whose comment had led Thayer to re-examine cadets. Poinsett had no rancor concerning that event and remained a great admirer of the Academy and Thayer. His sentiments reflected those of Van Buren, who had met Thayer often at Gouverneur Kemble's dinners. Van Buren's son, Abraham, graduated in the Class of 1827. After serving in the Florida wars as a captain in the 1st Regiment of Dragoons, he resigned his commission in early 1837 to become his father's private secretary.

It soon became apparent that the new administration was not pleased with the way DeRussy administered the Academy. In the summer of 1837, anticipating reassignment, DeRussy requested a transfer. General Gratiot and Secretary Poinsett approved the request but retained DeRussy until a replacement could be selected. A year would pass before the change was made.

Two officers were primary candidates, Thayer and Totten. Totten refused the appointment. Thayer's old friend, Gouverneur Kemble, urged Thayer to accept reappointment, and Thayer told Kemble that he would do so. However, General Gratiot would not agree to Thayer's selection because Thayer had attempted to make the Academy responsible directly to the Secretary of War, bypassing the Chief of Engineers. In November 1837, Poinsett wrote Kemble that he intended to relieve both DeRussy and Chaplain Warner in June 1883 and reappoint Thayer, but Gratiot convinced Poinsett to eliminate Thayer as a candidate.

This decision forced Gratiot and Poinsett to consider younger officers, the same group reviewed by Cass and Jackson when Thayer resigned. Poinsett used Kemble as a go-between to ask Thayer for his recommendations. The Secretary accepted Thayer's recommendation of Major Richard Delafield, Class of 1818, without any objections from Gratiot. Delafield was appointed superintendent in September 1838.

While these discussions were taking place, a near-disaster took place at West Point. Fire had been a problem from the time of the Burbeck academy. Despite careful planning and strict regulations, fires often broke out in cadet rooms, officers' quarters, and other buildings. After the Long Barracks on the edge of Execution Hollow burned to the ground in December 1827, a hand-operated fire "engine" designed to pump water from a main or a well to a fire was obtained.

On February 19, 1838, a fire in the Academic Building was discovered by a cadet at two o'clock in the morning. He had been awakened by the smell of smoke, saw flames in the fencing room on the first floor, and immediately gave the alarm. In a short time, the entire Corps of Cadets, the enlisted detachment, and most of the officers and civilians on the Post gathered to fight the conflagration. When the fire engine was attached to the water main near South Barracks, the engine would not function. Buckets passed from hand to hand were thrown at the flames, but, despite all efforts, the building and most of its contents were a complete loss.

While efforts were being taken to extinguish the flames, a group of cadets spontaneously dashed to the library on the second floor. Cadet Alfred Sully, son of artist Thomas Sully, wrote that Lieutenant Benjamin Alvord was the only officer to join them. Opening or breaking the windows, they hurled books out into the snow. Other volumes were carried to the stairs where they were passed down from hand to hand and out the front door. Another group carefully removed the Sully paintings of Jefferson, Monroe, Swift, and Williams and dropped them from the windows into the arms of cadets below. Young Sully reported to his father that only the Monroe portrait was damaged. "The stretching frame was broken," he wrote, "and he was scratched a little, but not in the face." This rescue effort saved the majority of the books and all of the paintings.

The valor and initiative of the cadets was praiseworthy. Ignoring flames in the eastern end of the building, they dashed to the upper floor shouting, according to Alfred Sully, "save the paintings." One can picture shouting cadets in various states of undress throwing books out of the windows, carefully lowering the paintings to cadets below, and passing other books down the stairs. When the fire spread to the adjutant's office adjoining the library, they were forced to leave the building; but their efforts had saved the portraits and most of the books.

The loss of the building and most of its contents must be attributed at least in part to DeRussy's negligence. Thayer had organized cadets into fire companies and drilled them periodically. Cadet Sully told his father that there was no organization of cadets to fight fires and "there is one thing in which Thayer is better than DeRussy; that is in having things in order. They say that when he was here the fire engine was in perfect order." He indicated that the fire had originated from a stove in the ground floor room where engineering models were stored, spreading rapidly throughout the building. Daylight revealed that only a heap of smoldering ashes remained, which Sully described as "a heap of black ruins."

Although the cadets' efforts saved most of the library, all of the paintings, and some of the chemical and philosophical apparatus, the records, apparatus, and models of three academic departments and the official papers in the adjutant's office were destroyed. With the exception of a few record books Adjutant Charles Smith had taken to his quarters, all of the Academy records and those of earlier years were burned. Their loss left a gap in Academy and West Point history only partially filled by the recent receipt of letters and personal records of the early period.

Loss of the Academic Building created a space problem. Rooms were needed for the library, classes, offices, and religious services. A few additional rooms in barracks were made available for classes by increasing the number of cadets in a room. In addition to the large room in the Cadet Mess already occupied by the drawing academy, smaller rooms were converted into classrooms, and the dining areas used for chapel services. Some classes were taught in instructors' homes. This was a temporary expedient used until the new Academic Building was completed in time for classes in the fall.

Library books, paintings, and apparatus saved by the cadets were taken to the hotel. Cadet Sully told his father that the hotel probably would not be available that summer because it was used for storage. Most of the books had been damaged by water and snow. They were carefully dried and placed on makeshift shelving. Congress provided funds in 1839 and 1840 appropriations to repair and rebind books damaged in the fire. Many old volumes in today's library still show evidence of water damage. Rebound books have very narrow margins as a result of being cropped prior to being rebound; many have water stains. A large atlas accompanying Jomini's *Traité des Grandes Operations Militaires* has many water-marked pages and a scuffed cover caused by falling against the building or on the hard surface below the library windows. The Sully portraits, repaired under the careful supervision of Professor Robert W. Weir, show no evidence of damage.

DeRussy's delay in approving plans for the new academic building proved to be a blessing in disguise. By the start of winter 1837, most of the exterior had been completed, and work was underway on the interior. Destruction of the old building necessitated a change in the plans. Originally, the new building was to have had classrooms for drawing, French, mathematics, and logic classes, eliminating the use of barracks rooms and mess hall facilities as classrooms. Living quarters were also to be provided for bachelor officer instructors.

Work was stopped and new plans drawn. The exercise room on the ground floor was retained, but the proposed officers' quarters were deleted. The second and third floors were redesigned for use by the Natural and Experimental Philosophy, Chemistry and Mineralogy, and Engineering departments, all of which required large laboratory areas and recitation rooms. After a slight delay, work was resumed, and the building was ready for use at the start of classes in September 1838. The library was given space on the second floor. Drawing classes continued in the mess building; French and mathematics in barracks rooms.

Destruction of the Academic Building was a hardship on most post personnel, cadets most of all. Use of barracks rooms for classes forced billeting six cadets in many rooms intended to be used only by three men, making sleeping uncomfortable. Studying was even more difficult because tables had to be removed to make space for added occupants. Mess steward Cozzens must have complained because the Cadet Mess was used for classes, chapel services, and recreation. With the hotel dining area filled with books, he had to feed official guests such as the Board of Visitors in the Cadet Mess. Officers in the departments whose files had been burned tried to reconstruct their records. Fortunately, copies of monthly reports were available in the office of the Chief of Engineers and at the War Department. Despite the inconvenience and added work, cadets and officers continued their normal routines.

In March 1838, the Commandant was reassigned, and the Adjutant, Captain Smith, was appointed to replace Fowle, who had been promoted to lieutenant colonel in the 6th Infantry after Alexander Thompson was killed in Florida. Fowle did not leave an enviable record at West Point. His inexperience and lack of administrative ability had placed an additional load on DeRussy, who was forced to assume many of the functions of the Commandant. En route to his new assignment, less than a month after leaving West Point, Fowle was killed when the boiler of the steamer carrying him down the Ohio River exploded.

June brought the annual examinations before the Board of Visitors. In its report, the Board commented on the need for additional academic space, noting that the destruction of the old Academic Building had nullified the planned increase in space that would have been available when the new building was completed. The curriculum was criticized by the Board, which recommended that history, geography, and composition be taught to cadets. It urged that a swimming school be established and cavalry instruction included in training by the Department of Tactics.

With the departure of the graduating class, the Corps moved into camp on the northeastern corner of the Plain. Infantry and artillery instruction and parades occupied most of each day, but cadets found time for swimming and hiking. Two dances were held each week in the Mess Hall. Cadets prepared for these hops by attending dancing classes. Cadet Bushrod Johnson, Class of 1840, wrote to his friend Dr. J. H. Brown to describe preparations for the final ball before moving back into barracks. He told Brown that two thousand invitations had been sent by cadets and that they anticipated attendance by "the most fashionable beauties of the country." Johnson and other cadets enjoyed dancing with the "beautiful belles" who attended.

Other popular forms of recreation were band concerts and theatricals. Concerts were scheduled every Saturday evening, out of doors during the summer and in a large section room in North Barracks during the winter. Alfred Sully told his father that the theatrics were "short pieces, generally of comic order." Only the First Class cadets took part in these skits, "much to our amusement as well as that of the officers and the rest of the inhabitants of the Point."

Altercations with Great Britain concerning the border between Maine and New Brunswick caused Army units to be sent to northern Maine. British units moved to face them on the New Brunswick side of the border. The "Potato War" excited cadets, and many wrote home, expressing the hope that United States forces would push back the British. Cadet Isaac Stevens wrote to his father, severely criticizing the administration for not taking more forceful steps to resolve the dispute. The peaceful solution of the problem did not please eager cadets yearning for action.

September 1, 1838 brought Major Delafield to West Point to replace DeRussy. DeRussy's five-year superintendency had not benefitted the Academy. Discipline had lessened under Major Fowle's supervision as commandant. Administrative procedures had worsened despite the efforts of Adjutant Smith.

Destruction of the old Academic Building disrupted classes, caused severe over-crowding in barracks, and emphasized the lack of planning and supervision by DeRussy and Fowle. The curriculum remained unchanged from the Thayer period. Perhaps the greatest change was a result of DeRussy's wavering inaction; the Academic Board increased in stature and became a body that governed almost every Academy activity. Firm guidance was needed; Delafield would provide that guidance.

14

Preparing for the Ultimate Test

The combination of Delafield as Superintendent and Smith as Commandant provided what DeRussy and Fowle had lacked: teamwork and leadership. Commissioned in the 2nd Artillery when he graduated in 1825, Smith had been on duty at West Point since 1829. He had taught cadets infantry tactics from 1829 to 1831 when Thayer had appointed him Adjutant; DeRussy retained him in this position. When Fowle was promoted and transferred, Smith became Commandant, undoubtedly with Delafield's concurrence. Perhaps better than any of his predecessors, Smith fully understood the interlocking relationships of the functions of the Superintendent, the Commandant, and the Academic Board. He had been an assistant to Worth and Hitchcock during their tours as Commandant, enabling him to observe and absorb the techniques and disciplinary principles used by Thayer's two outstanding assistants. His service as Adjutant to Thayer and DeRussy provided him with a firsthand comparison of two completely different men and their supervision of Academy operations. Smith probably possessed more knowledge of the Commandant's functions and duties than any Commandant before or since.

By contrast, Delafield, who had graduated at the head of his class in 1818, had never been stationed at West Point. All of his duty after graduation had been as a supervisory engineer. He had been Astronomical and Topographical Draftsman for the American Commission that determined the northern boundary of the United States in accordance with the Treaty of Ghent. What he had learned in drawing classes at the Academy benefitted him greatly during this tour of duty. His other assignments included construction, repairs, or surveys at Hampton Roads, Virginia; along the Mississippi and Ohio rivers; Fort Delaware south of Wilmington; and Fort Mifflin near Philadelphia. His engineering and building experience would prove to be a great asset during his superintendency.

Six weeks after Delafield assumed his new duties, Augustus Pleasanton, Class of 1826, visited West Point. He had resigned his commission in 1830 to become a Philadelphia attorney. His diary recorded impressions of both Delafield and Smith. Pleasanton noted that Professor Church told him that the discipline of the Corps was better than it had been since Thayer's departure. Pleasanton joined the Commandant in inspecting the cadets, commenting in his diary that much credit was due Smith for returning the Corps to its former state of discipline in the short period of six months.

"Major Delafield," wrote Pleasanton, "will make an excellent Superintendent. He is a man of exceeding good sense, great singleness of purpose, and perfect honesty." He noted that Delafield was already a favorite with the cadets, and "I am inclined to think that their fondness for him will increase with their knowledge of him." This observation would prove to be wrong. Delafield, in Pleasanton's opinion, was not only pleased with his command but preferred it to any other assignment. "His whole soul seems wrapped up in the success of the institution," was his final comment about the Superintendent.

Pleasanton also recorded a conversation with Delafield concerning the Revolutionary War relics. During DeRussy's superintendency, Secretary of War Cass had directed that much of this equipment be sold. Only thirty links of the chain stretched across the Hudson River to prevent passage of British ships were retained. Many uniforms and personal weapons were sold. Pleasanton bemoaned the sale of "many barrels which were filled with papers, reports, order correspondence and other valuable information connected with our Revolutionary struggle." The barrels were sold as waste paper, disposing of "thousands of letters, orders, instructions, and reports in the handwriting of General Washington, of Lafayette, of Knox, Arnold, and a host of others." Pleasanton was deeply disturbed to learn of this loss. The links of chain, several brass cannon, and a few other items were the only relics retained.

Much of Smith's initial effort was devoted to improving the comfort of cadets and restoring discipline to the Thayer level. Delafield gave full support to Smith's proposals. For the first time, beds were a mandatory item. Iron bedsteads narrower than present army bunks were obtained from the West Point Foundry at Cold Spring. Cadets were charged twenty cents a month to cover the costs of these beds; appropriated funds were not made available until much later. New plebes were required to sleep on pallets on the floor until after the entrance examinations. From reveille to tattoo, mattresses were folded and bedding in a bed bag was placed on top of the mattress. The bed bag was eliminated in 1842, but bedding was still folded and placed on the mattress, a requirement continued for over a century. This arrangement was considered to be a way of preventing cadets from sleeping during study hours.

Each cadet was required to purchase a mattress, sheets, pillow, pillow cases, four blankets, leather trunk, chair, clothes brush, hair brush and comb, toothbrush, and glass tumbler. Roommates jointly procured a mirror, washstand, pitcher, broom, scrub brush, tables, and candlesticks or lamps as prescribed by the Superintendent. All of these items were obtained from the store operated for cadets. The uniformity of these furnishings enabled Captain Smith to establish a similar arrangement for all cadet rooms, similar but not identical because rooms differed in size and shape.

The number of cadets billeted in a room varied. Some of the larger rooms in North Barracks housed six cadets. A few very small rooms were assigned only two occupants, usually cadet officers. Because of the almost universal crowding, the partitions dividing many of the rooms in North Barracks were removed to provide more space. Conditions had been even worse after the February fire until the Corps moved to camp for the summer. The completion of the new Academic Building did not eliminate the use of barracks rooms for mathematics and French instruction, offices, and quarters for company tactical officers. As a result, the barracks were inadequate to properly house cadets.

Water was carried from the outdoor taps or wells to the rooms. Enterprising cadets devised a small yoke to enable them to carry at least two large buckets of water at a time. Pails in each room were filled from the buckets, and the buckets and yoke were then hidden from inspecting officers. One of the cadet yokes was displayed in the office of the supervisor of barracks police (janitors) as late as 1944. No bathing facilities were provided in barracks. Cadets still used the primitive shower near the cemetery or the river in good weather.

Rooms were heated only by a fireplace. Wood was stacked on the stoops of South Barracks and near the entrance to North Barracks. To provide better heating, Delafield authorized the use of anthracite coal. Cadets considered this a mixed blessing. Heating was more efficient. Coal fires were better for cooking unauthorized meals, but the burning coal provided less light for studying.

Both barracks were drafty; wind whistled through window frames and doors. Cadets studied wrapped in blankets, often sitting or lying in front of the fire instead of using chairs and tables in much colder parts of their rooms. Because of the continuing danger of fires, cadets were again organized into fire companies and drilled frequently. Two new fire engines were authorized; and the old engine, which had been inoperable at the time of the February fire, was repaired.

Rooms were inspected several times each day and at least once each evening. Cadets were required to be in their rooms when not in class or attending formations. Authorized absence required the prior written approval of the Superintendent. The only free time available was on Saturday afternoons and Sundays after chapel.

Proper uniform was required at all times from reveille to tattoo, even when a cadet was in his room studying or working on equipment. In an effort to lessen cadet expenses, Delafield directed that only a white vest be an optional part of the uniform, eliminating the gray vest formerly required for winter wear. Cadets complained about the uncomfortable shako, a five-pound leather hat with a tall feather pompon. Realizing the validity of these complaints, Delafield authorized wear of the forage cap instead of the shako when not in formation. Another irritating feature of the uniform was a black leather stock that chaffed a cadet's throat, especially in hot weather. Delafield directed that a black bombazine stock be used instead.

Parades were scheduled every afternoon, Sundays included. Special reviews were often held for distinguished visitors. Formal guard mount took place every morning during the summer and on weekends during the academic year. Cadets marched to classes, meals, chapel, and even to recreational activities such as swimming in the river, all under the supervision of cadet officers or officers of the Tactical Department. A cadet's life was regimented from the time he was awakened by the reveille call until he went to bed at taps. Taps was a signal on a drum, not the familiar bugle call adopted after the Civil War.

Recreational activities were limited. Cadets were prohibited from playing any game of cards, chess, or checkers in their rooms or elsewhere. Athletics were limited to informal games of baseball and football, the latter probably a version of soccer. The exercise room on the ground floor of the new Academic Building included a small gymnasium and fencing facilities, which many cadets used during their free hours on Saturday and Sunday. Swimming and boating were commonplace during the summer months. Hiking, fishing, and hunting were the favorite recreation of many cadets.

Winter found many cadets skating on the large pond near the Superintendent's quarters, on a large low marshy area near South Barracks, or on the river. Occasionally, cadets built snow forts near Execution Hollow and put their classroom tactics to practical use in mock battles. There were no snow plows, although oxen were used to pull a flat, shovel-like scraper to remove heavy drifts. Professor Weir left an excellent oil showing oxen scraping snow near the barracks during a blizzard.

Dancing classes continued during the summer encampment, and three dances were scheduled each week. A few special balls were held each year. Cadets sent invitations to friends at home, even though it was unlikely that they would attend. Often, more than 300 guests attended these balls. Cadet Samuel French described the ballroom in September 1840, probably a large classroom in the Academic Building or the dining area in the Cadet Mess decorated with flags, ensigns, pennants, greenery and flowers, swords, bayonets, guns, hats, and other equipment. At 8:00 P.M., a signal gun was fired and dancing began. Shortly after midnight, refreshments were served. Dancing continued until after 3:00 A.M. French left before the end of the ball, saying that he "was wearied out."

Cadets selected by classmates served as "managers" at each dance. Their duties included supervising the start and ending of each dance, arranging for the music to be played by the orchestra, welcoming officers and their wives or escorts, and making certain that cadet dates had an opportunity to dance with as many cadets as possible. Cadet managers supervised refreshments to make certain no intoxicating liquor was added to the fruit punch. They also had the unenviable task of making certain all cadets left the dance hall for camp or barracks when a long drum roll signaled the end of the evening.

Frequent dances and dancing classes were an excellent means for teaching cadets the social graces of the times; most cadet hops were formal. Cadets wore full dress uniform; their young ladies, formal gowns. Customs used at cadet hops reflected the current practices of society and the officer corps of the Army. A reception line was commonplace with an officer and his wife and the cadet floor manager and his escort welcoming cadets and their escorts. A cadet learned the proper way to pass down a reception line and how to introduce his young lady. Dances were an enjoyable recreation, and they were a means of preparing a cadet to take his place in the Army and in society.

Music played at the dances reflected the popular pieces of the time. The Academy Band, a versatile group of enlisted musicians known for their excellence on the parade ground, provided an orchestra for cadet dances, a concert orchestra for recitals, and smaller groups for parties. The band leader, also the music teacher, taught interested cadets and families of post personnel. Thayer's bandmaster, Richard Willis, was nationally known for introducing the Kent bugle to the United States, for his accomplished ability to play that instrument, and for his many compositions, including marches, ballads, and quick steps. The words for his ballad, "Rose! Pretty Rose," were written by Cadet George W. Patten, Class of 1830.

Other cadets wrote the words or composed the music for popular pieces. Jonathan G. Barnard, Class of 1833, published many pieces, including "The Round of the Waters," "The Splendor Falls on Castle Walls," and "Sweet and Low," a ballad or cradle song still popular today. Cadet Daniel M. Beltzhoover composed the music for the song of the Class of 1847, which had words written by Mrs. Winfield Scott.

Music by other musicians—marches, polkas, schottisches, and waltzes—was dedicated to the Corps. "The Florida March" by Gustave Blefsner was dedicated to Major Delafield. Professor Weir provided cover drawings for many songs. The great number of songs concerning or dedicated to the Academy and its cadets is an excellent indication of its prestige and popularity despite continued political attacks generated by Partridge.

The Academy began to appear in popular literature about this time. One of the first novels about cadet life, *The West Point Cadet or, the Young Officer's Bride*, by Harry Hazel was published in 1845. The small, paperback volume described cadet life and service in the Florida Indian wars. Periodicals and newspapers often published cadet letters, providing a more accurate and less flowery description of Academy life.

Another way of introducing a cadet to the proper social graces was by asking him to tea or to dinner. Most of the married officers, including the Superintendent, hosted cadets at social functions in their quarters. Thayer had initiated this practice shortly after his new quarters were built in 1821. All of his successors followed his example. Professors, instructors, and tactical officers did the same. Whether this was a mandatory requirement or whether it was done at the initiative of the individual officer is not known, but cadet letters and diaries do indicate that invitations to the homes of officers were quite common.

Delafield was even more opposed to the use of intoxicants than Thayer and made every effort to stop cadet drinking. Cadets still slipped out to Benny Havens' establishment. A few made a trip across the river to a tavern at the boat landing at Cold Spring, by boat during the warm months or by walking across the ice in winter. Occasionally, cadets were stranded in Cold Spring when ice broke during early spring. Cadets caught drinking were subject to dismissal. James Ramsay was one cadet tried for intoxication. His classmates pledged themselves to abstain from drinking if the Secretary of War would reinstate Ramsay; Poinsett accepted the pledge. Delafield announced the decision to the Corps, concluding his announcement by saying that he hoped that the action of the Secretary would never "be hereafter abused by the committal of an act looked upon by the whole nation as brutal, degrading, and ungentlemanly." Ironically, Ramsay did not graduate despite the support of his classmates.

Popular Benny Havens had a competitor during this period. A retired bugler named Avery opened a tavern about a half mile south of the Kinsley house, much closer to the Academy than Havens, and many cadets frequented Avery's establishment. Cadet Hatch told his sister that Avery was willing to accept shoes, clothing, or blankets from cadets who had no money. This, of course, was contrary to regulations, and Delafield and Smith constantly reviewed cadet accounts, looking for cadets purchasing unnecessary equipment. A subsequent inspection would bring severe punishment to cadets who were unable to account for all of their belongings.

Both Thayer and Delafield were concerned by the temptations available to cadets on furlough passing through or stopping in large cities such as New York, Boston, and Philadelphia. Both realized that cadets on their first extended leave after two years of near-monastic existence would be very susceptible to urban attractions. This concern undoubtedly contributed to their efforts to teach cadets to avoid alcohol. That there was reason for this feeling was a report by Cadet Derby, who told his mother that three cadets were under arrest and would probably be dismissed for "contracting a horrible disease" while on furlough. A year later, he wrote that only one man in his class faced similar punishment.

It was customary for cadets to wear civilian clothing on furlough, probably because the gray uniform was uncomfortable for normal wear. To lessen the cadet tendency to succumb to temptation by marking each cadet as a representative of the Academy, Delafield prescribed a new uniform for wear only on furlough. This consisted of a blue frock coat, cut in a design similar to a civilian coat, with brass cadet buttons and a standing collar. The cap had a gold wreath in front and U.S.M.A. in silver letters. White trousers and vest were worn because furloughs always were scheduled during July and August of a cadet's Second Class year. Many cadets carried a gold-headed cane. One of the earliest photographs of a cadet shows Derby in his furlough uniform during his 1844 leave.

Derby's letters, which were given to the Library in late 1989, provide an unusually detailed account of cadet life during the 1840s. Derby wrote to his mother at least once a month, often more frequently, during his four years as a cadet. His candid comments about fellow cadets, instructors, and enlisted men and his vivid descriptions of events provide one of the best and most intimate accounts available.

Most civilian colleges awarded diplomas to graduates at a special ceremony. This was not done at West Point until many years later. After the examinations, the chairman of the Board of Visitors often addressed the Corps. Diplomas were either given to the graduating class informally or mailed at a later date. Each diploma indicated the branch of the Army to which the individual was assigned and was signed by the members of the Academic Board, the Commandant, and the Superintendent.

During Delafield's superintendency, several traditions developed. One was a special parade honoring the graduating class and fireworks that night. Plebe Derby described the parade as very imposing. After the lower three classes marched onto the Plain behind the band and formed a line of companies, the First Class marched on with the Colors and took their places in ranks. The band played "Auld Lang Syne" and "Home Sweet Home" with, according to Derby, "not a dry eye among them." When the parade was dismissed, the new graduates all "screamed and screeched, took off their caps, kicked them around, and left them on the ground." This ceremonial formation evolved into today's Graduation Parade when the graduating cadets leave their companies, move forward, and watch the Corps pass in review in their honor.

Another event that became a tradition took place the night before cadets moved back to barracks from the summer encampment near Fort Clinton: illumination of the camp. This later became the traditional Camp Illumination continued until summer camp was moved to Lake Popolopen in 1943. Derby described the fete in 1843, his Yearling summer. Each tent had at least six candles flickering in the dusk. Tents of cadet officers were decorated with transparencies showing the name of the company. Another transparency in the Commandant's tent carried the motto "Essayons." Rockets were discharged every three minutes. Derby told of an immense "stag" held between rows of 200 candles on the parade ground. A stag was a form of country dancing performed by cadets. Derby recorded that the evening was a brilliant event witnessed by over 500 ladies and gentlemen, including officers and visitors at the hotel.

Cadet John Hatch said that Delafield was almost universally hated by the Corps, which Hatch considered to be the lot of all superintendents. Delafield, he said, merited that dislike more than any other because he pried into cadet activities and took unfair advantage of cadets. Derby wrote to his mother that cadets disliked Delafield because he was parsimonious and unfair in treating cadets; his punishments varied from case to case. The many benefits initiated by Delafield were outweighed by his rigid supervision, at least in the eyes of cadets.

Delafield was a complex individual. At times he was almost a tyrant in his disciplinary actions against offending cadets. At other times, he showed extreme leniency. One example was his punishment of Cadet Lucien Bibb, who missed a drawing class because he was "tired of drawing." Instead of referring Bibb to a Court Martial, the normal punishment for being absent without permission, Delafield punished him by requiring him to spend two hours of his recreational time drawing under the supervision of the drawing instructors. Needless to say, this instruction was resented by the instructor more than the cadet.

Another example of Delafield's leniency was a change in Cadet Regulations making it permissible for cadets to have food in their rooms, a restriction in force since Thayer's time. The change was made to enable cadets to legally accept food from home instead of smuggling sweets and snacks into barracks. The regulation was not intended to authorize cadets to cook over their fireplaces. Derby's letters frequently described cadet feasts with turkeys, ducks, or chickens as the main course. He also mentioned gourmet items brought from New York by cadet friends: oysters, seafood, cakes, pies, and pastries.

Cadets were restricted to limits encompassing the level of the Plain. Written permission was required for a hike to Crow's Nest, Fort Putnam, or elsewhere in the hills. Swimming in the river was always a supervised activity. Aware that prescribed limits were overly confining, Delafield extended the authorized area to include the Chain Walk and a path extending along the northern and eastern river fronts to Kosciuszko's Garden. This path later became Flirtation Walk with its famous Kissing Rock.

Over the years, it had become traditional for the tactical officers to ignore cadet cooking on Christmas Eve when many fine meals were prepared in cadet fireplaces. Delafield decided to end this in 1843, possibly because it was inconsistent to prohibit cooking in rooms at all other times while tacitly permitting it on one day. He announced that refreshments would be served in the exercise and large recitation rooms that evening. Cadet Derby wrote that "oyster men, pie men, turkey men, & the storekeeper" were there, all with food for cadets to purchase." Delafield made it possible for cadets not in debt to draw coupons valued at one dollar to purchase food. The band provided music for dancing. Derby said, "the halls were brilliantly illuminated, the oysters, pie, and turkey all fixed, all was ready, the ladies, the Major." Few cadets attended because most of the Corps considered Delafield's action an invasion of their privileges. Derby said that this left "the Major in a very unpleasant and ridiculous fix."

Cadets periodically raided fruit trees in the yards of officers' quarters. Occasionally, they would appropriate chickens to cook in their rooms. There were always complaints by the owners, but these were insignificant compared to Delafield's reaction when two pet ducks disappeared. Barracks inspection found the head and feathers of one duck. Delafield ordered all room orderlies to be questioned to determine if they had known if food was cooked in their rooms the night the ducks were taken.

Most cadets answered, but six refused because they believed the questioning to be improper and that any reply might be incriminating. Delafield interviewed the six and ordered them to answer his questions, pointing out that Cadet Regulations required that a room orderly answer the questions of an officer or cadet officer acting in the performance of his duty. The cadets still refused, and submitted letters to be forwarded to the Secretary of War, complaining about Delafield's actions. The Superintendent forwarded the letters to General Totten with a cover memorandum explaining the reasons for his treatment of the cadets. Nothing official occurred, but Delafield had lost whatever respect cadets may have had for him. One can only guess what Totten's reaction may have been; neither man left any record of the episode.

The complexity and ambiguity of Delafield's supervision of the Corps is shown in one way by his handling of the duck incident but in an entirely different manner by his fatherly attitude toward cadets. Augustus Pleasanton told of a cadet coming to Delafield's quarters while the Superintendent was having tea with guests. His servant informed him that Mr. Holt was calling; and Delafield, assuming it was a guest at the hotel, told the servant to ask the visitor to join the group. Although surprised when a cadet appeared, Delafield welcomed him as a guest. Pleasanton assumed that the young man had appeared because of a deficiency report, but Delafield did not raise the issue at the time, although he may have taken appropriate action later.

Delafield tried to provide cadets with outlets for their energy and talents. He either approved or at least condoned the publication of a small periodical by Cadet James W. Schureman in March 1842. Editor Schureman stated his editorial policy in the first issue of *The West Pointer*: the publication would be "devoted to literature, the fine arts, and everything else that can be thought of." This issue included an excellent sketch of the Cadet Monument in the cemetery to illustrate an article giving its history and describing some of the grave markers. A fictional story, "Anthony Prime, the Plebe," portrayed the life of a new cadet. One column was devoted to comments on current fiction. Rumors of a pending Mexican invasion of Texas were reported. Schureman included editorial remarks countering attacks on the Academy; this defense was expanded in the second issue, which also continued the story of Anthony Prime. Only two issues have been preserved; whether others were prepared is not known.

Other cadet publications of the period, definitely approved by Delafield, were distributed by the Dialectic Society. Two pamphlets containing cadet writings were published in 1839, "The Talisman" and "The Rover." An address by Benjamin Butler, prominent jurist and chairman of the Board of Visitors, on the military profession in the United States and the means of promoting its usefulness and honor was printed the following year. Another Dialectic Society pamphlet summarized the address by Lieutenant Benjamin Alvord commemorating the gallant conduct of nine graduates and other officers killed in the Seminole Wars. Delafield also arranged to have cadet Fourth of July orations published.

Classes followed the system established by Thayer. All subjects except drawing required extensive use of blackboard recitations. Each classroom had a single, large slate blackboard. The instructor would call two cadets forward at a time. One would go to the board to prepare his answer to an assigned problem; the second was examined orally. They would be followed by two other cadets who were tested in the same way.

Although a blackboard was available in the drawing classrooms, it was used only by the instructor to demonstrate lesson features, not for recitations by cadets. Professor Weir and his assistants taught terrain sketching, architectural graphics, map making—surveying was part of the Engineering instruction— drawing the human figure, portraiture, and some mechanical drawing. Cadets were taught to use charcoal, pen and ink, and watercolors. A few advanced students learned to use oils. This instruction developed skills and techniques that could be used in the field after the cadet graduated. Terrain sketching and map making were of vital importance at a time when photography was in its infancy and few maps were available from Army sources. Charcoal, pen and ink, and watercolors were media readily available or easily carried in the field.

The instructors in scientific classes used models to demonstrate various principles being discussed. Most of the models or apparatus came from France. After the fire, the advisability of employing a model maker at the Academy was discussed, but it was decided that better apparatus could be obtained in France at less cost. During this discussion, Professor Mahan emphasized the difficulty in finding a model maker with sufficient background knowledge to make scientific apparatus, a decided contrast to the ready availability of models and apparatus in Paris.

English composition and grammar, added to the curriculum in 1839, were taught by the Chaplain as Professor of Ethics. Time for English classes was taken from hours allocated to French, Drawing, and other subjects taught by the Department of Ethics. Nearly three-fourths of the time allocated to instruction was devoted to mathematics, engineering, topographical drawing, chemistry, mineralogy, geology, and natural philosophy. In determining the relative merit for graduation, scientific subjects comprised 55 percent of the total; French, Drawing, and Ethics 17 percent; tactics 14 percent; and conduct 14 percent.

In 1838, Thayer had written to Delafield to urge that he make no changes in the curriculum, deeming it ideally suited to its purpose of educating cadets to become officers. Apparently the Academic Board agreed with Thayer's recommendation, for no major changes were made to the curriculum from Thayer's departure in 1833 until the Civil War. Even the institution of a five-year curriculum in 1854 brought no major changes. Although there were many modifications during this quarter century, they were refinements rather than major alterations. Modifications were determined by the Academic Board, not the

Superintendent; Delafield did not interfere with Board supervision of all academic matters.

The Superintendent was chairman of the Academic Board and could vote on any proposal being considered. Unlike his civilian contemporaries, he was a temporary appointee. The professors, by contrast, had tenure. They were appointed for an indefinite term by the President, and Congress approved each appointment. A civilian college president was responsible to a supervisory group, possibly a state legislature, board of governors, or corporation. If he had problems with a professor, it was a simple matter to obtain approval to dismiss the professor, for there was no such thing as tenure. Consequently, the college president exerted considerable power over his faculty and could apply personal influence in academic activities.

This was not the case at West Point. The Superintendent could not replace a professor unless he resigned or died. Although a voting member and chairman of the Academic Board, he had no direct control over its members. What control he exerted came from leadership, logical argument, persuasion, and personal prestige. Thayer had used all of these with his Academic Board to initiate and influence many Board decisions. Because Board membership changed often during his superintendency, Thayer had the added advantage of providing continuity. A poor leader, DeRussy had little control over the Board, did not use logical argument or persuasion, and had little prestige in the eyes of the professors. Delafield took a middle road, permitting the Academic Board to control most academic matters. He was able to persuade them to support proposals that he submitted for consideration.

Delafield was fortunate to have professors who were scholars of national and international renown. The entire Academic Board, with the exception of the Professor of Geography, History, and Ethics, had been groomed by Thayer. The chaplains who headed this department were also appointed by the President with congressional approval. Their tenure normally was only a few years. Troublemaker Thomas Warner, after serving ten years, resigned when Delafield became Superintendent. His successor, Jasper Adams, left after two years. Chaplain M. P. Parks, at West Point from 1840 to 1846, was followed by William T. Sprole, who served until 1856. Assistant professors were Academy graduates.

Jacob W. Bailey, Professor of Chemistry, Mineralogy, and Geology, graduated from the Academy in 1832. After two years service with the 1st Artillery, he returned to West Point as an assistant professor. The State College of New Jersey at Princeton conferred a Master of Arts degree on him in 1837. A member of many scientific societies, he was noted for his inventions and improvements of the microscope. Bailey would hold his professorship until his early death in 1857 at the age of forty-six.

Professor of Mathematics Albert E. Church was an 1828 Academy graduate. After duty as an assistant professor from 1828 to 1831, he served two years with the 3rd Artillery, returning to West Point in 1833. He was Professor of Mathematics from 1838 until his death in 1870. Author of many mathematical works and a member of several scientific societies, Church was awarded an honorary M.A. degree by Washington College of Connecticut in 1837, another M.A. by the State College of New Jersey the same year, and an honorary doctorate by Yale in 1852.

William W. C. Bartlett, Professor of Natural and Experimental Philosophy, graduated at the head of the Class of 1826. An Engineer, Bartlett remained at West Point as an assistant professor until 1829. After three years supervising harbor fortifications and two years as assistant to the Chief of Engineers, he returned to the Academy in 1834 to become professor in 1836, remaining in this position until his retirement in 1871. Bartlett authored many scientific works concerning optics, mechanics, acoustics, and astronomy. He was awarded an honorary M.A. degree by the State College of New Jersey in 1837 and a doctorate by Geneva College of New York in 1847. A member of many scientific associations, he was a Corporator of the National Academy of Science.

The Teacher of Drawing, Robert W. Weir, was not a college graduate. He left a mercantile chief-clerk position in 1821 to devote himself to painting. The support of friends enabled him to study in Italy for three years. He was appointed to head the Academy Drawing Department in 1834 at the recommendation of William Cullen Bryant. Weir was noted for his portraits, landscapes, architectural drawings, and etchings. His best-known work is *The Embarkation of the Pilgrims* in the Capital rotunda in Washington. After the Teacher of Drawing became the Professor of Drawing in 1846, Weir held the position until his retirement in 1876. Many cadets whom Weir taught became noted artists. Seth Eastman, an assistant teacher under Weir, became known for his landscapes. Whistler and George Derby benefitted from Weir's instruction; both earned reputations as artists after putting their uniforms aside.

Claudius Berard, Teacher and, after 1846, Professor of French, was educated in France before coming to the United States in 1807. He was Professor of Greek and Latin at Dickinson College from 1812 until his appointment to the Academy in 1815. Berard was also the Academy Librarian. An able instructor, he prepared texts for cadet use until his pupils were able to read French technical publications. Cadet letters often mentioned his insistence that cadets learn to speak correctly as well as translate accurately, although there was no formal requirement to teach cadets to speak French. He remained professor until his death in 1848, when he was succeeded by his assistant, Hyacinthe R. Agnel, who would head the department until his death in 1871.

Perhaps best known of the professors was Dennis H. Mahan, who headed the Department of Engineering from 1832 until his death in 1871. Graduating first in the Class of 1824, Mahan remained at West Point for the rest of his life, except for four years of study in Europe arranged with Thayer's support. In addition to studying military instruction in Germany and Great Britain, Mahan studied at the French School of Engineers and Artillerists at Metz with special approval of the Minister of War. After completing the course, he returned to West Point in 1830. Mahan authored many scientific works on engineering, industrial drawing, architecture, fortifications, and military science.

Throughout his forty-one years as a professor, Mahan did his utmost to keep his courses in engineering and military science as up to date as possible. An excellent example of his efforts was a letter to Delafield four days after Delafield became superintendent. He explained the need for an additional assistant professor to assist in preparing changes in the course necessitated by new developments in engineering. He asked that models and apparatus lost in the Academic Building fire be replaced and requested the purchase of models for architecture studies. He suggested that models of the Parthenon and its molding and friezes be purchased, explaining that they could also be used by the Drawing Department. Complaining that books and periodicals in the Library were five years behind current publications, he asked Delafield to require the librarian to obtain current books and periodicals concerning civil and military engineering, architecture, and the science of war whether published in Europe or the United States "at the earliest period after publication so that the instructors, and even the pupils, in my Dept. may be enabled to keep up with the state of these arts and sciences, both at home and abroad."

During his long tenure, Mahan produced many books, articles for newspapers and periodicals, and lithographed texts for use by his students and faculty. Many of his texts on civil engineering, industrial drawing, architecture, and descriptive geometry were used by civilian colleges. His books on field fortifications, permanent fortifications, and military science were used by officers in the Army and by foreign military schools. His *Advance Guard, Outposts, and Detachment Service of Troops . . . with a Historical Sketch of the Rise and Progress of Tactics*, first published in 1847, became an essential part of every officer's personal library. Without his permission, it was reprinted in 1861 by the Confederate Army. The book included discussions of tactics and strategy and a brief history of military science from the time of the ancient Greeks through Napoleon's campaigns. This small volume probably had more impact upon American military concepts than any other single publication of the time.

Mahan became the principal Academy spokesman in countering attacks on West Point. He provided the Chief of Engineers with a constant stream of information negating antagonistic charges by Congressmen, state legislators, and journalists. Mahan was deeply interested in all Academy activities and did not hesitate to correct cadet behavior inside and outside the classroom. Despite his dedicated efforts, he was not liked by cadets, who considered him to be cold, unnecessarily demanding, sarcastic, and even unfair. Not until many years later did they realize his intention and see that his efforts had helped create professionalism in the officer corps.

These were the professors, the Academic Board, that led the faculty during what has so often been called the Golden Age of the Military Academy. They formulated academic doctrine, influenced the officers of the military staff, and developed cadets for decades.

Actions of an Academy superintendent were complicated by his chain of command, the Chief of Engineers and the Secretary of War and, through them, the President. In some instances, there was no problem as evidenced by Thayer's relationships with General Swift, Secretary Calhoun, and President Jefferson. Often, however, efforts of a superintendent could be made extremely difficult, as Thayer learned during conflicts with General Gratiot, Secretary Cass, and President Jackson. Thayer's unsuccessful attempt to have the Chief of Engineers removed from the Academy chain of command had aroused Gratiot's animosity.

Delafield's association with the Chief of Engineers improved when Gratiot was summarily dismissed in December 1838 for alleged financial irregularities. Joseph Totten, now the senior Engineer officer, was named his replacement. An 1805 Academy graduate, Totten had never served at West Point, although he had been a member of several Boards of Visitors. He had served with distinction during the War of 1812 and had been awarded two brevet promotions for gallantry and meritorious service. After the war, he had supervised the fortification and harbor construction in Florida, Rhode Island, and New York. Totten would serve as Chief of Engineers until his death in 1864, providing continuity and support of the Academy in his capacity of Inspector of the institution.

This support immediately became apparent to Delafield when he asked for approval to build a library building that would include additional classroom space and an observatory. Totten obtained Secretary Cass's approval; funds requested were approved by Congress in 1839. Delafield's design and location would influence all later construction at West Point.

Experience gained in previous assignments enabled him to take a direct and personal role in planning the new building. So interested was he in this project that he drew sketch plans during much of his free time, using whatever paper was available. One such plan is drawn on the end sheets of his personal copy of Cadet Regulations. He drew detailed architectural drawings and asked cadets in the first section of Drawing to prepare variations of his plans. His drawings and many of the cadet plans are in the USMA Library Special Collections today.

Delafield faced a problem in determining the architectural style to be used. The 1836 Chapel followed the neo-classic style so popular at the time. The new Academic Building, completed in late 1838, had no distinct style, although its Grecian columns and semicircular arches over the windows demonstrated some effort to blend with the classic Chapel across the street. Delafield considered the classic style unsuitable for a military institution.

He selected English Tudor as a style more fitting to a military institution. Developed in medieval England where homes necessarily became small forts, the style was basically military with battlements, corner towers, sallyports, and narrow windows. As warlike conditions lessened, gothic arches, larger windows, and other modifications softened the harsh appearance of the structures. The original functions of the building probably influenced Delafield's selection of the Tudor Gothic style. The new library was designed to house the headquarters staff, classrooms, and an astronomical observatory.

While Delafield studied architectural styles, undoubtedly with Mahan's assistance, Professor Bartlett, head of the Department of Natural and Experimental

Philosophy, went to Europe to visit leading astronomical observatories. He was the logical individual to make this survey because his department was responsible for teaching astronomy to cadets. On his return, he recommended that the Academy follow the prevalent European system of housing the equatorial, transit, and mural telescopes necessary for complete astronomical observations in three separate towers. The castellated towers used in Tudor structures were ideal for this purpose.

Delafield established a criterion that would influence future construction at West Point when he decided to use granite quarried locally for the library walls. The bleak gray walls were softened with brown stone embellishments and rain-stops above the windows. In original Tudor buildings, windows were flush with the outer walls, and the rain-stops were used to channel water away from the windows. Delafield added the stops to break the severe lines of the building. The three towers on the north face of the building had no windows and enclosed concrete foundations to bear the weight of the observatory apparatus. Domes that could be opened topped the towers. The equipment in the center tower was mounted on twenty-four large cannon balls, which served as bearings when the telescope was traversed.

Offices and classrooms were placed in the west wing on both the ground and second floors. The library occupied the east wing on the ground floor with a mezzanine on the second floor. Approximately 14,000 volumes were shelved in this area. Eighty percent of the books concerned engineering, science, and military science; the total number compared favorably with the holdings of college libraries of the period. Claudius Berard, Teacher of French, was also the librarian. In 1841, a young enlisted man, Andres Freis, was detailed as his assistant. Freis served with the library until his death in 1894.

The library remained unchanged for forty years. By that time, the library was entirely inadequate for its 36,000 volumes. Books were on tables, chairs, and the floor. In 1881, the West Shore Railroad tunnelled under the Plain to provide a clear way north. The rumble of trains going through the tunnel caused intense vibration that distorted astronomical readings. The railroad arranged for the construction of a new observatory near Lusk Reservoir, and a massive renovation of the library building was completed in 1901 under the supervision of George W. Goethals, then an assistant professor in the Department of Engineering. Classrooms and offices were modified to provide more library space. The domes were removed, and windows were placed in the three towers. The renovated building housed the library until it was replaced by a new structure in 1964.

The new library and observatory were soon in full use. George Derby wrote in 1843 that Professor Bartlett watched a comet in April and "probably discovered many important facts with regard to it." Bartlett made photographic images of an eclipse, one of the earliest experiments of this type. In 1845, cadets under Bartlett's supervision observed the planet Mercury moving across the sun and recorded its progress. Derby wrote that he had watched Mercury through "the great telescope; it looked about as large as a five cent piece." Bartlett recorded data on sunspots. Derby mentioned exercises in optics and magnetism, including the use of a magic lantern, camera obscura, and solar microscope. He was intrigued by "a flea magnified to the size of a horse." Bartlett published results of many Academy experiments and tests in professional journals and texts.

Delafield was not content to design only one building. While plans for the library were being processed, he designed a compound to house badly needed workshops, storehouses, and military equipment. His plans were quickly approved, and the compound was completed by 1840. Its style was also Tudor Gothic, and local granite was used in its construction.

The Superintendent had other plans. He realized that the old barracks were inadequate and deteriorating. As early as 1839, he asked General Totten to support the construction of new barracks. A subsequent request attached a plan of the 1815 North Barracks; today it is the only surviving accurate illustration of that early structure. Delafield proposed erecting barracks and a mess building on the bluff above the Hudson River, approximately on the present site of Cullum Hall. Old Fort Clinton would be modified to become an ordnance laboratory; both proposals were included in the report of the 1839 Board of Visitors. Fortunately, Major Smith and Professor Mahan convinced him that this was not a good location because it would be difficult for cadets to march to class during the snowy winter months. Delafield then selected a site adjacent to and west of the Academic Building, which was approved by Totten. Delafield began the design of new barracks using the Tudor Gothic style and local granite. Although Delafield departed before funds were available, the barracks erected in 1851 were based on his plans.

Cadets were aware of Delafield's plans. Like the British navy where sailors learned of their captain's plans by an underground information network, cadets were fully informed of the Superintendent's proposals. Sinkoids—latrine rumors—quickly spread information throughout the Corps, sometimes inaccurate but more often quite true. One source of facts about Delafield's building program was cadet assistant instructors in drawing and engineering. Cadets Bryant Tilden and DeLancey Jones drew plans of the proposed library building. Other cadets provided elevation and plan drawings of the barracks Delafield proposed.

Using cadet instructors or cadets with high academic standing for special projects was not unusual. Church, Bartlett, and Mahan had cadets prepare drawings and diagrams for use in class or to illustrate their publications. George Derby told his mother that he was drawing some large astronomical instruments for Professor Bartlett's book on astronomy. Other cadets made detailed drawings of cannon and artillery equipment for a text lithographed in the Academy printing plant. The professional quality of these drawings reflects the excellent instruction given cadets in art, engineering drawing, and architectural sketching.

In September 1841, Lieutenant Irvin McDowell, Class of 1838, reported for duty as a tactical officer. After graduating, McDowell had served with the 1st Artillery on the Maine frontier during the "potato war." British artillerymen invited their American contemporaries to dinner at their regimental mess. The formal dinner with all of the Royal Regiment of Artillery traditions impressed the American gunners. They had no formal mess and invited the British to an informal dinner and barn dance instead. After several visits with the British, the 1st Artillery officers established the first formal officers' mess in the American Army.

McDowell remembered this after he reported for duty at West Point and found that bachelor officers boarded with the Kinsley family or cooked their own meals in a makeshift kitchen in barracks. After discussing this, McDowell and the other bachelor officers submitted a request to Delafield to form the West Point Army Mess. Delafield concurred. Although an area of the Cadet Mess was reserved for officers, they requested that a mess building be erected because they felt it was not good for discipline to be messed with the cadets. Delafield approved the request and asked Totten to obtain funds for a building that he proposed to locate between the quarters of Professor Mahan and Captain Alexander Smith, across the road from the Cadet Mess. Because the mess was an unofficial organization, Totten refused the request, and Delafield was denied the chance to design still another building.

Delafield's great interest in building did not keep him from other projects. In June 1839, he was able to begin riding instruction for cadets when the War Department assigned six dragoons and twelve horses to West Point. Boards of Visitors had made such a recommendation constantly, beginning during Thayer's superintendency. Delafield and Totten were able to convince Secretary Poinsett that it was essential that cadets learn to ride and at least be familiar with the rudiments of mounted tactics. In September, Delafield was authorized to appoint a riding master. The following year, thirty additional horses and equipment for a mounted artillery battery were provided. The horses were initially stabled in buildings below the Plain until new stables were built in the 1850s.

While outdoor riding classes were taught during the summer, the ground floor exercise rooms in the Academic Building were modified for use as a riding hall. Floors and interior walls were removed, leaving only a small area at the north end of the building enclosed and floored for use as a fencing room. Large metal pillars in the center of the area were shielded to prevent injuring horses or cadets who might bump into them. When academics began in September, the new riding master, James McAuley, was able to train cadets indoors in bad weather. The area north of the Library was used for outdoor drill.

The riding hall was too small for extensive training, and pillars were a hazard, particularly for cadets riding for the first time. Cadet Derby wrote of an accident that injured his classmate, Darius Couch. Couch was thrown by his horse and hit his head against a pillar. He was unconscious for several days, apparently suffering a concussion, but recovered to graduate in the upper fifth of his class. Derby described later riding classes, pleased at jumping five-foot hurdles, practicing saber drill, and galloping in pairs. Outdoor classes included formation drill and occasional rides through the countryside. Derby told of one ride "through a wretched village called Buttermilk Falls" into the valley west of the Academy.

No qualifications for the position of Commandant of Cadets were specified by law. Appointment was made by the Secretary of War, usually with the concurrence of the Superintendent. Smith was an Artillery officer; most of his predecessors had been infantrymen. There was surprise and criticism when Smith was appointed. Many graduates and other Army officials maintained that the Commandant should be an infantryman because of the emphasis on infantry drill and tactics in cadet instruction. Totten and Delafield discussed this criticism and decided that the best qualified tactical officer at the Academy should be selected as Commandant regardless of his branch. Totten persuaded Secretary Poinsett to make this policy. Totten was also able to obtain approval for the instructor of Artillery tactics to be the instructor of Cavalry because the same horses were used for mounted artillery drill and cavalry instruction. He obtained assignment of a tactical instructor in practical field engineering. Previously this instruction had been supervised by the Professor of Engineering. Professor Mahan agreed to this change; it would not have been considered without his concurrence. Having no responsibility for supervising field engineering during the summer enabled Mahan and his assistants to concentrate on classroom instruction, a decided advantage for the department. The Commandant could now include field engineering as a part of overall tactical instruction.

Totten convinced Poinsett that the Commandant should have the same pay and allowances as the Professor of Mathematics and that the pay of other tactical officers should equal that of assistant professors. This raised the status of the Commandant to the same level as the professors regardless of his actual rank. A proposal to place tactical officers directly under the Superintendent was dropped because it would separate the tactical officers from the head of their department—if the Commandant were considered to be the head of the Department of Tactics—and place them on a level with the professors.

Totten became more and more involved with Academy affairs as time passed, far more than any of his predecessors. He became the spokesman countering attacks on the Academy, often using information sent to him by Mahan. He was the means for Academy officials to get information to government officials and Congressmen, both officially and informally. Totten told the Superintendent when the time was right to submit formal requests for funding various projects. His long tenure as Chief of Engineers enabled him to provide continuity not possible by changing superintendents. His friendship with the professors, especially Mahan, kept him fully informed of Academy activities and problems and gave him direct insight into the morale and actions of cadets. Historians have not given Totten credit for his many services to the Academy during his quarter-century tenure as Chief of Engineers. Without his help, superintendents, professors, and commandants would have had a much more difficult time improving the Academy and its curriculum. Whatever accolades were earned by superintendents from 1838 until Totten's death in 1864 deserve to be shared with him. His efficient handling of Academy affairs in Washington, diplomatic liaison with Congress, and ability to persuade both Secretaries of War and Presidents helped superintendents improve the Academy and its curriculum.

Many changes were made during this period to improve administrative procedures and to formalize various routine actions. For the first time, candidates for admission were required to pass a physical examination by a medical board assembled at West Point. After passing physical and academic examinations, a new cadet was required to take an oath of allegiance and agree to serve for eight years. A lithographed certificate of discharge was given to cadets dismissed for academic deficiency. The form for cadet official communications was specified in detail, including the format for a signature block. Even the delinquency report form was changed with a specific routine to be followed. Forms were prescribed for academic reports by the professors, financial statements by the Treasurer, and supply accounts of the Quartermaster and Ordnance officer. The mess steward and the hotel manager had to submit periodic reports. These procedural changes were not restricted to the Academy. The Army was going through a period of administrative change resulting from the increased professionalism that developed during the forty years after the War of 1812.

Not all of the changes at West Point were popular. Cadet Richard S. Ewell, Class of 1840, wrote to a friend that Delafield "seems to pride himself on having everything different from what it used to be." Ewell noted that ration costs had declined from fourteen dollars a month to seven but that meals were much better. He told his friend that some of the women who made pies were afraid of Delafield and that "Godfrey, our shoemaker, refused to make three holes in a leather strap for pants because it was customary to make but two" by order of the Superintendent.

Cadet John Hatch in May 1841 wrote to his sister, giving cadet opinions of Delafield. Stables and a new woodyard had been built. Hatch described the woodyard as "something like a fort or castle to which the name of Fort Punster has been given by cadets in honor of the Major"; Delafield was called "Dick the Punster." A cadet scrapbook of the period includes a caricature showing Delafield as a horned devil carrying a pitchfork on which a cadet is impaled. Hatch indicated that some uniform changes were unpopular with cadets. They were pleased not to have to wear the heavy, leather shako that Delafield had replaced but did not like the cotton trousers that replaced the linen trousers previously worn. Another unpopular action was charging cadets for damages to government property. This had been done by Thayer but not by DeRussy, and the cadets resented this regulation. It served its purpose; serious damage to rooms and equipment decreased.

Delafield did not restrict close regulation of Academy activities to cadets; he prescribed requirements for officers as well. He issued two sets of regulations, one for cadets and one for other personnel. Several officers were admonished for sending communications directly to the Superintendent instead of through the Adjutant. Delafield was following Army Regulations, but he was considered the instigator by the young officers at West Point. A devout man, Delafield directed all officers to attend chapel services. Assistant Surgeon Charles Hitchcock was required to explain in writing why he had not attended chapel services in May 1842 as prescribed by Post Regulations.

Cadet interests were not restricted to academics, social affairs, and other Academy activities. Discussions and debates in the Dialectic Society concerned subjects of military, political, and national interest. An 1840 debate on whether or not officers under the rank of captain should be permitted to marry brought a negative vote from the judges. In 1841, the right of a state to secede from the Union was debated. A tie vote resulted, and the Society president, Cadet Samuel Jones, a Virginian, cast the deciding affirmative vote. An 1843 topic questioned whether Texas would be justified to conquer Mexico. State rights was the subject for another 1843 debate, "Has a State under any circumstances the right to nullify an act of Congress?"

The Corps was aware of anti-Academy feelings in some sections of the nation. Cadet letters condemned bills passed by the Maine, Connecticut, and New York legislatures recommending that the Academy be abolished. Many cadets commented on state elections in letters to their families and friends. George Derby wrote during the 1844 presidential campaign that he had heard that if Polk were elected he would be "death to the Academy and to the Army generally" and expressed the hope that Polk would "be beaten out of sight" and Whig Henry Clay elected.

The annexation of Texas in early 1845 excited the Corps. The dedication of the Dade Monument to the victims of the Seminole massacre added to the excitement generated by General Zachary Taylor's move into Texas in May. It was apparent that fighting could break out at any time. Cadets eagerly read newspaper accounts and watched instructors leave to join their regiments. In August, Derby wrote to his mother that "the rumor now is that the First Class will all be commissioned and sent to Texas early in the fall." It was only a rumor, and Derby and his classmates did not graduate until the following June.

Delafield, reassigned in August 1845, was replaced by Captain Henry Brewerton, Class of 1819. Although cadets welcomed the change, their letters had little to say about the new Superintendent, apparently withholding judgment until they knew about him and how he would supervise the Corps. Derby and his classmates—including George B. McClellan, Jesse Reno, Edward Boynton, Thomas J. Jackson, George Stoneman, and George Pickett—left West Point on July 1, 1846, to join units destined for Texas and the war with Mexico, assignments in coastal defenses, or units on the Indian frontier.

Delafield's first tour as Superintendent—he would be reappointed in 1856—marked a revival of Thayer's program, a revival tempered by fatherly concern for cadet comfort and welfare. Discipline was rigid, as strict as under Thayer; but Delafield eroded its benefits by inconsistency. He left an indelible record as a builder, establishing an architectural pattern continued in the future. Academics were raised to an even higher quality level by professors groomed by Thayer. The underlying objective of all of Thayer's plans and efforts—development of professionalism in the officer corps—was soon to be tested in the ultimate military laboratory: war.

15

We Follow, Close Order, Behind You

News from Mexico was of more interest to cadets than the arrival of the new Superintendent. Zachary Taylor's victories over Mexican forces with a force composed primarily of Regulars brought excitement and cheers, which ceased abruptly when casualty lists appeared. Rankin Dilworth, Class of 1845, died of wounds received at Monterey where his classmate, James S. Woods, was killed storming enemy entrenchments. Only eight months after leaving the Academy, Francis T. Bryan, 1846, was wounded at the battle of Buena Vista. Several members of the Class of 1846 accompanied Kearny's column on its march from Fort Leavenworth to California and others were with Taylor. The majority of the Class, thirty-seven men, joined Winfield Scott's invasion of Mexico and his subsequent advance to Mexico City. Casualty lists from Scott's headquarters saddened the West Point family for many of the Class of 1846 were included. Twenty percent of the Class were wounded. Other classes also had heavy casualties. Of the 714 graduates in service, 48 were killed in battle or died of wounds, a percentage of battle deaths nearly 3 times the percentage of losses for other Regulars and over 7 times greater than the percentage losses of volunteer and militia units. As Cadet Thomas J. Haines wrote to a family friend, they had "seen and felt the elephant," a phrase that became prevalent during the Civil War to indicate that an individual had been in battle.

Other word about graduates was more exciting. Many received brevet promotions, the only way to recognize outstanding service because decorations were not authorized until many years later. Thomas J. Jackson, the awkward cadet who kept to himself, was promoted to permanent first lieutenant, an unusual recognition. He also received brevet promotions to captain and major. The Class of 1846 earned fifty-one brevets. George McClellan earned three promotions; seventeen of the Class received two. Other classes received similar recognition.

News of military activities thrilled the cadets and pleased the faculty. Word of the loss of two guns in the company commanded by Lieutenant John Paul Jones at Monterey saddened the cadets and enlisted men. Their recovery many months later at Cerro Gordo brought cheers of elation. Eventually, the two guns were taken to West Point. Today they greet a visitor to the Administration Building, where they flank the stairway to the Superintendent's office, "lost without dishonor, recovered with glory."

Humorous anecdotes were a welcome change from casualty lists. Zachary Taylor's instructions to Braxton Bragg at Monterey to "double shot your guns and give 'em hell" brought chuckles and ribald comments. In after years, Taylor's order became the mythical "A little more grape, Mr. Bragg."

A less well known incident caused even more hilarity. Captain Francis O. Wyse, Class of 1837, wrote about the unusual steps he had taken to replenish his ammunition west of Tampico. When his round shot and powder had been almost completely expended near the village of Tantinea and a large Mexican force stood between him and Tampico, he went to the village to look for shot. After ransacking dwellings, he found a large amount of powder and musket balls but no shot. When it was suggested that the musket balls could be used as cannister, a second search was made for containers. The village cantina provided a solution—wine bottles that were approximately the diameter of the gun tubes. Wyse had his men empty the bottles and fill them with ball shot. One wonders how many bottles were emptied on the ground and how many were disposed of in another manner. Still needed were powder bags. These were made from the flannel shirts of his men. With this supercharged ammunition available, the little force was able to fight its way back to Tampico, where more normal ammunition was obtained—and new shirts for the cannoneers.

The record of graduates assigned to the 1st Artillery illustrates the contributions that arm made throughout the conflict. Six of fifty officers assigned were killed in action or died of wounds. Over forty brevet promotions were earned by the forty officers serving in Mexico; one to brigadier general, one to colonel, six to lieutenant colonel, four to major, seven to captain, and others to first lieutenant. The regiment served first with Taylor and then joined Scott in the landings at Vera Cruz and the move to Mexico City. The experience gained in every battle of both campaigns was a benefit to these officers, many of whom are remembered for later service: Edward C. Boynton, Henry Coppee, Abner Doubleday, A. P. Hill, Joseph Hooker, Thomas J. Jackson, John B. Magruder, Irvin McDowell, James B. Ricketts, and John H. Winder.

The exploits of other graduates in other regiments and other branches—Beauregard, Bliss, Davis, Garnett, Grant, Lee, McClellan, Meade, Sherman, Thomas, and Totten, and two former commandants, Worth and Hitchcock—excited the cadets and pleased the faculty, Professor Mahan perhaps most of all. He more than others realized that both Scott and Taylor had vindicated his emphasis on mobility as a tool of battle. Worth had been a brigade commander with Taylor and a division commander with Scott. Totten, as Chief Engineer for Scott, planned and supervised the landings at Vera Cruz. Most engineers and artillerymen with both forces were graduates. The rapid movement of artillery units and their dominance on the battlefield proved that American artillery was equal to that of any other army. The skill of Academy engineer officers in repairing bridges, clearing roads, and reconnoitering routes of advance toward objectives or around obstacles contributed to the successes of Taylor and Scott.

Staff work of graduates such as William W. S. Bliss, who served as Taylor's Chief of Staff, assured troops that necessary supplies would be available. Concise, clear dispatches sent units to the battle zone in rapid time and ready to fight. The seeming ease with which units moved from one area of the battlefield to another was another indication of good staff work. Militia and volunteer units commanded by graduates performed well, particularly the Mississippi regiment under Colonel Jefferson Davis. After Buena Vista, where Davis was severely wounded leading his regiment in a charge that changed possible defeat into victory, he was offered a regular commission as a brigadier general instead of the usual brevet promotion. Davis declined; one wonders what would have happened in later years had he accepted.

The record of Academy graduates in all campaigns stifled the most adverse criticism of the institution. Their gallant conduct in battle and professional staff work developed as part of their education and training contributed much to the quick victory in a foreign campaign. The Academy, the Army, and the nation could look on their accomplishments with pride and satisfaction.

At West Point, routine continued almost unchanged. Cadets still devoted most of their time to study and drill. Although no new subjects were added to the curriculum, additions and changes within the existing structure caused the Board of Visitors in 1848 to urge that the course be extended to five years. The Board also recommended that Spanish be taught, a law department be established to teach cadets both military and civil law, and logic be dropped from the curriculum. The five year course would be established six years later; Spanish would be added in 1856; but law continued to be a subject taught by the Department of Geography, History, and Ethics until 1871.

Cadet letters described some of the added academic work. Thomas J. Haines wrote about an experiment conducted by Professor Bailey to test the properties of carbolic acid frozen under pressure. William Dutton told a friend about Professor Bartlett's classes using the new observatory telescope. Cadets made gunpowder, built small bridges, and learned stone cutting as part of their engineering course. Architectural drawing was a part of that course, supplementing the art instruction of Professor Weir. The new riding classes and these additions to the already full curriculum required more cadet time and provided the basis for the recommended course extension to five years.

Curriculum-related activities increased. In 1848, Professor Mahan and a group of officers established the Napoleon Club to foster the study of Napoleon's campaigns. A room in the Academic Building was set aside for its use. Large maps of Napoleonic campaigns lined the walls. Cadets studying military art under Mahan were taken to this room, where critical analysis of campaigns could be made. The club was an indication of the stress on French techniques advocated by Mahan, an emphasis that was reflected in the Army until after the Civil War.

Superintendent Brewerton took an interest in cadet welfare shortly after replacing Delafield. Concerned that cadets were not exercising properly, he directed in February 1846 that exercises be conducted for an hour each afternoon except Saturday and Sunday "in order to counteract the injurious effects likely to arise from too sedentary habits of the Corps of Cadets." The First Class was excused from exercise sessions. Classes were held only during the winter after drill was suspended. The small gymnasium at the north end of the Academic Building was inadequate and poorly equipped. Space and equipment improved after the new Riding Hall was completed in 1855.

Exercise classes were unpopular with the cadets who felt that they had been deprived of an hour of free time. Cadet Thomas J. Haines wrote to his friend, A. R. Hatch, that he thought "the gymnasium would be a fine thing if we were not required to go, but this spoils it all." Haines and other cadets who had used the gymnasium before Brewerton's edict resented being compelled to do what had previously been optional.

In November 1847, Brewerton directed cadets to form cricket clubs and ordered the riding and fencing halls to be made available for the daily exercise classes. Brewerton's effort to emulate the sports clubs of the British army was unsuccessful. Cricket at West Point lasted only a single season. Cadets preferred their rude games of football and baseball.

Another of Brewerton's changes was enthusiastically received by cadets; they were not required to attend dinner. Many cadets took advantage of this new privilege. Some "ran it" to Benny Havens or Avery's tavern, carefully avoiding tactical officers who would report them for being off limits. Most headed for the bootblack's abode. Joe Simpson, a mulatto who served as both bootblack and barber, occupied a small brick building east of North Barracks.

The strange building had an octagon center and two pentagonal wings. Its brick exterior had been painted yellow, the standard Quartermaster paint color, which had faded over the years. At one time it had been an officer's quarters and then the office of the post quartermaster that was relocated in the new service compound during Delafield's superintendency. Simpson was moved from his old location near the present Field House to save cadets the long walk across the Plain in bad weather.

Proximity to barracks and Brewerton's lenient order led the enterprising bootblack to provide an additional albeit unauthorized service to the young cadets: food, either cooked or uncooked. Cadet William P. Craighill in his diary mentioned obtaining turkeys, ducks, and chickens from Simpson. Most cadets preferred to roast their fowl in the fireplaces in their rooms; only a few purchased cooked food. Simpson kept erratic hours, and cadets often found him away when they wanted to buy food. When this happened, they either went without dinner or tried to forage something from friends in the barracks. Craighill mentioned several instances when Simpson was not in his shop and he and his companions made a meal of cheese, bread, nuts, and dried fruit.

Brewerton's leniency extended to cadet possession of money. Tactical officers made little effort to prevent cadets from writing home for funds. Most used these contributions for food from Simpson, but some spent their money at the taverns. Others used money from home to purchase clothing in order to keep a credit in their official accounts. Plebe August Plummer wrote to his aunt for help, explaining that there were many things "which we cannot get orders for and which we cannot do without," adding that he had been forced to borrow money from one of his roommates.

Class rings were now an established tradition. First Classmen wrote home enthusiastically describing their rings. There was no special ceremony when they put their rings on for the first time. Rings arrived individually by mail, and the recipient put the ring on his finger immediately. Many cadets asked for financial help to pay for their rings; even the few dollars involved was more than their official accounts could bear. All tried to keep sufficient funds available to pay for officers' uniforms and equipment, well over $200, an extremely large amount at that time.

Normally, a band concert was held each week, out of doors during the warmer months, in the fencing room during the winter. Bandmaster and Professor of Music Apelles always presided. Mrs. Theophile D'Oremieulx, whose husband was a civilian French instructor, in her memoirs praised Apelles for bringing the band to a high standard. She remembered him playing his violin at small social functions. The band reflected Apelles' personal musical interest with a large string section for the concerts.

Plebes were given dancing lessons during summer camp. They were not permitted to attend any of the three weekly dances, however, as Plummer complained in one of his letters. Dances were held in the Engineering laboratory in the Academic Building. Furniture, apparatus, and blackboards were removed, and the room decorated. All dances were formal with cadets in full dress uniforms and their young ladies in ball gowns.

Married officers invited cadets to dinners and other social functions in their homes. Mrs. D'Oremieulx said that she often invited cadets to supper, especially when she had young ladies as guests. Officers and cadets were rarely invited the same evening. Mary O'Maher, daughter of Commissary Officer Timothy O'Maher, who later married Quincy A. Gilmore, Class of 1849, wrote to a friend about a musical evening with Cadet Andrew Donelson, grandnephew of Andrew Jackson, "taking his place beside the piano with his flute." She also described rides and trips on the river. One of her escorts was Cadet James McNeill Whistler. Cadet William Morris wrote to his father of an evening he spent at the home of Hyacinthe Agnel, another civilian French instructor. Mrs. Agnel played opera music on her piano, and the group sang several songs to her accompaniment.

Life for officers' families was indeed pleasant. Mrs. D'Oremieulx described her home, a small wooden house next to the hospital, possibly part of the old North tavern moved there after the new hospital was built. Most families had one servant; she had two, a cook and a maid. The cook received eight dollars a month; the maid, four. Food costs for her family averaged fifty dollars a month. Provisions were purchased from farmers; bread, from the cadet bakery. During winter months, when farmers were unable to bring their foodstuffs to West Point, supplies were available at the Academy storeroom. Mrs. D'Oremieulx said that she often substituted cold pork or veal for chicken salad at parties during the winter, although "hot whiskey punch was always on hand, even when the lemons were scarce." Bootblack Simpson also operated a confectionery for Mrs. D'Oremieulx who mentioned that his wife, "our excellent confectioner," provided sweets for parties, one of the earliest accounts of the forerunner of the cadet "Boodlers." Wives frequently shared their specialties with their neighbors, "passing many a plate of hot biscuits, gingerbread, or seedcake over the fence which separated our quarters," recalled Mrs. D'Oremieulx.

Social affairs were exchanged with civilians living on the east shore. Gouverneur Kemble hosted West Point families and often included junior officers as well as the Superintendent, Commandant, and professors. His whist parties were famous, with distinguished guests joining local gentry and West Point visitors. General Scott enjoyed the game and hosted whist parties at the hotel. Kemble's dinners were famous for outstanding cuisine and excellent wines. A friend of the Academy since Thayer's day, Kemble supported it actively in good times and in bad and was considered to be almost a member of the West Point family.

Despite the many social activities, there was no attempt for one lady or officer to outdo others in their entertainment. Older wives helped newlyweds become more accustomed to their new way of life by providing advice and assistance when needed. Because all lived under the same regulations and with the same relative pay, there was little effort to vie with one another or attempt to live better than one's neighbors. Any such attempt was considered to be a sign of poor breeding and was not tolerated. Those with an outside income conformed to accepted practice. The result was a closely knit official family. Years later, one lady commented that she remembered only the good times and friendships, not any unpleasantness or ill will.

There were two elementary schools, one for officers' children and one for children of enlisted men. Officers' children attended school in a wooden building in the rear and south of the superintendent's quarters. The building had been a wing of the military storekeeper's house. When Mrs. Thompson moved there from her bungalow, one wing was moved and renovated as a school. William W. Bailey, son of Professor Jacob Bailey, many years later remembered fellow students Robert E. Lee, Jr.; the three Mahan boys; Professor Weir's sons; John

French, son of Chaplain French; and sons of other officers. Apparently the school was not coeducational, for Bailey mentions no girl students. The number of students rarely numbered more than fifteen.

The children, at least the boys, had a lively time and heckled both cadets and enlisted men. Growing up within sound of the reveille gun and bugler's notes forced the youngsters into a schedule paralleling the cadet routine. Up and fed at an early hour during the summer months, they headed for the cadet area to, as Bailey recorded, "devil the poor plebes till even a yearling's attention, by contrast, was delightful." Bailey once was thoroughly spanked by Fitzhugh Lee for calling him a "Beast," or an "Animal" or "Thing," titles reserved for plebes. Lee was a yearling at the time. Bailey's record is one of the earliest indications that "Beast" applied to plebes, a term later to be applied to plebe training, Beast Barracks.

Another Bailey recollection involved George Derby and the cadet fire engine. The boys hurried to the barracks area when fire call was sounded and watched the cadets go through their drill. During one test, Derby as "captain of the pipe" inadvertently directed the hose nozzle toward the Commandant, completely drenching him. Bailey did not record the results of that unplanned shower.

A favorite game was a form of tag played around the edges of Execution Hollow. The boys would slide down the banks to avoid being caught. They also played "seek" near the Library, often bringing the custodian out to chase them away or, when he managed to catch one of the culprits, exact a promise of better behavior.

The Bailey family worshiped at the Church of the Holy Innocents, the Episcopal church in Buttermilk Falls. Other West Point families, including the Mahans, also preferred Episcopal services to those in the Cadet Chapel. When the Superintendent directed all faculty members to attend Chapel regardless of their religious preferences, he aroused immediate and vociferous objections. Brewerton merely pointed out that Paragraph 127 of Academy Regulations required every member of the staff to attend Chapel and refused to make any exceptions. Professor Mahan wrote to the Secretary of War, citing his objections and reasons in a four-page letter. Secretary Conrad agreed that faculty members should be permitted to attend other services if the chaplain was of another persuasion. He also extended that right to cadets. Initially, cadets were required to study in their rooms if excused from Chapel. Later, they were permitted to attend services at the Church of the Holy Innocents or a Catholic parish.

Family life at West Point was enjoyable but not always easy. Fireplaces and stoves provided the only heat in quarters. Winter mornings were always cold, even though fires were banked the night before. Whale lamps and candles provided the light at night, although a few fortunate families possessed the new kerosene lamps. There was no running water in the quarters; most had a pump-and-pipe connection to the water mains running from the reservoir to the cadet area. Indoor bathrooms did not appear until the 1860s. Despite these disadvantages, life was pleasant, particularly for the children and young ladies.

Cadet uniforms since 1816 had always been strikingly attractive. The simple dignity of cadet gray, brass bullet buttons, white trousers, and the relatively unadorned shako was a decided contrast to the extremely gaudy uniforms of the period. Brewerton realized that the full-dress uniform was not suitable for wear at all times. His efforts, seconded by Totten, brought some changes. The collar of the full dress coat was lowered slightly, and a white collar was worn folded over the upper edge of the collar. A fatigue jacket, a brown linen coatee, was authorized for summer wear. Another welcome change was the cap provided for wear with the fatigue jacket. This was a variation of the cap worn by troops in Mexico, a stiff blue cloth base with visor and a floppy, enameled leather upper. The top, flattened by inserting a rattan grommet, extended over the base of the cap. With hard use, grommets cracked and many cadets removed them. Cadet Joseph Tidball in his unpublished memoirs described "airy cadets who pulled these tops over to one side, giving themselves a rakish appearance." Air Corps officers in World War II often did the same. Cadets liked the caps because they were ideally suited for smuggling food out of the mess hall.

The greatest uniform change, a very controversial matter, was the introduction of the fly-front trousers to replace the broad, front-flap pattern. The latter resembled the legendary sailors' bell-bottom trousers. Fly-front trousers were common in the civilian community but were considered inappropriate for cadets on the grounds of proper decorum. Tidball described a test involving trousers that opened in the rear. The concept was abandoned because the tails of the full dress coat often became tangled in the trouser opening. Despite objections from many of the ladies of the Post, the new style was adopted, much to the delight of the cadets.

West Point in the late 1840s and early 1850s became a tourist mecca. The Hudson River Railroad, built along the east bank of the Hudson River during this period, made the Academy much more accessible. By 1851, it had become common for New Yorkers to take the train to Cold Spring and a small ferry across the river to West Point. The railroad also ended the four-month isolation during the winter when ice blocked the river.

There were breaks in the routine. The death of former President John Quincy Adams in February 1848 canceled all normal activities for the day. The cadet battery fired a national salute in his honor. Martin Van Buren visited West Point in 1849, and the cadet battery again fired a salute of twenty-one guns. Other distinguished visitors always required a special parade. The annual Board of Visitors review of all cadet activities added to cadet duties. Cadets were well aware of the importance of that group and often wrote home expressing hope that the Board would recommend improvements, such as obtaining approval for the much-needed Riding Hall.

An unusual and exciting event for both cadets and families occurred on New Year's Day 1849. Winfield Scott arrived, bringing to West Point flags and trophies captured in Mexico. The Corps and band marched to the dock and formed a hollow square. Forty cadets, each carrying a flag, marched into the center of the square. Cadet George S. Hartsuff described the flags: "They must have passed through some hard fighting" because many of them were torn and covered with blood. The color bearers, escorted by the Corps and the band playing "Santa Ana's March," marched up the hill to the Library as the cadet battery fired a salute. A message from President Zachary Taylor was read to the assemblage and Scott again repeated his statement that but for the "science of the Military Academy . . . the army, multiplied by four, could not have entered the capital of Mexico." The flags were placed in the Library, where Hartsuff said, they "break down the arguments and remove the prejudices against the Military Academy by proving that its graduates were not mere mushroom soldiers afraid of the smell of powder."

Later, the flags were moved to the Chapel and the trophies to the service compound near the relics of the Revolutionary War. One, a howitzer captured at Monterey, was the subject of a cadet prank in 1872. It was taken from the compound and fired from the fourth floor of barracks. The flags were returned to Mexico in 1948; most of the trophies remain at West Point.

Cadet slang developed more during this period than in earlier years. "Find" or "found" became routine argot used by officers and cadets alike. Cadet David S. Stanley provided a very humorous account of such use in answering a Cullum questionnaire. Cadet Louis Guesnon, a Louisianan of French descent, ran into trouble during a calculus recitation to instructor Jesse Reno. According to Stanley, he turned to Reno and, in broken patois, said, "Captain, I cannot explain him; since I passed the general remark, I is losht." Reno, trying to stifle a laugh, replied, "Oh, never mind, Mr. Guesnon. If you are lost now, you will be found in January." Reno was correct; Guesnon did not graduate.

Changes were in process. Officers who had served in Mexico gradually replaced members of the staff and faculty. Simon B. Buckner, Erasmus D. Keyes, Fitz-John Porter, and George Thomas were assigned to the Tactical Department between 1848 and 1850. James W. Abert, George W. Cullum, Jesse Reno, Joseph J. Reynolds, Edmund K. Smith, and Gustavus W. Smith were among the officers assigned to academic departments. They brought with them practical experience learned in the field, experience that improved tactical instruction and gave cadets an opportunity to discuss military matters with men who had been through the confusion of combat. Professor Mahan, of course, was delighted to have a sounding board for his theories and spent many hours discussing Mexican campaigns with his former students.

These assignments were made by General Totten, who had returned to his Washington post as Chief of Engineers. Assignments were discussed with Winfield Scott, for most of the officers were not Engineers and Scott controlled assignments for other branches.

In 1848, the construction of new barracks was started. Recommendations by several Boards of Visitors and constant requests by Delafield during his superintendency had failed because Congress refused to provide the required funds. The postwar change in attitudes concerning the Academy was exemplified by the immediate appropriation of construction money. Delafield's plans were res-urrected and, with changes made by Totten's engineer staff, used as the basis for construction.

The Tudor Gothic style of the Library was used for the barracks. Battlements and castellated towers emphasized the military motif. Added features not found in the Library were a sallyport and external moats along the north side. Stone quarried in the area near the reservoir was used throughout. The somber gray tone was softened by brown stone as a trim above the windows. The initial construction provided for an L-shaped building with a sallyport in the center of the north wing.

Rooms were arranged in a manner similar to that of old South Barracks, a vertical organization with a "division" consisting of a section of four floors, four rooms on each floor opening onto a hall. The ground floor had exits on the north and south sides. Each of the four companies was assigned three divisions, a total of forty-eight rooms. Two rooms were assigned to each company tactical officer for use as an office and living quarters. Rooms in the northwestern tower and the west wing were used as family quarters. Two first floor rooms in the west wing were assigned initially to the Commandant. Later that year, he moved into the new guardhouse on the south side of the barracks area.

The large, vaulted room over the sallyport was occupied by the Dialectic Society. It was used for meetings, often attended by most of the officers, some family members, and many visitors. The Society library was quite large, over 600 volumes. Built-in bookcases were provided for books, which included essays, reference volumes, novels, memoirs, plays, poetry, travel works, and biogra-phies. Magazines and newspapers were available. A disastrous fire in February 1871 destroyed the library and the roof and fourth story of the barracks.

Despite fireplaces in each room, the barracks were heated by boilers in the basement of each division. Why were fireplaces included? Facetiously, this might be explained by the statement that Delafield's original plan had included fire-places and that alteration would involve too much red tape to make any change worthwhile. There are two logical reasons for leaving fireplaces in the rooms. If the heating system in any division failed, fireplaces could be used to keep cadets warm. Boilers probably were not used during cool months in the spring and fall. A sudden, temporary drop in temperature, all too frequent in March and October, would justify the use of fireplaces. In 1867, the division boilers were replaced by central heating provided by a heating plant on the south side of the barracks quadrangle.

Cadets did not like the new system because it ended most of the cooking "hash" in fireplaces. Many letters commented about the heating grills in each room. Some cadets complained about the odor. Others disliked the dust raised by warm air coming out of the ducts. Most agreed that rooms were much warmer than in the old barracks.

There was no running water. Cadets, usually plebes, still carried water to their rooms from the old main across the road. Since there was no way for them to have a shower or bath in barracks, cadets still used the primitive bathing facilities near the cemetery or strolled to the river in warm weather for a combination swim and bath. Eventually, a bath house was built across the area near the Academic Building, and cadets were able to bathe indoors.

There were no toilet facilities in the barracks. Latrines were located in a building on the south side of the area. As a part of the massive building program beginning in 1904, water pipes were installed in the barracks. Large sinks were placed in the hall on each floor. Toilets and bathing facilities were installed in the basement of each division.

There was one welcome omission in the new barracks. A room in old South Barracks had been used as the cadet prison. The half of the room with windows was the "light prison." The smaller portion was the hated "dark prison." Neither confinement area was actually uncomfortable, but cadets detested them anyway. After the move to the new barracks, confinement to one's room replaced confinement in either the light or dark prison. That a cadet could be expected to remain in his own room when under confinement restrictions indicated that he was honor bound to obey the limits imposed.

As each wing of the barracks was completed, cadets moved into their new rooms. North Barracks was vacated first, and A and B Companies moved into the first six divisions of the new structure. Cadets complained in their letters about guard duty on the stoops of Central Barracks for they were posted outside the building instead of in the halls as they had been in old North Barracks. By the time the next wing was completed, complaints had ended. Both of the old barracks were razed as soon as their occupants moved. The excavations were filled, and the ground was leveled.

Cadet initiative being what cadet initiative was—and still is—they soon found a place to cook their unauthorized meals. An unknown and enterprising cadet discovered a way into the attic area above the fourth floor. He found that there were fireplaces at the end of each wing, much larger fireplaces than those in the rooms. The attics soon became assembly areas for cadet escapades. Many turkeys and other fowl were roasted there. It became customary for the inhabitants of the "cockloft" to scratch their names or initials and their class year on the bricks of the fireplaces. A few tables and chairs were carried into the lofts unnoticed by the tactical officers. The cockloft was a place to go for a smoke, a meal, a game of whist or euchre, and even a bit of rum. Eventually, the tactical officers discovered the hideout, and the entries were sealed.

Another building was erected in 1851; a new Mess Hall south of the Academic Building. Delafield had not prepared any plans for the structure, and it differed somewhat from his Tudor Gothic style. It did have battlements, castellated towers, and windows similar to those in the Academic Building. One wing was turned over to the West Point Army Mess for use by bachelor officers. In addition to the dining area, the wing had a recreation room. The large cadet dining room, capable of seating the entire Corps at one time, was decorated with portraits of graduates and other distinguished military men.

The kitchen area was equipped with every convenience of the period. Hand pumps were used to pump water into the sinks instead of carrying it in buckets from outdoor mains. The building was heated by its own hot-air system. Large baking ovens were used to bake bread and occasional desserts for the cadet and officers' messes and for sale to post families. Quarters were provided for the mess steward and his family. In 1887, the building became Grant Hall, the first West Point structure to be given a specific name.

Despite improvements made by Brewerton, neither Scott nor Totten was pleased with the relaxed atmosphere of the Academy. Discipline in the Corps had lessened; it seemed to oscillate like a pendulum. Under Partridge, there was little discipline. Thayer developed the strict but fair discipline admired by Scott. With his departure in 1833, the pendulum had started a backward swing, and discipline eased with DeRussy. Under Delafield, the pendulum turned back as discipline stiffened, but Delafield was too strict on both cadets and the staff, rousing open resentment. Under Brewerton, discipline again lessened, too much so. The time had come to tighten the reins with a new superintendent.

The first steps had already been taken with the assignment of the Mexican War veterans. Knowing the value of discipline in battle, they quietly began to bring the Corps back to the desired level. Their instruction in infantry, artillery, and cavalry tactics also improved the training of the cadets. Methods used by George H. Thomas were typical of this instruction. As senior artillery and cavalry instructor, he taught cadets what he had learned in Mexico. In cavalry drill, he emphasized the role of the dragoon who moved to a battle area on horseback and then dismounted to fight as infantry. Thomas also stressed the shock value of the cavalry charge with troopers standing in their stirrups yelling, bare steel of sabers flashing overhead. Artillery instruction highlighted the need for artillery to move forward rapidly and constantly to support the infantry. As a battle-tested artilleryman, he taught that the guns should be with or ahead of the infantry, emphasizing the need for accurate and rapid fire. Speed and mobility were important, but accuracy was the key to successful support of the infantry.

The success of this instruction can be measured by the accomplishments of the cadets in a conflict not too distant in the future. George Crook, John Bell Hood, Oliver O. Howard, James McPherson, John Schofield, Philip Sheridan, Henry Slocum, and J.E.B. Stuart were among the cadets trained by this select group. They learned well their tactical lessons and Mahan's theories.

Thomas managed to get himself into trouble with Brewerton within a week after reporting for duty. Surveying the horses and riding equipment, Thomas was shocked at what he found. Most of the horses were old—one was nineteen, lame, and sullen—and worn out. Many were diseased, several far gone with glanders. One was blind; another had an affliction that caused him to fall unexpectedly and often. Saddles and sabers were obsolete. New stables were badly needed.

Thomas submitted a request for new horses and better equipment through channels. A second requisition followed, asking for curry combs, brushes, and other equipment. Brewerton's method of endorsing Thomas's requests did not satisfy Thomas. When no results were obtained, he sent another requisition directly to the Quartermaster General, Thomas S. Jessup. Irritated, Jessup reported the matter to General Totten, who officially reminded Thomas of the requirement to follow normal military procedures. Thomas replied, "For the future, my letters shall be sent through proper channels."

Another young officer assigned at this time would make a different contribution to the Academy. Captain George W. Cullum, Class of 1833, had reported for duty at West Point in 1846 to prepare a manual concerning rubber pontoon bridges. He remained as supervisory engineer during the construction of the new barracks and then successively as commander of the Sapper detachment, Treasurer of the Academy, and instructor of Practical Military Engineering. During these assignments, Cullum became interested in the history of the Academy and the careers of its graduates. In late 1849, he decided to publish a record of the service of graduates. He began a nineteen-year search for graduates no longer in service, sending a questionnaire to all living graduates he could locate. The project was completed with the 1868 publication of the first two volumes of *The Biographical Register of the Officers and Graduates of the U.S. Military Academy*. Seven additional volumes were published at ten year intervals. The series has been continued by the USMA Association of Graduates.

Cullum returned as Superintendent from 1864 to 1865. He prepared a history of the Academy and a biography of Sylvanus Thayer as part of Volume III of his *Register*. Through his efforts, graduates contributed funds for the statue of Thayer unveiled in 1883. Cullum's final contribution to the Academy was a bequest for the construction of the Memorial Hall bearing his name.

Although discipline had lessened under Brewerton's supervision, his superintendency had benefitted the Academy on the whole. His interest in cadet welfare made their uniforms more comfortable. The academic curriculum was improved. Horace Mann in 1849 stated that he had "rarely, if ever, seen anything that equalled either the excellence of the teaching or the proficiency of those taught." Brewerton had actively sought and obtained the funds for a major building program. Like his predecessors, he had to contend with the reinstatement of dismissed cadets by the Secretary of War. Neither he nor the Chief of Engineers was able to convince the Secretary that the policy was damaging to discipline and equally bad for the cadet concerned.

All things taken into consideration, the time had come to take the final step needed to raise discipline to the desired level. With the building material in place—the young veterans assigned to the Academy—Totten and Scott took that step: Brevet Colonel Robert E. Lee was appointed to succeed Brewerton on September 1, 1852.

Son of Revolutionary War hero Light Horse Harry Lee, Robert E. Lee entered the Academy in 1826. His cadet record was exemplary; he graduated second in his class. He was Acting Assistant Professor of Mathematics as a yearling and Second Classman. In his final year, he served as cadet adjutant. His most outstanding record was graduating without receiving any demerits during his entire cadet career. Other cadets during this period frequently had no demerits for a single year; a few for two years; but no other cadet equalled Lee's record. As a cadet, he had been subject to and learned to admire the stern but fair and fatherly discipline of Worth and Thayer, a lesson he followed throughout his life. He also absorbed thoroughly the Thayer concept of honor; and, many years later, he would establish a comparable honor system at Washington College in Lexington, Virginia.

Lee returned to find the Academy much changed since his graduation in 1829. Very few of the old buildings remained. The new Barracks, Hospital, Chapel, Ordnance and Artillery laboratories, Academic Building, Library, Mess Hall, and Band Barracks had been built long after his cadet years. Many of the depressions in the Plain had been filled, and most of the large rocks had been removed. Trees that which had been saplings were approaching full growth. The monument to Kosciuszko, for which he had assisted in raising funds, was in place on the parapet of Fort Clinton. Wood Monument had been moved from the barracks area to the small hillock near the road to the dock. The monument to Dade's Command stood on the east side of the Plain overlooking the river.

The curriculum had progressed since Lee's graduation. Thayer's basic framework was still intact, but the subjects taught had moved forward rapidly as new theories were proven and scientific discoveries made. New equipment, such as the telescopes in the Library observatory, provided cadets and faculty members with greater opportunity for research. The books in the Library, which Lee had used extensively as a cadet, had increased greatly in number and scope. Practical work was included in the engineering instruction. The value of the technical and scientific education inherent in cadet instruction was known nationwide.

Of his professors, only Church and Bartlett remained. He may have seen Mahan before Mahan left for Europe shortly after Lee entered the Academy, but Lee certainly was aware of Mahan's reputation as an engineer and exponent of military tactics and strategy. Church, whom he remembered as an upperclassman, was also well known for his mathematical treatises. Lee had known many of the young officers on the faculty and staff in Mexico. He did not return to a strange group; it was more a return to the family.

There was one significant change. The Academy had been under constant attacks from critics when Lee wore a gray uniform. Now it was praised from all sides for the accomplishments of its graduates in the War with Mexico. As a cadet, Lee had seen state legislatures calling for the abolishment of the Academy. Now he observed states praising the work of graduates. The respect and esteem with which the Academy was viewed was not restricted to military accomplishments. Graduates had contributed to almost every field of national endeavor.

Books and texts written by faculty members were used extensively in other academic institutions. Bartlett, Davies, Mahan, Church, and Bailey had all contributed to knowledge in their respective fields. At least two colleges had been founded by graduates, Virginia Military Institute by Francis H. Smith and Norwich by Alden Partridge. West Point was no longer the only engineering school in the United States, but graduates were a part of every other college teaching engineering or scientific subjects.

When Harvard founded the Lawrence School of Engineering in 1846, Henry L. Eustis, Class of 1842, was selected as its first dean and professor of engineering. Yale followed a year later by naming William A. Norton, Class of 1831, as the first professor of civil engineering in the Sheffield School of Engineering. The University of Michigan made William G. Peck, Class of 1844, its first professor of physics and engineering in 1852. Two years later, he became professor of mathematics at Columbia. The United States Naval Academy, established in 1845, based much of its original organization on a report and recommendations of Midshipman S. Marcy, who had made a detailed study of West Point's methods at the direction of Secretary of the Navy George Bancroft. Graduates who became professors at the Naval Academy included Henry H. Lockwood, 1836; William F. Hopkins, 1825; and Richard S. Smith, 1834. Seven of eight civilian institutions involved with technical education (Brown, Columbia, Brooklyn Polytechnic Institute, Lehigh, Harvard, Union, and Yale) had West Point graduates on their faculties. Only Rensselaer had no direct connection with the Academy, but it used mathematical and engineering texts prepared by West Point graduates.

The period between Lee's graduation and his return in 1852 was the era of railroad building and expansion. Academy graduates were involved in the building of almost every railroad line in the country. William G. McNeill, Class of 1817, and George W. Whistler, Class of 1819, father of artist James McNeill Whistler, were instrumental in planning for and building the Baltimore and Ohio Railroad, the earliest important railroad in the United States intended for general transportation. Whistler designed a locomotive more suitable to American terrain than its British forerunner. Other early graduates who contributed to the railroad expansion included Joshua Barney, 1820; Isaac Trimble, William Cook, and Walter Gwynn, 1822; and John Dilahunty and R. Edward Hazzard, 1824. Nearly forty railroads had graduates as engineers or supervisory officials. Some early graduates remained in service while working for the new railroads, the War Department giving them permission to do so. Later, this dual interest was not condoned, and graduates resigned to join the rapidly expanding number of railroad companies. Graduates later would be involved in the surveys and construction of the transcontinental railways.

Whistler was perhaps the best known of these railroad engineers, not only in the United States but also in Europe. So great was his reputation that the Czar of Russia personally invited him to build a railroad from St. Petersburg to Moscow. Whistler did not live to complete the project. After his death in 1849, his work was completed by another graduate, Thompson S. Brown, Class of 1825.

Graduates also aided in the construction of canals, bridges, and roads. The famed Cumberland Road was the work of Richard Delafield, Henry Brewerton,

Joseph Mansfield, and George Dutton, a Corps of Engineers project; all were still on active duty. Other Corps of Engineers projects included the Chesapeake and Ohio and the Erie Canals. Several graduates were involved with the development of the Croton reservoir to provide water for New York City. Harbors and rivers were improved by the Corps and its Academy graduates. They constructed breakwaters, lighthouses, and levees. Silted areas in harbors were dredged clear, and harbors were deepened to permit their use as major ports. Along the Mississippi River, periodic floods had disrupted commerce and destroyed farmlands. Silt carried into the Mississippi threatened to ruin river ports such as St. Louis. Periodic dredging was only a temporary measure; silt soon blocked the area again. An unusual, self-scouring solution developed by a Corps of Engineers officer, Lieutenant Robert E. Lee, enabled St. Louis to survive and become a major artery for both river and railway traffic.

Some graduates who resigned their commissions became elected officials. Jefferson Davis, 1828, was elected to the House of Representatives in 1845. After his return from Mexico, he was elected to the Senate, where he served as Chairman of the Military Affairs Committee from 1849 to 1851. He would shortly be appointed Lee's superior as Secretary of War. Robert M. McLane, 1837, was a Congressman from 1847 to 1851 and Chairman of the House Committee on Commerce from 1849 to 1851. Robert F. W. Allston, 1833, was a South Carolina state legislator from 1828 to 1856 and governor from 1856 to 1858. Many other graduates also held state or city elective offices or filled appointed positions.

Most graduates who resigned entered the engineering profession and participated in various state and local engineering projects. A great number became attorneys. Several served as state judges. A few graduates became physicians. Strangely, more West Pointers became clergymen than doctors. Joseph S. Worth, 1825; William Bryant, George Woodbridge, Martin P. Parks, all from the Class of 1826; Leonidas Polk, 1827; Francis Vinton and William N. Pendleton of the Class of 1830; and Roswell Park, 1831, were among the many graduates who became Episcopal rectors. Polk served as Bishop from 1841 until the beginning of the Civil War. Martin Parks was Academy Chaplain from 1840 to 1846. Although elected Bishop of Alabama, he declined the honor. Francis Vinton declined the position of Bishop of Indiana in 1847. Other graduates became clergymen in the Methodist and Presbyterian churches. Michael S. Culberton, 1839, became a Presbyterian missionary in China and translated the Bible into Chinese. James Clark, 1829, became a Jesuit priest in 1847. A leading Catholic educator, he served as professor at Georgetown and Holy Cross colleges. George Deshon entered a Catholic seminary in 1851.

Other graduates became planters and farmers. A few turned to manufacturing. Robert W. Parrott, 1824, became superintendent of the West Point Foundry at Cold Spring in 1836, a partner of the Academy's old friend, Gouverneur Kemble, and the inventor of the Parrott gun. Joseph R. Anderson, 1836, became proprietor and superintendent of the Tredegar Iron Manufactury and Cannon Company in Richmond, Virginia. Guns and projectiles made by these two graduates would be fired at each other in the Civil War. Another graduate, Henry Dupont, 1833, also entered the arms industry in 1834, becoming the proprietor and director of the Dupont Powder Mills at Wilmington, Delaware.

Graduates and cadets on active duty assisted in the exploration and surveying of territory acquired by the purchase of Louisiana in 1803. Three graduates— John R. Bell, 1812; James D. Graham, 1817; and William H. Swift, 1819—accompanied Major Stephen H. Long on his three-year exploration of the west. Swift, still a cadet, returned in 1821 to find that his class had graduated. He was commissioned, one of the very few cadets not to be examined for a commission after the Partridge era. Benjamin E. L. Bonneville, Class of 1815, led an exploration from 1832 to 1835 that traveled from Missouri through Wyoming to Utah and then on to California. He also moved through Idaho to the Columbia River. His trip led to the claim of the Oregon territory and a later dispute with Britain. Another cadet, Richard Delafield, 1818, served for two months before his graduation as a member of the Board of Commissioners determining the boundary between the United States and Canada. He too was commissioned without being examined.

The diplomatic field attracted some graduates. Andrew Jackson Donelson, nephew of Andrew Jackson, was the United States representative to the Republic of Texas and Envoy and Minister Plenipotentiary to Prussia and the Federal Government of Germany from 1846 to 1849. Nicholas P. Trist, a former member of the Class of 1822, was President Polk's personal representative at peace discussions with the Mexican government, accompanying Scott on his advance from Vera Cruz to Mexico City. Graduates also served on many international commissions.

Of all the graduates who returned to civil life, Alexander D. Bache, 1825, was perhaps the best known nationally and internationally. Resigning his commission in 1829, he became a professor at the University of Pennsylvania and then president of Girard College. After reorganizing and serving as superintendent of Philadelphia's public schools, he became a member of the Assay Commissioners of the Philadelphia Mint and Superintendent of the Geodetic and Hydrographic Survey of the Coasts of the United States, a project taking twenty-four years to complete. He was a regent of the Smithsonian Institution from its organization until his death. Many honors were conferred on him: honorary degrees from Harvard, Yale, the City of New York College, and the University of Pennsylvania; medals of honor from Great Britain, Sardinia, Denmark, and Sweden; honorary membership or fellowship in most of the learned societies of Europe.

Contrary to all of the allegations made by Partridge so many years before, graduates of the Academy did not become a military elite restricted to sons of the wealthy or influential. When Lee returned as Superintendent, Academy records showed that more graduates came from what must be termed the lower classes—farmers, workmen, and clerks—than the wealthy. Graduates who returned to civil life often became members of local militia units. The Mexican

War experience had shown that units led by or including graduates were better trained, better disciplined, and more reliable than militia troops without West Point influences. The best example, perhaps, was the Mississippi Rifle Regiment commanded by Jefferson Davis. This, too, countered another of Partridge's allegations.

Brevet Colonel Robert Edward Lee brought with him his own personal record of excellence. He found an Academy much changed physically in the years since his graduation, an Academy with a greatly enlarged curriculum, an institution respected throughout the nation. Behind him stretched a line of 1,578 graduates and many former cadets who had all contributed to the development of the United States in many fields. He faced a challenge, a challenge to further improve the Academy to enable its graduates to continue to serve the country in uniform or in mufti. Scott and Totten had selected one of the most outstanding officers of the Army to be the superintendent in a critical period of Academy history. Sectional feelings were beginning to seethe outside the gray walls and inside as well, for the cadets reflected the customs and feelings of their contemporaries at home. Lee was expected to move forward, improve discipline, and curtail any sectionalism at West Point. Above all, he would supervise the education and training of cadets, preparing them to follow in the footsteps of earlier graduates. As Bishop H. S. Shipman stated in the words of the Cadet Hymn, "The Corps," the cadets had to be prepared to "follow, close order, behind you where you have pointed the way."

1852–1865

We few, we happy few, we band of brothers,
For he today that sheds his blood with us
Shall be my brother.

WILLIAM SHAKESPEARE
HENRY V, ACT IV, SCENE 3, LINE 40

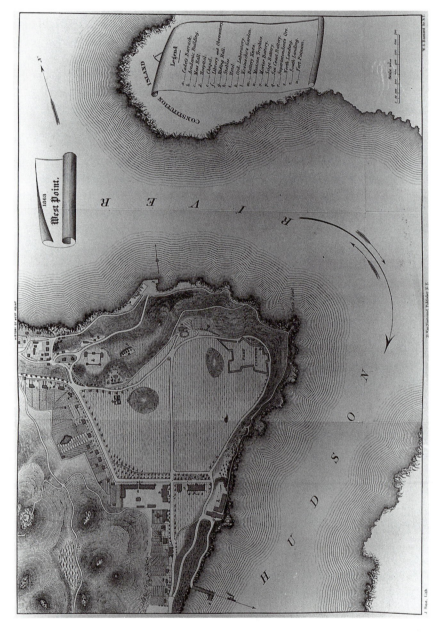

West Point in 1863. This map from Major Edward C. Boyton's *History of West Point*, shows the 1851 Cadet Barracks (a), the 1855 Mess Hall (c) south of the 1838 Academic Building (b), the Hospital (d), the Riding Hall (g), stables (h), and the many quarters and service buildings erected in the 1850s. Demolition of the Old Mess Hall cleared the Plain of all structures and established a pattern followed thereafter.

16

The Ante-Bellum Army

As the Military Academy entered its second half-century, the Regular Army was undergoing many changes. Despite its outstanding accomplishments during the Mexican War, Congress in 1848 reduced its wartime strength from approximately 31,000 men and officers to 10,317, over 2,000 less than its authorized strength ten years earlier. This minuscule force was tasked with a multi-faceted mission. Coastal fortifications had to be manned and improved. Frontier posts had to be garrisoned. New attention was drawn to the immense lands west of the Mississippi when gold was discovered in California in 1849. The Army now had to provide protection for settlers moving westward as well as surveying and mapping routes across the plains and mountains.

Many civil engineering projects—roads, bridges, canals, and river and harbor improvements—were made under Army supervision. Although other educational institutions such as Yale, Harvard, Rensselaer, and Norwich began to offer engineering degrees in the 1830s, Academy-trained officers still set an example for their civilian contemporaries.

The Regular Army of this period had an unwieldy and somewhat inefficient organization. Morrison in his history of the Military Academy from 1833 to 1866 divides the Army into three groups: the scientific or technical services consisting of the Corps of Engineers, the Topographical Engineers, and the Ordnance Corps. What would today be considered the general staff included the Adjutant General, Inspector General, Subsistence, Quartermaster, Medical, Pay, and Judge Advocate General Departments. The third group consisted of combat units of artillery, infantry, dragoons, cavalry, and mounted riflemen.

The Corps of Engineers was considered the elite organization of the Army. Until 1846, the Corps included only officers, all of whom had graduated high in their respective classes at the Military Academy. In that year, Congress authorized a 100-man company of Sappers, Miners, and Pontooners, the only Engineer company until the Civil War. The Engineers were much envied by officers in other arms because most of their assignments, except for occasional tours of exploration and surveying in the West or constructing railroads, roads, and canals, were in the eastern urban areas where the Corps continued to add to coastal fortifications or improve rivers and harbors.

The second of the scientific services, the Topographical Engineers, had the primary task of surveying and mapping, although other branches assisted in this work. The Topographical Engineers consisted only of officers throughout its existence from 1821 to 1863; its strength increased from ten officers in 1821 to thirty-seven in 1855.

The Ordnance Corps, the third scientific service, had a varied existence. Initially a separate service, it had been consolidated with the Artillery in the reorganization of the Army in 1821. This merger did not function efficiently, and the Ordnance Corps again became a separate service in 1832. The Corps did not function as a separate unit; it had detachments at various posts where large numbers of troops were stationed. Except for the period of the Mexican War, its peak strength was 250 enlisted men and 52 officers.

The Corps of Artillery was part scientific service and part combat arm. It continued to man and assist in the construction and improvement of coastal fortifications. Beginning in 1838, emphasis began to be placed upon mobile artillery companies capable of providing support to advancing infantry units. The value of these mobile units was proven during the Mexican War. The 1st Artillery, for example, today carries battle streamers for every battle of that conflict. After the war, Artillery regiments included two companies of light artillery, each with four horse-drawn guns, and ten companies manning seacoast fortifications. Artillery often fought as infantry in skirmishes with Indians. Two companies of the 1st Artillery, for example, were sent to Washington and Oregon in 1848 for this purpose, while its other ten companies were scattered at posts in New York, New Jersey, Delaware, Pennsylvania, Maryland, and Florida. In 1855, the strength of the Corps of Artillery was approximately 3,000 officers and men.

Largest of the combat arms in the 1850s was the Infantry. Seldom stationed in the East, its units were garrisoned in company-size posts in the West. Life for officers and enlisted men was far from comfortable. Housed in log buildings or adobe structures, they had few comforts when compared with the more fortunate Artillery and Engineer officers in eastern suburban posts. Their primary mission was scouting along trails to keep Indians away from wagon trains headed westward. In 1855, Secretary of War Jefferson Davis added two regiments to the Infantry, making ten regiments totaling approximately 5,500 men and officers.

The inability of foot soldiers to keep up with their mounted Indian adversaries led to the organization of additional mounted regiments. By 1855, Davis added two regiments of cavalry to the two regiments of dragoons and one regiment of mounted riflemen. Their designations made no difference in their tactical use. All rode to the scene of conflict, dismounted, and fought on foot, a distinct change from the use of similar units in European armies. Before the Civil War, a U.S. mounted unit seldom if ever charged its opponents. The primary mission of these mounted units was reconnaissance, security, raiding, and pursuit. By 1855, the total strength of all mounted units was approximately 3,000 officers and men.

For the most part, both infantry and mounted units were stationed at small, company-size posts. Their activities were restricted to patrols and small skirmishes. Occasionally, larger forces were assembled, as was done during the Brule Indian uprising in Nebraska in 1855 and the Mormon expedition in 1858. The Brule expedition included units of the 2nd Dragoons, the 4th Artillery, and the 6th and 10th Infantry. Work for the units stationed at these small posts consisted of post maintenance, patrolling the areas between posts, and keeping Indians from attacking settlers moving westward.

To administer this widespread force, the Army was divided into departments. By 1860, there were seven departments: the Departments of the East, the West, Texas, New Mexico, Utah, Oregon, and California, commanded by either general officers or colonels. The colonels simultaneously commanded their respective regiments. This loose, almost uncoordinated organization gave each department commander maximum freedom of action, a necessity because of the communications of the time. In a way this was fortunate; troop and department staff officers were not involved in the political bickering taking place in Washington.

Overseeing the Army was its senior officer, the Commanding General, Winfield Scott, who had held this position since 1841. Although Scott never openly challenged the authority of the Secretary of War, he constantly opposed many of the actions of the secretaries under whom he served. He preferred to operate from his headquarters in New York rather than in Washington. This obviously would cause problems: it led to department chiefs working directly with the Secretary of War as well as causing the Secretary to send orders directly to department chiefs or to field commanders. Scott's dislike of Jefferson Davis, a dislike returned by Davis, caused friction between department heads and the Commanding General. Many of Davis's reform were accomplished without Scott's approval or, all too often, even without his knowledge.

The Army general staff, as discussed by Morrison, was a nebulous grouping of staff departments organized by their primary functions. Although the general staff was charged with advising, planning, and coordination under the supervision of the Commanding General, the departments never functioned as a true general staff. Each department or bureau chief acted as a separate entity within his own specialized area of administrative or logistical support. Although they were responsible to the Commanding General, department chiefs continued to work directly with the Secretary of War or, as was often the case, with the President. Secretary of War Floyd complained bitterly about this and the reduction of the authority of the Commanding General in 1857, but no change resulted.

The exceptionally long tenure of department chiefs enabled them to isolate themselves from the direct control of their superiors. Thomas Jessup, Quartermaster General, held office from 1818 until his death in 1860. Adjutant General Roger Jones was appointed in 1825 and served until 1852. His succesor, Samuel Cooper, served nine years before resigning to join the Confederacy. Inspector General George Crogan held office for twenty-four years; his successor, George Churchill, from 1841 to 1861. Judge Advocate General J. E. Lee served in that capacity from 1849 to 1862. Even the Surgeon General had long tenure; Thomas Lawson held that office from 1836 to 1861. Joseph Totten was Chief of Engineers from 1838 to 1864; John Abert, Chief of Topographical Engineers from 1834 until his death in 1861; and George Talcott, Chief of Ordnance from 1851 to 1861.

Long tenure was not restricted to the department heads and bureau chiefs. Senior officers in line regiments often remained in grade for long periods of time. For example, Colonel Ichabod B. Crane commanded the 1st Regiment of Artillery from June 1843 until his death in October 1857. Long time in grade is undesirable when promotion is based upon rank within the entire officer corps. The situation in the 1850s was far worse because promotions were made within a regiment, not within a branch and not Army-wide. Consequently, promotions were available only when an officer died, transferred to another regiment or branch, or left the service.

In many cases, there were no vacancies for second lieutenants when cadets graduated and were assigned to a regiment. As a result, they were commissioned either as brevet second lieutenant or "additional" lieutenants until a vacancy occurred. Graduating cadets who were given regular commissions often ranked their less fortunate classmates in regular rank by months and even by years. New officers assigned to the elite Corps of Engineers and the Topographical Engineers suffered this disparity more than officers in the combat arms because of the small number of officers in these two corps compared to the number of officers in an artillery, infantry, or mounted regiment.

Perhaps the best example of stagnation in the officer ranks because of the long tenure of senior officers was one of the most outstanding officers in the War with Mexico: Captain and Brevet Colonel Robert E. Lee. An 1829 Academy graduate, Lee was still only a captain on the Regular Army list in 1855. After twenty-six years of service, he was still ranked by three captains, four majors, two lieutenant colonels, and one colonel. There was little indication that the senior officer and Chief of Engineers, Colonel Joseph G. Totten, had any inclination to retire despite the fact that he was sixty-seven years old in 1855 (Totten was promoted to brigadier general in 1863 and remained on active duty until his death in 1864). Significantly, no graduate of the Military Academy became a general officer until Joseph E. Johnston, Class of 1829, was appointed Quartermaster General in 1860, fifty-eight years after the Academy was founded.

Most officers were apolitical; few even voted. This is understandable for, except for engineers and artillerymen stationed near eastern urban centers, units in the West were usually far from any cities or even villages. This was not true of Army men in Washington. All of the department heads played political poker with elected officials and the party powers. Zachary Taylor and Winfield Scott vied for the Whig presidential candidacy in 1848. Taylor was selected and then elected President. Scott was selected as the Whig candidate in 1852 but lost to Franklin Pierce. Both Taylor and Scott were on active status. Taylor, of course, resigned his commission after the election, but Scott continued as the Army's Commanding General until 1861.

This was the Army that graduating cadets joined in the 1850s. It was small; 13,000 men and officers were required to safeguard more than 3,000,000 square miles of territory. The Army was responsible for manning and improving coastal fortifications, surveying and mapping the vast territory west of the Mississippi, building canals and roads, improving harbors and navigable rivers, and safe-guarding settlers moving across the plains to the far West. Engineers explored the plains and mountains to determine the best routes for continental railroads. The overall mission of the ante-bellum Army differed greatly from that of the pre–Mexican War forces. The changes in Army missions required the Military Academy to modify its curriculum to meet the demands of its parent. As early as 1844, Superintendent Richard Delafield realized that the Academy could no longer restrict its teaching to educating future engineers and artillerymen. In a report to the Secretary of War, Delafield cited the mission of the Academy to be: "To provide capable and well instructed officers for the several arms com-posing our Army." While this mission differed from the stated purpose of the Academy in Thayer's time, it only emphasized that the Military Academy must change its teachings to meet the needs of the Army regardless of what those requirements might be.

17

When Shall We Meet Again?

The Academy to which Lee returned in September 1852 had observed the fiftieth anniversary of its founding earlier that year. Much of those fifty years had been filled with conflict and crisis after crisis. The inborn distrust of the military coupled with a belief that a citizen army composed primarily of state militia would meet all military requirements, both legacies of the Revolutionary War, brought initial objection to its establishment and then a constant effort to have the Academy abolished. By 1852, however, criticism about the Academy and attempts to abolish it had almost disappeared. The military services of graduates, both those who had remained in uniform and those who had returned from civil life during the War with Mexico, had earned the gratitude of the nation. Their contributions in other fields—education, engineering, exploration, surveying, and science—had aided the growth of the United States from a small, East Coast nation to a sprawling giant extending from ocean to ocean.

Lee inherited an Academic Board whose members were known and respected throughout the country. The curriculum still followed the mold established by Thayer with emphasis upon mathematical and engineering studies. Most of the professors were Thayer men whom Lee remembered from his cadet days. Dennis H. Mahan had been a mathematics instructor from 1824, Assistant Professor of Civil and Military Engineering from 1825, and Professor and head of that Department since 1830. Albert E. Church had served as Assistant Professor of Mathematics from 1828 to 1831 and from 1833 until he was appointed Professor in 1837. William H. C. Bartlett, Professor of Natural and Experimental Philosophy since 1834, had also served as an Assistant Professor of Civil and Military Engineering from 1826 to 1829. Robert W. Weir had been Professor of Drawing since 1834; and Hyacinthe R. Agnel, Professor of French since 1848. Professor of Chemistry, Mineralogy, and Geology Jacob W. Bailey had been at the Academy in various capacities since 1834. Even Chaplain William T. Sprole, also Professor of Geography, History, and Ethics, had been at West Point since 1847. Their long tenure and academic ability has led many historians to call this period the Golden Age of the Military Academy.

The Corps of Cadets of 1852, however, was little changed from the Corps in 1829. Its authorized strength was still 250. Newly appointed cadets reported in June to take the entrance examinations: simple testing in reading, writing, and mathematics. Despite the very basic examinations, many appointees failed and returned home. Approximately half of those who passed did not graduate, failing academically or being separated for other reasons. This, strangely enough, was not a greater percentage of failures than that of civilian colleges, whose average percentage of graduates for this period varied from 18 to 73 percent with an average approximating the graduating percentage of the Academy. The percentages of other military schools—Norwich, Virginia Military Institute, the Citadel, and the U.S. Naval Academy—were higher, from 49 to 77 percent.

Even the cadet uniform had changed little. The basic uniform, the gray coatee and trousers adopted during the War of 1812, had been altered only slightly, primarily in cut and fit. The white collar in 1852 extended over the outer, gray collar of the coatee, a change from the almost swallow-tailed collar of 1829. The insignia of rank, cloth chevrons much like those of today, had been adopted in 1830 with the point of the chevrons pointing upward instead of the reverse used before that date. The ornate "Austrian" knot on the gray pantaloons had been abolished in 1838, undoubtedly because of the cost of having this braid sewn on the pantaloons. The full dress hat changed from the awkward, heavy, bell-shaped leather shako to a lighter, felt shako called the "stovepipe" because its circular configuration approximated that of a stove pipe. The insignia on the hat changed from the diamond worn in Lee's cadet years to an eagle over crossed cannon in 1839 and then to an eagle over the Engineer castle in 1843. Legend maintains that the Engineer castle insignia was patterned after the design of the USMA Library. Such is not true; the castle was the insignia used on the seal of the Corps of Engineers by 1839, if not earlier. Stocks were still worn, although black cloth replaced the leather stock in 1838; stocks continued to be required until 1862, long after the Army had discontinued their use. The single-breasted overcoat adopted in 1828 was replaced by a double-breasted coat in 1851. In 1849 the first riding uniform was introduced, gray trousers and a gray jacket that resembled the Eisenhower jacket of the World War II period. Forage caps had been used since the late 1830s, first a leather cap similar to that worn by artillerymen in the Mexican War period and then to a cap patterned after the French chasseur design. The normal wear for almost all formations, including classes, was the full dress coat and either gray or white trousers. Despite these changes, the cadet uniform of 1852 closely resembled that of 1829.

Lee possessed one attribute not shared by his predecessors nor by many of his successors; he understood cadets and realized the great pressures under which they studied and lived. This understanding was due to some degree because his son, George Washington Custis, was a member of the Class of 1854 and his nephew, Fitzhugh Lee, had entered the Academy in June 1852 with the Class of 1856.

Custis had entered the Academy in June 1850 and, initially, had worried Lee because he had not fully applied himself to his cadet duties. Lee had visited Custis in December 1850 to counsel him. He was pleased to find that Custis had improved in his studies and stood well in his class academically. His conduct had improved, and he had been reported for only two minor offenses. Six months later, Lee was shocked to learn that liquor had been found in Custis's room. The boy and his roommates maintained that they had not known the liquor was there, that some other cadet had hidden the liquor without their knowledge. Custis's mates offered to sign a pledge if the charges were dropped, a common practice at this time. Custis wrote to his father, telling him that he was reluctant to accept the offer and asking for advice. Lee replied that one should not hesitate to sign a pledge to help a classmate if it "could be done without loss of faith & honour, but to receive the pledge of the Class in *my own* behalf is another matter." Custis had decided to refuse the offer, and, essentially, his father agreed with that decision even though it could result in Custis's dismissal. Fortunately, the Superintendent, Captain Brewerton, had decided that the charges did not warrant a court martial and awarded the cadets only eight demerits; the Secretary of War approved this decision.

Lee's nephew, Fitzhugh, entered the Academy in June 1852, three months before Lee became superintendent. Lee questioned Fitzhugh's ability to adapt to the rigors of cadet life even before the boy became a cadet. In May 1851, he had written to Custis that "he [Fitzhugh] thinks he might get through the Academy, though he would not stand as well as Boo [Custis]. I tell him he would get 200 demerits the first year and that would be an end to all his military resources." Lee's estimate proved to be true. High-spirited Fitzhugh was in trouble during most of his cadet career, was almost dismissed for misconduct, but did graduate in 1856 fifth from the bottom of his class.

The concern he had felt during Custis's plebe year convinced Lee that other parents undoubtedly had similar worries. Knowing that cadets all too often failed to write to parents about their problems, Lee became almost a surrogate parent to every cadet. Thayer's cadets in later years often maintained that Thayer knew everything about every cadet: his standing in each subject, his financial status, his physical well being, his military aptitude, and his conduct rating. Lee took even greater interest in his cadets. If a young man did well, he was complimented. If he had trouble with his studies or incurred too many demerits, Lee advised the young man of ways to improve himself.

Lee often wrote to parents to explain the reason cadets were not doing well academically or were in trouble because of excessive demerits or serious violations of regulations. Letters to parents explained conduct problems, often assuring them that the conduct of the cadet was not disgraceful or immoral. When a cadet had trouble with his studies—weekly reports submitted by every instructor clearly showed cadets who were having difficulty—Lee consulted the instructor concerned and often called the cadet to his office to discuss the situation and to offer advice. He contacted parents to inform them of their son's problems and to ask their help in persuading the young man to better apply himself. If a parent wrote that a cadet had not written home, Lee talked to the young man to determine why he had not.

Lee was often asked to grant leave to a cadet, to attend a wedding for example, a request always denied. His answer always explained the reason, as was done in a letter to Henry A. DuBois in February 1853:

> I regret that I cannot with propriety grant the leave of absence to your son you desire to attend a wedding in your family on the 17th. I have been obliged to refuse many similar applications; for what is granted to one must be given to all; & you can readily see the serious interruptions that would take place to their studies & duties. The whole time of the Cadets is necessary to master their Course at the Academy, & any withdrawal of their attention affects them injuriously.

If a cadet was ill, Lee often wrote to his parents to explain the nature of the illness and the care the cadet received in the hospital. As an example, he wrote to the mother of James A. McNeill Whistler to inform her that Whistler was sick in the hospital with a rheumatism problem. "He does not suffer from much pain," wrote Lee, "but his attack does not seem to yield to remedies and the surgeon has this morning informed me that he fears his lungs are seriously involved." Whistler recovered and returned to his studies and drills, but his indifference to everything except his drawing lessons soon resulted in his dismissal for academic failure.

Lee's consuming interest in his cadets extended beyond their academic and military activities. Occupying the Superintendent's Quarters built during Thayer's tenure, the Lees brought with them furniture and artifacts, including George Washington's silver service, from their Arlington home. Having Custis in the Corps enabled Lee to introduce other cadets to the social graces, an important but seldom stressed part of a cadet's education. "We always have a no. of cadets at our house every Sat. evening," noted his daughter Agnes in her journal. The frequent dinners and other entertainments for cadets gave Lee and his family an unusual opportunity to know cadets as individuals. Agnes wrote, "We know almost all of Custis' class, the 1st, & many in the other three." Cadets continued to be welcomed to the Lee home after Custis graduated, first in his class, in 1854.

The Lee children were kept busy with school and with art and music lessons. William Bailey, son of Professor Jacob W. Bailey, wrote in his memoirs that "Robert and I both attended the little School for Officer's children [enlisted children attended a separate school near the enlisted quarters], then in charge of Mr. W. F. Whiting. Some of our companions should be mentioned. Among them were Alfred T. Mahan, the famous naval writer, and his two brothers, John F. Weir now the distinguished head of the Yale Art School, John French, afterwards a colonel in the Regular Army, and Charles F. Roe, now the General commanding the N.Y. National Guard." Younger students were taught Latin, spelling, reading, geography, mathematics, history, penmanship, grammar, and composition. Older students were taught Greek, spelling, geography, history, algebra, and geometry. The grading system was the same as that used by the Academy faculty: 3.0 was a perfect grade; 2.0 passing. Bailey's report card for May 1855 showed that he had received 3.0 in spelling, reading, writing, geography, history, English composition, and deportment but only 2.0 in grammar, Latin translation, and Latin parsing, 1½ in Latin grammar, and 0 in arithmetic. One wonders what his father's reaction was to the last grade!

Apparently only boys attended the school; the girls probably were taught at home by their parents, although they did receive some lessons from others. Agnes noted in her journal that "Annie & I take music & french [*sic*] lessons. Our music master is Mr. Apelles, leader of the band, an excellent teacher no doubt but he gives me such long hard exercises & makes me *thump* so I don't enjoy his lesson much. 'French' is ever so nice. We go three times a week to Mr. Agnel [Hyacinthe R. Agnel was Professor of French]. He is not strict but teaches so thoroughly. There are three in the class besides ourselves."

Although they attended services in the Cadet Chapel, the Lee family also worshipped at the Church of the Holy Innocents in Buttermilk Falls. Mrs. Lee was Episcopalian, and the children had been brought up in this faith. Lee himself belonged to no particular denomination. As a cadet, he had been greatly impressed by Chaplain Charles E. McIlvaine, a young Episcopal clergyman who later became Bishop of Ohio. As he grew older, Lee's religious beliefs deepened, and he was confirmed in the Episcopal faith in July 1853. His son Robert noted that his father often nodded during sermons in the Cadet Chapel. Cadets often did the same—or worse. Agnes Lee noted in her journal that "the cadets as a body behave very well, but some few—I hope very few—bring books to read during the sermon, which is certainly very wrong."

The Lees' social life was not restricted to entertaining cadets. Faculty and staff officers and their wives were often guests. There were parties for young people of various ages—from Robert's very young friends to Agnes's teen-age group. New Year's Day was, as Agnes noted, "a great day. From morning till night the house was filled by officers & cadets, dinner was dispensed with by most of us while 'sweets' of all kinds supplied its place." The commander's New Year's Day reception is a tradition continued to the present time. There were Valentine parties for cadets and smaller, informal gatherings for plebes after the Corps had moved back into barracks in the fall. Every distinguished visitor—and there were many—was entertained in the Lee home. The constant entertainment schedule was tiring for Lee. Mrs. Lee wrote to their son William, whom they called "Rooney," that the family had attended a concert but that "we left the Superintendent stretched out full length on the sofa, too poorly to go out to the concert."

Agnes noted that her father "had a large dinner party for some of his classmates." Although the plan was for a "he dinner," according to Agnes, it became a mixed affair when one of the classmates brought his wife. Agnes did not list the guests, although she commented that "it is such nice work to fix a handsome dinner, but to be present is not to my taste."

An inconspicuous but important event took place at West Point in July 1853: the first known alumni reunion. Five of the eighteen survivors of the more than fifty men who became cadets in 1817 returned to commemorate their entry into the Academy. Unfortunately, little is known about that reunion. Robert Allston had written to the survivors in 1851 to suggest that they honor their Superintendent, Sylvanus Thayer, by having a presentation sword made. All agreed that this should be done, hoping that the sword could be given to Thayer at West Point on the twenty-fifth anniversary of their entry into the Academy. Thayer, however, wrote that he would be unable to join them—significantly, Thayer never returned to West Point after his 1833 departure. The group then decided to meet at the Academy in July 1853. Allston wrote to Thayer and gave him an extremely brief report of the reunion. No other record of reunion events has been found, but the following description is what may have transpired.

The five men—Allston from North Carolina, Major John Scott of the 4th Artillery, Louisianan Seth Capron, and New Yorkers Joshua Baker and Washington Wheelwright—would undoubtedly have stayed at the West Point Hotel on the northern edge of the Plain. Old memories would have returned as the five old gentlemen watched the Corps march from camp to the new Mess Hall. In all probability, Lee would have invited them to tour the cadet barracks and the Academic Building. They might have been honored by standing in the reviewing line as the Corps paraded. Although Lee might have asked them to dinner in his quarters, it is more probable that the five men would have invited all of Thayer's former cadets present at West Point to dinner at the hotel. The following is an interpretation of what might have transpired at that dinner. Comments ascribed to various individuals, especially those of Lee, and the description of the dinner at the hotel have been taken from other writings and slightly amended to fit the occasion. The ceremonious toast after dinner followed the customs of the lst Artillery Mess, the first mess in the U.S. Army, which were adopted when Irwin McDowell established the West Point Army Mess in 1841. The five would have invited Lee; Professors Bailey, Bartlett, Church, and Mahan; the Commandant of Cadets, Captain Bradford Alden, and Captain George Cullum, commander of the Sapper, Miner, and Pontonier Detachment, all of whom had been cadets during Thayer's superintendency.

After welcoming the guests, Allston led them to the table, seating Lee on his right and Captain Alden on his left. The Professors and the other four old grads sat on either side of the table with Cullum, the junior graduate present, at the foot. Allston began conversation by telling Lee and Alden, "I was impressed with the precision of the drill at parade. You have done a superb job with the new plebes. They've been here only a month yet it was hard to tell the plebes from the upperclassmen."

Wheelwright added, "It was considerate to have the band play 'Home Sweet Home' and 'Auld Lang Syne.' I understand that special version is normally used only at graduation parade. I wonder what the cadets thought about five old codgers being honored with their music."

Major Scott was talking with Professor Mahan, "We enjoyed touring the new Academic Building and the Library this morning. Your Napoleon Club room was impressive indeed, but the telescopes in the observatory were even more impressive."

Professor Bartlett answered this comment, "We are fortunate to have that equipment. With such magnificent apparatus, we are able to improve our instruction of cadets and contribute to scientific knowledge. I have heard of a new process for copying astral observations, an adaptation of imprinting an image or thing on paper or metal. I hope that we can test this concept during the solar eclipse next May."

The meal was served: oysters, a tasty bisque, a fish entree, roast turkey, and a marmalade cream desert. Allston told Lee that Gouverneur Kemble had sent the turkey. "Kemble," he added, "asked Colonel Thayer to stay with him but the Colonel was unable to join us."

Lee replied that he was not surprised for Kemble often sent foodstuffs to officers as well as including many as guests at his whist-dinners. "He has certainly been a good friend of West Point and all of us," said Lee. "His efforts did much to counter the antagonistic criticisms so prevalent before the war. We try to match him in kind, but it is difficult to equal his generosity and hospitality."

When the table had been cleared, Allston rose and said, "Gentlemen, while we are waiting for the port, I want to show you the sword we are presenting to Colonel Thayer." He nodded to an orderly who smiled and brought a long, rosewood box to him. Opening the case, Allston took out an ornate weapon and held it up for all to see. He pointed to the hilt and told his audience that the gold head was an excellent likeness of John Calhoun, Secretary of War at the time the five had entered the Academy. He pointed to the West Point scenes on the scabbard and the names etched on the gold medal. "Of the more than fifty young men who entered in 1817, only eighteen of us survive. Our names are etched here. We are proud to say that we were the first class to enter the Academy after Colonel Thayer became superintendent. We feel privileged to recognize in this way how much he contributed to our development by stressing the importance of duty and honor in all that we did."

As the sword was passed from hand to hand, the orderly placed glasses at the right of each man and two decanters of port before Allston. When the sword had been returned to Allston, replaced in its case, and removed from the table, Allston poured wine in his glass and then passed a decanter down each side of the table. When all the glasses had been filled, he stood and said, "Mr. Baker, the President."

They all stood and raised their glasses as Baker toasted, "The President of the United States." When they were again seated, Allston explained that he had asked Baker to make the first toast because he was the senior member of the class entering in 1817, graduating in 1819. He then called on Major Scott to toast the Secretary of War. Again, they all stood as Scott said, "Gentlemen, the Secretary of War, Jefferson Davis." Each man echoed, "The Secretary of War."

"Colonel Lee," said Capron, "As you know, Allston is from North Carolina, and my home is in Louisiana. All of us in the South are concerned about the growing feeling of sectionalism fostered by the disagreements about slavery. Is there any sectional attitude within the Corps?"

Lee frowned for a moment before replying, "I wish that I could answer that question with a strong NO, but I cannot. There is sectional feeling in the Corps, but we and the cadets themselves discourage it. There is an unspoken ground rule that sectional discussions will not take place. The Dialectic Society—yes, it still exists, stronger than ever—no longer debates any issue concerning sectionalism. We encourage cadets from northern and western states to room with young men from southern states. We carefully watch to avoid putting too many cadets from any section into any one company. I know that many southern youngsters resent the comparatively high academic standings of northern cadets. This is to be expected because most of the northern cadets had better and more extensive schooling before receiving their cadet appointments."

He paused for a moment before continuing, "I feel most deeply that the best way to discourage sectionalistic feelings here—and throughout the Army—is by stressing duty and by fostering strong and fair discipline. We try to teach our cadets the importance and necessity of duty. To me, duty is the sublimest word in the English language. The most that we can do, however, is to follow the unwritten rule and not discuss sectionalism here at West Point."

Allston rapped the table and said, "Mr. Capron, the Chief of Engineers." All joined Capron in the toast to Colonel Joseph Totten. After a short interval, Allston again rapped the table and asked Wheelwright to toast the Superintendent. All except Lee rose, raised their glasses to him, and again took seats. Allston then rose and said, "Gentlemen, Colonel Thayer." All rose for the toast.

When they were seated, Allston addressed Lee, "Colonel Lee, my friends and I thank you for joining us tonight to honor the man who has done and continues to do so much for the Academy. We thank you too for your cordial reception of this group of old codgers, especially for honoring us at parade."

Lee smiled—Allston afterward insisted that his moustache actually twitched—and said, "Gentlemen, you and all other graduates are always welcome to our alma mater. Mr. Allston showed me a letter he received from Colonel Thayer. May I read part of that letter to you now? Colonel Thayer wrote, 'The example set by your class will doubtless be followed by succeeding classes wherein would result the most important consequences to the welfare of our alma mater.' I fully agree with this sentiment, and I hope that the reunions of various classes will become an annual event. I know that every class, including those who had no direct contact with Colonel Thayer, will toast him as we have done tonight. Every man who has worn cadet gray knows how much all of us owe that wonderful man. His seventeen years as superintendent made an indelible impression upon this institution and upon the Army as well. More than any other single individual, he has made West Point what it is today."

Amid cries of "Hear, hear," Lee smiled again and said, "I must apologize, gentlemen, *for my sermon. I intended only to read that one sentence, but my personal feelings made me say more. My apologies, gentlemen."*

At the foot of the table, Captain Cullum stood quietly and said, "Mr. Allston, Colonel Lee, I am the junior graduate present, and I think that I must stand on my rights for I have been ignored in making any of our toasts. I am compelled to protest." A smile hovered on his face as he continued, "We have toasted the President, the Secretary of War, the Chief of Engineers, the Superintendent, and Colonel Thayer. Those toasts are all well deserved. But I must protest that we have forgotten the most important toast of all. More to the point, Gentlemen, TO THE POINT."

Eleven glasses were raised as eleven voices rang out, "To the Point."

The presentation sword, which was later taken to Thayer, was acquired from his descendants in the late 1890s and given to the West Point Museum. Thayer's prediction that "the example set by your class will doubtless be followed by succeeding classes" has proven to be true. Alumni today return to West Point each year to honor the man who is today revered as the Father of the Military Academy.

Lee was fortunate to have inherited a faculty whose professors were known nationally and internationally. He also inherited problems, the same problems that had plagued his predecessors, primarily actions generated in Washington over which neither he nor the Chief of Engineers, Joseph Totten, had any control. First was the tendency of Congressmen and Senators to appoint unqualified young men as cadets. Simple as the entrance examinations were—actually little more than a check of a candidate's ability to read, write, and do simple mathematics problems—too many appointees failed to qualify for admission. The requests of superintendents from Thayer on and the efforts of various Chiefs of Engineers had little influence on Congress, whose members insisted that only simple examinations be required in order to assure a democratic selection of cadets. Political requirements negated the need for better qualified appointees. There is little doubt that the relatively high rate of non-graduates can be attributed at least in part to the admission of many candidates with a very minimum qualification. Many of these young men could not absorb the technical subjects taught at the Academy and failed to graduate.

The second major problem inherited by Lee was an outgrowth of the number of cadets who either failed academically or were dismissed for misconduct. It had become almost traditional for the President or the Secretary of War to reinstate many cadets discharged for these reasons. This tendency was well known to cadets, and many who had failed academically or been discharged for other reasons immediately went to Washington to get help from members of Congress or to appeal directly to the Secretary of War or even the President for reinstatement. Again, political requirements negated the action taken by the Academic Board and the Superintendent.

A third problem encountered by Lee was not generated in Washington. Although the basic curriculum was virtually unchanged from Thayer's time, additional requirements had been added in every course taught by the various professors. This was true in the scientific courses, which were constantly up-dated to keep pace with the many new discoveries and new techniques developed during this period. Additional requirements had been added to the course taught by the Professor of Geography, History, and Ethics; he now was required to provide instruction in constitutional and international law as well as the additional subjects of English composition and grammar and history. More topography was added by the Drawing Department. Spanish was an added requirement after the Mexican War. The Department of Tactics added more requirements. Equitation and fencing received more emphasis; additional time was devoted to artillery drill. Practical Military Engineering was taught from 4:00 P.M. until sunset during the fall and spring terms and as a routine part of summer instruction.

Cadets were overloaded with work and had very little time to themselves. More than a few wrote parents short notes stating that their study load was so heavy that they had little time to write letters. Many veiled their windows with blankets in order to continue studying after taps had sounded. Many devoted their free time on Saturday and Sunday afternoons to studies. Perhaps cadets in the upper sections and those at the bottom of their respective classes studied harder than cadets in the middle sections. Those at the top studied harder, hoping to rank high enough academically at graduation to be commissioned in the Corps of Engineers or in the Artillery. Cadets in the lower sections studied equally hard or even harder, trying to avoid being found for academic deficiencies. The middle group had neither incentive. They knew that they could get by without dropping many files or risking failure. They were aware that they had little chance of being commissioned as an Engineer or Artilleryman, realizing that in all probability they would be assigned to the Infantry.

Many of the additions to the curriculum were generated by changing requirements of the Army. Actions in the Mexican War had clearly indicated the value of mobile artillery. Drill with horse-drawn artillery pieces was increased, and cadets spent as much time wheeling caissons into position to fire as they did practicing with the seacoast artillery guns on the bank of the Hudson. The lessons the Army learned when its infantry units, marching as fast as possible, could not keep pace with their more mobile Indian foes led to increased emphasis of mounted drill at West Point. Cadets were not only taught to ride, they received instruction in cavalry movements and the use of the saber by mounted troops. This emphasis on mobile artillery and cavalry tactics required additional horses to replace the old and relatively feeble animals used by cadets. Lee's requests were finally approved, and better cavalry and artillery mounts were sent to the Academy. As Army units were stationed in the Southwest, the need for Spanish-speaking officers became apparent. The Academic Board almost reluctantly agreed to add Spanish to the curriculum, a change urged by several Boards of Visitors. The establishment of many small Army posts west of the Mississippi revealed how little was known about that vast territory. Maps were few and often inaccurate. To cope with this problem, more surveying and topographic drawing was added to the curriculum. The Academy, as always, reacted to the needs of the Army, but initially this was done by adding to the curriculum without eliminating existing requirements.

Lee's major problems lessened greatly after Jefferson Davis was appointed Secretary of War in 1853 by President Franklin Pierce. Davis essentially stopped the reinstatement of cadets and persuaded the President to do the same. Very few cadets were reinstated during his tenure; most of these were sent back to the Academy at the recommendation of the Academic Board and Lee. However, even Davis, ably assisted by Chief of Engineers Joseph Totten, could not persuade Congress to stiffen the entrance requirements. Davis and Totten supported most of Lee's requests and thus contributed to the progress of the Academy during what has so often been called its Golden Age.

The fact that Davis was a West Point graduate brought objective and understanding judgment to the Secretary of War's handling of Academy matters. For example, when Lee revised the 1839 cadet regulations, Davis's predecessor, Charles Conrad, objected to what he considered to be self-incrimination. The regulations indicated that a cadet was expected to answer official questions concerning his conduct and performance of his duties and that he was required to report that he had accomplished all required duties when on guard or other duty. To Conrad this was self-incrimination. Lee considered these regulations nothing more than codification of his concept of an officer's duty. He explained his concept to the Chief of Engineers in a March 1853 letter, stating that he considered it his duty to answer every official question concerning his duties even though a truthful answer might mean the end of his Army career. When Davis replaced Conrad, he supported Lee's concept and ended that problem.

Significantly, the Board of Visitors in its 1852 report to the Secretary of War commented on this very point. "The regulations of the academy . . . are admirably adapted to produce the morals that seem to exist," it stated, "whilst the system of military education, addressing itself to the pride and honor of the pupil, habituates him to a course of conduct that challenges the admiration of every beholder. The crime of telling an untruth or prevaricating in the slightest degree is punished by dismissal." This supported Lee's contention that discipline required truthful answers to official questions.

Despite Lee's strict discipline, cadets made little complaint, primarily because he was fair, treating all alike. He was not a harsh disciplinarian and appeared to believe in the concept that there was no such thing as poor discipline. Discipline might be stern; discipline might be hard; but discipline could not be poor because it then ceased to be discipline. Lee added justice to his treatment of disciplinary problems involving cadets. He preferred to administer punishments other than subjecting the cadet to trial by court martial. There was one exception involving his nephew Fitzhugh Lee. Fitzhugh had proven Lee's prediction that he would have a hard time surviving cadet discipline to be true. He was constantly in trouble and, as a result, had an extremely high number of demerits annually. When he was reported for being off limits at Benny Havens' tavern, it was recommended that he be tried by court martial with the undoubted finding that he be dismissed. Lee would not intervene or recommend other punishment. Fitzhugh was saved when his classmates pledged themselves to refrain from imbibing alcoholic spirits if Lee was permitted to remain. Chief of Engineers Joseph Totten approved the request, although the Superintendent had made no recommendation one way or other. Young Lee graduated in the Class of 1856, thanks to the generosity of his classmates—and the understanding of Secretary of War Davis who had himself often run into trouble as a cadet.

Another young cadet who seemed to be constantly in trouble because of his carefree view of life in general was John M. Schofield. Beginning early in his plebe year, he seemed to collect demerits in the same way that a magnet attracts iron filings. On his first tour as a sentinel in camp, only a few weeks after he entered the Academy in 1849, Schofield literally crossed bayonets with the corporal of the guard when the corporal tried to cross Schofield's post without giving the countersign. Although he was not reported for his action, upperclassmen made his life uncomfortable for a good share of his plebe year. As a yearling, Schofield often covered his window with a blanket—not to study, but to smoke his pipe and play cards. As a result of many demerits for such escapades, he accumulated a total of 196 demerits for the year; four more would have meant dismissal. Schofield seldom turned down a challenge. In his memoirs, *Forty-six Years in the Army*, he told of a discussion about the possibility of a cadet going to New York and back without being caught. Several cadets challenged him "to undertake it for a high wager, and that challenge overcame any scruple I may have had." Not having any money, Schofield borrowed five dollars from Jerome Bonaparte, persuaded Benny Havens to row him across the river to Garrison, took the train to New York, and returned to "walk across the plain in full view of the crowd of officers and ladies, and appeared in ranks at roll-call, as innocent as anybody." Schofield never collected the wager, although he did repay the loan from Bonaparte. Despite his high total of demerits, he graduated seventh in the Class of 1853.

Like many other superintendents, Lee refrained from interfering with the Academic Board in academic matters. The Academic Board was a Thayer creation. Consisting of the professors, the Commandant of Cadets, and the Superintendent, who was the *ad hoc* chairman, the Board was a powerful group whose influence often extended far beyond the limits of academic affairs. The long tenure of the professors and their professional reputations both within and outside the Army often created problems. Several of the professors had little reluctance in writing to former students, the Chief of Engineers, or the Secretary of War to urge adoption of favored proposals. Mahan, for example, wrote to Chief of Engineers Joseph Totten, urging that professors not be required to teach a class, as had been customary since Thayer's day. It remained for Lee, however, to adopt Mahan's concept. This he did as part of his revision of the 1839 regulations. Unfortunately, the wording of this change was vague enough to cause problems when Delafield returned as superintendent in 1856.

The working relationship of any superintendent with the Academic Board was a delicate matter. Although the superintendent was chairman of the Board, he had only one vote. This could—and did—prove to be embarrassing because the Board might vote against proposals of the superintendent. Some superintendents tried to restrict the Board's activities to academic affairs but with little success. Delafield, for example, had objected in 1842 to the Chief of Engineer's request for the opinion of the Academic Board on recommendations made by the Board of Visitors, stating his opinion that the Board should concern itself only with academic matters. In his opinion, involvement of the Board in other matters interfered with the superintendent's authority. Joseph Totten, who was Chief of Engineers from 1838 to 1864, informed Delafield that he and the Secretary of War, although they valued the opinions of the superintendent, wanted the advice of the Academic Board, indicating that the Board because of its tenure, academic ability and accomplishments, and overall interest in Academy affairs was well qualified to present its "considered opinions on many of, if not all, matters pertaining to the course of discipline as well as instruction." Totten did not hesitate to write to a professor directly, asking questions or commenting upon actions of the Board. The professors—particularly Mahan—often corresponded directly with Totten, completely bypassing the superintendent and his staff. Although other superintendents had difficulty with this situation, Lee with his tact and gentlemanly attitude toward others had few problems with the members of the Academic Board or with Totten. His concept of duty did not include criticizing his superior for his actions, even though Totten's tendency to work directly with various professors might well be considered ignoring the chain of command. Lee showed no resentment of Totten's actions, nor did he complain to or about the professors' discussions with Totten. Mahan was one of Lee's closest associates, and the two men developed a mutual admiration for the dedication and ability of each other.

Despite the interest of Mahan, Bartlett, and Bailey in keeping abreast of the newest developments in their respective fields, some cadet instruction was not based upon current technology and practices. This was especially true of instruction in tactics. Several Boards of Visitors complained that cadets were required to drill with obsolete artillery pieces. Lee, with help from Totten and Davis, was able to obtain more current artillery guns, including mobile field pieces. Artillery instruction included making projectiles, repairing field carriages, and controlling fire of an artillery company (the term "battery" did not come into general use until much later).

Although the first regiment of dragoons was established in 1833, cavalry tactics were not made a part of the course until 1853 during Lee's superintendency. New and better mounts were provided and cavalry tactics made a part of mounted drill. The old riding hall on the ground floor of the 1838 Academic Building was completely inadequate. Iron pillars supporting the upper floors were dangerous, and cadets were often injured, despite padding around the pillars, when horses tossed them during riding instruction. Lee cannot be considered a builder; he did not design buildings as had Delafield, but he was able to obtain authorization for a new Riding Hall and quarters for officer and enlisted families. The new Riding Hall, completed in 1855, was considered to be the largest structure of its type in the country.

The Department of Practical Military Engineering improved its instruction. Initially cadet instruction was strictly theoretical. Beginning in 1851, practical as well as theoretical techniques were taught. Cadets at first only observed the enlisted engineer detachment build roads, bridge, and field fortifications. The Academic Board, however, considered this insufficient, and cadets then actively participated in field work. They surveyed positions, built field fortifications, constructed small bridges, and built military roads.

Infantry training was expanded. Instead of concentrating on close order drill, tactical officers taught cadets company and battalion tactics, including forming a square to hold off mounted charges. Although the Corps was not large enough to form a regiment, the tactical officers taught cadets drills based upon regimental and division maneuvers. Firing was an important part of their instruction, and they learned to fire their muskets as individuals, as a platoon, and as a company.

All of these changes reflected the needs of the Army after the Mexican War. Troops west of the Mississippi often were required to build posts, bridges, and roads. Young graduates found themselves designing small buildings and fortifications, which were then built under their supervision. The increased need and use of mounted troops clearly indicated the need for improved cavalry instruction. Although artillery was not extensively used against Indians, the lessons learned in Mexico and observation of the development of artillery tactics in European armies dictated the need for cadet instruction in the latest artillery pieces being obtained for Regular Army units.

The most outstanding of the professors of the 1850s, certainly one of the most outstanding in the Academy's entire history, was undoubtedly Dennis Hart Mahan. From his graduation in 1824 until his death in 1871, except for four year's study in Europe from 1826 to 1830, Mahan was either an instructor, an associate professor, or the professor of the Department of Civil and Military Engineering. Unable to find suitable textbooks, he wrote his own. Lithographed by the West Point press, these books were used at West Point for over forty years; they were reproduced in England and translated into French, German, and Spanish. The subject matter encompassed subjects taught by his department: field fortifications, attack and defense, mines, architecture, and civil engineering. Two of his better-known works concerned the art of war: *Engineering and the Science of War* and *An Elementary Treatise on Advanced Guard, Outpost, and Detachment Service of Troops*. Most of the men commanding major units on both sides in the Civil War studied these works as cadets. Mahan was a member of the Geographical Society of Paris and one of the founders of the U.S. National Academy of Sciences.

Mahan was not well liked by cadets, although he was deeply respected by them. As an instructor, he seemed to be able to select the least prepared cadet to recite and did not hesitate to embarrass that individual by caustic remarks concerning his poor recitation. Consequently, cadets in Mahan's classes were exceptionally well prepared to recite—and learned his principles thoroughly and with understanding.

To further the study of the art of war by officers of the Post and visitors, Mahan organized the Napoleon Club shortly after the Mexican War. Strangely, Mahan was the only professor who was a member. In today's terminology, the meetings of the Napoleon Club would be called a graduate seminar. As chairman, Mahan assigned topics to various officers and commented on their later presentations, giving "the members the benefit of his keen incisive criticism and instructive analysis of their studies," remembered Peter S. Michie. Lee made a room available for club meetings, and the members painted a large map of Europe on the wall to facilitate their discussions of Napoleon's campaigns and the battles of Frederick the Great. Examples of papers presented include George McClellan's discussion of Napoleon's Wagram campaign, George Thomas's review of Frederick's battles, Gustavus W. Smith's analysis of Napoleon's Russian invasion, and George Cullum's study of the French actions in Spain. Lee presented at least one paper and became a close friend of Mahan. There is little doubt that Mahan must have taken cadets to the club room at times to emphasize some of Napoleon's strategy covered in their classes.

Mahan corresponded with many individuals in and outside of the Army. Many of his former pupils wrote to tell him of their experiences. Grant, Sherman, and Halleck wrote often during the Civil War to provide Mahan with firsthand information of their activities. Mahan did not hesitate to rebut any and all criticism of the Academy. Congressmen, educators, and the press all received his terse and pertinent arguments against criticisms of the Academy and its graduates. Mahan, in actuality, was the unofficial spokesman for West Point during much of his tenure as professor.

Mahan's teaching and theories of the art of war were reflected in the tactical instruction of cadets. Despite his interest in and emphasis of Napoleonic methods, he did stress mobility, the need for field engineering, and the use of field fortifications for troop security. The principles he expounded in his course on military art were reflected in the tactical instruction by the Commandant and his assistants.

Mahan was not alone in keeping abreast of the latest scientific developments. Jacob W. Bailey, Professor of Chemistry, Mineralogy, and Geology, obtained a daguererrotype camera in 1840 when he reported to the Superintendent that he had "received from Mr. Weir the Daguererrotype Apparatus, the purchase of which for the Chem. Dept. was authorized by the Superintendent." Unfortunately, none of the photographs taken by Bailey are in the possession of the USMA Library nor is their exact location known. Cadet photographs of the *carte vista* type began to be taken in the late 1840s. The George Derby papers in the West Point Library Special Collections include a portrait of Derby in furlough uniform taken in 1844 (it was regulation at that time for cadets to wear a special uniform on furlough, a blue frock coat and light-colored trousers). Another early cadet photograph shows Cadet Philip Sheridan with Lieutenants George W. Crook and John Nugen. This photo was probably taken in 1852 for both Crook and Nugen graduated that year; Sheridan is in cadet uniform, Crook and Nugen in officer uniforms.

The earliest known scenic photographs of West Point were taken in 1854 by noted photographer Victor Prevost. The West Point Museum has five of the Prevost photos: the Mess Hall, a general view taken from the observatory tower of the Library, a view up the Hudson, and two of officers' quarters, possibly the home of French instructor T. D'Ormeleulx, whom Prevost was visiting. The Library Special Collections has three additional Prevost photographs: Central Barracks from the area, a view down the Hudson from the Riding Hall, and a view of officers' row taken from across the Plain.

While at West Point, Prevost cooperated with W.H.C. Bartlett, Professor of Natural and Experimental Philosophy, in photographing the solar eclipse on May 28, 1854. The Library Special Collections has an album of nineteen photographs of that eclipse. The Smithsonian Institute has a duplicate album of these photographs, which are considered to be among the earliest eclipse photos. After the Library was built in 1841 and its observatory equipment installed, Bartlett increased cadet instruction in astronomy. The West Point Observatory was considered one of the finest in the country for many years. Cadets spent much time under Bartlett's tutelage, taking stellar observations and learning to determine locations based upon their sightings. This was important to officers of that period because, with very few maps available, it was important to be able to determine their exact location in the unsurveyed lands west of the Mississippi.

The additions to academic and tactical instruction were made without deleting any major part of the previous courses. Additions to the various academic courses meant that cadets had to cover more material in the allotted time. The added tactical instruction, especially practical military engineering, was added to the already full cadet schedule. Tactics were taught during summer camp and during the academic year as well. Practical military engineering was scheduled from 4:00 P.M. to sundown. What this meant was that a cadet was in class or studying—during the day, he was required to remain in his room studying at any time he was not in class—from breakfast until taps. His only free time was on Saturday afternoon or after chapel services on Sunday until evening parade at 5:00 P.M.

The increased academic schedule led to some unfortunate inequalities insofar as allocating time to the various departments was concerned. The scientific and mathematical subjects were not curtailed in any way despite the addition of many new developments in their field of interest. The primary loser was the Department of Geography, History, and Ethics whose professor was also the chaplain. International and constitutional law and English grammar and rhetoric had been added to its instruction, but no additional time was made available.

Mahan and Church headed every committee appointed by the Academic Board and actually dominated much of the policy discussions of that group. The addition of Spanish to the instructional load of the French Department and the increased emphasis on topographical sketching by the Department of Drawing were made without providing additional time to those departments. As a result, although there was no lessening of the high academic quality of instruction in mathematics and the sciences, the liberal arts subjects, with the exception of drawing, were substandard.

Morrison lists three solutions considered. The first—requiring proficiency in English, history, geography, and speech as a requirement for appointment as a cadet—was deemed highly desirable because Congress insisted that the entrance examinations be kept as simple as possible in order to enable any young man appointed to enter the Academy. Boards of Visitors from Thayer's time on had urged that the entrance examinations be stiffened, but these recommendations were constantly ignored. The second consideration involved dividing the curriculum into separate courses. One course, intended for cadets whose backgrounds clearly indicated that they would be commissioned in the Infantry, Dragoons or Cavalry, would include more literary and military subjects and less mathematics, engineering, and science. The second course essentially would be the Thayer curriculum updated with the traditional emphasis on technical and scientific subjects, which would qualify cadets for commissioning in the Corps of Engineers, the Topographical Engineers, and the Artillery. Lee, the Academic Board, Chief of Engineers Totten, and Secretary of War Davis unanimously agreed that adopting this alternative might destroy the Academy because it would produce two grades of graduates, the "haves" and the "have nots." This left the third option: changing the course to five years instead of four. Adding a year would provide the time required to bring all parts of the curriculum to the high level desired as well as adding more instruction in law, history, geography, and English.

Several Boards of Visitors had recommended that this be done, but no definite action was taken by the Academic Board until 1846 when it recommended that a five-year course of instruction be adopted. Although Totten favored the five-plan, he considered 1846 to be the wrong time to make the change. The Mexican War had increased the need for officers. Because the proposal included splitting a plebe class into two groups with one instructed in the four-year curriculum and the other in the five-year course, Totten wanted to wait until a large enough group of cadets entered to be divided into two classes. In 1852, a large class was appointed, and Totten recommended that the five-year course be implemented. Secretary of War Conrad vetoed the proposal because he believed that the purpose of the Academy was to produce good officers, not scholars or "accomplished gentlemen." The appointment of Jefferson Davis as Secretary and the appointment of a large plebe class in 1854 led Totten to recommend that the class entering that year, 103 new cadets, be divided and the five-year course initiated. Contrary to the accounts of some historians, Lee played no prominent part in this decision. Although he and the Academic Board must have been consulted, the decision was made by Davis and Totten.

The Academic Board made a simple decision in dividing the new cadets: age would be the determining factor in deciding whether a plebe would take the four-year or five-year course. This decision was based upon the desire to avoid having no class graduate in any one year. Forty-seven plebes who were eighteen or older were selected to join the three upper classes in the old, four-year curriculum as the new Fourth Class. The remaining fifty-six appointees became the first Fifth Class.

The five-year course—perhaps "experiment" should be used instead of "course"—was short lived. Only three, five-year classes were graduated: the classes of 1859, 1860, and May 1861. As might be expected, the change was not welcomed by cadets. Letters to parents and friends complained about being required to spend an additional year as a cadet. Many cadets wrote Congressmen; their parents and friends did the same. Although these complaints and resultant comments by Congressmen had little impact on Jefferson Davis, his successor, John B. Floyd, capitulated and ordered a return to the four-year course in August 1858.

Floyd was not influenced by cadet complaints and congressional disapproval alone. The Academic Board recommended a return to the four-year course because it considered the effort to incorporate humanities into the curriculum to be a failure. Geography taught cadets, in the Board's opinion, was no better than that offered by schools, and history was little more than a chronological listing of events. The Board also argued that a five-year program would probably result in graduates not studying independently. Another statement, however, may have given a truer reason for the recommendation made by the Academic Board. In the opinion of the professors, the humanities taught had resulted in cadets paying more attention to these studies than to the scientific courses. The Board recommended eliminating or curtailing the study of the humanities and concentrating instead on the old curriculum with its emphasis on mathematics, science, and engineering.

Only the Professor of Geography, History, and Ethics, Chaplain John French, did not agree with the Academic Board recommendation. He maintained that the five-year program had not been given sufficient time to prove its merits. He argued that cadets would always select the easiest courses of study if left to make the decision themselves. Of course, this argument only strengthened the stand of the Academic Board by showing that cadets actually did concentrate on these subjects instead of the scientific, mathematical, and engineering courses. French's arguments failed to convince Floyd, and the five-year course was abandoned in October 1858. To compensate for the change, both of the classes that had entered in 1854 were programmed to graduate in 1859.

This flip-flop from four-year to five-year and back to four-year courses must have added to the workload of the faculty, although no written record can be found to verify this opinion. The change to the five-year program meant that instructors had to teach the four-year curriculum to the classes already enrolled as well as beginning instruction of the five-year curriculum to the classes that entered from 1854 to 1858. The return to the four-year course meant additional work to make certain that all of the critical core subjects were covered fully in the time remaining for the five-year cadets. Losing a full year required a concentrated effort by instructors and cadets to compensate for the loss of time involved.

In April 1859, Floyd abruptly ordered a return to the five-year curriculum, using the arguments of Chaplain French to explain his change of heart. Why it took several months for French's position to convince the Secretary was not explained. Morrison maintains that pressure from Jefferson Davis, now Chairman of the Senate Military Affairs Committee, may have convinced Floyd that he had made the wrong decision. Although Morrison states that this premise cannot be proven, it is logical to assume that Davis, who had been so much in favor of the program when he was Secretary of War, would have done everything possible to have it reinstated. Cadet Henry Dupont in a June 1859 letter to his mother cited another possible reason for Floyd's action. Dupont maintained that Floyd wanted to appoint civilians as officers; and, if two classes were graduated in June, "he will be unable to make any appointments at all." Therefore, Dupont asserted, Floyd had ordered the return to the five-year program, "pretty certain that if only twenty-two men graduate in June he will have a chance" to make his desired appointments.

The sudden reversal had a profound impact upon everyone at West Point. Cadets were extremely unhappy and upset, especially those who would have graduated in June but would now have to spend another year studying. Superintendent Delafield, the Academic Board, instructors, and tactical officers were perplexed. Cadet Dupont summarized the situation in his June 10 letter to his mother:

> The whole affair is certainly enough to disgust even the most reasonable man with the miserable, shuffling, vacillating way of doing business at Washington which now seems to be the order of the day. The professors here are all disgusted and do not scruple to say so. Old "Del" [Delafield] pretends to be, but whether he really is or not, is a matter which remains to be proved, as he long since forfeited any claim to confidence in him on our part. As to the Secretary the anathema of the whole Corps are now heaped on his head and justly too in my opinion.

What Colonel Lee thought of this situation is unknown. His tenure as superintendent ended in May 1855 when Davis offered him a lieutenant colonelcy in one of the two new cavalry regiments being organized. Lee hesitated in accepting because it meant leaving the Corps of Engineers and ending his tour of duty at West Point earlier than he had anticipated. His decision was based upon permanent promotion to lieutenant colonel, two grades higher than his permanent rank of captain in the Corps of Engineers.

The Lee family was swamped with invitations from officers of the Post. A constant stream of cadets called at their quarters every afternoon and evening to say goodbye to Lee—and to his daughters, Agnes and Anne. Agnes wrote in her diary about attending their last Saturday parade, "I looked out on parade that evening for the *last* time. How strangely it sounded as I repeated to myself 'my last parade.' I couldn't realize it." Sunday morning the two girls attended Chapel and then joined Colonel and Mrs. Lee for Communion at the Church of the Holy Innocents in Buttermilk Falls, it being Easter Sunday. After lunch, the girls walked to the "lower church," the enlisted chapel in Camptown below the level of the Plain. Because the Lee quarters were filled with people, the girls walked to the cemetery and back, joined by cadets. That evening the Corps serenaded the Lees, ending with "Home Sweet Home" and "Carry Me Back to Ole Virginny." The next evening the band arrived for an impromptu concert. The Lees left in the morning, crossing the river to take the train from Garrison. Agnes noted that "the Heavens seemed to sympathize with us, it shed torrents of tears & as we crossed the river in open boats everything was pretty well soaked." The wharf was crowded with officers and their ladies who had come to "bid a last, a long farewell" to Robert E. Lee and his family.

It is difficult to assess Lee's impact upon the Academy. He was not a builder in the Delafield manner, but the new Riding Hall, quarters for officers and enlisted men, and service buildings were built during his superintendency. The old riding hall on the ground floor of the Academic Building was renovated into an improved fencing room and a gymnasium. The entire Plain, west of the artillery and cavalry drill area near Fort Clinton, was sodded. Lee made no academic innovations of note. He was aware, however, of the stress placed upon cadets by their heavy academic workload. Although there is no indication as such, Lee probably agreed with Davis's and Totten's decision to extend the course to five years. Three men served as Commandant of Cadets during Lee's tenure: Bradford Allen, Robert Garnett, and William Walker. Under their supervision, cadet drill reached a new high of perfection, probably at Lee's insistence. Although he believed in strict discipline, he was sympathetic to cadet effervescent spirits and often imposed lesser punishments than might have been justified. He showed no favoritism and would not shield even his family members in the Corps from punishment if such was required. Lee was an administrator who delegated authority to his subordinates while retaining the responsibility for their actions. The Commandant was in charge of the Corps; Lee did not interfere with his actions. Each professor controlled his department, and the Academic Board met to determine overall policy for operation of the Academy. Lee did not attempt to assert his desires over those recommended by the Board. His tact, gentle manners, and understanding enabled him to cooperate and work closely with his West Point associates and with the Chief of Engineers and the Secretary of War as well. His interest in the welfare of his cadets is best shown by his many letters to their parents. Robert E. Lee was well liked by cadets, officers, enlisted men, the ladies, and the children at West Point. Credit must be given to Lee for his efforts to graduate cadets who were gentlemen versed in the social graces and military courtesy; he believed that each graduate should be well-rounded in academics, military subjects, and the niceties of off-duty life. The Academy improved during his superintendency. If, as has so often been stated, this was the "Golden Age" of the Military Academy, Lee must be given some of the credit for guiding it in that direction.

Lee was replaced by Captain John G. Barnard, but he remained for only eighteen months. Little of significance occurred during Barnard's term of office. He did, however, take one action to ease the hardships of cadet life; he authorized cadets to play chess in camp! In September 1856, Richard Delafield returned for his second tour as Superintendent. He had recently returned from a two-year tour in Europe as a member of the Military Commission to the Crimea. Another member of the group was Captain George B. McClellan, Class of 1846. Delafield's report, *Report on the Art of War in Europe in 1854, 1855, and 1856* was published by order of Congress in 1860. There is little doubt that Mahan discussed the Crimean War in detail with Delafield, and it is quite possible that Delafield may have reported his observations to the Napoleon Club.

Delafield's second tour did not include any large building programs. It was, however, marked by seemingly constant strife with Secretary of War Floyd. The return to the four-year course and the reversal of that decision were only one of several problems generated by Floyd. In 1858 Sylvanus Thayer, Acting Chief of Engineers during a temporary absence of Totten, received the recommendation of the Academic Board to return to the four-year course. Thayer concurred in the Board's request, although he had himself recommended a five-year program in 1832. He recommended to Floyd that a permanent board be established to oversee the activities of the Academy. Floyd accepted Thayer's recommendation and appointed a commission consisting of Delafield, Major Alfred Mordecai, and Captain George W. Cullum. Their first mission was to review the curriculum and recommend a length for the course of instruction. The commission met for several months in early 1860 and then was suddenly dissolved by Floyd, possibly because the Secretary was concerned that the commission would recommend a return to the four-year course, which would have been more than a bit embarrassing.

Not surprisingly, both houses of Congress were concerned about the length of the Academy course of instruction. Letters from cadets and complaints from parents and other constituents resulted in bicameral studies to determine what the length should be. The Senate group, questioning whether or not the Secretary of War had the authority to vary the course of instruction, prepared legislation fixing the course length at four years. Jefferson Davis was able to prevent action on the proposed bill but was not able to obtain outright approval of his favored five-year course. He did, however, succeed in having an investigation committee appointed.

Committee members were Davis as chairman, Senator Solomon Foote, Representatives Henry W. Davis and John Cochrane, Artillery Major Robert Anderson, and Topographical Engineer Captain Andrew A. Humphreys. The committee met at West Point from summer to November 1860. During this period, it interviewed personally or by written questions Superintendent Delafield, all of the Academic Board, Commandant William J. Hardee, other instructors and tactical officers, cadets, Winfield Scott, and other senior Army officers. After months of investigation and interviews, the committee submitted its report to Congress in December. Its recommendations were extensive. Retention of the five-year course was the first recommendation made. A committee similar to the Thayer group would be appointed to supervise Academy activities and to approve any changes recommended by the Academic Board. This committee would include members of the House and Senate, the Chief of Engineers, a line officer, another officer from one of the scientific branches, a civilian noted for his scientific accomplishments, and another civilian recognized as an outstanding mathematician. Another recommendation was to enable an officer of any branch of the Army to become superintendent, breaking the long-standing monopoly requiring the superintendent to be chosen from the Corps of Engineers. Professors would be required to retire after twenty-five years of service, although they might be removed at any time by the President acting on the recommendations of the supervising committee. Although the Academic Board was to retain its function of arranging classes based upon academic merit, it would be required to submit all curriculum changes to the supervisory committee for approval. The committee recommendations were incorporated in a proposed bill submitted to the Senate Military Affairs Committee in January 1861. Before any action could be taken, the firing on Fort Sumter in April directed Senate attention to far more important matters, and the proposed legislation was forgotten. Of the committee recommendations, only the removal of the requirement that the superintendent be chosen from the Corps of Engineers was adopted, this in July 1866.

During the time the committee was at West Point, Captain Anderson wrote many long, diary-like letters to his wife, commenting on various committee actions. Jefferson Davis apparently was against making it possible for the superintendent to be chosen from any branch of the Army. "Col. Davis," Anderson wrote, "says that the law is clearly that no one can be appointed Supt. unless he belongs to the Engineer Corps. Whether our commission will recommend the opening of that to the Army at large or restrict it to certain Corps, etc. and then whether the Congress will meet our recommendation in a law—are all questions for the future." In the same August 4 letter, Anderson wrote "I am very much afraid from turn the investigation is taking that our report will, if adopted, not do the Academy much good." A week later, Anderson was even more specific, saying, "We have now too much politics in securing appointments and promotions. Our only safety is to try and keep the Army free from such influences." Anderson commented on the many social activities held for the committee, including band concerts, cadet hops, dinners, luncheons, and receptions. The group was invited to dinners by Gouverneur Kemble several times. In return, the committee hosted dinners at the hotel. He commented frequently on the testimony given by various officers, giving special emphasis to the value of suggestions made by Captain George Cullum. Anderson was a bit surprised when Sylvanus Thayer declined to answer the questions of the committee, although Thayer informed Anderson that he would answer any specific questions that Anderson might ask. Anderson did not hestitate to criticize Academy officers. He was particularly outspoken about Professor Bartlett: "I was a little annoyed by the manner in which one of the young officers spoke about Bartlett. It appears that B. has made some very violent enemies here by something he has done within the last years. The fact is that he has a son in the Corps whose conduct is bad, and the Prof. to save him has had the discipline of the Corps interfered with and injured by getting the interposition of the authorities in Washington. This with some other causes has produced a bad state of feeling towards him." In his last letter, Anderson summarized his opinion of the committee's activities, "All are pushing to get through—I am sorry for it, on many accounts, as our Report will in all probability be marked by hurry, that it will not be worth as much as it should be. I am very much afraid that we will make a botch of our work. It is a great pity as we have collected a mass of most excellently well digested material."

Floyd's term as Secretary of War brought more turmoil and frustration to the Academy than at any time since Andrew Jackson's presidency. He appeared to be unable to make a permanent decision. The flip-flop fiasco involving the five-year course caused problems for and resentment by cadets and officers alike. Appointing the investigative committee to study the overall activities at West Point and then suddenly dissolving the committee without any notice added to the antagonistic attitude of Academy officials. The apparent friction between Floyd and Jefferson Davis did little to ease the problems resulting from Floyd's actions. Although it might seem that Davis attempted to continue to control the War Department by his efforts as a senator and chairman of the Military Affairs Committee for personal aggrandizement, it is more probable that Davis was motivated by a sincere desire to improve the Academy. Contrary to opinions expressed by some historians, there is little evidence that his actions were motivated by the intent to lessen the quality of Academy training or to increase the number of southern cadets graduating, in anticipation of the coming secession of southern states. As Secretary of War, Davis refused to authorize the building of a second military academy in a southern state, and, in so doing, praised the nationalistic attitude of West Pointers and their dedication to their duties as officers in the U.S. Army. Davis in a Senate debate in 1859 asserted vigorously that Academy graduates served the country without any limitations caused by sectionalism.

In addition to the turbulence caused by Secretary Floyd, Delafield faced another, growing problem: the increased sectional feeling within the Corps of

Cadets. Delafield must have contrasted the new sectionalism with that he had encountered during his first superintendency from 1838 to 1845. There was sectionalism at that time, but it was more resentment on the part of southern cadets who felt that their northern contemporaries had an advantage because of better schooling. If there was any great difference, other than earlier education, between northern and southern cadets, it was a tendency for the southern young men to take a greater interest in politics, both regional and national. The increased interest in the slavery issue led to the authorities—and the cadets themselves—deciding to eliminate sectional issues from the debates and study presentations of the Dialectic Society.

Intense sectional attitudes by cadets did not lead immediately to isolation of one group from another. Oliver Howard, an outspoken abolitionist, became a close friend of Jeb Stuart, an equally outspoken advocate of slavery. As the 1850s passed, however, sectionalism in the true sense became more and more prevalent at the Academy. This was only a reflection of the growing sectionalism of the nation as a whole. At West Point, the growth was marked by an increasing tendency for cadets to get themselves assigned to a company predominately southern or northern in composition. There were many exceptions to this unofficial segregation. George Custer, for example, spent his four cadet years assigned to a company composed primarily of southern cadets. There was no lessening of the close friendships between cadets regardless of whether their homes were in the North or the South. Throughout this period of turmoil, there was no lessening of the efforts by Academy authorities to instill dedication to country in their charges. This was commented upon most favorably by several Boards of Visitors. Cadet Jeb Stuart probably expressed an accurate view of the situation in a March 1851 letter, "there seems to be a sentiment of mutual forbearance" in the Corps to acknowledge sectionalism existed outside the gray walls.

But a catalyst changed that feeling. John Brown's raid on Harper's Ferry in October 1859 caused great excitement at West Point. Some cadets made adult and objective judgments of what had taken place. Henry Dupont, for example, wrote to his mother, "What an outrageous affair was that at Harper's Ferry. . . . The most disgusting part of the business though, I think, are the meetings of the republicans of Chicago and of various towns of Massachusetts to express their sympathy with Brown and regret at the failure of his plans. A great deal of political capital will I suppose be made of the affair." The Brown raid polarized feelings in the Corps. Southern cadets denounced abolitionists and anyone in the North who sympathized with them. Northern cadets criticized slavery and its evils. There were discussions; there were arguments.

Morris Schaff in his memoirs indicated that the first "collision of a political nature" resulted: a fight between Pennsylvanian Emory Upton and South Carolinian Wade Hampton Gibbes. Upton had attended Oberlin College, which admitted negro students, before entering the Academy and was an admitted abolitionist. Schaff asserted that Upton was probably the only cadet who "ever had the temerity to plant himself squarely in the ranks of that unpopular band of liberty-loving dreamers." After the Brown raid, Gibbes made some highly derogatory and inflammatory remarks about Upton who, hearing about Gibbes' statements, challenged him to a fight. The bout took place after dinner in a room on the second floor of barracks. Other cadets crowded into the room around the fighters, out into the hallway, on the stairway, out onto the stoops of barracks, and into the area. Although the cadet guard called for the corporal of the guard, no one paid any attention to his efforts. Both combatants fought hard with little inclination to stop; Schaff noticed that Upton's face was bleeding and Gibbes' eye was blackening. One of Schaff's companions, Texan Willis Robertson, yelled at Gibbes to use his bayonet. In the silence that resulted, an ice-cold voice at the head of the stairs called out, "If there are any more of you down there who want anything, come right up." It was John Rodgers, Upton's roommate and second. Cooler heads prevailed, the fight ended, and the crowd dispersed. But the unspoken truce that had existed had ended; sectionalism was no longer pushed away but became clearly evident.

Despite this change in cadet attitudes, there were few if any outright confrontations in the months following John Brown's raid. The tranquillity and deliberate return to friendly relationships between cadets from all parts of the country seemed to be a quiet, unspoken admission of shame that political and sectional feelings had caused the Upton-Gibbes fracas. Whether or not officials learned of the fight is unknown; if they did, no official action was taken. The Corps policed the Corps to prevent another outbreak.

The comradeship of cadets was best shown perhaps in their recreational activities. Northern and southern men skated together on the Hudson or on one of the ponds still existing on the level of the Plain. Debates sponsored by the Dialectic Society continued to avoid sectional topics. "Hashes"—cookouts—in cadet rooms brought cadets together informally, and the bull sessions during these feasts included friendly discussions of many subjects—but not those of political nature.

A definite indication of the return to genuine friendship is to be found in class photograph albums. Beginning in the late 1850s, cadets began to assemble class albums containing portraits of classmates, instructors, and some scenic views. Other colleges adopted this custom about the same time. Yale, for example, had initiated the preparation of class albums in the early 1850s, using lithograph or engraved portraits of class members; about 1860, the Yale albums used photographs.

The earliest West Point album was assembled about 1856. The contents of the albums in 1859 and 1860 show no sign of sectional emphasis; both northern and southern cadets included photographs of all of their classmates. No two of these albums are identical; each reflects the interests and desires of the cadet to whom it belonged. Many of the albums include the signatures of the officers and cadets whose photographs were used. Among the photographers taking these photos were representatives of the Pach and Brady Studios in New York City. This custom continued until the appearance of the cadet yearbook, *The Howitzer*, in 1896.

Cadets often gathered at Fort Clinton parapet, near Execution Hollow, or in the area of barracks for a singing session during the period between supper and call to quarters. Popular songs and traditional ditties were sung with vigor and, at times, with comical motions. These song fests led to the development of another custom: the writing of songs for furlough and graduating classes. Words for the Class of 1848 graduation song were written by Mrs. Winfield Scott. The last lines of the chorus were very popular in that sentimental age:

> "Hurrah for the merry bright manly flame
> That opens a life so new.
> When we doff the Cadet and don the Brevet
> And change the Gray for Blue."

Eleven years later, the Class of 1859 used similar wording, starting their class song with:

> A few days more, a few days more,
> To toilsome study given.
> A few days more—we'll reach that shore
> For which we long have striven.
> With pipe and song we'll jog along
> Till these few days are through,
> And all among our jovial throng
> Have donned the Army Blue.

These words were catching, and many classes used them in one form or another for their own songs. The music, however, varied from year to year. Some tunes were composed by cadets, others by Bandmaster Apelles. Then in 1865, Cadet George T. Olmstead wrote words for his class song that have become a West Point tradition:

> We've not much longer here to stay,
> For in a month or two,
> We'll bid farewell to Cadet gray
> And don the Army Blue.
>
> Army Blue, Army Blue,
> Hurrah for the Army Blue.
> We'll bid farewell to Cadet gray
> And don the Army Blue.

The words were set to the music of a popular southern song, "Aura Lea," made nationally popular in modern times by Elvis Presley with words called "Love Me Tender." Countless verses have been written since—"To the Ladies who come up in June, we'll bid a fond adieu"; "Here's to the man who wins the cup . . . and may he bring our godson up to join the Army too," and "Army Blue" remains one of West Point's most popular songs. It is by tradition the last song played at a hop, coupled with "Goodnight, Ladies." Old grads often sing it to express their sentiments of missing their cadet days, although the original intent of the Class of '65 was to joyfully celebrate their approaching graduation.

Religion was important to cadets, officers, enlisted men, and their families. The Cadet Chapel was attended by cadets and many officers. Cadets were permitted to attend church services in Buttermilk Falls if their denomination differed from that of the chaplain. Catholic services were held on post or cadets were given permits to attend the local parish church. A separate chapel for enlisted men was in the vicinity of the barracks and quarters in Camptown. In the late 1850s, a religious revival occurred, paralleling that of the late 1820s and 1830s. Credit for this must be shared by Chaplain John French and Lieutenant Oliver Howard, Class of 1854. Howard returned to West Point in 1857 as a mathematics instructor. Intending at that time to leave the Army and enter the ministry, Howard organized twice-weekly prayer meetings, which were held in "the angle of barracks," the seventh and seventh-and-a-half divisions. At first, only five cadets attended these classes, but the number increased until the meeting rooms were no longer adequate. To prepare himself to teach at these meetings, Howard learned Hebrew, studying with the Episcopal pastor of the Chapel of the Holy Innocents in Buttermilk Falls, a church erected by the contributions of Professor Mahan from funds he received from his many published works. In addition to the barracks prayer meetings, Howard held Bible study in "the little church under the hill," the enlisted chapel. The chapel was arranged in such a way that Catholic services could be conducted in the morning and Protestant services in the afternoon and evenings. A Methodist clergyman often held evening services, and representatives of other denominations often were guest preachers. Howard often stressed his sincere belief that a paternal system of discipline was far more advantageous than the martinet system currently enforced in the Army. His autobiography expressed his concept: "I endeavored to show that the general who cared for his men as a father cares for his children, providing for all their wants and doing everything he could for their comfort consistent with their strict performance of duty, would be the most successful; that his men would love him; would follow him readily and be willing even to sacrifice their lives while enabling him to accomplish a great patriotic purpose."

Few other officers at West Point agreed with Howard's concepts. When he wrote an article entitled "Discipline in the Army" for a New York monthly, Superintendent Delafield was annoyed because he considered the article to criticize his supervision of Academy affairs. Although a few faculty and staff officers agreed with Howard, most felt that his ideas were "contrary to a proper military spirit." One officer who did side with Howard was Lieutenant Edward P. Alexander, commander of the Sapper Detachment. When the Detachment was sent to join the expedition against the Mormons, Alexander gave Howard two religious books and money to expend in Christian work. Alexander told Howard that he wished "to be remembered by my men to be a Christian and have their sympathy and interest during the expedition to Utah." Alexander later joined the Confederate Army and became Longstreet's Chief of Artillery.

A new task was given to the Corps by the Commandant, William H. Hardee, who was completing a new manual of tactics. To test his regulations, Hardee used the cadets as a test battalion. The Corps was moved through various maneuvers at the normal pace, at quick time, and then at double time. Needless to say, this drill was not popular to the cadets because it took more of their time than the old drill. Parades lasted longer, for it took more time to pass in review three times instead of the one time at the normal pace. Hardee's drill was approved by the War Department and was used at West Point until the mid-1860s.

The tranquillity of the unspoken truce lasted only a short time. Jefferson Davis unknowingly initiated the return to outspoken sectionalism in the Corps when he submitted six Southern extremist resolutions to the Senate in early February 1860. These resolutions stated that no state had the right to interfere with domestic institutions of other states, that any attack on slavery was a violation of the Constitution, that it was the duty of Congress to oppose all discriminatory action against persons or property in the territories, that neither Congress nor any territorial legislature could impair the right to hold slaves in the territories, that a territory could not make any decision regarding slavery until it had been admitted to the Union as a state, and that all states interfering with the recovery of slaves were violating the Constitution. The resulting intense and violent debates in the Senate and the widespread and vociferous comments in the press were reflected by outspoken criticism by both northern and southern cadets in an increasingly volatile division of sectional feelings.

The political conventions in the spring increased tension in the Corps of Cadets because of the split of the Democratic party with the Douglas-Johnson ticket of northerners and the Breckenridge-Lane representation for the southern group. The secession of southern Democrats now appears to have been a forerunner of what would occur after the election in November. Douglas adherents favored nonintervention by Congress and abiding by Supreme Court decisions. Breckenridge supporters in eight southern states adopted a platform that supported slavery in the territories and admission of new states into the Union on an equal basis with the other states. The young Republican party nominated Lincoln and Hamlin with a platform that, among many other statements, condemned any renewal of the African slave trade and maintained that neither Congress nor any territorial legislature could give legal status to slavery in the territories.

The reaction of the Corps of Cadets was a reflection of the action of cadet parents and friends at home. The furlough class returned from leave at the end of the summer, bringing firsthand information of attitudes at home. Although increased tension was evident, it seemed to draw cadets from all sections of the country closer together instead of lessening the ties of friendship. William Harris wrote to his father that "the greatest excitement prevails, but it does not lead to any open rupture but rather tends to draw out our individual sympathy for each other." A New Yorker, Harris expressed some thoughts that may have shocked his father. "Slavery may be a curse," he wrote, "but I cannot help thinking that Anti-Slavery is a greater one. Perhaps not in theory but it certainly seems so in practice. The resistance to the execution of the Fugitive Slave Law, the measures which are being taken in some parts of the country to allow negroes to vote, and others of a similar nature, spring from heads to whom I should not like to be subjected." Harris ended his political discussion with "I know that I have as much sectional pride and love my own state as much as any other man, but I cannot help feeling that the United States has a prior claim upon me, especially since the solemn oath I took three years ago [the oath taken when he became a cadet]. The every day, reckless talk about Disunion is particularly disgusting to me."

Harris was not alone in his opinions. Stephen Lyford, whose home was in New Hampshire, wrote to his father in early October 1860 that he believed that his home state would vote for Lincoln but that "I only wish that some of those rampant abolitionists might have a few filthy, greasy . . . niggers to hug to their bosoms—They would soon be sick of their bargains and wish them back to their southern homes." Perhaps George Custer was the most outspoken northern cadet—he came from Michigan—to support his southern friends. Custer's best friend was Thomas Rosser from Texas; his company was composed mostly of southern cadets. Detesting Republicans and Abolitionists alike, Custer wrote home denouncing both, especially the "black- brown Republicans who will either deprive a portion of their fellow citizens of their just rights or produce a dissolution of the Union." In his opinion, southerners had been subjected to insult after insult and were determined to no longer submit to such aggression.

There were some events that interrupted political discussions. The Commandant, Colonel William J. Hardee, was replaced by Artillery Captain John F. Reynolds. Other tactical officers and instructors were also relieved. Cadet Samuel Benjamin wrote to his mother to describe the departure of Lieutenant Rufus Saxton, his Artillery Tactics instructor: "Lt. Saxton was relieved from duty to-night. He was Officer in Charge and as it was his last parade we *raised* our hats to him when we marched to the front and saluted. He looked surprised and pleased and raised his hat too. It is the first time I have ever seen that compliment paid to an officer on his being *relieved*. I do not believe there has ever been an officer more popular than Lt. Saxton." Although Hardee had not been too well liked by the cadets—he was a strict disciplinarian and cadets remembered all too well his using the Corps to test his new manual—they serenaded him in front of his quarters the night before his departure, following a long-established tradition.

The Senate commission headed by Jefferson Davis met at West Point during the fall of 1860. In addition to holding its sessions, the commission members were entertained by officers and returned the social obligations by dinners at the hotel. Cadets were often invited to these affairs and to other social activities sponsored by General and Mrs. Winfield Scott and other distinguished visitors. Not all visiting dignitaries were as welcome to the cadets. William Harris wrote to his father about the visit of Governor John Letcher of Virginia, who visited the Academy while arranging for the purchase of arms from the West Point Foundry at Cold Spring and "contracting for arms for that State, to be procured at Springfield." Superintendent Delafield had the Corps pass in review for the Virginia visitors. In December, Harris also told his father of the visit of Colonel Hardee, former Commandant of Cadets, "to buy cannon at Parrott's foundry [the West Point Foundry] in Cold Spring for the State of Georgia. He is drawing pay from the *United States* & at the same time executing a contract for the State of Georgia." Samuel Benjamin reported to his mother that "Colonel Cook of the dragoons [Philip St. George Cooke, Class of 1827] is here. He is revising the cavalry tactics and is going to adopt a 'one rank formation.' He was at our drill yesterday trying some of his new maneuvers. It made the ride miserably stupid, for it took him a long time to explain and then we would only walk through the maneuver."

October 1860 brought much excitement to West Point. Edward, Prince of Wales, visited the Academy at the invitation of the Superintendent and General Winfield Scott. A huge crowd arrived from New York and cities to the north to see the royal visitor. Edward arrived on the revenue cutter, *Harriet Lane*. He was met at the dock by the Academic Board, the Superintendent, and the Commandant, all in full dress uniform. A detachment of cavalry escorted him up the hill to the Superintendent's quarters as a cadet battery fired a royal salute. Tully McRae wrote that he "was with the rest of the cadets under arms for three precious long hours. This too upon damp ground and without our overcoats. But we had some fun watching the police and dragoons trying to keep the crowd back off the parade ground." McCrae continued, "When the Prince did come he saw the prettiest military spectacle he ever will have the chance to see. Every cadet had his pride aroused and did his best. The result was we outdid ourselves."

The Corps was disappointed when a scheduled hop was cancelled. The First Class had planned to hold a ball in his honor, but Edward declined the invitation. Tully McRae wrote that "one excuse was that he left his baggage in New York. Another was that he was too tired, but this was not likely for he rolled ten-pins at the hotel until 12 o'clock. The fact of it was," he added, "the Prince himself was very anxious to have the ball, but the old Duke of Newcastle would not let him."

Cadet officers were introduced to Edward after the review and were impressed by his pleasant attitude. Emory Upton wrote to his sister that "I can now say my rustic hand has grasped the hand of royalty." The royal party visited classrooms and the Riding Hall. Llewellyn Hoxton remembered his classmate James Kennard losing a stirrup and almost being tossed. When he regained his seat and put his foot back into the stirrup, he was applauded by the visitor's gallery, the Prince joining in the applause.

A day or so after the visit ended, cadets laughed at the coverage in New York weekly magazines, especially the illustrations in *Harper's Weekly*. Henry Dupont wrote to his mother that the illustrations "existed only in the artist's imagination [he was referring to a drawing of artillery exercises]. There were no military exercises in his honor excepting the review, which the *Weekly* calls 'a parade.' As to the only one of the illustrations founded on fact, that is full of the grossest errors of detail—all the muskets at a left shoulder shift, a position not in the tactics."

Visitors and political discussions did not interrupt instruction. Professor Bartlett increased his emphasis on teaching cadets to determine their exact location using lunar and stellar observations. The instructors in the Department of Practical Military Engineering added new material to teach cadets additional field fortifications, the making of gambians for example. For the first time, cadets were taught bayonet drill. William Harris wrote to his father that "Lt. Kelton [John C. Kelton, Class of 1851] drills us every day in *bayonet exercise*, a new art borrowed from the military school in France. It has never before been taught here & the graduating class & our own are the only ones learning it. For my own part I like it very much, although it is very severe exercise for the limbs & makes us very tired, keeping the body in the same position nearly all the time but vaulting, charging & retreating constantly." Harris illustrated a cadet at drill, wearing a full dress coat and kepi, musket and bayonet at the thrust position. Even Professor Weir and his Drawing Department placed more emphasis on practical drawing, and William Harris wrote to his father, "A certain number of our class is detailed daily to go out and take topographical sketches of the country from measurements made in the field. I think it is a good idea, as it may be of much use to us some day." Studying Napoleon's campaigns might not be teaching practical tactics, but Mahan stressed Napoleon's maxims and actions even more during this trying period. Cadet Harris, who often discussed academic methods in his letters home, wrote that "we have a large room in the Academic Building, on the walls of which are painted very large maps of Napoleon's campaigns. It is called the 'Napoleon Room' & cadets are taken in there & study his marches & battles. The officers are very particular about the study of all military campaigns & they are generally well 'posted' on them so that the study is interesting." Although nothing was said officially to the Corps, it is quite evident that the faculty and tactical officers were extremely concerned about increased talk of secession in southern newspapers, hence the increased emphasis upon practical military instruction.

At least one individual at West Point tried to persuade Jefferson Davis to take a stand against secession. Chaplain John French, himself a Virginian and long-time friend of Davis, talked with Davis many times during the Davis commission's long stay at West Point. Oliver Howard noted in his autobiography that

French "worked day and night in anxious thought and correspondence with him with ever-decreasing hope that he might somehow stay the hands which threatened a fraternal strife." Howard also reported that French had offered all of his funds to the government after Fort Sumter was fired upon by the Confederates. Although no evidence has been found, it is entirely probable that other faculty members who knew Davis— Mahan, Bartlett, Bailey, and Church— undoubtedly urged him to do what he could to quell the mounting move toward secession in the South.

As the November election neared, the campaign fervor taking place throughout the United States was reflected to some degree at West Point. Although there were no torch-lit parades led by resounding bands and chanting marchers, cadets did show their enthusiasm for one candidate or another by singing patriotic songs and cheering during the interval between supper and call to quarters, actions far more comparable to one of today's football rallies than a political gathering. Morris Schaff many years later made some extremely acute judgments of the Corps at that time. He noted that, although politics and national affairs were not discussed at the time, letters and local papers from home kept cadets abreast of events throughout the country. "Representing, however, as we did, every Congressional district, we were in miniature the country itself." Schaff felt that the entire situation caused "a state of recklessness as to discipline and a new indifference to class standing, were more or less noticeable in the conduct of the entire corps." He also noted that "the effect on the conduct and temper of some of the Southern cadets was marked by increasingly provoking arrogance; and strangely enough, savage encounters took place between Southerners themselves." He and others did not report any physical encounters between northern and southern cadets, however.

"In October 1860," Schaff wrote, "some evil spirit stole his way into West Point and thence into the room of a couple of bitterly partisan Southerners in my division. The next day—as a result of his visit—a box was set up at a suitable place, with a request that cadets should deposit therein their preferences for President of the United States." Schaff considered the straw vote a deliberate attempt to embroil the Corps and cause trouble. Schaff did not record the total number of votes cast; Ambrose in his history of the Academy states that 214 of the 278 cadets voted: 99 for Breckenridge, 47 for Douglas, 44 for Bell, and 24 for Lincoln. Schaff, however, cited 64 votes for Lincoln, with the statement that "it was always a peculiarity, almost childlike, in simplicity, for the old South, to take it for granted that every one was going its way; never understanding the silence of the Puritan." Angered by the results of the poll, the supervisors appointed tellers for each division of barracks to find cadets who had voted for Lincoln. Only thirty-odd cadets admitted supporting the Republican candidate, all from west of the Hudson River and most from north of the Ohio. Schaff was astounded that there was not a single vote from New England for Lincoln and attributed it to Puritanism or "What business is it of yours how I voted? You get out of this!" The reaction in the Corps was violent; several fights occurred.

The unspoken truce following John Brown's raid was over. Schaff summarized the change by saying, "In one way, I really think it took more courage to vote for Lincoln than to face Picket."

As the November election neared, political fervor increased throughout the country. There were torch-lit parades led by bands and cheering marchers. Candidates addressed constituents at every possible opportunity. At West Point, in contrast to the heated arguments that had taken place during the straw vote, little enthusiasm was expressed. Perhaps the cadets and officers realized the true seriousness of the situation. Would Lincoln be elected? Would any southern states attempt to secede? It was clearly evident that the Army anticipated trouble. Eighteen tactical officers and instructors were returned to their regiments in the latter part of 1860; some of the enlisted men were also transferred. The major indications of cadet interest in the election were a lessening of discipline and increased indifference to their studies—and more frequent forays to Benny Havens' tavern.

On November 4, 1860, William Harris wrote to his mother about cadet concern. "I think it would pain you, as it has me, to witness the effect which this struggle has produced in the Army & especially in the Corps of Cadets. Some of my own class who are appointed from South Carolina have received positive orders from home to come there immediately in the case of Lincoln's election. The greatest excitement prevails, but it does not lead to any open rupture but rather tends to draw out our individual sympathy for each other. It seems inevitable that we must lose some of the finest fellows in our class." Harris indicated that most of the South Carolina cadets and some from other southern states had already written their resignations, intending to submit them to the Superintendent if Lincoln was elected. Henry Dupont commented that "I am glad that the elections will so soon be over, though there is not much uncertainty as to their result in my estimation, though I feel a great deal of uncertainty as to the consequences of this result at the South. There is an insane spirit here rampant on the secession question."

Cadet McCrea wrote, "It [the election] has been the cause of much ill feeling among cadets for the last few weeks. Nearly all take an active interest and are in favor of one or the other of the candidates. . . . [T]he southerners swore (as is customary with a great many of them), they threatened to do all kinds of terrible things and blustered around at a great rate. They were all going to resign, they said, if Lincoln was elected." Many southern cadets wore a blue ribbon cockade tied to a button on their caps, which McRae called a "South Carolina cockade." "Although a Republican," McCrea wrote, "I still remember my native state [Mississippi] and am concerned in its welfare and prosperity. I think it would lose everything and gain nothing by seceding from the Union." Cadet Samuel Benjamin wrote to his sister that "I tried to vote, but they decided in Buttermilk that we could not vote. At first they said we might vote and I had made arrangements to get my name registered, and then was going to run it [go off post without permission] on election day and vote, coming back in a carriage so as to be in time for Parade." Benjamin was disappointed when the Buttermilk Falls authorities decided that being stationed at West Point did not qualify individuals as New York State residents.

The election results did not surprise many cadets. Henry Dupont wrote to his mother that "the elections have turned out precisely as I anticipated, and have had the results too which I expected at the South and where people have gone too far now to retrace their steps, unless some concessions are made. I disapprove of secession simply on the ground of Lincoln's election." One South Carolina cadet, Henry S. Farley, resigned on November 19, although South Carolina did not secede until a month later. Virginia cadet Thomas Rowland wrote to his mother about Farley's resignation, "The excitement here with regard to the Presidential election was not much abated, you may imagine, by the result. Cadet Farley of South Carolina is the only one, however, who has actually resigned thus far. I think there will be no further resignations until some of the Southern States actually secede."

Governors and senators from several southern states were asked by cadets to advise them what to do. Thomas Rowland told his mother that Virginia Governor Letcher in a letter to Cadet Edmund Kirby "advises all cadets from Virginia to remain here and do their duty until their native State shall absolutely require their services." Sam Houston replied to a letter from Cadet Tom Rosser with advice Rosser may not have liked, telling Rosser that "much as excitement has wrought on the public mind, I cannot for a moment entertain the belief that any cause for disunion exists, or that the masses of the people would be ready or willing to precipitate the country into all the horrors of civil war. Such a picture should not be contemplated, but we should look to the union as the main pillar in the temple of our independence. Under her wise protection we hold our dearest rights and enjoy our chiefest blessings. My advice is that you give your whole time and attention to your studies in order that you may be prepared to assume that position to which your graduation would entitle you." John Pelham wrote to family friend Alabama Judge A. J. Walker for his advice and was told "I advise you to resign immediately after Alabama secedes and tender your sword to her." Some southern cadets who wrote home for permission to resign— parental approval was required—were told to remain at West Point for there would be no disunion.

Southern cadets were in a quandary. If their states did secede, would they be able to remain at West Point until graduation? Were they still citizens of the United States or would they become aliens? Resigning would mean leaving the Academy and giving up the prestige of receiving its diploma. The First Classmen, the seniors, had devoted almost five years to their studies; leaving would be especially hard for them. Morris Schaff expressed their problem clearly when he wrote many years later that "it meant at last a dismal alternative—either to stand by the Government or to obey the commands of States in rebellion. Should they yield to the natural pleas of home and blood, or should they meet the eye of that thoughtful face called duty."

Like their home state, South Carolina cadets were outspoken in their criticism of the new President. In mid-November, these cadets sent a letter to the *Columbia Guardian* swearing to stand by their state if it should secede, adding that "we cannot so stifle our convictions of duty as to serve under such a man as Mr. Lincoln as our commander-in-chief." James Hamilton, another South Carolinian, resigned on November 23. Mississippian John W. Lea, George Custer's close friend, followed on December 11. Four days after South Carolina seceded, another Mississippi cadet, Joseph C. Dixon, informed his governor that "the war has begun. I leave tomorrow." These early resignations had shaken the Corps, but the resignation of Alabaman Charles P. Ball brought the truth, the hard facts, before every cadet and officer. Ball was one of the most popular men in the Corps, ranked high in his class academically, and was the first sergeant of A Company. Had he not resigned, he might have been selected as the first captain of the Corps. Ball said good-bye to the Corps at breakfast; and, when he left for the afternoon boat to New York, he was carried on the shoulders of his classmates, who waved their hats until the boat pulled around the bend.

There were attempts to ease the tense feelings at West Point. The venerable Dialectic Society abandoned its normal debate meeting in mid-December to present an amateur theatrical. Cadet Thomas Rowland wrote to his mother, "The play was 'Toodles.' It was admirably performed and elicited enthusiastic support from the audience." Plebe John M. Wright was cast as Mary, Mr. Toodles' daughter; and Toodles was played by First Classman Eugene B. Beaumont. Rowland believed that although "Wright made a very pretty girl; you know he is small, fair and quite handsome," the star of the production was Beaumont, who "possesses a wonderful talent for comedy." As far as can be determined, this was the first theatrical presented by the Dialectic Society and may be considered to be the forerunner of today's Hundredth Night shows.

The decision of Major Robert Anderson to concentrate his garrison forces in Fort Sumter brought even more reality and soberness to West Point. Most of the cadets and all of the officers understood Anderson's reasons for moving troops from Fort Moultrie to Sumter. Henry Dupont told his mother that "Major Anderson has certainly acted with great judgement and good-sense. Had he remained in Fort Moultrie I think blood would have been spilt before this." Stephen Lyford wrote to his father that "I had not believed until today that this trouble would amount to anything but it is my firm conviction that S. C. will go at it [Fort Sumter] before January and that civil war will be the consequence." In another letter, Lyford expressed his disdain for the secessionists—and for President Buchanan: "In my opinion which may not be worth much no state has any cause for seceding as yet and the right of secession cannot be considered trouble as I look upon the matter. It constitutes treason and if we had a *man* like Jackson in the Presidential chair something would be done—But an old woman that decides that a state cannot secede and if one does he cannot help or prevent it cannot be expected to accomplish any great deeds. What an old fool."

Even cadets from the southern states understood Anderson's action. Virginian Thomas Rowland wrote to his father at the end of December 1860 that "It seems to me to have been a most excellent move on the part of Major Anderson, though he has been somewhat condemned. His orders were to act upon the defensive. He would not have been *acting on the defensive* had he remained quietly in an untenable position until an attack had made it too late to prepare for a proper defense." In the same letter, Rowland expressed strong doubts about secession, "What is to become of our glorious Union? Everyone seems to despair of its perpetuation, but I cannot give it up. I will catch at the last straw, and stand by the Union until all is hopelessly lost. Then we must cast our lot with Virginia and hope for the best."

By the end of December, all but one of the South Carolina cadets, three from Mississippi, and two from Alabama had resigned. There was little question in the minds of the cadets and even less in the opinion of the officers that more resignations would come with the New Year. Chaplain French, Virginian loyal to the Union, had the hymn traditionally sung at the last chapel service before graduation included in the Christmas songs. The words, so appropriate for graduation services, were even more fitting in December 1860:

> When shall we meet again?
>   Meet ne'er to sever?
> When will Peace wreath her chain
>   Round us forever?
> Our hearts will ne'er repose
>   Safe from each blast that blows
> In this dark vale of woes,—
>   Never—no, never.

18

Adhere to Your Purpose

New Year's Day 1861 at West Point was marked in the traditional Army manner. Virginia Cadet Thomas Rowland called it a gala day. "The officers families," he wrote to his mother, "all kept open houses, well filled tables, and a plenty of toddy. Ramsay [George W. Ramsay, Jr.] and I made about twelve calls and enjoyed the day very much." That evening, Rowland joined a group making a "hash" in barracks, using the gas lamps as a stove. "About 11 o'clk," he wrote, "I just got to bed ahead in time for the inspecting officer who came around with a dark lantern, caught a great many fellows out of bed."

Resignations continued in January but at a much reduced pace with only two cadets, John T. Wofford of South Carolina and Felix H. Robertson of Tennessee leaving the Academy. Even the secession of Alabama, Florida, Georgia, Louisiana, and Mississippi by the end of January had little impact on the southern cadets. Only four resigned after Texas seceded on February 1.

Another, very brief change came when Major Pierre G. T. Beauregard became the twelfth superintendent on January 23. Three days after his arrival, his native state, Louisiana, seceded from the Union. Two days later, the Secretary of War relieved Beauregard and ordered Delafield to resume the superintendency. In his history of the Academy, Thomas Fleming asserts that the primary reason Beauregard agreed to accept the appointment was to assist in blocking a congressional attempt to enable officers of all branches of the Army to be appointed superintendent. At the time, Beauregard was supervising the construction of the New Orleans Customs House for which he received a percentage of funds expended, about $5,000 a year. En route to West Point, he stopped in Washington and made it known that he would resign his commission should Louisiana secede. Nevertheless, Beauregard objected to his relief, stating that he would only resign if Louisiana joined in a war against the United States. His statement to the War Department, however, was not reflected in his advice to a Louisiana cadet asking if he should resign. "Watch me," Beauregard replied, "and when I jump, you jump. What's the use of jumping too soon."

It is not difficult to understand the quandary facing southern cadets, especially the First Classmen who would graduate in six months. Every day, every cadet paraded in the late afternoon and presented arms when the Post flag was lowered. This simple ceremony emphasized the respect of the Corps and the spectators to the flag, the symbol of unity.

Every man had left his home for the austere regimented life of a cadet. Plebes had been at the Academy for six months; First Classmen—seniors—for nearly five years. In the small Corps of about 250 cadets, every man knew every other man. Each had experienced the same discomforts, the same academic challenges, the same Spartan existence. Each man suffered when a classmate or friend lost a family member. Each cadet laughed at the antics of others and cheered those fortunate enough to have made the run to Benny Havens without being detected.

The Corps had been torn by the viciousness of the election campaign. Despite each cadet's personal preference, there was for the most part an understanding of the beliefs of his counterpart who came from a different part of the country. Living intimately with cadets from another area had taught most of the Corps to appreciate the feelings and convictions of others. And with the secession of so many of the southern states, this understanding, coupled strangely enough with each cadet's own loyalty to country or to state, became deeper. The schism of states seceding only strengthened the bonds of friendship among the young men in gray uniforms.

Cadets did not hesitate to express their personal feelings in letters home. When Kentucky Senator John J. Crittenden introduced a resolution that would have extended the Missouri Compromise to the Pacific, Cadet Stephen Lyford wrote to his father, "I wish Crittenden's propositions would be adopted but I doubt they will. I am in favor of reasonable concessions, as respecting the Nullification Laws, granting the right of entering territories, and the enforcement of the Fugitive Slave Laws, but further than this would not be honorable and should not be submitted to. How they can hold any successful war I cannot imagine and I see by the papers that they are already advocating peaceable secessions. If this Institution is suspended as it may be for lack of funds, I shall join some Army for the Union." Lyford was referring to the shortage of Academy and personal funds. Officers at West Point had not been paid for several months, and Academy expenses were curtailed because the government was unable to or would not provide the funds required for its full operation. Henry Dupont also commented on Crittenden's resolution, "I don't see how any possible adjustment can be effected except by adopting Mr. Crittenden's plan, and I have no idea that the Republicans will ever allow them to be voted on by the people."

In the southern states, United States arsenals, forts, and other public property were seized. South Carolina forces fired on the *Star of the West*, an unarmed ship carrying reinforcements and supplies to Fort Sumter, forcing it to return without resupplying the Union forces. These actions were condemned by cadets. Samuel Benjamin wrote to his father, "But hating civil war as I do I would rather have seen it inaugurated by 'shelling' Fort Moultrie or Morris Island battery than had our country disgraced as she was by the return of the Star of the West. We have heard that Lt. Snyder [George Snyder, Class of 1856] trained a heavy gun on Morris Island, and stomped up and down (in his shirt sleeves) begging Major Anderson for 'God's sake, let me have one shot.' "

There were visible manifestations at West Point of the actions elsewhere. Eighteen officers of the faculty, tactical department, or staff were returned to their regiments in early 1861. Some were replaced by officers wounded in western actions with the Indians. Benjamin described two of these officers. Lieutenant George Bayard had been wounded in a skirmish with Kiowas at Bent's Fort, Colorado. Benjamin told his father that "poor fellow his cheek is badly swollen from an Indian arrow which entered just below the eye and passed down into the throat. It was last spring when he was shot and he had to ride some hundreds of miles before he could get it cut out." Another young officer, Lieutenant William Hazen, Class of 1855, was wounded in a hand-to-hand struggle with a Comanche, killing his assailant but being badly cut in the hand and arm, so badly, wrote Benjamin, "that it is probable he will never have full use of that arm again." He then exclaimed, "So you see we have some tried officers here."

Even the assignment of invalids did not fill the depleted ranks of the staff and faculty. Additional cadet instructors were appointed. Henry Dupont and Samuel Benjamin were among those selected. Cadet instructors had many privileges. Receiving ten dollars a month in addition to their regular pay, these cadets were excused from many duties and did not have to march to class or meals. Benjamin told his father that he walked to the Mess Hall and "I do not have to wait in the Mess Hall until the battalion rises, but enter and leave when I please." Unfortunately, there were more cadet instructors than the venerable Thompson sisters could board, their number being limited to twelve. Best of all, Benjamin said, "I also have the grand pleasure of sleeping until breakfast, unmindful of Reveille and Inspection."

Another evidence of the approaching crisis was related by Henry Dupont, "Orders have been received here to organize a light battery, and they have relieved four artillery officers from duty here and set them to work drilling the dragoons who are to be converted into artillerists." Dragoons were drafted into the battery because they and the Sapper detachment were the only troops at West Point. The dragoons were familiar with driving artillery teams since they did so in training cadets, but they had to be taught the duties of cannoneers. Sappers were not used because they were already alerted to be ready to move to Washington. Dupont told his father, "The battery has orders as well as the sapper company to hold themselves in readiness to march at a moment's notice and a train has been engaged and is in readiness at Garrison's to take them off whenever the order comes." The Sapper unit left on January 19. Tully McCrea commented on the record of the artillery unit in the Mexican War, "This battery is celebrated by its exploits . . . under the famous Captain Bragg." Thomas Rowland wrote to his mother on January 31 that "the Light Artillery Company left this morning for Washington, carrying several field pieces and all the horses from the stables so that there will be no instruction in riding. The latter is much regretted by the cadets; it is the most agreeable duty they have." McCrea and Dupont also commented on the loss of the horses. Harris had a different comment, "If soldiers were the only ones affected by this trouble, we wouldn't care a fig, but I cannot bear to think of such a war. I hold myself bound to the Government, only as long as the Stars & Stripes remain its flag. They may cover up 3 or 4 stars for a year or so, but when it ceases to be the Star Spangled Banner I shall *secede* myself."

Despite these momentous events elsewhere, the Academy kept to its routine. January examinations were conducted on schedule, and cadets who failed were dismissed. Classes were resumed; the seeming indifference that had existed before and after the November election seemed to have disappeared. Cadets applied themselves to their studies as though nothing had happened to disrupt their routine. Although there were no riding lessons, cadets concentrated on sword drill taught by Sword Master Antone Lorentz. During cold spells, cadets skated on the Hudson River or on the small ponds on the level of the Plain. On warm days, they took long walks, along Flirtation Walk or into the hills. Officers invited cadets to dinners or teas. Hops were held in the Mess Hall. The Dialectic Society resumed its periodic debates, but avoided any topics having the slightest bearing on the increasing rupture between the southern states and the remainder of the country.

There were runs to Benny Havens or across the river to Cold Spring when the Hudson froze. Cadet pranks continued unabated. George Custer lived in the 8th Division barracks facing Lieutenant Henry Douglass's quarters. Douglass kept a flock of chickens and a rooster whose raucous crowing often irritated Custer. As Morris Schaff recalled many years later, "But he crowed too often. Custer slipped down one night, took him from his perch, and later he was in a kettle boiling over the gas-burner [cadet rooms were lighted by gas lamps], his feathers on an outspread newspaper." After a tasty meal, one of the group was delegated to dispose of the feathers in trash bins across the area in back of the bathhouse. Hastening across the area to avoid being detected by an officer, he left a trail of feathers behind him. Luckily, the feathered trail did not lead to Custer, and no deficiency was ever charged to him or any other cadet. Had Custer been reported, the demerits resulting would probably have been enough to push him over the maximum number permitted, and Custer, who ranked near the bottom of his class in conduct, would have been dismissed.

And yet there was an underlying tension on the Post. A few more southern cadets resigned. Officers made a point of not discussing the national situation with cadets, undoubtedly to avoid any charges of unduly influencing cadets in one direction or the other. Outwardly there appeared to be no change in Academy activities; inwardly there was tension, apprehension, and confusion.

Outgoing President James Buchanan ordered the Corps to march to the Chapel on Washington's Birthday to listen to his farewell address; Abraham Lincoln concurred with the order. That morning, the Corps was awakened by the entire band playing patriotic airs instead of by the field music sounding reveille. Southern cadets hissed in objection; they were answered by cheers from the northern and western men. All, however, were happy because academics for the day had been canceled.

At eleven-thirty, the Corps and the majority of the officers and their families assembled at the Chapel. The Corps had formed in a column of platoons, each company led by its tactical officer: Lieutenants Fitzhugh Lee with A Company, Alexander McCook with B, Robert Williams with C, and William Hazen with D. The Commandant, John F. Reynolds, led the battalion, which marched behind the band. Arriving at the Chapel, the Corps saluted as the Colors were marched in and placed beside the altar beneath Weir's mural of War and Peace. The band took its place in the choir loft and played patriotic pieces until Chaplain French went to the lecturn to read the Farewell Address. Parts of that address must have hit the listeners as a prediction:

> Such is our situation, and such are our prospects; but not withstanding the cup of blessing is thus reached out to us, not withstanding happiness is ours, if we have a disposition to seize the occasion and make it our own; yet it appears to me there is an option still left to the United States of America, that it is in their choice, and depends upon their conduct, whether they will be respectable and prosperous, or contemptable and miserable as a Nation. This is the time of their political probation, this is the moment when the eyes of the whole World are turned upon them, this is the moment to establish or ruin their national Character forever, this is the favorable moment to give such a tone to our Federal Government, as will enable it to answer the ends of its institution, or this may be the ill-fated moment for relaxing the powers of the Union, annihilating the cement of the Confederation . . . which may play one State against another to prevent their growing importance, and to serve their own interested purpose. For, according to the system of Policy the States shall adopt at this moment, they will stand or fall, and by their confirmation or lapse, it is yet to be decided whether the Revolution must ultimately be considered as a blessing or a curse: a blessing or a curse, not to the present age alone, for without fail will the destiny of unborn Millions be involved.

The simple commemoration over, the Corps was marched back to barracks and dismissed for the day. Although none of the cadet letters during this period described activities for the remainder of the day, it can be assumed that cadets walked around the Post, studied, discussed matters with other cadets, or simply relaxed by getting a little extra "sack time." Call to Quarters sounded on schedule after supper, and cadets returned to their rooms to study for the next day's classes. By 9:30 P.M., the band had formed near the signal gun on Trophy Point to take the place of the drums that normally sounded Tattoo and Taps. The drum major raised his baton, and the band marched off, across the Plain, playing "Washington's March," as Morris Schaff recalled, "pouring forth their tones, now with resounding depth and now with pathos." Windows facing the Plain opened, and cadets watched the band approach. As it reached the line of elm trees planted during Thayer's superintendency, the band struck up "The Star Spangled Banner," the stirring notes echoing as it passed through the sallyport and into the area of barracks. Schaff was on the third floor of the 8th Division with Custer, Elbert, and Sanderson. Across the hall were a group of southern cadets. "Every room fronting the area was aglow," recalled Schaff, "every window filled with men." As the band entered the area, and "a thundering cheer broke . . . begun at our window by Custer, for it took a man of his courage and heedlessness openly to violate the regulations." An answering cheer for "Dixie" came from the southern cadets. Cheer followed cheer. "Ah," wrote Schaff, "it was a great night."

On March 1, cadets were at dinner in the Mess Hall when they were ordered to leave immediately to assist in fighting a fire in Cozzens' hotel in Buttermilk Falls. Cadet companies formed up quickly and marched to the engine house to get the pump engines housed there. Henry Dupont raced into barracks to get his overcoat—as a cadet instructor, he was not required to march with his company. Running full speed he soon passed cadets towing the heavy pump equipment and reached the hotel in advance of most of the Corps. "The flames were then bursting out in the window of the main building," he wrote to his father. "There was a high wind, so that there was no hope of saving the house which was of frame, all that could be done was to get out the furniture." Edward Willis wrote to his father that the engines could not pump water enough to be of much use. Tully McCrea described the efforts of cadet fire teams that stayed in the building or on the roof until they had to be ordered out by the Commandant. One of the areas cleared was the wine cellar. The cadet fire teams assigned to that duty worked enthusiastically to save as much of the bottled stock as possible—and many bottles were waylaid under cadet overcoats. Willis wrote that two of his classmates were in arrest charged with drunkenness. His class was the only class that had not pledged to refrain from using any form of alcohol; but, said Willis, "I fear half the corps would be in the same predicament. . . . The result of this little escapade will probably be nothing more than getting my class on pledge with the rest." It was not unusual for a class to make such a pledge. Shortly before the hotel fire, Thomas Rowland wrote that he had signed the pledge being made by his class, "We the undersigned members of the fourth class hereby pledge ourselves to abstain from, and exert our moral influence against, the use of intoxicating liquor, while on duty, as cadets at West Point." Every member of a class had to sign; even one omission would make the pledge invalid. Rowland predicted that "the Commandant is delighted, of course, and will have the fifth class on pledge, they say, before the winter is over, if he has to drink one of them drunk himself."

Three days later, Abraham Lincoln was inaugurated. His first address to the nation was a peace offering and a gauntlet. "I have no purpose directly or indirectly to interfere with the institution of slavery in the States where it exists," he said, a statement which should have—but did not—please southerners. However, "no State, upon its own mere action, can lawfully get out of the Union," should have met northern desires—but did not. Lincoln tried to heal the early wounds with "though passion may have strained, it must not break our bonds of affection." And his speech included a warning, "in your hands, my dissatisfied fellow countrymen, and not in mine, is the momentous issue of civil war. The Government will not assail you. You can have no conflict without being yourselves the aggressor."

The reaction of the Corps was a reflection of the reaction of people in the South, the North, and the West. Schaff and his roommate, Georgian John A. West, discussed Lincoln's address "over and over again, sometimes long after 'taps' had sounded." West bitterly criticized all "fire-eaters and abolitionists." Henry Dupont was more forthright. "I will not talk of politics," he wrote to his father. "I am sick of them. . . . Mr. Lincoln's speeches are certainly among the poorest I have ever read. Most schoolboys could do better." He expressed his hope that the administration would "have firmness enough in spite of the howls of the radical wing of their part, to adopt a peace policy and thus give an effectual coup de grace to the secessionists of the border states, as well as enable conservatives of the cotton states to make a stand against the fire-eaters there and thus pave the way to an eventual reconstruction of the Union." Thomas Rowland was more concerned with Virginia's interests. "Socially," he wrote, "our sympathies are certainly with the Southern States, and for my part I see no reason why the commercial interests of Virginia will not be quite as secure in a Southern Confederacy as in a Northern Union. I have been so long in suspense between Union and Secession that my mind is almost equally prepared for either event."

A week after the inaugural, Georgia cadets had a meeting. When Schaff's roommate West returned, he told Schaff that he and several other Georgians had resigned. Resigning had been a hard decision for West to make. His Congressman and family friend, Joshua Hill, was among the southern legislators who tried to keep southern states from seceding. West's family, noted Schaff, "were all of a peaceful tenor, too, brimming with fear and misgiving for the outcome." As was true of newspapers in other southern states, the Georgia press had published lists of officers being commissioned and these lists included the names of all of the Georgia cadets whether they had accepted or not. West and several other Georgians were not even aware that they had even been offered commissions.

West and Schaff waited for official acceptance of West's resignation. Several days later came the order from the Chief of Engineers, Joseph Totten: "Cadet John Asbury West, of Georgia, having declared that he would not be willing to bear arms against the Southern States is hereby discharged from the service of the United States." Schaff helped West pack his trunk and waited while West said good-bye to his friends, "returning with moist eyes." Schaff walked with West to a point east of the Library where the road to the small ferry dock began, the boundary of cadet limits. The two friends embraced; West headed down the road, pausing to wave a handkerchief, then moved on, around a curve, and out of sight.

As April approached, President Lincoln was flooded with proposals from members of his cabinet and from Congressmen and Senators, all trying to avoid open conflict. Secretary of State William Seward proposed that Sumter be evacuated, Gulf ports be reinforced, and a strong stand be taken toward interference by foreign nations. Lincoln replied that he intended to run his own administration. Another proposal to yield Sumter if Virginia would pledge its loyalty to the Union was also rejected because Lincoln considered it to indicate a fatal weakness. He decided instead to send provisions and other supplies to Major Anderson and his troops, notifying South Carolina of his intention on April 16. Five days later, South Carolina demanded that Anderson, who did not know supplies were on the way, surrender Fort Sumter immediately. Anderson replied that he would do so only after his provisions were gone, which would be a matter of days. That offer was rejected, and the next morning at 4:30 A.M., shore batteries under the command of General Pierre P. T. Beauregard opened fire. Ironically, the first round was fired by Wade Hampton Gibbes, the same Gibbes who had fought Emory Upton after John Brown's raid. After thirty-four hours of constant shelling, Anderson surrendered Sumter at 2:30 P.M., April 13. The outbreak of hostilities was followed by the secession of Virginia, Arkansas, Tennessee, and North Carolina, North Carolina being the last to leave the Union on May 20.

The New York papers arriving at West Point shortly after 8:00 A.M. on April 12 brought the first word of the attack on Sumter, although official notification may have been received by Colonel Delafield. When classes were dismissed at 9:30, the sections marching out of the Academic Building found groups of cadets gathered in the area, talking seriously and anxiously about the news. Little attention was paid to anything else that day. Classes were a disaster; cadet thoughts were anywhere but on the subject for the day. The discussions continued into the night, and there was little attempt to prepare for the next day's recitations. Tully McCrea wrote later that "when the news of the firing on Fort Sumter was received the effect was instantaneous, every Northern cadet showed his true colors and rallied that night in Harris' room [William Harris] in the Fifth Division. One could have heard us singing 'The Star Spangled Banner' in Cold Spring. It was the first time I ever saw the Southern contingent cowed. All of their Northern allies had deserted them, and they were stunned." Cadets marched about the area to the tune of "Yankee Doodle" or "Our Fair Flag," but now there was no countering cheer for "Dixie." Schaff summed up the feeling in the Corps: "It was a great political blunder on the part of the South to strike the first blow." The reaction of cadets only reflected that of the entire North; antagonism toward the Lincoln administration was forgotten, and sympathy for the South disappeared.

The faculty and tactical officers had problems trying to keep cadets at least partially in line. Tully McRae noted that the professors "complain bitterly about the deficiency of cadets in their recitations and the Superintendent says that something will have to be done about it. I imagine the only way to prevent it is to stop the war, for it is impossible to confine the mind to dry abstractions in philosophy when our country is passing through the most trying ordeal since the Revolution." Textbooks and lessons were put aside; the daily New York papers were read and re-read by every cadet. Southern cadets also read the papers. McCrea said that "the Secessionists that are still here are disappointed and look a little frightened, for they were not expecting such a universal outburst of patriotic indignation."

Some cadets tried to show their support by displaying small flags in their rooms. This, of course, was against regulations, and regulations had to be enforced, war or no war. Lieutenant Fitzhugh Lee ordered his cadets in A Company to remove the flags. This was done, but several cadets painted their leather water buckets red, white, and blue. Apparently this was not contrary to regulations for Lee did nothing about it. Other tactical officers ordered the flags removed even though they themselves approved of the display.

Henry Dupont was one of the cadets who had supported southern actions to some degree. Now he too abandoned that stand. Writing to his father three days after Sumter was fired upon, he said, "Though I regret now that I am at this juncture in the service of the U.S., I see no honorable mode of leaving it, avoiding a participation in this unnatural contest, and I expect, therefore, to remain in it, and conscientiously endeavor to perform my duty as well as I know how."

Schaff's comment that the South had made a political blunder proved to be true as men throughout the northern states rushed to enlist. At West Point, although cadets of course were already in military service, there was a miniscule rush to enlist. Cadet Stephen Lyford wrote to his father, "It seems everybody is enlisting. The son of our chaplain, a clerk in N.Y., enlisted in the famous 7th and is now gone. Our Prof in Philosophy also has a son in the same Reg't. Also our Prof of Drawing."

In some ways, what might be called "enlistments" in southern units took place at West Point and elsewhere in the North as well. Robert E. Lee regretfully resigned his commission in Washington shortly after Virginia seceded. That news hit officers and cadets hard. Professor Mahan went to his quarters, exclaiming to his wife, "Lee's gone!" Many southern officers in the U.S. Army also resigned their commissions, but many did not. Of the 343 officers on active duty who were not graduates of the Academy, 99 (28.8%) resigned to join Confederate forces. This contrasts with the 161 (24.6%) of the 655 graduates from classes of 1830 through 1860 who were on active duty and resigned. Even more indicative of the loyalty of most graduates is the percentage of all living graduates from 1830 to 1860 (a total of 1,033 men) who remained loyal. Only 275 (26.6%) joined the Confederacy; 661 (64.0%) served on the Union side. The remaining 97 men (9.4%) did not fight on either side, probably because of age.

By the end of April most of the southern cadets had resigned or been dismissed. Eighty-six of the 278 cadets had entered from southern states. Sixty-five left to join the Confederacy; twenty-one remained at the Academy. This contrasts with the departure of southern students from Columbia, Yale, Harvard, Princeton, and Union Colleges where the vast majority returned home. At Princeton every southern student departed. Civilian students, of course, had not taken an oath to support the government of the United States and had no matters of conscience to cause them to delay their departure. A far more significant statistic negating any argument that the Military Academy influenced its graduates to desert to their home states is the number of resignations of officers stationed at West Point between 1850 and 1861. Of the 155 officers assigned there during this period, only twenty-three (14.8%) resigned to join the Confederacy. More than one third of the southern officers who were at West Point during the period remained loyal to the Union. Not one of the seven permanent professors resigned. General George Cullum, later to become superintendent, maintained that the southerners who remained loyal were "rescued from treason by West Point influences." Even if one ignores Cullum's claim because of his all too evident fixation to show that the Academy had nothing but good influence on its cadets and officers, one must admit that the percentage of desertions by graduates to the Confederacy was less than that of non-graduates in the Army.

The day after the surrender of Fort Sumter, cadets were excited about a report that the senior class at the Naval Academy had volunteered for immediate active duty and would be graduated at once. Henry Dupont reported to his father that he hesitated to sign a letter to the Secretary of War from his class stating that "we the undersigned members of the graduating class at the Military Academy do respectfully request to be graduated now, and take our places among those who are serving their country and defending its flag." Dupont hesitated to sign the request because he felt that the letter might have the opposite of the desired result for there was a distinct possibility that the Secretary might disapprove the request. Dupont went to the new Superintendent, Major Alexander Bowman, who had replaced Delafield in early March, to ask his advice. Bowman informed him that he was not in favor of forwarding the request but that he had informed the Chief of Engineers of its content, leaving the decision to General Totten. Two other cadets, Robert Eastman and Franklin Harwood, had the same reluctance to sign a class request, and the three classmates submitted a letter to the Secretary of War "merely saying that like our class-mates we would apply for permission to graduate at once lest our motives for not joining with them be misinterpreted and that as soldiers we were willing and ready to do our duty in any contingency." Totten disapproved both letters and neither was forwarded to the Secretary.

On the day that Dupont wrote to his father, Secretary of War Simon Cameron ordered that the oath of allegiance be administered to all cadets immediately, this despite the fact that all had taken the oath after passing their period of probation as plebes. The entire Corps marched to the Chapel to observe the oath being administered to the plebe class. The ceremony was made as impressive as possible; all the officers present were in full dress uniform. Goshen County Clerk Charles Drake administered the oath. A group of five cadets were taken to a table on which rested a Bible. Each cadet took the oath with his hand on the Bible and sealed it with a kiss. Tully McCrea indicated that it was anticipated that many of the southern cadets would refuse to take the oath. He described what happened: "Ten of the class refused to take the oath and of course will be dismissed. When the first one refused, a few southern cadets tried to applaud him by stamping on the floor, but he was immediately greeted with such a unanimous hiss that he could clearly see the sentiments of the great majority. This shows what a change has come over the country, for never before did a cadet refuse the oath of allegiance, but on the contrary was proud of the opportunity and hailed with delight the day when he was a plebe no longer."

Henry Dupont had advised plebe Edward Anderson to take the oath, but he refused. He wrote to his mother to describe the anguish his action caused him. He indicated that he refused to take the oath because he considered the United States, as it had existed when he received his appointment, to no longer exist, and he felt that he could not therefore be expected to uphold what had already been dissolved. Thirty-two southern cadets refused to take the oath, which was administered by class, and were dismissed.

There was much concern that dismissed cadets might be mobbed as they passed through New York. Major Bowman recommended that they leave by way of Albany instead; some did, but some did not. McCrea noted that some were "getting red white and blue ribbons before they left here to make rosettes of to wear in New York. I would have preferred by far to have been mobbed than to have carried false colors and wear a lie on my breast. But I have found 'Southern chivalry,' since I have been at West Point, to be something not worth bragging of."

There were other departures. Lieutenant Alexander McCook, tactical officer of B Company, was ordered to Ohio to muster state volunteers. The night before his departure, cadets and officers gathered outside his quarters to serenade him, a longstanding tradition at West Point. Two days later, they gathered again to serenade Captain Truman Seymour, a member of Anderson's garrison at Fort Sumter, who was visiting his father-in-law Professor Weir. Tully McCrea reported that when the Captain came to the window cadets applauded him with vigor. The Captain made a "patriotic speech . . . and cadets applauded him from beginning to end. But he would have been been applauded if he had not said a word, for actions speak louder than words, and his actions at Fort Sumter had preceded him and endeared him to every true American heart."

The night of April 26, cadets were joined by officers and their ladies in serenading a departing officer. Lieutenant Fitzhugh Lee was leaving for Virginia. He was one of the most popular officers at West Point, well liked by cadets, officers, ladies, and enlisted men. McCrea indicated that "it was a bitter day for him when he left, for he did not want to go and said that he hated to desert his old flag." Lee had been outspokenly against secession and, like his uncle, Robert E. Lee, reluctantly submitted his resignation because he felt it his duty to follow Virginia. The evening before he left, Lee went to each room in A Company to say good-bye to his cadets. He shook hands with each cadet and, according to McCrea, "with tears in his eyes ... hoped, he said, that our recollections of him would be as happy as those that he had of us." After breakfast the next morning, cadets lined the street in front of barracks waiting for him to start for the road down the hill to the ferry dock. As he passed, cadets removed their hats in farewell, an unusual gesture of their respect.

There were other southern officers at West Point who did not resign their commissions. One, Lieutenant William Craighill, a Virginian who graduated in 1853, wrote a long, ten-page letter to his mother explaining his decision. It is one of the most poignant letters of that troublesome period. He began his letter with "The sad difference of opinion that now exists between us can never change in the smallest degree my love for you all & my willingness to do anything consistent with honor & right which would in the smallest degree gratify you." He reminded his mother of how strongly she and his father had opposed the lead of South Carolina in planning to secede. "Ask yourself," he continued, "if we were not happy before this war began & if we not have continued so if it had not begun. Ask yourself again who began it. The answer must be So. Ca." After more comments on the actions of South Carolina, Craighill said, "But when Virginia turns around & does if anything worse than So. Ca. I am a traitor to her, a hardhearted, cold creature because I do not give myself over hand & foot to the guidance of madmen such as Wise etc. who deceived Viriginia into secession." He tried to explain his feelings, stating that the United States had taken him "as a boy of sixteen, educated me, fed me, and has taken care of me from that day to this." He pointed out that his family had urged him to retain his commission during good times but now maintained that "in its adversity I must leave this munificent government. I cannot take that view, but on the contrary am going to cling to it." After emphasizing his personal dislike of the Republican administration, he pointed out that Lincoln and his cabinet had only a temporary position, depending on the will of the people for tenure. Craighill expressed his opinion about the possible outcome of the war, "But suppose that the war ended & the independence of your confederacy acknowledged, how long can such a rope of sand cling together like a parcel of states with clashing interests when each may at pleasure secede from the confederacy. You must have in ten years after your independence either a civil war among yourselves, or a strong government a monarch or military despotism. . . . When the outside pressure of war is removed which now keeps together the states of your confederacy, it will crumble into atoms & the fragments will one by one return to the original Union." By far the most poignant comment made in his long letter was Craighill's simple but eloquent explanation of his reasons for not resigning: "When I look around our once happy but distracted land, I think no longer of north or south, but I look for something substantial in the shape of a govt. to cling to & I find it in the Constitution of the United States to which I have more than 12 years ago [taken] a solemn oath of allegiance, another at Charlestown before a Virg. magistrate when I graduated at the Mi. Acady. & again this spring I repeated the same oath. This oath, so help me God, I shall keep to the best of my ability, be the consequences what they may." After expressing his love for Virginia and its beauty, Craighill wrote, "Henceforth I know no north, no south, think of no state, but only what will conduce to the stability of the Nation to which I belong. Much as I love the south and her people I am not going to lift a finger in her defence." The Chief of Engineers had told Craighill that he would remain at West Point for a reasonable period. He stayed as the Principal Assistant Professor of Engineering until June 1863 when he joined the armies in the West. He retired as brigadier general and Chief of Engineers in 1897.

Another southern officer who remainded loyal to the Union was George Thomas. His family never forgave him for refusing to resign his commission, even long after the war. His sister turned his portrait to the wall and never reversed it during her lifetime. One wonders why she had not removed the portrait instead.

The letter signed by the First Class may have been pigeonholed by Chief of Engineers Totten, but Secretary of War Cameron took action independently. He ordered the Class of 1861 to be graduated immediately and, at the same time, returned the curriclum to the four-year course desired by the Academic Board. One of these two orders would have been enough to cause problems; the two together placed much of the Academy staff and two classes of cadets into turmoil. The Class of 1861, which was being graduated immediately, fortunately had already ordered uniforms and equipment from New York firms. Frantic requests from the cadets brought most of their orders to West Point before the Academic Board had completed the final testing of the class—not even a war could change the requirement that each graduate be examined by the Board before receiving his diploma! On May 6, the Class of 1861 marched to the Library as the remainder of the Corps was going to lunch. The Goshen County justice of the peace was there to administer the oath of allegiance in the presence of the officers and some of their ladies. Not one cadet refused to take the oath, although several were from southern states. They were then given their diplomas by Superintendent Bowman.

After the ceremony was concluded, the cadets marched to the Mess Hall, where the remainder of the Corps awaited their arrival. When it was learned that there had been no refusals to take the oath, pandemonium broke out in the dining area. Tully McCrea described what took place: "They . . . entered the Mess Hall and were received by the other classes with such rounds of applause as was never heard there before. The oldest waiters and employees about the Mess Hall, who are used to seeing such demonstrations on the departure of graduating classes, were perfectly astonished." McCrea was so excited that he knocked his stool to pieces, "which will cost me a few dollars," he said. Henry W. Kingsbury, the Cadet Adjutant, made a brief speech on behalf of the class. Then the new graduates walked around the dining area saying good-bye to their friends. "As they bid us goodbye," wrote McCrea, "the tears rolled down their cheeks as if they were boys. The parting words of a great man . . . were to stand by the old flag and do credit to the institution they were leaving."

Cameron's order had also directed the class to report to Washington immediately. After leaving the Mess Hall, the new lieutenants walked down the hill to the ferry dock as the cadets near the Library cheered their departure. When they arrived in Washington, they were amazed to find a large police force waiting for them. Emory Upton wrote to his sister to tell her what had happened. The group were escorted to the Rogues Gallery in Independence Hall and required to surrender their swords and revolvers. Calm members of the class kept the group from attacking the police and asked for a city official to talk with them. The mayor arrived and was shown a copy of their orders from the War Department. He immediately apologized, ordered their arms to be returned, and had them put up at the Continental Hotel at city expense. The cause of this embarrassing error was a telegram he had received from the mayor of Jersey City informing him that forty southern cadets were on the train, armed and heading for the South. Apparently some well-meaning and patriotic citizen had heard some of the class talk about their departure from West Point when the train stopped in Jersey City. Putting together what he had heard, the well-meaning man drew the wrong conclusion and informed city authorities that rebels were on the train, resulting in the telegram to the mayor of Washington. Six members of the class resigned in less than two months. Five were from border states and one from Virginia. All were later commissioned in the Confederate army.

Even before the Class of May 1861 was graduated, the Academic Board and faculty members were preparing a greatly condensed course for the old Second Class who, by Cameron's order to return to the four-year curriculum, were to be graduated as soon as possible. The class was delighted and assumed that Cameron's action had resulted from their April 24 letter requesting early graduation. The first step was to examine the class on the subjects taken during the year. Cadet Francis Parker wrote to his father that the class would be given a short course "taking only the most important and practical part of our 1st class course." Two weeks later, Parker told his father that "this method of cramming a years course into two months time is rather hard on us. I never studied so hard and did so poorly as I am doing now." Stephen Lyford expressed similar thoughts, "Imagine yourself in my circumstances, studying night and day to cram a full years course into forty-five days, and you will not be surprised that I am irritable." The seven weeks between the graduation of the Class of May 1861 and June 1861 were busy times for the cadets. In addition to suffering through the cram course, they were measured for uniforms and boots, selected photographs for their class album, and packed for their departure. Many, including Lyford, wrote home for money to pay for their uniforms. He told his father that it would be easy for him to repay the amount needed for he would receive monthly "Pay $53, Rations $31, Forage for 2 horses $16, Subsistence for Servant $23.50." Lyford did not intend to have a servant and therefore computed his monthly pay at about $100 since he had "accounted for 4 rations which are allowed by law but will not of course be drawn as I cannot well eat as much as four able bodied men."

Graduation exercises were held in the Chapel on June 24. The entire Corps accompanied the class; the band led the way followed by the graduates and then by the remainder of the Corps. Each man marched to the front of the Chapel to receive his diploma from Superintendent Bowman, who stated the man's name and the branch in which he was being commissioned: "Patrick Henry O'Rorke, you are recommended for the U.S. Corps of Engineers with the rank of second lieutenant." O'Rorke was the first man in his class and returned to his seat to a thunderous ovation from the spectators. Bowman continued with each man, "Alfred Mordecai . . . Topographical Engineers, Alonzo Hersford Cushing . . . Artillery, ... George Armstrong Custer . . . Cavalry." Custer had managed to graduate despite his 192 demerits, only eight less than the maximum normally permitted.

Custer did not accompany his classmates to Washington. The day before graduation, he was the Officer of the Day in the encampment. A fight broke out; and, instead of stopping the brawl, Custer had the spectators form a circle around the fighters and then acted as referee. Custer and the two fighters were soon in arrest, pending a court martial. Custer was released a day later to go to Washington and report for duty.

The departure of the Class of June 1861 left the Corps at its smallest size since Thayer's early days as superintendent. Captain Edward C. Boynton, Adjutant of the Academy during the war years, prepared a study of the size of the Corps for his 1864 history of the Academy. There were 278 cadets on the rolls in November 1860. Sixty-five southern cadets resigned or were dismissed for refusing to take the oath of allegiance or other war-related causes. Forty-five cadets graduated in May 1861; thirty-five, in June. The Corps thus had a strength of only ninety-eight cadets. Twenty-five members of the Class of 1863 left on furlough—strangely, leave was not curtailed during the war—leaving only seventy cadets at West Point to train eighty-eight new plebes.

At the same time that he ordered the early graduation of the two upper classes, Secretary of War Cameron alerted Academy officials to prepare to graduate the Third Class later in the summer of 1861. As the Academic Board frantically tried to devise another condensed course for that class, essentially incorporating subjects normally covered in a two-year period into a few months, Cameron reversed himself. Instead of graduating in 1861, the class would remain at West Point until the following summer. Cadets were unhappy about that decision; the Academic Board and instructors were much relieved. Cameron's decision prevented the turmoil that would occur during World War I caused by the early graduation of all classes except the plebe class that had been at the Academy for only a few months.

The curriculum adopted by the Academic Board during the summer of 1861 essentially was the same curriculum taught before the five-year course was instituted. The Fourth Class, plebes, were taught mathematics, English, U.S. geography, French, fencing, and bayonet exercise. Third Classmen studied French and mathematics and started classes in drawing and riding. The course for Second Classmen included natural and experimental philosophy, chemistry, drawing, infantry tactics, artillery tactics, and riding. First Classmen studied military civil engineering, practical military engineering; the science of war; ethics; constitutional, international, and military law; mineralogy and geology; cavalry tactics; Spanish; and equitation.

Congress recommended that German be introduced into the curriculum, believing that the ability to speak this language would better prepare graduates to command the large number of soldiers who spoke German more fluently than English. The Academic Board refused to adopt this recommendation, stating that German could not be added without deleting other subjects of more importance. In many ways, this decision must be considered to be an indication that the Academic Board considered its curriculum to be the only course that should be taught at the Academy. This attitude would become much more apparent in the 1870s when the Academy lost its reputation of being the primary school of engineering and mathematical sciences in the United States. The refusal of the Academic Board to include German in 1861 was the harbinger of similar actions the Board would take in later years.

The Chief of Engineers, however, recommended and obtained the addition of a course in military signaling. Perhaps General Totten, as Inspector of the Academy, had greater ability to convince the Academic Board of changes needed than did a congressional committee. Even Totten, however, was not able to have signal instruction taught during the academic year. Instead, the Academic Board used the summer camp training period: Third Classmen were given practical instruction in visual signaling, using semaphore flags or signal lanterns; Second Classmen studied telegraphy. This was the only change made in the curriculum during the war years.

Congress had been shocked and outraged at the resignations of graduates and cadets from the southern states. In August 1861, a law was passed to insure that this would not happend again. The law required each cadet to take an oath of allegiance when he received his warrant, stating in addition to the existing oath to defend the national government and the Constitution that he would "maintain and defend the sovereignty of the United States paramount to any and all allegiance, sovereignty, or fealty I may owe to any state, county, or country whatsoever." A second act, passed in July 1862, required the new cadet to swear that he had never borne arms against the United States, given aid to her enemies, held office under any authority hostile to the United States, or supported any "pretended government, power or constitution within the United States, hostile thereto."

The two acts were but one manifestation of a new and vehement antagonism toward the Military Academy. The defection of southern cadets and graduates, termed treason by many antagonists, was used as a stepping-stone for criticizing West Point in general and its graduates in particular. Arguments used fifty years before were resurrected: the Academy developed an elite officer corps; worthy enlisted men were prevented from becoming officers because Academy graduates were given priority; cadets were appointed only from the upper classes; the sons of average Americans were unable to obtain appointments or pass the entrance examinations; graduates did not remain in service but resigned to take positions with industry to gain prominence and wealth; and, because the country could rely on state militia units for defense, there was no need for a standing, regular army. Speeches on the floor of Congress and reports in the press of the period led to defense by graduates—and by non-graduates as well. Dr. Edward Mansfield, Class of 1819 and son of Professor Jared Mansfield who served at West Point from 1802 to 1828, defended the Academy in the scholarly *American Journal of Education*. Brigadier General Truman Seymour, Class of 1842, was less scholarly than Mansfield in his rebuttal published in the *Army and Navy Journal*. He blamed political appointees to high commands for which they were unqualifed for many of the problems encountered during the early years of the Civil War: "And over the heads and upon the hearts of those who had long been carefully taught in a hard school at least the rudiments of a general's duties stepped or were thrust perfectly uneducated and incompetent men." Seymour concentrated on his theme that politics was at fault for the very being of the Civil War, not the resignations of southern graduates and cadets. One fortunate result of the criticisms was the history of the Military Academy by its adjutant, Edward C. Boynton. This first and remarkably scholarly history countered step-by-step and without any emotion all of the allegations made by Academy opponents. Vehement during the early war years when Union victories were few and the Confederacy seemed to be winning, the attacks dwindled as Grant, Meade, Sherman, Thomas, and other generals beat back continued Confederate campaigns.

Fortunately, efforts in Congress to abolish the Academy, the first since pre-Mexican War days, were not approved. Instead, a series of acts were passed that strengthened the Academy; many pleased Sylvanus Thayer for they vindicated the position he had taken thirty years earlier. The same August 1861 law that required the oath of allegiance to renounce loyalty to any state included what was possibly a far more important requirement: no cadet dismissed or discharged from the Academy could be commissioned until after his class had graduated. But the successes of the Union forces in the war and recognition of the part played by Academy graduates brought even more important laws in 1866. The Act of June 8, 1866, stated that "cadets found deficient at any examination shall not be continued at the military academy, or be reappointed except upon the recommendation of the academic board." How Thayer must have chuckled when he learned of this! The same act provided that no person who had served the Confederacy in any military capacity could be appointed a cadet or midshipman. Cadets must have been overjoyed at another section of that act, which provided that "the annual pay of cadets at the military academy at West Point shall be the same as that allowed to midshipman at the naval academy."

In July 1866, another act was passed containing a provision important to the well-being of the Academy. Prescribing that "the superintendent of the United States Military Academy may hereafter be selected and the officers of that institution detailed from any arm of the service; and the supervision and charge of the Academy shall be in the War Department under such officer or officers as the Secretary of War may assign to that duty." This ended the domination of Academy affairs by the Corps of Engineers and finally recognized what had been intended from the very institution of the Academy in 1802: it had the mission of training potential officers for all arms, not the Corps of Engineers alone.

In recognition of the services of many young men during the war, Congress increased the age limit for appointment of cadets, realizing that many men in uniform who would have been eligible to become cadets were unable to seek or accept appointments during the conflict. The law specified that a cadet appointee was to be between seventeen and twenty-two years of age; but "any person who has served honorably and faithfully not less than one year as an officer or enlisted man in the army of the United States . . . shall be eligible to appointment up to the age twenty-four years." The same law required each appointing official to nominate five candidates for each vacancy with selection to be made based upon "their respective merits and qualifications." The act also authorized the President to appoint fifty candidates instead of the ten previously authorized.

Officer personnel at West Point changed often during the war years. Major Alexander Bowman served as Superintendent from March 1861 to July 1864. He was replaced by Major Zealous B. Tower, who remained for only two months. Lieutenant Colonel George W. Cullum held the office from September 1864 to August 1868. Individuals assigned as Commandant of Cadets rotated even more rapidly. Captain John F. Reynolds was replaced in June 1861 (he would die at Gettysburg on the first day of that battle) by Christopher C. Augur, who successfully volunteered for line duty, leaving in December 1861. He was followed by Captain Kenneth Garrard; Garrard had been captured by Texas insurgents and paroled until an exchange for a southern officer of equivalent rank could

be made. Garrard remained at West Point until September 1862, anxiously awaiting the exchange that would enable him to return to regimental duty. Major
Henry B. Clitz, his successor, had been wounded three times during the Peninsula Campaign, was captured at Gaines Mill, and imprisoned in Libby Prison
in Richmond. He too was paroled, pending exchange, and sent to West Point,
where he remained until July 1864. Captain John C. Tidball, who replaced Clitz,
was at West Point for only ten weeks. Tidball had been part of the garrison at
Fort Pickens, Florida, which successfully defended the fort against Confederate
attacks, and had then fought in every campaign in the eastern theater from Bull
Run to Petersburg. He had command of the 2nd Corps Artillery when assigned
to West Point; exactly three weeks later he was promoted to Brevet Brigadier
General of Volunteers, the first officer of general-officer rank to serve at the
Academy. The undoubtedly embarrassing situation of having the Commandant
of Cadets senior in rank to the Superintendent may possibly have had some
bearing on his relief on September 22, when he returned to command the 9th
Corps Artillery. The last wartime Commandant was Major Henry M. Black, who
had been stationed in California where, as colonel of California volunteers, he
had trained state units to join forces in the East.

During the four years of war, the Academy had three superintendents and
six commandants. The turnover of tactical officers and instructors was equally
drastic. Young graduates became tactical officers immediately after graduation,
but left within months. Approximately fifty officers served as assistant instructors in artillery, infantry, and cavalry tactics and as cadet company tactical officers. More than eighty instructors served at West Point between April 1861
and June 1865. Most of these officers had combat service; many had been
wounded. Only the professors had assurance that they would remain at the
Academy indefinitely. In all probability, this rapid turnover of instructors and
tactical officers may have influenced the Academic Board to return to the same
curriculum used before the five-year course was initiated, although no official
substantiation of this possibility has been found. It is a logical assumption,
however, for most of the officers who returned had graduated from the four-
year course of instruction and could therefore more easily assume classroom or
tactical responsibilities.

Cadets were proud of the combat records of their tactical officers—"tacs"—and
instructors, all of whom were called "Ps." Little recognition has been given to the
way that these young officers moved from vigorous combat duty to the academic
environment at the Military Academy. In the early days of the war, officers were
paroled pending an exchange for an officer of equal rank; these men, some
wounded and some not, were all eager to return to their units. Later, when officers were not paroled, the majority of those assigned to the Academy were recu-
perating from wounds, most serious enough to require long periods of conva-
lescence. Their ability to take their places as instructors or as tactical officers is an
excellent indication of the quality of the education they had received as cadets.

Another change occurred during and after 1862: enlisted men and officers were appointed cadets. More than seventy-five veterans entered the Academy between 1862 and 1868; forty-five graduated. Many had been lieutenants; one, Robert M. Rogers, had been a captain in the 82nd Ohio Volunteer Infantry, seeing action in the Shenandoah Valley, 2nd Bull Run, Chancellorsville, and Gettysburg. Many years later, Charles King recalled "that in '64 and '65 there sometimes came bearded men with a record of a dozen pitched battles behind them." King related how he and William "Pirate" Vose, Class of 1865, were on guard "chatting in front of the coal fire in the guardhouse when there came a knock at the door and, as it swung open, there stood revealed a young officer in the dress of the cavalry. Instantly Vose and I sprang to attention and faced him at the salute. . . . The next moment he had lifted his forage-cap, bowed gracefully and . . . addressed us, 'Pardon me, gentlemen. I have only just come from the army and am ordered to report here as a new cadet.' " At least one cadet saw some action while still in cadet uniform. George W. Greenough, Class of 1865, served as volunteer aide to Major General W. H. French at the battles of Wapping Springs and Manassas Gap, Virginia, while he was on furlough in July 1863. There may have been other cadets who had similar experience, but no documentation was made of their service. Others saw combat service, although they were not officially enlisted or commissioned at the time. Loyall Farragut, son of Admiral David C. Farragut, Class of 1868, served as his father's secretary or aide at Port Hudson and Grand Gulf in 1863, a year before he entered the Academy. Before entering the Academy in 1862, Charles King had seen combat in Virginia while acting as an unofficial aide and courier for his father, Brigadier General Rufus King, Class of 1833. President Lincoln had appointed several of these veteran soldiers to become cadets. He also named Charles King as a candidate in 1862.

Lincoln's relationships with the Military Academy and its graduates—younger graduates, not the senior general officers—has never been thoroughly researched. It is quite probable that the Academy was discussed during his conversations with Secretary of War Cameron and General Winfield Scott at the time Robert E. Lee and southern officers and cadets resigned. There can also be little doubt that Scott, ever a strong supporter of West Point, spoke highly in favor of the Academy to counter the adverse comments being made in Congress. In June 1862, Lincoln made an unexpected visit to West Point. Winfield Scott, who had retired the previous November, was notified that the President would arrive at Garrison's the evening of June 23. General Scott, in full-dress uniform, waited until 3:00 A.M. the next morning to greet the President and escort him to Cozzen's Hotel in Buttermilk Falls. Lincoln immediately calmed Scott and others by stating that he had come to see Scott "to avail himself of the experience and profound military science of the greatest captain of the age," according to the *New York Herald*.

Lincoln had apparently become concerned with the overall military situation. McClellan was in the midst of his Yorktown Peninsula campaign, bogged down and making little headway. Stonewall Jackson had driven federal forces out of the Shenandoah Valley. In the western theater, Thomas had moved into Kentucky and Grant had won a costly victory at Shiloh. Admiral Farragut had taken New Orleans. The discussion between the two men later the morning of June 24 related to the overall strategic situation. After four hours poring over maps and reviewing possible actions, Lincoln asked to be taken to West Point.

Escorted by the Superintendent, Major Bowman, and General Scott, the President visited summer camp, the Academic Building, the Riding Hall, and the Library. Professor Mahan was extremely pleased when Lincoln, during the tour of the Academic Building, came to the Napoleon Club room where he asked for an explanation of the large map of Europe painted on the wall. After Mahan had demonstrated how the map was used to discuss Napoleonic campaigns, Lincoln asked that a copy be made and sent to him. He also asked for a copy of Mahan's *Outpost Service. . . .* The party then moved to the adjacent barracks where the entire First Class waited to be introduced. Lincoln then asked if he could meet the ten plebes he had recently appointed to the Academy. Fortunately they were still in barracks, having only recently completed the entrance examination and were awaiting its results. Among the ten plebes were William H. Upham and Charles King. Upham later wrote that Lincoln "asked if I had passed my examination and I told him he would have to ask Mr. Bowman, the superintendent, as he had not yet informed me. I saw Mr. Bowman nod to Mr. Lincoln and so I knew 24 hours before publication that I had been successful."

The relationship between Cadets King and Upham was unusual. Upham had been severely wounded at First Bull Run and left for dead on the field. Captured by Confederates and hospitalized, he recovered, spent time in Libby Prison, and was finally exchanged. His Wisconsin Senator recommended him to the President for appointment as a cadet, but Lincoln had already promised the appointment to King. When sixteen-year-old King learned of this, he wrote to Lincoln offering to step aside so that Upham could be appointed, stating that he was proud to give up his chance to become a cadet to enable Upham to enter. Lincoln then appointed Upham, telling King he would be given the next at-large appointment. That appointment came sooner than expected. Professor Mahan's son Frederick had been nominated but could not accept the appointment because he was below the minimum age for admission. King was given that appointment.

The presidential party then moved to the West Point Foundry at Cold Spring, which was turning out cannon at an expedited rate. Colonel Robert Parrott had a crew fire rounds from various sized cannon across the river at Crow's Nest to demonstrate the capabilities of these artillery pieces. After a brief stop for refreshment at Gouverneur Kemble's home, the party returned to West Point and reviewed the Corps at parade. Lincoln returned to the hotel, leaving the next morning for Washington. Thus ended the first West Point visit of a President since Monroe's trip in 1817 to personally investigate the Partridge situation.

Five days later, Lincoln received a letter from Mrs. Lincoln's cousin, Mrs. Ann Todd Campbell, telling the President that her son Quinton, a classmate of King and Upham, was unhappy at the Academy. Lincoln took the time to write to young Campbell to assure him that he would very soon feel better. "Adhere to your purpose," wrote the President, "and you will soon feel as well as you ever did. On the contrary, if you falter, and give up, you will lose all the power of keeping any resolution, and will regret it all your life."

During the war years—the exact year cannot be determined—an unfortunate practice became a part of cadet life. The life of a plebe during the summer months had never been easy, but now treatment of plebes went beyond playful trickery. From the time that plebes successfully passed the entrance examinations and moved to camp until graduation and their promotion to the Third Class, they were bedeviled and forced to perform menial tasks. They cleaned the tents of upperclassmen, polished brass belt plates, kept muskets in good shape, filled water buckets, folded bedding in the morning, and made down beds at night. The move back to barracks at the end of the summer did not end their year of purgatory, as had been true before the war. They had added duties, including sweeping rooms and carrying boots to the shoe black or running errands for upperclassmen. Only one word describes their ordeal: hazing. Abuse of plebes became so flagrant that the West Point authorities were unable to cope with it. Finally, in November 1863, a War Department order was read specifying, according to Charles King, "that hereafter no cadet would be granted the customary furlough at the end of his second year unless he could certify on honor that he had in no manner or way interfered with, molested, or harassed a new cadet." The cadets were quite upset, not only because many would lose their coveted leave, but also because they felt that cadets who did not make the required certificate might be charged with hazing.

What were the origins of this hazing? One can only speculate because cadet letters of that period make no reference to how the practice started. Can the blame be directed at the wounded tactical officers who undoubtedly had a difficult time inspecting barracks at all hours? The barracks were organized in "division" form: each division had four floors with four rooms separated by the hallway on each floor. Each division had doorways leading to the area of barracks on the south and opening toward the Plain on the north. Inspecting the two divisions assigned to each company required the company tactical officer to climb four flights in each division, a difficult and painful task for some of the wounded officers. Both King and Paul Dahlgren noted that company officers were often absent from guard mount or inspections on the Plain because of physical incapacity.

There were other possible contributing factors. Before 1862, the number of plebes entering each year was always greater than the number of yearlings, the Third Class or sophomores. In 1862, the plebe class was very small, primarily because no cadets were appointed from southern states. A Company, Charles King noted, had only eight plebes compared to thirty yearlings and seven First Classmen (the Second Class, on furlough, also had only seven members). The preponderance of yearlings would have made it more difficult for the First

Classmen to supervise them at all hours, day and night. Did the appointment of former enlisted men and officers contribute to the development of hazing? Possibly; one must remember that the Army of that era had a distinct separation of officers and enlisted men. Former enlisted men who had seen their officers living in better circumstances than the enlisted men may have used that differentiation in treating plebes as inferior beings, far more so than had been true from Thayer's time on. Conversely, former officers, particularly those from state volunteer units, might have considered the plebes a lower form of life in the same way that they had considered enlisted men an inferior group. There is a third possible contributing factor. Many of the new cadets had attended college and may have encountered hazing there. The seed planted in 1862 flourished in 1863 when the small new yearling class made up for its paucity in numbers by increased harassment and molestation of the new plebe class, the largest to enter the Academy since 1842.

In a very short time, cadets assumed that hazing plebes was a longstanding tradition and resented any effort of the West Point officers or the War Department to ban the practice. It is difficult for an older person, Academy graduate or not, to understand the sense of time of a young cadet. To these young men— and, today, young women—the past encompasses only a few years; the future even less. Cadets often consider a Corps habit to be a tradition even though it may have been in use only five or six years. For many years after the Civil War period—to the present day, in fact—cadets maintained that hazing plebes was a longstanding tradition, that it had existed for years. This has been a constant problem to the staff and faculty when steps were taken to end hazing practices. The same reasoning would be used by cadets in the 1870s, the late 1890s, the early 1920s, and even in 1990 and 1991.

Despite the harsh treatment of plebes in the 1860s, there were many comical results. King recalled one episode from his plebe year. When the second group of new plebes arrived in September, they were quartered in barracks until after they had taken the entrance examinations. A group of yearlings slipped out of camp, went to barracks, and brought two plebes back to camp to spend the night. Here, wrote King, they "noiselessly rolled them in their blankets in the Colonel's 'marquee,' bidding them stir not till they should come again; then roused everybody in camp to tell of the splendid joke they had on the Com— 'what fun it would be to watch him at reveille.' " They were disappointed, however, for Colonel Garrard only ordered the unfortunate plebes to be taken back to barracks.

The Chief of Engineers, General Totten, and Secretary of War Stanton took some positive steps in 1864 to curtail this abuse. Although it was not feasible to replace wounded officers with physically strong young graduates, they took the next best step and assigned Lieutenant Colonel George Cullum as Superintendent and Major Henry M. Black as Commandant of Cadets. Cullum had been stationed at West Point from 1846 to 1850 as an instructor, commander of the Sapper detachment, and supervising engineer of the new barracks construction. He had a deep understanding of cadet problems and the stress generated by the rigid Academy curriculum and discipline, an understanding very similar to that of Robert E. Lee. Like Lee, Cullum was a disciplinarian, but his disciplinary requirements were tempered by a deep sense of justice that was often shown by his lenient treatment of errant cadets when leniency was more desirable than harsh punishment. Colonel Black had served as a tactical officer for a short time after his graduation in 1847. He had been with Scott's forces when Mexico City was taken, and had fought Seminole and Yakima Indians. From 1861 to 1864, Black had supervised the training of California volunteers.

The two men instituted many policies to ease cadet stress. Breakfast and supper were optional. This enabled cadets to take a hot bath between reveille and class or to exercise in the gymnasium or take a brisk walk. Paul Dahlgren often mentioned getting food from "the Dutchman," the proprietor of the soda and sweet shop below the edge of the Plain near the path leading to the north dock. Cadets were able to get cheese, crackers, and even a roast chicken or a turkey there. Cullum also made it possible for families to send packages of food and other items to cadets. The practice of using extra guard duty for punishment had been reinstituted; this Black stopped, and cadets instead were given punishment tours in the area of barracks. Normally, tours were walked from 2:00 to 5:00 P.M. on Saturday afternoons. There were exceptions; Captain Jared A. "Lanky" Smith received special mention from Dahlgren, "Lanky was officer in charge today and made the 'extra' men walk from 9 A.M. until tattoo. Blessings showered down on his head by the dozen." Prior to Cullum's arrival, inspections and guard mount were always held on the Plain regardless of weather. Cullum and Black nullified the tradition that cadets could stand any battle of the elements and ordered such formations to be held in the area of barracks if the weather was threatening. If it rained or snowed, the formation was held on the covered stoops of the barracks. To emphasize the status of the First Class, Black and Cullum removed First Class privates from duty as sentinels. Instead, they would be added to the duty rosters for officer of the day and officer of the guard.

One change proved to be very popular with cadets. Instead of being restricted to using the Library only on Saturdays or Sunday afternoons, Cullum authorized them to go to the Library at any time they were released from quarters. This enabled cadets to study or read for pleasure every afternoon or early evening. Paul Dahlgren noted in his journal that he often went to the Library to read the New York papers. He also commented on going to the Library after dinner on Wednesday, November 13, 1864, where he "saw some splendid photographs of the scenes of Sherman's operations in the south-west, among others, Atlanta, Lookout Mountain, Knoxville, Nashville, Florence, and many other places." He also mentioned following the 1864 campaign and election by reading newspapers. Many cadets favored McClellan, but the majority wanted Lincoln to be re-elected.

Officers also watched the progress of the campaign. Professor Mahan in late September 1864 wrote to his old friend Gouverneur Kemble to give him comparison of the two candidates. "I do know," he said, "that he [Lincoln] has conducted a war on the largest scale, administered a government of most delicate compromises, under difficulties far greater than history presents any example of; and this in the face of a large and infuriated party, both in and out of the Army, decrying his acts, and censuring his judgment." He then went on to give his impression of McClellan, "Mr. Lincoln is a man of far greater experience, and has far more of that knowledge that goes to form a civil ruler than Gen. McClellan. I believe him to be both mentally and morally a stronger man than General McClellan; and am prepared to back my assertions with facts. I believe, that, with the exception of Fremont, the Country has never had a name before it less qualified for the Presidential office than General McClellan, both from education and a deficiency of cardinal moral traits." If Mahan was referring to McClellan's cadet education, his comment can hardly be considered complimentary to the Military Academy; he may, however, have referred to education gained by experience rather than formal college instruction.

Permitting cadets to make free use of off-duty time was extended even further. They could walk off post on Saturday and Sunday afternoons. Dahlgren recorded that he walked across the frozen river to Garrison's and from there to Cold Spring, taking only an hour and a half for this trek, returning to West Point "just in time for parade." Cadets, including plebes, were permitted to take short leaves at Christmastime if they were not undergoing punishment or were not deficient in their studies. Dahlgren could not take leave because he had punishment tours to walk, but he and others in the same situation celebrated Christmas Eve 1864 in an exemplary manner. After a special "hash" in barracks, they started a song fest in the area, which eventually got out of hand. "A lot of us," noted Dahlgren, "got hold of Brady's photograph wagon [Brady was at West Point to take photographs of cadets and scenes for class albums] & hauled it all around, kicking up an awful noise & yelling, setting off cartridges, etc." Because Christmas and New Year's Day fell on Sunday that year, Cullum specified that the following Mondays would be the official day of observance. This was a hit to cadets because it meant two days with no official duties. Another change appreciated by cadets was necessitated by the physical condition of wounded officer-instructors. At times, some were unable to make it to class. Normally, a cadet section would go to the classroom and remain there until the end of the scheduled recitation period whether the instructor was present or not. Cullum had this changed, recognizing that it was a waste of cadet time and often led to hilarity in the Academic Building. Instead, as Paul Dahlgren entered in his journal, when the instructor "was not present to hear us . . . after waiting ten minutes, we 'decamped.' "

Wartime restrictions apparently had little impact upon travel between New York City and West Point. Both the West Point Hotel and Cozzens' Hotel in Buttermilk Falls were normally full during the spring-to-fall period. Three hops a week continued to be scheduled during the summer camp and one each week during the remainder of the year.

December 26, 1864, was marked by the news that Sherman had captured Savannah. When they learned of this at noon, "the delight of the cadets was not to be controlled. For hours nothing could be heard but deafening cheers one after another," noted Dahlgren, "and finally the officers were obliged to get some of us, preferably 3rd class-men to go over to the battery & fire a national salute in honor of the event."

New Year's Eve was celebrated in a more tranquil fashion. Apparently the first dramatic performance sponsored by the Dialectic Society had been so successful as to warrant its continuance. The 1864 production was described by Paul Dahlgren, "But the grand excitement at night was the 'Nigger Show' which took place down at our mess hall. . . . All the officers stationed here were present & many ladies & gentlemen came from N.Y. to see the fun. The acting was excellently original [Dahlgren made no comment about its quality, however!] and many good hits were got off on the institution & some connected with it." From that description, it can be acknowledged that the longstanding tradition of the Dialectic Society 100th Night Show with its satirical parody of West Point life had its origin at this time.

There were other effects of the war in addition to cheering Union victories. The cost of cadet uniforms and equipment had increased astronomically. Both King and Dahlgren commented on how much they were in debt and the fact that they were not alone; the vast majority of cadets owed the commissariat at least $50, many as much as $200. Cullum tried to stop their going into debt by adopting Thayer's principle that a cadet could not buy anything unless he had a positive balance in his account. To offset this, knowing full well that very few cadets were out of debt, Cullum authorized and urged the receipt of funds from home, the first time in Academy history that this had been permitted. Charles King much later gave a vivid, albeit too colorful, description of the Corps during this period: "More than one-third of our membership were excused from all military duty as being shoeless and in rags. Men made caps by utilizing discarded 'shakoes,' cutting them down and roofing the frame with oilskin. Pillow cases were made to do duty as shirts, armless, of course, but cadet collars and cuffs were then attachments of the coat, not of the undergarment." King may have used poetic license because none of the other letters of that time make any similar description. Paul Dahlgren, whose journal recorded the general indebtedness of cadets, did not note any of the steps described by King, and other letters only mentioned the shortage of funds.

To inspire cadets to study harder, Cullum initiated special awards for the first five men academically in the upper three classes. Gold medals were awarded to the First Class; silver, to the Second; and bronze, to the Third. The order authorizing the medals specified that "these badges of eminent attainments in their Academic Course will be worn by the recipients on the left breast at dress-parades, guard mounting, reviews, and all occasions of ceremony." Paralleling this recognition of academic achievement, Cullum authorized an award for military merit based upon exemplary conduct, soldierly deportment, and attention to duty. The award, called a "chevron" was actually one or more gold lace stripes on the outer half of the coat cuff, running diagonally from seam to seam of the sleeves. First Class cadets were authorized three stripes; Second Class, two; and Third Class, one. Strangely, these awards are essentially identical to the stripes used to differentiate classes today. Cullum's innovations did not last long, however. Two years later, the Secretary of War directed that the awards be discontinued.

The celebration of Sherman's victory at Savannah paled in comparison to the riotous clamor that greeted the April 10 news that Lee had surrendered at Appomattox. Charles King compared the Savannah celebration as being "a mere whisper of the thunderous uproar that bellowed along the Hudson the soft April day that brought us the tidings of the close of the war." Every gun was manned; and, when a signal gun was fired from Fort Putnam, "all the batteries turned loose at once, and presently the gray battlements of the beautiful old Point were wreathed in sulphur smoke." The First Class manned the seacoast battery with its large Columbiad and Parrott guns; the Second Class, Battery Knox on the shore below Trophy Point; and the Third and Fourth Classes fired the Napoleon and Rodman three-inch field guns. King believed that a one-hundred gun salute was intended. Dahlgren stated that the salute was twice that number of rounds. The celebration continued into the night and even the next day. King's class tried to be excused from reciting by stating that they had cheered so much the day before that they were unable to talk.

Five days later that joyful attitude turned to sorrow when the news of Lincoln's assassination reached West Point. Word came with the arrival of the New York papers at about 9:00 A.M. Shortly afterward, Superintendent Cullum ordered all classes to be dismissed for the day. Cadets marched out of the Academic Building and poured out of barracks. Charles King was handed a copy of the *New York Herald* by an officer and told to read it to the cadets. The Officer in Charge tried to dispel the cadets by ordering them to their rooms but, as King later recalled, "Never before or since have I known that official to be utterly ignored by the corps of cadets." King climbed on the sundial pedestal (the dial itself had been removed when the clock was installed in the Academic Building in the 1830s) and began to read the newspaper account. Even the Officer in Charge stopped trying to order cadets to dispel, falling silent to listen instead. "When I finished," wrote King, "I had one glance at that little 'sea of upturned faces,' white, awe-stricken, and, most of them, quivering." The crowd broke into small groups, some going to their rooms, others sitting on the steps leading to the stoops of barracks.

On April 19, the Corps was formed and marched to the Plain, where they were joined by the enlisted detachments to hear Adjutant Captain Boynton read the official Army order announcing the death of the President. At noon, the Corps assembled in the Chapel for a memorial service held at exactly the time the funeral ceremonies were held in Washington. A week later, the Corps and the enlisted detachments were taken to Garrison's by ferry to form a long line on both sides of the railroad tracks. King described the scene, "With our colors and drums draped in black, [we] stood at the 'present' as the day was dying and a long funeral train rolled slowly by. On the platforms and at the car windows were generals famous in song and story, but we had eyes for only that solemn pile on which was laid all that was mortal of him, whose words and whose wisdom gain in worth and power with every added year."

The Corps returned to West Point, much subdued and solemn. Not until graduation neared did West Point begin to put aside its mourning. The ten days before graduation were gay and colorful. There were parades and hops. King recalled that the hop the night before graduation was, for the first time, hosted by the Second Class in honor of the graduates, a custom that continued until the turn of the century. Graduation parade was stirring with its music of "Auld Lang Syne" and "Home Sweet Home." After retreat had been sounded, the graduating class moved forward, doffed their hats to the Commandant, and received his congratulations. The next day, they formed in front of the Chapel to receive their diplomas from the Superintendent.

West Point had survived the turmoil of war, not unchanged, but with its fundamental principles untouched. The resignation of southern graduates and cadets had not weakened its dedication to duty; instead their departure only strengthened the belief in country. Letters and diaries of the period stressed the continued importance of honor to cadets; they would not condone lying or stealing of any form. Friendships made as cadets survived fratricidal conflict. Union General George Custer was best man for his former classmate, Confederate Colonel John W. Lea after Lea had been wounded and captured at Williamsburg in 1862. When Confederate Stephen D. Ramseur, former member of the Class of 1860, was fatally wounded and captured at Cedar Creek, Custer, Wesley Merritt, and Alexander Pennington stayed with him until he died. Despite the physical incapacities of many instructors and tactical officers, the level of instruction and discipline did not lessen materially. West Point survived attacks throughout the early days of the war. Attempts to abolish the Academy failed; and the accomplishments of graduates strengthened its esteem in the eyes of the American people. Lincoln's words to Cadet Quinton Campbell might well have been directed to his alma mater: "Adhere to your purpose . . . if you falter . . . you will regret it." West Point did not falter, but adhered to its purpose of preparing the future officers of the Army.

1865–1902

Time does heal and
The World does change . . .

GEORGE BUSH
Pearl Harbor, Hawaii
December 7, 1991

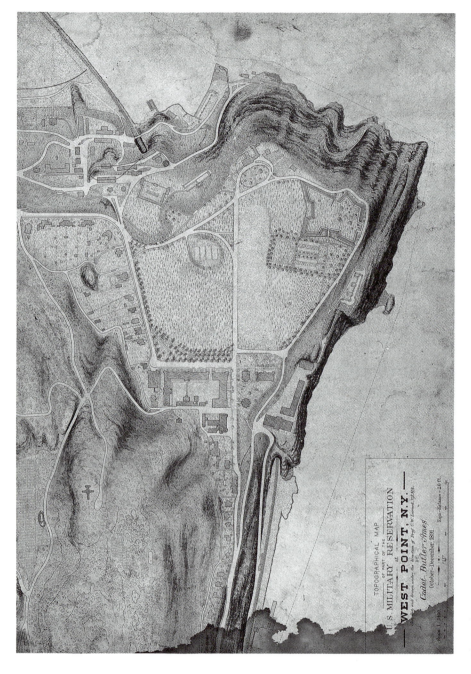

The Military Academy in 1891. This map was prepared by Cadet Butler Ames, Class of 1894, as part of his studies. The Cadet Barracks was enlarged by an addition to the west wing in 1882, the new 1895 Academic Building (it was being built when Ames drew this map in 1891), the 1870 Administration Building south of the Cadet Chapel, the 1885 Gymnasium west of the Barracks, and the 1885 Hospital.

19

All Institutions Are Imperfect and Subject to the Law of Change

Graduation is always exciting and impressive at the Military Academy. It was more so on June 23, 1865. More than one cadet firebrand regretted the end of the war, for that meant he would not see combat; fighting Indians was not considered to be civilized warfare. When the traditional graduation ceremony in front of the Chapel began, Superintendent George Cullum called the first man in the Class forward and announced, "Charles Walker Raymond, you are commissioned a first lieutenant in the Corps of Engineers." Applause came from the Corps and other spectators. Cullum continued, "Lewis Cooper Overman, you are commissioned a first lieutenant in the Corps of Engineers." More applause. The first nine men were all assigned as Engineer first lieutenants, not uncommon during the war years. The next four graduates were commissioned second lieutenants of Artillery. But the fifteenth graduate, John K. Heslep, was assigned to the 7th Infantry as a second lieutenant and was immediately promoted to first lieutenant. When Cullum announced his promotion after handing him his diploma, a roar came from the Corps; this was most unusual. This continued; man after man was commissioned a second lieutenant in the Infantry and then immediately promoted to first lieutenant. Only the six Artillery and nine Cavalry assignees were not promoted. The lowly infantrymen, the graduates ranking lowest in the class academically, all ranked the elite artillerymen who ranked next to the engineers in graduation order.

What caused this unusual situation? There were two factors. The wartime army was rapidly disbanding, and regular units were being reconstituted. During the war, the number of regular Infantry regiments had been increased from ten to nineteen. The number of Artillery regiments, five, and Cavalry regiments, six, remained unchanged. In the Corps of Engineers, which had no regiments, the number of lieutenants increased from twenty-one to thirty-six. During the war, assignment to these units often went to volunteer officers because many regulars accepted temporary appointments with state regiments, usually in much higher rank than they would have held in a regular unit. This force was expanded by the Act of July 28, 1866, to forty-five Infantry regiments, ten Cavalry regiments, and five Artillery regiments; included were black regiments—38th, 39th, 40th, and 41st Infantry and the 9th and 10th Cavalry. Only two black Infantry regiments were retained in the 1869 reorganization, the 24th and 25th Regiments. Most of the officer positions were filled by appointments from volunteer officers and some enlisted men promoted from the ranks.

These forces were stationed at more than 250 posts. Many company-sized units were stationed in the South as a police force to prevent any renewal of the conflict. Larger units were sent to the western states to subdue Indians left much to themselves during the war. The two mobile companies of each Artillery regiment were included in the western garrisons; the remaining eight companies manned fortifications on the eastern and western coasts. To administer and control these scattered units, departments and divisions were established, each with a sizeable staff. Without exception, units of the postwar Army required retraining and reorganization. Officers and men accustomed to fighting a conventional "civilized" war now faced a mobile enemy using hit-and-run guerrilla tactics. This was the Army the Military Academy trained cadets to serve in after the Civil War.

The Class of 1865 has two distinctions that set it off from any other West Point class. Its class song has become the traditional "Army Blue" played at the end of each hop and sung by graduates the world over. The second Class of '65 distinction was its decision to award a "Class Cup" to the Class godson, the first son born to a member of the Class. An ornate silver cup was presented to Allen Dwight Raymond, son of Charles W. Raymond, the first man in the Class academically. Succeeding classes followed the lead of '65. Many years later, the custom developed of having a class cup made from silver napkin rings used in the Cadet Mess.

There were some immediate changes at West Point. Twenty-seven instructors, tactical officers, and staff members were relieved between April 1865 and January 1866. Many had been assigned to convalesce from wounds and were now able to return to their units or were separated for physical disabilities. Artillery pieces were replaced with more modern weapons, surplus now that active conflict was over. More men who had seen combat service were appointed cadets. One, Charles A. Woodruff, had been severely wounded and retired physically with a pension. He gave up his pension to accept an appointment; his failure to pass the physical was waived by the Secretary of War to enable him to enter the Academy. Signal training during the summer months, instituted at the recommendation of the Chief of Engineers, continued; but this was one of very few changes to the curriculum.

The Academic Board resisted the changes recommended by various Boards of Visitors, Congressmen, and graduates. In their opinion, the course of instruction that had produced Grant, Sherman, Sheridan, Schofield, and many others who had led the Army to victory against forces led by many other graduates needed little improvement. Almost every committee appointed by the Academic Board to study curriculum content was headed by either Professor Mahan or Professor Church. Seldom did their reports recommend any major changes, only that additional material should be added to existing courses.

Despite the efforts of superintendents and commandants, hazing continued unabated. Charles King many years later provided a vivid description of treatment of plebes immediately following the war. Sons of distinguished officers were marked for special treatment. Ulysses Grant's son Frederick, said King, was "worked and worried . . . to the verge of exasperation, but with that everlasting grin on his broad, good-natured face he plodded along, patiently awaiting the day when he too should be a yearling and privileged to devil someone else." Professor Mahan's son received similar treatment with the same good-natured grin. The son of the Chief of Engineers, General Totten, was another plebe doomed to have such treatment. General Sheridan's son received special treatment, which King described as "small wonder that Phil Sheridan's gallant boy should be bestriding a broomstick and doing his father's famous ride from Winchester town." The roll of plebes during this period was almost a listing of distinguished officers. King listed among the sons of famous fathers "Charley Breckenridge, 'Bricks' Farragut [young Farragut had to demonstrate his father's actions when he made his famous statement 'damn the torpedoes, full speed ahead' at Mobile Bay], 'Scrubs' Heintzelman, 'Monitor' Jack Worden [one wonders what special treatment he received], George Meade, Schofield, Augur, Tommy Townsend (son of the Adjutant General), Baird, Rucker, Mitchell, Casey, Reynolds—sons of men famous in war days—but not a word of their woes did the papers get!"

There were many indignities encountered by every plebe; some were not hazing but official requirements. After passing the entrance examinations, plebes were taken to the cadet commissary, where they were issued their equipment: blankets, mattress, bedding, bucket, broom, washbowl, and some ready-made uniform items. As King described what took place, a plebe was sent "laden like a beast of burden, the long tramp across the hot Plain to barracks or camp in full view of throng of visitors, jeered by all the small boys about the post and 'guyed' generally by civil as well as military observers." Plebes began their military training—learning to march and handle a rifle—in front of the Library "with pretty girls and jaunty cadets looking on and tittering at their misery."

After moving to camp at Fort Clinton, yearling "supervision" took over. King wrote, "We were worked and drilled from dawn till dark and devilled from dark to dawn." Plebes who had seen combat were given special treatment because they were supposed to have "presupposed knowledge of the proper care of camp, of arms and equipment." "Yanking" was a favorite treatment by yearlings who pulled plebes out of their blankets into the company street or took them to a drainage ditch beside the camp and tossed them into it. King remembered one night when he was yanked constantly by yearlings who had decided to yank him forty times between taps and reveille—they missed their goal by only three. This treatment, however, generally ended when the Corps returned to the barracks at the end of August.

Life in barracks was much easier, but some upperclassmen required "their" plebes to perform menial tasks: sweeping rooms, making beds, and caring for equipment. Although this was forbidden by cadet regulations, as was hazing of any type, some cadets ignored the regulations in the same way that they ignored being prohibited from visiting Benny Havens' tavern. Another form of hazing occurred in September when a second group of plebes arrived. These "seps" were appointees to fill vacancies left after the June examinations. Strangely, the chief instigators were June entrants who were determined that their September classmates would receive the same treatment that they had endured the entire summer.

West Point authorities and Washington supervisors periodically clamped down on hazing. The pledge required for a leave to be approved was reinstituted. Every cadet going on furlough or even a short leave of only a few days was required to sign this pledge: "Upon the honor of a cadet and gentleman, I certify that I have in no manner or way improperly interfered with, or molested, harassed, or injured new Cadets, from my admission as a Cadet to the present time; and I do further pledge my honor, that, during my absence from West Point, I will abstain from all intoxicating liquors, and every dissipation or excess, for three days immediately following my departure from, and preceding my return to the Academy." Cadets reported for hazing whom investigation proved had done so were subject to mandatory dismissal. When restrictions were increased, the practice decreased. After a period of time, cadets revived it again, often with new torments for the unfortunate recipients.

Writing in 1901—after a more recent hazing scandal—King maintained that hazing at the Military Academy was no worse, and in fact better, than similar practices at many colleges and universities. "Every few years," wrote King, "when nothing else is pressing, West Point comes in for an overhauling at the hands of the papers and the people. 'Hazing,' as it is called today; 'deviling,' as it was more descriptively called in the old days, is the usual text." King described some college pranks—branding fraternity candidates, using electric shock treatment, shaving heads, paddling— to draw a comparison with what he felt was the more humane treatment of plebes by upperclassmen. Like many old grads, he maintained that "The Corps Has [gone to hell]," by stating that plebes had a much harder time when he was a cadet in the 1860s. King also asserted that the rigorous life of a cadet and his near-Spartan existence justified hazing as a means of easing the monotony of cadet routine. Almost ignored in his article was the fact that most of the treatments faced by plebes were demeaning. In today's Army, an officer or a non-commissioned officer does not demean or embarrass an enlisted man in his unit. Admittedly, the Army of the

1860s and 1870s differed greatly from the Army of today. Lower grade enlisted men were a gulf away from their corporals and sergeants and had few contacts with their officers, none socially. Treatment of privates was little different from the Beast Barracks of that period; it was harsh, personal, and often demeaning. What King ignored in his attempts to justify hazing was the impropriety of harassing and demeaning subordinates. He and other old grads perpetuated the practice by efforts to justify its existence instead of condemning it as unnecessary.

Cadets themselves sought better ways of easing their daily routine. Walking, swimming, riding, and skating were the most popular recreational activities. Ten pins or bowling had become popular during the war years. Various recommendations that bowling alleys be installed had been made as early as 1848. Surgeon Charles McDowell recommended that two alleys be obtained that year to provide exercise for cadets and "to lessen the inclination to gambling and other vicious habits." In 1856, Secretary of War Jefferson Davis urged that two alleys be installed on the ground floor of the Academic Building, vacated when the new Riding Hall was built, as a "means of winter amusement and exercise for cadets." The first two alleys were installed in that space in 1859 and proved to be extremely popular with the cadets. Cadet Elbridge R. Hills noted in his diary that he often bowled between reveille and breakfast.

Cadets were—and still are—an ingenious group, especially when unauthorized recreational matters are concerned. One of the best examples of this ingenuity occurred in the winter of 1865. Bored with inactivity during the cold winter, a group of Second Classmen decided to form a billiards club. They ordered a billiard table from a manufacturer in New York with instructions to have it delivered to an individual in Garrison's across the river from West Point. While awaiting its arrival, the cadets commandeered a coal cellar in the basement of the 6th Division with the willing acquiescence of the barracks policeman responsible for that division, cleaned it thoroughly, boarded up the windows with a double layer of wood insulated with tan-bark to deaden the sound of clicking balls as much as possible, and installed lights and a stove.

When the word came that the table was across the river, the group "borrowed" a sled and team belonging to the mess steward and drove across the ice to get their table. Bringing it carefully into barracks in the small hours of the morning, they mounted the table on saw horses, levelled it, and were ready to play. Three or four weeks later, the check sent to the manufacturer in payment in some strange way came to the office of the Academy treasurer. He, of course, informed the tactical officers who made a careful search of barracks but met with no success. The search even extended to other buildings near the barracks, including some officers' quarters. As usually happens, the ladies of the Post learned about the table and teased the tactical officers unmercifully.

Extreme care was taken when going to or coming from the "billiard room" to avoid being seen by any officer. About thirty cadets became members of the billiard club, paying an entrance fee of ten dollars, this going to the cadets who had paid for the table originally. The table was much used during the winter and spring, but it waited patiently during the summer encampment. During the fall of 1866, cadets enjoyed their unauthorized privilege.

In late November, two cadets clad only in bathrobes and slippers crossed the sallyport en route to the billiard room. Unfortunately, two officers saw them move across the passage and followed them stealthily, hoping that the cadets would lead them to the hidden game room. They crept down the steps after the cadets and watched them go to the door of the supposed coal cellar, give a special recognition knock, and clearly heard balls clicking on the table when the door was opened. When the cadets had entered the room and the door closed behind them, the two officers held a whispered conversation to decide whether to make their presence known immediately or to wait until later when more officers could join in the raid. They decided to wait until the next night and went on to their quarters.

What the two officers did not know was that they in turn had been quietly followed by a single cadet. He had kept as close to them as possible and had overheard most of their conversation. After their departure, he hurried into the billiard room to report what he had discovered. A meeting of all the club members was called the next morning to decide what should be done. Because it was obviously nearly impossible to move the table to another location, the cadets decided, according to Cadet Oliver E. Wood, "to make a virtue out of necessity and yield in a handsome manner."

That evening, the room was thoroughly cleaned, the lamps polished, a fire lit in the stove, and the billiard balls carefully racked on the table with cue sticks ready to be used. A carefully worded note was placed on the table, the door locked, and the cadets went home to their rooms. Shortly after Taps, almost all of the officers on duty at the Academy assembled in the guardroom, marched across the area to the billiard room, chuckling at the coup they were making. When several knocks on the door were not answered, they forced the door open only to find no cadets present. One read the note to the others:

> the members of the Billiard Club of the First Class of the Corps of Cadets, desire to present this billiard table, with all the appurtenances, to the officers on duty at West Point, as a slight token of our gratitude to them, for the generous courtesy displayed by them toward us, in allowing us for so long a time to enjoy the privilege of the Club. The table was manufactured in New York nearly a year ago, and the room furnished at our own expense. From that time to the present, we have freely indulged in this amusement, and we cannot but feel most grateful to you for your generous forbearance. Hoping that you will be pleased to accept this little token of regard, we are,
>
> Very respectfully yours,
> By Order of the Committee.

Wood wrote several years later, "One can imagine their mortification at being so completely outwitted by the cadets." The tactical officers were never able to learn the names of the cadet members of the billiard club, and the matter was eventually dropped—but not forgotten. The officers were "for a long time twitted by the ladies at their grand failure in 'hiving' the cadets," and the cadets themselves chuckled for months at the great victory won in the basement of the 6th Division.

Normal routine at the Academy was sadly interrupted in May 1866 when General Winfield Scott died at the West Point Hotel. Superintendent Cullum notified the Secretary of War and General Grant by telegraph and was directed by Secretary Stanton to render appropriate honors. All officers in the Army were directed to wear a crepe band on the left sleeve and to attach a black knot to their swords for six months, an honor far exceeding the normal mourning period of a few days. Six officers, headed by the Commandant of Cadets, Colonel Henry M. Black, formed a guard of honor in the room where Scott had died, remaining in attendance for three days. On Friday, June 1, half-hour guns were fired from Battery Knox and the seacoast battery from sunrise until after the interment. At eleven o'clock, twelve enlisted men carried the casket across the Plain to the Chapel, where a distinguished group of mourners waited. General Grant and the heads of all the Army staff departments were present, as were official representatives of most eastern states and many cities, and many of Scott's friends. Militia officers of New York, New Jersey, and Connecticut appeared in full dress uniform with a badge of mourning on the left sleeve. More than fifty press representatives battled for good positions outside the Chapel—they were not permitted to enter. The Vice President headed a delegation of ten senators, and the Speaker of the House, a group of five Congressmen. One New York newspaper estimated that more than 200 officers had come to pay their respects. In addition to the staff department heads, they included Generals Grant, George Meade, Dan Butterfield, Oliver Howard, Ethan Allen Hitchcock, George Thomas, and Robert Anderson. Admiral David G. Farragut headed a Navy delegation. Without any doubt, this was the largest, single group of distinguished personages ever to gather at West Point at one time.

After the services conducted by Chaplain French, the Reverend Warren of Elizabeth, New Jersey, the Reverend Hoffman of Brooklyn (Scott had been a communicant of both of their parishes), and Episcopal Bishop Potter, a procession was formed to march to the cemetery. An estimated 15,000 spectators watched the procession. Led by the West Point Band, the entire Corps of Cadets marching with reversed arms, six companies of Artillery, and a battery of Light Artillery were followed by Scott's family, the official delegations, all of the officers stationed at West Point, and a host of individual officers. Scott was buried near the present site of the Old Chapel. Although not a graduate, Scott had asked to be buried at the Academy he had loved so well, among friends with whom he had served for so many years.

By the following Monday, although the flag remained at half-staff for the mourning period, West Point had resumed its normal routine. Cadets attended classes in preparation for the scheduled end-of-year examinations. General Cullum, Colonel Black, and most of the staff tried to relax after the hectic days spent preparing for Scott's funeral. Most of the Academy officers had been involved to some degree, but Cullum, Black, and the Adjutant, Major Edward Boynton, had carried the weight of planning and executing most of the details. Now they had to prepare for the Board of Visitors, examinations, and graduation.

The Board of Visitors was welcomed with a review and participated in the examinations. Artillery and cavalry drills were a part of the program for the Board. Cadet Robert Fletcher described artillery drill with the cadets going through "various movements and maneuvers, fired by piece, section, half-battery, and battery." On June 8, General Grant was welcomed with a fifteen-gun salute fired by the Third Class. Fletcher described the infantry drill conducted for Grant by Colonel Black "on horse back." Immediately after the drill, noted Fletcher, "we had dress parade, in order to save the trouble of marching out on the plain again this evening." After the parade was dismissed, the First Class fell out to be introduced to Grant. The General later rode by the Barracks in a carriage and, according to Fletcher, "was cheered long and loudly by a group of cadets assembled in front to see him pass."

Demonstrations continued for a week. Included were bayonet exercises and sword movements under the supervision of Sword Master Antone Lorentz. There were more artillery demonstrations, including firing large mortars at a target about a mile up river. Parrot guns were fired at a target on the west bank. Fletcher estimated that about thirty rounds were fired and that "about one-third of the shots went right through the canvass [target], the rest . . . came so near the mark that they were almost as good as hits." Evenings were busy for the Corps. Studying for the next day's examinations occupied most of cadets' time, but this was interrupted by what Fletcher described as "a band from Camptown that came up and serenaded the Corps giving three pieces of very fine music. It was a string band. They probably serenaded the officers also."

Graduation Parade was held on Sunday, June 18. Fletcher left one of the best descriptions of the colorful ceremony. When the Corps formed for parade, First Class privates formed in the rear rank without rifles. The battalion marched onto the Plain to the tune of "The Dashing White Sergeant." After the lowering of the flag at retreat, the band played "Auld Lang Syne" and "Home Sweet Home" before the Corps passed in review. Instead of returning to barracks, the battalion returned to its position facing the reviewing party headed by the Commandant. At the command of the cadet adjutant, all the First Class moved front and center, First Class privates forming a line in rear of the cadet officers. The Class then moved forward to the reviewing stand, halted, and raised their hats to the Commandant who, after doffing his hat in return, addressed a few words to the Class. The Corps was dismissed, and the graduating cadets broke ranks to join the spectators. The ceremony that Fletcher described was the genesis of today's traditional Graduation Parade. First Classmen other than cadet officers still form in the rear of their companies. "The Dashing White Sergeant," "Auld

Lang Syne," and "Home Sweet Home" are still a part of the ceremony. There has been one decided change, however. The First Class move forward after retreat, before the remainder of the Corps pass in review. They do not doff their hats to the reviewing party—now the superintendent and, possibly, visiting dignitaries—but salute instead. The Class then forms a line stretching from one end of the path of march to the opposite end of the Plain. At the command of "Pass in Review," the Corps marches before the First Class, whose members remove their hats in final salute to the Corps in which they have served for four years.

Graduation week ended with the traditional Graduation Hop the night before the presentation of diplomas. There were actually two hops. One, held in the Mess Hall, consisted of waltzes, polkas, and other similar dances. The other, held in the Academic Building, was a "german," a series of intricate dance maneuvers conducted by a large number of couples. Included was the Grand March so often featured in western military films by John Ford and other directors.

Congress passed several acts affecting the Military Academy in late 1865 and 1866. In addition to authorizing veterans to enter up to the age of twenty-four years, Congress specified that "no person who has served in any capacity in the military or naval services of the so-called Confederate States during the late rebellion shall hereafter receive an appointment as a cadet of the Military or Naval Academy." The reasons for this are obvious; its impact was negligible.

Far more important was the act authorizing the selection of an officer from any branch of the Army as superintendent. From 1802 to 1866, every superintendent had been selected from the Corps of Engineers. Superintendents and members of the Academic Board had carefully retained a curriculum designed to produce engineers and, to a lesser degree, artillerymen fully competent technically. When news of the proposed act reached West Point, members of the Academic Board reacted violently. Professor Mahan, once again their spokesman, campaigned to have the act defeated. In one letter to Senator William Pitt Fessenden, Mahan wrote, "I learn, through the public press that Generals Grant, Sherman, Meade, and Thomas have agreed to recommend that the national military school at this place shall in future be provided with a Superintendent taken from any corps in the army, instead of confining this office, as at present, to the corps of engineers." Mahan indicated that his tenure of over forty years "unless indeed they have been unproductive of any of the results of experience— entitles my views upon the subject of the Superintendency, full sustained, as they are, by my only two colleagues who were appointed to their professorships from the Line of the Army—Professors Church and Kendrick—to as much consideration as those of Generals Grant, Sherman, and Meade, who neither have been at the school in any capacity but as cadets." He continued that he had only one purpose in writing Fessenden, "I have no object in keeping the office where it is but to ensure a competent head for the school, and to keep it out of the hands of mere politicians, both outside of and within the Army." Mahan warned of problems that would develop if a line officer were selected to be the superintendent. And then he took direct aim at Grant, saying that "I am aware that General Grant will use his endeavors to secure the head man for the place, but General Grant's bases of influence are the two of most instability in this country—that of life and that of popularity." Mahan's efforts were unsuccessful; the act became law in July 1866.

Another 1866 act required each Congressman and Senator to nominate five candidates for cadet vacancies. The act specified that the "selection of one shall be made from the candidates according to their respective merits and qualifications, under such rules and regulations as the Secretary of War shall from time to time prescribe." The President was authorized to nominate fifty candidates, instead of the ten previously authorized. Ten would be selected following the procedures used for selecting congressional appointees. No more than two of the fifty nominees could be appointed in one year from one state. It was hoped that having five men nominated for each appointment would cause Congressmen to select better qualified candidates, considering the competition among each group of five nominees. Unspoken was the thought that Congressmen would not be pleased if any or all of their nominees failed to qualify.

In early July, orders were received indicating that Cullum would be replaced as superintendent in August by Colonel Thomas Pitcher, an Infantry officer, the first non-Engineer to be appointed. He would head the Academy for nearly five years. Cullum prepared to turn over the superintendency. Another order irritated Mahan and his fellow Academic Board members. By direction of the Secretary of War, the Chief of Engineers was relieved from duty as the Inspector of the Military Academy. The Corps of Engineers had lost its last control over Academy activities. What Thayer had recommended more than thirty-five years earlier had finally come to pass. The Academy now truly was able to prepare cadets for service in the Army without undue stress on Corps of Engineer requirements.

One of Cullum's last acts as superintendent was the presentation of medals for academic merit to the first five men in each class and chevrons for general merit to five cadets in each class standing highest in general order of merit. Cadet Fletcher described the ceremony, "The 'merit' or 'good boy' chevrons were awarded. They bring the usual privileges, vis: public lands from reveille to retreat [cadets awarded chevrons were authorized to walk about freely on the Post during this period], visiting the hotel from 3 P.M. until retreat, escorting ladies to band practice, etc.." Cullum's innovative awards had lasted only two years. It would be many years before academic achievement was again recognized by authorizing cadets to wear stars on the collars of their dress and full dress coats for academic achievement and even longer for recognition of general merit with a wreath worn similarly.

From Thayer's time on, honor had been stressed in all cadet activities. Lying or stealing were not tolerated by either cadets or officers. From time to time, a cadet was dismissed when it was shown that he had lied or, in a few instances, stolen the property of another cadet or officer. Strangely, cheating was condoned at this time. Several writings describe cadet efforts to get copies of final examinations from enlisted clerks or even by copying copies in an office or even at an instructor's quarters. The use of an "All Right, Sir," reply in answer to a question—for example, to indicate that a cadet leaving the barracks during call to quarters was authorized to do so—was an accepted way of cadet life. It was permissible for a cadet to stuff his bunk while he "ran" to Benny Havens—IF he did not give the "All Right, Sir," to the sentinel on duty in each division of barracks. Giving the pledge, however, and stuffing a bunk were considered dishonorable.

Cadet monitoring of the honor of the Corps was tacitly approved by Academy authorities. A cadet reported for an honor violation—usually, the report was made to the Commandant by the Cadet Adjutant—resulted in the offender's being given an opportunity to resign or, if he refused, his being tried by court martial and dismissed for conduct unbecoming an officer (cadet in this instance). The Corps had increasingly taken direct action with honor offenders. During the war, Charles King recorded one instance when a cadet who had stolen the property of another cadet was escorted to the South Gate, tarred and feathered, and sent on his way. King also cited two other instances. One had brought prompt dismissal by the Commandant and Superintendent. The second, involving a classmate of King, was investigated by cadet officers; there was no Cadet Honor Committee at this time. The culprit, said King, "equivocated, in fact lied" and was promptly dismissed.

At this time, the Cadet Adjutant, the senior captain equivalent to today's First Captain, was the primary link between the Commandant and the Corps. During the summer of 1865, when King was Cadet Adjutant, a number of reports were made that jewelry and money had been stolen from various cadets. Although cadets were not authorized to have either money or jewelry, King reported the thefts to the Commandant, who promptly informed King and other cadet officers, "In my time, young gentlemen, we never would have rested until we found the thief and had handled him as he deserved." This unfortunately caused the cadets to take steps that caused a tragic result.

Several new treasury notes, which were marked or their numbers recorded, were left in tents obviously visible. Nothing happened until the Corps had returned to barracks, when the thefts began again. A surprise search during lunch one December day found some of the marked bills inside books in the room of a cadet ostracized by the remainder of the Corps for undue hazing and bullying of even his own classmates. That afternoon, all of the cadet officers met to determine what action should be taken. Three cadets were sent to question the suspect. Returning in less than an hour, they unanimously agreed that there was no question that he was guilty. They reported that he had told "a dozen different stories and had contradicted himself in a dozen different ways."

The cadet officers now faced the question of what to do with the suspect, Cadet Orsemus B. Boyd. His classmates, of the Class of 1867, had formed a committee that wanted to tar and feather him. King and his fellow cadet officers did not agree with this intent and, to prevent such action, decided to drum Boyd out of the Corps at the next undress parade in the area of barracks. This formation was chosen because the Officer-in-Charge did not normally attend; and King, as Adjutant, would serve as troop commander. After King had published the day's orders, all of the cadet officers moved to his side and faced the Corps. Robert Fletcher graphically described what happened at parade on December 18, 1865.

> The Adjutant, King, after publishing tomorrow's detail, said that any one who left ranks at this parade, on any pretext whatever, would be immediately put in arrest by any first class officer. Immediately after, to the astonishment of almost every member of the Corps, Cranston, Murphy, Wright, and two or three others came out of the third 'div' leading Boyd, who was white as a sheet, dressed in citizen's clothes, one having hold of each hand by a strap tied thereto, and a huge placard on his back, on which was written the word "Thief." Taking him in front of the battalion, King commanded the 'Rogues March' to be beaten, when he was marched along the front of the whole line and then released to escape the vengeance of the Corps if possible.

Boyd disappeared in the passageway between the Academic Building and the Mess Hall, assumedly heading for the landing, where he could catch the afternoon ferry to Garrison's. King held the Corps in formation until the whistle of the ferry indicated that it had left West Point; King took this action to prevent Boyd's classmates from carrying out their tar-and-feathering plan. When King dismissed the Corps, a group of cadets ran toward the road leading to the dock only to encounter the Superintendent, General Cullum. In the meantime, King had gone to the Commandant to report what had been done.

As King related many years later, "Several hours later, the Superintendent had the fugitive brought back under guard." Apparently, Cullum had been at the dock to see visitors off on the ferry and had ordered Boyd to remain there until he sent for him. Boyd was taken to the Commandant's home, where he remained overnight, according to Cadet Fletcher's diary. Fletcher made an astute comment, "It is suspected that another is in the Corps for a great deal of money was taken in camp when Boyd was on furlough. We hope for the honor of the Corps that such is not the case. That [the money taken in camp] might have not have been stolen by cadets." He added that the entire affair had been "well managed, not an officer knowing anything about it, until it all was over."

The next day, Fletcher reported that Boyd had protested his innocence and asked for a Court of Inquiry. Two days after he was drummed out of the Corps, the court began its inquiries. The Court continued its investigation until January 9 when it submitted its findings to the Superintendent. Although the results were not announced, it was evident that the Court had found Boyd innocent because King and the four company commanders, wrote Fletcher, "were put in arrest this afternoon for complicity in the Mr. Boyd affair. The charge is 'conduct prejudicial to good order and military discipline.' Mr. Boyd is also put in arrest for 'conduct unbecoming a cadet and gentleman' or something of the sort." Fletcher's use of "Mr. Boyd" was significant because it indicated that the Corps considered him guilty regardless of the findings of the court, "Mr." never being used in addressing or writing about a fellow cadet under normal circumstances.

Within a week, Secretary of War Stanton had reviewed the findings of the court and declared the evidence to be inconclusive. The charges against Boyd were dismissed. Stanton also ordered King and his fellow captains to be tried by court martial for their "unwarrantable outrage on Mr. Boyd in the presence of the Corps of Cadets." The action of the court was announced on February 19 with Fletcher commenting, "The 'findings' of the court martial in the 'Mr. Boyd' case were published at parade. King, Soule, Wright, and Murphy, charged with conduct prejudicial to good order and military discipline, to which were appended specifications as to . . . treatment of 'Mr. Boyd,' all pleaded guilty." All five were sentenced to be dismissed, but the sentences were remitted. Only King was reduced to the grade of private and, as he later wrote, "went back to the ranks of Company 'A'." Fletcher's final comment was, "It seems as though there is some injustice."

Boyd was reinstated and graduated with the Class of 1867. He lived alone and, according to King, was often abused by his classmates. He resented no insult, however, accepting his solitude quietly. After graduation, he was assigned to a regiment in a western garrison and served in an outstanding manner. The few graduates at that post, however, would not speak to him. Nevertheless, he was a model officer and, according to King, reserved, dignified, and studious. The Boyd story, however, does not end here. Many years later, the real culprit admitted to a classmate that he had stolen the money, not Boyd. He had been secretly married, a dismissal offense then as now, and his wife was blackmailing him, threatening to report the marriage to the superintendent unless he sent her money and jewelry. To avoid suspicion, he had hidden the stolen money in books in Boyd's room. His action preyed upon his mind, and he had two mental breakdowns after his graduation. "Then," reported King, "practically by his own hand he died." Boyd was informed of this before his death in 1885.

Most of the officers at West Point sympathized with King and believed that the Corps was doing the right thing by shunning any contact with Boyd. Although instructions were issued concerning cadet action in the case of honor violations, little was done to systematize the cadet honor system. There appeared to be little if any awareness of West Point authorities that cadets were young men and that young men often permit emotion to overcome common sense in cases such as the Boyd incident. That the Academy administration supported cadet honor supervision was admirable; that nothing was done to systematize the use of the honor system was inexcusable. Positive steps would not occur until 1920 when General Douglas MacArthur became Superintendent. He approved recommendations of a cadet committee and formalized the honor system of the Corps.

Winters were—and are—cold at West Point. Cadet Fletcher recorded a temperature of minus fifteen degrees the winter of 1865. All formations were marched at double-quick time instead of quick time, almost a dead run. Fletcher noted in his diary that the Commandant "had double windows put up today on the north side of barracks in order to keep out the cold wind. It seems not to be any warmer." The attractive diamond-shaped pier glass panes included in Delafield's design for the barracks provided added authenticity for the Tudor-style barracks but only added additional cracks for the wind to blow through.

The bitter cold led to a water shortage when some of the conduit pipes froze. Fletcher mentioned taking a bath, "the first one for over two weeks. The Superintendent published an order recently, by which, owing to the scarcity of water, the bathrooms are only open on Saturday afternoons." Two companies bathed on one Saturday, the other two the following week. Fletcher complained that he could only take one bath every two weeks instead of his usual bath twice a week.

Cold did not hamper cadet relaxation activities. Instead of walking around the Post or down Flirtation Walk, many cadets visited the Museum in the Academic Building. Fletcher told of seeing the model of a Mexican silver mine, shells, trophies, mementos, and models, which he termed "all very interesting." Forts were built on the edge of the Plain, and mock battles fought, some lasting for several hours.

New Year's Eve was celebrated in the usual manner. The Dialectic Society presented its theatrical production in the fencing room, which had been arranged as a theater. General Cullum and most of the officers and ladies of the Post were present. Fletcher estimated that the entire Corps, other than cadets under arrest or on guard, also attended. Two farces were featured, which "kept the audience in roar of laughter a great deal of the time." There were also fancy dances and recitations of poems written by cadets. The two-hour entertainment was only a prelude to the additional celebration.

Shortly after midnight, the area of barracks erupted in a cacophony of noise from horns and tin pails rolling down the iron staircases in barracks. "Somebody had the nozzle from the [fire] engine and others horns of frightful sound," wrote Fletcher. Shouts and bursting fire crackers, which had been surreptitiously made in the Ordnance laboratory, added to the din. When officers appeared from the guardhouse, the noise abruptly ceased, except for one last blast on the nozzle-horn. At the same time, the reveille gun was dismounted and rolled into Execution Hollow. Shortly after quiet returned, Fletcher recalled that "we had a serenade by the string band from Camptown. They played music which was really enchanting, and I was perfectly willing to be waked up to hear the New Year ushered in by such manner."

One evening, cadets were awakened by a sentinel firing a pistol and yelling

"Fire! fire!" Cadets streamed out of barracks to form their fire-fighting companies. The engine was dragged to a store shed near the Mess Hall. Water was piped through hoses, and bucket brigades passed pails of water from hydrants along a line of cadets to the flames. General Cullum and the Commandant were among the officers who came to supervise. An enlisted detachment from Camptown arrived and took over from the cadet teams. The prompt action by cadet fire fighters stopped the fire from reaching the stores inside the shed, including about "150 firkins of butter," as Fletcher estimated. "The affair showed," he wrote, "that our fire organization is very good."

A new tradition developed during the postwar years. First Classmen gathered to observe the date of "100 days until graduation." This was a class function that included a special meal and short skits. Often liquor was distributed quietly but freely, sometimes with resulting reports and punishments. From this one-class celebration has evolved today's Hundredth Night Show, a combination of the early observance and the Dialectic Society entertainments on New Year's Eve.

Professor Mahan spent many hours during this period studying campaigns of the Civil War. He had the distinct advantage of being able to discuss battles with the men who had fought them at all levels of command. The frequent visits of Grant, Sherman, Sheridan, Schofield, Meade, Thomas, and other senior commanders enabled Mahan to obtain information from the men who had planned and conducted most of the important campaigns. One of his earliest lectures was given to the entire First Class in May 1868. The three-hour lectures included recitation on previous lessons and questions about Mahan's lecture. Apparently, Mahan discussed one campaign in each lecture, as Fletcher noted the lecture on the Atlanta campaign on May 23 and the Nashville campaign a few days later. Unfortunately, Mahan's maps and lecture notes do not appear to have survived the passage of years. It would be interesting to learn what changes Mahan may have made from his instruction based on Napoleon's tactics and strategy to the science of war evolved from the actions of Grant, Lee, Sherman, and Jackson. Did he compare Sherman's march through Georgia with Napoleon's move forward to Moscow? Was Jackson's rapid movement from the Shenandoah to join Lee on the Yorktown peninsula compared to the many times Napoleon rapidly assembled his forces from many areas to confront his opponents? Was Murat compared to Jeb Stuart or Sheridan? Mahan may have criticized Grant for his dogged attacks, pushing Lee toward Richmond with tremendous losses incurred in the process. He may have praised Lee for time and time again forcing Union forces to fight on ground he had selected when he wanted a battle to be fought. Without doubt, Mahan did not change what he considered the most important military axiom, "To do the greatest damage to our enemy with least exposure to ourselves."

An unusual visit took place during the 1868 Board of Visitors stay at West Point. Three ships brought the graduating class of midshipmen from Annapolis to the Academy. Neither cadets nor midshipmen were particulary happy with the visit; both graduating classes and the furlough class at West Point were kept from departing until after the visit. Anchoring near the south dock on Sunday, midshipmen went ashore, where they were informally greeted by cadets who guided them on a tour of Academy facilities.

At eight o'clock the next morning, the three ships fired a twenty-one gun salute honoring the Academy. A return salute was fired by cadets from Battery Knox at nine o'clock. No formal ceremonies were scheduled until two o'clock that afternoon when the Corps marched to the dock, where they formed ranks on both sides of the road to the Plain. The battalion of midshipmen and the Naval Academy Band, which had already landed and formed in ranks, marched between the lines of cadets to the Plain, halting near the Library to form a double rank along which the Corps, led by the West Point Band, marched. The midshipmen followed the Corps to the center of the Plain, formed a half-circle in front of Generals Grant, Meade, Shriver, and Superintendent Pitcher. The First Class stacked arms and moved forward to form two ranks. General Grant presented them with their diplomas. After the ceremony, the two battalions marched to the front of the Barracks; and, after being formally dismissed, cadets and midshipmen wandered off together.

The flotilla remained at West Point until Saturday. The entire week was filled with one joint activity after another. Graduation Hop had both midshipmen and cadets seeking partners, which was apparently no problem, for Edward Fletcher estimated that over 700 young ladies had come to West Point for the Hop. The midshipmen marched in review for the Corps with every cadet watching from the sidelines. The Corps marched in honor of the Naval Academy visitors. Drills were conducted to show the midshipmen what Army infantrymen and artillerymen could do. The Navy responded with demonstrations, firing the ships' guns upriver. Cadets were surprised when midshipmen offered them sherry or claret during shipboard visits. Fletcher reported several cadets "went too far" and were ill but not from being seasick. Two final events marked the end of the visit. The first was Graduation Parade, where the Corps and the graduating cadets were cheered by the midshipmen spectators. That night, the Navy hosted a hop aboard the three ships, which had been lashed together and lighted for the occasion. Fletcher commented that many cadets and midshipmen exchanged clothing "to avoid detection, cadets wearing 'mid's' clothes and vice verse." Thus ended the first known exchange visit of midshipmen and cadets, a congenial meeting that formed many friendships that lasted for years.

In January 1869, Robert Anderson, the hero of Fort Sumter, wrote Sylvanus Thayer to propose the formation of an Association of Graduates of the Military Academy. Thayer replied, endorsing the concept, using a sentiment similar to that he had expressed to Robert Allston when Allston had invited Thayer to join his classmates at the first alumni reunion in 1853, "I hope that reunions of various classes will become an annual event." Thayer wrote to Anderson that the proposal "will fulfill a wish I have long entertained." He concurred in the Washington's Birthday date selected by Anderson for a meeting to organize an association, indicating that he hoped the same day would be used for the annual meetings since "no time would be more appropriate."

Thayer made one comment that was not directly related to organizing an association, a comment that was almost a policy pattern for the continued development of the Military Academy:

> That the Institution has existed for fifty-one years, viz., since 1817–18, with scarcely a single change in its organization, its system of instruction, or its administration, or general regulations, may be regarded as pretty good evidence that the edifice was not badly planned and constructed, and need not now to be taken down from top to bottom, and built over again; yet all human work and institutions are imperfect and subject to the law of progress. To stand still, or not to advance, is to retrograde.
>
> Our Alma Mater has done a good work, and the nation is proud of her, or ought to be, but this should not blind us to her shortcomings if any there be, or dampen our zeal to make her still more useful, and beautiful, till she shall become the beau ideal I have dreamed of for half a century.

This comment was made in response to Anderson's suggestion of the purpose of the association: "perfect and perpetuate the Military Academy." Both Thayer and Anderson envisioned the proposed association to be involved—and even having a major role—in determining and making changes or improvements in Academy operations. Fortunately, the Association of Graduates has never formally followed Thayer's recommendations. It does not take much imagination to see the problems and consternation that would exist if graduates directly influenced the operation of the Military Academy. Without any doubt whatsoever, any superintendent, commandant of cadets, professor, or tactical officer already has sufficient problems in answering the recommendations, complaints, and demands of "DOGs"—Distinguished Old Grads, Disgusted Old Grads, Damned Old Grads!

Anderson's organizational meeting was not held until May 22; Anderson could not attend because of illness. Dr. Horace Porter, Class of 1815 and President of the City College of New York, served as chairman, being the oldest graduate present. Others attending were General Alexander S. Webb, Class of 1855 and soon to replace Porter as President of the City College of New York; Thomas J. Leslie, Class of 1815; Abraham Van Buren, Class of 1827 and son of President Van Buren; Francis Vinton, Class of 1830 and Assistant Minister of Trinity Church, New York City. Five men could hardly be considered a quorum of the more than 2,000 graduates to that date. This they realized because only two major decisions were made. Sylvanus Thayer was asked to be the first president of the association. Thayer replied a few days later, indicating how honored and pleased he was to be selected. His inherent humor was shown by his comment that he "was not unaware that I am indebted for the distinction mainly and perhaps entirely to the accidental circumstance of being the senior surviving graduate." He declined the position, feeling that because he was in his eighty-fifth year with all of the infirmities of old age, he would be unable to fulfill the duties of the office. His refusal was negated by the simple expedient of including in the association constitution the proviso that the senior living graduate would be president. Thayer served as the first president from 1870 until his death in 1872.

The second major decision was to write all living graduates, asking for their opinion and an indication if they would join the proposed association. Fortunately, the group was able to obtain addresses from General George Cullum, who had traced most living graduates in preparing the first two volumes of his *Biographical Register of Officers and Graduates of the United States Military Academy*. Most of the answers received in the next two years approved the concept, some enthusiastically, some in a routine manner. Many graduates, however, objected to the entire concept. A seven-page letter came from Lieutenant Colonel George A. Custer at far-off Fort Hays, Kansas (Custer typically signed the letter "G. A. Custer, Brevet Maj. Genl.). Although he considered the objects of the Association—to cherish the memories of our Alma Mater and to promote the social intercourse and fraternal fellowship of graduates—favorably, Custer asked, "Is the organization of such a Society either necessary or advisable? To my mind the answer is most decidedly in the negative." In Custer's opinion, he already cherished the memory of his cadet days, and he had never encountered a graduate who did not. Consequently, he could see no advantage in organizing a society to cherish already held memories. This in his opinion was the equivalent of the members of a family forming a society for the purpose of "cherishing their memories of a common parent." Custer also objected to the Association purpose of promoting social intercourse and fraternal fellowship, asserting that simply being a graduate "was in itself a certificate of 'fraternal friendship' stronger than any society could formulate." He also questioned the desirability of a society formed by "a mere fraction of the entire number of graduates." He closed these two arguments with an impassioned statement: "Have we lived to see the day when, forgetful of the historical romances which surround the spot, of the importance of the latter during and since the revolutionary struggle, of the steady but permanent growth of the Military Academy, and last but not least of the enduring triumphs won by her sons in the Mexican, as well as in our late, unhappy, war; have we, I repeat, lived to see the day, when, unmindful of these glorious traditions, the Graduates of the Military Academy deem it necessary in order to cherish the memories of our Alma Mater, to form an Association?" Custer also stated that he felt the establishment of the Association would increase the gulf between officers who were graduates and those who were not. In his opinion, non-graduates would resent the very existence of the Association, stating that "when the Military Academy, by legal enactment, or otherwise, is abolished, or is no more, then and not until then would the formation of such an association as it is proposed be necessary or advisable; but as long as our Alma Mater continues to exist, it of itself, in the eyes of all her sons, will be the noblest of all Societies!!!" Custer maintained, without citing names, that many fellow graduates on active duty shared his sentiments.

Objections of an entirely different nature came from Simon Bolivar Buckner, Class of 1844 and Lieutenant General of the Confederate Army. Writing a far less florid and impassioned letter than had Custer, Buckner indicated that he agreed with the concept with which the Association was being formed and that the objects of the Association were "as dear to me as they can be to any who have received its diploma. Entertaining these sentiments as fully as I do, it is with reluctance that I feel compelled to state that I cannot, at this time, think it proper to become a member of the Association." Buckner based his decision on actions of the federal government, "which extends its fostering care to one class of the graduates of our Alma Mater; and at the same time proscribes the other." He referred to the First Reconstruction Act passed by Congress in March 1868, which excluded former Confederates from voting. "Outside of such an organization," wrote Buckner, "I can conceive, even under existing circumstances, of the most friendly personal relations based upon ideas of equality and upon the recognition of mutual respect and esteem." Other southern graduates undoubtedly had similar reservations concerning the proposed Association. The majority of replies, however, supported the establishment of the Association of Graduates, and its first annual meeting was held in New York City in 1870.

It is possible that Buckner may not have been aware of George Cullum's sentiments about graduates who had served the Confederacy; it is equally possible that he did but did not mention Cullum in his letter for diplomatic considerations. Cullum did not hesitate to strongly condemn southern graduates who "forgot the flag under which they were educated, to follow false gods." In the first edition of his *Register of Officers and Graduates . . .* , Cullum ignored the wartime service of southern graduates. He did make a slight concession in the second and third volumes by including the statement, "joined in the Rebellion of 1861–65 against the United States." Cullum refused to even listen to requests to include Confederate service in his biographical register by saying, "I could not by such an act give even the semblance of my approval of their taking up arms against the flag under which they were educated." To insure that his format for the *Register* remained unchanged, Cullum provided funds in his will for continuing its publication with the stipulation that the present text "as prepared by me to include the year 1890" were to be retained unchanged. His bitterness was not restricted to his publications. His will also left $125,000 for the erection of a memorial building. To prevent former Confederates from being memorialized, Cullum specified that the Academic Board would select individuals to be appropriately recognized and "to prevent the introduction of unworthy subjects into this Hall." Cullum's desires have been followed; the only Confederate officers memorialized in the memorial hall are Robert E. Lee and Pierre G. T. Beauregard, both as former superintendents. Not for many years would the bitterness vanish. In 1869, time had not healed nor had the world changed enough to bring together old friends who had fought on opposite sides during the Civil War.

The Corps was unaware of the activities involved in organizing the Association of Graduates. There appears to have been little antagonism toward the South; cadets from the southern states would not be appointed until after the rebellious states had been readmitted. By June 1868, only Mississippi, Texas, and Virginia had not met congressional requirements; they were re-admitted in 1870. Cadets from the southern states were welcomed again into the Corps, suffered the same plebe agonies as cadets from other sectors, and participated fully in all cadet activities.

The year 1870 would be remembered as the year that troubles began to assail the Academy. Congress and the entire nation were shocked early in the year by allegations that appointments to West Point were being sold by members of the House. Although the Academy was not directly involved in this misdemeanor or in the resulting investigations, the charges indirectly impacted on West Point and its cadets and staff. Hearings conducted by the House Armed Forces Committee revealed that many Congressmen had appointed young men in return for direct or indirect payments. The *Philadelphia Inquirer* of February 21, 1870, recommended, as a means of stopping this practice, the nomination of several young men with the nominee making the highest grades in the entrance examinations being appointed. The liberal *Nation* magazine went a step further, recommending that appointments and reinstatement of cadets dismissed for academic or conduct deficiencies be completely taken away from Congress, "Break up this unconstitutional custom . . . apportion the cadet appointments, if you will, among the States according to their Congressional representation; leave the selection of candidates to each State, and throw upon each the responsibility of selecting its best men." The investigation continued for nearly two years and ended with no change to the system of appointing cadets.

Late that spring, the Corps, West Point officers, and many ordinary citizens throughout the country were surprised and even shocked when two "colored" young men were nominated to take the entrance examinations in June. The two applicants were dissimilar, greatly so. Michael Howard, nominated by a Mississippi Congressman, was eighteen years of age and had less than a year of schooling. His father was a member of the Mississippi State Legislature. James W. Smith, son of a former slave who became a prosperous carpenter, had attended a Freedmen's Bureau school until he was brought to Hartford, Connecticut by wealthy philanthropist David Clark. After his graduation from high school in the spring of 1870, Smith entered the newly established Howard University three weeks before he was nominated for a cadet vacancy. That blacks were appointed should not have been a surprise to West Point officials or to the general public. As Professor William F. Vaughn pointed out in his 1971 article, *West Point and the First Negro Cadet*, southern states were dominated by "radical Republicans, [a] coalition of blacks, carpetbaggers, and native whites. Negroes formed a majority of the population, and it was only a matter of time until some local Congressman rewarded his black supporters with an appointment to the Academy." Rabid abolitionist, Massachusetts Congressman Benjamin F. Butler had considered appointing a black in 1867. Despite an extensive search in cooperation with Oberlin College President James Fairchild, Butler was unable to find a black whom both men thought qualified to enter the Academy. Neither of the Congressmen appointing Howard and Smith made any effort to determine the capabilities of the two nominees.

Howard, who reported on May 30, was described by a correspondent of the *New York Sun*, who "had timed his arrival so accurately that he stepped into the Adjutant's office at West Point just as the ebony son of Mississippi was reporting himself for orders." When the reporter asked if he might talk with Howard, Major Edward C. Boynton replied, "Certainly, talk with him as much as you please." During the conversation Howard impressed the newsman by his simplicity and candor. However, Howard's replies gave him the impression that Howard "showed either unusual intelligence and gratitude on the part of the boy, or else careful coaching on the part of the benefactor or someone else." The latter assumption may have been correct. When Howard was refused a room in the West Point Hotel, the first time any appointee had not been welcomed, he made a comment concerning his rights and demanded to see "Colonel Jerry Black." When word reached "Colonel Black of the Regular Army," the Commandant of Cadets, he "respectfully asked that his equality be recognized." Colonel Black, according to the newsman, only waved him away. This is hard to believe. The *Sun* reporter also claimed that cadets wanted to throw Howard in the river and that "others talk of killing the black boy outright." It was also reported that many cadets wanted to resign and that one exclaimed, "Great God, what shall we do? He will have to drill with us for four weeks before the examination any way. He will have to be bilged." The report in the *Sun* is highly suspect, especially when compared to stories in other New York papers.

The New York Tribune the next day presented a far more conservative account of Howard's first day at West Point. Beginning his account, the *Tribune* reporter stated, "As far as I have read in the papers, I do not think that the whole truth has been told" about Howard's reporting for duty. Howard "stated to me most emphatically that the stories retailed about his being persecuted and cruelly dealt with by the cadets are wholly destitute of truth." Howard said that he had been treated the same as any other plebe; his only complaint was that he had been left completely alone. The reporter believed that, although cadets could be required to drill with Howard, they could not be forced to associate with him. He added, "From what I have seen of him I do not think he will be able to go through the severe intellectual examinations which every 'plebe' has to go through before he can don the gray."

James Smith, the second black, reported a day after Howard. Initially, newsmen paid little attention to him other than to describe his physical characteristics. Before either was subjected to the entrance examinations, the correspondent of *The Boston Globe* commented, "Seriously, the sudden intrusion of this negro

[Smith] into the West Point system may work a great deal that is bad; but I believe, from what I have seen and heard, that if people who are not prejudiced look at the thing in its proper light there need be no fear of A NATIONAL CATASTROPHE from the innovation. But there is just this about it, which is well understood here, and that is that there is a certain sect in the country who will cry out 'murder' no matter whether the colored boys are dealt with fairly or not." He predicted the "advocates of negro equality" would be outraged if either Howard or Smith were disqualified.

All of the newly arrived appointees were given the normal physical examination at the Cadet Hospital. Howard passed the testing without trouble. Smith, whom newsmen noted had a nervous affliction with his eyes that caused him to go almost blind at times and also had a "lung affection"—they must have obtained this information from Smith himself—also passed. Smith had no problems with the academic tests, but Howard made an extremely poor showing and was not accepted as a cadet. The *Globe* reporter's concern was apparently in error for little comment was made when Howard was disqualified. At the conclusion of the examinations and after Howard had departed, the *New York Tribune* commented that "these two colored boys have been treated with uniform kindness at the Academy, and the tricks that the boys usually play upon new comers have been omitted in their cases, because the cadets thought the people would say they were roughly handled because they were colored boys."

One reason for the apparent harmony was the insistence of the Superintendent and the Commandant, General Emory Upton, who had replaced Colonel Black. When cadets assigned to the same table as Smith asked to be seated elsewhere, Upton refused their request, indicating that their reasons for wanting a change would not be accepted under any circumstances. When Smith got into a fight with another cadet for taking food before the white cadet, Upton had the table commandant arrested for neglect of duty. By tacit agreement, the Corps decided to leave Smith completely alone and to speak to him only in the line of duty.

After this quick and forceful action by Upton, with the complete approval of the Superintendent, everything seemed to be moving ahead quietly and the training of the new cadets was no different than the training in previous years. Although there were many visitors who hoped to find fault with the handling of Smith, they found little ground for complaint. Comments in the press lessened; it appeared that the crisis was over.

Two weeks later, West Point was scathingly criticized in almost every newspaper in the country. The Hartford *Courant* published a letter that Smith had written to his benefactor, David Clark, complaining about the treatment he received from other cadets. He asserted that he had been cursed and abused day and night, so much so at night that he was unable to get more than two hours of sleep. He maintained that the only way he could get anything to eat in the Mess Hall was to grab for food like a dog. Academy officials, according to Smith, would do nothing to prevent cadets from abusing him. Perhaps his most damaging statement concerned the examinations. Only thirty-nine of eighty-six appointees passed the examination because, wrote Smith, "They had prepared it to fix the colored candidates, but it proved most disastrous to the whites."

General Pitcher acted wisely, initiating an immediate investigation by a West Point board and, at the same time, requesting the Secretary of War to order a formal Court of Inquiry. Before his own board had completed its investigation, Smith's letter was published in a majority of the daily press, sometimes without comment but more often with harshly critical words. Letters to the editors were printed in many papers. The Hartford *Courant* produced a letter from General Oliver O. Howard, President of the Freedmen's Bureau, to Smith, offering sound advice to "endure the insults without any show of fear. A prompt and able reply when off duty will sometimes avail you. A pleasant smile will win hearts to you." But Howard's comments about his alma mater in another letter to the *New York Tribune*—he said that "the thought occurs to me that I might perhaps influence high-minded cadets in his favor by giving you my letter [to Smith] for publication"—were far from charitable and quite evidently biased in favor of Smith. "If West Point has not power enough," wrote Howard, "to protect such a young man as Cadet Smith—quick, able, honest, noble-spirited as he is—then West Point will have a hard struggle against the returning tide of feeling that will reach it from the people." It is difficult to understand Howard's motive in writing this letter for publication. He had not asked for any information from West Point concerning Smith's letter. Were his charges true? Had he actually been treated as badly as he charged? Howard's letter was copied by other newspapers and brought immediate and vituperative response throughout the country. In Congress, Representatives Charles Sumner and Benjamin Butler of Massachusetts demanded a congressional investigation. Although Butler's resolution was adopted, no action was taken by the House at this time.

Secretary of War William W. Belknap and General in Chief William T. Sherman were quick to agree with General Pitcher's recommendation. A Court of Inquiry was formed with Oliver Howard as president and another general officer and two majors as members. Within a week, the Court met at West Point. During interviews, Smith insisted that the letter published was different than the personal letter sent to Clark and that he had not intended the letter to be published. Smith also cited a number of minor harassments by white cadets and stated that Academy authorities had always treated him justly and kindly. The Court noted that cadet regulations prohibited them from writing to newspapers or periodicals. The Superintendent emphatically stressed the falseness of Smith's charges that the Academic Board had "fixed the examinations" against the two black candidates. Emory Upton reported that, acting upon complaints by Smith, he had interviewed the cadets alleged to have harassed Smith to make certain there would be no further abuse. In addition, he told the entire Corps that federal laws assured Smith was entitled to "precisely the same rights and privileges as all other cadets and that the law should be strictly enforced."

Although the board met for only four days, it interviewed Smith at length, talked with other cadets and members of the staff and faculty, and questioned the Superintendent and the Commandant thoroughly. Its findings were released on July 21, stating that most of the allegations made by Smith were either unfounded or exaggerated, that there was no evidence whatsoever that the Academic Board had tried to "fix" the examinations against the black candidates, and that there had been some mistreatment of Smith by other cadets. The Court stated that the Academy authorities had no responsibility for Smith's troubles, that they had treated Smith with complete and scrupulous fairness. The Court recommended that Smith be tried by general court martial. When the recommendation was reviewed by Secretary Belknap, he discarded the recommendation and instead ordered a severe reprimand by the Superintendent. In addition, Belknap warned Smith and Academy officials that should any further harassment occur, rigorous action would be "devised and enforced for their suppression."

A month later, Smith again caused trouble. During an argument about using the water tank in summer camp, Smith had assaulted another cadet with a metal water dipper. Two days later, Smith was reported for replying disrespectfully to correction by a "file closer," an upperclassman marching in the rear to the two-rank formation. Smith wrote a denial of these charges, but the cadet reporting him produced witnesses to verify his report. General Upton preferred charges against Smith for making a false official statement. Superintendent Pitcher referred the recommendation to Secretary Belknap, who convened a Court Martial in October. The Court consisted of eight senior officers with General Howard again serving as president. Trying Smith for creating a disturbance in camp and for making a false official statement, the Court found him guilty of hitting another cadet but innocent on the false statement charge. It recommended that Smith walk punishment tours on "six consecutive Saturdays." Secretary Belknap, with the concurrence of President Grant, set aside the recommended punishment because it was completely insufficient. However, he could not increase the recommended punishment of the courts; Smith went unpunished.

Cadets could not understand the actions of Academy officials. To them, Smith's actions were proven violations of the honor code—making false official statements. They did not consider the pressure on the officers and their need to be extremely careful in their dealing with Smith. Cadet James Fornance wrote to his brother that the officers were making a pet of Smith, giving him far more lenient punishments than those given to white cadets for similar violations of cadet regulations. After the announcement of Smith's second court martial results, Fornance wrote, "The nigger was sentenced by the recent Court-Martial to walk six extra tours of Guard duty for his lying, knocking down, &c while white men are sent away. But—the Attorney General has made some remarks on the Court-Martial. I do not know what he will do. The President has disapproved the sentence so he gets no punishment at all unless the nigger is court-marshalled [sic] again for the same offense." Many cadet letters expressed a strong dislike of Smith. Eben Swift, Class of 1876, left a memoir that stated that Smith, "the colored cadet, [was] a repulsive looking, freckle-faced negro, who had probably been appointed by an enemy of the Academy as a living caricature upon its lofty ideals and standards."

Plebe Hugh Scott, later Superintendent and Army Chief of Staff from 1914 to 1917, was more emphatic in his description of any feelings about Smith. Writing to his mother in June 1871, Scott stated, "We came near having trouble because it was reported that Cadet Smith [would] drill some of us and the whole class . . . swore that they would all leave before they would be bossed around by the nigger." In July, Scott wrote that "I cannot imagine why you are so anxious about the 'Niggers,' for meaner niggers you never saw. Yesterday, we were to take dancing lessons but, when the drum beat, the nigger came out and fell in with the rest, and all the rest of us fell out." Smith marched to the dancing class by himself; the other cadets marched as a group. Smith did little to win friends among his classmates. Scott, in his description of the march to dancing class, said that Smith's reaction was a mean and leering smile.

Less than two months later, Smith was in trouble again. Reported by a cadet for inattention in ranks, he denied the charges; the cadet had witnesses; Upton preferred charges; and Smith was brought before a general Court Martial in January 1877. This time the Court found him guilty of conduct unbecoming a gentleman and sentenced him to be dismissed from the Academy. The findings of the Court remained in limbo in Washington for six months while Belknap, Grant, the Army Judge Advocate General, members of Congress, and others battled to arrive at a decision. The black press—even at this early time, only five years after the Civil War, there were many black newspapers—began to clamor for the abolition of the Academy, maintaining that such an institution was a dishonor to the nation and that its graduates would prove to be a curse in case of any emergency. Finally, in mid-June, Belknap announced the administration's decision. The sentence of dismissal was too severe and reduced Smith's punishment to be turned back to the next class.

This cannot be considered strict punishment; it meant that Smith had to repeat his plebe year, which was not a problem to him for he had had little trouble with academics. Smith's remaining cadet career was not marked by the sensationalism and periodic outbursts of his first plebe year. His academic standing improved during his second year but began to drop the succeeding year. In June 1874, his existence as a cadet became more pleasant when another black, Henry Flipper, entered the Academy. However, Smith's academic standing continued to drop; in the June 1875 examinations, he failed to pass the Natural and Experimental Philosophy testing and was dismissed.

Shortly after the second Smith Court Martial in January 1871, a distinct and momentous change took place: the architects of West Point's Golden Age began to leave the Academy. First to depart was Hyacinthe Agnel, Professor of French since 1848, who died in May. In March, William H. C. Bartlett retired after serving as Professor of Natural and Experimental Philosophy since 1836; his successor was Brigadier General Peter S. Michie, Class of 1863. The death in July of Chaplain John W. French, Professor of Geography, History, and Ethics since 1856, brought about the appointment of the Reverend John Forsyth as his replacement.

The loss of these three members of the Academic Board was felt greatly by the West Point family. But tragedy was ahead. In September, Professor Dennis Hart Mahan either fell or jumped overboard from the paddle steamer *Mary Powell* en route to New York City to consult his physician. The story making its rounds in the Corps was that Mahan, despondent at being forced to retire, had deliberately jumped overboard. After forty-five years at West Point as an instructor and head of the Department of Engineering, Mahan had tired visibly. Headaches incapacitated him for days at a time. So apparent was his deteriorating condition that the Board of Visitors recommended that he retire. Mahan, the senior professor, had been appointed in 1830, three years before Thayer's departure. He and Church had dominated Academic Board affairs for many years. He had seen eleven superintendents appointed and replaced. His writings were known internationally; many of his engineering texts were used by other colleges. During criticisms before the Mexican War and during the Civil War, Mahan had been the self-appointed spokesman defending the Academy, its educational system, and its graduates. His tragic death shocked Academy personnel and graduates throughout the nation.

At Braintree, Brevet Brigadier General Sylvanus Thayer—he had been promoted in June 1863—mourned the tragic death of his old friend and protégé. One week less than a year later, Thayer died quietly. He was buried at Braintree but his remains were returned to West Point in 1877. The remaining three professors of the "old guard" retired within a few years. Professor of Drawing Robert Weir left the Academy in 1876; Albert E. Church, Professor of Mathematics died in 1878; and Chemistry, Mineralogy, and Geology Professor Henry L. Kendrick retired in 1880. Thayer had chosen his professors well, including two non-graduates: Agnel of the French Department and Drawing Professor Weir.

The replacements were all graduates with questionable qualifications to become professors heading their respective departments. The new Profesor of French, George L. Andrews, had resigned his commission in 1855, four years after graduating; he earned promotions from lieutenant colonel to major general during the Civil War. Charles W. Larned's sole qualification to head the Department of Drawing was one tour as an instructor under Weir. Apparently no attempt was made to find a qualified civilian artist as Thayer had done in bringing Weir to West Point. Junius P. Wheeler, Mahan's successor, Class of 1855, had earned three brevet promotions during the Civil War and had been an assistant professor for six years prior to his appointment after Mahan's death. Peter S. Michie, second man in the Class of 1863, had earned four brevet promotions during the Civil War, the last the rank of brigadier general. He had been Assistant

Professor of Engineering for six years when he was appointed Professor of Natural Philosophy when Bartlett retired. Kendrick's successor, Lieutenant Samuel E. Tillman, Class of 1869, had been an assistant professor for six years before his appointment as Professor of Chemistry, Mineralogy, and Geology. Edgar W. Bass, Class of 1868, had served as assistant professor for six years after graduating. He was appointed Professor of Mathematics after Church's death in 1878. With the departure of the Thayer Academic Board, whose tenure as professors averaged nearly forty years per man, the Military Academy entered a new era with new and younger guidance.

The turmoil and anguish caused by the Smith problem and the departure of the old professors was increased by another critical problem in 1871, almost a repeat of the cadet honor fiasco in 1866. While the Smith court was still in session, Cadets William Baird and McDowell Barnes apparently made periodic trips to Buttermilk Falls on what the *New York Tribune* called "whiskey frolics," often bringing liquor back to Baird's roommate, Enoch Flickinger. During the night of January 2, 1871, Baird left his room before Tattoo for several hours, going to Buttermilk Falls wearing civilian clothing. While he was gone, his roommate, Enoch Flickinger, twice reported "All right, Sir," to the cadet guard making his periodic inspections. The "All right," which had been adopted shortly after Thayer left West Point in 1833, meant that any absentee was on an authorized absence, that all the individuals in the room were authorized to be there, and that a cadet challenged by a sentinel was authorized to be out of his room. Flickinger's reply meant a violation of the cadet honor code—an outright lie. Baird had asked his roommate to cover his absence; it is not known whether he specifically asked Flinkinger to give an all right for him. While he was gone, their classmate, McDowell Barnes, had left his own room to join Flinkinger, reporting "All right" to the sentry, and had spent the evening with Flinkinger. The sentinel apparently believed that something was not proper about the reports given and included the incident in his report to the cadet Officer of the Day, who in turn included the sentry's comment in his own report to the Commandant.

At parade the next afternoon, orders were read placing the three cadets under arrest pending investigation of charges of making false official statements. The First Class was outraged. That evening, the entire First Class (less eight men who were absent: one on guard, one in the hospital, and six who refused to participate) met to determine a course of action. The thirty-eight men were organized in squads and about midnight went to the rooms of the cadets under arrest; there was no challenge by a guard because the guards were dismissed at Tattoo. Awakening the three culprits, they ordered them to make no noise and waited while they put on civilian clothing. President Grant's son Frederick was leader of one squad and, when Flickinger said he had no civilian clothing, brought him a coat. The class marched the three up the hill toward Fort Putnam to a road leading southward to Buttermilk Falls, where they were told to leave and never to return to West Point, emphasis being placed on the fact that the entire First Class was taking this action. The three spent the night in Buttermilk Falls before proceeding to friends' homes in Poughkeepsie and New York City.

The next morning at reveille, all three were reported absent without leave. A quick investigation proved them to be absent, and they were reported to the War Department as deserters. In the meantime, the three evictees wrote to the First Class to ask that their clothing and other valuables be sent to them. This was done with an additional warning not to return. Baird and Flickinger sent a notarized statement to the Superintendent describing what had happened. General Pitcher immediately sent an officer to arrest the three as deserters and return them to West Point. The *Tribune* reported that the three, "instead of receiving the sympathy and support of the officers of the Academy, were urged to sign resignations. Shortly thereafter, Pitcher issued a statement to the Corps, condemning their action and restricting the First Class to the area of the Plain; only the group who had not participated were exempted.

Initially the daily press contained reports about the "outrage," but within days emphasis returned to the Smith court martial. Within three weeks, nothing was reported about the First Class action against the three plebes. Reaction in military circles was relatively mild; most officers understood what had happened and the reasons for the First Class arbitrary action against Baird, Barnes, and Flickinger. The quasi-official *Army and Navy Journal* condemned the action taken but stated that "in characterizing the conduct of the first class as violently insubordinate, we do not forget that the members were actuated by a high sensitiveness for cadet honor; but it will never do to allow them to assume the office of judge, jury, and executioner in a case of this kind." Reaction in Congress was more outraged. An investigating committee went to West Point to hold hearings on the honor case. One of the first things the committee learned was that the Fourth Class cadets, classmates of Baird, Barnes, and Flickinger, had taken a pledge to refrain from taking any alcoholic beverage if the three were re-admitted to the Academy. The First Class justified its action by stating that lying had become so prevalent at the Academy that it felt obligated to make an example of the three offenders in order to maintain the honor of the Corps. There is little doubt that this claim tacitly referred to Smith's false official statements at two different times. The Class also stated that twenty-one of twenty-two cadets who had been dismissed by court martial rulings were reinstated by Washington authorities, this to them meaning that a Court Martial could not be relied upon to punish offenders. The *Tribune* summarized the subcommittee hearings with the statement that "there seems to be but one opinion on the subject among the members of Congress and that is that the conduct of Academy officials should be censured and such punishment inflicted on the offending class as will insure the academy against any future introduction of mob law among the cadets." It also reported the rumor that the House would take action to remove all of the officers at the Academy and to expel the entire First Class.

Fortunately, that rumor proved untrue. The three cadets were reinstated.

Barnes was found academically deficient at the January examinations and discharged; Flickinger resigned. Baird graduated with the Class of 1875. The congressional committee severely criticized the handling of the case by Academy authorities, for giving the First Class such lenient punishment, and for first persuading the cadets to resign and then for accepting the resignations without concurrence of the parents; Baird and Flickinger were both under age. The Committee demanded that a military Court of Inquiry determine exactly which members of the First Class had been involved and that these cadets be dismissed.

The Secretary of War ignored these recommendations. Strangely, the strongest supporter of the Academy in Congress proved to be Benjamin Butler, who maintained that the Committee resolutions were unjustified. However, when Pitcher and Upton demanded a Court of Inquiry, which they hoped would find the Committee censure unwarranted, Secretary Belknap did appoint an inquiry panel. This essentially was the result of the Court of Inquiry, which also chose to ignore the recommendations of the congressional committee.

Both the Boyd incident in 1866 and the 1871 case emphasized the feeling of the Corps that cadets should handle honor violations, taking severe action against offenders who did not meet the standards of the Corps. Lying and stealing were not condoned. The *Boston Globe* in June 1870 tried to explain cadet honor to its readers, stating that the cadet sense of honor had never been fully explained to the general public. "A pledge is the most sacredly esteemed matter that can be imagined," stated the reporter. When the newsman was unsuccessful in getting information from a cadet, he insisted because "no one will know that you told it; I'll see that that never comes out." The cadet replied, "Sir, honor here is not what it is elsewhere. It is honor. *Honor is a sacred thing with us!*" The reporter went on to explain that a cadet under arrest and restricted to his room or to the guardhouse was not locked up or even watched as a civil prisoner would be. "He is simply made acquainted with his sentence. He observes the penalty as strictly as among a cordon of bayonets hemmed him in. This is honor. If such a system could be infused into the discipline of civil education, what a marvellous improvement that would be in the system! Oh, for more of such *honoring of honor!*"

What was needed was a formal code for the cadet honor system. Had such a code been instituted in 1866 after the Boyd incident, the 1871 problem might not have taken place. Any attempt to codify the honor system at this time was nullified by the report of the congressional committee statement that cadets should never be permitted to take action on their own. Both incidents also indicated that West Point authorities and the War Department did not want to permit cadets to take action on their own. There is no question whatsoever that this attitude was completely correct; cadets should not be able to force honor violators to leave the Academy. What was needed was official recognition of a cadet honor group that would review reported violations of the honor code, determine the guilt of an accused, and then report the case to the Commandant and Superintendent for final action. This would have placed the responsibility for monitoring the honor code on the Corps, with the full understanding that the Academy authorities would support the cadet committee recommendations when its findings were justified. This was not done, not even started, until the 1890s.

Four black cadets entered the Academy in the 1870s. Only one, Henry Ossian Flipper, graduated; the other three were dismissed for academic deficiencies. Flipper and John Washington Williams (Williams was a cadet for only six months, failing the January examinations) were Smith's roommates during Smith's last year as a cadet. One would expect that Smith, as an older cadet, would guide Flipper and Williams into following his own attitudes toward his fellow cadets and Academy officials. If Smith made such an attempt, it had no influence on Flipper. He had decided, even before entering the Academy, that he would do everything possible to avoid antagonizing his fellow cadets, adopting a course that would today be described as "not rocking the boat" or "not upsetting the apple cart." This decision was made before he left his home in Atlanta. When a local newspaper wanted to publicize his appointment with a detailed biography, Flipper refused to give the editor permission lest "too great a knowledge of me should precede me, such, for example, as a publication of that kind would give."

Upton's advice to cadets concerning a black cadet's rights and the definite probability of dismissal for harassment had convinced the Corps that the best policy was to leave black cadets completely alone. Smith had lived by himself until Flipper arrived. A year later, Smith had been dismissed for academic deficiency; and, although he had occasional black roommates, all of whom were dismissed for academic failures, Flipper lived alone for the greater part of four years. Smith had tried to impose himself into white cadet activities with dire results; Flipper made no effort to impose himself upon his white classmates. Spoken to only in line of duty, he suffered through his lonely years in silence, hearing his own voice only when he recited in class.

Flipper had little trouble with academics. His schooling in the American Missionary Association school and his four years at Atlanta University had given him a solid academic background, which enabled him to meet Academy academic criteria. In a way, his solitary life may have helped him academically, for he was able to concentrate on his studies with no distractions. He graduated fiftieth in his class of seventy-six.

During his four years at West Point, many cadets gradually began to accept his presence and to admire his fortitude and willingness to live his lonely life without complaint. Although most cadets followed the Corps' tacit agreement to associate with Flipper only in the line of duty, some cadets quietly made their support known to him. In his autobiography, Flipper told of one incident when he was walking post at camp. He heard his name called softly; and, when he neared the spot where he thought the call had originated, he found a classmate, also on guard at the next post. They talked quietly, and the cadet expressed regret at the treatment he had received and "assured me that he would ever be a friend and treat me as a gentleman should." Others expressed similar feelings. At graduation, he was the only graduate greeted with cheers.

Many cadets and faculty members congratulated Flipper. Cadets went to his room to shake his hand. Flipper wrote of how much these gestures meant to him, "I prized these good words of the cadets above all others. They knew me thoroughly. They meant what they said, and I felt I was in some way deserving of all I received from them by way of congratulation. . . . All signs of ostracism were gone. All felt I was worthy of some regard, and did not fail to extend it to me."

One wonders why there was so much resistance to blacks entering the Academy and why they were treated in this manner. Professor George Andrews in an 1880 article in *International Review* maintained that the West Point reaction "is a feeling everywhere prevalent, at least in this country, and is to be found in those who are loudest in condemning the same feeling in others." Andrews asserted that the cadet attitude toward the black cadets had been established "in their respective homes scattered throughout the country. That Southern cadets, with their opinion of the colored race, would kindly welcome such newcomers was not to be expected," he continued, "but most, if not all, of even the Northern cadets had similar and almost equally strong feelings." The cadet from a northern state, in Andrews' opinion, might be willing to admit the legal rights of the black, but he was "but little, if at all, more inclined to admit them to social equality." Andrews told of a father, bringing his son to West Point to enter the Academy as a classmate of Smith and Howard, who was enthusiastic about the two blacks becoming cadets. When a tactical officer told him that his son would be welcome to room with one of them, he "sputtered with alarm and indignation."

Flipper, in his autobiography, provided a different analysis of the problem, an analysis that truly shows the intelligence and keen insight of the man. His statements might have been made in far more recent years.

> Now in these recent years, there has been a great clamor for rights. The clamor has reached West Point, and, if no bad results have come from it materially, West Point has nevertheless received a bad reputation, and I think an undeserved one, as respects her treatment of colored cadets.
>
> Among those who, claiming social equality, claim it as a right, there exists the greatest possible diversity of creeds, instincts, and of moral and mental conditions, in which they are widely different from those with whom they claim this equality. They can therefore have no rights socially in common; or, in other words, the social equality they claim is not a right, and ought not to and cannot exist under present circumstances, and any law that overreaches the moral reason to the contrary must be admitted as unjust if not impolite.
>
> But it is color, they say, color only, which determines how the negro must treated. Color is his misfortune, and his treatment must

be his misfortune also. Mistaken idea! and one of which we should speedily rid ourselves. It may be color in some cases, but in the great majority of instances it is mental and moral condition. Little or no education, little moral refinement, and all their repulsive consequences will never be accepted as equals of education, intellectual or moral.

Flipper had little adverse criticism of his four years as a cadet. "I expected all sorts of ill-treatment," he wrote, "and yet from the day I entered till the day I graduated I had not cause to utter so much as an angry word. I refused to obtrude myself upon the white cadets, and treated them all with uniform courtesy. I have been treated likewise." Professor Andrews certainly made a profound statement when he said that "the story of the colored cadets at West Point might have been quite different if Flipper had been the first instead of Smith."

There were unusual events involving the Corps. In late February 1873, Secretary of War Belknap ordered the Corps to Washington to march in Ulysses Grant's inaugural parade. The trip was long and tiring. Crossing the river by marching on the ice, the Corps entrained for New York, where a ferry carried them to New Jersey and another train ride. Despite intense cold on March 4, the cadets paraded without overcoats. Many attended the inaugural ball; others were guests of Washington residents. This was the first appearance of the Corps in an inaugural parade; it has marched before every new President since that date.

Equally of note, possibly much more important to the cadets, was the Corps' participation in the Centennial Exposition in Philadelphia in 1876. A camp was set up for the cadets on the exposition grounds. The seven-day stay was the longest time the Corps had spent away from West Point as a group since its march to Boston in 1821. Cadets enjoyed themselves despite the twice daily parades and extremely strict discipline imposed by the Commandant. Their letters reflect a keen interest in the exhibits and their enjoyment of the change from the normal routine of summer camp at West Point.

Their time in Philadelphia ended all too quickly, and they returned to their summer instruction. Young ladies visiting the Academy often had difficulty finding lodging, especially when special events, such as Camp Illumination, were scheduled. Both the West Point Hotel and Cozzens Hotel in Highland Falls (Buttermilk Falls had changed its name to Highland Falls when the area was incorporated as the town of Highlands) were full for much of the summer, and several other lodging establishments were made available. Advertisements of the time carried notices of at least ten boarding houses in every issue. There were three hotels in addition to Cozzens, and several cottages were offered for rent. These advertisements carried names familiar to West Point in earlier years. M. Appel operated a shop that featured "Domestic and Imported Segars" and daily and weekly newspapers. The proprietor was a descendent of Band Master

Appel. Another familiar name was R. A. Berard, who offered rooms in his boarding house. W. M. Berard advertised "Ice Cream, Confectionery, and Stationery, etc. on call and supplied on order." Both Berards were descendants of Claudius Berard, Professor of French from 1815 until his death in 1846. Two preparatory schools were operated by retired graduates. Many enlisted men also retired in the area. The proximity of the village to the Academy enabled them to maintain West Point contacts and to participate in Academy activities.

The newly formed Association of Graduates held annual meetings at West Point. Although the first two meetings were attended by few graduates other than those stationed at West Point, increased numbers were present each year. In 1874, Charles Davies, Class of 1815 and former Professor of Mathematics, urged the passage of a resolution the following year for a reunion of all graduates, both those who served the Union and those who fought for the Confederacy. Davies eloquently asserted that "from the sunny memories of many joys common to them all, and from the grave of all painful recollections never to be disturbed by thought, by word, or by deed, there will spring up a closer brotherhood, a purer patriotism, and a more abiding love of country." Unfortunately, the reunion envisioned by Davies did not take place for many years. Memories of the war were still too poignant, not only among graduates but most of the country as well. Typical of the still existing feel were the words of the oath required of officers as late as 1881. Emory Upton, when promoted to Colonel of the 4th Artillery, was required to state that "I have never voluntarily borne arms against the United States since I have been a citizen thereof; that I have voluntarily given no aid, countenance, counsel, or encouragement to persons engaged in armed hostility thereto; that I have neither sought, nor accepted, nor attempted to exercise the function of any office whatsoever, under any authority, or pretended authority, in hostility to the United States; that I have not yielded a voluntary support to any pretended government, authority, power, or constitution within the United States, hostile or inimical thereto." Time had not yet healed the wounds left by that conflict.

The first decade after Appomattox had seen the Academy face one crisis after another. Reports of hazing, despite Academy officials' effort to stop the practice, were highly critical. Two instances of cadets taking direct action to force honor code offenders to leave West Point were disastrous. The problems caused by the entry of the first black cadets brought unwanted and adverse publicity in the majority of the daily press. The departure of the Academic Board, Thayer's "old guard," created a void not completely filled by the newly appointed professors. What was needed was a tightening of the belt and the joint resolve of the Corps and the faculty to close ranks and move forward together.

20

Guard Well Your Heritage

The turmoil caused by problems at West Point was not unnoticed by graduates. The obvious mishandling of the black cadet problem, hazing incidents, and the cadet attempted punishment of honor code violations caused much concern. Near the end of his second term, President Grant and General in Chief William T. Sherman, both graduates of the Academy, realized that strong and effective action had to be taken immediately. Their first step was to persuade Major General John M. Schofield, Class of 1853, to be superintendent. This was unusual. Schofield was the third ranking general officer in the Army; although brevet general officers had served as both commandant of cadets and superintendent, this was the first time a general of regular rank was named superintendent. Schofield had little to gain from this appointment and realized that without major support in Washington he would be unable to improve the Academy operations and academic activities.

Schofield realized that his efforts would be hampered by three different groups: Congress, the Academic Board, and the War Department, specifically the Secretary of War. Difficulties with individual Congressmen and Senators had plagued superintendents since Thayer's time. Congressmen too often appointed cadets who did not have the educational background to pass even the simple entrance exams, let alone maintain proficiency in Academy studies. Efforts by superintendents, including Thayer, to have Congress enact legislation making entrance examinations more difficult were fruitless. As a result, only a small percentage of each class graduated four years later. Congressmen insisted that simple examinations were necessary if every young man was to have equal opportunity to enter the Academy. They also pressured the Secretary of War and the President to reinstate cadets dismissed for academic deficiencies or misconduct. The aftermath of the Civil War found many Congressmen still maintaining that West Point and its graduates were disloyal. Led by Benjamin Butler and John Logan, this group constantly criticized the Academy. Logan recommended abolishing the institution and replacing it by commissioning graduates of colleges and universities, which would be encouraged to establish military programs as part of their curriculum.

The Academic Board presented a different problem. Appointed by the President for an indefinite period, the professors were not officers, although they did receive the equivalent pay of regular officers. Consequently, a superintendent could not give them orders. As a member of the Academic Board and ad hoc chairman, he had only one vote and could only recommend and persuade. Schofield considered this unmilitary. The long tenure of the men Thayer had groomed to become professors was criticized by graduates and by many Boards of Visitors. Emory Upton wrote to General Sherman in October 1871, expressing his belief that the "new professors" would join the Superintendent, Colonel Thomas Ruger, in preventing the Academy from "sinking back into the mire of the past four years." Upton blamed the postwar lethargy on the tendency of the Thayer professors to forget that "to his [Thayer's] vigor and resolution the prosperity of the Academy was then due," indicating that the old professors thought that they, not Thayer, were responsible for the successful status of the Academy. The departure of Thayer's "old guard" did not lessen the complaints because the newer members of the Academic Board continued to resist curriculum changes. Despite the changed needs of the Army, the professors insisted that the basic engineering composition of Academy studies remain the same. Unquestionably, their belief that emphasis on mathematics engendered logical reasoning in the cadets was true, but the Army no longer needed the heavily weighted engineering subjects.

Equally criticized was the indefinite tenure of the professors appointed by the President. Schofield advocated appointing professors for a specified and limited tenure. To accomplish this objective, he also urged that the professors have rank as officers of the Army instead of civilian status with the pay of officers. If this system was adopted, a superintendent would truly be in command of West Point and the Academy. Schofield's concept would have limited the Academic Board to the control of curricular activities only, removing them from acting on other West Point affairs. It would also have lessened the tendency of various professors to write to former pupils—and even the Secretary of War and the President directly—to negate efforts of superintendents to improve or change Academy operations. Unfortunately, Schofield's concept was not adopted for many years and then only in a sporadic manner.

The 1866 Act authorizing the appointment of the superintendent from branches other than the Corps of Engineers and the subsequent order relieving the Chief of Engineers as Inspector of the Military Academy caused an unexpected problem. The Superintendent now reported directly to the Secretary of War, a chain of command that soon became ponderous and troublesome. Trivial matters, from approval of the selection of new textbooks to scheduling leave for officers required secretarial approval. Far more important, however, was the removal of the Chief of Engineers as an Academy advocate in Washington. General Joseph Totten during his long tenure as Chief of Engineers had served not only as an intermediate link between the Superintendent and the Secretary of War, but also as a direct link with Congressmen and Senators—what would today be called "legislative liaison." After the Chief of Engineers was stripped of his role as Inspector of the Academy, the Secretary of War often took action on Academy matters without informing the General of the Army, General Sherman.

Writing to Secretary of War James Cameron in December 1876, less than four months after his appointment, Schofield informed Cameron that the 1876 Board of Visitors "strongly recommended the appointment by Congress at an early date of a commission to revise the course of study and discipline." The Board had commented on its opinion that "neither the Secretary of War nor the Academic Board nor both together can be expected to determine upon the changes to be made." Such a commission would make a one-time study of the curriculum and determine necessary modifications. The Board of Visitors, stated Schofield, further recommended the appointment of a board of trustees similar to those of other institutions.

Schofield informed the Secretary that "such a mode of supervision and control would not be compatible with the military principles which should govern the Military Academy as a school for the Army. I understand it was the purpose of the President in selecting a General Officer for the command to give the Academy a Military Government." Schofield placed the blame for the well-justified comments of the Board of Visitors primarily on the Academic Board and, to a lesser degree, on the various superintendents since the Civil War. "I accepted the Superintendency," he continued," with the understanding that I was to regulate these things under the supervision and with the assistance of the General Commanding the Army, and subject to the approval of the Secretary of War as required by law." In accordance with those instructions, Schofield had recommended changes to the academic regulations, which he urged the Secretary to approve.

"I did not seek this duty nor do I yet desire it," wrote Schofield. "If I am to do it I beg to be informed with no unnecessary delay." He emphatically stated that the 1873 Academic Regulations "will show you that the Superintendent has less authority in many respects than the Commander of the least important military post in the Army. The most minute details of 'Interior Police and Discipline' even down to the office hours of the Superintendent are regulated by the 'President of the United States.' " Schofield formally requested that President Grant be asked to approve the authority he had promised Schofield before he appointed him Superintendent. This essentially would enable Schofield to conduct Academy activities with no supervision other than that of the General in Chief, General Sherman.

The War Department solution to this dilemma was to establish the Military Academy as the Department of West Point, one of the major divisions of the Army under Sherman's direct command. As a department commander, Schofield was able to appoint officers to serve on courts martial, approve personnel actions such as officers' requests for leave, and—at least theoretically—command all activities within his command. Although this did solve many of his command problems, he still had to contend with the reinstatement of cadets by the Secretary of War, the same dilemma that had plagued every superintendent. Even this problem was lessened to some extent by his complete support from General Sherman.

Schofield, with Sherman's help, was able to obtain approval of his recommended change to the Academic Regulations that gave him authority to direct the studies. Although he was able to initiate changes in the curriculum, approval of the Academic Board was still required. He might propose a change, but he had only one vote in the approval by the Academic Board. He was handicapped, as had been many previous superintendents, by the reluctance of the members of the Board to change the emphasis on engineering by providing more time for liberal arts subjects and by the even stronger determination of the professors to leave the basic curriculum unchanged.

Schofield, however, was able to keep the Academic Board from interfering with matters of discipline and command of the Corps of Cadets—but only with the direct intervention and support of Sherman. The Board maintained that the Superintendent could not remove demerits once they had been awarded cadets for various infractions and that it, not the superintendent, had sole authority to recommend the dismissal of cadets who were deficient in conduct. Schofield asserted that he and the Commandant of Cadets had the authority to discipline cadets. Unspoken was his belief that the professors, all civilians who had not served in the Army for years, did not understand the Army's requirements for qualified leaders. He and the Commandant considered a cadet's overall character and leadership ability in considering dismissal for disciplinary reasons; the Board did not. Despite support from both the Secretary of War and General Sherman, the matter was never fully resolved, and the Academic Board eventually regained its control of dismissals for either academic or disciplinary deficiencies.

Although approval of academic matters still remained with the Academic Board, Schofield was able to make some changes to the curriculum. Noteworthy was his recommendation that English studies be added to the curriculum and be placed under the Professor of French. Approval came from the Board—by one vote; essentially this meant that Schofield's vote brought that approval.

Schofield, however, was able to institute many changes in military instruction because control of these subjects rested with him and the Commandant of Cadets. Improved instruction in cavalry tactics was emphasized by Schofield; this was needed in his opinion to improve Army actions against Indians. Riding classes for the First and Second Classes were combined to provide cadets an opportunity to drill as company-sized units. Artillery instruction was also improved by obtaining more modern guns. Infantry drill—field drill and rifle marksmanship, not close order marching—emphasized marksmanship and skirmishing. He was responsible for initiating instruction in the use of barges and large boats in military operations, a concept unknown before this time. Cadets were taught to signal by semaphore, heliograph, and telegraph. In all of the tactical instruction, cadets were required to learn the duties of privates and non-commissioned officers as well as those of junior officers. Schofield believed sincerely that a commander had to understand enlisted men and their work if he was to properly command, teach, and correct his men.

Off-duty life at West Point was pleasant in the 1870s and 1880s. Officers and their wives took part in amateur theatricals and tableaux. Many belonged to card clubs that met weekly for games of whist or euchre. During the winter months, officers' dances were held in the Officers' Mess in the south wing of the Cadet Mess Hall. During the summer, officers and their wives attended the cadet hops. Riding in the hills was a favorite recreation for the more athletic. Rides often included a picnic stop at Fort Putnam. There was little swimming; it was not considered ladylike for a young woman to swim in these years. Winter provided an opportunity to skate or enjoy a long ride in horse-drawn sleighs, bells jangling merrily as the team trotted along trails. The ladies enjoyed frequent trips to New York City. One young wife wrote that she and several friends left Garrison at 8:00 A.M., spent the day "examining rugs & chairs & curtains & furniture & walked & saw & chose & selected," returning by the 5:30 P.M. train. There were many guests, and attending the daily parades became almost routine. At times, a young wife accompanied her husband on his last inspection, as one young lady wrote, "I walked his tour with him in the moonlight & we got home at ten minutes past one. It was so much fun—I'd like to do it every time!"

Schofield believed that an officer assigned to duty at West Point should improve his own professional knowledge as well as working with cadets. Using the Thayer Club, which had been founded in 1873, as a study vehicle, officers met once a month to discuss military topics: campaigns, new equipment being considered by the Army, and foreign military doctrine. Attendance was voluntary, however, and many young officers found that preparing for their cadet classes took most of their free time. The Thayer Club continued to meet monthly until World War I, although in its last years it competed with the West Point Chapter of the Military Service Institution for members. In many ways, the Thayer Club was an outgrowth of Mahan's Napoleon Club, the primary difference being that its activities were not restricted to the study of Napoleon's campaigns.

Cadet recreational activities were more limited, primarily because their only free time was on Saturday afternoons and Sundays after Chapel, inspection, and parade. Cadets played a form of baseball, a sport that had started at West Point in the late 1820s. Letters mention windows in barracks being broken when a ball was batted into the area. The Commandant issued an order that ball games were not to be played near barracks. First Classmen often rode into the hills or through Highland Falls on weekends. Rowing on the Hudson and swimming near Washington Valley were summer delights. Fencing, bowling, and exercise were available in the makeshift gymnasium on the ground floor of the Academic Building.

Hops were scheduled three times weekly during the summer and were attended by many young ladies from throughout the eastern seaboard. The hops were more formal; a receiving line was headed by the Commandant and his wife or one of the tactical officers. Hop cards and invitations had changed from the simple listing of dances in the 1860s to ornate programs, often in the shape of uniforms, full dress hats, cannon, or tents. These cards were made by outstanding firms: Bailey, Banks, and Biddle of Philadelphia and Tiffany of New York City, for example. Cadets had the cost of the cards taken from their accounts by the Academy treasurer.

Forays were still made into Highland Falls for an unauthorized dinner and a bit of liquor. The more adventurous rowed across the river to Cold Spring during the summer months or walked across on the ice during the winter. Many were caught by tactical officers and joined other delinquents walking punishment tours in their free time. Cadets were able to obtain food from the confectioner, although supper was no longer optional. The Dialectic Society "dramatic" presentation on New Year's Eve had been moved to one hundred days before graduation, the origin of today's Hundredth Night Show. Most of the presentations parodied minstrel shows with the audience delighted at the ironic comments about other cadets, instructors, and tactical officers. The presentations were attended by most of the Corps and by many officers and their families.

The many official and unofficial visitors to West Point added to the social activities. Official guests almost always received a special review by the Corps and often demonstrations of cavalry and artillery drill. Presidents Grant and Hayes, Secretaries of War, and Generals Sherman, Sheridan, Thomas, Hancock, and other noted graduates were honored during their visits. General Schofield hosted the twenty-fifth reunion of his 1853 Class in 1878. The initial suggestion for this reunion came from William P. Craighill, the same Craighill who had written to his mother of his decision to remain loyal to the Union many years before. Schofield, delighted with the suggestion, wrote to many classmates to invite them to attend. A June 1877 letter to Confederate General John B. Hood stated, "There is no member of the class whose welcome by all would be more cordial than yours. To me especially it would be the greatest pleasure to renew the warm brotherhood of 1853. Let us have a real genuine reunion on the ground where we formed our early attachments." Hood, unfortunately, did not attend. Little is known of the reunion. The group had a dinner at the West Point Hotel the night before graduation with Secretary of War George McCrary, General Sherman, and General Hancock as guests. The next day, the group attended graduation, heard Hancock address the graduating class, and applauded as Secretary McCrary awarded diplomas. One wonders if Craighill and Schofield remembered the 1853 reunion of the graduates who had entered the Academy in 1817. Perhaps Thayer's hope that other classes would follow the example of that group was now being realized.

Cadets noticed changes in academic procedures with varying degrees of interest. Charles Noyes wrote in April 1877 that "Professor Larned has instituted a new feature in his department of Drawing. He is going to give practical instruction in making military surveys. Work started with cadets following the road from the South Gate to Fort Putnam, making notes as they progressed. A month later, Noyes reported that he was "getting very much interested in my drawing. We are now engaged in making the topographical sketch of the survey which was made last month." Because only two or three drawing days remained, Noyes and several classmates took their sketches to their rooms, where they could complete their drawing. Other classmates, however, were not so conscientious and "proposed to bump the malefactors." Noyes said that "after supper I was caught and bumped. It was not pleasant and my pants were badly torn."

Another change was also noted by Noyes. His class was given a demonstration of the phonograph "now in course of development by its inventor Edison, and when complete we will be enabled to bottle up our conversation and have it ground out afterwards from the machine whenever we wish it." Noyes felt that the phonograph would "work wonders one of these days." He also noted that frequent games of baseball were played in front of the barracks and, by contrast, weekly prayer meetings were well attended. He also commented that he "received a little volume of tales from Miss [Anna B.] Warner." Miss Warner lived on Constitution Island for many years and often entertained cadets at her home on weekends. The island and all of her possessions were willed to the Academy after her death.

Normal routine was interrupted in 1877. Schofield extended an invitation to "the officers and students of Vassar College" to visit West Point in early June. The group came by boat on a Saturday and was escorted by cadets and officers to the review and dinner at the hotel. Cadet Charles Noyes wrote in his diary that about 400 young ladies came to West Point and that cadets "put on their best clothes and best looks and went out to try to catch some. Most of them would not admit any approach; a few however were captivated by the pretty coats and shiny buttons, and allowed themselves to be entertained and escorted to parade by a cadet." A number of cadets ran to Gee's Point to give a final cheer as the Vassar boat steamed up river. The Vassar visit became an annual event for several years, much to the enjoyment of the cadets who escorted the young ladies.

Less pleasant were other changes of routine. On October 10, the entire Corps was the escort for George Custer's remains. Cadet Frederick Abbot, Class of 1879, recalled the large number of officials and civilians attending the interment. "The road was almost blocked with the crowd of civilian visitors, the policemen were at their wits' end making a path for the procession and the guides had many a chance to give a severe knock with the butt of a gun to the unsuspecting 'cits' who were strolling along exactly in their path without regard to the 'customs of war in like cases.' " The Corps marched at slow time, their rifles carried at the reverse. After firing three volleys over the grave, the Corps marched back to barracks. Abbot wrote that "it will be long years before they forget the agonies they suffered at Custer's funeral."

Two years later, a bronze statue of Custer was erected on a knoll across the road from the Mess Hall. More than 3,000 visitors attended the dedication, many coming from New York City on an excursion boat. Congress had authorized the use of twenty bronze cannon for the larger-than-life-size statue. Custer was shown in full dress uniform, wearing jack boots, and holding a saber in his right hand and a pistol in his left. His long hair was shown blowing in a breeze. From the outset, the statue was controversial. Schofield was astounded to learn from Mrs. Custer in April that she had not been consulted about sculptor Wilson MacDonald's work. She objected to the selection of MacDonald as sculptor because, in her opinion, he did not have sufficient reputation to execute Custer's statue. Mrs. Custer tried to persuade Schofield to refuse to accept the statue, but this could not be done because the work was almost completed. Mrs. Custer did not attend the dedication nor, as far as is known, did she ever see it.

The controversy did not end with the dedication of the monument. An effort to duplicate the monument and have it placed appropriately in Washington, D.C., failed when a congressional committee, influenced by Mrs. Custer's objections, voted against the project. She continued to voice her objections in many places and to many government officials. Maintaining that the statue had "the face of a man of sixty," was in improper uniform, and that Custer "is armed like a desperado in both hands," Libby Custer continued for years her efforts to have the statue removed. Finally in 1884, Secretary of War Robert Lincoln ordered the Superintendent, General Wesley Merritt, to remove the monument. Eventually, the base was placed on Custer's grave; Mrs. Custer had a granite obelisk added in 1905.

What happened to the statue is unknown. For many years, it rested in a supply shed at West Point. In 1906, Mrs. Custer asked Superintendent Colonel Mills to have the bust removed, and Mills assured her that this would be done. No trace of either the bust or the torso has been found. In 1951, Cadet John Byers became interested in the monument. His research found no record after the 1910 correspondence from Mrs. Custer. It is possible that the body of the statue may have been added to other West Point metal relics contributed to the World War II scrap metal drive. If the bust was placed "in an appropriate place" for permanent display, that place has not been found. All that remains is the base of the monument now on Custer's grave in the West Point cemetery.

A month after the Custer funeral, the Corps escorted the remains of Sylvanus Thayer to the cemetery. The ceremony was similar to the Custer rites. The Corps escorted the casket from the Chapel to the ceremony, followed by a large number of official mourners, mostly graduates. There was, however, no repetition of the civilian crowd present at the Custer funeral. Thayer was not known to the public, although he was revered by Academy graduates. There was another parallel to the Custer incident. In June 1883, a statue of Thayer was erected immediately west of the Cadet Barracks in the grove of trees Thayer and Walker Armistead had planted in 1802. General George Cullum headed a committee that raised funds for the granite statue. Not all graduates showed enthusiasm for the project. General Sherman, for example, refused to contribute to the fund drive, replying to Cullum that "I honestly think it is not incumbent on me to subscribe for the Thayer monument—he was not *my Superintendent*, nor did I ever see him in my life." The attitude of most graduates was best expressed by John Latrobe, non-graduate of the Class of 1822: "There is no memory of a long life that I cherish more affectionately, or that is greener, than the years that I passed under the eye of the kind and just, able and accomplished man, whose form and features will now be perpetuated . . . at the institution which his intelligence and rare Executive and administrative skill brought from chaos into order, and gave to it the impetus . . . which has made it what it is today." The statue remained in this spot until the major building program in the 1970s. It now stands at the northwest corner of the Plain, facing the Academy buildings as though Thayer has a perpetual eye on the institution, which now recognizes him as "Father of the Military Academy."

Another unusual incident had Schofield send copies of Academy textbooks and regulations to Said Pasha, Minister de la Marine at Constantinople. Reporting the shipment to the Adjutant General in Washington, Schofield requested that the cost of the books, $73.27, and the Wells Fargo express charge of $17.30 be paid to the Academy Treasurer! A third unusual event took place during a yellow fever epidemic in the South. Officers and cadets contributed $515.50 to assist relief efforts. Schofield sent this contribution to Secretary of War McCrary, saying that "I beg you will do us the favor to direct it into the proper channel." Another unusual letter in December 1879 asked Lieutenant Charles A. L. Totten to come to West Point to demonstrate his game "Strategos." Totten's game had created so much interest that an Army Board of Officers, headed by Colonel August Kautz, had studied the game. Totten's concept may have been an early form of what is today known as "war gaming." Unfortunately, a description of the game cannot be found.

Schofield was besieged with requests to re-admit cadets discharged or turned back to the next class for academic or disciplinary deficiencies. His replies were quite firm in refusing to take any action. A letter to Judge W. W. Lyston in October 1877 indicated that, despite sincere regret not to comply with the judge's wishes, Schofield had "dealt with the present cases quite as mildly as the circumstances would justify, and I am unwilling that any subsequent action in respect to them shall leave Cadets any ground for hope that the same offense in future will not be followed by irrevocable dismissal."

The widow of Confederate General Archibald Gracie, Jr., wrote to Schofield to ask his "candid opinion" of why her son had so many demerits. Schofield replied, "This is surely a 'conundrum' which I verily believe no one can 'find out.' In my search for a solution of the question, I find from the ancient records that both Cadets Gracie & Schofield of 1854 and 1853 were about as *bad boys* as your son seems to be—perhaps worse. Why we got so many demerits I cannot tell and do not believe either of us could have told at the time. I am certain we did not do it 'on purpose.' " Schofield indicated that "Mothers will worry about them, but it does not do the least bit of good. So, dear Madam, I beg you do not be anxious about your son. He seems to be doing as well as he can & he will come out 'all right' in the end." Schofield was wrong; young Gracie was dismissed the following year.

Far more serious was the Congressional Military Academy Bill of 1878, which specified that the graduating class would not be assured of commissions in the Army. Schofield wrote to General Sherman of the probable impact of that bill on the Academy. "Young men," asserted Schofield, "have obtained their Cadet appointments and spent nearly four years of hard work in the hope and expectation of gaining commissions in the Army. Now, at the last moment, when they are about to graduate, it is proposed to deny them the commissions they have earned and turn them adrift." For many years, newly graduated officers often were not given regular commissions until vacancies occurred in their regiments through deaths, resignations, transfers, or promotions. Instead, these graduates were given brevet second lieutenant commissions or were carried as "additional second lieutenants" on their unit rosters. In some cases, permanent ranks of classmates originally commissioned in this manner were one or two years behind the date of rank of their more fortunate classmates. This would be stopped by the 1878 bill; the graduating class would receive commissions only to fill definite vacancies; those not commissioned would be, as Schofield stated, "turned adrift."

If Congress decided to educate more cadets than were required for the Army, this should be made known in advance, asserted Schofield. Cadets would then know that they were competing for commissions and that a definite number could rely upon receiving commissions. This would benefit the Academy and would increase the general excellence of its classes. "But," continued Schofield, "to make the success of those who reach a high degree of excellence depend upon the accidental number of vacancies in the Army, 'on the first day of July in each year' would certainly break down the West Point standard of education and reduce it to the common level."

The 1878 Board of Visitors also criticized the proposed bill in a different way. The Board report pointed to "a fact which is little familiar, and that is, that the graduates of the Military Academy at West Point do not, as is popularly supposed, hold the largest proportion of commissions in the Army . . . but 42.1 percent being West Point graduates; while the present number of annual graduates from the Academy is not sufficient to supply the annual vacancies occurring in the list of officers." Schofield, in an August 1877 letter to a young man desiring an Army commission, supported this statement by the Board, "There are now some thirty or forty additional second lieutenants of the Class of 1877, who are awaiting absorption into regiments," between 40 and 50 percent of a class of seventy-six graduates. The Board then discussed the reason there were insufficient vacancies for the graduating classes, "The reason why the Academy is now apparently furnishing a surplus of graduates is not because there is not a sufficient annual demand for officers in the Army, but because vacancies occurring in commissions have been and are applied by appointments, and by promotions from the ranks."

Schofield's arguments, aided by firm support from General Sherman, the Secretary of War, and the Board of Visitors were successful. The bill, amended and passed in June 1878, provided that "hereafter all vacancies in the grade of second lieutenant shall be filled by appointment from the graduates of the Military Academy so long as any such remain in service unassigned; and any vacancies thereafter remaining shall be filled by promotion of meritorious non-commissioned officers of the Army."

By coincidence, a similar situation exists in 1992. A bill sponsored by Senator Sam Nunn of Georgia will eliminate regular commissioning of Academy graduates and ROTC Distinguished Military Graduates beginning in 1996. No individual may be eligible for a regular commission until one year after his commissioning as a reserve second lieutenant. The impact of the current legislation upon the Academy is only a matter of conjecture at this time. It may result in a lessening of applications for appointments. Young men today, as in Schofield's time, may not be willing to devote four years of discipline and hard work, of near-monastic existence and comparative isolation, followed by a minimum of four years of obligatory service after graduation if only a reserve commission is available at the end of four years of study. Under this act, the graduate would receive the same commission as that given any ROTC graduate, the young man who took military science as little more than a sidelight to his regular college education. Amazingly, even the percentage of graduates given regular commissions between 1964 and 1992 was about 40 percent of the total number of officers commissioned, approximately the same percentage cited by the 1878 Board of Visitors. Perhaps Schofield's comment to Sherman applies equally to the present situation, "This mania for tinkering with established institutions is one of the greatest evils of our government."

The suppression of hazing in the immediate years after the Civil War was only temporarily successful. The harsh measures taken by West Point authorities and the War Department greatly decreased the mistreatment of plebes for several years, but when Schofield was appointed superintendent in 1876, cadets had resumed many of the unauthorized and unwarranted practices of the late 1860s. Schofield took prompt action against offenders by having them court martialed and dismissed. His letters reveal his concern and describe his efforts to not only curtail but eliminate cadet hazing.

Replying to a letter from Pennsylvania Congressman Sam J. Randall, Schofield told Randall that he had interviewed Cadet Louis Ostheim and that Ostheim denied that "he has been hazed to any degree worthy of notice." Schofield described Ostheim as a timid youth who might be afraid to reveal the true situation. To Schofield this case illustrated the difficulty of trying to totally eradicate hazing. "I have tried to encourage Ostheim and others of like character to defend themselves, at least so far as to expose those who annoy them. Unless their manhood can be developed, their brightness and intelligence can be made of very little use in the Military service."

Hampering Schofield's efforts were the tendencies of the Secretary of War and the President to reinstate cadets dismissed for hazing. Returning from leave in July 1877, Schofield reported to Sherman that "all goes well here, except the matter of hazing and that will be righted in due time if the President will firmly sustain me in my efforts to enforce obedience. Unfortunately, the cadets rely upon the President's well known kindness to save them from extreme penalties." He reported that the new Fourth Class had already shown "some manhood in resisting the outrageous treatment of a few rowdies in the Third Class and will probably enable us to get rid of some of the latter."

The steps taken by Schofield were unusual for that time. He informed cadet officers that it was their duty to protect plebes from mistreatment; those who did not do so were subject to the same punishment as cadets hazing plebes: trial by court martial and dismissal. He instructed the Commandant that a tactical officer would be present at all times during new cadet drills and that the officer would be assisted by as many cadet officers as necessary. "Constant care should be taken to *instruct the drill-masters themselves* and to correct their errors; to require them to properly regulate the tone and character of the voice in which commands and instructions are given; to avoid harsh, improper, or even unnecessary words in reproving or correcting the errors of those under their instruction." This was a new concept, a radical departure from the prevailing practice in the Army and the Academy. New enlisted men were under the supervision of a non-commissioned officer; their training verged on being brutal in many instances. Schofield's approach is remarkably similar to current Army practices, although it was truly unusual in the late 1870s. "One of the most important elements of military education," Schofield continued in his instructions to the Commandant, "respects the manner and the language which may and ought to be held by superiors toward their inferiors, both when on or off duty." Schofield emphasized that the important object of this instruction was, not only to teach the new cadets, but also "to teach the older cadets how to *instruct* and *to command*—the latter being in fact the great end of West Point education."

Realizing that directing the Commandant, his tactical officers, and cadet officers only would be insufficient to accomplish his purpose, Schofield addressed the entire Corps of Cadets on August 11, 1879. At the outset, Schofield drew their complete attention by stating, "I am taking this mode, rather than that of a printed order, of saying what I wish to strongly impress upon your minds, partly because I am doing my duty toward you as your instructor, quite as much as my duty toward the Government as your commander." Attempting to convince the cadets that hazing was an immoral practice, Schofield compared it with arson and slavery. Slavery, "inherited from our ancestors," he commented, was now condemned "because it is a violation of the natural rights of man and because it is injurious to all concerned." In the same way, hazing deprived fellow cadets of the rights given him by his appointment and guaranteed by laws and regulations. "It is therefore," strongly asserted Schofield, "nothing more or less than ROBBERY."

Schofield discussed the development of hazing at the Academy, pointing out that thirty years earlier, hazing at West Point was restricted for the most part to comparatively harmless sport. There was no use of demeaning names or epithets when speaking to a new cadet. "Thirty years ago," he said, "if a new cadet had been assailed with the words 'you d——m slimy beast,' he would have done his best to kill his assailant on the spot. Any one who would have addressed another in such words would have been denounced and 'cut' even by his own class."

After reviewing the development to the current injurious practices, Schofield discussed the impact of harsh treatment when imparting military instruction. His words have endured to the present day; a bronze plaque in the barracks area cites a part of Schofield's address to the Corps, which plebes have been required to memorize for decades:

> The discipline which makes the soldiers of a free country reliable in battle is not to be gained by harsh and tyrannical treatment. On the contrary, such treatment is far more likely to defeat than to make an army. It is possible to impart instruction and give commands in such a manner and in such tone of voice as to inspire in the soldier no feeling but an intense desire to obey. While the opposite manner and tone of voice can not fail to excite strong resentment and a desire to disobey. The one mode or the other of dealing with subordinates springs from a corresponding spirit in the breast of the commander. He who feels the respect which is due to others can not fail to inspire in them regard for himself. While he who feels, and hence manifests, disrespect toward others, especially his inferiors, can not fail to inspire hatred against himself.

The wise advice given the Corps appeared to have impressed and been accepted by the cadets. Writing to the President on another matter, Schofield told President Hayes that he had "read to the cadets a pretty sharp lecture upon the subject of hazing." In his estimation, the result of that lecture could be determined in September when the remainder of the new plebe class arrived. "Strange as it may appear," he wrote, "the habit has prevailed for several years among fourth classmen who were hazed in June and July to haze their own classmates in September." He expressed his hope of stopping that practice as a result of his lecture and the instructions he had given the Commandant and the cadet officers.

The entry of Johnson C. Whittaker in 1876, a black, had caused few problems in the Corps; he was simply ignored by other cadets. During his plebe year,

Whittaker roomed with Henry Flipper. After Flipper graduated with the Class of 1877, Whittaker had another black roommate, Charles A. Minnie until Minnie was dismissed for academic deficiency in January 1888, and Whittaker roomed alone for the remainder of his time as a cadet. One would think that living with Flipper for a year would have benefitted Whittaker, that Flipper would have convinced him to follow his example of quietly tolerating his loneliness and avoiding any possible problems with white cadets. Whittaker instead generally patterned his demeanor after the behavior of the first black cadet, James Smith.

In early 1878, Whittaker was struck by Cadet John B. McDonald. Their classmate George W. Goethals wrote to a friend of the episode: "In the gymnasium one day McD went to get his hat and overcoat when the darkey went in front of him and stood in his way. McD told him to get out of his way. Mr. W. replied that he wouldn't, after we broke ranks McD hit him in the mouth and drew 'claret.' Mr. W. immediately went to see 'Grandma' [the cadet nickname for Commandant Henry M. Lazelle]. McD was immediately put in arrest and confined to light prison; he was court martialled, found guilty, and dismissed the service of the U. States."

Almost immediately, efforts were made to have McDonald reinstated. McDonald, according to Goethals, after leaving West Point, "immediately went directly to General Sherman explained matters, and Gen. S. gave him a paper of some kind and said if Gen. Schofield would sign it, he would reinstate him. I don't know if the Sup. signed the paper or not but it's thought that he did." No documentary evidence has been found to support Goethal's statement; it must be considered a cadet rumor or "sinkoid." Congressmen and Senators, however, did attempt to have the Secretary of War reinstate McDonald. When these efforts failed, they went to President Hayes. Hayes wrote to Schofield in December 1879, "The friends of John B. McDonald, cadet, are very anxious that he should not be put back one year. Any other punishment thought suitable to the case would be preferred. If they can be accommodated in this matter, it would be agreeable to my feelings if in your judgment not prejudicial to the Service."

Although Schofield had already informed Sherman that he was convinced that McDonald should not be reinstated, he maintained that his offense was "essentially the same in the degree of offense" of five other cadets who had been dismissed for hazing. Despite Schofield's opinion, the entire group was reinstated but turned back to join later classes. Of the six, only McDonald and one other cadet graduated; the others were later dismissed for academic deficiencies. Several nights after the reinstatement was announced, there was a riotous New Year's Eve celebration in barracks, so much so that Schofield "heard the firing, got up and saw the rockets." Reporting to General Sherman, Schofield indicated that the majority of the Corps and almost all of the First Class had been involved. He indicated that he intended to take prompt action "in accordance with my own legal authority." Schofield believed that it would be senseless to court martial the cadets responsible because they obviously believed that they would be reinstated. Instead, reductions in rank, restrictions to their rooms, and punishment tours would be proper. This action was followed by Schofield's momentous lecture on hazing.

Relative quiet resulted. For nearly eighteen months, Schofield faced few problems involving hazing or other ungentlemanly conduct. The calm degenerated into a storm in early April 1880. Cadet Whittaker was absent from reveille, and the cadet Officer of the Day immediately went to his room to investigate. He found Whittaker unconscious on the floor with his hands and feet tied. A bloody Indian club and a small pool of blood beneath him indicated that he had probably been hit with the club. Both of his ears had been cut with small notches. Whittaker maintained that he had been assaulted by three masked cadets.

Schofield, after ordering the Commandant to make an immediate investigation, telegraphed Sherman, informing him of what was known about the incident. Colonel Thomas F. Barr of the Judge Advocate General's Corps was sent to West Point to determine what assistance the War Department could provide Schofield in his investigation. Barr and Schofield after hearing Colonel Lazelle's report decided that a formal Court of Inquiry was necessary. It was noted that, although Lazelle had questioned Whittaker in detail, he had only asked other cadets if they had any knowledge of the incident. His report indicated his belief that Whittaker had himself staged the supposed assault.

Schofield ordered a formal Court of Inquiry to determine exactly what had happened if at all possible. The Court began its inquiry within a few days. The inquiry was fully covered by the press from its beginning. Initially, newspaper accounts indicated the belief that Whittaker had planned the incident. Criticism did increase, but the press comments were not as vindictive as those published during the Smith episode in 1870. Whittaker had produced a note of warning, which he claimed to have received several days prior to the attack. The Court submitted the note to five handwriting experts, who compared it with samples of writing by Whittaker and several other cadets. Three of the five experts definitely matched it with the Whittaker sample. Over a period of several weeks, the Court interviewed cadets, instructors, tactical officers, and civilian employees. On May 29, the Court found that Whittaker had planned the entire incident. He was placed under arrest until the War Department determined what action would be taken.

Political pressure demanded that Schofield be replaced by a superintendent who could better handle the problems of black cadets. President Hayes called Schofield to Washington to inform him that he would be replaced later in the year. Among the officers considered were Oliver O. Howard, former head of the Freedmen's Bureau, and Indian fighters Nelson A. Miles and Alfred M. Terry. Neither Miles nor Terry was an Academy graduate. Hayes asked Schofield's advice concerning the Whittaker case; Schofield recommended that Whittaker be placed on leave until a court martial could be prepared. Shortly afterward, Whittaker left West Point on leave, and Hayes ordered a court martial to be convened.

Secretary of War Alexander Ramsey directed that extreme care be taken in selecting the officers to serve on the court to avoid any possibility of racial bias. Brigadier General Nelson A. Miles was appointed president of the court. The majority of its members were not Academy graduates; all were northerners. Ramsey also directed that the court meet in New York instead of at West Point. Whittaker was charged with conduct unbecoming an officer and gentleman and with actions prejudicial to good order and discipline, both charges involving false official statements before and during the Court of Inquiry. No new evidence was produced during the trial; testimony was the same as that given at the earlier investigations. Once again, primary stress was upon the findings of handwriting experts.

It had been anticipated that the trial would be of short duration, several weeks at the most. Instead, the examinations and testimony extended from early February to mid-June. The intense coverage in the press and widespread public interest, which had existed when the trial started, waned as weeks went by. By the time the Court had concluded its examinations, the press and the public were no longer greatly interested in its procedures, and newspapers no longer carried daily accounts of testimony.

Whittaker was found guilty as charged. The Court did modify the first charge, which had been worded in such a way as to indicate Whittaker had himself devised the alleged beating to bring discredit to the Academy because he was afraid that he would not pass academic requirements. The revision indicated that Whittaker's action was designed to bring him public sympathy because of the Corps' policy to have no social contacts with him. The Court recommended clemency because of Whittaker's youth and inexperience. When the proceedings were reviewed by the Army Judge Advocate General, he questioned the actions of the Court. Astoundingly, he declared that the trial was unconstitutional because the President was authorized to appoint a Court Martial only when the commander concerned had so requested; this had not been done by Schofield. The Judge Advocate also questioned the legality of using samples of Whittaker's writing to compare with the note Whittaker maintained he had received before the incident; he maintained that these examples should have been submitted as evidence. Most importantly, the Judge Advocate stated that no positive evidence had been presented to prove that Whittaker had mutilated and tied himself, that all evidence given had been circumstantial. He recommended that the court proceedings, findings, and sentence be set aside. Secretary of War Robert Lincoln (appointed by the new President Chester Arthur in March after the trial had begun) referred the case to the Attorney General, who agreed with the Judge Advocate's recommendation. President Arthur accepted these recommendations and ordered the court sentence to be revoked and Whittaker reinstated.

Whittaker did not return to West Point. In June 1880, two months after the incident occurred, he had failed to pass the June examination in Natural and Experimental Philosophy. The Academic Board, after reviewing his test and other records, had recommended that he be dismissed. The War Department, however, took no action, maintaining that this was necessary to retain Whittaker's military status until his trial had been concluded. Now, on the same day that the President approved the recommendation to revoke the sentence of the Court, the War Department, with the approval of Secretary Lincoln, ordered Whittaker to be dismissed for academic deficiency.

There is little question that the findings and sentence of the Court Martial officers was based primarily upon circumstantial evidence. Other than the testimony of handwriting experts that Whittaker had written the warning letter, nothing offered at the trial directly proved that he had engineered the incident nor, if he had, was any proof presented to show reasons for his actions. The Judge Advocate and the Attorney General had every reason for their recommendations that the findings and sentence be set aside. However, the actions of President Arthur and Secretary of War Lincoln caused bitter resentment throughout the Army.

Schofield, the Army's third ranking general officer, was relieved without Sherman's being consulted and certainly without his concurrence. His successor, Oliver Howard, was selected by Arthur and Lincoln primarily because of his known sympathy for blacks. His appointment was also made without consulting Sherman. Both Sherman and Schofield were upset, actually bitter, about the manner in which these decisions had been made. Although neither officer objected to civilian control of the military in any way, both felt that Schofield's relief was unnecessary. Sherman for a while considered resigning as General in Chief "to protect Schofield," as he wrote to Howard in December 1880 shortly before Howard became superintendent. The impact on Academy personnel was equally bitter. For once the Academic Board staunchly supported the Superintendent. Cadets and other officers, convinced that Whittaker had indeed planned and executed the entire incident, were amazed that he received no punishment. The admiration for Flipper's enduring social ostracism might have led to improved black-white relationships; the Whittaker case strengthened cadet intentions to have nothing to do with black cadets, an intent that would last for nearly seventy years.

Sherman, Schofield, and members of the Academic Board maintained that black cadets would not be able to compete successfully with white cadets until their educational opportunities were improved. Nevertheless, black cadets were given every opportunity to succeed. Professor Peter Michie in an article in the *South American Review* stated that in any altercation with a black cadet, white cadets were more certain to receive more severe and speedy punishment. His assertion was supported by punishments administered to cadets who had tangled with Smith and Whittaker. Considering the tenor of the times, the Academy had been given an almost impossible task of eliminating racial prejudice and social ostracism when both were common throughout the United States. Dillard Scott in his history of the Academy from 1864 to 1900 stated that "preservation of the legal rights of these first black cadets was not enough; strict guardianship of their human rights was the only proper course." He then maintained that, although segregation had become an accepted part of American life by 1900, "West Point had the opportunity to stand as a bulwark against it, and had abdicated the responsibility." Scott may have made his judgment based upon the standards and conditions of the 1970s rather than those that existed in the 1880s. Schofield was closer to actuality when he stated in his last report as superintendent that "it does not seem a reasonable expectation that young men of a race so recently emerged from a state of slavery could compete successfully with those who have inherited the strength gained in the many generations of freedom enjoyed by their ancestors."

Oliver Howard replaced Schofield in January 1881; he served less than two years. Within a month, he was faced with the same problem Schofield had encountered regarding the reinstatement of cadets dismissed for deficiencies in studies or conduct. The Academic Board had recommended the discharge of First Class Cadet James A. Patterson for failing to pass the January examinations in law. While Secretary of War Ramsey considered restoring Patterson, he did direct the reinstatement of three other cadets. Howard objected strongly to the Adjutant General, Brigadier General R. C. Drum, who did not forward Howard's concern to Sherman or the Secretary of War. Howard again emphasized that the Academic Board by law had the right to dismiss cadets and that their reinstatement by the Secretary therefore was illegal. Drum did forward Howard's objections to the Secretary, but not to Sherman, another instance of a bureau chief bypassing the General in Chief. Drum continued to insist that the Secretary could reinstate cadets even if the Academic Board and the Superintendent objected.

By this time a new Secretary of War, Robert Lincoln, had been appointed. Sherman informed him of the controversy involving Patterson, and Lincoln wisely referred the entire matter to the Attorney General of the United States. His findings supported Howard and the Academic Board. He supported the dismissal of Patterson, informing Lincoln that he could not be reinstated. The Attorney General in making this decision added that dismissal of any cadet by the Academic Board for deficiency in studies or conduct was binding upon the President and the Secretary of War. This ended the practice that had plagued superintendents from Thayer's time on. Although there were many requests from Presidents and Secretaries of War for the Academic Board to reconsider dismissals, there was no effort to override the Board's recommendations. Not until the honor scandal of 1976 shocked the nation was this prerogative of the Academic Board revoked.

Many historians have labeled the 1880s and 1890s as the period of "stagnation." Weigley in his *History of the United States Army* did not use that term, instead stating that the "technical engineering part of the curriculum was somewhat constricted, and the genuinely military was expanded to include about one-third of the curriculum by the turn of the century. But with these changes the Academy lost its eminence among American engineering schools without commensurate gain in the quality of its military instruction." Ambrose was more scathing; in his chapter entitled "Stagnation," he maintained that "Self satis-faction was complete . . . neither Superintendents nor faculty looked forward; rather they assumed the problems were still the same [as before the Civil War]." Ambrose commented on the changes in civilian colleges and universities; Weig-ley did not. This was the period of change from the old emphasis on the classical mode of education to the more modern stress on a multitude of fields of knowl-edge. This was the period when the number of college students increased dra-matically; at West Point, the Corps increased from 250 in 1861 to 492 by 1900. New findings in engineering, transportation, and communication resulted in additional emphasis on scientific studies. To Ambrose, the Academy did not keep pace with the changes made in civilian schooling. He applied the term "the Gilded Age" to American education during this period; Scott used that term to describe the Academy after the Civil War, possibly to show the difference from West Point's pre-war "Golden Age." Ambrose summed up his beliefs by stating, "America in the Gilded Age was bold and brash, always changing, living in and for the future. New ideas, new methods, new organizations dom-inated. With a few exceptions, the American colleges reflected this spirit as much as any other institution. The major exception to the rule was the United States Military Academy. . . . The more the intellectual and technological devel-opments demanded change, the more determined the Academy was to retain inviolate Sylvanus Thayer's system."

To some degree this allegation is true. The basic fundamentals established by Thayer as the foundation of the West Point system were retained. Cadets recited every day in every subject, although there were occasional lectures and dem-onstrations. Cadets were marked daily, and weekly grades were posted in the sallyport of barracks. Mathematics and the sciences were still stressed, but En-glish, Spanish, and history were added after the Civil War. Entrance to the Academy was by examination, but these entrance tests were kept extremely simple by legislators more interested in obtaining political benefits from their appointments with little concern for the educational and intellectual abilities of their appointees. Despite the simplicity of the examinations, a high percentage of candidates continued to fail to pass. Those that did enter the Academy often failed to complete the four-year course because they were unable to master the rigid academic requirements. More time was devoted to military-related subjects; engineering courses were still stressed. It is true that the Academy did lose its eminence among engineering schools. What neither Ambrose nor Weigley con-sidered was the change in the American educational scene between Thayer's superintendency and the 1880s. Significantly, educators of that period seldom criticized the Academy adversely for failing to follow the trend of the civilian colleges. Perhaps the comments of Dr. William R. Harper, president of the University of Chicago, at the Academy Centennial Observance in 1902 better portrayed the educational role of the Academy than do modern historians. He succinctly stated that the purpose was "a singular one with no disposition . . . to dissipate the effort of instructor or student by undertaking to do things other than those directly and absolutely involved in the particular purpose for which the school was founded."

When Thayer became superintendent in 1817, there were no other engineering schools in the United States. Almost without exception, colleges of that period still patterned their instruction in the classical manner, emphasizing Latin, Greek, and other liberal arts. Rensselaer Polytechnic Institution, founded in 1824, led the entry of colleges into engineering and scientific fields. By the 1880s many major civilian institutions offered engineering and scientific degrees; many became universities instead of colleges and conferred graduate degrees in many fields. West Point was not, and still is not, a university. It differed from its civilian contemporaries in educating its cadet students for a single field: the military profession. There was little reason for the Academy to sponsor graduate study in the sciences or in any other field. It was not the role of the Academy to support graduate study in engineering or any other field. Its mission was to educate and train its cadets to become second lieutenants. The Army parallel of civilian graduate degree study in various fields was the increasing attendance at various specialized schools: the Artillery School of Practice at Fort Monroe and Sherman's School of the Line at Fort Leavenworth. Within twenty years, this evolved into the Army educational program of branch training of young officers at infantry, artillery, and cavalry schools, staff training at the Command and General Staff College, and the ultimate education of senior officers at the Army War College.

There was another reason for the seeming decline of West Point's stature in educating engineers. In earlier years many graduates had left the Army for engineering work in civil life, a field that emphasized building roads, railroads, bridges, and communications systems. As the United States emerged into the age of manufacturing, a new type of engineering was required. Large buildings, manufacturing machines, and civic improvements were required using engineering techniques having no relationship to military engineering. The ability to meet these new needs came from civilian institutions and their engineering instruction. The Army gradually became divorced from civilian projects other than the public works programs of the Corps of Engineers.

There were organizational changes in the academic departments. The Departments of French and Spanish were combined into the Department of Modern Languages in 1882; about the same time, responsibility for teaching English was transferred from the Department of Geography, History, and Ethics, headed by the chaplain. As professor, the chaplain was tasked with teaching geography, history, constitutional law, English, ethics, and logic. In 1874, the Department of Law was established; for two years, from 1908 to 1910, the department also taught history and the chaplain had only religious duties. Practical military engineering and theoretical engineering continued as separate departments. The allocation of cadet time to scientific and engineering subjects declined, and more hours were allocated to English, history, law and military instruction.

Some phases of instruction gradually disappeared to be replaced by studies more appropriate to the time. The building of the railway tunnel beneath the Plain made use of the Library observatory impossible, and a new observatory was built on the edge of Lusk Reservoir below Fort Putnam. By 1900, celestial observation had almost been eliminated from the course of instruction. In the Department of Drawing, increased emphasis was placed upon surveying and terrain sketching; fine art instruction declined and was eventually replaced by engineering drawing. The Department of Artillery, which had for many years taught cadets how to make powder, flares, rockets, and projectiles as well as teaching the use of artillery pieces, became the Department of Artillery and Ordnance, which taught techniques for development of new artillery weapons. New methods of communication brought instruction in telegraphy, heliography, and signaling by flags. The Army experience in fighting Indians changed cavalry instruction. The leveled-saber charge was not stressed as it had been in prewar days. Instead, emphasis was given to rapid movement by mounted troops that would dismount and fight on foot when contact was made with an enemy. Company adminstration and supply functions were added to the instruction conducted by the Commandant. If there was any shortcoming in meeting possible Army needs, it was in the logistics field—both at West Point and elsewhere in the Army school system. The unfortunate result of this neglect was the fiasco involved in staging and supplying troops heading for Cuba during the Spanish War in 1898. This deficiency was one of the primary factors leading to the establishment in 1901 of the Army War College by Secretary of War Elihu Root.

The physical plant changed during the last three decades of the nineteenth century. In 1870, an adminstration building was built across the road from the Cadet Mess. It was built with gray stone to harmonize with other buildings, but its architectural design resembled a French Renaissance chateau with a mansard roof and wrought-iron railings, which contrasted with the severe military-Gothic style of the Delafield era buildings and the neoclassic Chapel. To provide additional cadet rooms, the west wing of Cadet Barracks was extended by adding a sallyport and two divisions of rooms, giving the building an L-shape. A new and much needed hospital was built south of the Cadet Mess in 1884; its architectural style can only be termed nondescript. In 1891 a gymnasium was completed on the present site of Washington Hall. Its gray-stone towers gave it the appearance of a small medieval Norman castle, another contrast with the Gothic architecture of the Cadet Barracks. The Cadet Mess was renovated in 1887 and renamed Grant Hall, the first West Point building named in honor of a graduate. A new academic building was finished in 1895. It replaced the old building of the 1830s. During its construction over a period of nearly four years, classes were held in the Library, the Administration Building, and the new wing of Cadet Barracks. Standing next to the barracks on the west and Grant Hall on the south and across the road from the Administration Building and the Cadet Chapel, the building designed by noted architect Richard Hunt combined Gothic, French Renaissance, and Classic styles in an effort to provide some architectural unity to the cadet area. Its battlements corresponded to those on the barracks; its small towers resembled those of

Grant Hall. For the first time, locally quarried stone was not used; instead, granite from Chester, Massachusetts, was used. Well designed with large classrooms, wide halls, and large windows that provided excellent natural light, the building was considered modern at that time.

Little effort was directed to improving or building other structures. Quarters for both officers and enlisted men were badly needed, but only a few new houses were added, notably a row of thirty duplex quarters for senior enlisted men. An inadequate building provided quarters for bachelor officers. There were never enough quarters for married officers and their families, which required more than one family to occupy the same set of quarters, an undesirable situation at best. Adding to the problem was the Army regulation of the time providing that an officer arriving on post could demand the quarters assigned to any other officer junior in rank. This caused countless moves as an officer "ranked" out of his quarters would do the same to another officer junior to him. Finally, in 1891, the Superintendent, Colonel John M. Wilson, realizing that most newly assigned officers arrived in late summer, directed that only one quarters drawing be scheduled in August each year, stopping the moves caused by "ranking" a particular set of quarters. Newly assigned officers could choose any vacant set of quarters. Officers already on post could "toss in" their assigned quarters if they thought they would be able to obtain a more suitable house. Once in a set of quarters, Wilson directed, the occupant would remain in those quarters until his departure or until he decided to participate in the annual quarters drawing. This system is still followed for the most part. The annual quarters drawing has become a festive event attended by many officers and wives not participating— they come to watch the joy of those who were assigned good sets of quarters and the agonies of those drawing less desirable residences.

The hodgepodge of architectural styles led to the use of the term "battle of the styles" in describing building programs at the Academy. Two new structures appeared in the 1890s. The will of General George Cullum provided funds for a memorial building to house trophies and memorial plaques, statues, and portraits honoring graduates of the Academy. An architectural competition led to the selection of the firm of McKim, Mead, and White to design and construct the memorial hall. Stanford White, who had already designed the Battle Monument honoring the officers and enlisted men of the Regular Army killed in the Civil War, designed the building in Neo-Greek style. Completed in 1898, the unadorned, windowless, classic building contrasted vividly with the other structures nearby. White was also selected to design the West Point Army Mess next to the memorial hall beginning in 1900. This building was badly needed; the officers' mess in Grant Hall was inadequate for the number of officers stationed at West Point, and the increase in the number of cadets required additional dining space for the Corps.

White's Battle Monument was completed and dedicated in May 1897. Selected in another architectural competition, White designed a polished granite, monolith shaft forty-six feet high and five feet six inches in diameter. The names of

188 officers and 2,041 enlisted men of the Regular Army killed during the Civil War appear on bronze plaques or on the base of the shaft. A bronze statue of Fame surmounted the shaft. Contrary to cadet legend, Evelyn Nesbit did not pose for the figure by sculptor Frederick MacMonnies; she was far too young at the time. The shaft was moved from Massachusetts to West Point by rail, except for a short move by boat across the river at Newburg. A temporary track was built from the railway station at West Point to the site selected for the monument on Trophy Point. Funds for the monument were donations from officers of the Army. Secretary of War Russell Alger, who represented the President, General Schofield, and former superintendent John M. Wilson, addressed the Corps and nearly 1,000 guests. Wilson, a member of the memorial committee, presented the monument to the Army. General Schofield accepted the gift and, in turn, presented it to the nation. Secretary Alger accepted in the name of the President. Both Alger and Schofield commented on the appropriateness of the roster of enlisted men; both emphasized the devotion, bravery, and dedication of the enlisted ranks of the Regular Army. Alger, however, in addressing the cadets directly, urged them to "guard well your heritage," stressing the need for integrity, honor, devotion, and patriotism in the Army.

There were other unusual events for the Corps. As a body, cadets camped at the St. Louis Exposition, the Columbian Exposition in Chicago, and the Jamestown Exposition. Marching in review for the new Commander-in-Chief after his inaugural became a tradition. There were parades in New York from time to time, visits that cadets enjoyed. Mark Twain visited West Point many times, enjoying informal discussions with cadets and giving an occasional formal lecture. Smoking his inevitable cigar, Twain walked freely about the Academy. Honored at a review after a lecture, he took his place beside the Superintendent still smoking his cigar. The Dialectic Society entertainments continued, and there were plays sponsored by the officers of the garrison. These paled in comparison to the presentation of *The Merchant of Venice* with noted actor Henry Irving as Shylock and Ellen Terry as Portia. Irving, a friend of Professor Michie, had offered to bring the Corps to New York on a special train provided by Chauncey Depew, but the Superintendent would not change regulations to permit the trip. Instead, Irving brought his troupe to West Point and staged Shakespeare's play in Grant Hall the night of the great blizzard of 1888. Cadet cheers continued long after the final scene. Finally, Irving came out and told the cheering cadets that a cable from London indicated that church bells were ringing because a Britisher had finally captured West Point. The blizzard continued all night and into the next day. Drifts covered both entrances to the north sallyport and reached the barracks windows on the second floor. Cadets enjoyed the blizzard for one reason: classes were suspended for the day. With all of these unusual events taking place, the adoption of a coat of arms and motto for the Academy went almost unnoticed. For the first time, the words "Duty, Honor, Country" were formally acknowledged as the keystone of West Point training.

But the event that excited the Corps more than any other was the first football game with the midshipmen from Annapolis. From its very inception, the Military Academy had encouraged athletic sports for its cadets, tacitly when applied to "baseball" in the 1820s, openly in later years when boating, gymnastics, and track and field brought interclass rivalry to the Plain. Early cadet letters mention football games in front of barracks; it is doubtful that this "football" ever resembled the sport developed in the last decade of the nineteenth century. Dennis Michie, son of Professor Peter S. Michie, and his classmate Leonard M. Prince are credited with bringing modern football to West Point. Young Michie had been at school at Lawrenceville and had seen and played the new sport. After he entered the Academy in 1888, he and Prince organized class teams, approved by the Academic Board after intercession by Professor Michie. Three games were played against visiting teams in 1890: the Philadelphia Merriams, the New York Sylvans, and the Governors Island Atlantics. In October, the Naval Academy challenged the cadet team. The first game on November 29, 1890, brought the first victory to Annapolis, 24–0. Coached by Michie, the Army team was no match for the flying wedge of the Navy eleven. The next year, seventeen cadets made the trip to Annapolis, eager for revenge. Coached by Yale graduate H. H. Williams and captained by Michie, the cadets rolled over the midshipmen 32–16. The same year, Army played Tufts, Rutgers, Stevens Institute, and Princeton. Interest in the new sport led to the organization of the Army Athletic Association in 1893.

The football excitement was nothing compared to the reaction of the Corps when the battleship U.S.S. *Maine* was blown up in Havana Harbor in February 1898. War with Spain was declared on April 15; the next day the Class of 1898 graduated and left to join their regiments. The Class of 1899 also graduated early on February 15, 1899. Its early departure made it impossible for its yearbook, *The Howitzer*, to be produced, breaking the continued series begun in 1896 and continuing to the present day. The victories in Cuba were cheered by the cadets, but their elation was subdued by casualty lists. Among the graduates killed in action was Dennis Michie. Southern cadets were ecstatic over the news that "Fighting Joe" Wheeler and Fitzhugh Lee, both generals in the Confederate Army, had been given general officer commissions to lead troops in Cuba.

One cadet saw action in those campaigns. At the Centennial Observance in June 1902, President Theodore Roosevelt related that "I had at that time in my regiment as acting second lieutenant a cadet from West Point. He was having his holiday; he took his holiday coming down with us, and just before the assault he was shot, the bullet going in, I think, into the stomach, going out the other side. He fell over, and we came up. I leaned over to him, he said, 'All right, Colonel, I am going to get well.' I didn't think he was, but I said, 'All right, I am sure you will,' and he did; he is all right now." Roosevelt did not give the cadet's name. A search of cadet letters and the news letters of the Class of 1900— any cadet on leave in 1898 would have had to be a member of that class— revealed that Cadet Ernest E. Haskell had indeed been with the Rough Riders at San Juan Hill. Haskell had been sent to a Washington, D.C., hospital earlier in the year. His doctor was Captain Leonard Wood, who brought his friend Theodore Roosevelt to meet the young cadet. When Wood told Haskell that he and Roosevelt were organizing a volunteer cavalry regiment, Haskell asked to join the unit. Told that he could not without approval of the Secretary of War, Haskell went to the Secretary and obtained approval if the regimental commander would agree to accept him and would assign him actual duty with the unit. Haskell accompanied Wood and Roosevelt to Texas and assisted them in training the lst Volunteer Cavalry Regiment. When the regiment went to Cuba, Haskell went with it as an acting second lieutenant wearing his cadet dress gray uniform, leggings, and a campaign hat. After the Cuban campaign was over, Wood, now a brigadier general, and Roosevelt urged the Secretary of War to give Haskell an immediate commission. They learned that this could not be done, that any member of a West Point class that did not graduate could not be commissioned until after his class had graduated. When the Class of 1900 learned of the situation, they unanimously signed a petition to the Secretary, indicating that they had no objection to Haskell being given an immediate commission. A few days later, Haskell replaced his cadet gray with an officer's blue uniform.

The military successes in Cuba and later in the Philippines brought new accolades to graduates and the Academy. Media coverage was ostentatious in its praise of West Point and the education given its cadets. Seemingly, the adverse reports concerning the treatment of black cadets and hazing were forgotten. Within the gray walls, however, hazing continued to be a problem despite the assertions of successive superintendents—Schofield, Howard, Merritt, Parke, Wilson, and Ernst—that it had been eliminated or at least curtailed to within reasonable boundaries. Typical of the comments of superintendents was Colonel John M. Wilson's statement in 1892, "I believe what is known as 'hazing' in the old acceptance of that term has been broken up at the Academy although minor teasing to a limited extent still continues, receiving prompt punishment when detected." That "minor teasing" reached such epidemic proportions by 1895 that dismissal became the standard punishment. Despite political pressure on the Secretary of War and the President, cadets dismissed for hazing were not reinstated.

Colonel Albert L. Mills, who became Superintendent in April 1898, was determined to stop cadets from ignoring regulations against hazing. Mills and the Commandant, Lieutenant Colonel Otto L. Hein, instituted grading First Classmen on their enforcement of regulations as a part of a new program for improving discipline and developing leadership. The Cadet Officer of the Day, a roster duty for First Classmen, was required to sign a statement at the end of his tour of duty that he had reported all hazing that he had observed. Sixteen senior cadets objected to the statement because their signature as Officer of the Day used their honor to enforce regulations (the interpretation being that a man's signature was his bond, that everything it attested to was true). Mills reacted promptly and sternly, informing the cadets that failing to sign the report was refusing to obey regulations and that he would have them tried by court martial if they continued to refuse to sign their reports. The cadets, faced with probable suspension, reconsidered and agreed to follow instructions. Mills reported to Secretary of War Elihu Root that he had eliminated an attempt to disobey orders and oppose authority.

This was the first of a series of events bringing an outright clash between the Mills-Hein concept of duty and discipline and the cadet sense of honor. The simple basis for this serious controversy was hazing. Cadets considered hazing to be a traditional prerogative; it was their right to require plebes to perform menial tasks, assume exaggerated military posture, learn inconsequential definitions, and provide amusement for upperclassmen's enjoyment. If a plebe was disobedient, he was expected to endure verbal abuse and physical exercise without complaint and without reporting his discomfort or, if questioned, the identity of his abusers. Mills and Hein, following the Schofield definition of military discipline, maintained that supervision, instruction, and correction of plebes would be done without verbal or physical abuse; that menial tasks would not be assigned to Fourth Classmen; that physical abuse was absolutely forbidden; and that plebes who failed to report being hazed were as guilty of condoning the practice as were the upperclassmen who abused them. This completely opposite viewpoint was compounded by a paragraph of regulations that stated that a cadet need not make self-incriminating statements during an investigation conducted by the Superintendent.

As Roger Nye points out in his history of the post-1900 Academy, hazing had never been as severe as it was in 1900. It appeared that the start of the new century had resulted in a consolidation of and addition to all of the hazing techniques used in the last fifty years. Mills and Hein obviously were aware of the situation, tried to stop the practice, but were generally unsuccessful. An August 1899 article in the *New York Sun*, supposedly written by a cadet floridly described treatment of plebes in detail, 5,000 words of detail. Although Mills later learned from the *Sun's* editor that the letter had been written by the father of an ex-cadet, the damage was done. The daily papers spread the letter nationwide; public furor was raised in tone and vehemence. Mills appealed to cadets, emphasizing the damage their actions was bringing to the Academy; his appeal was successful and the Corps agreed by pledging no further ill-treatment of new cadets. This soon proved to be only a temporary truce.

Mills realized that in all probability hazing would again emerge, but he was determined to at least minimize its growth if not prevent it completely. He prepared for the seemingly inevitable in several ways. Secretary Root agreed that the Superintendent, not a cadet, would determine whether answering questions during an investigation of hazing would be self-incriminating. Mills then rescinded the regulation that made a plebe being hazed as guilty as the hazer. This made it possible for a plebe to admit that he had been hazed without incriminating himself. Mills also dropped his intent to revive the old requirement that cadets certify they had not been involved in hazing any Fourth Classmen in order to be eligible for furlough or to receive his diploma.

In July 1900, Lieutenant Julian Lindsay reported a Third Class cadet, a yearling, for hazing a plebe. The Class of 1903, Third Classmen at the time, resented this and decided to silence Lindsay. When Lindsay on his next tour as Officer in Charge—a roster duty for tactical officers—entered Grant Hall for lunch, he was ostentatiously met with complete silence. So obvious was this action that Lindsay ordered the cadets to leave their meal immediately. Mills was outraged and ordered an investigation. The Board of Officers reported that the cadet action showed disrespect and insubordination. Mills could have ordered the ten leaders tried by court martial; instead he gave each of these ten cadets nine to twelve months of confinement and punishment tours on the area for the entire period. Anyone who has walked the area for punishment can attest that this punishment was indeed severe. The attitude of the Third Classmen while testifying before the Board of Officers was sullen and clearly reflected contempt for the Board. Mills again took prompt action; twenty-one yearlings were confined for nine months and lost half of their three-months' furlough the following year (confinement was not incarceration but restriction to their rooms and specified limits in the cadet area).

Seven weeks later, Mills was convinced that any problem concerning discipline had been solved and that hazing was under control. The Corps moved back into barracks and began the academic term. In November, the Academy and the entire nation were rocked by newspaper articles maintaining that former cadet Oscar Booz was dying because of maltreatment during his plebe summer camp the previous year. His father had written to a newspaper describing the boy's abuse in summer camp, stating that he had been forced to fight an upperclassman, had been required to exercise until he dropped, and that he had been forced to drink a bottle of tabasco sauce. While an official Court of Inquiry investigated the charges, newspapers and magazines published lurid accounts of Booz's hazing. Previous reports from several years earlier were reviewed. Thomas Nast directed sarcastic cartoons at the Academy and its cadets. Mills and other West Point authorities were condemned; many editors demanded his immediate relief, a demand echoed in many letters from irate citizens. One paper demanded that the cadets involved be tried in civil court for manslaughter.

The Court of Inquiry reported that Booz had been hazed but that his treatment had nothing to do with his death from tuberculosis in December 1900. A congressional committee conducting another investigation at the same time drew similar conclusions. Both investigating groups reported that plebes were routinely required to drink a spoonful of tabasco sauce from time to time; Booz had been required to drink a bottle in the period of a week. Other cadets, including Douglas MacArthur, had been physically exercised to exhaustion; MacArthur had convulsions. But MacArthur and other plebes were reluctant to testify against their upperclass hazers, an attitude that was admired by other cadets.

Booz had resigned in September, nine days before Colonel Mills became Superintendent; Mills inherited a condition that his later actions would have prevented.

The congressional committee report brought strong action from Congress. A rider to the Academy appropriations bill required that regulations be devised to prevent hazing and directed that any cadet guilty of hazing or condoning hazing by others be summarily dismissed. The reaction from the Corps reflected their chagrin, their resentment of public humiliation and the failure of the press to fairly report the findings of the Court of Inquiry and the congressional committee, and their resentment at the steps Mills had taken to prevent hazing prior to the first report of the Booz incident. They informed the Superintendent that they were willing to stop physical exercise for plebes but that they would not accept restrictions against annoying, harassing, or bracing plebes. Mills continued to take prompt action by punishing cadets interfering with plebes taking examinations or bracing plebes at any time. By April, cadets were seething at what they considered to be unjust punishment. Punishment of a cadet for gross neglect of duty brought what must be considered to be outright mutiny, something unheard of since the legendary "Eggnog" mutiny at Christmastime in 1826. The evening of April 16, 1901 began with a demonstration in the north sallyport of barracks, spread into the area, and then onto the Plain north of barracks. Most of the Corps participated; and, as misdirected enthusiasm increased, the cadets marched to the Superintendent's quarters, cheering cadets who had been recently punished for hazing, jeering their tactical officers, and shouting profane comments about Mills. The reveille gun was hauled from Trophy Point and pointed at Mills' quarters; fortunately it was not fired.

An irate Mills took prompt action. Class meetings were prohibited. The Class of 1902, the senior class, was singled out for special punishment; as First Classmen they were expected to set an example for the underclasses, and as cadet officers were expected to maintain proper discipline in the Corps at all times. Mills declared that the First Class had caused the hazing problems of 1899, had permitted unruly cadets to overrule those with cool-headed stability, and had ignored their responsibilities as First Classmen and cadet officers. Five First Classmen were dismissed; six others were suspended for one year; and thirty more were confined and walked punishment tours for many months. This strong and well-justified action ended the two-year conflict between Mills and the cadets. The authority of the Superintendent had been supported and strengthened by Secretary of War Elihu Root; the infantile belief by cadets that hazing represented manliness and that honor required physical combat had been rejected by the cadets themselves. Even the humiliation of being embarrassed publicly by the newspaper accounts was soon forgotten or, if not forgotten, at least eased as time passed. Mills was able to almost eradicate hazing *per se*, and the discipline so well defined by Schofield fifteen years earlier prevailed. Credit for this change must be given to Colonel Mills. Fortunately, in contrast to the reassignment of Schofield in 1881, Mills was retained as Superintendent for another five years, enabling him to continue his improvements. Firm in punishing malfeasance, Mills tempered that firmness by adding to cadet privileges. More frequent visits to other cadet rooms or officers' quarters were authorized. Cadets were given more opportunity to "dine out," have dinner as a guest at the hotel or at officers' homes. Short leaves at Christmastime were authorized for deserving cadets. All of these privileges were based upon good conduct as shown by a low number of demerits received. By late summer 1901, the Board of Visitors was able to report to Secretary of War Root that Mills should be retained, that he had succeeded in eliminating hazing, a practice contrary to good discipline and military professionalism.

During this period of turmoil, discontent, and humiliation, one profound and important change occurred: the cadet honor system was more clearly defined and, to some extent, codified. Honor had been considered one of the most important aspects of cadet life and training since Thayer's time, so much so that it was a central part of the new Academy motto, "Duty, Honor, Country." The cadet honor code then—and now—was not understood by the general public. The keystone of the cadet honor code was simple: an honorable man did not lie; his word was his bond; his signature certified that what appeared above it was correct. This, of course, was understood by the public; no one could argue that lying should be condoned. But the cadet tenet that one did not condone lying in others was not understood outside the gray walls of the Academy. Stealing was not condoned in any way. Cheating had not been considered a violation of the honor code in earlier years; by 1900 cadets considered cheating as dishonorable as lying.

From time to time, cadets had taken direct action to punish honor-code violators. Steps taken by Superintendents Cullum and Schofield had convinced the Corps that it was far better to report honor violations to the Commandant and Superintendent for official action. Mills had supported cadet recommendations in a February 1899 incident involving two cadets who had altered demerit records in the Commandant's office, stolen examination papers, and lied by denying their guilt. A committee of nine cadets had investigated the rumor of these activities, found them true, and reported the two cadets to Mills. They were promptly dismissed from the Academy, action supported by the Secretary of War. The cadet committee was an *ad hoc* group formed within a class organization. It was not a standing honor committee but was selected and convened only when honor violations were reported. This temporary committee later became an unofficial vigilante group and then developed gradually over a long period into the Cadet Honor Committee of the present day.

The 1890s were a period of turmoil and transition, a decade of embarrassment and chagrin, and an era of reaffirmation of the ideals of good discipline and character building. The Corps had increased in size; the physical plant was no longer adequate. Much of the abuse of what cadets considered a traditional right was shown to be an unfounded myth and hazing in the old, violent, abusive manner was essentially eliminated. Another war had shown the value of West Point training—not because graduates had led the successful campaigns but because the tremendous turmoil resulting from inexperience and disorganization of many civilian soldiers had clearly proved the need for professionalism in the armed forces. The Military Academy approached its second century as changes and modifications were being made to better enable West Point to meet the changing demands of the Army.

1902

The long gray line of us stretches
Through the years of a century told . . .

THE CORPS
BISHOP H. S. SHIPMAN
FORMER CADET CHAPLAIN

21

The Corps and the Corps and the Corps

On March 16, 1902, the United States Military Academy entered its second century. The first fifty years of that century had been a struggle for the Academy and its graduates, a struggle to survive, a struggle to grow and mature, a struggle to overcome antagonistic governmental officials and an indifferent public. Not until the War with Mexico did the true value of the West Point education and training become apparent. Although the graduates who fought in that conflict did not have senior rank and did not command any major forces, their contribution was a major factor in the successes attained in the field. As Winfield Scott commented—in words since memorized by countless plebes—"I give it as my fixed opinion, that but for our graduated cadets, the war between the United States and Mexico might, and probably would have lasted some four or five years, with, in its first half, more defeats than victories falling to our share; whereas, in less than two campaigns, we conquered a great country and a peace, without the loss of a single battle or skirmish."

The gratitude of the nation enabled the Academy to progress further along the road so ably mapped by Sylvanus Thayer. During the next decade, West Point entered what has been termed its Golden Age. It was in the foremost ranks of scientific and engineering schools. Textbooks authored by its professors were used in most of the technical schools of the time. Graduates who had left the Army built railroads, headed colleges, mapped rivers and harbors, and supervised countless engineering projects throughout the country.

A dozen years after the Mexican War, the Academy faced its most bitter test in a war where brother fought brother and West Point classmates faced each other on the battlefield. Graduates led the armies of both sides; and, when the conflict neared its end, they showed compassion and understanding for their opponents. The Academy itself had continued its disciplined routine during the conflict and welcome back cadets from the southern states when the war was over.

The following decades found the Academy struggling to overcome the intense problems of young black men becoming cadets at a time when blacks were not accepted as a part of American social life. Compounding this period of turmoil was the growing practice of upperclassmen hazing plebes, a practice that developed in the last years of the war and increased in severity and brutality as each year passed. Successive superintendents fought to end hazing; many announced that they had done so. But, inevitably, the practice was resumed within a very short time. Not until Colonel Albert Mills became Superintendent in 1899 was any effective and enduring stop made. The Academy and the Corps suffered humiliating comments in the daily press each time hazing reached epidemic proportions. Each time, the Corps agreed to stop mistreating plebes. Almost on a timed schedule of five years another episode would occur—five years saw all cadets participating in the agreement to cease hazing graduated. The actions taken by Mills were severe with no leniency given to offenders.

In the postwar period, the cadet honor code led cadets to take direct action to oust offenders. Youthful vigor did, at least in one instance, result in mistaken action against an alleged offender. By supporting the cadet honor concept and taking action against violators of the honor code, superintendents quietly and efficiently assisted cadets to improve their honor system. By 1900 an *ad hoc* committee, based on class organizations, was functioning when a reported violation occurred. Colonel Mills accepted cadet recommendations and, after his own investigations substantiated the cadet committee report, dismissed the offenders for dishonorable conduct.

In the postwar period, civilian colleges gradually—in some cases suddenly—changed their curricula from the old classical system to a more modern program incorporating study in specialized fields. This led to graduate study and the conferring of graduate degrees. The Academy has been criticized for "stagnating" during this period. Such was not the case. Its curriculum remained much the same in overall subject content, but, within the studies conducted by each academic department, the content changed and developed to meet the changing needs of the Army. The superintendents, commandants, and academic instructors all emphasized the need for military professionalism.

This emphasis was fully justified in the War with Spain. Although the major forces were not commanded by graduates, the turmoil, confusion, and misdirection of troop movements and logistical support brought clearly into focus the need for professionalism in the Army. Leonard Wood, who was not a graduate, and Secretary of War Elihu Root recognized the importance of a West Point education as the keystone of lifelong development of professionalism in the officers of the Regular Army. The development of various branch and service schools initiated by General Schofield and fostered by Secretary Root would bring the desired professionalism into being before the United States entered the conflict in Europe less than twenty years later.

The official observance of the Centennial of the Academy's founding was held during June Week 1902. Activities began on Alumni Day, Monday, June 9. The meeting followed luncheon in the new Cullum Memorial Hall. Graduates who had fought in the Mexican, Civil, Indian, and Spanish American Wars spoke to invited guests and the entire Corps. The address by Edward P. Alexander, Class of 1857 and Brigadier General of the Confederate Army, brought cheers from his audience; his participation truly indicated a beginning of the end of the animosity that had continued between Yankee and Rebel since 1861.

The second day of the Centennial observance was devoted to athletic contests. Class field and track competitions were held during the morning. In the afternoon, Army hosted Yale in a baseball game on the diamond in front of cadet barracks. The traditional Graduation Hop was held in Cullum Hall that night. Many distinguished guests, including Secretary of War Root, attended the ball.

Wednesday was Centennial Day. Events began with the arrival of President Theodore Roosevelt, who was escorted from the train station to Colonel Mills' quarters by the entire Corps of Cadets. A review in his honor was held shortly afterward. Roosevelt informed a surprised Superintendent that he would award the Medal of Honor to plebe Calvin P. Titus for "gallantry at Peking, China, August 14, 1900." Titus had been a bugler with the 14th Infantry and was the first man to scale the city wall. Changes were hastily made to properly present Titus to the President during the review. Normally, this would have had Titus move front and center to be escorted by the Colors to the reviewing stand. Instead, in an unusual ceremony, Titus was escorted by the entire Corps of Cadets. This was the first and only time that the Medal of Honor has been bestowed personally upon a cadet by his Commander-in-Chief. After the review and luncheon at Colonel Mills's quarters, the President was escorted to Cullum Hall by the entire Corps of Cadets. Addresses were made by Roosevelt, Secretary Root, and General Horace Porter, Class of 1860. The traditional graduation parade was followed by a banquet in the cadet mess, Grant Hall. Brief comments were made by dignitaries: Dr. William Harper, President of the University of Chicago; Speaker of the House David H. Henderson; Lieutenant General Nelson A. Miles, General in Chief of the Army; Captain French E. Chadwick, U.S. Navy; and Major General Henry C. Corbin, Adjutant General of the Army. The Centennial exercises ended the next day with the graduation of the Class of 1902, who received their diplomas from President Roosevelt.

Roosevelt and Secretary of War Root perhaps made the most important and cogent comments during their talks. Roosevelt stated that warfare was changing and that "the man who is going to be a good officer should meet those changes." It would be more of a challenge than ever for each graduate to prepare himself for the future. He added, "We had the right to expect that West Point would do well, we could not have expected that she would have done so well as she has. . . . During this century no other educational institution in the land contributed so many names as West Point to the honor roll of the nation's greatest citizens."

Elihu Root spoke more briefly than the President. In one sentence, he summarized the services of West Point Graduates over the last century but, most importantly, presented the challenge of the future: "The Military Academy is more necessary now than one hundred years ago."

Appendix A

Superintendents, U.S. Military Academy[1]

1. Major Jonathan Williams   April 15, 1802–June 20, 1803[2]
2. Lieutenant Colonel Jonathan Williams   April 19, 1805–July 31, 1812
3. Colonel Joseph G. Swift   July 31, 1812–March 24, 1814
4. Captain Alden Partridge   January 3, 1815–July 28, 1817[3]
5. Captain Sylvanus Thayer   July 28, 1817–July 1, 1833
6. Major Rene E. DeRussy   July 1, 1833–September 1, 1838
7. Major Richard Delafield   September 1, 1838–August 15, 1845
8. Captain Henry Brewerton   August 15, 1845–September 1, 1852
9. Captain Robert E. Lee[4]   September 1, 1852–March 31, 1855
10. Captain John G. Barnard   March 31, 1855–September 8, 1856
11. Major Richard Delafield   September 8, 1856–January 23, 1861
12. Captain Pierre G. T. Beauregarde   January 23, 1861–January 28, 1861
13. Major Richard Delafield   January 28, 1861–March 1, 1861
14. Major Alexander H. Bowman   March 1, 1861–July 8, 1864
15. Major Zealous B. Tower   July 8, 1864–September 8, 1864
16. Lieutenant Colonel George W. Cullum   September 8, 1864–August 28, 1866
17. Colonel Thomas G. Pitcher   August 28, 1866–September 1, 1871
18. Colonel Thomas H. Ruger   September 1, 1871–September 1, 1876

19. Major General John M. Schofield   September 1, 1876–January 21, 1881

20. Brigadier General Oliver O. Howard   January 21, 1881–September 1, 1882

21. Colonel Wesley Merritt   September 1, 1882–July 1, 1887

22. Colonel John G. Parke   August 28, 1887–June 24, 1889

23. Lieutenant Colonel John M. Wilson   August 26, 1889–March 31, 1893

24. Major Oswald H. Ernst   March 31, 1893–August 21, 1898

25. First Lieutenant Albert L. Mills   August 22, 1898–August 31, 1906

26. Major Hugh L. Scott   August 31, 1906–August 31, 1910

27. Major General Thomas H. Barry   August 31, 1910–August 31, 1912

28. Colonel Clarence F. Townsley   August 31, 1912–June 30, 1916

29. Colonel John Biddle   July 1, 1916–May 31, 1917

30. Colonel Samuel E. Tillman   June 13, 1917–June 11, 1919

31. Brigadier General Douglas Mac-   June 12, 1919–June 30, 1922
    Arthur

32. Brigadier General Fred W. Sladen   July 1, 1922–March 23, 1926

33. Brigadier General Merch B. Stewart   March 24, 1926–October 5, 1927

34. Major General Edwin B. Winans   October 23, 1927–February 25, 1928

35. Major General William R. Smith   February 26, 1928–April 30, 1932

36. Major General William D. Connor   May 1, 1932–January 17, 1938

37. Brigadier General Jay L. Benedict   February 5, 1938–November 17, 1940

38. Brigadier General Robert L. Eichel-   November 18, 1940–January 12, 1942
    berger

39. Major General Francis B. Wilby   January 13, 1942–September 4, 1945

40. Major General Maxwell D. Taylor   September 4, 1945–January 28, 1949

41. Major General Bryant E. Moore   January 28, 1949–January 17, 1951

42. Major General Frederick A. Irving   February 1, 1951–August 31, 1954

43. Lieutenant General Blackshear M.   September 3, 1954–July 15, 1956
    Bryan

44. Major General Garrison H. David-   July 15, 1956–July 1, 1960
    son

45. Major General William C. West-   July 1, 1960–June 25, 1963
    moreland

46. Major General James B. Lampert   June 28, 1963–January 6, 1966

47. Major General Donald V. Bennett   January 10, 1966–June 15, 1968

48. Major General Samuel W. Koster   June 26, 1968–March 22, 1970

49.	Major General William A. Knowlton	March 23, 1970–July 18, 1974
50.	Major General Sidney B. Berry	July 19, 1974–June 13, 1977
51.	Lieutenant General Andrew J. Goodpaster	June 13, 1977–June 30, 1981
52.	Lieutenant General Willard W. Scott, Jr.	July 1, 1981–July 28, 1986
53.	Lieutenant General Dave R. Palmer	July 28, 1986–July 22, 1991
54.	Lieutenant General Howard D. Graves	July 22, 1991–

NOTES

1. Rank given is rank individual held at time appointed Superintendent.

2. Williams resigned his commission on June 20, 1803, because of a dispute with the Secretary of War concerning his ability to command line troops stationed at West Point. In the interim until the dispute was settled and he was recommissioned, no permanent Superintendent was appointed, the senior Corps of Engineers officer at West Point serving as Acting Superintendent.

3. Partridge was never formally appointed Superintendent but served as Acting Superintendent during extended absences of Colonel Swift on duties elsewhere as Chief of the Corps of Engineers.

4. Captain Lee also held the brevet rank of colonel.

Appendix B

Commandants of Cadets[1]

1. Second Lieutenant George W. Gardiner   September 15, 1817–April 2, 1818

2. Captain John Bliss   April 2, 1818–January 15, 1819

3. Captain John R. Bell   February 8, 1819–March 17, 1820

4. Captain William J. Worth   March 17, 1820–December 2, 1828

5. Captain Ethan A. Hitchcock   March 13, 1829–June 24, 1833

6. Major John Fowle   July 10, 1833–March 31, 1838

7. First Lieutenant Charles F. Smith   April 1, 1838–September 1, 1842

8. First Lieutenant John A. Thomas   September 1, 1842–December 14, 1845

9. Captain Bradford R. Alden   December 14, 1845–November 1, 1852

10. Captain Robert S. Garnett   November 1, 1852–July 31, 1854

11. Captain William H. T. Walker   July 31, 1854–May 27 1856

12. Major William J. Hardee   July 22, 1856–September 8, 1860

13. Captain John F. Reynolds   September 8, 1860–July 25, 1861

14. Major Christopher C. Auger   August 26, 1861–December 5, 1861

15. Captain Kenner Garrard   December 5, 1861–September 28, 1862

16. Major Henry B. Clitz   October 23, 1862–July 4, 1864

17. Captain John C. Tidball   July 10, 1864–September 22, 1864

18. Major Henry M. Black   September 22, 1864–July 1, 1870

19. Lieutenant Colonel Emory Upton   July 1, 1870–June 30, 1875

20. Lieutenant Colonel Thomas H. Neill   July 1, 1875–June 30, 1879

21. Major Henry M. Lazelle   July 1, 1879–August 4, 1882

22. Captain Henry C. Hasbrouck   August 22, 1882–February 1, 1888

23. Major Hamilton S. Hawkins   February 1, 1888–September 1, 1892

24. Captain Samuel M. Mills, Jr.   September 1, 1892–June 15, 1897

25. Captain Otto L. Hein   June 15, 1897–June 15, 1901

26. Captain Charles G. Treat   June 15, 1901–June 15, 1905

27. Captain Robert L. Howze   June 15, 1905–February 1, 1909

28. Major Frederick W. Sibley   February 1, 1909–January 19, 1911

29. Major Fred W. Sladen   January 19, 1911–January 23, 1914

30. Captain Morton F. Smith   April 3, 1914–June 16 1916[2]

31. Captain Guy V. Henry   June 16, 1916–September 6, 1918

32. Colonel Jens Bugge   November 8, 1918–July 17, 1919[3]

33. Lieutenant Colonel Robert M. Danford   August 20, 1919–July 1, 1923

34. Colonel Merch B. Stewart   July 1, 1923–March 23, 1926

35. Major Campbell B. Hodges   April 15, 1926–March 25, 1929

36. Lieutenant Colonel Robert C. Richardson March 26, 1929–June 13, 1933

37. Lieutenant Colonel Simon B. Buckner, Jr. June 13, 1933–June 30, 1936

38. Lieutenant Colonel Dennis E. McCuniff   July 1, 1936–June 30, 1937

39. Lieutenant Colonel Charles W. Ryder   July 1, 1937–January 15, 1941

40. Lieutenant Colonel Frederick A. Irving   January 15, 1941–February 25, 1942

41. Colonel Philip E. Gallagher   February 25, 1942–November 5, 1943

42. Brigadier General George Honnen   November 6, 1943–January 30, 1946

43. Brigadier General Gerald J. Higgins   January 30, 1946–June 15, 1948

44. Colonel Paul D. Harkins   June 15, 1948–June 10, 1951

45. Colonel John K. Waters   June 11, 1951–July 19, 1952

46. Brigadier General John H. Michaelis   August 1, 1952–August 10, 1954

47. Brigadier General Edwin J. Messinger   September 1, 1954–April 19, 1956

48. Brigadier General John L. Throck- April 19, 1956–August 31, 1959
    morton

49. Brigadier General Charles W. G. August 31, 1959–June 30, 1961
    Rich

50. Brigadier General Richard G. Stil- July 1, 1961–March 9, 1963
    well

51. Brigadier General Michael S. Davi- March 9, 1963–March 19, 1965
    son

52. Brigadier General Richard P. Scott April 17, 1965–August 20, 1967

53. Brigadier General Bernard W. Rog- September 15, 1967–September 22, 1969
    ers

54. Brigadier General Sam S. Walker October 15, 1969–September 17, 1972

55. Brigadier General Philip R. Feir September 17, 1972–April 13, 1975

56. Brigadier General Walter F. Ulmer, April 15, 1975–1977
    Jr.

57. Brigadier General John C. Bard 1977–1979

58. Brigadier General Joseph P. Franklin 1979–1982

59. Brigadier General John H. Moeller- 1982–1984
    ing

60. Brigadier General Peter J. Boylan, Jr. 1984–1987

61. Brigadier General Fred A. Gorden 1987–1990

62. Brigadier General David A. Bramlett 1990–1992

63. Brigadier General Robert F. Foley 1992–

NOTES

1. Rank shown is rank at the time the individual was appointed Commandant of Cadets.
2. Died at West Point, June 16, 1916.
3. Died at West Point, July 17, 1919.

Appendix C

Deans of the Academic Board

The position of Dean of the Academic Board was formally authorized by Act of Congress on June 20, 1946. However, the senior professor was referred to as the Dean of the Academic Board or Dean of the United States Military Academy from at least the late 1880s. It can be assumed that this practice may have originated much earlier. If such is true and the senior professor was so designated from the Academy's earliest years, the following individuals, as Professor and Head of their respective deparments, would have had this honorary title.

Jared Mansfield, Department of Natural and Experimental Philosophy, 1818–1827
David B. Douglass, Department of Civil and Military Engineering, 1828–1830
Charles Davies, Department of Mathematics, 1831–1836
Thomas Warner, Department of Geography, History, and Ethics, 1837–1838
Dennis H. Mahan, Department of Civil and Military Engineering, 1839–1871
Albert E. Church, Department of Mathematics, 1872–1877
Henry L. Kendrick, Department of Chemistry, Mineralogy, and Geology, 1878–1880
Patrice de Janon, Department of Spanish, 1881–1882
Peter S. Michie, Department of Natural and Experimental Philosophy, 1883–1900
Charles W. Larned, Department of Drawing, 1901–1911
Gustav J. Fieberger, Department of Civil and Military Engineering, 1912–1921
Charles P. Echols, Department of Mathematics, 1922–1931
Clifton C. Carter, Department of Natural and Experimental Philosophy, 1932–1940
Roger G. Alexander, Department of Drawing, 1941–1945 and Acting Dean, September 2, 1945–July 20, 1946

• • • • •

The following individuals have been formally designated as Dean of the Academic Board. Included is the department in which each was Professor before being appointed Dean; all held the rank of brigadier general.

1. Roger G. Alexander, Department of Drawing, July 22, 1946–July 3, 1947
2. Harris Jones, Department of Mathematics, September 1, 1947–July 31, 1956
3. Thomas D. Stamps, Department of Military Art and Engineering, August 1, 1956– July 31, 1957
4. Gerald A. Counts, Department of Physics and Chemistry, August 1, 1957–September 30, 1959
5. William W. Bessell, Jr., Department of Mathematics, October 1, 1959–May 31, 1965
6. John E. Jannarone, Department of Physics and Chemistry, June 1, 1965–December 31, 1973
7. John S. B. Dick (Acting Dean), Department of Mathematics, January 1, 1974–August 15, 1974
8. Frederick A. Smith, Jr., Department of Mechanics, August 16, 1974–July 30, 1985
9. Roy K. Flint, Department of History, August 1, 1985–June 30, 1990
10. Gerald E. Galloway, Jr., Department of Geography and Computer Science, 1 July 1990–

Appendix D

The 1780 Map of West Point: An Unintentional Historical Hoax

For many years, historians and history buffs alike have cited a map of West Point dated 1780 as being one of the most accurate and detailed maps of the period. This map first came to prominence in the early 1900s when Dr. Edward S. Holden, the USMA Librarian, included the map in the two-volume *Centennial of the United States Military Academy at West Point, 1802–1902*. Although no definite record can be cited, one can assume that Holden "discovered" this map while researching the history of the Military Academy, using primarily sources in the USMA Library. So important did Holden consider the map that he included it in a list of maps of West Point and in his chronological bibliography of important events concerning the Post and the Academy.

The map was published in France in 1816 as an illlustration for *Complot d'Arnold et de Sir Henry Clinton contre Les Etats-Unis d'Amerique et contre le General George Washington* by F. Barbe-Marbois. The text of the book discussed the Arnold conspiracy only; there was no description of the post conforming to the buildings shown on the map. Holden apparently accepted the map as genuine and, adding two and two together, declared in his *Centennial* bibliography that "at this time there was an engineering school, a library, and a laboratory lodged in three buildings at West Point." Unfortunately, the sum that Holden obtained by adding two plus two did not add up to four; today, it is all too evident that the map is not an accurate depiction of the post of West Point in 1780.

Equally unfortunate has been the tendency of later historians to accept Holden's statement as fact. For example, Aloysius A. Norton used this map in his 1989 *History of the United States Military Academy* as proof that there was a library at West Point in 1780. Other historians have also used the map, indicating it to be an accurate portrayal of 1780 West Point. Significantly, historians who have carefully researched the period do not cite the document or use it as an illustration. Miller, Lockey, and Visconti do not use it in their 1988 USMA History Department publication, *Highland Fortress: West Point during the American Revolution, 1775–1783*, nor did Dave R. Palmer cite the map in his 1969 book, *The River and the Rock*.

The first serious questioning of the authenticity of the map was raised by Colonel Merle G. Sheffield, USMA Class of 1948, during his assignment to the USMA Physics

Department. A history buff, Sheffield devoted much time to a careful study of West Point during the Revolutionary period. His noting that other maps of the period did not agree with the 1780 drawing led him to compare that map with others drawn a quarter-century later. His conclusion left no doubt that this map was completely inaccurate and should be considered an unintentional historical hoax.

Sheffield compared the 1780 map with the Villefranche map in Boynton's *History of West Point*; there is little similarity between the two. He then studied the 1783 map prepared and attested to by S. DeWitt, Geographer to the Army, and again found little similarity. Sheffield also studied the L'Enfant panorama drawn about 1783. This drawing clearly shows Fort Clinton, the "Old Provost" on the edge of Execution Hollow, and barracks on the present site of professors' quarters. Other than the Old Provost, none of the Barbe-Marbois map's buildings are shown in L'Enfant's panorama. The findings derived from these comparisons, however, were not sufficient to definitely state that the 1780 map was not accurate because the other Revolutionary War maps showed only a few of the buildings known to have been erected at West Point before the end of the conflict. If the Barbe-Marbois map did not agree with the other period maps, where did he get that map or the information included on it?

The next thing Sheffield did was to compare the 1780 map with authenticated maps of the early Military Academy period. He found that a map drawn by the first Teacher of Drawing, Christian E. Zoeller, in 1808 appeared to agree with the Barbe-Marbois drawing. Sheffield carefully labeled buildings on the Zoeller map and then labeled similar structures on the 1780 drawing. He found that, after translating the French titles into English, the two maps were compatible. "The map [by Zoeller] was copied, rather poorly," stated Sheffield, "and Zoeller's English titles carefully replaced and nicely tabulated in French. There are no other essential differences between the two maps." Every building shown and tabulated by Barbe-Marbois is shown on the Zoeller map and identified in English.

As far as is known, Sheffield's short paper on the 1780 map was not published and consequently was not known widely. The authors of this article, while studying maps in the USMA Library and Museum as part of their research for a projected West Point Atlas, read the Sheffield analysis. They compared the 1780 maps with same Revolutionary period maps used by Sheffield and agreed with his conclusions. To further substantiate the difference between the Barbe-Marbois map and authenticated Revolutionary drawings, they also compared it with maps drawn by Greenleaf, Kosciuszko, Bourg, McDougall, and Romans. These drawings had no similarity with the Barbe-Marbois map.

To confirm Sheffield's conclusions that the 1780 map was copied from other maps subsequent to 1802, the authors compared it with drawings by Cadet John Webber in 1815, the George Whistler 1816 map, the Joseph G. Bruffs map (circa 1816), and the T. B. Brown map of 1826. Although the post-1815 maps also show the new barracks and mess buildings, the pre-1815 structures definitely correlate with the buildings on the Barbe-Marbois map. The only possible conclusion, based on this additional research, is that Merle Sheffield was correct in his statement that the 1780 map is incorrect and that it was copied from a map drawn after the establishment of USMA.

Why did Barbe-Marbois use post-1802 information for his 1780 map? One can only guess at his reasons. One thing, however, is certain: he had no intention of deceiving anyone into believing that there actually was an academy at West Point in 1780. Barbe-Marbois had served in the Continental Army during the Revolutionary War. He later became an official of the French government and was Napoleon's Minister of the Treasury, negotiating the sale of the Louisiana Territory to the United States in 1802. As Sheffield stated in his paper, "Since the main events in the conspiracy [Arnold's intent to turn West Point over to the British] occurred in 1780, it was only natural that Barbe-Marbois wanted his illustration to reflect that period. We can only regret that he was unable to find a map of West Point suitable to his needs."

All of this can be summarized in a very simple statement: the map in the 1816 work by Barbe-Marbois is not an accurate portrayal of West Point in 1780. Contrary to assumptions based upon that map, there was no Ecole de Genie at West Point; there was no library; there was no hospital at West Point in 1780. In fact, only two things are shown which actually were there in 1780 *and* in 1808: the Old Provost building [identified by Barbe-Marbois as the "Prisons Caserne"] and Kosciusko's Garden. An unintentional historical hoax was initiated, one that has been accepted as fact for over a century. Merle Sheffield certainly deserves thanks for detecting the inaccuracy of the 1780 Barbe-Marbois map.

One must pose another question, however. The Zoeller 1808 map shows the "Long Barracks" built on Trophy Point in 1795. Why did Barbe-Marbois neglect to include the barracks on his map? Is it possible that he copied another map drawn before the barracks were erected? If so, what map did he use and where is it today?

The above article by George S. Pappas and John K. Robertson was published in Assembly *in March 1992. Because it is important to lessen the chance of the 1780 map being considered authentic and used in future writings about Revolutionary War West Point, the entire article is included as an appendix to this work.*

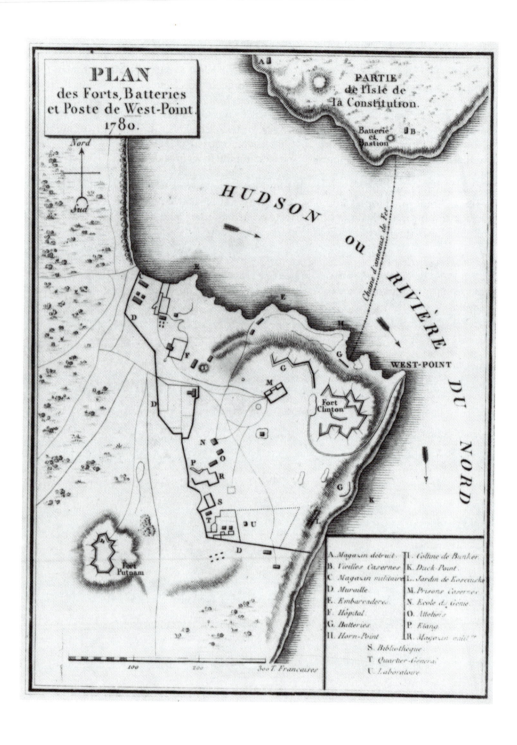

PLAN
des Forts, Batteries
et Poste de West-Point.
1780.

Nord
Sud

PARTIE
de l'Isle de
la Constitution.

Batterie
et
Bastion

HUDSON OU RIVIÈRE DU NORD

Chaîne d'anneaux de Fer

WEST-POINT

Fort Clinton

Fort Putnam

A..Magasin detruit.
B..Vieilles Casernes.
C..Magasin militaire.
D..Muraille.
E..Embarcaderes.
F..Hôpital.
G..Batteries.
H..Horn-Point.
I..Colline de Bunker.
K..Duck-Point.
L..Jardin de Koscuisko.
M..Prisons Casernes.
N..Ecole du Génie.
O..Attelier.
P..Etang.
R..Magasin milit.
S..Bibliothèque.
T..Quartier-Général.
U..Laboratoire.

100   200   300 T. Françaises

Appendix E

Comments on Sources

Rather than burden the reader with the hundreds of footnotes required in a work of this nature, I prefer to discuss the major sources used in a short bibliographic essay for each chapter. For those historians interested in a detailed attribution of comments included in this text, I have fully anotated a copy of the manuscript, which is available in the Special Collections Division of the United States Military Academy Library.

Reasons for my decision against footnoting are readily apparent when one looks at the bibliography of sources used. I have consulted hundreds of letters, diaries, and unpublished memoirs. Journal articles, books, and official documents have been extensively and carefully reviewed. The notes that follow discuss only those sources that are considered to be the most noteworthy.

Several works have been consulted in preparing the text of almost every chapter. Instead of mentioning these references in each of the chapter essays, I am citing these in this preface. Boynton's *History of West Point* has been used in all chapters covering the periods from 1802 through 1863. Cullum's *Biographical Register of Officers and Graduates*, Volumes 1 through 5 have provided information about graduates and, in particular, their assignments to the Military Academy staff or faculty. The USMA Association of Graduates' *Register of Graduates and Former Cadets* provided information supplementing the Cullum *Registers*. Colonel John K. Robertson's *Who Was Who, 1802–1990* has provided additional information concerning assignments to the staff and faculty and traces the various changes in academic departments from 1802 to the present day. To obtain information concerning the Army in various periods, I have used Weigley's *The History of the United States Army*, Dupuy's *Compact History of the United States Army*, and Jacobs' *The Beginning of the U.S. Army, 1783–1812*. Ganoe's *The History of the United States Army* provided details of Army history and its relationship to the Military Academy. Morris's *Encyclopedia of American History* has provided needed information concerning contemporary events in the periods covered in each chapter. *The Centennial of the United States Military Academy* provided summary information concerning development of the curriculum and the contributions of graduates to the development of both the Academy and the nation. An excellent summary of Congressional Acts concerning the Military Academy is Robert H. Hall's *Laws of Congress Relative to West Point and the United States Military Academy from 1785 to 1877*.

1775–1802

1. The Foundation Is Laid

Comments concerning the need for professional training of officers of the Revolutionary War army can be found in many discussions of that conflict. Although this work does not fully described the role of West Point in the Revolutionary War, I have consulted Palmer's *The River and the Rock* and Miller's *The Fortification of West Point during the American Revolution*, which provided detailed information concerning structures and personnel at West Point during the Revolution.

The most important sources used were the papers of Henry Burbeck in the Special Collections Division of the USMA Library and in the Fraunces' Tavern Museum in New York City. These two collections, which have no duplicatory materials, indicate that Burbeck—fortunately—was a pack rat and retained many military documents and copies of his official correspondence. The West Point collection includes muster reports, letters to subordinate commanders, and reports from officers at West Point responsible for the operation of the Artillerist and Engineer Academy. From these papers, it has been possible to obtain names of cadets and student officers and instructors. Some information concerning the curriculum of the pre-1802 academy can also be found in the Burbeck papers. Much of this data has been verified in other documents in the National Archives. Additional information has been obtained from unit muster reports and Court Martial records, Quartermaster and Ordnance Waste Reports, and other materials in the Special Collections. Gardner's *Memoir of Brevt. Brig. Genl. Henry Burbeck* provides an excellent summary of Burbeck's responsibility for establishing and maintaining the early academy. The importance of these materials concerning that academy cannot be overemphasized for they provide almost the only detailed description of the pre-1802 institution. Joseph Swift, first USMA graduate, was a cadet in the earlier academy; his *Memoirs* provide an informal description of cadet life and an excellent description of West Point's physical plant in 1801 and 1802. Swift's writings also assert that there were three graduates of the *U.S. Military Academy* before he graduated in 1802. The Swift papers in the Special Collections provide additional information about the pre-1802 Artillerist and Engineer Academy. Heitman's *Historical Register and Dictionary of the United States Army* provided biographical information concerning officers and cadets at the Artillerist and Engineer Academy. John Robertson's unpublished notes concerning the John Moore holdings at West Point and other land owners provided information concerning the use of West Point lands during and after the Revolutionary War.

1802–1817

2. Struggle for Survival

In addition to secondary sources used, I found that Special Collections possesses many primary source materials concerning the early U.S. Military Academy. The Sylvanus Thayer papers and the Alden Partridge papers provide some descriptive information. Documents in the Cullum Historical Files include early graduates' memoirs written in answer to Cullum's questionnaires. Also included in the Cullum Historical Files is the correspondence between Cullum and Thayer at the time Cullum was preparing his history of the Military Academy for Volume 3 of the Cullum *Register of Officers and Cadets*. In many letters, Thayer provided Cullum with information about the Academy when Thayer was a cadet. Thayer correspondence with Joseph Swift added additional information concerning the 1808 institution. The Edward Holden papers and scrapbooks contain many documents and papers collected by Holden during his research for the history of the Military Academy included in *The Centennial of the United States Military Academy*. Many of the documents were copied from records in the War Department now in the National Archives and from Corps of Engineer records, some of which are now in the West Point Library Special Collections. The USMA Archives include data in *Cadets Admitted Book* from 1800 to 1902, the *Register of Cadet Casualties* from 1802 to 1902, and the *Register of Officers and Cadets* from 1802 to 1849 (these archival records were also used in other chapters and will not be cited elsewhere). The small collection of Jonathan Williams' papers provide supplementary information concerning his superintendency. The personal papers of Abraham Wendell, Class of 1814, provide a description of his early cadet years. Maps of the period, especially the Zoeller 1808 map, provided factual information concerning the buildings at West Point.

3. Existence in Name Only

Joseph Swift's *Memoirs* and personal papers, Boynton's *History of West Point*, the Williams papers, and the Thayer papers provide much information about the turbulent existence of the Military Academy from 1805 to 1812. Forman's *West Point* summarizes the importance of the American Military Philosophical Society and its contribution to the development of the Academy. Some of the pamphlets published by the Society are included in the holdings of the West Point Library Special Collections. Correspondence between Jared Mansfield and the Secretary of War are included in the Mansfield papers. The Partridge papers provide some information about this period, although not in great detail. The Williams papers and the Holden papers detail Williams' efforts to have the Military Academy moved either to Washington, D.C., or to Staten Island. Swift's *Memoirs* and papers provide details concerning the court martial of Major Barron. Correspondence between Thayer and Swift indicate Thayer's efforts to correct Swift's description of the Academy during this period, intended as part of his *Memoirs*. Thayer's correspondence with Cullum provided Cullum with much of his description of the early Academy included in Cullum's history of the Academy included in Volume 3 of his *Register of Officers and Graduates of the United States Military Academy*. Information concerning Secretary of War Eustis's handling of Academy matters is detailed in the Holden papers. Unfortunately, no contemporary cadet letters were available to provide firsthand descriptions of cadet life in this period. The description of cadet uniforms was obtained in various publications of the Company of Military Historians and in Todd's *Cadet Gray*.

4. Right Man at the Right Time?

Materials in the Cullum Register files provide much information concerning Academy affairs and cadet life during the period from 1812 to 1814. Answers to Cullum's questionnaire by Harvey Brown, Class of 1818; George D. Ramsay, Class of 1820; Horace Webster, Class of 1818; and Simon Willard, Class of 1818, are worthy of special mention because of the many details included. Personal papers of John A. Webber, Class of 1815, provide additional information. The Jared Mansfield papers provide an excellent description of the Academy as Mansfield found it when he returned to West Point in August 1812. His daughter's descriptions of the Post are filed with the Mansfield collection.

Boynton's *History of West Point* and maps drawn in that period provide additional information. The Holden papers include many official papers concerning the relationship of Academy personnel with the Secretary of War. The Partridge papers add additional information concerning the curriculum, messing arrangements, and cadet discipline. Included in the Partridge collection are the papers of Henry Giles, Class of 1818; William Malcolm, Class of 1819; and John R. Vinton, Class of 1815. The Thayer papers and Thayer correspondence in the Cullum personal papers and the Swift papers provide additional information for this period.

5. Deliver Your Sword to the Bearer

The Partridge papers, the Swift papers and *Memoirs*, the Thayer papers, the Mansfield papers, the O'Connor papers, the Holden papers, and the Cullum Historical Files all contain much information about the turbulent period from 1814 until Partridge's arrest in 1817.

The records of both the 1816 Court of Inquiry investigating charges against Partridge and the 1817 Court Martial of Partridge include statements of the many witnesses who testified for and against him. Simon Willard's answer to the Cullum questionnaire (in the Cullum Historical Files) concerned his early cadet years. John Wright's (Class of 1814) correspondence concerning his cadet career is included in the Partridge papers. George Ramsay, Class of 1817, provided many details concerning the Partridge period in his answer to the Cullum questionnaire. Although Cullum included Ramsay's recollections in Volume 3 of his *Register*, he deleted all positive comments about Partridge. Researchers should use only the original Ramsay recollections. Details concerning the cadet uniform of this period are to be found in Todd's *Cadet Gray* and in the *Journal* of the Company of Military Historians.

1817–1828

6. The Rebuilding Begins

A wealth of information from primary sources is available for the period of Thayer's superintendency. The West Point Library Special Collections has many groups of personal papers and both published and unpublished memoirs. The personal papers of Thomas J. Cram, Class of 1826, include an analysis of Thayer's development of the Academy. The Cullum Historical Files include many answers to his questionnaires from graduates of this period. Cullum's personal papers include his extensive correspondence with Thayer, which provided Cullum with many details of Thayer's activities. The David B. Douglass papers include may items relating to curricular matters. Samuel P. Heintzelman's (Class of 1826) personal papers include his journal, which provides a daily account of cadet life. The Holden papers include many documents Holden obtained for his research concerning Academy history. Lucius Jone, non-graduate of the Class of 1818, described cadet life in his letters. The personal papers of Jared Mansfield and his sons, Edward D. Mansfield, Class of 1819, and Joseph K. F. Mansfield, Class of 1822, all contain descriptions of the Academy and of the Post of West Point. George Ramsay, Class of 1820, included comparisons of the Partridge era and the Thayer period in his answers to the Cullum questionnaire and other papers. The Swift papers and *Memoirs* and the Thayer papers include much material related to Thayer's superintendency. Horace Webster, Class of 1818, included descriptions of cadet uniforms and discipline in both the Partridge and early Thayer periods. Perhaps the best single description of the early Thayer superintendency is to be found in Albert E. Church's *Personal Reminiscences of the Military Academy from 1824 to 1831*, which was an address Church made to the Association of Graduates at its 1879 reunion. The many maps of this period provide details concerning the physical improvements made by Thayer. Other personal papers and memoirs provide additional information, but those cited above can be considered to be the most descriptive materials available.

7. Governed by the Rules and Articles of War

Albert Church's memoirs, the Cullum Historical Files, the Holden papers, and the Thayer papers provide many details concerning Thayer's development of the Academy during the first years of his superintendency. The personal papers of Edward Giles, William Malcolm, the Mansfield family, and George D. Ramsay provide information concerning cadet activities. Reports of Boards of Visitors mention the improvements made by Thayer and the excellence of instruction. The memoirs of John H. B. Latrobe give an excellent description of cadet life during this period.

8. Still in a State of Progressive Development

Reports of Boards of Visitors provide a yearly analysis and description of Thayer's progress in improving the Academy. More personal observations can be found in Church's *Memoirs*. Criticism of Thayer's methods are included in the Jared Mansfield papers. This collection also includes Mrs. Mansfield's comments about her husband's constant complaining. The Alexander Macomb papers include correspondence with Thayer, describing activities at the Academy. The National Park Service's *Historic Structures Inventory, West Point, New York* describes the building of the Superintendent's Quarters and other officers' quarters and traces the changes made to these structures during the ensuing years. Maps of the period, many drawn by cadets or officer instructors, provide a vivid indication of the changes from year to year. The description of Thayer's office in the basement of the Superintendent's Quarters is found in Church's *Memoirs* and also in the Thomas Cram personal papers. Most of the personal papers of cadets of this period mention various types of punishment and the recreation available to cadets. Cadet regulations state prohibitions against various activities and the punishment that could be expected if these regulations were violated. The Latrobe *Memoirs* provide a detailed description of the 1821 march to Boston, the festive treatment of cadets by Bostonians, the visit with John Adams, and the return to West Point.

9. Members of One Brotherhood

The memoirs of Church and Latrobe provide many details concerning cadet training and academic instruction. The Thayer papers include many letters expressing his desire to improve cadet living conditions. The Cram papers contain many statements describing cadet life and the spartan existence experienced by all. West Point Library records provide lists of books purchased each year and the list of books sent to the Secretary of War and the Artillery School at Fort Monroe. The Library still retains copies of many of the books authored by Academy professors. Copies of letters from Andrew Donelson, nephew of Andrew Jackson, can be found in the Thayer papers. Thayer's opinion of Jefferson Davis in a letter to George Cullum is in the Cullum Personal Papers. The letters of George Tichnor to his wife in 1826 provide perhaps the most complete description of the examinations attended by a Board of Visitors and the schedule prepared for them by Thayer and his staff. Tichnor's comments on the visitors' quarters in the mess building substantiated Thayer's insistence that a hotel was badly needed. The great involvement of members of the Board of Visitors and their thorough scrutiny of all Academy activities is in marked contrast to the procedures followed by today's Board.

10. Living Armory of the Nation

James Monroe's letter asking for advice concerning the University of Virginia and Thayer's reply are in the Thayer papers. Perhaps the most complete and detailed description of the Jefferson Davis instigated Christmas Eve revelry is James Agnew's *Egg Nog Riot*. Although Agnew did take some liberties with his descriptions of the events of those fateful hours, his comprehensive research and careful analysis provide a truly excellent and authentic account of the Egg Nog Riot and its aftermath. Material concerning Dennis Mahan's trip to Europe are included in both the Mahan and Thayer papers. Details concerning the changes to cadet uniforms is found in Todd's *Cadet Gray*. The Heintzelman papers provide an excellent description of the fire that destroyed the Long Barracks. The Andrew Donelson personal papers include his letters to Thayer; some of these are also a part of the Thayer papers.

1829–1833

11. I Have the Honor to Tender My Resignation

Weigley provides an excellent and comprehensive description of the militia in his *History of the United States Army*. The memoirs of Church, Latrobe, and Francis H. Smith provide many details about Academy activities during this period. The letters of Charles Mason, Class of 1829, describe cadet social activities. Hitchcock's comments on his appointment as Commandant of Cadets and his discussion with Andrew Jackson are provided in detail in Denton's *The Formative Years of the United States Military Academy, 1775–1833*. Church's description of the honor of the Corps of Cadets and its esprit de corps are found in the Cullum Historical Files. Copies of the Partridge pamphlet "The Military Academy at West Point Unmasked or Corruption and Military Despotism Exposed" are in the West Point Library Special Collections. Thayer's letters concerning this pamphlet to the Secretary of War and the Chief of Engineers are in the Thayer papers. Cullum's personal papers include his cadet letters, which provide excellent descriptions of cadet activities and political activities of that time. Thayer's correspondence with the Secretary of War during the month's prior to his resignation are in the Thayer papers.

12. I Believe It the Best School in the World

Letters in the Cullum Personal Papers provide an indication of cadet concern when word of Thayer's resignation spread throughout the Corps and the cadet reaction to the War Department order decreasing the amount of graduation leave and restricting visits to Washington, D.C. Much of the bias toward Andrew Jackson can be attributed to Cullum's analysis of the reasons for Thayer's resignation and Jackson's supposed antagonism toward Thayer. Cram's papers include comments concerning cadet reaction to and conjectures on the reasons for Thayer's departure. Cram also reported the interview with Thayer and his refusal to permit his portrait to be painted. Correspondence regarding the copying of the Sully portrait of Thayer is in the Holden papers. The descriptions of the Post in 1833 are found in cadet letters; maps of the period add to these descriptions. The Thayer correspondence with James Monroe concerning the University of Virginia are in the Thayer papers. Cram's papers include the description of Thayer's sudden unannounced departure.

1833–1852

13. A Firm Hand Is Needed

Comparative rank of Engineer officers in 1833 was obtained from the Cullum *Register of Graduates*. The summary of Major Fowle's career is found in Heitman's *Historical Register and Dictionary of the United States Army*, Volume 1. The West Point Library Special Collections has many collections of letters, diaries, and memoirs of cadets of this period, including John Bratt, Class of 1837; George Cullum, Class of 1833; William Frazer, Class of 1836; Bushrod Johnson, Class of 1840; James L. Mason, Class of 1836; Frederick A. Smith, Class of 1833; Walter Sherwood, Class of 1837; Isaac Stevens, Class of 1839; and Alfred Sully, Class of 1842. Although Special Collections holds papers of other cadets, these provide the most detailed descriptions of cadet activities during this period. The Sully papers include an excellent account of the fire that destroyed the Academic Building and the spontaneous action by cadets to save books and portraits. Correspondence in the Thayer papers includes letters from Gouverneur Kemble concerning Thayer's possible reappointment as Superintendent. The Special Collections also holds copies of the Court of Inquiry that investigated Cadet Sanders's charges against Professor Mahan. A Special Collections file of material on class rings includes details on the changes of rings in various periods. The Library has an extensive collection of rings donated by graduates or their heirs.

14. Preparing for the Ultimate Test

Personal papers, letters, diaries, and memoirs in the West Point Library Special Collections concerning this period include those of George H. Derby, Class of 1846; Samuel French, Class of 1843; John P. Hatch, Class of 1845; and Augustus Pleasanton, Class of 1826. The Derby letters are especially noteworthy, for they include weekly writings to his mother covering his entire four years as a cadet. Details concerning furniture and equipment each cadet was required to purchase are listed in Cadet Regulations and other official publications. The Library Special Collections possesses many plans and other drawings of Academy buildings. Many cadet drawings provide details of building architecture and interior arrangements. Special Collections also has an extensive collection of sheet music written by cadets, Band personnel, or dedicated to the Academy by other composers. Aloysius A. Norton's *A Study of the Customs and Traditions of West Point in the American Novel* discusses early fictional works concerning the Academy and its graduates. Details concerning the cadet uniform of the Delafield period are found in Todd's *Cadet Gray* and in the *Journal* of the Company of Military Historians. Two issues of *The West Pointer*, edited by Cadet Schureman, are in the Special Collections holdings, as are publications of the Dialectic Society. A description of the courtesies exchanged by British and American officers in Maine is found in Haskin's *First Regiment of Artillery*.

15. We Follow, Close Order, Behind You

Cadet letters from 1845 to 1853 are included in the papers of William P. Craighill, Class of 1853; George H. Derby, Class of 1846; William Dutton, Class of 1846; Thomas J. Haines, Class of 1849; David Stanley, Class of 1852; and Joseph Tidball, Class of 1848. The memoirs of Mrs. Theophile D'Oremieulx, wife of a civilian French instructor, provide an intimate and detailed description of family life and social activities during this period. The letters of Mary O'Maher, daughter of Commissary Officer Timothy O'Maher, complement the D'Oremieulx memoirs. The personal papers of William W. Bailey, son of Professor Jacob Bailey, and his *My Boyhood at West Point*, published in 1891, include excellent descriptions of the activities of young men and women of the time. His papers provide descriptions of many cadets and officers stationed at West Point. The Dennis Mahan papers include his letter to the Secretary of War complaining about the refusal of Superintendent Brewerton to permit officers to attend church services in Buttermilk Falls instead of attending chapel services on Post. Details concerning the changes in cadet uniforms are from Todd's *Cadet Gray* and Company of Military Historians' publications. Names of officers stationed at West Point are listed in John Robertson's *Who Was Who*. Crackel provides an excellent description of new buildings in his *The Illustrated History of West Point*. The accomplishments of graduates in many civilian fields is described in many *Assembly* articles and in Dupuy's *Men of West Point*. The promotion of graduates during the Mexican War to either brevet or permanent rank were obtained from the Cullum *Register of Graduates*. Account of First Artillery officers is in Haskin's *The First Regiment of Artillery*.

1852–1865

16. The Ante-Bellum Army

Material for this description of the Army before the Civil War was obtained from Ganoe's *The History of the United States Army*, Wiegley's *The History of the United States Army* and *The American Way of War*, and Dupuy's *Compact History of the United States Army*.

17. When Shall We Meet Again?

The West Point Library Special Collections has a great number of collections of letters, diaries, memoirs, and other personal papers of cadets at West Point between 1852 and 1865. Most noteworthy of these collections are those of the following cadets: Henry Dupont, Class of May 1861; William Harris, Class of June 1861; Stephen Lyford, Class of June 1861; Tully McCrea, Class of 1862; Thomas Rowland, non-graduate Class of 1863; Samuel Benjamin, Class of May 1861; and Emory Upton, Class of May 1861. The letters of Captain Robert Anderson to his wife provide an excellent description of the Post of West Point and social activities, as well as his comments on Jefferson Davis as chairman of the 1866 committee surveying Academy procedures. Morris Schaff's memoirs are a vivid and detailed description of events at West Point from 1857 to 1862. Oliver Howard's autobiography includes comments on the religious revival at West Point during this period. Assignment dates of officers and professors is from Robertson's *Who Was Who*. The descriptions of cadet uniform changes are from Todd's *Cadet Gray* and publications of the Company of Military Historians. Many of the descriptions of Robert E. Lee and his family are in Rhodes' *Robert E. Lee, the West Pointer*. Although not as well known as Freeman's superb biography of Lee, Rhodes' work concentrates on Lee's service at West Point as a cadet and as Superintendent. The small collection of Lee family letters in the Special Collections includes letters to and from Lee's son, Custis, and to his nephew, Fitzhugh Lee. Superintendent's Letter Books in the U.S.M.A. Archives, include many letters from Lee to parents of cadets. The journal of Lee's daughter, Agnes, and the letters and memoirs of William Bailey provide the views of young people growing up at West Point during the 1850s. Letters from Robert Allston to and answers from Thayer concerning the 1853 reunion of cadets who entered the Academy in 1817 are included in the Thayer papers. John M. Schofield's autobiography includes a description of the wager between Schofield and Jerome Bonaparte. The Special Collections holds Class Photograph albums from the late 1850s to 1896 when the first cadet yearbook, *The Howitzer*, was published. Sergeant's *They Lie Forgotten, The United States Military Academy, 1856–1861* includes many descriptions of cadet activities and reactions to political events during that period.

18. Adhere to Your Purpose

Letters, diaries, memoirs, and other personal papers related to this period include those of the following individuals: Samuel Benjamin, Class of May 1861; William Craighill, Class of 1853; Paul Dahlgen, Class of 1868; Henry Dupont, Class of May 1861; Charles King, Class of 1866; Stephen Lyford, Class of June 1861; Tully McCrae, Class of 1862; Francis Parker, Class of 1861; Thomas Rowland, non-graduate Class of 1863; and Edward Willis, non-graduate, Class of June 1861. Morris Schaff, Class of 1862, provided many details of cadet life in his *The Spirit of Old West Point*. The Cullum Register Files and the Cullum Historical Files include additional material obtained by Cullum from graduates. Boynton's history of the Academy includes a detailed statistical summary of the strength of the Corps before and after the secession of southern states. Two *Assembly* articles, Joseph O'Donnell's "Lincoln's Visit to West Point" and John Brinsfield's "When Lincoln Came to West Point," supplement Cadet Charles King's comments and newspaper articles concerning Abraham Lincoln's visit. The Mahan and Church papers provide the faculty viewpoint of these events. Charles King's many writings about the Academy provide much detail not found elsewhere.

1865–1902

19. All Institutions Are Imperfect and Subject to the Law of Change

Letters, diaries, memoirs, and other personal papers applying to this period include the collections of Robert Fletcher, Class of 1868; James Fornance, Class of 1871; Eldridge Hills, Class of 1866; Hugh Scott, Class of 1876; Eben Swift, Class of 1876; Emory Upton, Class of May 1861; and Oliver Wood, Class of 1867. Rank of graduates of the Class of 1865 is cited from Cullum's *Register of Graduates*. Information concerning active Civil War service of cadets also came from the Cullum *Register*. The strength of the Army immediately following the Civil War is cited in Ganoe's *History of the United States Army* and in Heitman's *Historical Register and Dictionary of the United States Army*. Information concerning the Class of 1865 "Class Cup" and the origins of the song "Army Blue" is in files prepared by the Special Collections staff. Many details concerning the 1868 visit of the U.S. Naval Academy flotilla are available in Special Collection holdings, including programs, menus, orders for formations, and hop cards, which supplement cadet descriptions of the visit. Information concerning the organization of the U.S.M.A. Association of Graduates is detailed in Association records. Copies of the correspondence to and from Thayer are in the Thayer papers. The comments of graduates are in Association material in the U.S.M.A. Archives. Details concerning Cullum's legacy are provided in his will; a copy is included in the Cullum personal papers. Information concerning black cadets was obtained from Andrews' "West Point and the Colored Cadets," Brown's "Eleven Men at West Point," the *Penman's Art Journal* article "Conclusion of the Whittaker Investigation at West Point," Gatewood's "John Hanks Alexander: Second Black Graduate of West Point," Marszalek's "A Black Cadet at West Point," and Vaughn's "West Point and the First Negro." Henry Flipper's autobiography, *The Colored Cadet at West Point* provides detailed firsthand information concerning his four years as a cadet. The Special Collections has collections of newspaper and periodical articles concerning the Whittaker and the Booz investigations.

20. Guard Well Your Heritage

Significant letters, diaries, memoirs, and personal papers of the following individuals provide firsthand descriptions of activities and events during this period: Frederick Abbot, Class of 1879; William Craighill, Class of 1853; George Goethals, Class of 1880; Charles Noyes, Class of 1879; John M. Schofield, Class of 1853; and Emory Upton, Class of May 1861. Lectures to the Ladies' Reading Club provide information concerning social activities of the period. The Elizabeth Custer papers contain letters concerning the statue of General Custer. Cadet John Byer's *Pointer* article "Custer's Last Stand" and Millbrook's "A Monument to Custer" provide information concerning the statue and its disappearance.

1902

21. The Corps and the Corps and the Corps

The description of events in June 1902 is taken from *The Centennial of the United States Military Academy*.

Bibliography

SECONDARY SOURCES

Abbot, Frederick V. *History of the Class of 'Seventy- Nine. . . .* New York: Putnam's, 1884.

Abbot, Henry L. *Half Century Record of the Class at West Point, 1850 to 1854.* Boston: Thomas Todd, 1905.

"Academy at West Point." *American Quarterly Review*, December 1834. Philadelphia: Key & Biddle, 1834.

Adams, Mary P. "Jefferson's Military Policy with Special Emphasis to the Frontier, 1805–1809." Ph.D. Dissertation, University of Virginia, Charlottesville, 1959.

Agnew, James B. *Eggnog Riot: The Christmas Mutiny at West Point.* San Rafael, Calif.: Presidio Press, 1979.

Aimone, Alan, and Aimone, Barbara. "The Civil War Years at West Point." *Blue and Gray Magazine*, December 1991.

Ambrose, Stephen E. "Dennis Hart Mahan." *Civil War Times Illustrated*, November 1963.

——. *Duty, Honor, Country. . . .* Baltimore: Johns Hopkins University Press, 1966.

——. *Upton and the Army.* Baton Rouge: Louisiana State University, 1964.

——. "The War Comes to West Point." *Civil War Times Illustrated*, August 1965.

——. "West Point in the Fifties: The Letters of Henry A. Du Pont." *Civil War Times Illustrated*, October 1964.

American State Papers: Military Affairs. 5 Vols. Washington, D.C.: Gales and Seaton, 1836–1861.

Ames, Blanche A. *Adelbert Ambes, 1835–1933.* North Eastern, Mass.: 1964.

Anderson, Edward W. "Letters of a West Pointer, 1860–1861." *The American Historical Review*, April 1928.

Andrews, George L. "Comments on 'The Military Academy at West Point and the Education of Officers [Article by Elmer W. Hubbard].' " *Journal of the Military Service Institute of the United States*, March 1895.

——. "The Military Academy and Its Requirements." Paper presented to the Military Service Institution, Governors Island, N.Y., March 17, 1883.

——. "West Point and the Colored Cadets." *The International Review*, November 1880.

Army and Navy Life and United Service. Vols. 8–13, January 1906–December 1909.

Arrington, Leonard J. "Willard Young: The Prophet's Son at West Point." *Mormon Dialogue*, 1969.

Assembly. Quarterly published by the USMA Association of Graduates, West Point, 1941 to date.

Bacevitch, Andrew J., Jr. "Emory Upton: A Centennial Assessment." *Military Review*, December 1980.

Bacon, Charles W. "Life at West Point." *Van Norden's Magazine*, November 1897.

Bailey, William Whitman. *My Boyhood at West Point*. Providence, R.I.: Providence Press, 1891.

Barnard, Major J. G. "Letter to the Editors of the *National Intelligencer*, in Answer to the Charges against the United States Military Academy in the Report of the Secretary of War, of July 1861." New York: Van Nostrand, 1862.

Barnes, James. "A Hundred Years of West Point." *Outlook*, July 1902.

Bass, Edgar W. "Comment and Criticism: The Preliminary Examination, West Point." *Journal of the Military Service Institution*, May 1865.

Bassler, Roy P., ed. *The Collected Works of Abraham Lincoln*, 9 Vols. New Brunswick, N.J.: Rutgers University Press, 1953–1955.

Baumer, William H. *Not All Warriors*, New York: Smith & Durrell, 1941.

———. *West Point: Moulder of Men*. New York: Appleton-Century, 1942.

Bayard, Samuel J. *Address at West Point before the Graduating Class of Cadets*. June 16, 1854, Camden *Democrat*, Camden, N.J.

———. *The Life of George Dashiel Bayard*, New York: Putnam's Sons, 1874.

[Berard, Augusta Blanche]. *Reminiscences of West Point in the Olden Time*. East Saginaw, Mich.: Evening News Printing and Binding House, 1886. Includes reminiscences of Miss Betsy Cox, George Tichnor, Mrs. Charles Davies (daughter of Colonel Jared Mansfield), and her own recollections.

Berman, Bennett H., and Michael E. Monbeck. *West Point: An Illustrated History of the United States Military Academy*. New York: New York Times Books, 1978.

Berry, L. G. "Comment and Criticism: The Preliminary Examination, West Point." *Journal of the Military Service Institution*, July 1895.

Bessett, John Spencer, ed. *Correspondence of Andrew Jackson*. Washington, D.C.: Carnegie Institute of Washington, 1929.

Beukema, Herman. *The United States Military Academy and Its Foreign Contemporaries*. West Point: USMA Printing Office, 1941.

Billingsley, John D. "Ordnance at West Point, 1802–1952." Unpublished manuscript. West Point, 1952.

Birkhimer, William E. "Can West Point Be Made More Generally Useful?" *Journal of the Military Service Institution*, November 1895.

———. "Comment and Criticism: The Preliminary Examination, West Point." *Journal of the Military Service Institution*, March 1895.

———. *Historical Sketch of the Artillery, United States Army*, Washington, D.C.: Thomas McGill, 1884.

Black, W. M. "Comment and Criticism: The Preliminary Examination, West Point." *Journal of the Military Service Institution*, March 1895.

Bonner, Thomas N. "The Beginnings of Engineering Education in the United States: The Curious Role of Eliphalet Nott." *New York History, Quarterly Journal of the New York State Historical Association*, New York, January 1988.

Boyd, Julian P., ed. *The Papers of Thomas Jefferson*. 19 Vols. Princteon, N.J.: Princeton University Press, 1950.

Boynton, Edward C. *Guide to West Point and the U.S. Military Academy*. New York: Van Nostrand, 1867.

————. *History of West Point. . . .* New York: Van Nostrand, 1871.

Brinsfield, John W. "Lincoln Comes to West Point." *Assembly*, February 1988.

Brown, Austin H. "Cadet Life at West Point." *Pall Mall Magazine* (London), January 1897.

Brown, Wesley A. "Eleven Men at West Point." *The Negro History Bulletin*, April 1956.

Brown, W. C. "Comment and Criticism: The Preliminary Examination, West Point." *Journal of the Military Service Institution*, July 1895.

Bryan, Roger B. *An Average American Army Officer*. San Diego, Calif.: Buck-Molina, 1914.

Buchwald, Donald M. "Chronological Listing of Significant Changes to Troop Units at West Point, New York from 1775 to 1978." Unpublished manuscript. West Point, 1978.

Budka, Metchie J. E. "Minerva Versus Archimedes." *The Smithsonian Journal of History*, Vol. 1, 1966.

Bushong, Millard Kessler. *Old Jube: A Biography of General Jubal Early*. Boyes, Va.: Carr, 1955.

Byers, John. "Custer's Last Stand." *The Pointer*, June 1, 1951.

Cadet Fine Arts Forum of the United States Corps of Cadets. *Robert Weir: Artist and Teacher of West Point*. Peekskill, N.Y.: Mills, 1976.

Carpenter, Hazen C. "Emerson at West Point." *Assembly*, April 1951.

Carter, William H. *The American Army*. Indianapolis, Ind.: Bobbs-Merrill, 1915.

————. "The Evolution of Army Reforms." *The United Service*, May 1903.

Catton, Bruce. *U.S. Grant and the American Military Tradition*. New York: Grosset & Dunlap, 1954.

Chartrand, Rene. "The US Army's Uniform Supply 'Crisis' during the War of 1812." *Military Collector and Historian, Quarterly of the Company of Military Historians, Providence, Rhode Island*, Summer 1988.

Church, Albert E. *Personal Reminiscences of the Military Academy from 1824 to 1831*. West Point: USMA Press, 1879.

Coffman, Edward H. *The Old Army*. New York: Oxford University Press, 1986.

Colton, J. H. (Publisher). *A Guide to West Point and Vicinity*. New York: J. H. Colton, 1844.

Commager, Henry Steele, and Morris, Richard B. *The Spirit of 'Seventy-six*. New York: Harper & Row, 1958 and 1967.

"Conclusion of the Whittaker Investigation at West Point." *The Penman's Art Journal*, June 1880.

Crackel, Theodore J. "The Founding of West Point." *Armed Forces and Society*, Summer 1981.

————. *The Illustrated History of West Point*. New York: Harry N. Abrams, 1991.

Crane, John, and Kieley, James F. *West Point. . . .* New York: McGraw-Hill, Whittlesey House, 1947.

Crary, Catherine S. *Dear Belle, Letters from a Cadet & Officer to His Sweetheart 1858–1865*. Middletown, Conn.: Weslyan University Press, 1965.

Craven, Avery. *"To Markie": The Letters of Robert E. Lee to Martha Custis Williams*. Cambridge, Mass.: Harvard University Press, 1933.

Crofut, W. A., ed. *Fifty Years in Camp and Field: The Diary of Ethan Allen Hitchcock, U.S.A.* New York: Putnam's, 1909.

Cullum, George W. *Biographical Register of Officers and Graduates of The United States Military Academy . . .*, 9 Vols. published between 1868 and 1950. Vol. III includes a history of the Military Academy from 1802 to 1833. Cullum's *Register* has been superceded by the *Register of Graduates* published annually by the USMA Association of Graduates.

Davies, Charles. *A Brief History of the Military Academy*. New York: Barnes, 1874.

Day, Robert S. "West Pointers as Educators." *Assembly*, Winter 1969.

De Butts, Mary Custis Lee. *Growing Up in the 1850s: The Journal of Agnes Lee.* Chapel Hill, University of North Carolina Press, 1985.

Degen, Robert. "The Evolution of Physical Education at the United States Military Academy." M.A. Thesis, University of Wisconsin, Madison, 1966.

Dialectic Society. *Cadet Life....* West Point, 1859.

――――. *Catalog of the Library of the Dialectic Society of the United States Military Academy.* West Point, 1855.

Dillard, Walter S. "The United States Military Academy, 1865–1900: The Uncertain Years." Ph.D. Dissertation, University of Washington, Seattle, 1972.

Dudley, Edgar S. "Was Secession Taught at West Point." *The Century Magazine,* August 1909.

Dupuy, R. Ernest. *The Compact History of the United States Army.* New York: Hawthorne, 1956.

――――. *Men of West Point....* New York: William Sloan, 1951.

――――. "West Point 100 Years Ago." *Assembly,* Summer 1961.

――――. *Where They Have Trod....* New York: Frederick A. Stokes, 1940.

Eagers, Sam'l W. *An Outline History of Orange County,[New York].* Newburgh, N.Y.: S. F. Callahan, 1846–47.

Esposito, Colonel Vincent J. *The West Point Atlas of American Wars.* New York: Praeger, 1959.

[Partridge, Alden]. *Exposé of Facts Concerning Recent Transactions Relating to the Corps of Cadets of the United States Military Academy at West Point,* Newburgh, N.Y.: Uriah C. Lewis, 1819.

Farley, Joseph P. *West Point in the Early Sixties.* Troy, N.Y.: Palfrey's, 1902.

Finke, Detmar, and McBarron, H. Charles. "Cadets, U.S. Military Academy, 1816–1817." *Military Collector and Historian, Quarterly of the Company of Military Historians,* Providence, R.I., March 1952.

Fleet, James W. *The Military Career of General Irving Hale.* M.A. Thesis, University of Denver, Denver, 1962.

Fleming, Thomas J. *West Point: The Men and Times of the United States Military Academy.* New York: Morrow, 1969.

Fleming, Walter L. "Jefferson Davis at West Point." *Metropolitan Magazine,* 1908.

Flipper, Henry. *The Colored Cadet at West Point.* New York: Homer Lea, 1878.

Forman, Sidney. "Brief Chronological History of the United States Military Academy." Unpublished manuscript. West Point, 1952. Digitized and updated by Robertson, John K., 1989.

――――. "Cadet Life before the Mexican War." *USMA Library Bulletin No. 1,* USMA Printing Office, West Point, 1945.

――――. "The First School of Engineering." *The Military Engineer,* March–April 1952.

――――. "Scandal among Cadets: An Historical Verdict." *Teachers College Record,* March 1966.

――――. "The United States Military Philosophical Society." *William and Mary Quarterly,* July 1945.

――――. *West Point....* New York: Columbia University Press, 1952.

――――. "West Point and the American Association for the Advancement of Science." *Science,* July 1946.

――――. "Why the United States Military Academy Was Established in 1802." *Military Affairs,* Spring 1965.

Freeman, Douglas Southall. *Lee's Lieutenants,* 3 Vols., New York: Scribner's, 1944.

――――. *Robert E. Lee,* 4 Vols., New York: Scribner's, 1947.

Fry, James H. "Admission to the United States Military Academy." *Journal of the Military Service Institution,* March 1895.

Gallagher, Gary W. "A South Carolinian at West Point, Stephen Dodson Ramseur, 1855–1860." *Assembly*, March 1986.

———. "Stephen D. Ramseur: A Biography." Ph.D. Dissertation, University of Texas, Austin, Texas: 1982.

Ganoe, William A. *The History of the United States Army*. New York: Appleton-Century, 1936.

Gardner, Asa Bird. *Memoir of Brvt. Brig. Genl. Henry Burbeck: Founder of the U.S. Military Academy*. New York: Barnes, 1883.

Garland, Hamlin. "Grant at West Point: The Story of His Cadet Days." *McClure's Magazine*, January 1897.

Gatewood, Willard B., Jr. "John Hanks Alexander: Second Black Graduate of West Point." *Arkansas Historical Quarterly*, February 1982.

Gibbon, John. "Can West Point Be Made More Useful?" *North American Review*, January 1895.

Gildart, Charles R. "Born to Be Brothers." *Assembly*, September 1973.

Gladstone, William. "Unpublished Prevost." *The New England Journal of Photographic History*, Summer 1990.

Godson, William F. H., Jr. "The History of West Point, 1852–1952." Ph.D. Dissertation, Temple University, Philadelphia, 1934.

Goodwin, Katherine Calvert. "A Hotel of Memories." *Daughters of the American Revolution Magazine*, June 1927.

Grant, Ulysses S. *Personal Memoirs of U. S. Grant*. New York: Charles L. Webster, 1885.

Grant, Ulysses S., 3rd. *Ulysses S. Grant, Warrior and Statesman*. New York: Morrow, 1969.

Gray, David W. *The Architectural Development of West Point*. West Point: Department of Military Topography and Graphics, 1951.

Griess, Thomas E. "Dennis Hart Mahan: West Point Professor. . . ." Ph.D. Dissertation, Duke University, Durham, N.C., 1968.

Hall, Robert H. "Early Discipline at the United States Military Academy." *Journal of the Military Service Institution*, November 1882.

———. *Laws of Congress Relative to West Point and the United States Military Academy from 1786 to 1877*. West Point: U.S.M.A. Press, 1877.

Hamilton, Stanislaus Murray, ed. *The Writings of James Monroe*, 7 Vols., New York: Putnam's, 1902.

Hamlin, Percy Gatling. *The Making of a Soldier: Letters of Richard S. Ewell*. Richmond, Va.: Whittet & Shepperson, 1935.

———. *Old Bald Head: General R. S. Ewell*. Strasburg, Va.: Shenandoah Publishing, 1940.

Hammond, Harold. *West Point: Its Glamour and Its Grind*. New York: Cupples & Leon, 1910.

Hancock, H. Irving. "For a New West Point." *Leslie's Weekly*, June 5, 1902.

Hart, B. H. Liddell. *Sherman*. New York: Praeger, 1960.

Hassler, William Woods. *A. P. Hill: Lee's Forgotten General*. Richmond, Va.: Garrett & Massie, 1957.

Hassler, Warren W., Jr. *General George B. McClellan: Shield of the Union*. Baton Rouge: Louisiana State University Press, 1957.

Hattaway, Herman. *General Stephen D. Lee*. Jackson: University Press of Mississippi, 1976.

Hazel, Harry [John Jones]. *The West Point Cadet or the Young Officer's Bride*. Boston: United States Publishing Co., 1845.

Headley, J. T. *The Life of Ulysses S. Grant*. New York: E. B. Treat, 1868.

Hein, Otto L. *Memories of Long Ago*. New York: Putnam's, 1925.

Hemphill, W. Edwin, ed. *The Papers of John C. Calhoun*, 15 Vols. Columbia: University of South Carolina Press, 1963.

Henderson, G.F.R. *Stonewall Jackson and the American Civil War*. New York: Longmans, Green, 1927.

Hewitt, John Hill. "Muskets and Music, A Cadet's Experience at West Point Military Academy over a Hundred Years Ago 1817–1922." Unpublished manuscript, circa 1922.

———. "Mutiny at West Point." *Emory University Quarterly*, December 1951.

Hill, Jim Dan. *The Minute Man in Peace and War. . . .* Harrisburg, Pa.: Stackpole, 1964.

Hinshaw, Ida C. "Whistler's First Drawings." *Century Magazine*, September 1910.

Holden, Edward S. "How Honor and Justice May Be Taught in the Schools." *The Cosmopolitan Magazine*, October 1900.

———. "The Library of the United States Military Academy, 1777–1906." *Army Navy Life and the United Service*, June 1906.

Holt, John E. "West Point, Something about Cadet Life in the Military Academy." *Rushville Republican*, March 1890.

Honeywell, Roy J. *The Educational Work of Thomas Jefferson*. Cambridge, Mass.: Harvard University Press, 1931.

Howard, Oliver Otis. *Autobiography of Oliver Otis Howard*, 2 Vols. New York: Baker & Taylor, 1907.

Howat, John K. *The Hudson River and Its Painters*. New York: American Legacy Press, 1983.

Howe, Edgar W. *The History of the Class of 'Seventy-Eight*. New York: Homer Lee Bank Note Co., 1881.

Hubbard, Elmer W. "The Military Academy and the Education of Officers." *Journal of the Military Service Institute of the United States*, January 1895.

Hughes, Nathaniel C. *General William J. Hardee: Old Reliable*. Baton Rouge: Louisiana State University Press, 1965.

Hunt, Ezra. "West Point and Cadet Life." *Putnam's Monthly Magzine*, August 1864.

Huntington, Samuel P. *The Soldier and the State. . . .* Cambridge, Mass.: Harvard University Press/Belknap Press, 1957.

The Illustrated American. "West Point's Commencement." June 27, 1891; "Students in the Art of War." June 23, 1894; "Fun at West Point." February 29, 1896; "Hundredth-Night Entertainment at West Point." April 10, 1897.

Jacobs, James R. *The Beginnings of the U.S. Army, 1783–1812*. Princeton, N.J.: Princeton University Press, 1947.

Janowitz, Morris. *The Professional Soldier*. New York: Free Press, 1960.

Johnson, William Preston. *The Life of Gen. Albert Sidney Johnston*. New York: Appleton, 1879.

Keep, Robert F. "The System of Instruction at West Point—Can It Be Employed in Our Colleges?" *The New Englander*, January 1869.

Kennedy, John P. *Memoirs of William Wirt*. Philadelphia: Lea & Blanchard, 1850.

Kershner, John William. "Sylvanus Thayer: A Biography." Ph.D. Dissertation, University of West Virginia, Morgantown, 1976.

Kindred, Marilyn Anne. "The Army Officer Corps and the Arts: Artistic Patronage and Practice in America, 1820–1885." Ph.D. Dissertation, University of Kansas, Lawrence, 1980.

King, Charles. *Cadet Days*. New York: Harper & Brothers, 1894.

———. "Cadet Life at West Point." *Harper's New Monthly Magazine*, July 1887.

———. "The Code of the Corps." *Stories of the Colleges, Being Tales of Life at the Great American Universities Told by Noted Graduates*. Philadelphia: Lippincott, 1901.

———. "Esprit de Corps." *The Army of the United States*, Theo. F. Rodenbough and William L. Haskins, eds. New York: Maynard, Merrill, 1896.

———. "Memories of a Busy Life." *Wisconsin Magazine of History*, March, June, September, and December, 1922.

————. *Noble Blood and a West Point Parallel*. New York: F. Tennyson Neely, 1896.

————. *Trials of a Staff Officer*. New York: Lippincott, 1895.

————. "West Point as It Was and Is." Philadelphia: Curtis, February 1901.

————. "West Point in the Old Days." *New York Illustrated Sunday Magazine*, July 10, 17, 24, 31 and August 7, 1910. Title of all articles except that of July 10 was "West Point in the War Days."

Krist, Bob. *West Point, United States Military Academy*. Prospect, Ky.: Harmony House, 1987.

Kuehne, Richard E., et al. *The West Point Museum: A Guide to the Collections*. West Point: The Class of 1932, USMA Association of Graduates, 1987.

Ladies Reading Club. *Research Papers*. West Point, 1967. A series of papers concerning West Point and USMA history presented to club members.

Lake, Virginia T. "A Crisis of Conscience: West Point Letters of Henry A. Dupont, October 1860–June 1861." *Civil War History*, March 1979.

Larned, Charles W. "Comment and Criticism: The Military Academy and the Education of Officers." *Journal of the Military Service Institution*, March 1902.

————. "The Genius of West Point." *The Churchman*, August 6, 1904.

————. *History of the Battle Monument at West Point*. West Point: Battle Monument Assn., 1898.

————. "Is Our Military Training Adequate?" *The Forum*, February 1892.

————. "West Point and Higher Education." *Army Navy Life and the United Service*, June 1906.

————. "West Point's Weakness." *The Evening Post* (New York), September 5, 1906.

Latrobe, John H. B. *Cadet Reminiscences*. West Point: USMA Association of Graduates, 1897.

————. *Journal of a March Performed by The Cadets*. N.p.; Newburgh, N.Y.: 1819, 1820, 1821.

Law Department, United States Military Academy. *Compilation of Laws (Annotated) Governing the United States Military Academy in Effect January 1, 1940*. West Point: U.S.M.A. Printing Office, 1940.

Lenney, John J. *Caste System in the American Army: A Study of the Corps of Engineers and Their West Point System*. N.Y.: Greenberg, 1949.

Leslie, Miss. "Recollections of West Point." *Graham's Magazine*, April 1842.

Lewis, Lloyd. "The Holy Spirit at West Point." *The American Mercury*, November 1930.

Liddell Hart, Basil H. *Sherman: Soldier, Realist, American*. New York: Praeger, 1956.

Lisowski, Lori A. "The Future of West Point: Senate Debates on the Military Academy during the Civil War." *Civil War History*, March 1988.

Longacre, Edward G. *From Union Stars to Top Hat: A Biography of the Extraordinary General James Harrison Wilson*. Harrisburg, Pa.: Stackpole, 1972.

————. *The Man Behind the Gun: A Biography of General Henry Jackson Hunt, Chief of Artillery, Army of the Potomac*. New York: Barnes, 1977.

Lossing, Benjamin J. "West Point." *Scribner's Monthly*, July 1872.

Lough, Frederick C., and DePaul, A. Kenneth. "A Legal Review and Analysis of the Relevant Federal Laws, Regulations, Judicial and Executive Opinions Pertaining to the United States Military Academy, Its Faculty and Student Body." Unpublished manuscript, West Point, 1967.

MacArthur, Douglas. *Reminiscences*, New York: McGraw-Hill, 1964.

McClellan, George B. *Oration at the Dedication of the Battle Monument Site*. New York: G. S. Westcott, 1864.

McElroy, Robert. *Jefferson Davis, the Unreal and the Real*. New York: Harper & Brothers, 1894.

McIlvaine, C. P. "Religion at West Point." *The Independent*, November 17, 1887.

McKinney, Francis F. *Education in Violence, the Life of George H. Thomas*. Detroit: Wayne State University Press, 1953.

McManus, Bernard T. "Cadet Life at West Point." *Godey's Magazine*, January 1895.

McWhiney, Grady. "Ulysses S. Grant's Pre–Civil War Military Education," in *Southerners and Other Americans*. New York: Rare Books, 1973.

Mansfield, Edward D. *Personal Memories*. . . . Cincinnati, Ohio: Robert Clark, 1879.

———. "The United States Military Academy at West Point." *The American Journal of Education*, March 1863.

Marsh, George P. *Address Delivered before the Graduating Class of the U.S. Military Academy at West Point, June 1860*. New York: Baker & Godwin, 1860.

Marszalek, John F., Jr. "A Black Cadet at West Point." *American Heritage*, August 1971.

———. "William T. Sherman on West Point." *Assembly*, Summer 1971.

Masland, John W., and Rodway, Laurence I. *Soldiers and Scholars: Military Education and National Policy*. Princeton, N.J.: Princeton University Press, 1957.

Maury, Dabney Herndon. *Recollections of a Virginian*. . . . New York: Scribner's, 1894.

Merritt, Westley. "United States Military Academy at West Point." *The Youth's Companion*, May 5, 1887.

Michie, Peter S. "Caste at West Point." *North American Review*, June 1880.

———. "Educational Methods at West Point." *Educational Review*, November 1892.

———. *Life and Letters of Emory Upton*. New York: Appleton, 1885.

Millbrook, Minnie D. "A Monument to Custer." *Montana, The Magazine of Western History*, Spring 1974.

Miller, Charles E., Jr., Lockey, Donald V., and Visconti, Joseph, Jr. *Highland Fortress: The Fortification of West Point during the American Revolution, 1775–1783*. West Point: USMA Department of History, 1988.

Mills, Samuel M. *A Valentine Party Given by Lt. and Mrs. S. M. Mills, 5th Artillery, West Point, N.Y., February 14, 1876*. West Point: 1876. Verses and comments by guests.

Mizell, Charles. "Battle Deaths of United States Military Academy Graduates." *Assembly*, December 1988.

Mordecai, Alfred. "Address," in *Eleventh Annual Reunion of the Association of Graduates*. East Saginaw, Mich.: E. W. Lyon, 1880.

Morris, Richard B. *Encyclopedia of American History*. New York: Harper & Brothers, 1933.

Morrison, James L., Jr. *"The Best School in the World."* Kent, Ohio: Kent State University Press, 1986.

———. "The Struggle between Sectionalism and Nationalism at Ante-Bellum West Point, 1830–1861." *Civil War History*, June 1973.

———. "The United States Military Academy, 1833–1866, Years of Progress and Turmoil." Ph.D. Dissertation, Columbia University, New York, 1970.

Morton, William J. "Sylvanus Thayer's Sons." *Assembly*, April 1957.

Moss, Michael E. *Robert Weir of West Point*. USMA Library Occasional Paper No. 4. West Point, 1976.

National Park Service. *Inventory of Historic Structures at the United States Military Academy*. Washington, D.C.: U.S. Department of the Interior, 1984.

Nevins, Allan, and Thomas, Milton H. *The Diary of George Templeton Strong, 1835–1875*, 4 Vols. New York: Macmillan, 1952.

Newell, Gordon, and McCurdy, H. W. *Duty, Honor, Country: The Biography of George H. McManus*. . . . Vancouver, British Columbia: Evergreen Press, 1950.

Norton, Aloysius A. *A History of the United States Military Academy Library*. Wayne, N.J.: Avery, 1984.

———. "A Study of the Customs and Traditions of West Point in the American Novel." Unpublished manuscript in Special Collections, USMA Library.

Nye, Roger H. "The United States Military Academy in an Era of Educational Reform, 1900–1925." Ph.D. Dissertation, Columbia University, New York, 1968.

O'Donnell, Joseph M. "Lincoln's Visit to West Point." *Assembly*, Fall 1971.

Oliver, Henry K. "West Point." *Salem Register* (Salem, Mass.), August 10, 1845.

Pahl, David. *West Point: The United States Military Academy*. New York: Exeter Books, 1987.

Palmer, Dave Richard. *The River and the Rock. . . .* Westport, Conn.: Greenwood Press, 1969.

Palmer, Frederick. *Bliss, Peacemaker: The Life and Letters of General Tasker H. Bliss*. New York: Dodd, Mead, & Co., 1934.

————. "West Point after a Century." *The World's Work*, June 1902.

Pappas, George S. *The Cadet Chapel: United States Military Academy*. Providence, R.I.: Andrew Mowbray, 1986.

————. "Hop Cards: Forgotten Tradition." *Assembly*, July 1990.

————. *Prudens Futuri: The U.S. Army War College, 1901–1967*. Carlisle Barracks, Pa.: Alumni Association of the U.S. Army War College, 1967.

————. "Walking the Area." *Assembly*, January 1991.

————. *West Point Sesquicentennial: A Pictorial History of the One Hundred and Fifty Years of the United States Military Academy*. Buffalo, N.Y.: Baker, Jones, & Hausauer, 1952.

Park, Roswell. *A Sketch of the History and Topography of West Point and the U.S. Military Academy*, Philadelphia: Henry Perkins, 1840.

Parker, John M. III. "The Life of Francis Henry Parker, 1838–1897." Unpublished manuscript, Raleigh, N.C.: 1986.

Parmely, Eleazor, III. "The Legendary West Point." *American Heritage*, Summer 1962.

Partridge, Alden [Americus]. *The Military Academy at West Point Unmasked*. Washington, D.C.: 1830.

Persy, N. *Elementary Treatise on the Forms of Cannon & Various Systems of Artillery. Translated for the Use of the Cadets of the U.S. Military Academy from the French of Professor N. Persy of Metz*. West Point: U.S. Military Academy, 1832.

Poore, Ben. *The Life and Public Services of Ambrose E. Burnside*. Providence, R.I.: J. A. & R. A. Reid, 1882.

Powers, Caleb. *My Own Story*. New York: Bobbs-Merrill, 1905.

Powers, Fred P. "West Point and the Army and the Militia." *Lippincott's Magazine*, July 1887.

Prucha, Francis Paul. *The Sword of the Republic: The United States Army . . . 1783–1946*. New York: Macmillan, 1969.

"Quiff." "A Pleib's [*sic*] Account of Himself." *The Military and Naval Magazine of the United States*, Washington, D.C.: Benjamin Homans, September 1833 to February 1834.

Rainey, James. "The Establishment of the United States Military Academy: The Motives and Objectives of President Jefferson." Unpublished paper, 1989.

Rapp, Kenneth. "The Legend of Fanny Essler's Pirouette by Moonlight." *Assembly*, February 1975.

————. *West Point, Whistler in Cadet Gray, and Other Stories*. Croton, N.Y.: North River Press, 1978.

Raynor, Kenneth. *Address Delivered to the Graduating Class of the United States Military Academy, June 17th, 1853*. New York: John F. Trow, 1853.

Reams, James P. "Astronomy and the Military Academy." Unpublished manuscript. West Point, 1975.

Reed, Hugh T. *Cadet Life at West Point*. Chicago: 1896.

Reed, William B. *Reprint of the Original Letters from Washington to Joseph Reed during the American Revolution*. Philadelphia: A. Hart, Late Carey & Hart, 1852.

Rees, James. "West Point." *United States Military Magazine*. Philadelphia: Huddy and Duval, January 1841.

Reeves, Ira L. *Military Education in the United States*. Burlington, Vt.: Free Press Printing, 1914.

Reynolds, Richard Derby. *Squibob: An Early California Humorist*. San Francisco: Squibob Press, 1990. The papers of George Derby.

Rhodes, Charles Dudley. *Robert E. Lee: The West Pointer*. Richmond, Va.: Garrett & Massie, 1932.

Robertson, John K. *Who Was Who, 1802–1990: A Researcher's Guide to the Occupants of Key Positions at the United States Military Academy and the Lineage of the Academic Departments*, 2d ed. West Point, April 10, 1991.

Roe, William F. "Church Call at West Point." *The Outlook*, August 22, 1908.

Rowland, Dunbar, ed. *Jefferson Davis, Constitutionalist: His Letters, Papers, and Speeches*. Jackson: University of Mississippi Press, 1923.

Rowland, Thomas. "Letters of a Virginia Cadet at West Point, 1859–1861." *The Southern Atlantic Quarterly*, July 1915.

Russell, J. Thomas. *Edgar Allen Poe: The Army Years*. West Point: USMA Library, 1972.

Ryan, Pat. "Sons of Thayer." *Assembly*, Summer, Fall, and Winter 1963.

Schaff, Morris. *The Spirit of Old West Point, 1858–1862*. Boston: Houghton Mifflin, 1907.

Schofield, John N. *An Address Delivered by Maj. Gen. J. Schofield to the Corps of Cadets . . . August 11, 1879*. West Point: USMA Printing Office, 1879.

———. *Forty-Six Years in the Army*, New York: Century, 1897.

Schulz, Edward H. *Reminiscences of Cadet Edward H. Schulz, Class of 1895, U.S.M.A.* Berkeley, Calif.

Schureman, James W., ed. *The West Pointer*, Vol. 1, Nos. 1 and 2. West Point: 1842.

Scott, Winfield. *Memoirs of Lieut.-General Scott . . .*, 2 Vols. New York: Sheldon, 1864.

Searles, William H. "The West Point Tunnel." *Journal of the Association of Engineering Societies*, February 1889.

Sergeant, Mary Elizabeth. "Classmates Divided." *American Heritage*, February 1958.

———. *They Lie Forgotten: The United States Military Academy, 1856–1861*. Middletown, N.Y.: Prior King Press, 1986.

Sheridan, Philip H. *Personal Memoirs*. New York: Charles L. Webster, 1888.

Sherman, William T. *Memoirs of General William T. Sherman by Himself*. Bloomington: Indiana University Press, 1957.

Simon, John Y., ed. *The Papers of Ulysses S. Grant, Volume 1: 1837–1861*. Carbondale: Southern Illinois University Press, 1967.

Simons, William E. *Liberal Education in the Service Academies*. New York: Institute for Higher Education, Bureau of Publications, Teachers College, Columbia University, 1965.

Simpson, Jeffry. *Officers and Gentlemen: Historic West Point in Photographs*. Tarrytown, N.Y.: Sleepy Hollow Press, 1982.

Sizer, Theodore, ed. *The Recollections of John Ferguson Weir. . . .* New York: The New York Historical Society and the Associates in Fine Arts at Yale University, 1957.

Smith, Dwight L. "Cadet Life in the 1860s." *Assembly*, June 1975.

Smith, Francis B. *West Point Fifty Years Ago*. New York: Van Nostrand, 1879.

Standish, Hal. "Fred Fearnot at West Point or Having Fun with the Hazers." *Work and Win*, May 1901.

Stevens, Hazard. *The Life of Isaac Ingalls Stevens*. Boston: Houghton Mifflin, 1900.

Stewart, George R. *John Phoenix, Esq. . . . A Life of Captain George H. Derby*. New York: Henry Holt, 1937.

Strode, Hudson. *Jefferson Davis: American Patriot*. New York: Harcourt, Brace, 1955.

Strong, George Crockett. *Cadet Life at West Point*. Boston: T.O.J.P. Burnham, 1862.

Sumner, Merlin E., ed. *The Diary of Cyrus B. Comstock.* Dayton, Ohio: Morningside House, 1987.

Swift, Joseph Gardner. *The Memoirs of Joseph Gardner Swift.* Washington, D.C.: F. Blanchard, 1890.

———. *A Statement of the Probable of Annual Expense of the Military Academy from the Year 1801 to 1816.* Washington, D.C.: William A. Davis, 1817.

Ticknor, George. "West Point in 1826." In *Report of the Annual Reunion, U.S.M.A. Graduates 1886.* West Point: Association of Graduates, 1886.

Tillman, Samuel. "The Origin of the Association of Graduates." *USMA Association of Graduates Annual Report,* West Point: 1931.

Todd, Frederick P. *Cadet Gray....* New York: Sterling, 1955.

The Tourist's Guide through the Empire State. Albany, N.Y.: Van Benthuysen & Sons, 1876.

Turner, Justin G., and Turner, Linda L. *Mary Todd Lincoln: Her Life and Letters.* New York: Knopf, 1972.

Turnley, Parmenas T. *Reminiscences.* Chicago: Donohue & Hennessee, 1892.

United States Military Academy. *The Centennial of the United States Military Academy at West Point, New York,* 2 Vols. Washington, D.C.: Government Printing Office, 1904.

USMA Class of 1867. *Fiftieth Reunion of the Class of 1867.* August 29, 1917.

USMA Class of 1870. *Fortieth Anniversary Reunion.* 1910.

USMA Class of 1873. *Record of the Class of 1873.* New York: Van Nostrand, 1875.

USMA Class of 1877. *The Class of '77.* Cambridge, Mass.: Riverside Press, 1878.

USMA Class of 1878. *The History of the Class of 'Seventy-Eight.* New York: Homer Lee Bank Note Co., 1881.

USMA Class of 1879. *History of the Class of 'Seventy-Nine.* New York: Putnam's Sons, Knickerbocker Press, 1884.

USMA Class of 1886. *25th Anniversary of Graduation of the Class of '86. USMA.* West Point: 1911.

USMA Class of 1887. *Class of 1887.* Washington, D.C.: P.S. Bond, 1938.

USMA Class of 1891. *Class of 1891: 35th Anniversary.*

USMA Class of 1892. Unpublished Class history. Seventy-five copies prepared in 1923 with periodic additions until 1927.

USMA Class Photograph Albums, 1854–1906.

Upton, Emory. *The Armies of Europe and Asia.* New York: Appleton, 1876.

———. *Military Policy of the United States.* Washington, D.C.: Government Printing Office, 1911.

Vaughn, William P. "West Point and the First Negro Cadet." *Military Affairs,* October 1971.

Viollet, Claude. "The Unusual Career of an American Officer in the Army of Napoleon III." *Assembly,* March 1987.

Wade, Arthur P. "Artillerists and Engineers: The Beginning of American Seacoast Fortifications." Ph.D. Dissertation, Kansas State University, 1977.

———. "Civil War at West Point." *Civil War History,* March 1957.

Wagner, Albert L. *Spy-Glass,* Vol. 1, No. 3, July 28, 1874. A cadet publication written by Wagner during Summer Camp 1874. Only this one issue is extant.

Walker, Harold S., Jr. "The English Department, 1802–1950." Unpublished paper prepared for the USMA English Department, West Point, 1950.

Warner, Ezra J. "A Black Man in the Long Gray Line." *American History Illustrated,* January 1970.

Washington, N. A., ed. *The Writings of Thomas Jefferson.* Washington, D.C.: Taylor & Maury, 1854.

Waugh, E.D.J. *West Point.* New York: Macmillan, 1954.

Webb, Ernie, Hart, John D., and Foley, James E. *West Point Sketch Book*. New York: Vantage Press, 1976.

Webb, Lyle A. *Captain Alden Partridge and the United States Military Academy, 1806–1833*. Northport, Ala.: American Southern Publishing, 1965.

Weigley, Russell. *The American Way of War. . . .* New York: Macmillan, 1973.

———. *The History of the United States Army*. New York: Macmillan, 1965.

———. *Towards an American Army. . . .* New York: Columbia University Press, 1962.

Weintraub, Stanley. *London Yankees*. New York: Harcourt, Brace, Johanovich, 1979.

———. *Whistler, A Biography*. New York: Webright & Talley, 1974.

Weir, Irene. *Robert Weir: Artist*. New York: Field-Doubleday, 1947.

West Point: A Selected Bibliography. Monticello, Ill.: Vance Bibliographies, 1983.

"West Point." *American Magazine of Useful Knowledge*, January 1835.

"West Point." *The Family Magazine*, January 1836.

"West Point." *Salem Register* (Salem, Mass.), August 14, 1845.

"West Point and Cadet Life." *Putnam's Monthly Magazine of American Literature, Science, and Art*, July to December 1854.

West Point and the War. St. Louis, Mo.: March 1863.

"West Point Cadets." *New-England Galaxy* (Boston), December 21, 1821.

"West Point Military Academy." *The New York Mirror*, July 20, 1823.

West Point Tic Tacs. New York: Homer Lee Bank Note Co., 1878.

"West Point Yearling: Cadets at Play." *The Illustrated American*, January 1895.

Wheatley, R. *West Point: United States Military Academy*. 1880.

Wheeler, Joseph. "West Point Fifty Years Ago." *The Golden Age*, February 1906.

White, Anthony G. *Military Architecture, U.S. Military Academy—West Point: A Selected Bibliography*. Monticello, Ill.: Vance Bibliographies, 1983.

Whitmore, Earle. "Artists at West Point before 1865." *Assembly*, December 1973.

Whittaker, Frederick. *A Complete Life of Gen. George A. Custer*. New York: Sheldon, 1876.

Wilkinson, Norman B. "The Forgotten 'Founder' of West Point." *Military Affairs*, March 1960.

Willcox, Cornelius DeWitt. "The Preliminary Examination: West Point." *Journal of the Military Service Institute of the United States*, March 1895.

Williams, Captain Charles W. *Quartermaster Report of Structures at West Point*. West Point: USMA Quartermaster Office, 1889.

Williams, T. Harry. "The Attacks upon West Point during the Civil War." *Mississippi Valley Historical Review*, March 1939.

Winton, George P., Jr. "Ante-Bellum Military Instruction of West Point Officers and Its Influence upon Confederate Military Organization and Operations." Ph.D. Dissertation, University of South Carolina, 1972.

Wood, Oliver E. *The West Point Scrap Book: A Collection of Stories, Songs, and Legends of the United States Military Academy*. New York: Van Nostrand, 1871.

Wood, Robert J. "Early Days of Benny Havens." *The Pointer*, February 16, 1937.

Wright, John R. "West Point before the War." *Southern Bivouac*, June 1885.

Young, Dorothy Weir. *The Life and Letters of J. Alden Weir*. New York: Da Capo Press, 1971.

Zogbaum, Rufus F. "A Morning at West Point." *Harper's Young People*, July 2, 1889.

Zotos, Helen. "Class of 1861." *The American Weekly*, September 3, 1961.

Zuersher, Dorothy J. S. "Benjamin Franklin, Jonathan Williams, and the United States Military Academy." Ph.D. Dissertation, University of North Carolina at Greensboro, 1974.

PRIMARY SOURCES

The following references are letters, diaries, scrapbooks, memoirs, answers to Cullum questionnaires, other personal papers, unpublished studies, and miscellaneous vertical file materials in the Special Collections of the USMA Library. Entries are cataloged under the name and USMA class of the individual concerned unless otherwise specified. *Note:* The Cullum number (C-   ) is provided to facilitate use of the Cullum Register Files in which materials are filed by graduation position of individuals in each class.

Ahrends, Arthur E. Class of 1903, C-4190. Scrapbook and personal papers.

Allen, Jesse K. Class of 1855, C-1780. Cadet letters.

Allston, Robert F. W. Class of 1817, C-271. Personal papers.

Anderson, George S. Class of 1871, C-2374. Personal papers.

Anderson, Robert. Class of 1825, C-406. Personal papers.

Association of Graduates. Book 1, Letters from graduates concerning forming the Association.

Ayres, Romayn B. Class of 1847, C-1352. Personal papers.

Bailey, Albert S. Class of 1878, C-2732. Personal papers and typescript memoirs.

Bailey, William W. Son of Professor Jacob Bailey. Personal papers and memoir of his boyhood days at West Point.

Barth, Charles A. Class of 1881, C-2910. Cadet diary.

Bayard, George D. Class of 1852, C-1721. Cadet letters.

Bedlinger, Frederick. Son of John B. Bedlinger, Class of 1879. Memoirs of boyhood at West Point, 1900–1903.

Bell, Ola W. Class of 1896, C-3710. Personal papers.

Bellinger, Frederick. Son of John B. Bellinger, Class of 1884. Memoirs of boyhood at West Point, 1900–1903.

Benjamin, Samuel. Class of May 1861, C-1899. Cadet letters.

Bennett, Clarence E. Class of 1855, C-1701. Cadet diary.

Berry, John A. Class of 1901, C-4035. Academic materials.

Berryman, Newton. Father of Henry Berryman, Class of 1817, C-174. Letters concerning his son; filed in Partridge papers.

Bigelow, John, Jr. Class of 1877, C-2686. Personal papers.

Bixby, William H. Class of 1873, C-2468. Scrapbook.

Bliss, Tasker H. Class of 1875, C-2557. Cadet letters; letters written from 1876 to 1880 when an instructor in French.

Bonaparte, Jerome. Class of 1852, C-1546. Cadet letters.

Booth, Charles A. Class of 1872, C-2439. Cadet letters.

Boynton, Edward C. Class of 1846, C-1283. Personal papers and scrapbook.

Bradford, Thomas C. Class of June 1861, C-1938. Cadet letters.

Bratt, John. Class of 1837. C-894. Cadet diary extract for 1837 and notebooks concerning period as purveyor of Cadet Mess.

Brister, Jane G. Unpublished history of Army Medical Service at West Point, 1802–1950.

Brown, Harvey. Class of 1818, C-185. Reminiscences, in Cullum Historical Files.

Brown, Walter C. Class of 1877, C-2681. Cadet diary, 1874–1875.

Brown, William S. Class of 1835, C-800. Personal papers.

Bruff, Mrs. Ada M. Wife of Lawrence L. Bruff, Class of 1895. Personal papers concerning activities at West Point, 1891–1900.

Buchwald, Donald M. Class of 1955, C-20435. Unpublished study concerning changes in troop units at West Point, 1775–1978.

Bullard, Robert L. Class of 1885, C-3084. Memoirs.

Bundy, Omar. Class of 1883, C-3018. Memoirs.

Burbeck, Henry. Personal papers and records concerning pre-1802 Artillerist and Engineer Academy. USMA Library Special Collections.

———. Personal papers and records. Fraunces Tavern, New York, N.Y. This collection supplements but does not duplicate the USMA Library Burbeck collection.

Burbridge, James W. Non-graduate, Class of 1831. Letters.

Burnett, Rogers L. Non-graduate, Class of 1878. Cadet scrapbook.

Burt, Reynolds J. Class of 1896, C-3723. Personal papers.

Burton, Oliver G. Correspondence, filed in Partridge papers. Burton was military store-keeper under Partridge and married Isaac Partridge's daughter.

Burtwell, John R. B. Class of 1860, C-1870. Personal papers.

Butler, William P. Class of 1866, C-2124. Cadet letters.

"Cadet letters. Class Rings and Miniatures." A file of reference material, journal articles, and excerpts from letters and diaries.

Chamberlain, John L. Class of 1880, C-2831. Cadet letters.

Chittenden, Hiram. Class of 1884, C-3023. Cadet letters.

Church, Albert E. Class of 1828, C-508. Personal papers.

Cleveland, John A. Non-graduate, Class of 1901. Personal papers.

Cole, Edwin T. Class of 1889, C-3316. Memoir concerning napkin rings and Ellen Terry's visit to West Point.

Cole, Haydn S. Class of 1885, C-3062. Personal papers.

Cook, Frank A. Class of 1885, C-3078. Memoirs.

Corps of Engineers, Letter Books, 1802–1890.

Craig, Mrs. Malin. Address to Society of Army Daughters, Washington, D.C., circa 1936, concerning military career of her father, Charles A. Woodruff, Class of 1871.

Craighill, William P. Class of 1853, C-1580. Personal papers.

Crain, Charles F. Class of 1894, C-3589. Personal papers.

Cram, Thomas J. Class of 1826, C-432. Personal papers.

Cullum, George W. Class of 1833, C-709. Personal papers.

Cullum, George W. Historical Files.

Cullum Register Files. Correspondence from graduates answering Cullum's questionnaire requests for data to be included in his *Biographical Register of Officers and Cadets of the United States Military Academy*. Special Collections includes three separate files of George W. Cullum materials. The *Cullum Personal Papers* include correspondence and other personal materials. The *Cullum Historical Files* contain research materials for and copies of Cullum writings, including questionnaires related to his history of the Military Academy and his biography of Sylvanus Thayer. The *Cullum Register Files* are materials collected by Cullum for his *Register of Officers and Graduates* and other materials concerning USMA graduates. USMA Library Special Collections maintains the files for classes having no living graduates; the Association of Graduates holds the files for all other classes.

Cushing, George W., Jr. Non-graduate, Class of 1858. Cadet letters.

Custer, Elizabeth [Mrs. George A. Custer]. Correspondence concerning Custer statue at West Point.

Custer, George A. Class of June 1861, C-1966. Cadet letters.

Dahlgren, Paul. Class of 1868, C-2238. Daily journal November 1864–November 1867.

Davis, Jefferson. Class of 1828, C-530. Miscellaneous letters.

Davis, William C. Class of 1890, C-3345. Scrapbook and personal papers.

Delafield, Richard. Class of 1818, C-180. Personal papers, primarily concerning his superintendency 1838–1845 and 1855–1861.

Derby, George H. Class of 1846, C-1278. Personal papers and drawings. This collection includes personal papers of his son, George McC. Derby, Class of 1878, C-2727, and his grandson, George T. Derby, Class of 1927, C-8033.

Derby, George M. Class of 1878, C-2717. Cadet letters.

Donelson, Andrew J. Class of 1820, C-233. Personal papers.

D'Oremieulx, Mrs. Theophile M. Wife of Lieutenant Theophile D'Oremieulx, Assistant Professor of French, 1839–1856. Recollections of West Point in 1853.

Douglass, David B. Professor of Mathematics, 1820–1823 and Professor of Engineering, 1823–1831. Correspondence. Materials concerning his conduct in answer to charges by Partridge are filed in the Partridge papers.

Drayton, Thomas F. Class of 1828, C-535. Personal papers.

Duncan, George B. Class of 1888, C-3161. Unpublished memoirs, "My Four Years at West Point."

Duncan, James. Class of 1834, C-755. Personal papers.

Dutton, William. Class of 1846, C-1286. Personal papers.

Edmunds, Frank A. Class of 1871, C-2376. Cadet letters.

Elderkin, William A. Class of May 1861, C-1909. Cadet letters.

Ellicott, Andrew. Professor of Mathematics, 1813–1820. Filed in Joseph Swift papers.

Eltinge, LeRoy. Class of 1896, C-3678. Memoirs.

Emory, William H. Class of 1831, C-642. Reminiscences.

Engle, James. Class of 1825, C-426. Personal papers.

Ernst, Oswald. Class of 1864, C-2035. Memoirs.

Ewing, Maskell C. Class of 1826, C-444. Personal papers.

Finley, Walter L. Class of 1879, C-2084. Cadet letters.

Fish, Williston. Class of 1881, C-1881, C-2885. Unpublished memoirs, "Memories of West Point, 1877–1881."

Fletcher, Robert. Class of 1868, C-2230. Cadet journal.

Fornance, James. Class of 1871, C-2398. Cadet letters and scrapbook.

Foster, Samuel A. Class of 1860, C-1863. Cadet letters.

Frazer, William. Class of 1836, C-875. Cadet letters.

French, Samuel G. Class of 1843, C-1180. Cadet letters.

Gardner, William N. Class of 1846, C-1326. Memoirs.

Garlington, Ernest A. Class of 1876, C-2622. Memoirs.

Giles, Henry. Class of 1818, C-201. Correspondence filed with Partridge papers.

Gillmore, Quincy A. Class of 1849, C-1407. Cadet letters.

Godfrey, Edward S. Class of 1867, C-2208. Memoirs.

Godfrey, George J. Class of 1886, C-3152. Cadet letters.

Goethals, George. Class of 1880, C-2828. Cadet letters.

Grant, Mrs. Gladys Edgerton. Daughter of Wright C. Edgerton, Class of 1874. Recollections of childhood at West Point, 1892–1898.

Grant, Ulysses S. Class of 1843, C-1187. Cadet letters.

Greene, Francis V. Class of 1870, C-2312. Letters from Professors Tillman and Kendrick.

Greene, George S. Class of 1823, C-327. Personal papers, includes notes as Civil Engineering instructor in 1825.

Haines, Thomas J. Class of 1849, C-1410. Cadet letters.

Haldane, Oswald. Non-Graduate, Class of 1873. Cadet papers and scrapbook.

Halleck, Henry W., Class of 1839, C-988. Personal papers.

Hardcastle, Edmund L. Class of 1846, C-1276. Personal papers.

Harris, David B. Class of 1833, C-713. Cadet letters.

Harris, William H. Class of June 1861, C-1940. Cadet letters.

Hartsuff, George L. Class of 1852, C-1554. Cadet letters.

Hartz, Edward L. Class of 1855, C-1700. Cadet letters.

Hascall, Milo S. Class of 1852, C-1549. Cadet letters.

Hatch, Evarard E. Class of 1884, C-3035. Memoirs.

Hatch, John P. Class of 1845, C-1247. Cadet letters.

Haupt, Herman. Class of 1835, C-816. Typescript autobiography of cadet experiences.

Havens, Benjamin. Legendary owner of tavern frequented by cadets. Miscellaneous reference papers including journal articles and recollections of graduates.

Hayman, Samuel B. Class of 1832, C-1161. Cadet letters.

Heinstand, Henry S. Class of 1878, C-2745. Cadet Letters.

Heintzelman, Samuel P. Class of 1826, C-445. Cadet journal.

Henry, Guy V., Jr. Class of 1898, C-3853. Memoirs.

Hersey, Mark L. Class of 1887, C-3232. Memoirs.

Hills, Eldridge R. Class of 1866, C-2141. Cadet diary.

Hodges, Henry C., Jr. Class of 1881, C-2901. Memoirs.

Holden, Edward S. Class of 1870, C-2314. Scrapbooks, personal papers, and research materials assembled for the Centennial history of USMA.

Horn, Tiemann F. Class of 1891, C-3393. Cadet letters.

Howard, Harold D. Class of 1891, C-3407. Cadet letters.

Howard, Oliver O. Class of 1854, C-1634. Cadet letters.

Hoyt, Ralph W. Class of 1872, C-2441. Cadet letters.

Jennings, Cortez A. Non-graduate, Class of 1880. Cadet letters.

Jesup, Charles E. Class of 1824, C-1858. Cadet letters.

Johnson, Bushrod, Class of 1840, C-1039. Cadet letters.

Johnston, Abraham R. Class of 1835, C-2314. Cadet letters.

Jones, Lucius. Non-graduate Class of 1818. Cadet letters.

Kendrick, Henry L. Class of 1835, C-801. Personal papers.

Kennon, Lyman W. V. Class of 1881, C-2928. Cadet letters.

Kent, Jacob F. Class of May 1861, C-1918. Cadet letters (filed in Holbrook collection).

King, William C. Class of 1863, C-1999. Cadet letters.

King, William R. Class of 1862, C-1990. Cadet letters.

Kinsley, Zebina J. D. Class of 1819, C-210. Personal papers.

Knowlton, Miner. Class of 1829, C-550. Personal papers.

LaMotte, Joseph N. Class of 1827, C-495. Reply to Cullum Questionnaire. In Cullum Register File.

Landers, George F. Class of 1887, C-3185. Scrapbook.

Lassiter, William. Class of 1889, C-3304. Unpublished memoirs.

Lee, Mary [Mrs. Robert E. Lee]. Letters to her nephew, prior to his entering the Academy in 1853.

Lee, Robert E. Class of 1829, C-542. Letters written to his family while USMA Superintendent, 1852–1855.

Lenihan, Michael J. Class of 1888, C-3230. Unpublished memoirs, "I Remember—I Remember."

Lord, James H. Class of 1862, C-1992. Cadet letters.

Lyford, Stephen C., Jr. Class of June 1861, C-1943. Cadet letters.

Lyle, David A. Class of 1869, C-2284. Cadet diary.

Mack, Oscar A. Class of 1850, C-1457. Cadet letters.

Macomb, Montgomery M. Class of 1874, C-2512. Personal papers.

Mahan, Dennis H. Class of 1824, C-361. Personal papers including correspondence as Professor of Civil and Military Engineering, 1821–1871.

Malcolm, William. Class of 1819, C-223. Cadet letters, filed in Partridge papers.

Mansfield, Edward D. Class of 1819, C-206. Personal papers.

Mansfield, Jared. Professor of Mathematics, 1802–1805, and Professor of Natural and Experimental Philosophy, 1812–1828. Personal papers.

Mansfield, Joseph K. F. Class of 1822, C-287. Personal papers.

Marcy, S. Past Midshipman, U.S. Navy. Special report to Secretary of the Navy George Bancroft concerning USMA instruction and discipline, July 18, 1845.

Marston, Ward. Non-graduate Class of 1818. Cadet letters, filed in Partridge papers.

Mason, James L. Class of 1836, C-843. Cadet letters.

McCauley, Charles A. H. Class of 1870, C-2333. Scrapbook and journal.

McCrea, Tully. Class of 1862, C-1980. Cadet letters.

McDowell, Irwin S. Class of 1838, C-963. Correspondence as USMA Adjutant, 1841–1845.

McGlachlin, Edward F., Jr. Class of 1889, C-3301. Memoirs.

Michie, Peter S. Class of 1863, C-1996. Correspondence while Professor of Natural and Experimental Philosophy, 1871–1901.

Miley, John D. Class of 1887, C-3153. Personal papers.

Miller, Harvey W. Class of 1898, C-3834. Cadet scrapbook.

Mitchell, Harry E. Class of 1900, C-3973. Unpublished memoirs, "As I Remember It" and cadet scrapbook.

Mordecai, Alfred. Class of June 1861, C-1941. Cadet letters.

Morgan, George H. Class of 1880, C-2858. Cadet diary.

Morris, William S. Class of 1851, C-1520. Cadet letters.

Morrow, Jay J. Class of 1891, C-3389. Memoirs.

Moseley, George V.W. Class of 1899, C-3904. Unpublished memoirs, "One Soldier's Journey."

Mott, Thomas B. Class of 1886, C-3128. Cadet letters.

Nichols, Thomas B. Class of 1872, C-2451. Cadet letters.

Noyes, Charles R. Class of 1879, C-2787. Cadet diary, letters, and scrapbook.

O'Connor, John O. Recorder for 1816 Partridge Court of Inquiry. Personal papers (filed in the Jared Mansfield papers).

O'Maher, Mary Isabel. Daughter of civilian USMA staff member. Later married Quincy A. Gillmore, Class of 1849. Letters to friends 1844–1847.

Parker, Francis H. Class of May 1861. Unpublished biography, "The Life of Francis Henry Parker, 1838–1897," by his grandson, John M. Parker III.

Parker, James. Class of 1876, C-2623. Memoirs.

Partridge, Alden. Class of 1806, C-15. Personal papers. Includes materials relating to his 1816 Court of Inquiry and 1817 Court Martial.

Patrick, Marsena R. Class of 1835, C-833. Cadet letters.

Patterson, Charles E. Class of May 1861, C-1903. Cadet letters.

Pearce, Thomas H. Class of 1826, C-468. Personal papers.

Pegram, John. Class of 1854, C-1640. Cadet letters.

Perry, James H. Non-graduate, Class of 1837. Cadet letters.

Pleasanton, Augustus J. Class of 1826, C-448. Diary entries concerning 1838 visit to West Point.

Plummer, Augustus H. Class of 1853, C-1626. Cadet letters.

Pope, John. Class of 1843, C-1127. Cadet letters.

Porter, Fitzjohn. Class of 1845, C-1238. Letters of 1855 concerning cadet equipment.

Potter, Stephen V. B. Non-graduate, Class of 1850. Cadet letters.

Ramsay, George D. Class of 1820, C-257. Memoir answer to Cullum Questionnaire. Filed in Cullum Historical File. Edited and abridged version included in Cullum history of USMA in Vol. III, Cullum's *Biographical Register of Officers and Cadets. . . .*

Raymond, Samuel. Non-graduate Class of 1846. Cadet letters.

Reed, Hugh T. Class of 1873, C-2503. Cadet scrapbook.

Rhodes, Charles R. Class of 1890, C-3307. Cadet letters and unpublished memoirs.

Robinson, William G. Class of 1858, C-1822. Cadet letters.

Robinson, Wirt. Class of 1887, C-3182. Natural History notes.

Roe, William J., Jr. Class of 1867, C-2209. Cadet scrapbook.

Ruger, Thomas H. Class of 1854, C-1633. Correspondence as USMA Superintendent, 1871–1876.

Scarritt, Jeremiah N. Class of 1838, C-945. Cadet letters.

Schofield, John M. Class of 1853, C-1585. Letters and personal papers. Also personal correspondence while Superintendent, 3 vols., 1877–1880.

Schulz, Edward H. Class of 1895, C-3617. Reminiscences and scrapbook.

Schureman, James W. Class of 1845, C-1152. Personal papers.

Scott, Hugh L. Class of 1876, C-2628. Cadet letters and unpublished memoirs.

Scriven, George P. Class of 1878, C-2721. Personal papers.

Shannon, James A. Class of 1903, C-4158. Personal papers.

Sherwood, Walter. Class of 1837, C-928. Cadet letters.

Shields, Hamilton L. Class of 1846, C-1295. Cadet letters.

Smith, Charles F. Class of 1826, C-410. Commandant of Cadets, letters 1842.

Smith, Frederick A. Class of 1833, C-707. Cadet letters and materials concerning construction at West Point 1846–1848.

Smoke, Samuel A. Class of 1887, C-3236. Cadet letters.

Sorley, Lewis. Class of 1891, C-3448. Memoirs and personal papers.

Stanley, David S. Class of 1852, C-1544. Memoirs of cadet experiences. Includes unpublished manscript by Miller J. Stewart, "No More Rivers to Cross, The Story of a West Point Cadet, 1842–1845," which describes Stanley's cadet exeriences.

Steele, Mathew F. Class of 1883, C-2992. Personal papers.

Stuart, J.E.B. Class of 1854, C-1643. Cadet letters.

Sully, Alfred. Class of 1842, C-1092. Cadet letters.

Sweet, John J. Class of 1860, C-1882. Cadet letters.

Swift, Eben. Class of 1876, C-2621. Memoirs.

Swift, Eben, Jr. Class of 1940, C-12165. Unpublished manuscript, "The Plebe System at West Point, 1872–1876 and 1936–1940, A Comparison." Cites memoirs of his father, Eben Swift.

Swift, Joseph. Class of 1802, C-1. Personal papers and records. Other Swift letters can be found in the Thayer, Cullum, and Partridge files.

Thayer, Sylvanus. Class of 1808, C-33. Personal papers, letters, and records. Typescript copies of letters available. Other Thayer materials can be found in various collections such as the Cullum Personal Papers and the Cullum Historical File.

Thomas, Orenzo. Class of 2823, C-342. Reminiscences in answer to Cullum Questionnaire. In Cullum Register Files.

Tidball, John C. Class of 1848, C-1379. Unpublished memoir, "Getting Through West Point by One Who Did and for Those Who Want to Know."

Tillman, Samuel E. Class of 1869, C-2275. Unpublished memoirs, "Backward Glances."

Totten, Joseph G. Class of 1805, C-10. Personal papers covering 1838–1863 period.

Tyler, Benjamin O. English instructor during Partridge period. Correspondence filed with Partridge papers.

Upton, Emory. Class of May 1861, C-1895. Correspondence written in 1880s.

Van Buren, Daniel T. Class of 1852, C-1536. Personal papers.

Vinton, John R. Class of 1817, C-168. Correspondence filed in Partridge papers.

Webber, John A. Class of 1815. Personal papers.

Webster, Horace. Class of 1818, C-183. Memoir answer to Cullum Questionnaire, in Cullum Register Files.

Weeks, Harrison. Class of 1868, C-2265. Cadet letters.

Weiss, Egon. USMA Librarian, August 21, 1962 letter concerning 1882 printing of Mark Twain's *1601* at West Point.

Wells, Briant H. Class of 1894, C-3610. Cadet papers.

Wendell, Abraham. Class of 1815, C-133. Personal papers.
Wessells, Henry. Class of 1833, C-735. Memoir answer to Cullum Questionnaire, in Cullum Register Files.
Wheeler, Joseph. Class of 1859, C-1843. Cadet letters.
Willard, Daniel. Traveling salesman for G&C Merriam Publishing Company. Correspondence regarding sales of books at West Point.
Willard, Simon. Class of 1815, C-125. Answer to Cullum Questionniare, in Cullum Historical Files.
Willcox, Cornelius D. Class of 1885, C-3061. Memoirs.
Williams, Jonathan. First Superintendent, USMA. Personal papers.
Wilson, Thomas. Class of 1853, C-1607. Cadet scrapbook and drawings.
Woodbridge, George. Class of 1826, C-442. Reminiscences in answer to Cullum Questionnaire, in Cullum Register Files.
Woodruff, George A. Class of June 1861, C-1948. Cadet letters and memoirs.
Workizer, John G. Class of 1897, C-3805. Cadet letters.
Wright, John. Class of 1814, C-99. Correspondence filed with Partridge papers.

OFFICIAL DOCUMENTS IN USMA ARCHIVES

Adjutant's Office: Letter Books, 1838–1902; Letters Received, 1838–1902.
Annual Report of the Superintendent, 1871 to 1992.
Cadets Admitted Books, 1846–1912
Casualties, U.S. Corps of Cadets, 1802–1915.
Department of West Point Letter Books, 1878–1882.
Office of the Superintendent: Letter Books, 1838–1902.
Post Orders, 1793–1833 and 1861–1904.
Quartermaster Waste Books, circa 1797–1801.
Records of the Academic Board: Correspondence, 1839–1905.
Records of the Department of Tactics: Orders, 1842–1899; Bimonthly and Seminannual Muster Rolls, October 1817–April 1839; Miscellaneous Book, 1813–1832; Register of Cadet Delinquencies, 1818–1829; Register of Punishment, 1837–1900.
Regulations of the United States Military Academy: Cadet Regulations, 1810–1991.
Reports of the Board of Visitors, 1819–1902.
Staff Records, 1818–1875.
Superintendent's Letter Books, 1861–1902.

Index

Abbot, Cadet Frederick, 393
Abert, James W., 272
Abert, John, 222, 284
Academic Board, 111, 119, 155, 249, 298–99, 303–4, 338, 388, 390
Academic Building, 78, 233–35, 255, 264, 407
Act of March 16, 1802, 28
Act of April 19, 1812, 62
Adams, Jasper, 249
Adams, John, 6, 11, 14, 15, 37, 146–47
Adams, John Quincy, 15, 173, 180, 268
"Additional" second lieutenants, 284
Agnel, Hyacinthe R., 250, 377
Alexander, Edward P., 421
Allen, Hannibal, 43
Ambrose, Stephen B., 405
American Military Philosophical Society, 47
Amosophic Society, 145
Anderson, Edward, 333
Anderson, Joseph R., 276
Anderson, Robert, 368
Andrews, George, 303
Armistead, Walker K., 17, 21, 25, 40, 125
Armstrong, John, 66
"Army Blue," 312
Army departments, 1860, 283
Army General Staff, 1860, 283

Army General Staff long tenure, 284
Army Geographical organization, 1865, 354
Army officers, involved politically, 285
Arnold, Benedict, 6
Articles of Confederation, 9
Artillerist and Engineer Academy, 10–11
Artillery, and emphasis on mobility, 1838, 282
Artillery School of Instruction, 128, 174
Associate Society of West Point, 191
Association of Graduates, 369–71
Atkinson, Col. Henry, 117
Avery's Tavern, 244

Bache, Alexander D., 277
Bailey, Jacob, 249
Bailey, William W., 266–67, 290
Barbe-Marbois, F., 26, 433
Barbour, Secretary of War James, 168, 170
Barnard, Cadet Jonathan G., 243
Barnard, John G., 307
Baron, George, 15, 20
Barracks, description of, 1818, 114–15
Barron, William Amherst, 15, 29–31, 33, 46, 51
Bartlett, William, H. C., 163, 174, 250, 377
Battle Monument, 12

Beauregard, Pierre G. T., 323–24, 330
Bell, John R., 126
Beltzhoover, Cadet Daniel M., 243
Benjamin, Cadet Samuel, 319, 325
Berard, Claudius, 106–7, 155, 250
Blackboard, use of, in class, 32, 41
Black cadets, 372–74, 377
Black Hawk, Chief, 227
Blair, Congressman James, 194
Blanco, Luis, 101, 139
Blanco, Mateo, 101, 139
Blaney, George, 130
Bliss, George, 117, 124–25
Bliss, William W. S., 263
Bloomberg, Joseph, 64
Board of Visitors, 83, 111, 127, 129–30,
    163–66, 263, 297, 389, 396, 415
Bombadier company, 143
Bomford, George, 46, 50
Booz, Cadet Oscar, 413–14
Bowditch, Nathaniel, 138
Bowling, by cadets, 357
Boyd, Cadet Orsemus B., 363, 365
Boynton, Edward C., 262, 337, 339
Bragg, Braxton, 262
Bratt, John, 228
Brevet 2nd lieutenants, 284
Brewerton, Henry, 258, 264, 267, 272
Brown, General Jacob, 123, 144
Brown, John, 310
Brule Indian uprising, 283
Buchanan, James, 327
Buckner, Simon B., 269, 371
Burbeck, Henry, 11, 14–17, 28, 46
Burton, John, 116
Butler, Attorney General Benjamin F.,
    224
Butler, Representative Benjamin, 375,
    381
Buttermilk Falls, 28, 384
Byers, Cadet John, 394

Cadet Acting Assistant Professors, 106–
    7, 162, 325
Cadet Chapel, 208, 230–31
Cadet Mess, 46, 78, 80
Cadet Monument, 89
Cadets: age limit, 1810, 55; age limit,
    1812, 62; assigned to Academy, 1812,
    62; assigned to Army units, 1807, 5;
    assigned to companies by height, 122,

142; attending officer social activities,
1830, 191; baseball games, 391; bond
of fellowship, 311, 324; branch selection, 103; at Columbian Exposition,
409; companies, 142; company officers, 113; complaining to Congress,
1819, 125; complaining about favoritism, 1816, 81; complaining about Mahan, 1834, 225; concept of honor, 174;
cooking in barracks, 79, 271; dances,
243; demanding arrest of commandant, 1819, 124; discipline deterio-
rates, 200; entrance requirements,
1810, 55; field trip to Long Island,
1814, 71; field trip to Philadelphia,
1820, 146; grades posted weekly, 103;
gray uniform, 1816, 71, 87; insignia of
rank, 1818, 113; interest in 1860 presidential campaign, 318; interest in Polish insurrection of 1830, 227; interest
in political affairs, 195; interest in
Texas insurrection against Mexico,
230; at Jamestown Exposition, 409; life
of, 1816, 72; life of, 1840s, 241–43;
march to Boston, 1821, 146–47; march
to Poughkeepsie, 1819, 146; mutiny
threat of 1819, 124; nicknames for officers, 214–15; number in various
branches, 31; officer responsibilities,
115; officers in 1824, 142; organized
into fire companies, 152; organized
into four companies, 1824, 123, 142;
pay in 1803, 41; pay accounts established, 1818, 115; permitted to resign
instead of being discharged, 100, 107;
petitioning Partridge for privileges,
80; petitioning Thayer regarding Bliss
brutality, 124; pledging abstinence if
classmates reinstated, 159, 244; prohibited from visiting Washington,
D.C., 204; punishments for, 1820s,
139–40; recreation, 145, 242, 311; reinstatements, 159, 197; resignations in
1860–61, 323, 329, 332; room furnishings, 241; room orderlies, 1822, 153; at
St. Louis Exposition, 409; saving library and paintings in fire, 1838, 234;
schedule, 1805, 45; sentenced to be
shot for mutiny, 180; shoes shined by
bootblack, 120, 142; shower formations, 1820s, 142; slang, 1840s, 230,

269; smuggling billiard table into barracks, 357; stealing Delafield's pet ducks, 246; taught to read but not to speak French, 155; uniform, 41, 45, 49, 72, 172, 176, 242, 268; visiting Benny Haven's tavern, 160–61; volunteering for duty in Florida, 1836, 228
Calhoun, John, 108, 125, 143, 158
Cameron, Simon, 333, 335, 338
Camp Illumination, 245
Candidate examinations, 87
Canfield, Cadet August, 115
Carter, Marshall S., 26
Catholic services, 52
Catlin, George, 191
Cavalry regiments added, 1855, 282
Centennial observance, 419
Central Barracks, 269–71
Chapel service in academic building, 156
Chemistry, Mineralogy, and Geology Department, 135
Church, Albert E., 106, 122, 133, 135–36, 149, 151–52, 186–87, 189, 191, 194, 249
Church of the Holy Innocents, 267, 313, 333
Ciceronian Society, 146
Civil War veterans, appointed cadets, 355
Clark, Cadet Silas, 17–18, 25
Class rings, 227–28, 265
Clinton, DeWitt, 83
Coat of arms, 409
Columbian Exposition, 409
Commandant of Cadets, 212, 340
Company of bombadiers and sappers, 62
Constitution Island, 12
Cooke, Philip St. George, 316
Coppee, Henry, 262
Copper beech tree, in superintendent's yard, 137
Corbin, Molly, 37
Corps of Invalids, 6, 37
Corps participation in Centennial Exposition, 1876, 384
Corps strength, 1808, 54
Corps strength, 1812, 62
Corps strength, 1815, 100
Cots, not required in 1822, 151
Courtenay, Edward H., 184
Cozzens, William B., 144, 178

Cozzens' Hotel destruction, 328
Craighill, William P., 264, 334–35, 392
Cram, Thomas, 136, 153, 156
Crawford, William, 79, 83, 86–87
Crockett, Davy, 193
Cross, Cadet Joseph, 17, 21
Crozet, Claude, 104–5, 155
Cullum, George, 30, 95, 195–97, 206, 209, 213, 221, 273, 275, 345–49, 361, 369, 371, 395
Cup for class godson, 354
Curriculum for five-year course, 303
Custer, George, 310, 326–28, 337, 370, 394
Custer, Mrs. George, 394
Cutbush, Surgeon James, 189

Dade Monument, 265
Dade's Massacre, 229
Dahlgren, Cadet Paul, 340, 346–47, 349
Dargan, Cadet Jeremiah, 180
Davies, Charles, 92, 155, 157, 193, 215
Davis, Jefferson, 161, 169, 263, 274, 297, 299, 303, 307–8, 357
Dearborn, Henry, 15, 34
De Kalb, Johann, 6
Delafield, Richard, 105, 107, 236, 239, 242, 245–47, 252–54, 257, 277, 307, 310, 323
Demerits, maximum permitted, 160
Demerit system, 159
Denton, Edgar, III, 38
Department of West Point, 390
Derby, Cadet George, 244–46, 253, 255, 258, 267
DeRussy, Rene, 62, 221–23, 226–27, 233, 312
Dialectic Society, 18, 146, 153, 229, 247, 278, 321, 351, 367
Donelson, Andrew, 112, 158, 193, 207
Donelson, Daniel, 206–7
D'Oremieux, Mrs. Theophile, 265–66
Doubleday, Abner, 262
Douglass, David B., 82, 100, 104, 138, 187, 193
Drake, County Clerk Charles, 333
Dransey, Peter, 15, 29
Dupont, Cadet Henry, 277, 305, 310, 320–21, 324, 325–26, 328–29, 332–33
Dutton, Cadet William, 263

Eakin, Cadet Constantine, 105
Eastman, Cadet Robert, 332
Edward, Prince of Wales, 316
"Eggnog" riot, 1826, 168–72
Ellicott, Andrew, 67, 83, 104, 138
Empie, Chaplain Adam, 67, 77
Engineering contribution of graduates, 275–76
Enlisted men, post–Civil War treatment of, 357
Enlisted men, recreation for, 14
Enlisted quarters, 66
Eustis, Henry, 275
Eustis, William, 54–56, 58, 158
Eveleth, William, 108
Ewell, Cadet William, 229, 257
Execution Hollow, 11, 26, 69

Fairfax, Cadet William, 116, 124
Fallen Timbers, Battle of, 10
Family life, 1840s, 264
Farley, Cadet Henry S., 322
Farragut, Cadet Loyall, 342
Featherstonhaugh, Cadet George W., 198
Fenwick, John R., 94
1st Artillery in Mexican War, 262
Five-year course, 304–5
"Flankers," origin of term, 122
Fleming, George, 25
Fleming, Thomas, 323
Fletcher, Cadet Robert, 360, 362, 364, 366, 368
Flipper, Cadet Henry, 382–83
Football, 410
Foreign cadets, 101, 193
Fornance, Cadet James, 376
Forsyth, Chaplain John W., 378
Fort Clinton, 10, 12, 26, 69
Fort Putnam, 10, 13, 27
Fourth of July, observance of, 120, 129, 160
Fowle, John, 223
France, threat of war with, 14
Frazer, Cadet William, 223, 227
Freeman, Constant, 11, 16
Freis, Andres, 253
French, Chaplain John, 317–18, 377

Gallatin, Albert, 52
Gardiner, George, 107, 228

Gardner, Asa Bird, 21
Gates, Cadet Samuel, 17, 21, 43
Gates, Cadet William, 17, 21
German Flats, 27
Ghosts in superintendent's home, 136
Gibson, Cadet Thomas W., 199
Gimbrede, Thomas, 122, 155, 191
Goethals, George W., 253, 400
"Golden Age" of USMA, 307
Grade posting discontinued, 1970s, 103
Graduation parade, 245, 360
Graham, James, 116
Grant, Ulysses S., 368, 384
Grant Hall, 271, 407
Gratiot, Charles, 51, 57, 180, 194, 221, 231
Grecian Society of Ladies, 169
Gridley's tavern, 27, 121, 134, 210
Gridley tract, 27
Griswold, Henry W., 138

Haines, Cadet Thomas J., 261, 263–64
Hamilton, Alexander, 8
Hardee, William H., 314
Harper, William R., 405, 421
Harris, Cadet William, 316–17, 319, 326, 473
Harvard College, 167, 216
Harwood, Cadet Franklin, 332
Haskell, Cadet Ernest E., 410
Hassler, Ferdinand R., 52
Hatch, Cadet John, 245
Havens, Benjamin ("Benny"), 84, 121, 134, 160
Havens, David, 117
Hayes, Samuel, 161
Hazing, 344–45, 356, 412–14
Hazing, in civilian colleges, 1860s, 345
Hein, Otto L., 412
Heintzelman, Cadet Samuel, 158, 177
"Hell Cats," 13
Hewitt, Cadet John H., 191
Hill, A. P., 262
Hills, Cadet Elbridge R., 357
Hitchcock, Ethan A., 105, 161, 169, 187–88, 201
Holden, Edward S., 210
Holmes, Cadet Charles, 124
Honor Code, 51, 114, 139, 363, 365–66, 379–80, 415
Hooker, Joseph, 262

Hospital, 189
House, James, 84
Houston, Sam, 163, 194, 320
Howard, Cadet Michael, 372–74
Howard, Oliver, 310, 317, 375–76, 403
Hundredth Night Show, 321, 367
Huntington, Ebenezer, 6

Infantry regiments, 282
Insignia, Corps of Engineers, 288
Instruction, 1801, 19
Irving, Major General Frederick A., 136
Izard, George, 33

Jackson, Andrew, 134, 185, 197, 203, 206–8, 224, 324
Jackson, Cadet Henry B., 17, 21, 40
Jackson, Major Daniel, 35
Jackson, Thomas J., 261–62
Jamestown Exposition, 409
Jefferson, Thomas, 10, 16, 36
Jessup, James S., 94, 131
Johnson, Cadet Bushrod, 227, 234
Johnston, Joseph, 169

Kemble, Gouverneur, 266, 276, 343
Keyes, Erasmus D., 269
Kilian, A. J., 154
King, Charles, 34, 342–45, 348–50, 356, 365
Kingsley, Zebulon, 27
Kinsley, J. D., 28
Kinsley, Zebina, J. D., 138
Kirby, Cadet Edmund, 320
Kirkland, John T., 67
Knox, Henry, 8, 9, 10
Kosciuszko, Thaddeus, 6
Kosciuszko Monument, 179
Kosciuszko's Garden, 27

Lafayette, Marquis de, 157
Landais, Cadet Louis, 19, 21
Latrobe, Benjamin H. B., 106, 144–45, 150–51, 395
Lawrence School of Engineering, 275
Lee, Agnes, 290–91, 306
Lee, Charles, 4
Lee, Cadet Fitzhugh, 289, 298
Lee, Cadet George Washington Custis, 289

Lee, Robert E., 169, 174, 193, 215, 273–74, 289–90, 294, 297–99, 305–6
L'Enfant, Pierre, 67
Leopard fires on *Chesapeake*, 1807, 53
Levy, Cadet Simon M., 17–18, 21, 29, 36, 38
Lillie, Cadet John, 17–18, 46
Lincoln, Abraham, 329, 342–44, 349–50
Lincoln, Secretary of War Robert, 344
Livingston, John, 40
Logan, Representative John, 388
Long, Lt. Stephen, 78
Long Barracks, 26, 27, 70, 78, 177–78
Lyford, Cadet Stephen, 315, 321, 324, 331, 337

MacArthur, Douglas, 413–14
McAuley, James, 255
McClellan, George, 261
McCrae, Cadet Tully, 316, 319, 325, 328, 330–31, 333–34, 336
McDonald, Cadet John B., 400
McDowell, Irwin, 254–55, 262
McIlvaine, Chaplain Charles P., 175–76
Macomb, Alexander, 17, 26, 29, 45, 47, 134, 168
McRee, William, 46, 77
Madison, James, 54, 86
Magruder, John B., 262
Mahan, Dennis H., 174–75, 186, 225, 250–51, 263, 301, 331, 347, 361, 367, 378
Mansfield, Edward, 105, 145, 339
Mansfield, Jared, 29, 40, 42, 55, 63, 70, 83, 104, 128, 134–35, 186
Mansfield, Mrs. Jared, 134
Marcy, Senator William, 185
Mason, Cadet Charles, 174, 190
Mason, Cadet James, 229
Masson, Florimond, 64
Mexican War, 262
Michie, Dennis, 410
Michie, Peter S., 378, 403
Military Academy, 3, 5–7, 10
Military Service Institution of the United States, 48
Militia, 186
Mills, Albert L., 414–15
Mitchell, Senator Samuel L., 131

Model yard, 19
Monroe, Cadet James, 80
Monroe, James, 75–76, 88, 90–91, 94, 126, 158, 168
Montgomery, Richard, 4
Moore, John, 27
Mormon expedition, 1850, 283
Motto, "Duty, Honor, Country," 409
Mulhallon, Cadet Daniel, 68
Murray, Cadet William, 17, 21

Napoleon Club, 263, 301, 317
Nast, Thomas, 413
Negro cadets, 372–74, 377
Nicholson, Cadet Edward L., 124
Norris, Cadet H. Ariel, 198
North Barracks, 78, 152, 156, 271
North's tavern, 12, 28, 52, 71
Norton, William, 275
Noyes, Cadet Charles, 393

O'Brien, Dr. Lucius, 161
O'Connor, Capt. John, 84, 90
Officer in Charge, 162
Old Provost, 11, 26, 33
Olmstead, Cadet George T., 312
O'Maher, Mary, 265
O'Maher, Timothy, 136
Ordnance Corps, 282
Osborn, Robert Weir, 25

Parker, Cadet Francis, 336
Parks, Chaplain M. P., 276
Parrott, Robert W., 276, 343
Partridge, Alden, 45, 49, 65–67, 69, 72, 75–77, 80–81, 85, 88–89, 91–95, 116, 126, 158, 193, 231
Partridge, Isaac, 69, 78, 82
Partridge Court of Inquiry, 83–84
Patten, Cadet George W., 243
Payne, Cadet John, 77
Pelham, Cadet John, 320
Perez, Juan, 193
Perkins, Capt. Samuel, 84–85
Philomatheu Society, 146
Photography at West Point, 245, 301–2, 311, 347
Pickering, Thomas, 7
Picton, Chaplain Thomas, 122
Pitcher, Thomas, 362, 365

Pleasanton, Augustus, 240
Plebes, on probation, 102, 150
Plummer, Cadet August, 265
Poe, Edgar Allan, 198
Polk, Cadet Edward, 68
Polk, Leonidas, 175
Porter, Cadet Ambrose, 17, 21, 40, 46
Porter, Commodore Horace, 101
Forter, Fitz-John, 269
Princeton University, 217
Proveaux, Cadet Joseph, 17, 21
Pulaski, Casimir, 6

Ragland, Cadet Thomas, 116, 124
Railroads, contribution of graduates to, 275
Ramsay, George D., 68, 73, 77, 79, 81, 95, 104, 119
Reed, Joseph, 4
Regulations, 34, 141
Religion, 52, 313
Reno, Jesse, 269
Renwick, James, 131
Reunion of cadets entering, 1817, 292
Reynolds, Joseph J., 269
Ricketts, James B., 262
Rivardi, John, 11–12, 26
Robertson, Cadet Felix H., 323
Rochefontaine, Stephen, 11, 12
Roe, Stephen, 178
Roosevelt, Theodore, 410, 421
Root, Elihu, 414, 422
Rowland, Cadet Isaac, 188
Rowland, Cadet Thomas, 320–23, 326, 328–29
"Runts," origin of term, 123

St. John's College, 167
St. Louis Exposition, 409
Sappers, miners, and pontooners, company of, 282
Saxe-Weimar, Duke of, 158
Schaff, Cadet Morris, 318, 326, 328–31
Schofield, John M., 216, 296, 298, 387–88, 390–92, 395–97, 399–401, 403–4
Schools for Post children, 266–67
Schureman, Cadet James W., 247

Scott, Cadet Hugh, 377
Scott, Winfield, 67, 93, 129, 144, 156–57, 167, 266, 268, 359, 419
Scott, Mrs. Winfield, 227, 243, 312
"Seps," origin of term, 356
Seymour, Thomas, 339
Shays, Daniel, 9
Shays' Rebellion, 9
Sheffield, Merle, 433
Sheffield School of Engineering, 275
Shepherd, William, 9
Shuler, Cadet John J., 68
Simpson, Joe, 264
Smith, Cadet James W., 372, 374–77
Smith, Charles F., 226, 236, 240
Smith, Edmund K., 269
Smith, Gustavus W., 269
Smith, Henry, 181
Smoking banned in 1820s, 141
South Barracks, 78, 152, 271
Southerland, Cadet Samuel, 139
Springfield Arsenal, 9, 123
Sprole, Chaplain William T., 249
Stanley, Cadet David S., 269
Steuben, Friedrich Von, 7
Stevens, Cadet Isaac, 103, 225, 229
Stuart, J.E.B., 310
Sully, Cadet Alfred, 233–35
Sully, Thomas, 54, 65, 104, 210
Summer camp, 63, 120, 143
Sumner, Charles, 375
Superintendents, 340, 423
Swift, Joseph G., 17, 20, 25, 29, 35, 38, 53, 65–67, 76–77, 83, 90, 92–93, 129
Swift, Cadet William H., 277

Talcott, Andrew, 105
Taylor, Cadet Josiah, 17, 21
Taylor, J. W., 195
Taylor, Zachary, 262
Tennessee legislature, 193
Texts translated from French, 102
Thayer statue, 395
Thayer, Sylvanus, 53–54, 57, 77, 91, 99–101, 106–8, 112–13, 124, 130, 156, 159, 161, 167–68, 172, 176, 188–89, 205–6, 208–9, 213–18, 222, 233, 294, 349, 378, 394

Thomas, George, 229, 269, 272, 335
Thomas, Pierre, 71, 145
Thompson, Benjamin, 15
Thompson, Mrs., 41, 79
Thornton, William A., 171
Ticknor, George, 103, 162–66
Tidball, Cadet Joseph, 268
Titus, Cadet Calvin P., 421
Topographical Engineers, 282
Totten, Charles A. L., 395
Totten, Joseph, 36, 46, 84, 233, 252, 256, 269, 284, 333, 338, 345, 383, 389
Touard, Lewis, 11, 15, 18–20
Tower, Zealous B., 340
Trescot, George, 70
Twain, Mark, 409
Tyler, Benjamin O., 67

United States Military Philosophical Society, 36
University of Virginia, 216
Upham, Cadet William H., 343
Upton, Emory, 305, 310, 316, 336, 374–75, 388
U.S. Marine Corps, 162
U.S. Naval Academy, 275, 322, 367–69, 410
U.S. and State officials, 376

Van Buren, Abraham, 233
Vance, Joseph, 194
Vassar College, 393
Visitor accommodations in mess building, 1816, 109

Wadsworth, Decius, 29, 35, 39, 44
Walsh, Samuel, 67
Warner, Anna B., 393
Warner, Chaplain Thomas, 226, 249
Washington, George, 3–4, 7–8, 10, 27, 327
Wayne, Anthony, 12
Wayne's Legion, 12, 18
Webb, Cadet George, 106, 116
Webber, Cadet John, 81
Webster, Cadet Horace, 79
Weigley, Russell, 404
Weir, Professor Robert W., 210, 250
Welcker, Cadet George L., 192

Wendell, Cadet Abraham, 79
West, Cadet John A., 329
West Point Hotel, 144, 178
West Point Library, 17, 33
West Shore Railroad, 253
Wheaton, William V., 226
Whistler, George, 275
Whistler, Cadet James A. McNeill, 265, 290
White, Stanford, 408
Whittaker, Cadet Johnson C., 399–403
Wilkinson, Major General James, 35
Wilkinson, Cadet Joseph B., 18
Willard, Cadet Simon, 72
Williams, Cadet John Washington, 382
Williams, Jonathan, 16, 20, 25, 29, 31, 33, 39, 44–45, 50–51, 55, 57, 64

Willis, Cadet Edward, 328
Willis, Richard, 243
Wilson, James, 29
Winder, John H., 262
Wirt, William, 126
Wofford, Cadet John T., 323
Wolcott, Cadet Alexander, 199
Wood, Leonard, 410
Wood, Cadet Oliver E., 358
Wood Monument, 123
Woodruff, Cadet Charles A., 354
Worrell, Stephen, 15
Worth, William, 138, 180, 214
Wright, John, 100, 116
Wyndham, John, 195
Wyse, Francis O., 262

Zoeller, Christian, 39, 54, 64, 78, 122

About the Author

GEORGE S. PAPPAS is a retired U.S. Army Colonel who was founder and first Director of the U.S. Army Military History Institute in Carlisle, Pennsylvania. He is the author of *Prudens Futuri: History of U.S. Army War College* and *The Cadet Chapel, United States Military Academy*. He has published articles in military journals, including *Assembly*, *Military Review*, and *Parameters*.